6 00

D0222294

The Explorers of South America

The Explorers
of South America

by Edward J. Goodman

University of Oklahoma Press
Norman and London

To my wife, Jeanne,

and to our children,

Jim, Steve, Karen, and Patrice

Library of Congress Cataloging-in-Publication Data

Goodman, Edward J. (Edward Julius), 1916–
    The explorers of South America / by Edward J.
    Goodman.
        p.   cm.
    Originally published: New York : Macmillan,
    c1972.
    Includes bibliographical references (p.   ) and
    index.
    ISBN 0-8061-2420-2
    1. South America—Discovery and exploration.
2. South America—History. 3. Explorers—South
America—History. 4. South America—Exploring
expeditions. I. Title.
F2233.G66   1992
980'.01'0922—dc20   91-50856
                                               CIP

Contents

vi   *Contents*

Foreword

Thirty-seven years ago, John Bartlet Brebner wrote an engaging and scholarly volume entitled *The Explorers of North America, 1492–1806*. Despite the wealth of material available, no comparable volume has ever appeared to recount the fabulous tale of the explorers of South America. It is hoped that this work will remedy that deficiency. It is the story of the brave and the foolhardy, the saints and the scoundrels, the learned and the unlettered, the aristocrats and the lowborn—the men who for four and a half centuries have explored the "green continent."

Insofar as possible, I have relied on the accounts of the explorers themselves—works of great detail, careful observation, and great human interest. These have been supplemented by the writings of distinguished historians in the field, whose works on various facets of the subject are invaluable to anyone undertaking a study of it. The selection of explorers, aside from the obviously great ones, was necessarily arbitrary, but it is hoped that it will be agreeable, and that none will feel slighted should his favorite explorer somehow fail to make an appearance in these pages. Nearly everyone whose contribution has been significant or whose work and experience is of unusual interest has been included.

In the preparation of this volume, I have owed much to many others. Perhaps I should begin with my father, the late Edward J. Goodman, Sr., whose interest in the unusual and whose extensive collection of *National Geographic*s first aroused my interest in exploration at an early age. Professor Brebner's book provided a challenge to do for South America what he had done for North America. But more recently I have been greatly helped through the interest and assistance of many scholars, students, and friends. To Professor Charles E. Nowell of the University of Illinois I am especially indebted. His suggestions during the early stages of my research were invaluable; he read the entire manuscript, and it has benefited much from his vast knowledge and critical eye. For whatever deficiencies or errors the work may contain, I alone, of course, am responsible. I am also grateful to the University of Illinois for a visiting professorship which permitted me to make use of the vast resources of its library, to the Catholic University of America for a summer appointment which permitted me to do research in the Library of Congress, to the Fredin Memorial Scholarship Committee of Xavier University in Cincinnati for a grant which allowed me to do research on the French explorers in the Bibliothèque Nationale in Paris, to the Fundação Calouste Gulbenkian in Lisboa for a generous contribution of books, and to the many Colombians whose kindnesses to me and to my family made our stay in their country such a memorable and rewarding experience.

In the early stages of planning this work, Professor Lewis Hanke of the University of Massachusetts and Professor William Manger of Georgetown University, as well as Professor Nowell, helped me to set reasonable limits to my research. During the course of my investigations I have received valuable suggestions from Professor John Thompson of the University of Illinois, Professor Ronald Hilton of Stanford University, Dr. Enrique de Gandía, Vice-Rector of the University of Olivos in Argentina, my colleague Dr. Matías G. Vega of Xavier University, and Mr. Peter V. Ritner, and much encouragement from two friends, Dr. Edward J. Devins and Mr. William S. Curran, of Cincinnati, whose interest could not have been greater had it been their own work. I have had much assistance from the staffs of the Library of Congress, the Bibliothèque Nationale, the Newberry Library, the Columbus Memorial Library of the Pan-American Union, the University of Illinois Library, the Oliveira Lima Library of the Catholic University of America, the library of the National Geographic Society, the Cincinnati Public Library, and the library of Xavier University. I am especially indebted to Mr. Carl Deal and Mr. Robert C. White of the University of Illinois Library, Mr. Yeatman Anderson III, Curator of Rare Books in the Cincinnati Public Library and his staff, Mr. Thomas Addison and Miss Gail Petersen, Mrs. Kathryn Dick of the Xavier University Library, Mr. Gordon Dunkley, and to Mr. Thomas Mandel of the Macmillan Co. for invaluable editorial help. For assistance with the illustrations, I thank Mr. Arthur Gropp of the Columbus Memorial Library and Mr. William Bradshaw Benesch of Cincinnati. I also owe a debt to several of my students at the University of Illinois and Xavier University, whose researches have been helpful, particularly Mr. Paul Brinkley-Rogers, Mr. Edward Keller, Miss Dwalia Nelson, and Mrs. Peggy Walters. And to the members of my own family, I am especially grateful for their long patience.

Edward J. Goodman

Part One

The First Century:

Discovery and Conquest

1 *Columbus and the*
Age of Discovery

On the fifth day of August, 1498, three vessels of the fleet of Christopher Columbus, on his third voyage to the New World, lay at anchor off the south coast of the peninsula of Paria in modern Venezuela. Since it was Sunday, and, as his son Ferdinand records, "from motives of piety [he] did not wish to set sail that day," [1] the Admiral dispatched several small boats which landed in a sheltered cove. In so casual a manner did the first Europeans set foot on the continent of South America. The exact location of this first landfall may never be known; it is clear, at least, that it was made somewhere between Bahía Celeste, at the eastern tip of the peninsula, and Ensenada Yacua, several leagues to the west. [2]

Columbus had organized his third voyage [3] for the specific purpose of discovering the mainland, which the king of Portugal believed to exist in the equatorial region, [4] and to determine whether it lay east or west of the line of demarcation of the Treaty of Tordesillas (1494) between Spain and Portugal. Such a region, it was believed, should be more profitable than the Antilles, and should equal the wealth of Guinea; according to the Aristotelian theory, similar products are found in similar latitudes. Moreover, one Jaime Ferrer of Balnes, a gem collector, advised Columbus to seek a land where the inhabitants were black or tan in color, since most precious stones came from such lands; accordingly, the Admiral decided to sail for the latitude of Sierra Leone. It was essential that some source of great wealth be found, lest their Catholic Highnesses, who had never seemed to be wholly satisfied with the results of Columbus' earlier voyages, decide to give up the Indies enterprise entirely.

After a long delay occasioned by Spanish involvement in wars and marriage alliances, a royal order was issued on April 23, 1497, authorizing preparations for the third voyage. Columbus was to take three hundred persons at royal expense and up to fifty more at their own expense, his original rights and privileges were confirmed, and he was to receive a percentage of the profits of the voyage. Despite considerable difficulty in raising funds and procuring ships, the fleet weighed anchor at Sevilla at the end of May, 1498, and was joined by the Admiral at Sanlúcar de Barrameda. On June 10 the ships reached Funchal in Madeira, where they were well received, and remained six days to take on supplies. Nine days later they anchored at San Sebastián in the Canaries and took on cheeses. Here Columbus decided to send three of his ships directly to Española, and departed with the rest, two caravels, *El Correo* and *La Vaqueños*, and the flagship Columbus referred to only as *la nao* (the ship), for the Cape Verde Islands, which he reached on Wednesday, June 27, anchoring at Boa Vista, which Ferdinand described as "a miserable and melancholy place." The Admiral reported that because of a thick and warm haze which hung over the islands three-quarters of the inhabitants were sick and the rest pallid.

On Thursday, July 5, Columbus left the island of São Tiago, and took a southwesterly course toward the equator. Because of very light winds, he did not clear the islands until July 7, and six days later entered the doldrums. For eight days the ships were becalmed, and the heat was so excessive that, according to Ferdinand, "it scorched the ships." Part of the food spoiled, and casks of wine and water burst. During the calm, Columbus took many observations of the Pole Star, whose apparent variation in position puzzled him. An unseasonal wind mercifully sprang up at last, and the vessels continued on course. With the exception of this trying experience, Columbus had less trouble on this than on any other of his voyages.

By the end of July, with food supplies spoiling and water diminishing, and fearful lest some uprising might occur in Española, Columbus decided to shift course to the north, in which direction he believed the Antilles lay. At noon on July 31, Alonzo Pérez Nizardo, who had climbed into the crow's nest, sighted land fifteen leagues to the west, "extending northwestward as far as the eye could reach," according to Ferdinand Columbus. After the crew said prayers of thanksgiving, the Admiral named the island Trinidad in fulfillment of a decision to give this name to the first land he saw, and because it seemed so appropriate for a land which showed three mountains joined at the base.

The immediate need was water, so Columbus sailed westward along the coast in search of a river. Anchoring at a place he named Punta de la Playa, he sent sailors ashore. They found a brook and found more as well—fishing tackle, huts, and villages. But where were the evidences of wealth—the gold and precious stones? Was this new land inhabited only by the same primitive people encountered on the earlier voyages—or were the great cities of wealth still ahead? Resuming their journey, the Spaniards sailed southward, sighting the continent on the left about 25

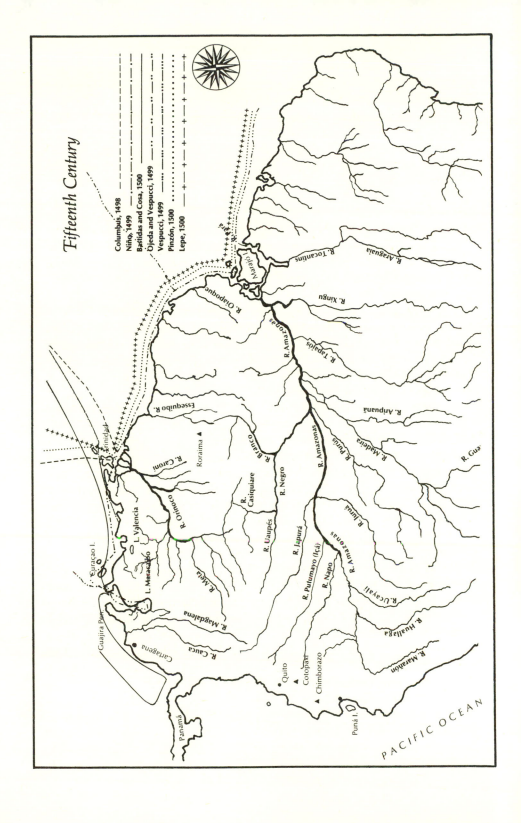

Fifteenth Century

Columbus, 1498
Niño, 1499
Bastidas and Cosa, 1500
Ojeda and Vespucci, 1499
Vespucci, 1499
Pinzón, 1500
Lepe, 1500

Pará

R. Oiapoque

Marajó

R. Tocantins
R. Araguaia
R. Xingu
R. Amazonas
R. Tapajós
R. Arinaná
R. Madeira
R. Gua
R. Purús
R. Juruá
R. Ucayali
R. Huallaga
R. Marañón

Essequibo R.

Trinidad

Roraima

R. Caroni

R. Branco

R. Casiquiare
R. Negro
R. Uaupés
R. Japurá
R. Putumayo (Içá)
R. Napo
R. Amazonas

R. Orinoco

Curaçao I.

L. Valencia
L. Maracaibo

R. Meta

R. Magdalena
R. Cauca

Guajira Pen.

Cartagena

Panamá

Quito
Cotopaxi
Chimborazo

Puná I.

PACIFIC OCEAN

leagues distant, and, believing it to be an island, Columbus named it Isla Santa. On the following day, August 2, the fleet anchored off Punta del Arenal on the south coast of Trinidad, where a canoe with 25 Indians appeared, apparently to ascertain who the Spaniards were and whence they had come. These were the first inhabitants the Spaniards had seen. Attempts at communication failed, and the Indians kept at a distance, so Columbus attempted to entice them by having some of his crew members perform a dance, to the accompaniment of pipes and drum. But despite the Admiral's good intentions, this seemed to have but one meaning for the Indians; it must be a war dance, and they quickly brought it to a halt with a volley of arrows. Not to permit such ill-mannered behavior to go unchallenged, Columbus returned fire, but the Indians without hesitation (apparently firearms inspired no fear in them) made for another vessel, *La Vaqueños*, whose pilot managed to enter the canoe and present some trinkets. But nothing was gained from this contact; having nothing to exchange, the Indians made off and the Spaniards saw no more of them.

On August 4 the vessels began to weigh anchor; Columbus had decided to attempt to sail through the narrows separating the southwestern tip of Trinidad from the mainland, a passsage which he subsequently named the Boca de la Sierpe ("Serpent's Mouth"). Suddenly a great wave approached from the south. The crews were terrified, afraid of being swamped, but the wave only raised the vessels up and dropped them down again, with no more harm than the snapping of the *Vaqueños'* cable. Continuing on course, the Admiral passed through the Gulf of Paria during the day, approaching the northern narrows, and reached the coast of Paria, where the first landing on the continent occurred. The region around the point of landing was mountainous, and apparently populated only by monkeys. In the belief that more level land lay to the west, Columbus followed the coast to the Río Guiria, where he anchored on August 6, went ashore, and took possession for Castile. When a canoe appeared alongside the *Correo*, the ship's pilot, knowing Columbus' anxiety to communicate with the Indians, jumped into it, overturned it, captured three Indians as they were swimming away, and brought them aboard the flagship. The Admiral treated them kindly, giving them beads, hawk's bells, and sugar, and sent them ashore. This favorable treatment brought more Indians out to the fleet to engage in barter, particularly for objects of brass, the smell of which they seemed to enjoy. The Indians appeared to have nothing of value except *guanín*, an alloy of gold, silver, and copper, which the Spaniards had never seen before.[5]

The Indians made known to Columbus that they called their land Paria, and that it was more densely populated to the west. On August 8, ordering six Indians to be taken along as guides, the Admiral sailed west along the coast to a point which he called La Aguja (The Needle), where he anchored at night. Daybreak revealed a beautiful, cultivated, and well-populated country, abounding in fruits, grapevines, and birds of brilliant plumage. The air was mild, and fragrant with the scent of flowers; struck by the beauty of the place, Columbus named it Los Jardines (The Gardens). The Indians were friendly. Banquets were served by the cacique and his son, consisting of bread, fruits, and beverages made from various fruits. The Spaniards noticed that the women wore strings of pearls, which they indicated came from the seacoast on the north side of the peninsula. Columbus saw that all the Indians were of a rather fair skin, which was something of a puzzlement to him, since he expected that, living so near the equator, they must necessarily be dark. The pearls he had seen and the warmth of his reception led him to believe that Spain would gain great wealth from this area, and that many converts would be made.

Continuing on a westerly course on August 10, the Admiral found the depth of the sea diminishing, and decided to return to the eastern tip of the Isla de Gracia, as he had originally named the peninsula in the belief that it was an island. A survey by the caravel *Correo* located a westward passage on August 11, and the ships sailed through the strait, which Columbus named Boca del Dragón (Dragon's Mouth), and coasted along the north shore of Paria on August 13. By now the Admiral was convinced that he had found the continent he sought, and so indicated in his journal. Considering the great beauty of the land he had discovered, the inaccuracy of his astronomical observations which led him to believe that the discrepancies in the apparent position of Polaris was caused by the fact that the earth was pear-shaped, with the high part below the equator near the land he had found, and his essentially medieval outlook, it is not surprising that Columbus should have assumed that near here was the Earthly Paradise. If this may seem strange and highly unrealistic today, it is of interest to note that such a realist as Amerigo Vespucci was willing to admit that if there were an Earthly Paradise, it would surely be there. Leaving the coast of Paria on August 14, Columbus passed by the island of Margarita, and headed for Española. It was a cause of regret to him that his log book could not be more complete, but long periods of watch had made his eyes bloodshot, a problem which, along with repeated attacks of gout, had been a constant trial to him on his voyage. After leaving the coast of South America, he was not to see it again until his fourth voyage in 1503, when he reached the coast of Darién.[6]

Less than a year after Columbus discovered the continent of South America, one of his former officers, Alonso de Ojeda, a native of Cuenca, undertook a voyage to the same area.[7] He was able to enlist the valuable support of the bishop of Burgos, Juan Rodríguez de Fonseca (who had been decidedly unfriendly to Columbus), the celebrated cartographer Juan de la Cosa, and the Florentine merchant Amerigo Vespucci, which enabled him to raise sufficient funds to equip four vessels at Puerto de Santa María. Cosa joined as pilot, but Vespucci insisted on command of two of the ships and a certain degree of independence with respect to the route. The expedition sailed May 18 (or 20), 1499, touched at the Canary Islands and, using a copy of Columbus' map, proceeded to follow his course across the Atlantic. After twenty-five days they reached the coast of the continent at 3° or 5° north latitude, where the expedition separated, Ojeda sailing to the northwest, Vespucci to the southeast. Of the latter's voyage we shall have more to say subsequently. Without disembarking, Ojeda followed the coast toward Paria, passing the mouths of many rivers; two of these merited a special mention since their waters flowed far into the sea before mixing with the salt water—the Essequibo and the Orinoco, in all probability. The first populated land he saw was his landfall, Trinidad, where he met some "Caribs or cannibals of gentle disposition"; on entering the Gulf of Paria, he met more friendly Indians and encountered signs of Columbus' visit there. Passing through the gulf, Ojeda sailed along the coast of Paria, through the Gulf of Cumaná (or Barcelona) to Chichiriviche, which he named Puerto Flechado, for upon landing the Spaniards were attacked by warlike Indians, losing twenty-one men in the skirmish, and one more who subsequently died of his wound. Putting to sea again, Ojeda sailed to the island of Curaçao, then to the Paraguaná peninsula, which he thought was an island, and entered the green waters of the Gulf of Venezuela, which the Indians called Coquibacoa. Entering Lake Maracaibo (which he called Lago y Puerto de San Bartolomé) on August 24, Ojeda noticed Indian dwellings built on stilts in the lake, and was inspired to call the place Venezuela (Little Venice). Returning to the gulf, he discovered Cape de la Vela on the peninsula of Grajira. From this point the expedition proceeded eastward, gathering slaves and pearls en route, and reached Santo Domingo on September 5, sailing ultimately for Spain in June of 1500. The voyage was a financial success; sale of the pearls and those slaves who survived the return trip netted 500 ducats, which were divided among fifty-five participants.

It remains now to follow the course of the other half of the expedition, under the command of Vespucci. Few explorers have been more vilified than Amerigo Vespucci, for whom the continent was eventually named; he has been described as a charlatan and a liar, whose aim was to rob Columbus of the glory of the discovery. While careful scholarship has established his reputation beyond question, some points are still subjects for controversy, among them his role in this voyage. One account describes him as a subaltern of Cosa, yet his most recent biographer, Pohl, asserts that Ojeda was only the nominal leader, and that Vespucci went along as a representative of the backers of the voyage, and hence "as director of the policy and the purpose of those ships which his merchant backers had supplied." [8] Since the voyage was essentially a commercial enterprise, a handsome profit indeed could be realized if the vessels could reach India, which had thus far eluded Columbus despite his firm conviction that he was somewhere near it. The existence of two large land masses of continental proportions was completely unknown at the end of the fifteenth century. Geographical concepts rested on the Ptolemy map as reinterpreted by Martin Behaim and Heinrich Hammer, which represented the Indian Ocean as bounded on the east by a long peninsula, evidently the Malay peninsula, whose eastern outline rather resembled the east coast of South America. The peninsula (quite inaccurately) extended south of the equator, and was separated from a large island by the Sinus Magnus, a strait which was entered by turning Cape Catigara. When Vespucci separated from Ojeda, who was interested primarily in seeking pearls, it was his intention to find this cape and get around it.

Sailing to the southeast with a favorable wind, Vespucci's ships reached a point on the coast about 5° north twenty-seven days after separating from Ojeda. Attempts to land and penetrate the country were frustrated by mudflats and the density of the forest, which in many places grew down to the water's edge; the water, Vespucci noted, was fresh. A few days later, on July 2, the ships entered a wide gulf—possibly the Amazon estuary—which was named Santa María, following the prevailing custom of naming places in accordance with the calendar of saints. Sailing up a wide river which flowed from the west, the explorers penetrated a distance of twenty-four leagues in four days without seeing any place to land. Nor did they see any inhabitants, only smoke in the distance. Taking to a small boat, Vespucci and twenty armed men rowed twenty-four leagues farther, marveling at the great beauty of the place, and the colorful parrots. Upon their return to the ships, the expedition penetrated yet another great river which flowed from the south—possibly the Pará. Here Vespucci noted the disappearance of Polaris. Despite careful observations for many nights, in the course of which he discovered the importance of the Southern Cross for navigational purposes, he was unable to find a southern counterpart.

The size of the rivers indicated that this was no relatively narrow peninsula but a land mass of considerable magnitude, so Vespucci resumed his search for the strait. By July 24, after they had sailed some forty leagues to the southeast, it became evident that their geographical concept did not conform with reality. Here they began to encounter a current so strong that little or no progress could be made against it; Melón believed this to be the Guiana current, which bifurcated at Cape São Roque. Marco Polo had made no mention of the ships of the Great Khan encountering any such difficulty in sailing to India, so Vespucci was understandably dismayed. Unable to progress, he could do little but sail with the current in a northwesterly direction; according to Magnaghi, Vespucci probably reached a southern limit of six degrees and thirty minutes. The remainder of the voyage parallels fairly well the route of Ojeda; after sighting Cape Orange, Vespucci sailed through the Gulf of Paria, visited islands which were probably Curaçao and either Aruba or Bonaire, and proceeded west to Lake Maracaibo. Here his spirits were raised, for this might be the Sinus Magnus; when it was evident that it was not, he named it Deceitful Gulf. The ships were by now becoming unseaworthy, so the expedition sailed to Española, rejoining Ojeda.[9]

A few days after Ojeda and Vespucci had departed for the New World, another expedition set sail to exploit the pearl trade, headed by Per Alonso Niño, a native of Moguer, Spain, who, like many of his crew of thirty-three, had previously sailed with Columbus.[10] Lured by the prospect of riches, he obtained a license from the Court to discover, with the proviso that he keep fifty leagues away from the lands discovered by Columbus. Lacking funds for providing a vessel, he finally succeeded in prevailing upon a merchant, Luis Guerra, to equip a caravel of fifty tons on condition that his brother Cristóbal be made captain. Niño had no alternative but to agree; nonetheless, credit for the voyage has always been assigned to him. The vessel followed the general route of Columbus to Paria, where a landing was made and brazilwood cut in violation of royal orders but at least with the approval of the Indians. Leaving this forbidden coast, Niño sailed westward to the island of Margarita, where he landed and traded for pearls; apparently these were the first Spaniards to land there. Proceeding back to the mainland, he put into a port along the coast called Curiana, or Cumaná, and came ashore among friendly Indians. Here Niño demonstrated his business acumen; within a few minutes he had traded bells, pins, bracelets, and strings of beads for fifteen ounces of pearls. He was able to repeat this feat in the days following, for the Indians were anxious to obtain what he had; for the sake of safety, he required that they come aboard his ship to trade. Niño left a somewhat detailed account of the people he visited—their dwellings, food, hunting practices, and domesticated animals and fowl, and he marveled at the noises in the forest at night.

The Indians traded some articles of gold, and indicated that they obtained these from a region to the west called Cauchieto, about six days' journey; this prospect was sufficient to cause them to weigh anchor and set a course to the west. After ten days they reached a very beautiful country where they made ready to land, only to be attacked by some two thousand naked cannibals, who made any further progress impossible. There was nothing to do but return to Curiana, where they remained for twenty days, trading for pearls—a lucrative enterprise indeed. More than 150 marcos (a measure of weight) of pearls appear to have been acquired on the voyage, yet when the expedition returned to

Spain only 96 marcos were placed on the market, which led to the belief that the rest had been hidden by the principals to defraud their companions and the king. Despite his denials, Niño was jailed, but managed to clear his reputation on his release.

Pearls and gold were to lure yet another Spanish explorer within a short time. Rodrigo de Bastidas, a notary of Sevilla, obtained a royal commission to discover islands and "Tierra-firme," with the express proviso that he was not to encroach on the lands discovered by "our Admiral of the Ocean Sea" or by Cristóbal Guerra (that is, the aforementioned Niño expedition), nor those lands belonging to "our very beloved son, the Most Serene King of Portugal." [11] The veteran pilot Juan de la Cosa joined the expedition, which finally got under way in October after a delay of several months. The two small vessels made an uneventful crossing and, following instructions, bypassed the area which Columbus had explored, beginning an investigation of the coast west of the Gulf of Venezuela, and continuing west of Maracaibo, which, it will be recalled, was as far as the Ojeda-Vespucci expedition had penetrated. Bastidas and Cosa pushed on as far as the Río Magdalena and the Gulf of Urabá, then coasted northwest to Cape San Blas, and eventually to Nombre de Dios, in present-day Panama. So badly had shipworms disabled the vessels that Bastidas was forced to put into Jamaica for repairs, and finally reached Santo Domingo, where extensive work was undertaken to make the vessels seaworthy. It was at this time that the fleet of Columbus, now on his last voyage, arrived at Española.

Bastidas and Cosa had scarcely begun the journey back to Cádiz when further troubles forced them back; a second start fared no better, for bad weather caused the loss of the ships, which, with their cargoes of slaves, gold, brazilwood, and fabrics, were worth about five million maravedís. Enough of the riches were saved, however, to make the voyage quite a profitable one. There was one discordant note, however; Bastidas was accused by the governor, Bobadilla, of trading illegally with the inhabitants of the island, but managed to clear himself in Spain. His reward was not inconsiderable; a royal *cédula* of February 14, 1504, gave him a lifetime annuity on the income from the lands discovered by him "in the Gulfs of Huraba and Barú." Juan de la Cosa shared equally in this largesse.

There was but one more Spanish voyage to the north coast of South America before the fifteenth century had run its course. Cristóbal Guerra, who had been with Per Alonso Niño, and his brother Luis sailed from either Cádiz or Sanlúcar in 1500 in two caravels, reached Paria, and proceeded along the coast to Margarita. This time the Indians were not as friendly, and while the Guerra brothers secured a considerable quantity of pearls and *guanín*, it was not always without violence. Bartolomé de Las Casas records that the Indians were treated with unbelievable cruelty, and that the death of Luis and the loss of one ship were God's punishment for this; yet Navarrete records that Luis was still living in 1503. The expedition proceeded west as far as the Paraguaná peninsula and the vicinity of the Gulf of Urabá, where Bastidas had so recently been. Here Cristóbal imprudently tried to rule over the Indians rather than confine his activities to trading, and it soon became apparent that the enterprise would have to be given up. The expedition returned to Cumaná and Margarita, and finally arrived, now with only one caravel, in Castile late in 1501, bearing a cargo of *guanín*, brazilwood, slaves, and pearls. The slaves were Guerras' undoing; for having captured and sold them contrary to the express terms of their license, Cristóbal was jailed, to be released later at his own and his companions' expense.[12]

There remains to be considered the discovery of Brazil. Little more than a year after the discovery of the continent by Columbus, his companion of the first voyage, Vicente Yáñez Pinzón, who had commanded the *Niña*, succeeded, with the help of relatives and friends, in equipping four caravels for a voyage to the New World. Taking with him Juan Quintero, Juan de Umbría, and Juan de Jerez, who had been to Paria with Columbus, Pinzón sailed from Palos in December of 1499, sailing to the southwest by way of the Canaries and the Cape Verde Islands. Despite the monopoly which had been granted to the Admiral, Pinzón secured royal permission without difficulty, so disenchanted had the sovereigns become with the results of Columbus' discoveries. Departing from Santiago Island (according to Peter Martyr), the caravels sailed southwest until they crossed the equator and lost sight of the North Star; Pinzón was unaware of the importance of the Southern Cross in navigation and searched in vain for a southern equivalent of Polaris. Following their course, the ships reached land on January 20, 1500, at approximately 8° south latitude, at a cape which Pinzón named Santa María de la Consolación. No Indians were seen for two days, although some large footprints, which seemed to be those of a giant, gave the Spaniards a fright. The course was altered to west and north, which brought the Spaniards to the mouth of a river where they had an encounter with the Indians which cost them ten lives and many wounded.

Returning to their ships, the Spaniards sailed along the coast toward the equator and noticed that the sea water was becoming fresh. Deciding to investigate, they found the mouth of a river of tremendous size, which Pinzón estimated at thirty leagues or more—the Amazon. The Indians in the area were gentle but had little gold or other valuables; some from the province of Marinatambal indicated that there was an abundance of gold in the interior, so Pinzón took thirty-six of them with him. Efforts to penetrate upstream were unavailing, since the ships were in great danger from the strong tides which caused waves of great height in the channels.

Sighting Polaris again, the Spaniards followed the coast some three hundred leagues to the Gulf of Paria, where the Indians who had treated Columbus so well appeared hostile and would not come aboard; Las Casas believed that they had been maltreated by others who had sailed the north coast after Columbus. The Spaniards followed the coast of Paria sufficiently far to assure themselves of the continental dimensions of the land, then proceeded to Española in June, and returned to Spain on September 30.[13]

While the account of Pinzón's voyage is relatively simple, it presents some serious geographical problems which have not yet been settled to the satisfaction of all. The facts of the voyage are not in question; they are well attested by Juan de la Cosa, Peter Martyr, and Angelo Trevisano. The major problem is the point of arrival on the South American coast. Pinzón is quite emphatic that the cape he named Santa María de la Consolación is the same one the Portuguese called Cabo Santo Agostinho; yet, he was there in 1509, and it has been suggested that he may have refreshed his memory too well.[14] But contemporary evidence and the opinions of several leading scholars provide considerable support for the belief that Pinzón was indeed the discoverer of Brazil and the Amazon.[15] Portuguese scholars, quite understandably, are unwilling to concede the discovery to a Spaniard despite the evidence, even to denying that Pinzón could have been in Brazil in 1500, and asserting that a storm mentioned by him could not possibly have occurred.[16]

The Portuguese claim to priority rests on the well-known voyage of Pedro Alvares Cabral, who is usually acclaimed as the discoverer of Brazil.[17] On Monday, March 9, 1500, a fleet of thirteen vessels sailed out of the Tejo under command to this captain, bound for Calicut, India. Vasco da Gama had prepared the sailing instructions for the voyage, directing Cabral to sail to São Tiago in the Cape Verde Islands, then to go south or southwest with the northeast trade winds astern, finally picking up the southeast trade winds. Then, sailing close to the wind, he could proceed to the Cape of Good Hope. Following these instructions, the fleet passed the Canaries on the fifth day out, finally reaching São Nicolau Island in the Cape Verde group.

Resuming a southwesterly course, Cabral was becalmed for a few days in the doldrums until rescued by the southeast trade winds, which moved the fleet far out to sea, past the northeast corner of Brazil. There the first disaster occurred; on Monday, April 20, at dawn, the ship of Vasco de Ataíde lost the fleet, and despite Cabral's diligence in searching for it, it was never seen again. The following day, which Cabral's chronicler, Pêro Vaz, reminds us was Easter Tuesday, a large quantity of grass was seen, indicating the presence of land not far off, and on Wednesday birds were sighted. Vaz continues: "On that day, at the hour of vespers, we saw land! First of all a great mountain, very high and round, and other ranges, much lower, to the south; then a lowland, with great forests: the captain named the mountain Monte Pascoal, and the land, Terra da Vera Cruz." [18] The peak, located eighteen and one-half miles inland, is 1,700 feet in height, and is visible at a great distance. [19] That night they anchored six leagues offshore, at about 450 leagues from Guinea at latitude 16° 53′ south. [20]

Unsure whether he had discovered a continental land mass or merely a large island such as Española, Cabral ordered the vessels to sail toward the shore on the morning of April 23, and they entered the mouth of a river. Nicolau Coelho was sent in a small boat to explore the area; he stepped ashore, becoming the first Portuguese known to have trod on the soil of Brazil, and saw a large number of Indians, all naked, whose behavior was peaceable. This was the expedition's first contact with the aborigines. That night a strong wind sprang up, accompanied by showers, and the ships dragged anchor; accordingly Cabral decided on the morning of April 24, Friday, to seek a better port where they could take on wood and water. After sailing ten leagues to the north, the Portuguese came upon a suitable bay, which they named Pôrto Seguro (Safe Port), on Saturday, April 25. This is a kilometer and a half from Coroa Vermelha, near the mouth of the Mutari River. [21]

A second encounter with the Indians occurred when two of them in a canoe were picked up by the Portuguese; Cabral ordered them dressed from head to foot and sent them ashore, where there suddenly appeared a great number of Indians, dancing, singing, and rejoicing. Cabral seemingly had quickly mastered the art of making friends of them. The following day, April 26, Low Sunday, the Portuguese landed on a small island in the inlet, and Mass was sung before an altar at the foot of a tall tree by Frei Henriques Soares de Coimbra, superior of the eight Franciscans who were aboard in addition to the nine secular priests. Throughout the Mass and sermon, the Indians sat in rapt attention and respectful silence, which led the Portuguese to believe that they were ripe for conversion to Christianity. [22] Afterward, a meeting was held on board ship to reach a decision concerning the discovery. It was agreed to send the supply ship back to Portugal with news of the event, and leave two men in the land to learn the language rather than take Indians with them by force. Lacking a *padrão* (stone pillar), Cabral had his carpenters construct a wooden cross to symbolize taking possession of the land, still not knowing whether it was a continent or an island. The cross was raised May 1; a new altar was set up, and Frei Henriques again celebrated Mass and preached. The following day the fleet set sail for the Cape of Good Hope. [23]

There remains to be considered one more fifteenth-century discovery of Brazil. Shortly after Pinzón sailed for the Indies in December of 1499, Diego de Lepe left either Cádiz or Palos with two ships. He had sought three, but was able to obtain only two, one equipped from his own savings, the other by Francisco Vélez of Moguer, known as "El Comendador." Accompanying him were three good cosmographers and Bartolomé Roldán, who had been a pilot for Columbus. The vessels departed for the Ilha do Fogo in the Cape Verde Islands, then proceeded along the same course followed by Pinzón, finally reaching Cape Santo Agostinho. There they turned and sailed on a little further, possibly as far as the Rio São Julião. Lepe landed and took possession in the name of the Castilian sovereign, inscribing his name on a tree he described as so large that sixteen men with arms extended could not encircle it. Coming about, the ships took a northerly course to the cape, then followed the coastline and subsequently entered the Río Marañón (Amazon), where the Spaniards heard the noise of the Amazon tide, the *pororoca*. Apparently the Indians remembered well Pinzón's visit, for they greeted Lepe with hostility, whereupon he assaulted them, plundering and killing many and taking slaves. Leaving this scene of devastation behind, Lepe followed the coast to Paria, where he hoped to find pearls. Unsuccessful in this, he contented himself with taking more slaves, and returned to Spain ahead of Pinzón. So reprehensible was his conduct in the eyes of Las Casas that the latter referred to him as a "destroyer."[24]

Who, then, discovered Brazil? We have solid evidence of the presence of four discoverers—Vespucci, Pinzón, Cabral, and Lepe—before the end of the century. What is more, claims have been made which antedate these, and even antedate the discovery of the continent by Columbus in 1498. Let us consider these before taking up the problem of the four major contenders. One of the earliest candidates was Jean Cousin, whom Gaffarel has hailed as the discoverer of America. According to his claim, Cousin, on a voyage west from the Azores in 1489, finally reached an unknown country and found himself in the mouth of a very large river. Unprepared to found a settlement, he returned to Dieppe and gave an account of his discovery. In view of the importance of such a voyage (if the account is to be accepted as trustworthy), why was it not known to his contemporaries? The claim seems to be unfounded, since no mention was made of it until 1785—a long time indeed to conceal so momentous a discovery. Furthermore, Cousin made the astonishing claim that he was accompanied by no less than Vicente Yáñez Pinzón, whom he claimed to have dismissed from service with the Dieppe fleet after a disagreement. Now either there were two Pinzóns with the same name, or Vicente Yáñez, who accompanied Columbus, was amazingly reticent about an earlier voyage which would have given him priority; this is highly unlikely.[25]

If Pedro Alvares Cabral was not the original discoverer of Brazil, there is certainly no dearth of candidates to keep the honor for Portugal; three of them will engage our attention here. First, we have the interesting case of the Bachelor of Cananéia. In 1531 Martim Afonso de Sousa, following the coast of Brazil to the Río de la Plata, put in at Cananéia (in the present state of São Paulo) and found a castaway, apparently a scholar (he is referred to as "O Bacheral da Cananeia"), who claimed to have been marooned there thirty years earlier; this would put him there in 1501, making him Brazil's oldest resident of Portuguese descent. But there is another reference, in a document of April 24, 1499, to a castaway also designated as *Bacheral*; it is expecting too much of coincidence to believe that there could have been two scholarly castaways. This would put him in Brazil two years earlier, and so the honor of discovery would obviously go to Portugal, since we have discounted the weak claim of Cousin. Various explanations have been advanced as to how he got there; the most interesting one for our purposes is the suggestion that he was left there by Bartolomeu Dias on a reconnaissance voyage in December, 1498, "as a living *padrão* of Portuguese sovereignty." [26] If true, this was a unique idea indeed!

What was Dias doing in Brazil in 1498? The hypothesis has been advanced that he could have discovered Brazil while on a reconnaissance or experimental voyage (or voyages) to prepare the way for Vasco da Gama and Cabral; it has been suggested that he probably sailed to São Tomé on such a voyage in December, 1498, with the result that we have already discussed above. Yet the author of this hypothesis readily admits that there are strong reasons for not accepting it.[27]

If we dismiss these hypotheses on the grounds of insufficient evidence, there still remains the claims of Duarte Pacheco Pereira. In his *Esmeraldo de Situ Orbis*, written for Dom Manuel in 1505–8, he wrote of a voyage in 1498 ordered by the king, and described a vast land mass which "has been found and navigated." Vague references as to its location, a reference to "this land of the Cross," and a mention of "much excellent brazil wood" south of the equator led some to believe that he had discovered the American continent or continents in that year. It has been suggested that the land mass might be Florida, or possibly Cuba; but Morison believes that Pacheco simply referred to all the land discovered prior to that year, and that his voyage was a failure. He rules out this and other Portuguese claims quite definitely: "That there was no Portuguese voyage to Brazil before Cabral's seems certain." [28]

The honor of discovering Brazil, then, must be divided between Pinzón (and perhaps Lepe, although Pinzón's discovery antedated his) and Cabral, who both reached its shores in 1500, and Vespucci. Since the Florentine apparently made a landfall in Brazil in the middle of 1499 and explored the Amazon, he would seem to have a six-month priority over Pinzón unless (an unlikely prospect) his account can be proved to be a complete fabrication, or, at least, a gross exaggeration. Yet all of these expeditions operated independently of one another, and so the credit must be divided. But since this part of the coast (or at least the major part of it) lay within the sphere assigned to Portugal by the Treaty of Tordesillas, and Spain repeatedly enjoined her navigators not to violate Portugal's rights, and since Cabral immediately detached a ship from his fleet to inform his king of the discovery (thereby being the first to report it to Europe), it does not seem improper to maintain that he must be counted as the *effective* discoverer of Brazil.[29]

But one major problem of priority remains, and this deals with the very important question of the discovery of the continent itself. Some of the claims of a pre-1498 discovery we have already discounted in discussing the discovery of Brazil, but two significant ones yet remain. There is, first of all, the problem of the alleged "first voyage" of Amerigo Vespucci in 1497–98, which would put him in the New World (on the continent, that is) a year ahead of the Admiral. There is considerable disagreement among Vespucci scholars as to whether this voyage must be accepted, or whether it must be completely disallowed.[30] Those who hold to the historicity of this voyage maintain that Vespucci, in the company of Juan de Solís and Vicente Yáñez Pinzón, cruised along the east coast of Central America, followed the coast of the Gulf of Mexico to Florida, sailed around that peninsula as far as Chesapeake Bay, then proceeded to Bermuda and back to Spain. Vespucci's mention of lands in the Torrid Zone would seem also to include the coast of South America, making this a remarkable voyage indeed and giving him the distinction of having discovered the continent.

It has hitherto been generally maintained that either this extravagant claim must be counted as true, or Vespucci must be branded a liar. But might there not be another solution? An interesting reinterpretation of the evidence has been made which accepts the veracity of the letters describing the "first" voyage, thereby removing the stigma of falsification from Vespucci, while at the same time demolishing the voyage.[31] In short, there was no such voyage; the geographical evidence has been grossly misinterpreted. By a careful investigation of the letters, it may be demonstrated that they actually refer to the "second" voyage in 1499, whose authenticity is nearly universally accepted. In this way such a puzzlement as reconciling the Gulf of Mexico and the Torrid Zone disappear, and the descriptions of the Indians and their customs tally with those usually attributed to the "second" voyage. Furthermore, Vespucci never claimed to have been in Central America or the Gulf of Mexico; this is the work of later scholars. There is still the problem of the date, 1497 instead of 1499. Since Vespucci was then in the service of Castile, the earlier date may have been given to claim priority over Duarte Pacheco rather than Columbus, as Las Casas believed.

The other claim is more unusual, for here we have no rival on the scene; this is a case of claiming for Columbus priority over himself, by asserting that he (or at least one of his ships) discovered the north coast of South America during the second voyage in 1494. The story first appeared, apparently, in López de Gómara's *Historia general de las Indias* in 1554,[32] and was based on a manuscript prepared in 1501 or 1502 by Angelo Trevisano, a secretary of the Venetian embassy to the Iberian kingdoms.[33] The claim attracted little attention until 1942 when an American scholar who had examined the manuscript (and much of the vast literature on Columbus as well) asserted that, on the basis of Trevisano's account, "The possibility must therefore be seriously considered that the South American continent was discovered on October 10, 1494." [34] According to the manuscript, Columbus sent five caravels from Española on September 28, 1494, to sail in a southeasterly direction in search of pearls. After twelve days of searching, their efforts were crowned with success; their purpose accomplished, they sailed along the coast for some 2,400 miles, returning eventually to Española on November 14.

Interesting as this may be, it is the sole account of such a venture, despite the rather extensive contemporary sources on the voyage of Columbus. The lack of a single shred of evidence in support of it, even in the lengthy *Pleitos de Colón*, where dozens of witnesses testified concerning the voyages, is certainly a compelling argument against the soundness of such a thesis.[35] Unless some corroborating evidence emerges to support the Trevisano document, which seems rather unlikely, we must disallow for Columbus, as we have for other claimants, any discovery prior to his landing on the coast of Paria on August 5, 1498.

NOTES

1. Fernando Colón, *The Life of the Admiral Christopher Columbus, by his Son, Ferdinand*, trans. Benjamin Keen (New Brunswick, N.J., 1959), p. 184.
2. Samuel Eliot Morison, *Admiral of the Ocean Sea* (Boston, 1942), Vol. II, p. 263; Antonio Ballesteros y Beretta, *Cristóbal Colón y el descubrimiento de América* (Barcelona, 1945), Vol. II, p. 377.
The exact location of this first landfall may never be known. Columbus himself, who did not realize at the time that Paria was a part of the continent, was not specific; Humboldt believed that the landing was made five leagues from Cape Lapa, and Morison, who made extensive personal investigations of the area, places the landing at Yacua inlet, about which Ballesteros expresses some misgivings. Navarrete favored Macuro inlet, which appears on today's charts as the Ensenada Cristóbal Colón, and boasts the small Puerto Cristóbal Colón. He cites Columbus' own account in his letter to his sovereigns. See Martín Fernández de Navarrete, *Colección de los viajes y descubrimientos que hicieron por mar los españoles desdel fin del siglo XV* (Madrid, 1825) Vol. I, p. 250. The Ensenada Cristóbal Colón and Puerto Cristóbal Colón may be located on the U.S. Navy Hydrographic Office Chart 5588 (Harbors in the Gulf of Paria) and 5586 (Island of Trinidad and the Eastern Part of the Gulf of Paria).
3. Morison, *Admiral*, Vol. II, pp. 223-288, gives an excellent detailed account of the voyage and its preparations.

4. On João II's geographical ideas, see Jaime Cortesão, *Os descubrimentos portuguêses* (Lisboa, 1962), Vol. II, Chap. III.

5. On the actual landing, see Morison, *op. cit.*, Vol II, pp. 258-63; Ballesteros, *op. cit.*, Vol. II, p. 377; Navarrete, *op. cit.*, Vol. I, pp. 249-50; Bartolomé de Las Casas, *Historia de las Indias* (Mexico, 1951), Bk. I, Chap. 133; Pedro Mártir de Angléria, *Décadas del Nuevo Mundo* (hereinafter cited as Peter Martyr), (Buenos Aires, 1944), pp. 64-65.

6. Accounts of the exploration of the coast may be found in Morison, *Admiral*, Vol. II, pp. 266-88; Colón (Keen trans.), *op. cit.*, pp. 185-87; Washington Irving, *A History of the Life and Voyages of Christopher Columbus* (London, 1828), Vol. II, pp. 381-87.

7. Accounts of Ojeda's activities may be found in Las Casas, *op. cit.*, Bk. I, Chaps. 164-66; Navarrete, *op. cit.*, Vol. III, pp. 4-11; Amando Melón, *Los primeros tiempos de la colonización* (Barcelona, 1952), pp. 6-10. There are also references in Spain, Ministro de Ultramar, *Colección de documentos inéditos relativos al descubrimiento, conquista, y colonización de las posesiones españolas en América y occidental* (Madrid, 1885-1932), 2nd ser., Vol. VIII, pp. 15, 30, 32 (hereinafter cited as *Documentos inéditos*).

8. Frederick J. Pohl, *Amerigo Vespucci, Pilot Major* (New York, 1944), p. 49. Manuel Ballesteros Gaibrois (*Historia de América*, Madrid, 1946, p. 158) mentions Ojeda's reference to a "Morigo Vespuce" in his correspondence between 1497 and 1504. The Portuguese Admiral Gago Coutinho (Portugal, Ministério do Ultramar, *A Náutica dos descobrimentos*, Lisboa, 1951, Vol. I, pp. 301-2) states that Vespucci's presence on the voyage is well attested by the Spanish archives, and asserts that he sailed under the command of Ojeda, as a subaltern to Cosa. He maintains that Ojeda reached a point north of the mouth of the Amazon, and that Vespucci, without mentioning Ojeda, falsified in claiming to have reached 8° south. In the *Décadas abreviadas de los descubrimientos, conquistas, fundaciones, y otras cosas notables acaecidas en las Indias occidentales desde 1492 a 1640* (*Documentos inéditos*, I Ser., Vol. VIII, p. 10), Vespucci is listed as a "merchant and as one learned in things of cosmography and of the sea."

9. Good accounts of Vespucci's part of the voyage can be found in Pohl, *op. cit.*, pp. 48-72, and Melón, *op. cit.*, pp. 144-46.

10. Contemporary accounts of Niño's expedition may be found in Las Casas, *op. cit.*, Bk. I, Chap. 170, and in Francisco López de Gómara, *Historia de las Indias* (in Andrés González de Barcia Carballido y Zuñiga, *Historiadores primitivos de las Indias Occidentales . . .* , Madrid, 1749, Vol. II). Navarrete's account (*op. cit.*, Vol. III, pp. 11-18) is based on the declaration of witnesses in the cause of Columbus, the *Pleito de Ojeda con Vergara y Ocampo*, and an Italian account printed in Milano in 1508. Perhaps the best contemporary account is that of Peter Martyr (Bk. VIII, Chaps. 1-3).

11. The text of the agreement between Bastidas and the sovereigns appears in the *Documentos inéditos*, I Ser., Vol. XXXVIII, pp. 433-38. There are repeated references to Bastidas as the discoverer of Darién and the Gulf of Urabá, rather than Columbus; see *ibid.*, I Ser., Vol. XIX, p. 407; I Ser., Vol. XXXIII, pp. 151, 201, 230-32; and II Ser., Vol. VII, p. 193 ff. A good account of the voyage appears in Navarrete, *op. cit.*, Vol. III, pp. 20-28.

12. The sources for this voyage are meager; cf. Melón, *op. cit.*, pp. 47-49. There is a brief account in Navarrete, *op. cit.*, Vol. III, pp. 24-25. On the supposed death of Luis Guerra and the loss of one of the ships, see Las Casas, *op. cit.*, Bk. I, Chap. 172.

13. For details of the voyage, see Las Casas, *op. cit.*, Bk. I, Chap. 172; Navarrete, *op. cit.*, Vol. III, pp. 18-21; Peter Martyr, Bk. IX, Chaps. I-II. There are references to Pinzón's discovery of C. Santa María de la Consolación (or C. Santo Agostinho, or Santa Cruz or Rostro Hermoso—all names are used) in the proceedings against Diego Colón (*Documentos Inéditos*, I Ser., Vol. XXXIX, pp. 346 ff.) in the *Décadas abreviadas* (*Ibid.*, I Ser., Vol. VIII, p. 10), and in Pinzón's capitulation (*Ibid.*, I Ser.,

Vol. XXX, p. 535-42). To the latter is appended an agreement with the sovereigns granting Pinzón four-fifths of the proceeds (deducting first the cost of the voyage) if he will return to the same locality within a year; there is the usual prohibition against taking slaves and encroaching on the lands of the king of Portugal, and one or two royal officials were to go along to ensure obedience, and share equally with the others.

14. Such is the belief of João Capistrano de Abreu, *O descobrimento do Brasil* (Rio de Janeiro, 1929), pp. 20-38.

15. Paul Vidal de la Blache (*La rivière Vincent Pinzon*, Paris, 1902, pp. 11-13) credits Pinzón with the discovery of Santa María de la Consolación, which he identifies as C. Santa Cruz or C. San Agustín (the Portuguese Santo Agostinho) and Rostro Hermoso, which Juan de la Cosa's map locates on the north coast of Brazil. The royal capitulation of September 1, 1501, refers to Pinzón's discoveries —"Santa María de la Consolación i Rostro-hermoso" and "Santa María de la Mar dulce" as well as the coast to C. St. Vincent. Peter Martyr spoke of the distance "from that point of land where the arctic pole is lost" to the Gulf of Paria as being about 300 leagues, and reported the discovery of a river of great width, the Marañón, by Pinzón; Navarrete proclaims him the discoverer of Brazil and the Marañón (Amazon). Cf. no. 13, above.

16. Jaime Cortesão (*Brasil*, Barcelona, 1956, pp. 216-19) rejects it, and cites Duarte Leite's *Descobridores do Brasil*, pp. 35 ff. in support of his contention. Leite challenged the report of a storm.

17. An eyewitness account of Cabral's voyage is that of Pêro Vaz de Caminha, which appears in modern Portuguese in Jaime Cortesão, *A carta de Pêro Vaz de Caminha* (Rio de Janeiro, 1943). Another good contemporary account is that of Las Casas, *op. cit.*, Bk. I, Chap. 173. Brief but satisfactory accounts can be found in Abreu, *op. cit.*, pp. 52-53; Cortesão, *Brasil*, pp. 194-204; Morison, *Portuguese Voyages to America in the Fifteenth Century* (Cambridge, Mass., 1940), pp. 95-119.

18. Cortesão, *A carta de Pêro Vaz de Caminha*, pp. 200-1.

19. Morison, *Portuguese Voyages*, pp. 111-12.

20. Las Casas (*op. cit.*, Bk. I, Chap. 73) states that the pilot's estimate was 10° S. —obviously a gross error!

21. Jaime Cortesão, *Cabral e as origens do Brasil* (Rio de Janeiro, 1944), p. 135.

22. Las Casas, *op. cit.*, Bk. I, Chap. 73.

23. Cortesão, *Brasil*, p. 204.

24. Las Casas, *op. cit.*, Bk. I, Chap. 73. This is the fullest account of the voyage. There is a short account in Melón, *op. cit.*, pp. 86-87, and Abreu, *op. cit.*, p. 39. Lepe's discovery of the Cape and the Marañón were attested to by members of the voyage in support of the Fiscal's action against Diego Colón in the *Probanzas* (*Documentos inéditos*, I Ser., Vol. XXXIX, pp. 357-8) and the *Pleitos* de Colón (*ibid.*, II Ser., Vol. VIII, p. 207).

25. Abreu (*op. cit.*, pp. 11-17) gives a careful and scholarly critique of Gaffarel's extravagant thesis.

26. Jaime Cortesão, *Os descobrimentos portuguêses*, Vol. II, p. 69. The whole affair of the bachelor, from which this account is taken, appears on pp. 64-69.

27. Gago Coutinho. The suggestion concerning the date of the voyage was advanced by Cortesão, (*Os descobrimentos*, p. 64).

28. Morison, *Portuguese Voyage*, p. 141. The whole Pacheco problem is discussed on pp. 132-41. Morison's conclusions would also rule out the suggestion in Peschel's *Geschichte des Zeitalters der Entdeckungen* (cited in Abreu, *op. cit.*, pp. 55-56) that Vasco da Gama passed along the coast of Brazil for some time in August of 1497, sighting birds and other signs of land, and would rule out this rather remote and tenuous contact as a discovery, even if it could be substantiated.

29. It has been suggested by several historians that Cabral's discovery was by no means accidental, but was planned. On this, see Cortesão, *Os descobrimentos portuguêses*, Vol. II, pp. 73-75 and especially Charles E. Nowell, "The Discovery of Brazil—Accidental or International?" *Hispanic American Historical Review* XVI (August, 1936): 311-38.

30. The American Pohl and the Italian Magnaghi do not accept the historicity of the "first" voyage, but the Argentine historian Levillier (*América la bien llamada,* 2 vols., Buenos Aires, 1948) is adamant in insisting that all four voyages must be accepted.

31. Arthur Davies, "The 'First' Voyage of Amerigo Vespucci in 1497–8," *Geographical Journal* CXVIII (1952); 331-37.

32. Cf. Morison, *Admiral of the Ocean Sea,* Vol. II, p. 290.

33. Known today as the Sneyd-Thatcher Manuscript; it may be found in the Rare Book Room of the Library of Congress, Washington, D.C.

34. William Jerome Wilson, "The Historicity of the 1494 Discovery of South America," *Hispanic American Historical Review* XXII (February, 1942): 193-205.

35. Such is the opinion of Charles E. Nowell in his "Reservations Regarding the Historicity of the 1494 Discovery of South America," *Hispanic American Historical Review* XXII (February, 1942): 205-10.

II *Sixteenth-Century*

Maritime Exploration: The Outline of

the Continent

THE NORTH COAST

Once the great discoveries of Columbus, Vespucci, Pinzón, and Cabral had been accomplished, subsequent navigators made rapid progress in exploring not only the coasts already discovered, but those of the remainder of the continent as well. With almost astonishing rapidity (given the distances and difficulties involved, as well as the comparative smallness of the vessels engaged), the general shape of the continent became known to Europeans. Beginning with a vague representation of the north and northeast coast, cartographers were able, within a few decades, to map both the Atlantic and the Pacific coastlines with a fair degree of accuracy.

We have already seen how the Caribbean coast was explored, subsequent to Columbus' discovery, by Alonso de Ojeda and Amerigo Vespucci, Per Alonso Niño, the Guerra brothers, and Rodrigo de Bastidas and Juan de la Cosa. In 1501 Ojeda sought the permission of his sovereigns to undertake a second voyage to the same area. Again he profited from the support of Bishop Juan Rodríguez de Fonseca, for in March of 1501 he was granted a royal license to cut thirty quintals (a quintal equaling a hundred-weight) of brazilwood in Española "and in whatever other islands of the Ocean Sea it might be found." [1] An agreement with the bishop was concluded and was found satisfactory to Their Highnesses, who then authorized him to equip up to ten vessels and sail to "the island of Coquibacoa" in "Tierra-Firme," investigate the pearl areas, and look for gold; he was also given the governorship of Coquibacoa (June 8), with full power to administer royal justice (June 10).[2]

Associated with Ojeda in the venture were Juan de Vergara and García del Campo, with whom he concluded an agreement on July 5, 1501, to share equally all the profits of the voyage, even his salary as governor.[3] Despite his efforts to equip the authorized ten ships, even with the aid of his companions he could only manage to fit out four, which were captained by Vergara, del Campo, Pedro de Ojeda (nephew of Alonso), and Hernando de Guevara.[4] The expedition sailed from Cádiz early in January of 1502, stopping briefly at Gran Canaria and later in the Cape Verde Islands for ten days to take on food. After reaching Paria in March, Ojeda dispersed his ships in the rivers for calking, and traded with the Indians for pearls. Resuming his course later, he sailed along the coast until March 12, when he was informed by the *veedor* that he had left the land forbidden to him in the royal *cédula*, and so he made provisions to land and exercise the full trading rights which were his.

At this point Guevara, in his light caravel, lagged several leagues behind the convoy. Ojeda, fearing this would slow him up, ordered the other vessels to set full sail, with the result that they lost Guevara, who sailed most of the night searching for them in vain, and finally headed direct for Codera, where Ojeda had intended to go. Upon arriving he found only the flagship, the *Santa María de la Antigua*—the others had been sent in search of him. The search vessels sailed in the waters around Margarita. Captain Vergara would not land or permit his crew to do so, but Captain Pedro de Ojeda was less troubled by rules and scruples and, landing on the island on the pretext of taking on water, engaged in a lively trade for pearls and *guanín*. Alonso de Ojeda, meanwhile, weary of waiting, sailed along the coast to a place he named Valfermoso, and which the Indians called Curiana, trading for pearls. The ships which had been on the search met him here; the leaders consulted among themselves over the shortage of provisions, and finally decided to gather the essentials for founding a colony elsewhere by the simple expedient of taking them from the neighboring Indians. Attacking them without warning, they killed seven or eight, burned their homes (despite Ojeda's strict orders), and confiscated hammocks, household goods, cotton, and some Indian women, most of whom they traded for *guanín*. This raid failed to produce enough provisions, so Ojeda, with the consent of the others, sent Vergara to Jamaica to buy what was necessary and join them at Maracaibo.[5] Ojeda then proceeded to Curaçao, and later to Coquibacoa, where he landed, took on water, an Indian woman, and a rabbit like those of Castile. But the country seemed so miserable that he did not linger; he proceeded instead to Santa Cruz (Bahía Honda), where he found one Juan de Buenaventura, who had been left there by Bastidas and had lived among the Indians, trading with them and learning their language. The Indians seemed peaceable enough until the Spaniards tried to make a settlement there; this attempt was greeted with a volley of arrows. When Ojeda appeared with a band of armed men the Indians sued for peace and got rid of the Spaniards by bringing them a little gold and *guanín* and telling them that a neighboring cacique (some distance to the west, naturally) had much more of it.

This cacique proved to be equally obdurate in the matter of a settlement, and Ojeda had to build a fort to maintain himself there. Santa Cruz was actually west of the limits assigned to Ojeda in the royal grant, and he was later accused of deliberately founding a settlement in lands discovered by Bastidas, although it is very doubtful that he was aware of it. When del Campo and Vergara finally arrived from Jamaica, they seized and shackled Ojeda on the charge of not paying the royal fifth, and took him to Española to turn him over to the governor. The date of his return to Spain in disgrace is not known, but he subsequently cleared himself by proving that Vergara and del Campo, rather than he, had helped themselves rather freely to the royal fifth, and he was restored to all his rights on November 8, 1503.[6]

On November 15, 1504, there was issued in favor of Ojeda an order of payment of 200,000 maravedís by the royal treasurer in consideration of his services to the crown, and to pay the salaries of fifty men for five months and equip two, three, or more ships to return to Coquibacoa, the isles of pearls, and the Gulf of Urabá.[7] A *cédula* of March 10, 1505, repeated the license and authorized the construction of a tower or fortress. The Casa de Contratación was ordered to prepare vessels for the voyage. One Portuguese caravel was obtained, and two others were built; the three were sent to Española in 1506, and the governor was told to make them available to Ojeda. Little is known about this third voyage. It apparently was of short duration, and was probably accomplished in one, or at the most two, vessels. Ojeda seems to have reached Coquibacoa and doubled Cape de la Vela, proceeding on to the Gulf of Urabá. There is no record of his having gone ashore, so the voyage could not have produced any pecuniary profit.[8]

Despite this apparent failure, Ojeda was able to undertake a fourth voyage. A capitulation of July 9, 1508, made him governor of "Tierra-Firme" from Cape de la Vela to the Gulf of Urabá, which land Queen Juana named Nueva Andalucía; Juan de la Cosa was named his lieutenant. At the same time Diego de Nicuesa was granted the governorship of "Castilla del Oro," which was to extend from the other half of the Gulf of Urabá to Cape Gracias a Dios—the land Columbus had explored on his fourth voyage. The expedition sailed from Española on November 10, 1509, ahead of Nicuesa (who was disputing the boundary of their respective domains) in two *navíos* and two brigantines, with a crew of

225. Because Ojeda was too poor to equip a fleet, Cosa and others chartered three of the ships, and Martín Fernández de Enciso provided the other.[9]

This expedition seems to have been one grand disaster. Despite the warning of Cosa that the Calamar Indians used poisoned arrows, and his recommendation to go on to Urabá, where they were less fierce, Ojeda insisted on attacking this coastal people in the hope of securing slaves. Meeting with a measure of success in a surprise attack, he next sought booty and attacked their neighbors, the Turbacos. This venture was to prove excessively costly: Ojeda lost seventy men, among them Juan de la Cosa, whose body was found the following day under a tree, badly disfigured from poison. Boats from the ships landed after the battle, and a search was begun for survivors. Ojeda was found, sword in hand, his shield showing more than three hundred dents from arrows. Fortunately Nicuesa was in the vicinity, and on learning of the disaster went to look for Ojeda. They joined forces for a surprise attack, killed every Indian they could find, regardless of age or sex, and appropriated a large amount of booty. This brief partnership proved to be profitable in another way, for Ojeda and Nicuesa settled their differences, and parted friends. Sailing now for Urabá, Ojeda went ashore upon arrival and founded the town of San Sebastián, the first Spanish settlement on South American soil.[10]

THE COAST OF BRAZIL

The first planned voyage to Brazil after Cabral's discovery was that proposed to Diego de Lepe by Bishop Fonseca, a good friend of his. A royal capitulation of September 14, 1501, licensed Lepe to discover lands and islands in the "Ocean Sea . . . and that part of the Indies where you went before," with the usual injunction to stay away from the domains of "the Most Serene King of Portugal, Our very dear and very beloved Son." [11] The line of the Treaty of Tordesillas did not extend farther west, by any interpretation, than the mouth of the Amazon, so much of the northern coast of Brazil was not included in this restriction. But the expedition never materialized, for in the midst of preparations, Lepe decided to go to Portugal to learn what he could about expeditions being prepared there for Brazil, and there he died unexpectedly.[12]

Spain proceeded to forget the Brazil project, but Amerigo Vespucci, who had planned to go with Lepe, did not; he had been there, it will be recalled, the year before, and was most anxious to return. With the death of Lepe he was no longer obligated to Spain, and so took service with the king of Portugal [13] and sailed from Lisboa with three caravels on

May 13, 1501. If the other voyages of Vespucci might be called into question, his presence on this "third" voyage seems beyond question; the uncertainty, as we shall see, is with respect to the extent, not the fact, of his discoveries. Again, the objective was to explore the coast until the "Strait of Catigara" could be found, which would open the way to India.[14]

The three caravels made their first stop at Cape Verde, where they encountered two ships of Cabral's, returning from India. From conversations with some members of the crew, Vespucci learned of the inadequacy of Ptolemy's geographical concepts with respect to India and the adjacent lands, and also of Cabral's discovery of Brazil, which he recognized as the same land he had previously explored.[15] Leaving the cape, Vespucci sailed some sixty-four days and reached the coast of Brazil; two of the ships made a landfall at about 5° south and found the bend of the coast, which they named Cape São Roque. The third vessel reached a point about 15° south and made a landfall near Santa Elena. This was near Pôrto Seguro, which had been agreed on as the destination and base of the expedition. Vespucci, with the other ships, left on a southerly course, reaching Cabo (Cape) Santo Agostino on August 28; they arrived at the Rio São Francisco on October 3, and entered the Bahia de Todos os Santos ("All Saints Bay") on November 1; it will be noted how the place names followed the calendar of the saints, in accordance with the custom of the time.[16]

By now Vespucci was convinced that Columbus' concept of what he had discovered was in error, and that the land he was exploring, whatever it might be, was not a part of Asia. We find no use of the term "Indians" to describe the "cannibals" with whom he tells us he lived for twenty-seven days (providing a detailed picture of their life and customs),[17] and subsequently he referred to this land as a "New World." The expedition then proceeded on to Cape Frio, near Rio de Janeiro, and this, according to some authorities, marks the southern limit of the voyage. One of the early historians of the Indies does not even put him this far; he mentions a voyage of "four ships" to Cape Santo Agostinho, stating categorically that they did not reach the Río de la Plata, as Vespucci claimed.[18] More recently it has been held that the voyage unquestionably never proceeded beyond Cape Frio;[19] others challenge the entire account of the voyage, referring to Vespucci as "that obscure merchant, . . . a very bad astronomer and incompetent sailor,"[20] and claiming to find too many errors and contradictions in his letters.[21]

Nonetheless, there is too much solid evidence favoring the veracity of the voyage and its accuracy (at least, in general), to dismiss it so lightly. To continue with the voyage as Vespucci reported it, we find him sailing into Guanabara Bay, and describing its striking landmark, Corcovado, quite accurately. He then proceeded to Cananéia, where Pohl believes he erected a *padrão* to mark the line of Tordesillas; it is significant that from here on he gave descriptive names to geographical features, rather than naming them formally for saints; apparently he was leaving this to the Spaniards, for this was land under their jurisdiction. Sailing still to the south in search of the strait, he encountered the Río de la Plata (which he named the Jordan River), and, recognizing it as part of a great river rather than a passage to the west, continued the search south. If we accept Vespucci's report as wholly reliable, we must then credit him with reaching and naming "Porto de San Giuliano" at latitude 49° south, in Patagonia, and then sailing north, because the approaching end of summer (it was February 27) made a further search to the south impractical. According to his letter to Lorenzo, he had sailed in the southern hemisphere nearly ten months.[22]

There remains to be considered the role of the Portuguese navigator Gonçalo Coelho at this time. Was he in command of Vespucci's "third" voyage in 1501, or the "fourth" in 1503? [23] And what of this "fourth" voyage? Did it ever take place? Not all the historians favorable to Vespucci accept it; two of them, Magnaghi and Pohl, limit the Florentine to two, in 1499 and 1501, doubting the authenticity of the letters referring to the "first" and "fourth" voyages. Levillier, Vespucci's most ardent supporter, insists that there were indeed four, and Gago Coutinho, who is loath to concede anything to Amerigo, does mention a voyage in 1503, which he describes as primarily a commerical venture in company with Damião de Góis. The commander of the expedition is not named, but is referred to as "incompetent." [24]

According to Varnhagen's account,[25] the king of Portugal organized an expedition in 1503 which was to sail along the coast of South America, find the strait, and proceed to the Orient to take on a cargo of spices. Six ships were readied, and Vespucci was given the command of two of them. Coelho, an experienced navigator, was placed in command of the fleet and, in Varnhagen's belief, Juan Díaz de Solís was probably along. The expedition sailed in the middle of 1503, took on supplies at São Tiago in the Cape Verde group, and reached an unknown island (Fernando de Noronha) on August 10, where the flagship was wrecked. Here the squadron separated. Vespucci's and one other ship sailed to Bahia de Todos os Santos to await the others there. After remaining for more than two months, they sailed south as far as Cape Frio and, taking on a cargo of brazilwood, set course for Europe, arriving in Lisboa on June 18, 1504. Coelho, meanwhile, sailed south to Guanabara Bay, where he set up camp near the present site of Rio de Janeiro, possibly on the stream called Carioca. Using this as a base of operations, Coelho directed explorations as far south as the Río de la Plata and the Bahía de San Matías before abandoning the search for the strait and returning home.

After Coelho's visit there is a hiatus of several years before ships again appear in the vicinity of Brazil. On March 22, 1508, a royal *cédula* was issued in Castile directing Vicente Yáñez Pinzón and Juan Díaz de Solís to sail to the New World in May.[26] A capitulation on the following day gave detailed instructions, including a directive to overhaul any vessels sailing west of the line of Tordesillas without a license, and to inform them that they are not to sail to any areas belonging to the crown of Castile.[27] The reality of this voyage is not doubted, but there is much disagreement concerning the route. Navarrete gives it its greatest extent, claiming that the ship sailed from Sanlúcar on June 29, 1508, to the Cape Verde Islands, then to Cape Santo Agostinho, then along the coast to about 40° south, which would put it near the mouth of the Río Colorado, south of the present site of Bahía Blanca. Dissensions brought an end to the expedition, which returned to Castile at the end of October, 1509. Herrera, on the other hand, mentions only that it touched Cape Santo Agostinho, while José Toribio Medina has it touch there, then continue along the Caribbean coast to Veragua, thence to Española; Melón is inclined to believe that it went to the coast of "Tierra-Firme" and then west and north to Honduras and the latitude of Tampico in Mexico.[28] In view of such disagreement, we can scarcely give the voyage an important place in the exploration of the littoral.

One more voyage deserves mention, that of Cristóbal de Haro in 1514; this was the last attempt, under the flag of Portugal, to seek the strait prior to its actual discovery. Haro was a business man, manager of the main office of his family's trading firm (which originated in Burgos) in Lisboa. Much interested in the spice trade, he sought a western route to the Moluccas (Spice Islands), and sent two ships to seek a passage. Sailing along the coast of South America, they seem to have explored the estuary subsequently called the Río de la Plata, and, in the belief that this was the strait (despite its fresh, muddy water which seems to have convinced Vespucci that it was not), they returned to Portugal. A subsequent globe made by Johann Schöner indicates a strait at this latitude, with a vast continent (generally believed to exist) to the south of it.[29]

THE DISCOVERY OF THE PACIFIC OCEAN AND THE STRAIT

The most important single discovery after Columbus found the continent of South America was the discovery of the Pacific Ocean by Vasco Núñez de Balboa in 1513, which was to prove that the lands of the "Indies" were not (at least, not the southern part) an extension of Asia but what Vespucci had suspected them to be—a new world. The antecedents of the discovery go back to the fourth voyage of Alonso de Ojeda, who, it will be recalled, had founded the settlement of San Sebastián on the Gulf of Urabá, named, appropriately enough, for the patron saint against arrows. Even here there was to be no repose; Ojeda was ambushed, wounded in the thigh by a poisoned arrow, and was saved only when he ordered the surgeon to bind two red-hot irons to the wound on the threat of hanging if he did not do so.[30] Hunger proved to be a worse problem; the settlement was saved only by the timely arrival of the scoundrel Bernardino de Talavera, who, fleeing from justice in Española, stole a ship laden with supplies and by chance put in at San Sebastián. Ojeda left the garrison in charge of Francisco Pizarro and returned with Talavera and Enciso (second in command of the garrison), who was to return with supplies. On reaching Española, Ojeda decided to give up the world and entered a Franciscan friary.[31]

On his return trip with supplies, Enciso found a stowaway hidden in a cask to escape his creditors in Española—Vasco Núñez de Balboa, who had previously visited the coast of "Tierra-Firme" with Rodrigo de Bastidas. This tall, vigorous, intelligent soldier was a godsend to Enciso, who could not handle his men; upon landing, Balboa took stock of the situation, and decided to move the settlement to Darién, a safer location with adequate supplies of food. There he founded the town of Santa María la Antigua. Eventually coming to a disagreement with Enciso, Balboa arrested and deposed him, and sent him back to Spain, assuming the office of Captain-General and Governor *ad interim* until a permanent assignment was made by the king. In this capacity he proved to be quite competent; he explored the coast some twenty-five leagues to the west, and enjoyed good relations with the Indians, baptizing two chieftains and marrying the daughter of one of them.[32]

Through this relationship Balboa first learned of Peru. While gold was being weighed for him by one of the caciques whom he had baptized, his son overturned the scale and told Balboa that to the south lay a land incredibly rich in gold, which he could conquer with one thousand men. Between them and this land lay the sea. Making preparations immediately, Balboa departed on September 1, 1513, with 190 Spaniards and 810 Indians in a chartered brigantine and ten large canoes, disembarking west of Puerto Bello in the domains of his father-in-law. Some of the members of the expedition tarried there, while the rest pushed on, led by Balboa, through a dense forest crossed by numerous arroyos, and subjected constantly to grave danger from the fierce caymans and large serpents in the region. Reaching the village of the cacique Ponca, Balboa presented him with gifts and asked directions. Ponca pointed to a distant range, from the crest of which, he said, the sea was visible. Ahead lay the land of Cuarecua, whose cacique, Torecha, was at war with Ponca; here the Spaniards were confronted with a very difficult passage through sloughs and a dense, murky atmosphere, with frequent torrential showers. It was five days before they were able to set up camp and build a fire, whereupon Torecha appeared with his army and ordered them out if they did not want to be killed to the last man. The Spaniards took up the challenge, and killed six hundred Indians, including Torecha; entering his house in the village nearby, they found his brother and others in women's clothes, and threw them to their mastiffs until Balboa appeared and put an end to it.[33]

Because of the illness of a number of his men, Balboa left them in the village and set out in the morning with a small force of sixty-seven to cross the cordillera. The summit was reached on the morning of September 25, Sunday; Balboa was first to see what he named the "South Sea" and got on his knees, as did the others, while a solemn Te Deum was intoned. A large tree was cut down, from which a cross was fashioned as a sign of taking possession, and a notary drew up appropriate documents. In the vicinity was the powerful cacique Chiapes, who took up arms against the Spaniards but finally submitted before Spanish shotguns, fierce mastiffs, and the timely eruption of a nearby volcano, which terrified his people. Balboa was given a hospitable reception after this show of force, and awaited the arrival of the remainder of his men who had been recuperating in the domains of Careta.[34] Meanwhile, three small parties pushed on to determine the shortest route to the sea. After two days Alonso Martín found three canoes, but no water. Shortly the tide came in and floated the canoes. Martín jumped into one of them, calling on his men to witness that he was the first to enter the South Sea.[35] The news was brought to Balboa, who quickly marched to the sea with his whole force, reaching it on September 29 (St. Michael's Day). With due (perhaps exaggerated) solemnity he strode into the water with drawn sword, took possession of the sea and all its coasts and islands for Castile, and offered to defend his sovereign's rights against any prince, Christian or infidel, from the Arctic to the Antarctic regions. A priest blessed the waters, which were named the Gulf of San Miguel, and appropriate documents were drawn up giving testimony of their priority.[36]

Once news of this discovery was communicated to Spain, the court became more anxious than ever to locate the strait that must connect the "North Sea" with the "South Sea." We find, in a royal *cédula* of August 20, 1514, addressed to the governor and Captain-general of Castilla del Oro, Pedrarias Dávila, a discussion of the importance of this discovery and the necessity of establishing communication between the two seas. Every inlet was hoped to be the strait, and the coast was carefully explored from Urabá to Florida and beyond, with negative results. The higher latitudes of North America were searched, and plans were even considered for digging a canal at Nombre de Dios in Panama, Nicaragua, or Tehuantepec in Mexico.[37] With nothing but failure in the north, a diligent search was conducted along the coast of South America, where Vespucci had sought in vain the strait leading to the supposed Sinus Magnus.

The first Spanish navigator to seek the strait when the news of the discovery of the South Sea had been made public was Juan Díaz de Solís, who, since the death of Vespucci, was Pilot Major of the Casa de Contratación. On November 24, 1514, he signed an agreement with the king "to discover along the other part of Castilla del Oro";[38] Solís was to go "a las espaldas de la tierra" (to the shoulders of the land[39]) with three vessels. The king would get one-third of the proceeds, Solís and those who had invested in the voyage one-third, and the remaining third was to go to those who accompanied him. It is believed by Capistrano de Abreu and Fortunato de Almeida that the expedition was motivated by news of the Haro expedition and the fear that the passage to the South Sea might be found by the Portuguese.[40]

The expedition suffered ill luck at the very beginning. Shortly before the scheduled departure the largest ship foundered, losing all the provisions. The king ordered immediate aid to Solís, who procured another vessel and was able to set sail from Sanlúcar on October 8, 1515. After a brief stay in Tenerife, the expedition sailed on to Brazil, reaching the reddish cliffs of Cape São Roque and then continuing on along the coast past Guanabara Bay, Cananéia, an island they named La Plata (Santa Catarina), and on to 35° south. Here, in February, 1516, they entered the "Mar Dulce" (Freshwater Sea—the Río de la Plata) believing that it might be the long-sought passage to India—a belief finally abandoned because water proved to be fresh so far as they proceeded. Solís and a small party went ashore on the left bank of the Arroyo de las Vacas, where they were attacked by Indians who killed all of them but a small cabin boy, who was to live with them until rescued later by Sebastian Cabot. Some chronicles describe the Indians as cannibals, and maintain that Solís and his companions were eaten in full view of those still aboard ship, but this is to be doubted strongly. The command now passed to Francisco de Torres, who decided to return to Spain immediately, and arrived in September with a cargo of logwood.[41]

The voyage of Solís, even though it failed of its purpose, revived Spanish interest in the Spice Islands, and on March 26, 1518, a royal capitulation revived "Hernando Magallanes and the Bachelor Luis Falero" (Fernão de Magalhães e Sousa and Rui Faleiro) to discover unknown lands within the Spanish sphere, and to seek the strait to the Spice Islands, with a share in the profits and the right of governing all lands discovered. Magalhães, or Magellan, was a Portuguese who, after an education at court, entered the Portuguese India service, sailing with Francisco de Almeida, Nuno Vaz Pereira, and Diogo Lopes de Sequera to Mombasa, India, and Malacca. In 1511 he had taken a part, along with Francisco Serrão, in the capture of Malacca (under Albuquerque), and may have made a voyage into the South China Sea and to New Guinea. Later he participated in an expedition against Morocco, where an unjust accusation led him to go to court to demand justice. Dom Manuel, who already had received an unfavorable report on him from Albuquerque, sent him back, where he discovered that he had been cleared. Nonetheless, the incident and the report were sufficient to cause the king to refuse to authorize his proposed voyage to the Moluccas, but he allowed him to seek the support of other monarchs. While preparing to leave Portugal, Magellan met one Rui Faleiro, who was piqued over not being named to the chair of astrology (i.e., astronomy) at the University of Coimbra, and they joined forces. Faleiro claimed to be a great astrologer, but there seems to have been considerable doubt concerning his ability; Las Casas, who met them both in Valladolid, remarked that "the Portuguese claim that he has a familiar demon and that he knows nothing of astrology." [42] Magellan, however, impressed him.

Assisted by the wealthy merchant Cristóbal de Haro, who had already made a voyage to the east coast of South America, as we have seen, Magellan arrived in Sevilla in 1517 and took up residence in the house of Diogo Barbosa (whose daughter he later married), a Portuguese with connections at the Casa de Contratación. One of these connections was the factor, Juan de Aranda, who took Magellan and Faleiro to Valladolid to meet the Grand Chancellor and Bishop Fonseca, both of whom were impressed by Magellan's idea. Aranda was willing to win the king over to the project for a price—one-fifth of the profits (which Magellan finally reduced to one-eighth). Magellan's idea was that the Moluccas lay within the Spanish sphere, and that he could reach them by sailing west without touching Portuguese territory. Carlos' doubts were finally resolved when Magellan offered to go personally and when Cristóbal de Haro expressed a willingness to fit out the fleet at his own expense. The king then decided to equip the fleet himself, and the capitulation was signed. [43]

Magellan's geographical concepts were based, according to Pigafetta, who accompanied him on the voyage, on a map he saw in the treasury of the king of Portugal, made by Martim Behaim, or perhaps by Heinrich Hammer and based on Behaim's globe. As we have indicated before, the map showed a long peninsula extending south from east Asia, separated from an island by a strait; the whole looked much like the east coast of South America, with Tierra del Fuego. This peninsula was actually taken from Ptolemy's map and represented the Malay peninsula. Magellan, who had been to Malacca, knew that the peninsula did not extend south of the equator as depicted, and so assumed that it must represent one farther east and lying within the

Spanish domains. Like Columbus, he felt that the Indies were not too far from Spain; his geographical concepts were more Columbian than Vespucian. Furthermore, he had received a letter from Francisco Serrão, now settled comfortably in the Moluccas, telling him of their fantastic wealth, and exaggerating the distance from Malacca, so that Magellan was more than ever convinced that they truly lay within the Spanish sphere.[44]

The voyage did not get off to a good start. The original sailing date of August 25, 1518, had to be changed, for the five ships authorized by the king had not even been purchased at that time. Capital for cargoes to trade in the East was provided by private investors, chief among them Haro, the only one to realize a profit on his investment. No maps of the proposed route were available in the Casa de Contratación, so three Portuguese cartographers were put to work to prepare charts. And there was further trouble. Dom Manuel had told his agent in Sevilla to prevent the departure of the fleet, and not to scruple concerning the means; his efforts, however, were unavailing. Then Faleiro, whose contact with reality was becoming more and more tenuous, began to make a nuisance of himself, and Fonseca replaced him with Juan de Cartagena and Andrés de San Martín, while the king provided busy work elsewhere for the deposed captain. Finally, after many delays, preparations were complete; the fleet left Sevilla on August 10, 1519, and after a long delay at Sanlúcar, departed on September 20 for the Canaries. The crew numbered 241 men from several European countries, and included two Malays. There was a large number of supernumeraries (among them Pigafetta), as well as Duarte Barbosa, cousin of Magellan's wife, who would eventually command the *Victoria*.[45]

After stops for a few days at Tenerife and Monte Rojo for provisions, the fleet sailed into the Ocean Sea at noon on Monday, October 3. Magellan sailed near to the coast of Africa as far as the equator, a decision which caused dissension between him and Cartagena. After nearly two months of almost continual rain, the fleet was becalmed in the horse latitudes for twenty days, with sufferings reminiscent of Columbus' difficulties. Finally, rescued by the trade winds, the fleet moved on, reaching the coast of "Verzin" (as Pigafetta called Brazil) in December; following the royal injunction to stay out of Portuguese domains, Magellan gave the coast a wide berth until he reached 20° south, where he believed the line of Tordesillas reached the sea. Putting to shore, the mariners traded trinkets for foodstuffs; one Indian even gave six fowls for a playing card (the ace of diamonds) and departed happy in the belief that he had got the better of the deal. After thirteen days in Brazil, the expedition sailed south to the vicinity of 35°, entering the "Río Solís" (Río de la Plata) after a thorough search of every inlet along the way. Magellan's hope that this was the strait (he had expected to find it at this latitude) was dashed after a careful exploration, and he continued south until he found a safe anchorage for the winter at Port San Julián, nearly 55° south—the presumed southern limit of Vespucci's earlier voyage.

Here, Pigafetta tells us, they found an abundance of "geese" (penguins) and "seawolves"; what is more interesting, however, is his account of "giants" so tall that the explorers came only up to their waists. (Another chronicler of the voyage, Maximilian of Transylvania, is not quite so generous in his estimate, assigning them only a height of ten spans— seven and one-half feet.) They had no homes, he said, only skin tents, and lived on a certain sweet root, and on the raw flesh of guanacos and rats, which they ate without skinning them. Either because of their large feet, or the skin coverings which they wore on them, Magellan called them *"Patagones."* [46]

At Port San Julián mutiny developed. The men, because of the severity of the winter and the barrenness of the land, sought an increase in the ration and urged Magellan to think of turning back; he only replied that the course had been laid down by Caesar himself and he would not think of altering it. Furthermore, Magellan had never taken Cartagena into his confidence, and he, who viewed himself as the guardian of Spain's interest, believed (and not without cause) that Magellan favored the Portuguese too much. The mutiny broke out on the *San Antonio* (whose captain, the Portuguese Alvaro de Mesquita was deposed in favor of Elcano) and the *Victoria*, but the latter vessel was recaptured by a ruse and taken over by Duarte Barbosa, whereupon the mutiny began to collapse. A trial was held under Mesquita; forty men were sentenced to death on April 7, but Magellan commuted the sentences of all but one, Quesada, who had killed a man. Cartagena and his accomplice, the priest Pedro Sánchez de Reina, were ordered marooned on shore with some biscuits and a few bottles of wine.[47]

It was proposed to Magellan by the pilot Estevão Gómes that he sail east to Malacca at latitude 50°, but Magellan stated that he proposed to go as far south as 75° before sailing east. Gómes nearly persuaded the men to put Magellan in irons until he suggested rescuing Cartagena, who would be restored to command. This they would not do. Finally, at 52° south, on October 21, the fleet rounded a cape named by Magellan for the Eleven Thousand Virgins, and entered what all thought to be an inlet, but which Magellan insisted was the strait he had seen on the map in Dom Miguel's treasury. The *San Antonio* and the *Concepción* were sent out to investigate, and only by chance discovered a turn which showed them that this was indeed the strait. At this point Estevão Gómes, pilot of the *San Antonio*, organized a conspiracy, seized Mesquita, and sailed back to Spain. Magellan, unaware of the desertion, sent Duarte Barbosa back to the entrance of the strait to look for him, but in vain. Meanwhile, after tarrying a few days in Puerto Deseado (as Magellan named the safe haven he found in the passage) and taking on fish, mussels, herbs, and wool (from the guanaco), they left the strait and on November 28, 1520, entered a great ocean which was so calm that Magellan called it the Pacific Sea. The way to the Orient and its fabulous wealth lay ahead.[48]

Magellan, of course, died in the Philippines, and only the *Victoria*, commanded now by Sebastián de Elcano, returned to Spain to complete the first circumnavigation of the globe. A few years later, in 1525, García Jofré de Loyasa prepared a fleet of seven vessels for the Moluccas trade and sailed out of the harbor of Coruña on July 24. So busy a waterway had the Atlantic become that the fleet met a Portuguese ship on the equator; amenities were exchanged, and letters taken back to Spain. After reaching the coast of Brazil, and sailing south for the Río de la Plata, a storm scattered the fleet and the flagship was separated from it. Farther south, near the Strait of Magellan, the *San Gabriel* got separated, and the captains, led by Sebastián de Elcano, decided to enter the strait and leave instructions for the missing vessels to meet them at "Puerto Sardinas" (Magellan's Puerto Deseado). Misfortune continued to dog the enterprise. While searching for the entrance to the strait, the vessels were driven near the shore by a violent storm, and the *Sancti Spiritus* ran aground and broke up. To add to the disaster, Captain Pedro de Vera of the *Anunciada*, frustrated by strong winds in several attempts to join the others, decided to try for the Moluccas via the Cape of Good Hope and was never seen again. And Captain Rodrigo de Acuña of the *San Gabriel*, on being given an order with which he strongly disagreed, disappeared with his ship; actually, he had tried in vain to reach the predetermined rendezvous at the Río Santa Cruz, then sailed north for provisions, met some French cruisers, and went aboard one of them to be informed that France and Spain were at war and that he could not return to his ship. The *San Gabriel* would not surrender, and sailed on to Spain. The remainder of the vessels finally passed through the strait in May, 1526, only to be scattered by a storm and never meet again. Loyasa died on July 30, and de Elcano produced a secret royal order naming him his successor; he died a few days later, on August 4, and successors were elected thereafter. Of the original seven vessels, two crossed the Pacific, and the pinnace *Pataca* reached Mexico.[49]

Undaunted by previous failures, which by now had cost hundreds of lives, yet another expedition undertook the passage of the strait in 1534, this one headed by Simón de Alcazaba, a Portuguese officer in the service of Spain whose friends at court had got him an extensive grant in the southern part of the continent. Almost from the very beginning the expedition suffered from short rations, and only those who brought their own food got enough to eat. After reaching the coast of Brazil, Alcazaba sailed south through the month of December, finally reaching Río Gallegos in Patagonia on January 13, where he took on water. On Sunday, January 17, he reached the mouth of the strait and entered it on the following day, sailing as far as the "Island of Ducks" (Penguin Island), but the ships were forced to turn back on February 5 because of strong winds. Sailing north to about 45°, at the Gulf of San Matías, Alcazaba established his headquarters and prepared his men for a march inland, which began on March 9. Being old and fat, he could not go far, and returned to the ships after covering twelve leagues. The rest of the party continued inland, fortunately meeting Indians who showed them how to survive on the seeds of wild beets, the roots of mountain thistles, and fish from the streams, all the while luring them on with tales of nonexistent gold. On Easter Sunday, 1535, after twenty-two days out, they decided to return, and after three days two captains, Arias and Sotelo, mutinied and seized the lieutenant-governor and his servants. Arias sent the squadron chiefs ahead, and upon reaching the ships they boarded them and threw Alcazaba and the pilot overboard. Arias arrived soon after and plundered the vessels. At this point the leaders quarreled; Sotelo wanted to go on to the Río de la Plata to await the arrival of Don Pedro de Mendoza, but Arias preferred to sail out in the *capitana* as a pirate, robbing the Portuguese India fleet. Only the seizure of Arias by the master of the flagship prevented him from putting Sotelo and the *veedor* Alonso in a small boat, boring holes in it, and sinking it. The mutineers were put to death as the survivors straggled in from the interior; by now the death toll was eighty. The new captain, Juan de Mori, reduced rations and sent the men to kill seals—no great help since eating the liver caused death at the worst or the loss of one's hair at the least. Only timely arrests and the use of the water torture forestalled another mutiny. The leaders, Captain Rodrigo Martínez, Nuño Alvarez, and Alejo García were left at the "Port of Lions" for ten years as the ships sailed away in June. After many subsequent misfortunes, the survivors reached Santo Domingo on September 11, with no food left.[50]

A little more successful was the expedition outfitted in 1539 by Dr. D. Gutiérrez Carbajal, bishop of Plasencia, which was suggested to him by his brother-in-law, Pedro de Mendoza. Two ships, under the command of a relative of the bishop, Captain Alonso de Camargo, sailed in August, 1539, and entered the strait on January 20, 1540; a fragment of the log, which has been preserved, mentions a very high cross visible on the shore—probably raised by Magellan. The flagship was wrecked in the first narrows on January 22 before dawn, but the crew was saved. Turning back to the entrance five days later, they were driven by a gale to the Cape of the Virgins. As they explored to the south later, they sighted a channel (Le Maire Strait) and anchored on the north coast of Staten Island, later moving to an enclosed port they named "Puerto de los Zorros" for the many foxes they saw. The captain believed this to be part of the mainland to the south of Magellan's strait; it was this strong belief in a great southern continent that impelled navigators to try the dangerous passage of the strait rather than seek another route farther south—they simply did not regard Tierra del Fuego (so named by Magellan for the fires the Indians kept constantly burning) as an island. After six months in port, the expedition returned to Spain—a success at least in the increased knowledge of the geography of the area which they brought with them.[51] By now, more than two thousand men had died in attempting the passage through the strait, victims of mutiny, foul play, shipwreck, and disease; twelve ships were lost in the passage, and only one, the *Victoria*, returned to Spain.[52]

THE PORTUGUESE IN BRAZIL

While Spanish navigators did battle with the elements to the south, the Portuguese undertook the far less spectacular task of exploring and colonizing their sector of the New World. In 1530 Dom João III, hard pressed financially, nourished the fond hope that Brazil might provide gold and silver in abundance, and sent Martim Afonso de Sousa to look for it. Leaving Lisboa on December 3, 1530, with five ships (two *naos*, one galleon, and two caravels) and five hundred soldiers and colonists, the expedition reached Cape Santo Agostinho at the end of January, 1531, and by a stroke of good fortune captured three French vessels and their cargoes of brazilwood. Sailing to the south, Sousa entered Bahia de Todos os Santos on March 13, and reached Guanabara Bay on March 30, where he remained for three months to build two brigantines for river exploration and to gather in supplies for a year.

On August 10, after resuming his voyage, Sousa reached Cananéia, and, as we have already seen, met the Bachelor who claimed to have been there for thirty years. He informed Sousa of gold and silver in the interior. Gathering eighty men, Sousa organized the first *bandeira* (pioneering expedition) to look for the precious metals, and sent the fleet south for further exploration. By mid-September the vessels reached Cape Santa María, where the flagship was lost in a storm. Because of this it was decided not to try to enter the Río de la Plata; instead, Pero de Sousa was sent in a brigantine to erect *padrões* and take possession in the name of the king. Since the Río de la Plata lay far to the west of the line of Tordesillas, it is evident that the king of Portugal was not quite so scrupulous about violating the agreement as was his Spanish neighbor. After exploring upstream for 115 leagues, the ships returned to São Vicente on January 20, 1532, and remained a year to organize a colony.[53]

THE WEST COAST

With the exception of the extreme southern portion of Chile, most of the early exploration of the west coast of South America was closely tied up with the conquest of Peru and Chile. We shall here be concerned only with the maritime aspects. It will be recalled that Balboa, in his quest for the South Sea, had been told of the existence of a land fabulously rich in gold, which could be reached by that sea. His untimely death at the hands of Pedrarias Dávila removed him as a potential conquistador of Peru, and the enterprise passed into other hands. In 1522 an expedition organized under the experienced captain Pascual Andagoya sailed south from Panama to the coast of modern Colombia and subjugated an area called Birú, which eventually seems to have been corrupted into Pirú. Dávila, on learning of this, wanted Andagoya to head another expedition there, but he was unable to go because of an injury, and the project was turned over to Francisco Pizarro, a Panama veteran who had served under Ojeda, Balboa and Dávila, Diego de Almagro, and Father Hernando Luque. Andagoya did not wish to be included, but gave freely what information he had of the country to the south up to the point where his injury had brought an end to the expedition.

Two small vessels were purchased for the enterprise; one of these had been built for Balboa, who, had he lived, would have undertaken the project himself. After considerable delay in recruiting even so few as one hundred men, Pizarro set sail from Panama in November of 1524. Almagro was to follow him as soon as possible. Despite Andagoya's advice, which he would have done well to heed, Pizarro, who distrusted him, sailed directly to the province of Birú, a rain-soaked, tangled morass at this time of the year. Two futile attempts to hack their way through this dismal jungle ended in failure, and the explorers returned to the sea, to look in vain for the arrival of Almagro to replenish their rapidly diminishing food supplies. Only the lure of gold, or, perhaps at the moment, the unwillingness to face bankruptcy and derision by returning to Panama as failures, kept them from abandoning the quest on the spot. Desperate now for supplies, Pizarro sent Montenegro and half of his men to return to the Isla de Perlas for food while he continued his search, finally finding an Indian village which the famished Spaniards plundered for food, finding also crude gold artifacts which indicated that they were on the right path. The eventual arrival of Montenegro with supplies encouraged Pizarro to forge ahead, and he landed at a place he called Punta Quemada, discovering there a much larger Indian town. These Indians proved to be warlike, and their attack cost the Spaniards two dead and many wounded. In this state, and with the vessel in poor condition, he decided to return to Panama. Almagro meanwhile sailed down the coast, and after suffering the loss of an eye in an encounter with the Indians, also returned.[54]

In 1526 Pizarro and Almagro persuaded the governor to authorize a new expedition, and on March 10, 1526, with great ceremony, they signed a contract to divide the territory to be conquered equally. Funds were raised for this second attempt, and the two captains were able to persuade 160 men to join them in seeking the riches to the south. Two ships were purchased, and this time they sailed under the direction of an experienced pilot, Bartolomé Ruiz, who went directly to the Río San Juan, the southern limit of Almagro's previous expedition. Here an Indian town was plundered of its gold, which Pizarro sent back to Panama as a lure to recruit the larger force he felt he would need, while Ruiz sailed south to explore, and soon encountered a large *balsa* under sail. Coming alongside, he noted the fine-textured woolen cloth the Indians wore, as well as their skillfully wrought gold artifacts— evidence of a higher civilization than the one they had previously encountered. The Indians indicated that they were from a rich city on the coast to the south, Tumbes, and two of them agreed to go with Ruiz, eventually to serve as interpreters. Continuing south, the Spaniards crossed the equator, then turned to sail north and join the others.

Meanwhile Almagro returned with reinforcements and provisions and the news that Pedro de los Ríos had succeeded as governor and strongly favored the enterprise. The ships set sail for Gallo Island, where they spent two weeks for repairs, and then continued on to the bay of San Mateo, noting the ever-increasing evidences of a higher civilization. The evident hostility of the Indians on shore made any thought of landing suicidal. Some favored abandoning the enterprise, but Almagro insisted that the only course was to go on; he would go back to Panama for reinforcements if necessary, while Pizarro remained where they were. This led to a quarrel between the captains, since Pizarro had been cast in this role too often, but they finally came to an agreement to take refuge back on Gallo Island, despite the mutinous attitude of some of the men. Almagro departed for Panama, but the governor, who by now had had enough of the venture, sent Pero Tafur, one of his officers, with two vessels to bring back those he would still find alive. Upon his arrival at Gallo Island, bearing also letters from Almagro and Luque urging Pizarro to hold firm, the latter dramatically drew a line in the sand, announcing that Panama, poverty, and disgrace lay to the north of it, Peru and its riches to the south. He stepped across, calling for support; thirteen joined him and he then led them to a better location on Gorgona Island, while Tafur departed for Panama, taking with him the rebel pilot Ruiz, who would join Almagro and Luque in trying to bring aid to Pizarro.

For seven months Pizarro remained on Gorgona. Ruiz and Almagro were able to return only because the governor sent with them an order for Pizarro to return in six months regardless of what befell the expedition. Picking up Pizarro's party, they cruised along the coast, entered the Gulf of Guayaquíl, and finally reached the rich Inca port of Tumbes; here they were given a most friendly reception, and gave the Indians gifts of pigs, chickens, and iron hatchets—all unknown in the New World —in exchange for gold and llamas. Pizarro departed with a promise to return soon, and sailed south to nine degrees, ever more impressed with the wealth and civilization of the Incas. On the return of the explorers to Panama, Governor Ríos was still unimpressed, so Pizarro and Pedro de Candía departed for Spain to secure royal authorization for a large expedition.

Meanwhile the southern portion of the west coast of South America had been discovered. Magellan, after leaving the strait, had sailed with the aid of favorable winds and currents to 45° south, where he found Cape Tres Montes and followed the coast to 35°, where his map indicated that the coast of Asia would be found. Encountering no such coast, he continued north to 32°, then changed course to strike out across the Pacific.[55] The only other recorded approach to Chile from the Atlantic at this time was that of the third vessel of the bishop of Plasencia's expedition, which appeared off the coast during Valdivia's conquest, to his great surprise. The ship touched at Valparaíso, and proceeded north to Callao, arriving there in 1541 in a pitiful condition.[56]

Much of the early exploration of the coast of Chile was undertaken under the impetus of the conquistador Pedro de Valdivia. The first of several expeditions was that of Juan Bautista Pastene, a Genoese captain who had been sent in an old vessel, the *San Pedro*, to protect Chile from the French, then at war with Spain. Valdivia decided that the French menace was trifling, and decided to send Pastene to explore the coast to the strait, to protect his rights by taking possession of the land if possible. The expedition was to be coordinated with that of Villagra by land, with Pastene in supreme command. Two vessels—all that Valdivia could spare—sailed on the night of September 4-5, 1544. Entering a port they named San Pedro on September 18, they met a few Indians who received them peaceably, and planted a cross, taking solemn possession of the land. At this point Pastene decided to return to Valparaíso, exploring the coast carefully as he sailed north.[57]

Still concerned over his claim to the land south to the strait, Valdivia organized another expedition in 1553 under Francisco de Ulloa, a lieutenant of Cortés who had explored the coast of Mexico north from Acapulco in 1539; with him he took the cosmographer Cortés Ojea and a skilled Flemish harbor pilot. This expedition was to work in conjuncion with Villagra, who made a sortie in the previous year with sixty-five men across the Andes. Leaving the port of Valdivia on October 27 or 28, they sailed south in two ships, entered the Gulf of Ancud on November 8 and discovered the island of San Martín and the Chonos archipelago a few days later. Subsequently they reached the Strait of Concepción, where they found a cross marking the location of a grave—possibly the remains of the Camargo expedition. One vessel entered the strait of Magellan and explored it part way; ultimately the expedition returned to Valdivia in February of 1554. Villagra did not penetrate by land beyond Concepción, for Indian troubles forced his return.[58]

In 1557, the new governor of Chile, D. García Hurtado de Mendoza, son of the second marqués of Cañete, D. Andrés Hurtado de Mendoza, viceroy of Peru, decided to organize an expedition to explore the strait and incidentally reinforce his claim to the governorship of that region. Two large vessels and a small brigantine, with seventy men, were placed under the command of Juan de Ladrillero, who was recommended by the viceroy; Francisco Cortés Ojea, who had served with Ulloa, was given command of one of the ships. Sailing from Valdivia on Wednesday, November 17, they encountered favorable winds for eight days, when a violent storm forced them to seek shelter in a bay they named Nuestra Señora del Valle, in the Fallos Channel between Campana and Wellington Islands. Continuing their voyage on December 6, the ships became separated by a storm on the night of December 9; the flagship *San Luis* was driven by the north wind, and the man-of-war *San Sebastián* under Ojea was unable to locate it. Ojea found himself in the midst of a labyrinth of islands and, despite the fact that it was midsummer, in danger from the cold, ice floes, and shifting winds. Unable to locate the strait, although he was probably very near to the entrance, and unable to obey his orders to "discover the North Sea" (the Atlantic), he held a council on January 23 and recommended that, in view of the loss of anchors and cables, their unknown position, scanty supplies, and lack of tools for repairs, they take the first favorable winds and return; the crew approved unanimously. Fearful of sailing the channel through the islands and the continent, they took the more dangerous route through the open sea, driven mainly by storms, since the tattered sails were all but useless. On February 14 an unusually violent storm drove them toward the shore. Entering a cove, they destroyed the ship and built a small brigantine under incredible conditions of almost constant rain. In this they finally reached Valdivia on October 1.

Ladrillero, meanwhile, unable to locate the *San Sebastián*, explored the Fallos Channel, the Madre de Dios archipelago, Concepción Channel, and Eyre Channel (where he found "islands of snow"), always seeking but never finding the entrance to the Strait of Magellan. By the end of December he had carefully explored the archipelago between 47° and 51°, leaving a very detailed account of the hydrography of the region. After entering Collingwood Strait, he spent all of January, 1558, before concluding that this was not what he sought. Going back to the Pacific, he finally entered the Strait of Magellan at Desolation Island, sailed to within a short distance of the Atlantic (after a long delay from March to July), and formally took possession for the king, the viceroy, and the governor on Tuesday, August 9. He then retraced his course, and returned to Concepción in the middle of 1559.[59]

Sixty years had elapsed since Columbus discovered the continent. In that relatively brief span of time, bold and courageous navigators, often suffering almost incredible hardships, particularly in the Strait of Magellan, surviving shipwreck, violent tempests, hunger and malnutrition, disease and human violence, had mapped with a surprising degree of accuracy the entire coastline of South America. It was clear by now that this was no extension of Asia, although cartographers were to show North America joined to Asia for some time to come. And centuries were to elapse before the outline of the northern continent would be known with anything approximating the accuracy of that of its southern neighbor.

NOTES

1. *Documentos inéditos,* I Ser., Vol. XXXVIII, pp. 466-67.
2. *Ibid.,* pp. 475-79.
3. *Ibid.,* pp. 484-91.
4. A list of the ships and their full complement of personnel may be found in Navarrete, *Colección de viajes,* Vol. III, p. 22, n. 4. A complete account of the voyage, on which this summary is largely based, may be found in *ibid.,* paragraphs 22-34, pp. 28-39.
5. The order may be found in *Documentos inéditos,* I Ser., Vol. XXXIX, pp. 34-36.
6. The many accusations against Ojeda, including the charge that twenty Christians had been killed because of his maltreatment of the Indians, appear in the "Ejecutoria en la cause de Hojeda," *Documentos inéditos,* I Ser., Vol. XXXIX, pp. 69 ff.
7. Navarrete, Vol. III, pp. 169-70.
8. Amando Melón, *Los primeros tiempos de la colonización* (Barcelona, 1952), pp. 37-39.
9. On this fourth voyage, see Navarrete, Vol. III, pp. 170-2 and Melón, *op. cit.,* pp. 289-91.
10. Cf. Bartolomé de las Casas, *Historia de las Indias* (México, D.F., 1951), Vol. III, Bk. II, Chap. 58.
11. *Documentos inéditos,* I Ser., Vol. XXXI, pp. 5 ff.
12. Melón, *op. cit.,* p. 148.
13. *Ibid.,* p. 149. Melón mentions Magnaghi's belief that Vespucci may have been a secret agent of Castile while serving Portugal.

14. Frederick J. Pohl, *Amerigo Vespucci, Pilot Major* (New York, 1944), pp. 111-12.

15. *Ibid.,* p. 110.

16. *Ibid.,* pp. 112-13.

17. "Letter of 1502." Amerigo Vespucci, *El Nuevo Mundo* (Buenos Aires, 1951), pp. 290-92.

18. Francisco López de Gómara, *Historia de las Indias,* p. 96 (in Andrés Barcín Carballido y Zuñiga, *Historiadores primitivos de las Indias occidentales,* Madrid, 1789, Vol. II).

19. Vicente Sierra, *Historia de la Argentina* (Buenos Aires, 1956), Vol. I, pp. 70-71.

20. Duarte Leite, *História .da colonização do Brasil,* Vol. II, p. 398 (cited in Armando Cortesão, *Cartografia e cartógrafos portuguêses dos séculos XV e XVI,* Lisboa, 1935, Vol. I, pp. 128-29, n. 2).

21. Portugal, Ministério do Ultramar, *A náutica dos descobrimentos* (Lisboa, 1951), Vol. I, pp. 302-5.

22. On this part of the voyage, see Pohl, *op. cit.,* pp. 118-25. Peter Martyr accepts a voyage "many degrees beyond the Equator" (*Décadas,* Bk. X, Chap. I, p. 189).

23. Robert Levillier (*América la bien llamada,* Buenos Aires, 1948, Vol. II, p. 20) says that Coelho was captain of the "third" voyage to 25° south, Vespucci afterward. F. A. de Varnhagen (*História geral do Brasil,* 4th ed., São Paulo, 1927, Vol. I, pp. 96-98) states that he was captain of the "fourth" voyage.

24. *A náutica dos descobrimentos,* Vol. I, pp. 306-7. Since de Góis was born in 1501, it is scarcely likely that he was voyaging as a business partner of Vespucci; perhaps Gago Coutinho intended to refer to Pero Góis da Silveira, who later accompanied Martim Afonso de Sousa to Brazil.

25. Varnhagen, *op. cit.,* Vol. I, pp. 96-98.

26. *Documentos inéditos,* I Ser., Vol. XXXVI, pp. 216-21. A list of everything to take is appended.

27. *Ibid.,* Vol. XXII, pp. 1-13.

28. Melón, *op. cit.,* pp. 180-81.

29. Charles E. Nowell, ed., *Magellan's Voyage Around the World: Three Contemporary Accounts* (Evanston, Ill., 1962), pp. 24-25.

30. Frederick A. Kirkpatrick, *The Spanish Conquistadores* (London, 1934), p. 48.

31. See Melón, *op. cit.,* p. 291, and Antonio Ballesteros y Beretta, *Historia de España* (Barcelona, 1948), Vol. V, p. 347.

32. On this portion of his career and the subsequent incident, see Kirkpatrick, *op. cit.,* pp. 49-53.

33. On the passage across the isthmus, see Peter Martyr, 3rd Decade, Bk. I, Chap. I and Melón, *op. cit.,* pp. 325-27. Las Casas (*op. cit.,* Bk. III, Chap. 47) says that Balboa doubtless thought that this punishment of deviates was right, but remarks that he had no right to set himself up as judge.

34. On the altercation with Chiapes, see Peter Martyr, 3rd Decade, Book I, Chap. 3.

35. Actually he was not, nor did Balboa discover it. António de Abreu entered the Pacific from Malacca near the end of 1511. See Charles E. Nowell, "The Discovery of the Pacific: a Suggested Change of Approach," *Pacific Historical Review* XVI (February, 1947): 1-10.

36. Melón, *op. cit.,* pp. 331-33.

37. Pablo Pastells, S.J., *El descubrimiento del Estrecho de Magallanes* (Madrid, 1920), Vol. I, pp. 17-22.

38. *Documentos inéditos,* I Ser., Vol. XXXIX, pp. 317-21.

39. That is, the Pacific side of Castilla del Oro (Central America); the coast was believed to bend west and connect with Asia. Cf. Nowell, *Magellan's Voyage,* p. 25.

40. Julián M. Rubio, *Exploración y conquista del Río de la Plata* (Barcelona: Salvat, 1942), p. 28.

41. On Solís in the Río de la Plata, see Rubio, *Exploración,* pp. 29-32; Sierra,

op. cit., Vol. I, pp. 75-76; and Lopes Vasques de Pestanha ("Lopes Vaz"), "A Discourse of the West Indies and South Sea" in Richard Hakluyt, *The Principall Navigations, Voiages, Traffiques, and Discoveries of the English Nation* (cited hereinafter as Hakluyt's *Voyages*), (Glasgow: Maclehose, 1905), Vol. XI, p. 252.

42. Las Casas, *op. cit.*, Bk. III, Chap. 101. On this portion of Magellan's career, see Nowell, *Magellan's Voyage*, pp. 33-50. For an excellent biography of Magellan in English, see Charles M. Parr, *So Noble a Captain* (New York: Crowell, 1933). The capitulation appears in *Documentos inéditos*, I Ser., Vol. XXII, pp. 46-52.

43. See Pastells, *op. cit.*, Vol. I, pp. 34-42; Nowell, *Magellan's Voyage*, pp. 50-55; Las Casas, *op. cit.*, Bk. III, Chap. 101.

44. Nowell, *Magellan's Voyage*, pp. 9-10, 28-36.

45. *Ibid.*, pp. 57-67; Parr, *op. cit.*, pp. 239-51. Peter Martyr gives a rather brief account of the voyage in Decade V, Bk. VII, Chaps. 1-2. He lists only 236 crew members.

46. On this portion of the voyage, see Pigafetta's account in Nowell, *Magellan's Voyage*, pp. 90-108. The story of the Patagonian giants is on pp. 102-8; Maximilian of Transylvania mentions the giants, p. 282. A lengthy, absorbing discussion of the "giants" may be found in Percy G. Adams, *Travelers and Travel Liars, 1660–1800* (Berkeley: University of California Press, 1962), Chap. II. Anthony Knivet's account of his adventures (Samuel Purchas, *Hakluytus Posthumus, or Purchas his Pilgrimes*, Glasgow, Maclehose, 1907–cited hereinafter as Purchas–Vol. XVI, pp. 205-6) mentions giants "of fifteene or sixteene spannes of height" and claims to have seen one buried who was "fourteene spannes long." Gaspar de Corrêa (Nowell, *Magellan's Voyage*, p. 319) mentions seeing "two men 15 spans high."

47. On the mutiny, see Pigafetta in Nowell, *Magellan's Voyage*, pp. 108-13; Maximilian of Transylvania, pp. 289-90; Gaspar de Corrêa, pp. 316-17; and Parr, *op. cit.*, pp. 293-304.

48. Pigafetta, *loc. cit.*, pp. 113-19; Parr, *op. cit.*, pp. 304-8; Pastells, *op. cit.*, Vol. I, pp. 82-83.

49. See Andrés de Urdaneta's account in Clements R. Markham, ed., *Early Voyages to Magellan's Strait* (London: Hakluyt Society, 1911).

50. See the narrative of Alonso (*veedor*) in Markham, *op. cit.*, pp. 141-56.

51. See the fragmentary account in Markham, pp. 158-68.

52. W. S. Barclay, *The Land of Magellan* (New York: Brentano's, n.d.), p. 41.

53. Jaime Cortesão, *Brasil*, pp. 347-49.

54. There are many excellent accounts of the conquest of Peru; a good contemporary account may be found in the narrative of Pascual de Andagoya (various editions); the classic account in English is William H. Prescott's *The Conquest of Peru* (various editions), the account of this portion appearing in Bk. II.

55. Parr, *op. cit.*, p. 323.

56. Clements R. Markham, ed., *Early Voyages*, p. 158.

57. Francisco Esteve Barba, *Descubrimiento y conquista de Chile* (Barcelona: Salvat, 1946), pp. 305-9; Pedro de Valdivia, "III Carta al Emperador Carlos V, Concepción, Oct. 15, 1550," in Robert B. Cunninghame Graham, *Pedro de Valdivia, Conqueror of Chile* (New York: Harper, 1927), Appendix, p. 199.

58. Esteve Barba, *op. cit.*, pp. 424-25.

59. On this expedition (both phases) see Diego Barros Arana, *Historia jeneral de Chile*, 2nd ed. (Santiago: Ed. Nascimento, 1937), Vol. II, pp. 193-207, and Rubén Vargas Ugarte, S.J., *Historia del Perú* (Lima, 1949), Vol. I, pp. 118-21.

III Sixteenth-Century

Penetration into the Interior:

West and South

While daring navigators were delineating the coasts of the continent, exploration did not stop at the water's edge. By midcentury most of the Andean cordillera had been at least partially explored, the Amazon navigated, the Río de la Plata system reconnoitered, and the Brazilian highland penetrated. By the end of the century the northeastern reaches of the Andes and the Orinoco system had been explored. This was the work of soldiers of fortune and representatives of banking houses, of knights-errant and scoundrels, of castaways and explorers. Their motives were many, but in most instances one was dominant—the search for gold and silver. In this quest men would bear the most extreme hardships, risk death and, too often, die. Vast territories would be traversed in the pursuit of such chimeras as the White King, El Dorado, and the fabled city of Manoa on the shores of Lake Parima. The lure was always the same—wealth beyond one's fondest dreams.

THE ANDEAN LANDS

Since Balboa explored the Isthmus of Panama, Spaniards had heard of the great wealth of the semilegendary province of Birú to the south. As we have seen, Francisco Pizarro had already ascertained the reality of these tales, and betook himself to Spain to inform his king. Presenting objects of gold, fine woolen cloth, and a llama as visible proof of the riches of Peru, he described the privations he had undergone in attempting to extend the dominions of Castile, and sought from the

45

king a grant of the government of the land he intended to discover, conquer, and populate. After a delay which nearly exhausted Pizarro's limited resources in Spain, a royal capitulation of July 26, 1529, conferred extensive powers and privileges on him. He was given the right to discover and conquer the province of Peru (or New Castile) with the rank of governor and captain-general, as well as adelantado and alguacil mayor for life, a salary of 725,000 maravedís, and extensive authority over the Indians. His associates were well provided for; Almagro was made a hidalgo and commander of the fortress of Tumbes, while Father Luque became bishop of Tumbes and was made protector of the Indians of Peru. Special tax exemptions were provided to encourage immigration into the province. Pizarro was further enjoined to raise a force of 250 men, well equipped, within six months, and to set out on the expedition within six months after returning to the New World. Armed with this great concession, he hastened to Panama, accompanied by his brothers Hernando, Juan Gonzalo, and Francisco Martín de Alcántara, and began making preparations for the conquest.[1]

At the port of Nombre de Dios, Pizarro met with his associates Almagro and Luque. The former was understandably discontented on learning of the relatively minor role assigned to him, and felt that he had been ill-used by the friend with whom he had shared equally the hazards of the enterprise thus far. But whatever Pizarro's explanations and promises might have accomplished in assuaging Almagro was undone by the haughty disdain with which he was treated by Hernando Pizarro, the only one of the brothers who could boast of legitimate birth. Only the intervention of Luque and the licentiate Espinosa kept Almagro from fitting out an expedition of his own; Pizarro, moreover, had to promise to give the office of adelantado to him (and seek royal confirmation of it), request a separate government for him (before seeking any for his brothers), and guarantee the tripartite division of the anticipated treasure as originally agreed.

Despite the prospect of dazzling wealth Pizarro held out, he found it difficult to augment his force in Panama; too many knew too well the privations of his earlier enterprises to be lured even by the promise of gold. In the end, including the force he had brought from Spain, he was able to raise only 180 men, with 27 horses, far below what the king had required of him. Leaving Almagro behind to raise a larger force, Pizarro resolved to depart. The expedition was blessed in the cathedral of Panama on December 27, 1530 (the feast of St. John the Evangelist), and early in January the Pizarro brothers and their force set sail in a vessel chartered by Hernando Ponce de León.[2]

Strong headwinds forced a change of course. Instead of sailing direct to Tumbes, the expedition put in about one hundred leagues north, at Bahía de San Mateo, and disembarked men and horses to proceed south

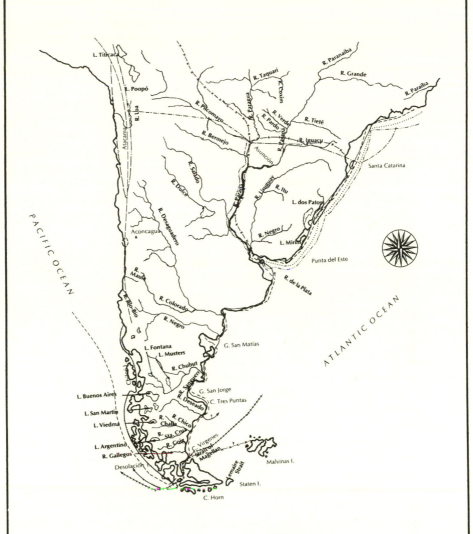

PACIFIC OCEAN

ATLANTIC OCEAN

L. Titicaca
R. Poopó
R. Loa
Atacama
R. Pilcomayo
R. Bermejo
R. Salado
R. Dulce
Aconcagua
R. Desaguadero
R. Maule
Bío-Bío
R. Colorado
R. Negro
L. Fontana
L. Musters
R. Chubut
G. San Matías
L. Buenos Aires
R. Deseado
G. San Jorge
L. San Martin
R. Chico
C. Tres Puntas
L. Viedma
Chalía
R. Sta. Cruz
L. Argentino
R. Coig
C. Vírgenes
R. Gallegos
Strait of Magellan
Desolación
Lemaire Strait
Staten I.
C. Horn
Malvinas I.

R. Taquari
R. Paranaíba
R. Coxim
R. Grande
R. Paraíba
R. Verde
R. Tieté
R. Pardo
R. Iguaçu
Asunción
Santa Catarina
R. Uruguay
R. Itu
L. dos Patos
R. Negro
L. Mirim
Punta del Este
R. de la Plata

Sixteenth Century

Vespucci, 1501 ——————
Solis, 1516 ·····························
Magellan, 1519-1520 — — — — — —
Barbosa, 1520? — x — x — x — x — x — x —
A. Garcia, 1524-1526 — . — .. — . — .. — . —
S. Cabot, 1526 —— . —— . —— . —— .
Almagro, 1534 — .. — ·· — ·· — ·· —
Ayolas, 1535-1539 — x — x — x — x — x —
Valdivia, 1540-1542 — — — — — — — —
Núñez Cabeza de Vaca, 1541 — + — + — + —
Ulloa and Villagrán, 1553 ·—·—·—·—·—·
Sarmiento de Gamboa, 1579-1580 + + + + + + +

along the coast. The march was difficult in the extreme; food was in short supply, and the swollen rivers formed at their mouths estuaries which they had to cross by swimming. Pizarro himself ignored personal danger to assist those who could not swim. The weary force finally reached the seaside town of Coaque, where they replenished their food and relieved the Indians of a considerable quantity of gold and silver ornaments. There were also precious stones—emeralds—which the Spaniards persisted in breaking with hammers, in the mistaken belief that the Indians were trying to deceive them and that true emeralds, like diamonds, would not break. After deducting the royal fifth, Pizarro divided the loot among his followers; indiscriminate plunder was not tolerated. More than 30,000 castellanos' worth of gold were sent back in three ships to Nicaragua and Panama, where they proved to be very effective recruiting agents.

From Coaque south the going was extremely difficult. The soldiers were blinded by the reflection of the sun from the sand dunes, and almost suffocated from the heat of its rays on their armor. An epidemic of huge skin ulcers, fatal to some, struck them with terrifying suddenness. But there were no Indians to trouble them; they fled at first sight of those whom they now viewed as a scourge. The small force, debilitated by fatigue and disease, finally reached Puerto Viejo to find that a ship from Panama awaited them, bringing supplies, reinforcements under Captain Belalcázar, and the royal officials of the treasury. While his weary troops might have preferred to remain in Puerto Viejo, Pizarro was determined to push on to Tumbes, and prepared to make his base on the island of Puná, offshore in the Gulf of Guayaquil. Despite his interpreters' suspicions of treachery on the part of the islanders, Pizarro got his forces safely ashore, intending to remain through the rainy season. Warned again of perfidy—this time a planned surprise attack at night—Pizarro struck first, seizing the leading cacique and his accomplices, and turning them over to their visiting rivals from Tumbes, who killed them. An attack was made on the Spanish camp immediately, but even far superior forces were no match for Spanish cavalry, guns, and pikes. Hernando Pizarro was wounded in the knee; many more were also wounded, but only a few were lost. Despite this victory, the Spaniards lived in a state of constant harassment; when Captain Hernando de Soto arrived with a hundred volunteers and some horses in a ship from Nicaragua, Pizarro decided that the time was opportune for crossing to the mainland. Before leaving, he liberated six hundred Indians, men and women from Tumbes, who had been held captive on Puná, and provided rafts to ferry them to the mainland. Three Spaniards accompanied them.[3]

As soon as the rafts landed, the three Spaniards were taken off and killed—sacrificed to idols, Zárate tells us, pointing out that Hernando de Soto, disembarking with only a servant, would have met the same fate but for the timely warning of Diego de Aguero and Rodrigo Lozano.[4] In view of Pizarro's gesture in returning the prisoners from Puná, and the friendly relations he had had with Tumbes on his earlier visit, this was strange behavior indeed; even stranger still was the condition of the city—deserted and nearly destroyed. Pizarro walked more than two leagues without seeing an Indian; finally he sent a small force to scour the hills, and they returned with a few captives who attributed the murders to lawless individuals (who would assuredly be punished!) and the destruction to invaders from Puná. The effect of this scene of desolation on the morale of Pizarro's new recruits might well be imagined, and he thought it well not to tarry in the place, but to seek out and settle some place which he could use as a base of operations. For some fifteen days a pitiless war raged between the Spaniards and the Indians with the inevitable result: the Indians offered peace, and returned to the city.

On May 16, 1532, Pizarro set out along the coast with his main force, sending Hernando de Soto to explore the foothills of the cordillera. The Spaniards came in peace, but any show of resistance was dealt with severely. For the most part the Indians seemed willing to accept the sovereignty of the mighty emperor Carlos V, which Pizarro duly proclaimed as he advanced. Finally, at a distance of some thirty leagues from Tumbes, at the Río de Poechos, Pizarro was met by messengers from the Inca Huáscar in Cuzco, informing him of the revolt of his half-brother Atahuallpa, and seeking his aid. Here was Pizarro's opportunity; selecting the site of the Indian pueblo of Tangarara in the valley of the Río de la Chira, he founded the fortified town of San Miguel as a base. Located near the sea, it afforded easy communication with Panama.[5]

Pizarro spent five months in San Miguel gathering intelligence of the civil struggle in the Inca empire and awaiting reinforcements that never came. Fearing the results of inaction, Pizarro set out from San Miguel on September 24, 1532, warning those remaining in the settlement of the absolute necessity of maintaining good relations with the Indians. The direction was toward Cajamarca where, he had learned, Atahuallpa was. After crossing the Río Piura, the Spaniards proceeded through relatively level land, forested except for barren spurs of the Andes which from time to time intersected it, and watered by the streams flowing from the mountains. By means of aqueducts and canals the Indians had made effective use of this water, and the land was filled with the color and fragrance of orchards. Five days out Pizarro took a bold step. Although he had but 177 men (of whom sixty-seven were cavalry), and less than twenty crossbowmen and arquebusiers, he called his men together, having suspected discontent, and gave them their choice of going on with him or, if they had doubts, of returning to San Miguel. In view of the small size of the garrison there, he added, they would be a welcome addition. Only nine returned: four infantry and five cavalry.[6]

Proceeding south, Pizarro learned of a large Indian city called Cajas, and dispatched a small force under de Soto to investigate; he would await him in the next town, Zarán. It was a week before de Soto appeared. He brought with him an envoy from Atahuallpa himself, who brought, among other things, a pair of painted shoes and some bracelets of gold for Pizarro to wear so that he might be recognized by the Inca. The envoy was entertained to the best of Pizarro's limited resources, given gifts, and told to inform his lord that the Spaniards represented a powerful king, and that they came to pay their respects to the Inca and to offer their services to him. Meanwhile, the conquistador learned from de Soto what he had gleaned in Cajas concerning the size, organization, and strength of the Inca empire.[7] Resuming his march, Pizarro reached the cordillera in three days. Here he saw the royal road of the Incas, the longest in the world, which stretched 3,250 miles from Quito to Talca. Here too he could see close at hand the wild splendor of the Andes, which he chose to cross through narrow defiles rather than take the highway to Cuzco. Not only was the passage difficult for the armor-clad Spaniards, but potentially dangerous in the extreme, so easily could the passes be defended. Apparently Atahuallpa did not intend to impede them; fortress after fortress was left undefended. As the Spaniards proceeded upward, the climate changed radically. Men and horses accustomed to the heat of the seacoast suddenly found themselves suffering from the cold. Lush vegetation gave way to pines and Alpine shrubs, and finally the Castilians found themselves in the windswept *páramos*, chilled to the bone. They had reached the crest; there remained the descent to Cajamarca.[8]

At their camp in the *páramos* the Spaniards were visited by an envoy of Atahuallpa to whom Pizarro made the same discourse as before. Two days later, as they descended the cordillera, they were visited by the earlier envoy, now arrived in great state, who introduced the Spaniards, probably for the first time, to the common Indian alcoholic beverage, *chicha*.[9] At this point one of Pizarro's interpreters, whom he had sent as a personal envoy to Atahuallpa, returned, voicing loudly his dismay and chagrin over the violent treatment he had received in comparison with the state reception accorded the envoy of the Inca. He reported further that Atahuallpa was encamped with a strong army near Cajamarca, which was deserted. Armed with this intelligence, the Spaniards continued their descent (which proved to be as difficult as the ascent), reaching after seven days the beautiful valley of Cajamarca, well irrigated and cultivated. The gleaming town lay below; nearby were the hot springs for which the place was famed. Most impressive was the vast expanse of tents. For here Atahuallpa's army was encamped, as Pizarro's envoy had said.

At this point Pizarro's forces became conquerors rather than explorers. Boldly entering the deserted city, Pizarro sent Hernando de Soto to Atahuallpa's encampment to invite the Inca to visit him in the city, which he consented to do. Cleverly concealing his men, he was able, at a given signal, to seize the Inca; several thousand Indian warriors were killed, but not a single Spaniard was lost. Meanwhile, Atahuallpa's brother Huáscar, the rightful ruler who was imprisoned at Cuzco, was murdered, probably at his brother's order. Sole ruler now, Atahuallpa offered Pizarro a room full of gold for his freedom, an offer which the Spaniard accepted with alacrity. The gold was collected and delivered, but the Inca was not released; despite his signed agreement, Pizarro charged him with conspiracy, had him executed, and began to move on the Inca capital of Cuzco.

Pizarro had seized Atahuallpa on November 16, 1532. A year later the Inca capital was in his hands; the inhabitants were cruelly treated, and the city was sacked. Desirous of locating his capital in a place more easily accessible from the Spanish centers of power, Pizarro chose a fertile area on the banks of the Río Rímac, not far from the sea. There, on January 6, 1535, the feast of the Epiphany, he founded his city, which he called "City of the Kings;" subsequently it would be known by a corrupted form of the river that flowed beside it—Lima. Within a year the Spaniards had overcome the last Inca resistance, and turned to fighting each other. Peru thus became, rather than an area for exploration, a base for the exploration of the surrounding country.

Shortly after Pizarro's entry into the city of Cuzco, one of Cortés' veterans, Pedro de Alvarado, at this time governor of Guatemala, decided to embark on the Pacific Ocean "for the discovery and conquest of the Indies and the mainland in the South Sea." Now he learned of Pizarro's conquest. Leaving his brother Jorge as his deputy, he sailed south and southeast with 500 Spaniards, 3,000 Guatemalan slaves, and 227 horses, hoping to conquer a northern kingdom in South America before Pizarro could turn his attention to it. The expedition disembarked at Puerto Viejo in modern Ecuador. Alvarado later reported to the emperor that he had been driven off course by storms. Exploring the vicinity, the party discovered a number of Indian villages which they looted and occupied. Alvarado's goal was Quito, but he could not anticipate the problems he would face in the attempt. As the party ascended the cordillera, moderate weather gave way to bitter cold, and the atmosphere was heavy with ashes from an eruption of Cotopaxi in the distance. Exposure and sickness took their toll; eighty Spaniards died, and of the Indians, accustomed to the warmth of Guatemala, at least 2,000 perished. There was nothing to do but abandon the attempt. Six months later the expedition reached the Inca highway, only to meet Belalcázar, who had conquered the area and founded Riobamba. Subsequently Almagro arrived. Facing desertions to the latter, Alvarado sold his arms and ships to him on August 26, 1534, and retired to Guatemala. The sum, 100,000 pesos de oro, was duly paid by Pizarro when Alvarado visited him later at Pachacamac (the site of Pizarro's new capital, Lima).[10]

Meanwhile, the struggle between Pizarro and Almagro for control of Peru had resulted in a complete victory for the former. In 1538 his brother Hernando, fearful of a renewed struggle between his followers and the Almagrists in Cuzco, granted permission to any captain to lead a force for the purpose of pacification, exploration, or conquest. By this clever device, Zárate points out, he rewarded his friends and got rid of his enemies. One of the first to go was a Greek gunner who had enriched himself, one Pedro de Candia. A slave girl had told him of a land called Ambaya, southeast of Cuzco, rich in gold and silver. Spending all he had and going into debt to equip an expedition, he departed with three hundred Spaniards and a large force of Indians, crossing the *páramos* of the eastern cordillera, and entered the rain-drenched forests of the *montaña*. Provisions ran out. They had to hack their way through the forests, covering at most a league a day. They crossed rivers, waded through swamps, ate their horses and llamas, and eventually concluded that Pizarro had sent them out deliberately to die. The fabled land of riches was never found; they were lucky to return in three months, with not a single *Spanish* life lost. Nothing was said about the Indians. Candia returned a poor man, and he became a poorer one; his aide was executed, and his command given to Pedro Anzures.[11]

Anzures, or Peranzures as he was sometimes called, was commissioned by Hernando Pizarro to enter the land of the Chunchos, barbarous Indians of the *montaña* east of Cuzco, beyond which lay a well-populated land rich in gold. It was easy to raise a force, and the expedition crossed the cordillera in September, 1538. Their experiences were harrowing. Provisions gave out and they were reduced to surviving on herbs and palm hearts. They had to hack their way through dense underbrush and wade through swamps, usually in torrential rain. But the lust for gold is a hard master. The Indians seemed less able than the Spaniards to cope with this environment, for many of them died, and were promptly devoured by the survivors. Where was the gold? Twenty-five days march to the east, the forest Indians assured them, obviously anxious to be rid of them. A constant deluge of water saved them from this fool's errand. Advance was impossible, so they retreated, slogging through constant rain, never seeing the sun, eating their horses, and finally returning, unrecognizable to their friends, their ranks frightfully depleted.[12]

More successful in exploring if not in finding gold was Alonso de Alvarado, one of the Guatemalans who had joined Almagro in 1534, and founder of the city of Chachapoyas, thirty-eight leagues northeast of Cajamarca. Undeterred by grim reports from a small exploring expedition he had sent into the *montaña*, he led a force of seventy men into the forest and reached the Río Huallaga, a tributary of the Marañón. Despite tales of level country fifteen days' journey away, where dwelt the wealthy Inca Ancallas, he found only forests and rivers.[13]

Three decades later a very successful attempt to explore the *montaña* was made by Juan Alvarez Maldonado. He had come to America in 1542, and escaped with his life in the civil struggle in Peru only through the intercession of many friends. Consequently he decided upon the safer career of exploration. In August, 1567, he was authorized by the officials in Lima to discover and explore lands up to the boundary of the Mojos, was promised the enjoyment of his discoveries for twenty years, and was given the title of governor and captain-general. Returning to Cuzco, he presented his authorization to the cabildo and sought recruits. With a small force he explored the Andes from Opatari to the Río Pilcopata, one of the headwaters of the Río Madre de Dios, and determined that it was navigable. Continuing his explorations in May, 1568, he reached the confluence of the Río Paucartambo and the Río Tono, and entered into the Manu, or upper Madre de Dios. The Indians were friendly, but when strife broke out among the Spaniards, the cacique Tarano, once host to Alvarez Maldonado, took advantage of the situation to lay siege to the fort constructed by his lieutenant Martín de Escobar. All the Spaniards but two were killed, and Alvarez Maldonado, hastening to the rescue but prevented by floods, nearly lost his life when his canoe overturned. Despite this untimely end to the venture, his survey of the upper Río Madre de Dios was the most comprehensive in colonial times.[14]

The country of the Mojos, which lay somewhat east of Cuzco, beyond the cordillera, had been forbidden to Alvarez Maldonado, but in 1582 Francisco de Hinojosa entered the territory with the intent of pacification. Subsequently, in 1590, with data supplied by Hinojosa, who had failed to colonize the area, Lorenzo Suárez de Figueroa was entrusted with the exploration of the territory. Some progress was made and a town founded, but his death ended the effort at colonization, which had to wait until the Jesuit attempt in mid-seventeenth century.[15]

We return to the southern Andes—that vast expanse southeast of Cuzco which contains some of the highest peaks and most beautiful lakes in the world—and the southernmost limits of the Inca world. It will be recalled that Diego de Almagro had never been satisfied with the royal capitulation Pizarro brought back from Spain, and had been promised an equal share. In 1534 a new capitulation authorized him to "discover, conquer, and settle the lands and provinces which are along the coast of the South Sea" two hundred leagues south from the limits of Pizarro's realm "to the Strait of Magellan." [16] Almagro, now an adelantado himself, set out in 1535 to explore and occupy his realm of Nuevo Toledo. Rodrigo Orgoñez led an advance party of 570 Spaniards and several thousand

Indians out of Cuzco, while Almagro himself followed with a second detachment of two hundred Spaniards and the Inca Paulu, whose presence was expected to facilitate passage. Despite the advice of Indian leaders to follow the coast,[17] the expedition proceeded along the Inca highway, taking the right fork at Lake Titicaca, around the southwest shore, to the *altiplano*. Almagro insisted in starting out in the winter, and his losses due to the bitter cold were staggering: 150 Spaniards, 10,000 Indians, and 30 horses. Entering the Salta valley, he waited for the summer, then crossed the cordillera at the high San Francisco pass; 1,500 Indians, 2 Spaniards, 150 Negroes, and 112 horses died in that pass, and many of the survivors were frostbitten. The expedition finally reached Copiapó on the plain of north Chile, forcing the submission of the Indians; an exploring party pushed to 36°, at the Río Maule (the southern limit of the Inca empire) but, finding no gold, reported that the land was sterile. News of the revolt in Peru caused Almagro to turn back, for he hoped to claim Cuzco. This time he followed the coastal route, crossing the forbidding Atacama desert, recrossing part of the cordillera (where his troops found their frozen comrades still standing) and returned to Cuzco; the men were snowblind for two days.

The bitter civil war for control of Peru ensued, culminating in the battle of Las Salinas April, 1538. After Almagro's defeat and subsequent execution, Pizarro gave the government of Chile to a thirty-eight-year-old colonel who had aided in the victory, Pedro de Valdivia. The following year, 1539, he was authorized to explore his province, and set about raising a force. He was greatly hampered by Almagro's poor description, but managed to recruit 150 Spaniards, with one thousand Indians as porters. Listening to the advice of the Indians, he crossed the cordillera to the Atacama, thence along the coast to the fertile Coquimbo valley. Farther to the south Valdivia's party came upon a bay and a beautiful valley in which almond trees were in full flower; he named it Valparaíso (Vale of Paradise).[18] A little to the south lay the valley of the Río Maipo. Following it inland, the conquistador came upon the magnificent central valley where on February 12, 1541, he founded the city of Santiago del Nuevo Extremo, calling the province Nueva Extremadura, for the place of his birth in Spain. To the south of Santiago was Araucanian country. Of this portion of the valley Lopez Vaz remarked: "But the other halfe as it was the richest and the fruitfullest part, so God had peopled it with the most valiant and furious people in all America."[19]

The Indians made every effort to starve out the Spaniards, and Valdivia had to guard his corn crop at all times from imminent destruction. But he was frequently away from Santiago. On one occasion the Indians took advantage of his absence to attack in force, and were repulsed largely through the heroic efforts of the chaplain, Padre Lobo, and Valdivia's mistress, Ines Suárez, who had accompanied him on the long journey from Peru. In these circumstances, Valdivia felt it urgent to establish communications with Peru, and sent Captain Alonso de Monroy to cross the Atacama with six men on horseback, some gold, and supplies. They left Santiago in January, 1542, and were ambushed in the Copiapó valley. Four men were killed; all the gold and all but two of the horses were taken. Monroy and one companion were allowed to live only if they would teach the Indians to ride. A Spanish soldier living with the Indians secretly gave Monroy a knife, enabling him to kill the chief and escape with his companion. Despite lack of provisions, he crossed the Atacama, reached Cuzco, managed to get seventy cavalry, money, and a supply ship, and made his way back to Valparaíso along the coast.

It was under such circumstances, as well as Valdivia's campaign south to and across the Bío Bío River in 1550–52, which ended in his tragic death, that the interior of Chile was explored. In a letter to the emperor, Valdivia remarked that never before had such a land been discovered for the Crown; it was, he said, well populated, "very healthful, fruitful, and pleasant, with most fair climate, very rich in gold." [20] Surely an encouraging report!

One significant expedition still requires attention. So vague was knowledge at that time of the southern part of the continent that Valdivia's grant was to have an east-west extent of one hundred leagues which would bring it well into Patagonia. In his third letter to the emperor, Valdivia sought to have the limits of his grant extended to include the Strait of Magellan, "and the land behind it up to the North Sea." [21] Just before his death he sent Francisco de Villagra from Concepción across the Andes to ascertain what was there. Villagra crossed the cordillera with only moderate difficulty, and came upon a great and rapid river flowing east—probably either the Río Colorado or the Río Negro. But difficulties in finding food put an end to his advance, and he returned to Concepción via the fertile Maguez valley.

THE WHITE KING AND THE RIVER OF SILVER

Three years before Francisco Pizarro first set foot in the Inca empire, a Portuguese explorer, Aleixo Garcia, penetrated the eastern borders of the realm in the company of Guaraní warriors, searching for the legendary White King. The dazzling exploits of Pizarro have almost obscured Garcia's accomplishment.[22] Garcia was one of eighteen survivors (four of them Portuguese) of one of the ships of the Solís expedition, wrecked off Santa Catarina Island, where he apparently learned the Guaraní language and heard rumors of the Inca empire and a White King who wore clothes like Europeans. Determined to find this wealth, Garcia, the mulatto Pacheco, and several others left the island and headed west, leaving two of the survivors for contact with ships that might stop. Their course took them across the Paraná, doubtless past Iguaçu Falls, and to the Paraguay near Asunción, where Garcia organized a Guaraní army, crossed the Chaco Boreal, arrived at the Andes, and penetrated the Inca frontier somewhere between Mizque and Tomina, an event duly recorded by Inca historians. The raiding party returned with considerable quantities of silver and copper objects. They had covered more than one thousand leagues. Garcia sent some of the treasure to the men on the coast, urging them to join in a new raid. But they refused and sometime after this, in 1525, Garcia was assassinated. The motive was probably robbery.

In 1526 the Venetian-born Sebastiano Caboto (or, to use the more familiar name, Sebastian Cabot), Pilot Major of Spain since the death of Juan de Solís, arrived in Recife, where he heard stories of the White King and the Sierra de la Plata. He could verify these, he was told, by checking with Enrique Montes and Melchor Ramírez, whom Garcia had left at Puerto de los Patos. There he found them in October, along with fifteen others left by the captain of one of García Jofré de Loyasa's ships, who had deserted the expedition. Most of Garcia's treasure was lost when a ship onto which it was being loaded sank. But enough remained to intrigue Cabot and to cause him to divert his course, for Montes and Ramírez told him that he could reach Garcia's starting point in Paraguay by sailing up the Río Solís.[23]

What was Cabot doing in Brazil? In 1524 he had won the approval of the Council of the Indies for an expedition to prove his claim that there was a shorter route to the South Sea than that taken by Magellan. The king seems to have contributed to the expedition. His major interest was in securing spices, but he was also desirous of having the west coast of South America more adequately mapped, since so little was known of it. Apparently Cabot was to explore the coasts of the continent first, then sail west toward the Moluccas.[24] For his services he was to receive from the royal treasury 25,000 maravedís for life. Four ships were provided for him, with a complement of somewhere between 214 and 224 men.[25] They were to discover "the islands of Tharsis, Ophir, and Eastern Cathay."[26] Sailing from Sanlúcar de Barrameda on Tuesday, April 3, 1526, they stopped at the Canaries and the Cape Verde Islands, and finally entered Recife on June 3; as they entered the bay Cabot and his men saw some seals, which they mistook for mermen. Small wonder, then, that they should be willing also to look for a White King.

The prospect of nearby silver quickly won out over distant spices. Cabot took on the castaways at Santa Catarina and hastened south, reaching the Plata estuary—forty-eight leagues away—in the remarkably brief time of six days. He entered the estuary, established a base, then set about a detailed exploration of the Río Solís, finally entering the Paraná, which he followed until it was joined by a large river he felt must flow from Peru (actually the Paraguay, which rises in Brazil) and entered it on March 31, 1528. Here Cabot discovered two of his men stealing from the Indians, and summarily executed them. Further probing led to an Indian attack in which eighteen Spaniards were killed and ten wounded. Cabot felt it advisable to return south to the Río Carcarañá, where he had built Fort Sancti Spiritus.[27]

At this point we come upon one of those chance meetings not uncommon in the history of the exploration of South America. Diego García, who had sailed around the world with Elcano, had left La Coruña in 1526 to explore the Río Solís. One can imagine his surprise and consternation upon learning that Cabot, who was supposed to be not there but on his way to the Moluccas, had built a fort and was in the vicinity. After visiting the fort in vain, he found Cabot some distance up the Paraná. Unable to come to any agreement concerning their respective rights, they decided to explore together and leave the decision to the king.[28] Together they explored the Pilcomayo in search of the White King and the silver mountain, but did not risk proceeding as far as Aleixo Garcia had gone. Indian attacks made retreat advisable. Subsequently a large force attacked and destroyed Fort Sancti Spiritus, leaving thirty-four dead and many wounded; the rest escaped to San Salvador, at the Río de la Plata. Cabot found the mangled bodies of the dead; the Indians had wanted to discover if they tasted as bad as the other Spaniards they had eaten, whom they found too salty.[29]

The help he had sought from Spain did not arrive, so Cabot held a council, which decided to return to the homeland. The only food available was seals; Cabot sent thirty-four men under Antonio de Montoya to look for some, but when, after a long wait, they failed to return, he set sail with the survivors early in November, 1529. As they left the estuary in January, they met Diego García, also bound for Spain. And so the enterprise, deflected from its original purpose, ended in failure. Had Cabot and García been able to continue, they might have reached the heart of the Inca empire several years before Pizarro. But the silver Cabot brought with him was the first Inca treasure to reach Spain, and the name he hopefully bestowed on the Río Solís has remained to this day—the Río de la Plata ("River of Silver").

Failure though it was, the Cabot expedition probably gave rise to one of the most enduring of the many myths which drove men to fantastic efforts in the New World—the Enchanted City of the Caesars (or Césares). As this version goes, Cabot had learned from the Querandí Indians of an Andean people, dominated by the Incas, whose culture was very superior to that of the lowland peoples. He decided to investigate, and detached a small force of fifteen men under Francisco César. There are two different accounts of his adventures. José Toribio Medina states simply that he left Sancti Spiritus in November, 1528, and returned in February, 1529, reporting that he had seen great riches in precious stones and metals, while the chronicler Ruy Díaz de Guzmán has César with only four men entering a rich province and meeting the prince (the White King?), who gave them gifts of gold and silver. Finding Sancti Spiritus in ruins on their return, (according to this version) they returned to this rich province, crossed the Andes, traversed the Atacama, and reached Cuzco just as Pizarro was meeting Atahuallpa at Cajamarca. Was Cuzco where he met the prince? He could not have gone back there, reasons Sierra, since he returned to Spain with Cabot and turned up in Venezuela in 1532, where, incidentally, he testified under oath that he had been in a very rich province and seen treasure, well-clad Indians, and llamas. Did his followers (the "Césares") return? And where was the province? A study of the route would seem to indicate that it was somewhere in northern Argentina; other versions place the "enchanted city" there, and men sought it there, for more than a century and a half.[30]

Despite Cabot's failure, the silver he brought to Spain spoke eloquently. In 1534 a royal capitulation of May 23 indicated that one Pedro de Mendoza (a native of Gaudix and a veteran of the Italian wars) had offered to conquer and populate the lands of the Río Solís (or La Plata), where Sebastian Cabot had been; accordingly the king authorized him to enter the Río de la Plata "to the South Sea," conferred upon him the rank of adelantado, and authorized him to govern two hundred leagues from the area given to Almagro to the Strait of Magellan, for life.[31] The reference to the "South Sea" is interesting; was this the shorter route Cabot thought he could find? A comparatively large fleet was assembled for Mendoza's expedition; there were fourteen large ships to carry 2,500 Spaniards, 150 Germans and Flemings, and 72 horses and mares, according to the account of a German soldier, Huldrich Schmidt (or Schmidel, as the Spaniards preferred to call him), who accompanied them.[32]

Bad weather dogged the enterprise, delaying its departure for several days and separating the vessels; two turned back, some went direct to the Río de la Plata, others put in at Rio de Janeiro where they remained for two weeks because of Mendoza's illness. Juan Osorio, his lieutenant, was given command, but was subsequently accused of mutiny and, despite the lack of positive proof, was executed on Mendoza's order. The expedition proceeded into the Río de la Plata, where, at the mouth of the Riachuelo, Mendoza founded a settlement which he called Santa María del Buen Aire, after a mariners' shrine in Sanlúcar. The neighboring Querandí Indians mistreated some of Mendoza's men and a battle ensued in which the Spaniards lost twenty-seven men, including Mendoza's brother Diego, a victim of the *boleadora*. Acute lack of food and constant harassment by the Querandís, Charrúas, Guaranís, and Chaneses made the settlement all but untenable, whereupon Mendoza sent Juan de Ayolas and Domingo Martínez de Irala up the Paraná to search for Peru. Of the 2,500 Spaniards who had left Sanlúcar, only 560 remained; most of the others had died of hunger. Hearing nothing from Ayolas, whom he had named captain-general, and now so ill that he could no longer move his hands and feet, Mendoza abandoned his colony and sailed for Spain, dying in mid-journey.[33]

Schmidel accompanied Ayolas' expedition, which numbered four hundred men; he gives us a graphic picture of their two-month voyage eighty-four leagues upstream. Fifty men died of hunger, and the rest would not have survived ten days had it not been for friendly Timbue Indians, whose cacique, in return for gifts sent by Mendoza, fed them abundantly. The expedition continued north, passing at times through well-populated areas, then for days not seeing any signs of human life. Schmidel was fascinated by the Indians, and describes them in detail—stature, clothing, food (most of them lived by hunting and fishing and gathering wild honey), ornamentation, and fighting qualities. The Carios in particular disgusted him; they were short and fat for the most part, energetic farmers and keepers of domesticated animals; they wore nothing, and seemed completely lacking in morals, for, he says, fathers sold their daughters, husbands their wives, and brothers their sisters. They ate meat including human flesh when available, which they salted and dried "as we do pigs." All captives—men, women, and children—taken in wars were killed with one exception: young and beautiful women were kept and spared if they submitted to the men—otherwise they were eaten in a solemn ceremony.[34]

The Carios, who lived along the Río Paraguay (the expedition had left the Paraná and continued north) had a fortified town which they called Lampiri at the confluence of the Paraguay and the Pilcomayo. When his efforts to establish friendly relations failed, Ayolas attacked the town with three hundred men, taking it with a loss of sixteen. The Carios immediately saw the wisdom of friendship, and offered the Spaniards food, and two women servants each. Ayolas entered the town on Assumption Day (August 15), 1539, and built a fort of stone, wood, and earth which he called Asunción. He remained there nearly six months, then, leaving a small garrison, pushed on upstream with three hundred men. From the Paiembos Indians he learned of a province rich in gold and silver, whose inhabitants were as learned as the Christians. He decided to find this fabulous place, and left fifty men under Martínez de Irala at Candelaria, with instructions to wait for him for four months, and then go to Asunción. Irala waited six rather than four months before returning, and in vain. As Ayolas entered the country of the Paiembos and Naperos, he was ambushed and his entire company killed.[35]

By 1540 Carlos V had been apprised of the failure of Mendoza's expedition and the sorry plight of the struggling settlement at Asunción. In answer to the call for assistance, the king issued a capitulation on March 8, 1540, conceding the right to explore the territories which had been granted to Mendoza, with the right of government and the titles of captain-general and adelantado, to Alvar Núñez Cabeza de Vaca. From the standpoint of exploration, at least, the choice was an admirable one, for Cabeza de Vaca's credentials were impressive indeed. He had served with distinction in Italy, Navarre, and against the *comuneros* at Toledo; he had spent ten years on an almost unbelievable odyssey from Florida through the southwestern states to Mexico City, which alone would have sufficed to rank him among the greatest explorers of all time. Now he would go to Asunción to assume the government, and find the way to the silver mountain and the White King.

The expedition departed from Cádiz in three vessels on November 2, 1540, sailed to the Canaries and the Cape Verde Islands, and followed the Brazilian coast from Cananéia past the Rio São Francisco to Santa Catarina Island, arriving on March 29, 1541. In May he dispatched a caravel to Buenos Aires, but winter winds prevented entrance into the Río de la Plata, and it returned to Santa Catarina. Meanwhile nine refugees from Buenos Aires, who claimed to be fleeing from bad government, briefed Cabeza de Vaca on affairs in Asunción. In the light of this information and the failure of the caravel to reach Buenos Aires, and relying on his experience gained in North America, he decided on an overland march to Asunción. On November 2 he departed with 250 infantry, 26 cavalry, 2 Franciscan friars, and Indians from the island. They reached the mountains in nineteen days, having cut their way through a trackless wilderness. What supplies they had brought with them had by now given out, but they came upon some villages of friendly Guaranís, who supplied them with food in exchange for items of trade the Spaniards had brought with them. On November 29 they took leave of their hosts, and on December 1 reached the Rio Iguaçu.

For the next two weeks, guided by a Christian Indian named Miguel, who had come from Asunción, Cabeza de Vaca and his party passed through Guaraní country in a generally west-northwest direction, maintaining excellent relations with the Indians by scrupulously paying them for all supplies—generally chickens, flour, corn, and pine nuts. The Spaniards marveled at the tall Paraná pines, and at the antics of the monkeys who would climb them, hang by their tails while knocking the cones to the ground with their hands and feet, and then rush down to devour them. Christmas was spent among friendly Indians at the town of Tugui, who were most generous with food, and the Spaniards indulged too freely, to their great discomfort. Cabeza de Vaca allowed a few days rest, then resumed the journey through pleasant country. For the next ten days they progressed through lands laced with rivers and arroyos, past mountains and through extensive cane fields.

At the end of January, traveling still by land, the Spaniards came again upon the Iguaçu and learned from the Indians that it flowed into the Paraná not far away, through hostile country. Accordingly, Cabeza de Vaca decided to divide his forces, part to continue by land, the remainder—eighty men and himself—to proceed by canoe to the Paraná. They had scarcely started downstream when they noticed a marked increase in the speed of the current, and discovered that they were approaching the spectacular Iguaçu Falls—one of the scenic wonders of the continent. Drawing their canoes out of the water, they made the hazardous descent safely, a distance of a league and a half. Continuing downstream below the falls, they reached the Paraná and, with the assistance of neighboring Guaranís (the first Indians they had seen for some time), whom they assured of their peaceful intentions, they were able to negotiate the crossing by rafts and canoes in two hours. One canoe overturned and a man was drowned: the only loss of life in the entire march—a remarkable record indeed.

Many were ailing, however, and unable to continue; Cabeza de Vaca had sought boats from Asunción to meet him at the Paraná, and hoped to transport the sick to the city in this manner, but they did not arrive. Finally he decided to send them downstream on rafts (in the expectation of meeting the boats) in the care of an Indian chieftain. Thirty embarked, with fifty arquebusiers and crossbowmen for protection. The rest continued overland, finally meeting a Spaniard from Asunción who advised them of the wretched state of affairs there, and of the abandonment of Buenos Aires. At 9 A.M. on Saturday, March 11, 1542, Cabeza de Vaca and his party entered the city of Asunción to the great relief of the inhabitants, who had almost given up hope of relief. A month later they were joined by the group sent on rafts via the Paraná and Paraguay rivers.[36]

Irala, who was in command at Asunción, recognized Cabeza de Vaca as his superior, and was appointed *maestre de campo* by him. After suppressing an Indian uprising, the adelantado made preparations to open a route to Peru; he selected four hundred Spaniards and two hundred Indian auxiliaries, and prepared four brigantines, six barks, twenty rafts and more than two hundred canoes. The expedition set sail early in September, 1543, and after several stops along the way in friendly country, reached Candelaria on October 12. Schmidel accompanied the explorers and has left us a detailed and graphic description of the country through which they traveled and the Indians they encountered; this German soldier seems to have had an eye for feminine beauty, since he seldom fails to inform us whether the women of the various tribes were beautiful or not. In the country of the Scherves they were guests of the king, who entertained them in the grand manner for four days. Learning on inquiry that they were seeking gold and silver, he gave them several objects fashioned from these metals, but said that he had no more, since these were the spoils of war with the Amazons. These female warriors (Schmidel's description of them is right out of classic Greek mythology), he informed them, lived on an island some two months' march to the north; they had no gold themselves, but got it from Tierra-Firme, which was inhabited by Indians who possessed much of the metal.

The mention of gold was enough to warm the heart and whip up enthusiasm for an immediate march to the Amazon country. The king advised against it, claiming that such a venture would be quite impossible because of the floods. Despite the warning, the Spaniards pushed on, and soon found themselves walking in water up to the knees, and sometimes waist-deep; frequently they went without eating, for their cooking fires and bowls often fell into the water. For fifteen days they waded through this flat, inundated country, with rain almost continuous, finally reaching the Orthuesen nation, whose cacique gave the same unwelcome warning—they would not make the Amazon country because of the floods. Sick and hungry, the Spaniards at length turned back to the country of the Scherves, and embarked in their boats for Asunción. They had not found the White King or the Amazons, yet they did not return empty-handed, having gained 200 ducats by trading. Cabeza de Vaca, it will be noted, never had trouble with the Indians, and was adamantly opposed to abusing them. The colonists, however, did not like his show of friendliness and when he returned in April, 1544, he was arrested—the victim of a conspiracy—and was sent to Spain in chains. He was absolved of all charges against him there, but never returned to America.[37]

Irala, who had a hand in deposing the adelantado, was chosen to succeed him as captain-general. In 1548 he organized an expedition to find the route to Peru; a force of 350 Spaniards (plus the ever-present Schmidel) and 2,000 Indians sailed up the Paraguay in 7 brigantines and 200 canoes, while 130 followed by land. A base was established at San Fernando, ninety-two leagues from Asunción, and the expedition pushed on into what is now Bolivia, Schmidel as usual keeping a detailed account of the Indians they encountered. Finally they met an Indian who greeted them in Spanish (they were now 372 leagues from Asunción), and informed them that he and his people were under Pedro Anzures. There they remained for twenty days, finally receiving orders from Gasca in Lima to proceed no further under pain of death. He feared, says Schmidel, that they would join the Pizarrists. Irala sent four men as envoys to Lima, but was unable to await their return, and proceeded back to Asunción, where he was forced to turn out a usurper.[38]

At this point our chronicler, Schmidel, received word from his brother Thomas telling him to return to Germany. Irala granted permission, and with a party of twenty Indians he hastened to Brazil via the Paraná, leaving Asunción on December 26, 1552. As usual, his account is a lively one; he tells of spending six months going through deserts and over mountains, through valleys full of wild beasts, and across the Rio Urqua, which contained (according to an informant) large serpents that ate men and beasts.[39] Eventually he reached a Christian settlement, and managed to get to São Vicente, where he was able to embark for Lisboa on July 13, 1553.[40]

Meanwhile Vaca de Castro, after establishing peace in Peru, "rewarded the services of his soldiers by sending them to conquer unexplored lands." [41] In 1543 a party consisting of Diego de Rojas, Felipe de Gutiérrez, Nicolás de Heredia, and Francisco de Mendoza with two hundred Spaniards, Indian auxiliaries, and horses left the plateau of Charcas and moved into the Salta valley seeking the "city of the Césares." In an encounter with Indians in the valley, Rojas died from a poisoned arrow, leaving the command to Mendoza, who promptly arrested Gutiérrez and sent him back to Peru. Following next the valley of the Río Carcarañá (or Tercero), Mendoza reached that ruined fortification known as Cabot's Tower, and met Indians who told him of Irala's rule at Asunción: the two streams of exploration—from the Río de la Plata north and west, and southeast from Peru—had finally converged. Summer rains forced Mendoza to turn back. Later he was killed in his tent by his own men and the rest of the force returned to Peru under Heredia.[42]

We hear of two more attempts to find the city of "los Césares" before the century was out. In 1581, Juan de Garay, who had refounded the city of Buenos Aires, traveled south with thirty men and some horses, and seems to have reached the vicinity of Mar del Plata. For lack of sufficient horses the expedition did not continue, but Garay wrote the king that he hoped to return and find the city.[43] In 1587 the viceroy of Peru learned from one Cristóbal Hernández, a soldier of long service, that he had encountered two Indians who told him of large cities along a lake, whose inhabitants mined large quantities of gold and silver. The place was no more than seventy leagues from Córdoba. This story was a new version of the origin of the fabled city, for there were references to lost Spaniards and a shipwreck. According to this account, with subsequent additions, the city was founded by survivors of the ill-fated expedition of the bishop of Plasencia. Those without mates married Indian women. The viceroy wrote the king that he had no doubts about the existence of the city, and wanted priests to be sent there. But much time was to pass before any serious attempt was made to try to care for the spiritual needs of those who were supposed to inhabit the city of "los Césares." [44]

NOTES

1. These events are described in many excellent histories of the conquest of Peru. See particularly the classic account in English, William H. Prescott's *The Conquest of Peru*, Bk. III, Chap. 1, and two contemporary accounts: Agustín de Zárate (Contador de Mercedes of Carlos V in Peru), *Historia del descubrimiento y conquista de la Provincia del Perú* (Antwerp, 1555), (reprinted in the *Biblioteca de los Autores Españoles*—hereinafter cited as BAE—Vol. XXVI) Bk. I, Chap. 3, and Francisco de Jerez, *Verdadera relación de la conquista del Perú y Provincia del Cuzco* (BAE, Vol. XXVI, pp. 320-21). Jerez was Pizarro's secretary.

2. Prescott, *loc. cit.* and Zárate, Bk. II, Chap. 1; Jerez, pp. 321-22.

3. On the march south to Tumbes from the point of debarkation, see Prescott, *loc. cit.* and Zárate, Bk. II, Chaps. 1-3.

4. Zárate, *op. cit.*, Bk. II, Chap. 3. Jerez gives a detailed account of this, pp. 322-23.

5. Prescott, Bk. II, Chap. 3; Zárate, Bk. I, Chap. 3; Jerez, pp. 323-24. Spelling of the Inca rulers' names varies; these also appear as Guáscar and Atabalipa. On the struggle between the rivals, see *The Incas of Pedro de Cieza de León*, ed. by Wolfgang von Hagen (Norman, Okla., 1959), Chaps. 20-24.

6. Jerez, p. 325; Prescott, *loc. cit.*

7. Jerez, pp. 325-26; Prescott, *loc. cit.;* Zárate, Bk. II, Chap. 4.

8. The crossing of the cordillera is treated by Jerez, p. 326, and vividly by Prescott, *loc. cit.*

9. *Chicha* is commonly made in this manner: Indian women chewed germinated corn, which was spit into a large bowl and allowed to ferment. The strength, of course, was determined by the length of fermentation. There being no distillation involved, the product is more reminiscent of home brew than the "corn squeezins" of Appalachia.

10. On this see Prescott, Bk. III, Chap. 9, and F. A. Kirkpatrick, *The Spanish Conquistadores* (Cleveland, 1962), pp. 114-17; also Zárate, Bk. II, Chaps. 10-13.

11. See Zárate, Bk. III, Chap. 12, and Kirkpatrick, pp. 204-6.

12. Kirkpatrick, pp. 206-7.

13. *Ibid.*, pp. 207-9.

14. Rubén Vargas Ugarte, S.J., *Historia del Perú* (Lima, 1956), Vol. I, pp. 175–78.

15. *Ibid.*, pp. 390-91.

16. "Capitulación que se tomó con el Mariscal Don Diego de Almagro," para descubrir doscientos leguas del Mar del Sur hacia el estrecho. Año de 1534 (*Documentos inéditos*, I Ser., Vol. XXII, pp. 338-50). It will be seen that geographical notions were quite hazy at the time.

17. Jean Descola, *The Conquistadors* (London, 1954), p. 299. A sixteenth-century writer, Lopes Vasques de Pestanha ("Lopes Vaz") in his "A Discourse of the West Indies and the South Sea" (Hakluyt's *Voyages*, Vol. XI, p. 274) believed that the Indians advised the route Almagro took: "being constrained in his way to goe over part of the snowy mountains, which way his Indian guides conducted him, to the end that himselfe and all his companie, might die for colde." On the Chilean expedition, see also Kirkpatrick, pp. 177-80, and *An Account of the Spanish Settlements in America* (Edinburgh, 1762), pp. 261-63.

18. There are several excellent accounts of Valdivia's conquests. Best known in English, perhaps, is R. B. Cunninghame Graham, *Pedro de Valdivia, Conqueror of Chile* (New York, 1927); briefer accounts may be found in Lopez Vaz, *op. cit.*, *An Account of the Spanish Settlements in America*, pp. 264-316; Kirkpatrick, pp. 272-91; and Descola, pp. 302-8.

19. Lopez Vaz, *op. cit.*, p. 274.

20. Pedro de Valdivia, "III Letter to the Emperor Charles V. Concepción, Oct. 15, 1550," in Graham, *op. cit.*, Appendix, p. 195.

21. *Ibid.*, p. 199. The "North Sea," of course, refers to the Atlantic Ocean.

22. Nowell, "Aleixo Garcia and the White King," *Hispanic American Historical Review* XXVI (1946): 450-66. Charles E. Nowell has succeeded in rescuing him from his "almost legendary" status and presenting him as the audacious and intrepid explorer that he was.

23. *Ibid.*, pp. 461-62.

24. Henry Harrisse, *John Cabot, the Discoverer of North America, and Sebastian, His Son* (London, 1896) p. 185. Harrisse is inclined to accept the view of the Venetian ambassador Contarini rather than that of Peter Martyr, who said that Cabot was to sail directly to the Moluccas via the Strait of Magellan, then recross the Pacific to Panama, explore the west coast, and return to Spain.

25. *Ibid.*, p. 195.

26. *Ibid.*, p. 203.

27. *Ibid.*, pp. 211-17.

28. In 1530, with both parties before him, the king decided, as he should have, in favor of García.

29. Harrisse, p. 221.

30. For these versions see Vicente Sierra, *Historia de la Argentina* (Buenos Aires, 1958), Vol. I, pp. 186-87.

31. "Capitulación que se tomó con Don Pedro de Mendoza, para la conquista del Río de la Flata" (*Documentos inéditos*, Ser. I, Vol. XXII, pp. 350–60). This document is undated; the date, however, may be ascertained from the Libro de Asientos i Capitulaciones, *Ibid.*, Ser. II, Vol. XVII, p. 40.

32. Huldrich Schmidel, *Historia y descubrimiento de el Río de la Plata y Paraguay* (several editions, including an English translation published by the Hakluyt Society, London, 1891). This writer used the Spanish version in Andrés González de Barcia Carballido y Zuñiga, *Historiadores primitivos de las Indias occidentales*, (Madrid, 1749), Vol. III. See also R. B. Cunninghame Graham, *The Conquest of the River Plate* (London, 1924); Enrique de Gandía, *Historia de la conquista del Río de la Plata y del Paraguay, 1535-1556* (Buenos Aires, 1932); and Kirkpatrick, Chap. 26.

33. Schmidel, Chaps. 1-14.

34. *Ibid.*, Chaps. 17-20.

35. *Ibid.*, Chaps. 23-26. Schmidel states (Chap. 27) that he learned of this from an Indian who had been a slave of Ayolas. Alvar Núñez Cabeza de Vaca in his *Comentarios*, Chap. 4 (BAE, Vol. XXII) states that this Indian was a Christian, named Gonzalo.

36. This account of the journey from Santa Catarina to Asunción is from Cabeza de Vaca, Chaps. 1-14.

37. *Ibid.*, Chaps. 44-73; Schmidel, Chaps. 34-40.

38. Schmidel, Chaps. 44-49. Nuflo de Cháves headed the mission.

39. Schmidel was not the only one to report river monsters; we shall hear more of them from the *monçoeiros*—those who made the journey by river from São Paulo to the mines of Cuiabá in the eighteenth century.

40. Schmidel, Chaps. 51-53.

41. Ricardo Levene, *A History of Argentina* (Chapel Hill, N.C., 1937), p. 35.

42. Cf. Kirkpatrick, pp. 336-37. An excellent account of Rojas' entry into Argentina, giving a valuable critique of the sources, may be found in Francisco de Aparicio, "Descubrimiento del Territorio Argentino: la 'Entrada' de Diego Rojas," *Revista Histórica Americana*, December, 1952, pp. 323-37.

43. Sierra, *op. cit.*, Vol. I, pp. 394-95.

44. *Ibid.*, pp. 466-68.

IV *Sixteenth-Century*

Penetration into the Interior:

East and North

THE AMAZON

Gold and silver were not the only kinds of wealth sought by the sixteenth-century explorers. Portugal had acquired a near monopoly on the spice trade of the east, but there were high hopes in Spain that the New World would also be productive of this valuable item of trade. In 1539 Gonzalo Pizarro, then governor of Quito, learned of a "cinnamon tree" which bore fragrant leaves and nuts. Indians claimed that these trees grew in profusion in the forests on the other side of the Andes. This source of spices would make Spain independent of the East Indies. Late in 1540 Pizarro began equipping an expedition to search for cinnamon; for 50,000 castellanos of gold he was able to raise 200 foot soldiers and 100 cavalry, 4000 Indians, and several thousand pigs, dogs, and llamas—partly at his own expense. If this seems an excessive outlay to find cinnamon, Pizarro's letter to his king indicated another (perhaps his chief) purpose—he intended to look for the "very populous and very rich land" around Lake El Dorado, about which he had learned "from prominent and very aged chiefs as well as from Spaniards, whose accounts agreed with one another." [1] Serving under him was one Captain Francisco de Orellana, lieutenant-governor of Guayaquil; he had volunteered his services, went to Guayaquil to resign his office and make preparations at his own expense, then returned to Quito to find that Pizarro had already left. With twenty-three men he took off in pursuit, and caught up with the governor in Motín province.

The enterprise was beset by so many difficulties—Indians, rain, earthquakes, and thunderstorms—"such that anyone but Gonzalles Pizarre would have abandon'd such an Enterprize as seem'd to be opposed by both Heaven and Earth." [2] The party crossed the cordillera in heavy rain, which turned to snow, and finally stopped at Zumaque, some sixty leagues from Quito. Pizarro then proceeded with 230 men, and found some cinnamon trees. Seeking to discover where they flourished in abundance, he tortured Indians and threw them to his dogs, but he learned nothing, for there was nothing to learn, and reported to the king that only the buds had the flavor of cinnamon and the paucity of trees did not make the search worth the trouble. With the whole country up in arms against him, he returned to Zumaque. There was still the prospect of gold. Pizarro's letter referred to a "Lake El Dorado," but there was also the tale, which Pizarro knew, of "King El Dorado"—the Gilded King—who went about clad only in gold dust, applied to his body with ointment, since he believed that to wear anything fabricated of gold was vulgarity. So abundant was gold in his realm that he washed off the gold dust every night and threw it away.[3] El Dorado was to join the White King, the silver mountain, and the Enchanted City of the Caesars as one of the most alluring of the South American legends.

Hearing of a well-populated land ahead, Pizarro sent his camp master with fifty men to investigate. He returned in fifteen days with a story of a well-populated province along a great river. The inhabitants, he added, seemed quite civilized. Leaving most of his force in Zumaque, Pizarro proceeded toward the river, hacking his way through the forest, often in heavy rain. On his arrival, the cacique of the settlement told him that the easiest way out was to embark on the river, which would lead to a larger one on whose banks lived people covered with plates of gold—certainly an appealing idea to Pizarro. He sent for the rest of his force. So frightened was the cacique by the sight of these troops in battle array that he gave Pizarro nearly all his provisions to get rid of him. The next morning the Spaniards took leave, and proceeded along the river, which was the Río Coca, a tributary of the Napo which flows into the Amazon. For forty-three days they followed along the shore, failing to find a ford, canoes, or provisions, until they came to a place where two rocks in the river some twenty feet apart made possible the building of a bridge. The other side of the river was no better, so they decided to build a brigantine to carry the sick and their provisions.[4]

After the expedition had sailed downstream fifty leagues, and found no more inhabited regions, Orellana approached Pizarro with an offer to leave him nearly all the food, and head downstream with a small force in the hope of finding a populated place and, most of all, more food. Pizarro was to wait three or four days or longer for his return. To this he gave his consent, and Orellana selected fifty-three men to accompany him. The first day out, no food was found; the second day the boat was damaged when it struck a log, but luckily it was near the shore and could be hauled out and repaired. By the end of the third day the swiftness of the current had carried them two hundred leagues, and they were nearly out of food; they decided to look one more day, then another, without success. They had now gone so far from their companions that to attempt to return without food seemed impossible; they were eating "nothing but leather, belts and soles of shoes, cooked with certain herbs." Orellana decided not to attempt a return, but, trusting to Divine Providence, to continue on downstream in the hope of finding food and eventually reaching civilization.[5] To Pizarro, who waited in vain, and to some of Orellana's own men this was desertion.[6]

Pizarro, unable to continue without boats, stole five canoes from the Indians and set out to look for food. Hunger had become acute. The men had been eating palm shoots and "various kinds of noxious wild beasts which they had been able to find," and had consumed more than one thousand dogs and one hundred horses. Going up to the Napo, and following that river upstream a short distance, Pizarro found food on an abandoned yuca plantation. He was now convinced that Orellana must have found provisions here and gone on without reporting it. Transporting his weakened forces across the Napo by canoe took eight days, but he succeeded in feeding his men and in laying in supplies for a journey. There was nothing to do but go back. The expedition returned up the Río Coca, and after an arduous journey in which many were lost, eighty emaciated, naked men finally stumbled into Quito in August of 1542, completely exhausted.[7]

Meanwhile, far to the east, Orellana's problem of food abated temporarily when the distant sound of drums told him that human life was near. Canoes appeared in the river. The Spaniards rushed into the first village in sight and ate everything possible while the Indians fled. Orellana himself approached, demanded to talk to the cacique, and convinced him that his party meant no harm, but sought only food. The relieved chieftain ordered it brought in abundance, and the Spaniards, true to their orders, made no effort to seize any of the gold objects they noticed the Indians were wearing. Convinced that they would eventually reach the sea by continuing downstream, and realizing that their present craft was quite unseaworthy, Orellana insisted that they build a larger brigantine, and spent so much time in the difficult task of making nails that his forces consumed nearly all their food and dared not ask for more. Fortunately, after their departure, the Spaniards were able to make known their wants, and the Indians they encountered as they progressed downstream seemed quite willing—even eager—to provide parrots, partridges, turtles, fish, and other items for which Orellana offered, as he had before, various articles from his supplies.

Orellana's acquaintance with the Indian language was of enormous

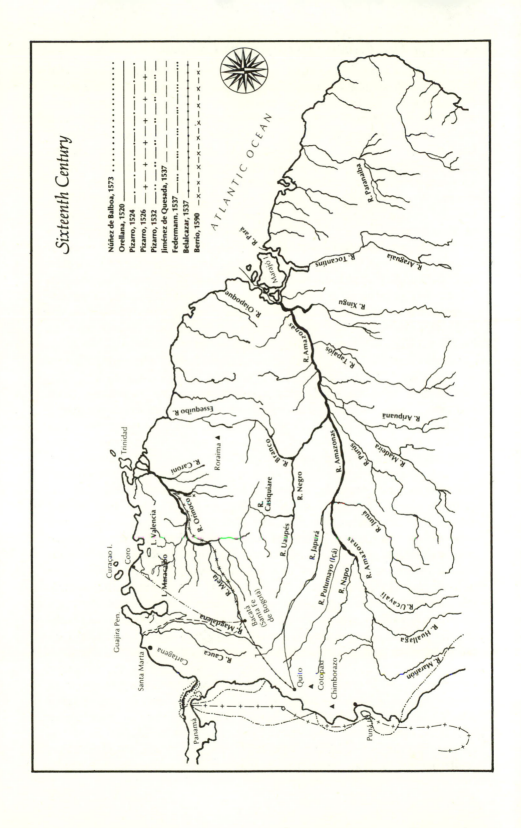

Sixteenth Century

Núñez de Balboa, 1573 ·······
Orellana, 1520 ——————
Pizarro, 1524 ·—·—·—·
Pizarro, 1526 —+—+—+—
Pizarro, 1532 ·—··—··—
Jiménez de Quesada, 1537 ———————
Federmann, 1537 ·············
Belalcazar, 1537 —×—×—×—
Berrío, 1590 —×—×—×—

ATLANTIC OCEAN

benefit to the expedition, since it enabled him to express his peaceful intentions and obtain food and supplies as they were needed. In one village, where the Indians were particularly friendly and there was a good supply of materials, he decided to build yet another brigantine, a task which consumed thirty-five days and happened to coincide with Lent; Father Carvajal, who accompanied Orellana tells of regular preaching during this period, and of renewed fervor among the men. On April 24 the brigantine was launched, and the expedition continued downstream. Several weeks passed. There were violent encounters with hostile Indians and the usual food-raiding parties by the Spaniards. On the eve of Trinity Sunday, Carvajal tells us, they saw the mouth of a large river on the left, whose waters were so black that they gave it the name Río Negro. Its current was so strong that the waters did not mix for twenty leagues. Two days later the Spaniards met some Indians who claimed to be subjects of a nation of women, Amazons, and still later, in an encounter with other Indians, Carvajal reports seeing a dozen very white and tall women warriors, fighting in front of the men as captains, and killing any men who turned their backs.[8]

Eastward from the Río Negro the Spaniards had several encounters with warlike Indians, some—Carvajal reports—of great stature and very dark. They found the river "cluttered with pirogues" on one occasion, and the Indians "began to attack us and to fight like ravenous dogs," but were driven off by the crossbowmen and arquebusiers, with some Spanish losses due to poisoned arrows. Further on they saw an unmistakable sign that their journey was near an end—the movement of the tide was discernible. The nature of the country began to change. Savannas and high ground gave way to low ground and numerous islands, through which "the tide comes up with great fury." Once they entered among the islands, says Carvajal, they never again saw the shore. There was still the problem of food, solved for the most part by occasional raids on villages, and the problem of repairing the vessels, which consumed several weeks. The last stage of the voyage was made under sails of blankets and rigging of vines. The expedition sailed out of the estuary, which Carvajal estimated was over fifty leagues wide, on August 26; lacking any navigational instruments, they clung to the coast until reaching the port of Cubagua near Trinidad. They had been eight months on the great river, and had traveled 1800 leagues to its mouth.[9]

After he reached Spain again, Orellana "so charmed the Emperor with the agreeable recital of his Adventures, and with the fair Promises he made, that he obtain'd three Ships of him in which to return from whence he came, with orders to build Forts and Houses in three places which he should find most commodious, and to take possession of the Country in the Name of this Prince."[10] He was unable to leave Spain until the end of 1549 when, proceeding to the Canaries, he lost many of his crew from sickness, and went on to Cape Verde, where he was advised to return. Unwilling to abandon the enterprise Orellana crossed the Atlantic, reaching the Amazon. So frightful were his losses that he ordered all the crews aboard his own ship. Yet the losses continued. An attempt to ascend the Amazon failed, and the course was changed to the coast of Tierra-Firme in vain; the last of the crew, and Orellana himself, perished on Margarita Island.

A second Amazon expedition began in 1558 when a Navarrese soldier, Pedro de Ursúa, presented himself to the viceroy of Peru, and received permission to explore the interior, with a grant of funds for the venture. Ursúa was a persuasive speaker and drew a substantial number of recruits to make a truly impressive expedition. Unfortunately, he did not take the trouble to sort out the undesirables, of whom he recruited a fair number; worst of the lot was Lope de Aguirre, fifty years of age, who led a gang of a dozen thugs into the expedition. Ursúa's plan was to follow the Río Huallaga to the Marañón, and then duplicate Orellana's feat.[11]

Although the expedition started off badly, nothing suggested that it would become one of the most bizarre and terrifying of all attempts to explore the interior of the continent. There were too few ships, requiring frequent stops to seek provisions. Ursúa had invited trouble by insisting on bringing along a beautiful widow, Inés de Atienza.[12] And as if to crown these blunders with a monumental—and fatal—act of stupidity, he gave the command to Aguirre when they reached the confluence of the Ucayali and the Marañón. The expedition continued downstream, finding "Synamon trees,"[13] abundant vegetables, and tortoises. But trouble soon arose. Aguirre hatched a plot with Fernando de Guzmán, and Ursúa was assassinated on December 31, 1560. It may have been Aguirre's ambition or Ursúa's complaints about his treatment of the Indians which led to the mutiny, but Acuña presents a more plausible explanation—Doña Inés: "thinking they had a favorable occasion to satisfy their Lust and Ambition together, [they] engaged Orsua's Troops to revolt, and assassinated him."[14] Doña Inés was killed soon after, Aguirre charging misbehavior on her part and claiming also that she took up too much room in the boat.

From here on the expedition became a nightmare. Guzmán was made leader, but Aguirre soon killed him, now proclaimed himself king, blasphemed wildly, and wrote an insolent letter to Felipe II. In what must have been a psychopathic delusion, he announced that he would master Guiana, Peru, and New Granada, and promised riches to all who would follow him. Yet he could not master the Amazon current, and drifted downstream to Margarita Island, where he killed the governor and his aged father, and plundered the isle. Fearing the consequences for his daughter, Doña Elvira, as the daughter of a traitor, Aguirre killed her when he was on the point of being captured. Taken prisoner himself, he was executed publicly, and his body was quartered. His house was razed and salt sown in the ruins.

THE INTERIOR OF BRAZIL

With the exception of the explorations already discussed, the exploration of Brazil was confined largely to the seacoast areas: few dared to venture into the unknown interior—the forbidding *sertão*— and it long remained a land of mystery. Geographical notions of the *sertão* were extremely vague and anthropological ideas even more so. Fantasy stocked the area with the strangest of peoples—men with no heads, but with faces in their chests; men with but a single eye, or a single leg; and others. It was easy to transport such oddities, once believed to inhabit the unexplored parts of Asia, to the forbidding wilderness of Brazil. And rumor told of white Indians, pygmies, and female warriors. If men could seek gilded chieftains and white kings in the interior of South America, could it not also contain such prodigies as these? Was this not, after all, an age of wonder?

The earliest explorations of any consequence were undertaken under the auspices of Martim Afonso de Sousa, who had been favored with a grant of extensive powers of government and the charge to mark the limits of Portuguese dominion according to the Treaty of Tordesillas. His vessels roamed from the Amazon to the Río de la Plata, where his men erected stone pillars (*padrões*) claiming the land for the Portuguese crown. They had heard rumors of gold and silver there, and interpreted the treaty to extend as far west as possible, laying the ground for a long struggle with Spain.

But expeditions into the *sertão* had a way of turning into disasters. Aleixo Garcia had been murdered. In 1531 Sousa had been influenced by a resident of Cananéia to order a force of eighty men under Pero Lôbo into the interior. The resident, Francisco de Chaves, gave his word that they would return in ten months with four hundred slaves laden with gold and silver. The entire party, however, was killed near the confluence of the Iguaçu and the Paraná. A ship sent under the command of Miguel Henriques to explore the Rio São Francisco never returned. Subsequent attempts in the *sertões* of the Rio São Francisco, Ilhéus, Pernambuco, and Espiritú Santo all failed.[15]

However, there were some successes. Several penetrations into the interior, although somewhat limited in their depth, did provide the outside world with considerable information about the land at this early date. Two French naturalists, the Franciscan friar André Thevet and the Calvinist Jean de Léry prepared studies of the flora and fauna of

Brazil. Thevet, incidentally, also introduced tobacco into France. A far more extensive study was the *Epistola* of Padre José de Anchieta, S.J., published in Latin in 1560. He described the climate, the monkeys, ant-eaters, porcupines; a great variety of birds, insects, and serpents; the mangrove swamps; and the luxurious vegetation of the country with the practiced eye of a true scientist. Gabriel Soares de Sousa, who operated a sugar *fazenda* in the interior, rounded out this scholarly exploration with his *Tratado Descritivo do Brasil* (1587), which was particularly valuable for its studies of geography, botany, and ethnography.[16]

It is interesting that some of the most colorful information about the interior came from men who were not Portuguese, and who were not there voluntarily in the first place. We have first the Hessian gunner, Hans Staden, who was in the service of Portugal. After being ship-wrecked near São Vicente, he took a job as a gunner at Fort Santo Amaro, built to defend the settlement from the Tupinambá tribe, deadly enemies of the Portuguese. As luck would have it, Staden went hunting one day and was captured by the Indians, who made known their in-tention of eating him. Efforts to rescue him were in vain, and he was taken to the Indian village and eventually turned over to an uncle of his captors in payment for a favor. His efforts to convince them that he was not Portuguese, but "kin to the French" (with whom they were friendly) failed miserably when a Frenchman in the area came to see him, and told his captors to eat him—he was Portuguese. When he was brought before the king, who boasted how many Portuguese he had eaten, Staden told him of an impending attack by an enemy tribe, which he had learned of before his captivity, and offered to assist in the defense. The attack came off as predicted, and the victory of Staden's captors enhanced his prestige somewhat. Subsequently sickness in the tribe, bad dreams by the tribal leaders, Staden's remark about divine vengeance and his prayers for the sick (many of whom recovered), plus his red beard (they had never seen a red-bearded Portuguese) combined to lend credence to his claim that he was not Portuguese, and to make the Indians wonder about his God.

Twice Staden almost escaped—once to a Portuguese, another time to a French, ship—but failed and was obliged to invent convincing ex-planations for his behavior. Christian captives were brought to the village and several were eaten before him; Staden managed to assist the rest in escaping, but could not get away himself. Eventually he contrived to get aboard a French ship with the king, who, overcome by the pleadings of the crew members—who pretended to be his brothers—that their aged father wanted to see him once more before he died, released him. The details of his almost incredible experiences are related in Staden's own absorbing account, *The True History of His Captivity* (1557).[17]

Two decades later, in 1578, an English sailor, Peter Carder, and seven companions were left in a shallop when Drake returned to the Strait of Magellan after passing it earlier. They lost sight of their ship, and after a search as far as the strait returned to the Río de la Plata, where all but two were killed in a skirmish with the Indians. For two months Carder and his companion, William Pitcher, stayed on a small island, with little food and almost no water. Finally they were able to reach the mainland on a plank, where Pitcher, finding water, drank so much that he died.

Carder proceeded along the coast, hoping to reach Brazil. Meeting some Indians from the very tribe which had attacked Staden's captors, he joined them and went to their town, where he remained for several months, learning their language and customs. They were moon worshipers, he relates, and killed their captives by splitting open their heads, often eating them afterward. Eventually he secured permission to leave, and was given an escort to Bahia de Todos os Santos, where he was surrendered to the Portuguese.[18]

Last of this trio of unintentional explorers was Anthony Knivet, who had served under Thomas Cavendish in a raid on Santos. Returning to that port after failing to get through the strait, Cavendish was engaged by the Portuguese, after which he decided to put the sick (including Knivet) ashore to shift for themselves. Knivet was soon the sole survivor, managing to stay alive on crabs and parts of a stranded whale until picked up by some Englishmen, who quickly lost him to attacking Portuguese. Knivet was eventually turned over to Martim de Sá as a servant ("slave," as he put it), and told of taking part in an expedition into the interior "there to trafficke with the Canibals for Women, Boyes, and Girles." The entry was a success; ninety slaves were brought back. Subsequently, in 1597, Knivet accompanied Sá, seven hundred Portuguese, and one thousand Indians in an expedition against a cannibal nation. They traversed meadows, pine forests, rivers, and mountains. At one point Knivet and Sá ate some poisonous fruit, and were saved only by Enefrio de Sá, "who had a piece of Unicornes horne"! Hunger, disease, and "Wormes in their fundament" caused the death of many. For a month they lived on leather and wild honey. On one occasion Knivet nearly met death by execution. While on watch he had left his post momentarily to kill some snakes, and was accused of deserting his duty. Only the captain's inability to produce royal authority to conduct an execution, when challenged by Knivet's friends, saved him.

The reduced party pushed on, evidently no longer concerned with its original project, for in several small streams in the mountains they had found gold nuggets "as bigge as an Hasell nut." A large mountain loomed ahead, and the party could find no pass; finally they followed the course of a river which passed through a cavern in the mountain, and emerged near an Indian village. Knivet had the presence of mind to identify himself as French, for the Indians killed and ate the Portuguese. Knivet joined the Indians, and persuaded them to migrate away from the Portuguese settlements and the Spanish areas, but word of it apparently reached the Portuguese. An expedition under Martim de Sá (who had left the earlier expedition) engaged the Indians, capturing twenty thousand slaves and Knivet. Back in Portuguese service, he was again off to fight the Indians. On one occasion he mentions a curious incident— some Indians showed him a rock from which they claimed that the Apostle St. Thomas had preached to them, even showing his footprints in the stone. After his return from this successful expedition, we find Knivet in a new role—that of a diver. Several pieces of ordnance from a fort had washed into the sea; Knivet agreed to go down and try to recover it for 10,000 crowns and his freedom. Weighted down by a heavy stone, he went into eighteen fathoms of water in a diving suit of greased leather, with air supplied by three bladders; the plan did not work, so Knivet cut the rope and surfaced so quickly that for a month he did not know what he was doing. Ultimately he was able to get to Recife, and sailed for Lisboa in 1599, planning to go from there to England.[19]

TIERRA-FIRME, THE ORINOCO AND THE SEARCH FOR EL DORADO

The first serious attempts to penetrate the interior of Tierra-Firme, along the Caribbean coast, were the work of Germans rather than Spaniards. The Emperor Carlos V, in order to win election to the imperial dignity, was deeply in debt to German bankers. To pay off this obligation, he conceded Venezuela to the house of Welser, agents of the Fuggers. As their agent, the Welsers chose one Ambrosius Ehinger (or Einger—the Spaniards called him Alfinger), twenty-eight years of age, who was named governor-general, displacing the Spaniard Juan de Ampués, founder of the settlement at Coro. He began by exploring Lake Maracaibo, and founded the city of the same name. Finding no gold, he seized Indians and branded them. In 1531 Ehinger sallied forth again, crossing into the land behind the Sierra Santa Marta, where he heard of a nation that possessed a golden idol the size of a man, which was carried in a hammock; this would seem to be a variant of the El Dorado legend. Ehinger surpassed all records for cruelty in America, pillaging, burning, and murdering indiscriminately, extorting gold in the manner of a barbarian.

Believing that he was approaching El Dorado, and needing more troops for the conquest, Ehinger sent Iñigo Vascuña with thirty-five men and 60,000 pesos of gold to get men and provisions in Coro. Not daring to return by the same route, they got lost, buried their gold at the foot of a ceiba tree, ate all their porters, and divided into small groups. The sole survivor was Francisco Martín, who was saved by a tribe whose language he knew slightly. He joined them, married several of their women, and became a warrior of their chief. Ehinger, meanwhile, had sent out exploring parties, and learned of a temperate valley. Leading his party along the swollen Magdalena River, he took them into the cold *páramos,* where, as so often happened, nearly all the Indians died. He was nearer to the Chibcha kingdom than he realized when he turned back, was ambushed and shot with a poisoned arrow, and died three days later in terrible agony.[20]

Meanwhile Nicholas Federmann, whom the Welsers had sent to America when they had heard nothing from Ehinger for a year, and who had already conducted an unauthorized expedition toward the Chibcha kingdom, for which he had been deported, was now back in Venezuela. He had arrived with the new governor, Georg Hohemuth of Speier, who was now calling himself Jorge de Espira, and had staged a slave raid immediately upon landing. Determined to find the buried gold, Hohemuth set out with 361 men, guided by that one-time Indian warrior Francisco Martín, who unfortunately could not remember under which ceiba tree they had buried it. Hohemuth pushed on, lured by stories of gold, through torrential rains, across the Río Meta and into the mountains, finally reaching a small village where he found salt and cotton, but missed the Chibcha kingdom, as Ehinger had before him. The troops would go no farther. The return journey was terrible. Martín died from an infected wound. The horses died and were eaten. So low did their hunger cause them to sink that they ate a year-old boy.[21]

When the starved remnants of Hohemuth's expedition reached Coro, Federmann was found to have left, despite orders to the contrary. Having failed before, he was determined to reach the Chibcha kingdom, this time by the Río Magdalena. But since the governor of Santa Marta was equipping Jiménez de Quesada for the identical project, and had expressly forbidden Federmann to go, he decided to leave from Venezuela in the hope of reaching the kingdom before his Spanish rival. Led by Pedro de Limpias, Federmann made an extraordinary ascent of the cordillera, in which his horses had to be hoisted by rope; Indians tried in vain to halt him by burning the grass before him, but Federmann put out the fires and crossed the *páramos* without further opposition. Ahead was the savanna of Bogotá; success would crown three years of effort. But all was in vain. As he entered the Chibcha capital, he was greeted by the conquistador Jiménez de Quesada, who had won the race. And as if to crown the ignominy, Belalcázar and his well-fed troops, carrying treasure with them, arrived from Quito. Federmann had nothing to show for all his effort.[22]

Gold, of course, was the chief objective of all these efforts. And intermingled with tales of gold there was nearly always a reference of some sort to "El Dorado"—the Gilded King. We have already noted one version of the story, which seems to be well-grounded in fact. Prior to 1480, when a conquest by another tribe ended the practice, the chief of a people around the sacred lake of Guatavita, near Bogotá, would anoint his body, roll in gold dust, enter a canoe, make a ceremonial offering of gold and jewels in the lake, then jump in and wash off the gold dust. Somehow in the telling, the idea of El Dorado as a place developed; for Ehinger it was the rich province of Xerira, in Santo Domingo it was believed to be a rich land between Peru and the Río de la Plata (the White King again?), while the Goahibo Indians of Tierra-Firme located it around the headwaters of the Río Meta, where they probably got gold objects from the "rich" Muisca Indians, craftsmen in gold. Ultimately we find El Dorado located in the Orinoco valley—it was the golden city of Manoa, on the shores of the great lake of Parima. Curiously enough, since silver was more highly prized at first in Brazil, legend there described Manoa as a city of silver, shimmering in the moonlight.[23]

One of the first Spaniards actively to search for El Dorado was the conqueror of Quito, Sebastián de Belalcázar (or Benalcázar). In 1536 he had taken it into his head to explore on his own. He left Pizarro and pushed north into the valley of the Río Cauca, founding the cities of Popayán and Cali. Here, apparently, he learned of El Dorado, and set out with three hundred Spaniards and a large number of Indians in search of it. Progress was slow, and there were frequent encounters with Indians who used poisoned arrows. As Belalcázar and his men entered the Magdalena valley, they were astounded and disappointed to be greeted by another force of Spaniards under Hernán Pérez de Quesada, brother of the conquistador, who had heard of their presence in the valley in Bogotá. Together they entered the city, as we have seen, and a division of some of the spoils was made among the three commanders.[24]

The expedition of the third of these captains has an interesting background. In 1535 Don Pedro Fernández de Lugo was made governor of Santa Marta, and sent his son Alonso to lead a party inland. Alonso proved to be a bad choice; he robbed the Indians, his father, and the king, and then fled to Spain. The governor now turned to a thirty-four-year-old lawyer from Córdoba who was attached to his staff, Gonzalo Jiménez de Quesada. There were rumors, as we have seen, of a rich kingdom to the south; Quesada was to conquer it. The plan was for him to proceed on foot with six hundred men and one hundred horses along the banks of the Río Magdalena, well protected against any poisonous arrows by coverings of thick cotton quilting. Forty leagues upstream they were to meet three hundred men in five ships. The meeting did not take place, for three of the ships were wrecked in a gale and the other two returned to Santa Marta. The governor sent word of the disaster to Quesada and built two more ships. Of the four which set out this time, three finally joined the conquistador many months later.

The expedition had started out from Santa Marta in April of 1536, and the Spaniards proceeded under great difficulties when the ships failed to arrive. Food ran out, and they resorted to eating snakes, lizards, rats and bats, dogs, leather shields and the hides of dead animals. Many died and others grew sick but Quesada refused to turn back. When the ships finally arrived with the supplies, the sick were sent back to Santa Marta, some dying on the way. In December, with supplies again running low, the Spaniards found a deserted Indian village. Luckily the nearby fields were filled with ripening corn, which Quesada rationed out. Again there were murmurings of discontent, but advance exploring parties discovered some abandoned huts and canoes and, what was more significant, salt and fabrics; furthermore, Indians told them of emeralds and powerful caciques. Quesada determined to go on, and in April of 1537 he reached a large basin between the mountains. But of the 900 who began the expedition a year before no more than 166 remained.

In August Quesada began a campaign against the king of Tunja, on the rather weak pretext that he had rebelled against the Christians. The Indians, who like most of their fellow aborigines throughout the continent lived in almost mortal dread of horses, offered no opposition, and the Spaniards rode directly into the "palace" and into the presence of the king. He was enormously fat and so unable to escape. The invaders appropriated all the gold they could find, and when they left a few weeks later made it quite plain to the king that henceforth he was a vassal of the emperor. Toward the end of the year and the beginning of 1538, Quesada's forces were able to bring under their rule most of the petty princes of Cundinamarca, and they entered the Chibcha realm. Here was wealth at last—gold, emeralds, and semiprecious stones—and the Spaniards appropriated it. The king of Bacatá (Bogotá) was accidentally killed, whereupon Quesada appointed his cousin as king, but he failed to reveal the hiding place of more treasure—if there was any— and subsequently died. Shortly thereafter Federmann arrived, and then Belalcázar. The German, who thus far had nothing, was given a share in the gold, and the question of the right of government was left to the king. Despite the gold that he had acquired, Quesada was not convinced that he had found El Dorado. Perhaps he still sought the Gilded Man.[25] Meanwhile gold had been found elsewhere. Francisco César, for whose "lost city" men would search, set out from Santa Marta in 1536 and some nine months later discovered a temple of the devil and tombs containing gold. Lacking enough men, he took what he could and returned.

Despite the failures of Ehinger, Hohemuth, and Federmann, the Germans had not yet given up. Anton Welser decided to send his son Bartholomew and a German knight named Philipp von Hutten (they were known to the Spaniards as Bartolomé Belzar and Felipe de Utre) to Coro to try to find gold. Some of Hohemuth's veterans were on hand and were anxious for another try, so Hutten was able in 1541 to recruit 130 volunteers. As camp master he chose Pedro de Limpias, who, recognizing the value of a good name and well aware of the legend, named the provinces they would seek "El Dorado." Indians recommended that they follow the course of the Río Meta and then head toward the Amazon, where they would find gold idols the size of a woman (had the legends of the Amazons and El Dorado become mixed?). Hutten did so, following the course of the Meta into the highlands where life became difficult and food scarce. Here he learned that Hernán Pérez de Quesada, brother of the conquistador, had passed recently in his search for the Temple of the Sun (which he never found). Against all advice, Hutten determined to follow Quesada's course. His guides deserted, so he finally decided to return to Coro, where he had been given up for lost. On the way back he encountered Juan de Carvajal, who had illegally seized power in Coro and refused to let him return. After a quarrel Carvajal arrested Hutten, who, with Welser, tried to escape. Carvajal finally caught up with them and had them beheaded. For this black deed Carvajal was finally condemned, dragged by horses, and hanged to a large ceiba tree, which promptly died.[26]

Two years after the death of Hutten and Welser, another Spanish attempt to reach El Dorado was made from Coro. In February of 1547 Alonso Pérez de Tolosa headed south, followed the Río Tocuyo up to the mountains, crossed over, reaching the Río Guarane, crossed the *llanos*, and made ready to ascend the Sierra Nevada. Seeing the height of the mountains, he feared his men would die of cold, and so returned to the *llanos*, eventually reaching the Río Apure, which he followed west in the hope of finding a pass. As he reached the valley of Cúcuta, still far short of his goal, Pérez de Tolosa was killed by Indians.[27]

A number of expeditions sought to reach El Dorado by way of the Orinoco River. One of the first of these entered the Orinoco quite by accident. Diego de Ordaz had contracted with Carlos V to explore the Amazon region, perhaps to find El Dorado. He sailed in November of 1530 and reached the Amazon estuary only to suffer shipwreck, but saved his force of five hundred men and thirty-one horses. Heading north to the Orinoco after repairs, he took on additional troops and decided to proceed up that river, constructing boats for the purpose. The voyage was difficult—hunger, rain, savages, sickness, insects—but was not the goal worth it? For ahead was untold wealth and people clothed in gold. Indian guides advised going up the Meta, but perhaps because of its shallowness at that season Ordaz headed south on the Orinoco until forced to halt at the falls of Atures. Returning to Paria, he planned an overland journey, but was unable to recruit followers.[28] His camp master, Alonso de Herrera, was able, with great difficulty, to penetrate farther up the Meta in 1533, finding Indians of higher culture, but died from a poisoned arrow.

Much later in the century, activity in this area was resumed. Pedro Malaver de Silva led several expeditions between 1565 and 1576, determined to find El Dorado. He entered the area from Peru, from Coro, and from the Orinoco before meeting his death at the hands of the Caribs in present-day Guyana. Another expedition led by Diego Fernández de Serpa in 1568 was equally disastrous; the explorer died in an Indian attack. In 1584 the dynamic Antonio de Berrio, a soldier who had married Quesada's niece, launched his first Orinoco expedition. Then in his sixties, he entered the Orinoco area from New Granada, explored the valley of the Meta, but was forced back by fever. Undaunted, he made a second attempt from New Granada in 1586, and explored the Sierra Parima, seeking El Dorado and the golden city of Manoa. He possessed a vivid description of the city, for a Spanish soldier told him of having been taken to it blindfolded, of enjoying its opulence, and leaving. Oddly, he could not remember the way back. An attempt by Berrio about 1589 to build ships for exploration along the river ended in mutiny, and in the abandonment of the project. Still Berrio would not give up. Bearing now the sonorous and impressive title of governor of El Dorado, he left Tunja in 1590 and went down the Meta to the Orinoco, exploring the right bank in the expectation of finding a valley which would lead to El Dorado. Learning of the Río Caroní, which enters the Orinoco from the south, Berrio hastened to it, only to find that a great cataract near its mouth prevented entry. Disillusioned, and hindered by hostile Indians, he gave up the search in 1591. Two years later, unable to try again himself, Berrio sent Domingo de Vera to explore the Caroní above the cataract; it was the usual story—the great lake, the golden city of Manoa, were always ahead. Exhausted from the fruitless search, Vera gave up.

An account Vera wrote of his experience eventually came to the notice of that eminent Elizabethan gentleman, Sir Walter Raleigh, who had previously learned of El Dorado from Pedro Sarmiento de Gamboa during the latter's imprisonment in England. Early in 1595 Raleigh arrived in Trinidad and captured Berrio, who provided him with much information, for the most part untrue or misleading. Raleigh believed that the Caroní was the route to El Dorado, but barely managed to reach the river when the flood season began, so he returned to England. The following year he sent Lawrence Keymis, who reached the same point only to discover that Berrio had constructed a fort; he had to content himself, then, with exploring various rivers in Guiana. Years passed, but the lure of El Dorado did not diminish. In 1617 Raleigh arrived in Trinidad and ordered Keymis to go to the Caroní. Several men were killed at the fort, including Raleigh's son; Keymis committed suicide, and Raleigh returned to England, soon to meet his own death.[20]

El Dorado remained undiscovered, as did the White King and the Enchanted City of the Caesars. That they should remain so occasions no surprise today, for a more sophisticated generation knows full well, or pretends to believe that it knows, that such marvels are but the figment of fertile imaginations, and could not possibly be true. Today we would people distant worlds across the void of space with exotic creatures of incredible achievements; in this sixteenth-century age of marvels, when a hitherto unknown world was thrust upon them, might we not excuse those people for flights of fancy which might prove true? Gold beyond men's dreams had already been found; was it expecting too much to hope to encounter even greater prodigies? Much remained to be learned of this New World; it does not seem far-fetched to suggest that had not these alluring legends enticed men into the unknown, many would long have hesitated before facing unknown perils with no promise of reward.

With the close of the sixteenth century, then, we reach the end of the great age of discovery and conquest. The outline of the continent, as we have seen, was quite well known by the middle of the century; by its end, daring and courageous men of amazing vitality and endurance had crossed its highest mountains, sailed on its greatest rivers, and poured out their fortunes and their lives in pursuit of myths. The conquest was over, and the continent had been crossed; cities had been founded, and men could enjoy the peaceful pursuits of a settled life. But there was still the lure of the unknown, the need to know what lay beyond each mountain and forest, around the bend of each river. And this made explorers of those who chased the myths, lusted after gold, baptized the heathen, hunted for slaves, sought high adventure, or studied the phenomena of nature. For them there was still much to learn, and much to be done.

NOTES

1. Letter of Gonzalo Pizarro to the King, dated September 3, 1542, in José Toribio Medina, ed., *The Discovery of the Amazon* (New York, 1934), Part III, Documents, pp. 245-49. The best longer accounts of the discovery are those of the eyewitness Friar Gaspar de Carvajal, whose *Account of the Discovery of the Orellana River* forms the core of Medina's study, Gonzalo Fernández de Oviedo, whose contemporary account, based on Carvajal, is in Part V of his *Historia general y natural de las Indias*, and Cristóbal Acuña, S.J., who wrote a century later *Nuevo descubrimiento del gran río de Amazonas* (English trans. in *Voyages and Discoveries*

in South America, London, 1698). See also Kirkpatrick, *The Spanish Conquistadores* (London, 1934), pp. 230-37.

2. Acuña, Chap. 2.

3. Fernández de Oviedo, Chap. 2. Cf. Enrique de Gandía, *Historia crítica de los mitos de la conquista americana* (Madrid, 1929).

4. Fernández de Oviedo, Chap. 2; see also Pizarro's Letter, Carvajal, *op. cit.*, pp. 168-69, and Acuña, Chaps. 2-3.

5. Carvajal, pp. 171-72. Fernández de Oviedo gives the names of all of Orellana's companions, Chap. 2.

6. Carvajal, who accompanied Orellana, presents the decision as the lesser of two evils. Pizarro calls him a "rebel" and charges him with "cruelty and faithlessness" in leaving the expedition unprovided for (Letter); Acuña charges him with faithlessness, occasioned by the sudden realization that he had found the great river and could not resist the temptation to exploit his discovery. Fernández de Oviedo, who heard both sides of the story, was inclined to believe Orellana could have returned had he desired to.

7. Pizarro, Letter.

8. P. 214. He relates more information reported by Indians, pp. 219-22. Acuña was skeptical, claiming that Orellana made up the story "that he might render his Discovery more considerable and glorious" (Chap. 7). Fernández de Oviedo had similar misgivings; he reports a number of such stories but adds "if I have been told the truth" and "if Amazons they ought to be called" (Chap. 4).

9. Carvajal, pp. 215-35.

10. Acuña, p. 20.

11. There are a number of accounts of this expedition; excellent brief versions may be found in Acuña (*Voyages and Discoveries*, pp. 24–27). Manuel Ballesteros Gaibrois, *Historia de América* (Madrid, 1946), pp. 238–40; and in Boies Penrose, *Travel and Discovery in the Renaissance* (Cambridge, Mass., 1952), p. 116.

12. Some doubt exists whether Doña Inés and Ursúa were married; Acuña believed so, referring to her as Inés de Ursúa.

13. So says Lawrence Keymis, *A Relation of the Second Voyage to Guiana* (Hakluyt's *Voyages*, Vol. X, p. 498).

14. Acuña, p. 24.

15. See Teodoro Sampaio, "The Sertão before the Conquest," in Richard M. Morse, *The Bandeirantes* (New York, 1965), pp. 39-47, and Sergio Buarque de Holanda, "As primeiras expedições" in his *História geral da civilização brasileira* (São Paulo, 1963), Vol. I, Part I, pp. 89-95.

16. Olivério Mário Oliveira Pinto, "Explorações científicas" in Buarque de Holanda, *op. cit.*, Vol. I, Part II, pp. 163-64. See also the commemorative volume *Anchietana*, published by the Comissão Nacional para as Comemorações do "Dia de Anchieta," São Paulo, 1965.

17. Trans. and ed. by Malcolm Letts (London, 1928).

18. "The Relation of Peter Carder of Saint Verian in Cornwall . . ." in Samuel Purchas, *Purchas His Pilgrimes*, Vol. XVI, pp. 136-45.

19. "The admirable adventures and strange fortunes of Master Antonie Knivet, which went with Master Thomas Candish in his second voyage to the South Sea. 1591." Purchas, Vol. XVI, pp. 177–289. Knivet's adventures are so remarkable as to cast some doubt as to his credibility.

20. On Ehinger's (or Alfinger's) career, see José Oviedo y Baños, *Historia de la conquista y población de la Provincia de Venezuela* (BAE, Vol. CVII), Bk. I, Chaps. 6-8; Germán Arciniegas, *Germans in the Conquest of America* (New York, 1943), pp. 104-18; and Kirkpatrick, pp. 304-07.

21. For the details of this expedition, see Oviedo y Baños, Bk. I, Chaps. 8-14, and Bk. II, Chaps. 2-6; also Arciniegas, pp. 154-67.

22. Oviedo y Baños, Bk. II, Ch. 8, and Arciniegas, pp. 170-81.

23. See Penrose, p. 113 for a brief account of the legend; for the sources of the concept of El Dorado as a place, see Juan Friede, "Geographical Ideas and the

Conquest of Venezuela," *The Americas* XVI (October, 1959): 145-59. A letter to Dom João V of Portugal located Lake Parima somewhere between Santa Fe de Bogotá and the Amazon; it related that the people of Manoa could field an army of fifty thousand, armed with gold and silver weapons—the only metals they had. See João Lucio d'Azevedo, *Os jesuitas no Grão-Pará*, 2nd ed., (Coimbra, 1930), p. 151.

24. For details of the several expeditions sent to intercept Belalcázar see Kirkpatrick, pp. 221-28.

25. *Ibid.*, pp. 313-20.

26. Oviedo y Baños, Bk. II, Chaps. 11-12, and Bk. III, Chaps. 3-4. Also Arciniegas, pp. 187-207.

27. Oviedo y Baños, Bk. III, Chap. 5.

28. López de Gómara, *op. cit., loc. cit.*, Vol. II, p. 80; Keymis, *loc. cit.*, Vol. X, p. 496; Kirkpatrick, pp. 301-02.

29. See Keymis, *op. cit.*, and Sir Walter Raleigh, *The Discoverie of the Large, Rich, and Beautifull Empire of Guiana.* Hakluyt's *Voyages*, Vol. X.

Part Two

The Age of Expansion:
For God, Slaves, and Gold

V · *The Missionaries*

The conquistadores may have established the dominion of the Spanish monarch in the New World, but it was another force which would win the hearts of men. Filled with a zeal born in the Reconquest, fired with enthusiasm for converting the heathen Indians, the work of the missionaries was the real glory of Spain and Portugal in the New World. They went everywhere; following the trails of the conquistadores, blazing new ones deep into the forests, crossing mountains, navigating unknown rivers, exposing themselves to countless dangers—often alone—in search of souls. Equipment was usually minimal: no tents, medicines, insect repellants, weapons, or extra clothing or provisions; they abandoned themselves completely to Divine Providence. Few, however, went without some writing materials, and some carried simple instruments; with the aid of these they mapped the areas through which they traveled "with full fidelity if not always with exactitude." [1]

Practically all the work of exploration by the clergy was done by members of religious orders. The secular clergy were confined for the most part to the parishes of the cities and the towns while the friars and Jesuits made *entradas* [2] in the back country, often where no European had been before, and many times where no European would come again for a century or more. Some missionaries explored in the latter half of the sixteenth century, and we find others traveling with the "monsoons" in Brazil and seeking the "lost city of the Caesars" in the south, but the seventeenth century was the great age of missionary endeavor, and it is with this that we shall be primarily concerned.

Early in the century two Jesuit missionaries, Diego de Torres and Alonso de Sandoval, went to Urabá with the intention of exploring the country thoroughly and founding a mission there; difficulties forced its abandonment. In 1628 five Jesuits headed by the Italian Daddei

(Dadey in Spanish) left Bogotá, crossed the cordillera by trails through passes, and finally saw ahead of them an "ocean of savannas" bordered by barren peaks. Mountain streams tumbled over precipices into the lush valleys below, and there the missionaries halted. Each took charge of an Indian pueblo, winning friendship by offering the Indians trinkets, and set about learning their language and preparing a grammar. Unfortunately merchants whom they forbade to swindle the Indians spread stories in Bogotá that the missionaries were enriching themselves at Indian expense, and they were called back to Bogotá.[3]

In 1656 the first mission was established in what is now Venezuela. A group of Recollect Fathers who had arrived in Cumaná on May 8 made an *entrada* into the interior around the pueblo of Piritú, accompanied by an armed guard and an interpreter who informed the Indians that "these Fathers came sent by our Catholic King as ministers of God to preach His holy law to them and to instruct them in the mysteries of our Holy Faith." [4] They were well received by the Indians, who remembered the good treatment they had received from some Capuchins who had spent two years with them earlier, and so the guard returned to Cumaná. Yet their treatment by the Indians did not measure up to their reception, for they received no support from them other than some manioc, poorly made cornbread, roots and bulbs, for which they were often asked to pay. The Indians tried their patience and chastity many times, and, stirred up by witchdoctors, even plotted their death. The area was hot and humid through most of the year, full of wild beasts, poisonous insects and disease. Such were the tribulations of those who left the settled areas to preach in the interior.[5]

Three years later the Jesuits made another attempt to found missions in the *llanos*, when some Jirara Indians appeared in Bogotá seeking missionaries. On April 13, 1659, Fathers Bartolomé Pérez, Francisco Jiménez, and Francisco Alvarez were sent to explore the land. After an uncomfortable and dangerous journey across the cordillera they reached the Río Panto, crossed the Casanare, proceeded through hot and extensive savannas, finally reaching the settlement of Tame, where Indians presented themselves for baptism. Their return trip, which took forty-nine days, was equally successful from the standpoint of baptisms.[6]

In 1663 an expedition of French Jesuits, who had come through Guyana to find that the colony had been destroyed by the Dutch, became discouraged and returned to France. With them had been Antonio de Monteverde and Antoine Maisland,[7] who decided to remain and separated. Both reached the *llanos*. We are told that Monteverde's journey was very difficult, since he traveled through unknown lands, had to cross swift rivers, and lived on wild herbs, sleeping in the hollows of rocks and tree trunks. Meeting missionaries from Bogotá in the *llanos*, Monteverde was struck by the difficulties of the long route from Cartagena via Bogotá, and felt that the Orinoco-Meta-Casanare route, over which he and Maisland had come, would be preferable as a direct water route between Spain and the Casanare reductions. He sent the plan to Bogotá, seeking also a priest for the Guyana mission (which he planned to restore), and received two—Fathers Francisco Ellauri (then sixty-two years of age) and Julián Vergara. Reaching the mission area, they found soldiers in tatters, who persuaded them that no successful missionary activity in the Orinoco area could function from there. Father Ellauri died of fever in 1665, and the enterprise was abandoned. Vergara returned in 1668, but a Carib attack destroyed his newly founded mission.[8]

The following year, on July 28, Monteverde made an *entrada*, with an escort of four soldiers, into Sáliva country. Despite a cool reception, he won them over with axes, beads and trinkets, and founded a mission. It was his last effort, for shortly after the assistant he requested arrived at the mission, both became gravely ill and died within a few days of each other. The mission continued, however, through the efforts of two Jesuits sent to replace them. In 1679 Fathers Ignacio Fiol and Felipe Gómez were sent to re-establish the Orinoco missions where Monteverde had worked earlier. After exploring the lands of several Indian peoples, Gómez remained while Fiol returned to Cartagena to organize an expedition. Luckily a number of German and Spanish Jesuits had arrived, and in 1682 Fiol and four of them, accompanied by some Spanish colonists, pushed into the interior and founded the town of Santa Rosa. An attack of the Caribs put an end to the expedition and destroyed the Sáliva mission; but one survivor remained, Father Julián de Vergara, who managed to reach the Casanare mission nearly four weeks later.[9]

In 1694 an effort was made to restore the Orinoco missions. Two Jesuits, José Cabarte and Manuel Pérez, reached the river on November 25, only to find that the Caribs had occupied all the area in which they intended to evangelize; the project had to be abandoned in January. Subsequently Father Cabarte returned, bringing with him another missionary, José de Silva, along with five or six soldiers and guides. Both were skilled in handling Indians, and Cabarte had the added advantage of being fluent in both the Sáliva and Achagua languages. One of their objectives was to attract these Indians to a safe place away from their hereditary enemies, which they sought to do by founding towns for them. The party finally reached the Río Meta, only to find it swollen from rains. When it failed to subside in a few days, Cabarte, an Indian guide, and two soldiers constructed a rather poor craft in which they managed to cross the river. The rest remained to found a mission. Cabarte continued, following no fixed direction. When food gave out the party resorted to using bows and arrows, and lived on monkeys and parrots. Finally they reached an Indian town, Quirosiveni, whose cacique, once a Christian, decided to kill the missionary. Father Cabarte happened to be carrying under his arm a rolled-up picture of St. Francis Xavier, and when the would-be assassin saw it, he apparently thought it was some kind of weapon—perhaps a new kind of gun—and stepped back. The padre rode on, unmolested, finally reaching Sabana Alta in December, where he founded a mission.[10]

Let us turn now to the Pacific coast of the New Kingdom of Granada, the province of Chocó. On March 18, 1648, a Franciscan lay brother, Fray Matías Abad, left the convent of Loreto de Cartagena with the intention of christianizing the Indians of Chocó. He went via Antioquia where his superior requested that he write everything of interest that happened to him. Two letters arrived not long after his departure, one dated May 16, from Remedios, and another July 21, from an outlying district of Antioquia. He then proceeded five hundred leagues into the heart of the forest, arriving at Buena Vista, where he secured an interpreter and continued on, finally arriving at the Río Atrato, where he built a mission on land given by the cacique. His third letter, dated October 6, was from the mission of San Francisco, and is filled with detailed information about the province—its geography, ethnography, and hydrography, and particularly its precious metals. Abad, who had been a miner before he became a friar, discovered gold in the area. With more enthusiasm than accuracy he excitedly described the coastal part of the province as "the richest land in the world." The Indians, he said, were very barbarous; they went about completely nude, had no concept of God (and so were not idolaters either) or of the immortality of the soul, and seemed to have no leaders whom they obeyed. An attempt on his life was frustrated by the interpreters. The land, he remarked, was rich in corn, plantains, boars, fish and palms; so abundant were the necessities of life that the Indians were quite indolent. The river, Abad said, was navigable up to the mission by frigates, and above it by canoes; it provided easy access to Popayán, and thus a short route to Quito. Unfortunately, Abad's career as missionary, geographer, and explorer was brief: an Indian killed him with a spear in 1650.[11]

Following that route to Quito, descending the eastern slopes of the cordillera just after crossing the border of modern Ecuador, toward the headwaters of the Río Aguarico, one would enter the country of the Cofanes. First to preach Christianity to these Indians was the Jesuit missionary, Father Rafael Ferrer. Once designated for the task, his preparations were minimal, for he took with him only his crucifix, the Bible, his breviary, and writing materials. After crossing the cordillera he tarried in the province of Quijos, where he learned what he could about the Cofanes. Hearing that they hated the Spaniards and wanted to kill them, he decided to enter their lands alone and unarmed, late in 1602 or early in 1603. Seeing him unarmed, they assumed his mission was peaceful, and he began preaching with some degree of success. The Cofanes lived in houses scattered over a wide area rather than in towns, which made preaching difficult and defense even more so. Ferrer persuaded them to organize a town, which he called San Pedro de los Cofanes, on June 29, 1604. So successful was the settlement that he founded two more, Santa María and Santa Cruz, with the help of Fathers Fernando Arnolfini and Estéban Páez of Quito. Learning from the Cofanes of other peaceful tribes east of the missions, Ferrer undertook a mission of exploration toward the Río Marañón, in territory completely unknown to him. From the Río de los Cofanes he entered the Aguarico, which flowed in the Río Napo. Following the Napo until it discharged into the Amazon, he explored that great river for some time, preaching to the riparian peoples, the Omaguas, and others, making extensive notes on them. He returned a year after his departure. As befell many of the early missionaries, Padre Ferrer was killed by a converted cacique whom he had denounced for reverting to polygamy.[12]

To the south of Cofanes country, and a bit to the east, lay the land of the Maynas Indians, in the relatively level country north of the Río Marañón after it makes its descent from the mountains. The first mission in this country was established among the Jeberos, a Mayna people, by the Jesuit Lucas de la Cueva, in 1637. He had some difficulty at first, when they assumed that a list of Christian names he was preparing for them was a list for distributing them among *encomenderos* and fled, returning only when hunger and fear of capture by Indian hunters induced them to trust the padre. A letter he wrote to his superior on April 16, 1638, gives an interesting picture of the Maynas country, which he explored on his mission tours. Most striking, perhaps, is his description of Lake Rimachuma, which lies west of the Río Pastaza near its confluence with the Marañón: it was "the most famous lake found in the whole conquest because of its size (the name 'Rimachuma' in the Maynas tongue means 'Big Lake') which they say is more than forty leagues in length, its many islands . . . , its great depth, which at some points they say is not measurable, and for such turbulence and waves that it appears to be a gulf in the high seas." Father Cueva seems to have been deceived as to the size of the lake, which, according to these measurements, would be the size of Lake Titicaca, which is strongly suggested by the description.[13]

Very active in exploring the upper reaches of the Amazon and in establishing missions there were the Franciscan friars of the province of Quito; "the glory of this missionary protoexploration of the Amazon, the taking possession of Amazonia for the crown of Spain and the firm foundation of Franciscan mission centers on both shores—very difficult, it must be said—was due to the intrepidity and extraordinary apostolic spirit of the famous Province of Quito."[14] Four Franciscan *entradas* were made into the upper Amazon area; the first of these got underway late in August of 1632, and included two priests, Juan de Casarubias [15] and Francisco Anguita, and three lay brothers, Domingo de Brieva, Pedro de Moya and Pedro Pecador. Their journey began, without soldiers or other religious, from Pasto, where they procured provisions; journeying next to Ezija in the Sucumbío country, they were given canoes and an Indian interpreter, Pata. After two days they reached the Putamayo, a major tributary of the upper Amazon, and followed it for eleven days to the country of the Seños (or Zuñes), whose cacique, Maroyo, received them joyfully. The interpreter, unfortunately, went back to Ezija, and hanged himself when he realized the importance of his defection; without him, the missionaries had to return to Ezija and then to Quito.[16]

The second Franciscan *entrada* into upper Amazonia was authorized by the provincial of Quito and the *audiencia* (court) early in 1634 or 1635, and included two priests, Fray Lorenzo Fernández and Fray Antonio Caicedo, and the lay brothers Domingo Brieva and Pedro Pecador, who had been on the first mission. They were outfitted for the journey at Ezija, where the lieutenant-general of the province gave them an interpreter and "four honorable Spaniards." Embarking on the Río San Miguel, they proceeded downstream for eight days, finally reaching the province of the Becavas, among whom they worked for three and one-half months, learning their language and baptizing many, when suddenly the Indians rose up against them, wounding all but Fray Pedro Pecador, who luckily had some knowledge of surgery and was able to help the others. They left the province soon after, some going to seek help in Quito, one remaining among the Sucumbíos, while Pedro Pecador went to Popayán seeking help, and, when none was forthcoming, went down the Río Aguarico into Cofane country to the mission of San Pedro de Alcántara. Here he was joined by Captain Juan Palacios, and together they entered the lands of the Encabellados (so-called because of their long hair), who had been terrorizing the area (between the Río Napo and the Río Putamayo). When they saw that the Spaniards came in peace, the Indians were willing to negotiate a treaty of peace with the crown. Pecador took the news to Quito, thus becoming the first to go to Quito via the Río Napo, and the audiencia authorized him to take thirty soldiers and found a town among them.[17]

After the Becava attack, as we have seen, the group of friars broke up. Two of them, Father Fernández and Fray Brieva went to Quito to seek aid in re-establishing missions in the east. The audiencia decided to send five Franciscans with Captain Felipe Machacón to found a town among the Avijiras Indians on the Amazon. They left Quito on December 29, 1635 (or 1636), reached San Pedro de los Cofanes, set out on the Río Aguarico, and in eight days reached the Río Napo, where they learned that the Avijiras had gone on the warpath. Realizing that the Encabellados were at peace as the result of the work of Pedro Pecador, they went among them. Several months later Friars Pedro Pecador and Andrés de Toledo arrived with the thirty soldiers sent by the audiencia and in a formal ceremony took possession of the land for the crown, founding the town of San Diego de Alcalá de los Encabellados. Unfortunately for the success of the mission, Captain Palacios maltreated a cacique and was killed August 25, 1636 (or 1637), six weeks after the town had been founded. Again the friars had to leave a mission area.

As they prepared to go, they met a Portuguese sailor who had been in Grão-Pará; he informed them that the Río Napo flowed into the Amazon and through Brazil; by following it they would find El Dorado and the Casa del Sol. Try as he would, the superior could not dissuade two adventurous friars, Domingo de Brieva and Andrés de Toledo, from taking advantage of a clause allowing any friar of the mission to leave if he wished; finally the superior resorted to having a soldier cut one of the large canoes adrift, but in vain—they took a small one and left on October 17, accompanied by six soldiers. A few days later they found the large canoe and took it, leaving the small one behind. For five months they proceeded down the great river system, never lacking food, despite having taken only a small ration of parched corn. In February they came upon the Portuguese Fort Curupá; the complement of the fort was very happy to see them, since they had been charged with exploring the Amazon to its source, but had ventured only this far—now the report of the friars, they felt, made their further penetration unnecessary. The friars continued to Grão-Pará, and then on to São Luís do Maranhão, whose captain sent Fray Andrés to Spain (the crowns of Spain and Portugal were still united at the time) to give an account of their journey, which proved the usefulness of the Amazon route.

What of those left behind? After the departure of the two friars and the soldiers, they searched for the large canoe, but found only the small one the explorers had exchanged for it. In this they journeyed up the Napo, with some following on shore, alternating from time to time. Eventually, on January 20, they reached Avila, where Pedro Pecador met them with letters ordering them back to Quito.[18]

While Fray Andrés de Toledo journeyed to Spain to report on the importance of the Amazon route, and Fray Juan Calderón and his group who remained behind were completing their journey to Quito, there still remained the other friar who had made the long journey to Grão-Pará and São Luís, Domingo de Brieva. It would be his experience to make the return journey up the Amazon and back to Quito as a part of the Teixeira expedition, the "fourth *entrada*"—this time from east to west—which will occupy our attention presently.

The eastern region of Peru—the *montaña*—attracted a few exploring expeditions in the sixteenth century, as we have already seen. This area, which occupies the eastern slopes of the cordillera as far as the jungle regions of the lowlands to the north and farther east, is a land of continual spring, a land of forests, flowers and meadows, of a temperate climate and great promise.[19] Through this area flow some of the tributaries of the upper Amazon, and it was here that the Franciscans turned after the Jesuits took over the lands watered by the tributaries flowing into the upper Amazon from the north. On August 3, 1641, Fray Pedro de la Cruz and Fray Francisco Piña departed from the town of Quimirí on the Ucayali, going downstream "as God willed." They entered the country of the Shipibo Indians, explored it, and labored among them for more than a year, when, for some unexplained reason, they were murdered by them at the Río Aguatía in 1643.[20] In that same year two other Franciscans, Fathers Gaspar de Vera and Juan Cabezas, were working farther to the west, across the mountains, among the Quidquidcanas and the Tepquis, who lived along the Río Huallaga, a tributary of the Amazon. They were particularly successful among the Tepquis, and in August, accompanied by Fray Agustín de Mendia, penetrated far into their country for the purpose of conversion and, equally important, it would appear, for the purpose of exploration. Joined by twenty-three Indians and adequately provisioned, they traveled to the country of the Comanahuas, who were three days' journey away, and who were neighbors of the Incas. The success of the venture—for they were received in friendship by a powerful cacique and entered into communication with the Incas—assured communication between the already settled lands of the western cordillera with the upper Amazon.[21]

Exploring the Huallaga region was no task for the weak or faint-hearted. In 1644 three Franciscans, Father Ignacio de Irarraga and the lay brothers Jerónimo Jiménez and Francisco Suárez with some laymen, both Spanish and Indian, explored the right bank of the river on foot. No advance was possible without the machete, for they had to cut their way through branches and brambles, with sharp thorns tearing their clothing. Frequently they had to ford swollen streams with water to their waists, and what rest they got was on muddy ground. Then there was the nightly vigil, to be on guard against wild beasts or unfriendly Indians. Food was anything but a gourmet's delight; basically it was the parched corn they brought with them, augmented by whatever they could find en route.[22]

The exploration of the headwaters of the Amazon continued after midcentury. In 1658 two Jesuit fathers, Francisco Figueroa and Domingo Fernández, descended the Marañón, ascended the Ucayali, then crossed over to the Huallaga and established the mission of Santa María on that river. In 1673 the Franciscans in Andamarca, high above the upper

Apurímac valley, were visited by Indians from the basin of the lower Río Pangoa who had heard much about the excellent treatment of the Indian converts by their missionary, Alonso Zurbano Rea. They asked him to accompany them back to their own land, but he could not be spared from the mission. Finally he was able to secure Father Manuel Biedma, who had for ten years been a missionary in the Huallaga and Ucayali valleys. Starting out from Andamarca on May 11, accompanied by Indians and three Franciscan brothers, he made the hazardous journey along precipices, across snow-covered plateaus, through heavy rains and through dense growth, living on cheese and parched corn, finally arriving at his destination after eight days. The cacique was an enthusiastic Christian, and so the missionaries were able to labor successfully in this area for some time.

Later, in 1676, a conspiracy against the missionaries and the gradual decay of the mission of Santa Cruz led all the friars except Biedma and one lay brother to seek more fruitful areas. Then both of them took sick, and Biedma had to make the dangerous journey back to Andamarca to convalesce, an experience which led him to seek a better route back to the basin. Upon his recovery he sought a water route, and searched the area watered by the Mantara, the Apurímac, the Tambo, the Ucayali, and the Pachitea. All this effort was in vain—there was no better route. But if he had not found what he sought, he greatly enlarged geographical knowledge of the region and its people, and returned with plans for a mission there.[23]

In 1684 the viceroy of Peru ordered the corregidor of the province of Jauja to cooperate with Father Biedma surveying a proposed new route, which the missionary envisioned, from San Buenaventura de Savini to the confluence of the Ene and Perené rivers; the mission ended in failure. In 1685 they prepared again, opening a path for mules to the banks of the Perené, where they established a settlement, and proceeded on to a point near the Río Tambo. The corregidor was elated—here was the entrance to the Ucayali and the Amazon which they had sought. Biedma was also impressed, but for a different reason: he was sure that many peoples lived along the banks of these rivers, awaiting evangelization, and was anxious to begin his work. The corregidor, remembering three missionaries recently killed, forbade him to go, but finally consented to send one lay brother, fluent in the languages of the area, accompanied by a tertiary and a layman (all three wore religious garb) and Indian rowers. For fifteen days they drifted downstream on a journey that was not only uneventful but monotonous. Finally they met a group of Cunivos who had already met Franciscans from Peru and Jesuits from Ecuador, and showed a strong disposition to become Christians. The missionaries raised a cross in their settlement, naming it San Miguel de los Cunivos, and returned late in October.

Biedma lost no time in sending these explorers to Lima to report on their work; the viceroy was pleased, and determined to send an official *entrada* into Cunivo country. Twelve soldiers and two Negroes were assigned, under Captain Francisco de Rojas y Guzmán (who was joined by two other volunteer officers), four Franciscan priests and three lay brothers were selected, and 4,000 pesos were provided for the expenses of the expedition. They departed from Concepción de Jauja on June 30, 1686, and drove their mules, heavily laden with tools, a forge, iron and steel over mountain trails to Savini, arriving on July 28. As rafts were being built for the journey downstream, two friars fell sick, and Father Biedma went in their place. The expedition departed on August 18, reached San Luis, where some were left, on August 25, and continued on to San Miguel de los Cunivos. When they arrived on September 4, they were astonished to find a church, complete with a bell—the Jesuits, learning of the settlement, had come and built it. Biedma's mission among the Cunivos was not to last long, for early in 1687, he and several others were ambushed and killed.[24]

South of Peru, perhaps the most significant Franciscan establishment was that on the island of Chiloé, in the southern part of Chile. This foundation was to serve as a base for several memorable exploring expeditions, both to the south and across the Andes. The earliest of these was that of Fray Antonio de Quadramiro and Fray Cristóbal de Mérida between 1574 and 1581, who explored the entire archipelago and then headed south toward the strait, hoping to find suitable locations for missions. Subsequently they left for Spain to gather missionaries, and Fray Quadramiro returned; after great hardships he came upon the town of San Felipe, which Pedro Sarmiento de Gamboa had founded, then proceeded east to work among the Huelches, where our knowledge of him comes to an end. Of the trans-Andean expeditions we shall treat subsequently.[25]

On the other side of the continent, in the region of the Río de la Plata, the Jesuits were active quite early. In 1619, on October 25, Father Roque González de Santa Cruz, who would be known as the apostle of the Uruguay, received permission from his superior to explore that river and establish reductions along it. His background well qualified him for the assignment; a Creole from Asunción, he had been ten years a Jesuit and had considerable mission experience in the Paraná area. His first mission was that of Concepción, founded on December 8; he was to spend six years in the region, exploring the course of the river and the territory eastward to the Atlantic. Assisted by the cacique Nicolás Neenguirú he went up the Río Ibicuí some fifty leagues, among Indians who had never seen a white man, and built the chapel of Nuestra Señora de Candelaria, which was subsequently destroyed. Other reductions were founded on the Río Tebicuarí, the Río Ijuí, and on the right bank of the Uruguay; to these González de Santa Cruz assigned missionaries, while he himself continued on in the role of explorer and founder. On November 1, 1628, with two companions, he entered the district called Caaró, between the Ijuí and Piratiní rivers, and founded a reduction there on the following day. Unfortunately it would soon come to grief. It happened that a neighboring cacique, Nheçum, maintained a harem in a certain house, a fact revealed to the missionaries by a small boy. When he discovered that his secret was out, Nheçum, prodded by an apostate from a neighboring reduction, had a slave kill the missionaries with a hatchet. The body of one of them was cut up and dragged around, and the chapel was destroyed.[26]

Farther to the south, across the seemingly endless pampas and beyond the Río Negro and the Río Colorado, we find missionaries engaged in exploring and preaching the gospel; their story, however, more properly belongs to an account of the exploration of Patagonia, which will engage out attention subsequently.

In Brazil missionary activity began early with the arrival of the first Jesuits in 1549 under the leadership of Manuel de Nóbrega; with him were six companions, among whom was José de Anchieta, who would eventually be known as one of the greatest of the missionaries in South America. A second group was to follow in 1553. Scarcely had the Jesuits established themselves in Brazil when they set out into the *sertão*, that vast backland away from the coast. We have an interesting description of this area in a letter from one of the missionaries, Father João de Azpilcueta Escripta, written to his "dearest brothers" from Pôrto Seguro, June 24, 1555. He had gone into the *sertão* some 350 leagues "always by little-known routes, over craggy mountains hitherto unknown, and so many rivers that in some areas, in a space of four or five leagues, we crossed over water fifty times by count." [27] For three months, he said, they went through very humid and cool country, full of groves of huge trees, whose foliage was always green. There was much rain, and often they slept completely drenched. For sickness there was no remedy but to go on, more often than not with no food but flour and water. Only God's mercy, he said, protected them from the many perils they faced.

For more than a century missionary activities were confined mainly to the coastal areas. After the Teixeira expedition of 1638-39 and the separation from Spain in 1640, Portugal took a decided interest in the Amazon Valley. In 1653 the Indians of northern Brazil were placed under a Jesuit monopoly, which lasted until the arrival of Capuchins, Mercedarians, and Carmelites in 1685. Subsequently, by a series of royal letters, the area was partitioned among all the orders, with the Franciscans responsible for the northern part of lower Amazonia, the Mercedarians in other parts of the lower river, the Carmelites along the Rio

Negro, Rio Branco, and Solimoes (upper Amazon), and the Jesuits on the Tocantins, Xingu, Tapajós, and Madeira rivers. Of these the Jesuits were perhaps most active in exploration; in the years prior to the division, they entered much of Amazonia. In 1668 we find two padres, Tomé Ribeiro and Ricardo, on the Araguaia, the following year Manuel Nunes led an expedition up the Tocantins to the present site of Carolina, and in 1668 there were two *entradas* to the Araguaia, led by Gaspar Misch and João de Almeida, and Gonçalo de Veras and Sebastiano Teixeira respectively.[28] The great age of the Amazonian missions, however, was the first part of the eighteenth century. With the role of the missionary explorers of this era we shall deal subsequently.

Neither Spain nor Portugal was able to establish control over much of the coastline between the Amazon and Orinoco rivers; consequently, such exploring as was done in this region of Guiana was undertaken by others, primarily by the French. As in Brazil, the missionaries were among the chief explorers, and two of them, both Jesuits, Jean Grillet and François Bechamel, penetrated quite far into the interior of what became known as French Guiana. Their expedition, of which they kept a careful journal, began in Cayenne late in December of 1673, when the visitor to the missions, Père François Mercier, who wanted to discover "those Nations that lie remote from the Sea" chose Grillet to go. Grillet asked for Bechamel, who was a zealous man and had a flair for languages. On January 25 they left Cayenne with Indian guides in a small canoe, following the Oyack through the country of the Galibis, a poverty-stricken people. On February 3, about forty leagues from Cayenne, they entered the country of the Nouragues, reputed to be cannibals; they proved to be courteous and affable, however, and the cacique allied himself with them and gave them porters. The wife of one of them had breast cancer; Bechamel instructed and baptized her before they left. A few days later they were joined by a French trader, whose Galibi guides, tired of carrying the ironware he had brought for trading purposes, mutinied and had to be replaced by Nouragues. For some time, while a canoe was being built for them, the missionaries remained at a cottage of a Nourague chieftain, learning the language, doing some preaching when they were able, and teaching a few hymns. The Indians, who had three wives, did them the courtesy of listening respectfully and not condemning a religion which permitted only one. The missionaries, under these circumstances, could count it a signal success when they persuaded two young men to pledge monogamy. On April 9 they departed in two canoes, with sixteen men. Along the route they baptized some dying children, and passed a place where three Englishmen, they were told, had been killed and eaten, justifying, apparently, the reputation of the Nouragues. They were in higher country now, having passed the falls of the Approuague, and by April 30 they reached the little Eiski river (which flows into the Inipi), followed it ten leagues to the Camopi, and went up this swift stream four leagues on May 3 and 4. The following day they reached their destination, the Acoqua country (2° 25′ N.), and were well received by the Indians, who listened to them and showed an interest in instruction. Legend comes in again as it nearly always does; the fathers inquired concerning the marvelous Lake Parima, but none of the Acoqua had ever heard of it. On May 25 they embarked on the Camopi, following it into Nourague country, and then undertook the difficult passage back, reaching Cayenne on June 27.[29]

Père Grillet, it appears, was something of a navigator and inventor as well as missionary and explorer. In describing a voyage across the Atlantic, he tells of an instrument he invented for determining the altitude above the sea during all the hours when the sun appears, without having to see the horizon. He further describes a method he invented for determining longitude by marking exactly the time the sun set and the time elapsed before the full moon rose; if the moon rose later, one had to be west of the line where sunset and moonrise occurred simultaneously. He counted the time by dividing it into minutes measurd by twenty-four pulse beats "when one is in health," a method, he admitted, difficult to execute and fraught with possibilities of considerable error.[30]

Of such stuff were the missionary explorers of South America. Men of a zealous—often heroic—stamp in the service of God, they emerge as men of many parts. Dedicated primarily to the conversion of the Indians, they also brought with them an intellectual curiosity and a sometimes amazing amount of skill in various fields of activity. While this may be said of nearly all the missionaries, the Jesuits in particular, who were the products of the finest traditions of European humanism and were well trained in science, were especially active in noting down everything of interest. They, and the friars as well, emerge as the first naturalists, the first anthropologists, the first geographers, and the first cartographers of the interior of the continent. Many maps of the continent had indeed been published by European mapmakers but as the first Jesuit cartographer in the Río de la Plata area, Padre Romero, pointed out, there was no substitute, if one would be accurate, for actually traveling through the land and recording faithfully what had been seen.[31] For our knowledge of many areas of the continent, we must rely on the missionaries alone, for there they were almost the only explorers. When the golden age of missions passed, there was no one to take their place, and many regions of promise became again virtually *terrae incognitae* until they were penetrated once more by the scientists of the nineteenth century.

NOTES

1. Martin Dobrtizhoffer, S.J., *Historia de Apibonibus* (Vienna, 1784), Vol. I, p. 3 (quoted in Guillermo Fúrlong Cárdiff, *Cartografía* Jesuitica del Río de la Plata, Buenos Aires, 1936, p. 10).

2. An *entrada* was an "entry" of missionaries, accompanied by a few soldiers for protection, into Indian country for the purpose of "reducing" it, that is, catechizing and persuading the Indians to lead an agricultural life in settled communities.

3. For details of this Jesuit endeavor see Daniel Restrepo, S.J., *La Compañía de Jesús en Colombia* (Bogotá, 1940), pp. 28-29; José Joaquín Borda, S.J., *Historia de la Compañía de Jesús en la Nueva Granada* (Poissy, 1872), Vol. I, pp. 85-92; and Antonio Ybot León, *La iglesia y los eclesiásticos españoles en la empresa de Indias* (Barcelona, 1963), Vol. II, p. 890.

4. Fray Antonio Caulín, *Historia de la Nueva Andalucía*, Bk. III, Chap. 2 (BAE, Vol. CVII, p. 395).

5. *Ibid.*

6. Borda, pp. 92-94; Restrepo, pp. 58-59.

7. J. Fred Rippy, whose *Crusaders in the Jungle* (Chapel Hill, N.C., 1936) is perhaps the best study on the missionaries in English, refers to a Dionisio Meland (p. 131); in view of the confusion in the spelling of proper names of the time, it is possible that he refers to the same man.

8. Borda, p. 99; Rippy, p. 131; Restrepo, pp. 75-82.

9. Restrepo, *ibid.* Vergara's own account of the massacre appears on pp. 79-81.

10. Restrepo, pp. 92-93; Borda, pp. 164-68; Borda spells the name Cavarte.

11. On Abad's career, see Gregorio Arcila Robledo, *Las misiones franciscanas en Colombia* (Bogotá, 1950), pp. 15-22.

12. José Jouanen, S.J., *Historia de la Compañía de Jesús en la antigua Provincia de Quito* (Quito, 1941), Vol. I, pp. 100-3; also Rippy, p. 200, and Ybot León, Vol. I, p. 885. Ferrer was killed in 1611.

13. Francisco de Figueroa, *Relación de las misiones de la Compañía de Jesús en el pais de los Maynas* (original title: *Ynforme de las missiones de el Marañón, Grán Pará, o río de las Amazonas*), (Madrid, 1901), pp. 36-37, also Rippy, pp. 203-4. A Map of Peru, Ecuador, and Bolivia in the Rand McNally *Indexed Atlas of the World* (Chicago, 1902) shows the lake as having an approximate length of twenty-five or thirty miles, with a width of perhaps five miles. It barely appears on the National Geographic Society's map of northwestern South America (1964). For a vivid description of this country, see W. H. Hudson's *Green Mansions*.

14. Arcila Robledo, p. 355.

15. Ybot León (Vol. II, p. 396) calls him Lorenzo Cararrubia.

16. Arcila Robledo, pp. 358-59; Ybot León, Vol. II, p. 386; and Fray Bernardino Izaguirre Ispizua, *Historia de las misiones Franciscanas y narración de los progresos de la geografía en el oriente del Perú*, (Lima, 1922), Vol. I, p. 181. In Brazil the river is known as the Içá rather than the Putamayo.

17. Arcila Robledo, pp. 359-60; Ybot León, Vol. II, p. 387; Izaguirre, Vol. I, p. 181. There is some discrepancy in dates; Arcila Robledo states that the *entrada* was made in 1634, Ybot León says 1635.

18. Arcila Robledo, pp. 360-61; Ybot León, Vol. II, pp. 389-90; Izaguirre, Vol. I, pp. 181-82. Note the discrepancy in dates, as above.

19. For a description of the *montaña* see J. A. Zahm (H. J. Mozans, pseud.) *Along the Andes and down the Amazon* (New York, 1923), pp. 379-97.

20. Izaguirre, Vol. I, pp. 183-84.

21. *Ibid.*, Vol. I, p. 125.

22. *Ibid.*, Vol. I, pp. 128-29.

23. *Ibid.*, Vol. I, pp. 192-95, 243.

24. On the career of Padre Biedma, see Izaguirre, Vol. I, pp. 249-60.

25. Ybot León, Vol. II, pp. 422-23.

26. Vicente Sierra, *Historia de la Argentina*, Vol. II, pp. 164-68; Pablo Pastells, S.J., *Historia de la Compañía de Jesús en la Provincia de Paraguay* (Madrid, 1912), Vol. II, pp. 513-14, n. 1.

27. *Cartas avulsas* (Rio de Janeiro, 1887), pp. 146-47.

28. On these explorations see Rippy, pp. 224-27; Buarque de Holanda, *op. cit.*, Vol. I, p. 265; João Luis d'Azevedo, *Os Jesuitas no Grão-Pará: suas missões e a colonização* (Coimbra, 1930), *passim;* Affonso d'Escragnolle Taunay, *História das bandeirantes paulistas* (São Paulo, 1953), Vol. I, pp. 193-94.

29. See Grillet and Bechamel, *A Journal of the Travels of John Grillet and Francis Bechamel into Guiana in the Year 1674,* (London, 1698), and "Pièces Justicatives No. 3. Voyage Geographique du P. Grillet," in *Lettres Edifiantes et Curieuses* (Paris, 1829), Vol. XIV, pp. 479-83. The latter presents certain problems for the historian; the text contains several printer's errors concerning dates of arrival at various stops, and as to the latitude of the falls of the Approuague River. Furthermore, the names of some of the rivers, as they appear in both works, have changed, making identification somewhat difficult.

30. "Lettre du P. Grillet, Prémier Supérieur de la Mission de la Compagnie de Jésus a Cayenne a un Religieux de la Même Compagnie (le frère Pierre de Saint-Gilles) a Paris," *Lettres Edifiantes*, Vol. XIV, pp. 185-86.

31. Fúrlong Cárdiff, *op. cit.* p. 9. A substantial number of Jesuit maps of South America may be found in the Archivo Histórico in Madrid.

VI *The Bandeirantes*

Half a mile above the port of Santos, in the cooler Brazilian uplands, just below the Tropic of Capricorn, lies the city of São Paulo. Today Brazil's largest city, a bustling, dynamic metropolis, in the seventeenth century it numbered but a few thousand souls living in a hundred-odd houses atop a small hill. Actually São Paulo was not the oldest settlement on the plains of Piratininga; that distinction belonged to Santo André, a roaring frontier town founded by João Ramalho, who took to wife the daughter of a local cacique, Tibiriçá. He sired a large brood, and was in a very real sense the father of his country. The nearness of the settlement (then called Piratininga) to the seacoast was one of the factors which led Martim Afonso de Sousa to found the first Portuguese settlement (the first official one, at least) at São Vicente in 1532. Twenty-one years later Governor Tomé de Sousa converted Ramalho's village into the town of Santo André, and in the following year the Jesuits of São Vicente, under Father Manuel da Nóbrega, seeking a location which had a better climate and was closer to Indian settlements, established the *colégio* of São Paulo nine miles away. The site was a better one than the original settlement, a fact recognized by Tibiriçá, and in 1560 Santo André secured permission to merge with São Paulo, completing the move in two years, in time to stave off an attack of the Tamoio Indians, the terror of the plateau.

As immigrants came to carve out a future for themselves on the plateau the settlement grew. Mainly Portuguese, there were also Spaniards and other Europeans; this they all had in common—they were poor, but ambitious. Society was essentially agricultural, and the area was basically self-governing—a kind of diarchy of town dwellers and neighboring planters. In this type of frontier society, large families were not only usually the rule but also a necessity. In addition to his legitimate family, many a Paulista fathered a numerous brood of *mamelucos*, whose mothers were Indian and, after the importation of Negro slaves at the end of the sixteenth century, occasionally some mulattoes. In view of the subsequent importance of these *mamelucos*, let us look briefly at their Indian forebears. They were Tupi-Guarani peoples, whose culture was neolithic; a number of them lived together in large houses in villages which were by no means permanent, for they moved when the soil, tilled by slash and burn methods, became exhausted. They were skilled woodsmen, and adept at the art of finding directions.

Thus we have the typical Paulista—the *mameluco*. From his Portuguese father he received the Catholic faith, to which he was attached more by belief than practice, often some degree of education, firearms, and Portuguese attitudes; from his Indian mother the skills that were to prove so useful in the *sertões*, as well as the Tupi language. His basic attitudes were Portuguese, as evidenced by his relentless hunting of Indian slaves, and his position in society just below the creoles. Many writers like to see a similarity between the Paulista and the *coureurs-de-bois* of seventeenth-century French Canada, but the movements of the Paulistas seem to have been more dynamic and better organized; we find no real analog to the *bandeiras* in French Canada.[1]

Just what was a *bandeira?* Various explanations of the term have been attempted; the distinguished historian Jaime Cortesão presents three origins: (1) a flag (*bandeira*) hoisted by the expedition, (2) a band (*bandeira*) of men under a leader, and (3) a small raiding party detached from a larger body of troops.[2] The third, he believes, is the proper meaning of the term. It was interchangeable at this time with the military company of thirty-six men; and in the seventeenth century, Cortesão points out, with the recruiting of both Portuguese and Indians, "the *bandeira* of militia comes to have a Luso-Tupi structure." It was this structure which distinguished the Paulista *bandeiras* from others in Brazil, and which is important to remember in view of the fact that most of the energy, drive, and accomplishments of the whole *bandeira* movement were essentially Paulista.

While the *bandeiras* were primarily a seventeenth-century phenomenon, there was considerable activity of this sort in the late sixteenth century. In 1560, for example, a large *entrada* was made by Brás Cubas and Luís Martins in search of gold; nothing is known of the route, and it apparently accomplished little or nothing, since the Crown does not seem to have attached any importance to it. A few years later Heliodoro Eobanos apparently discovered some gold-bearing deposits along the Iguape and Paranaguá, and João Ramalho explored the upper reaches of the Paraíba. In 1585 or 1586 Jerônimo Leitão led a *bandeira* of considerable size into the valleys of the Paranguá and Teitê, and spent six years there, during which he devastated the Indian *aldeias* which the Spanish Jesuits had built. If the anticipated gold could not be found, slaves made an acceptable substitute. But some gold was found, and much nearer to São Paulo, not by Leitão but by the Afonso Sardinhas, father and son, and Clemente Alvares. It was not much, apparently, but it was enough to lure the English pirates Fenton and Cavendish to the coast of São Paulo in 1583 and 1592.[3]

The first known *entrada* into the Goiás area seems to have been made by Sebastião Marinho in 1592 according to an entry on a Spanish map of the time which mentions mines discovered near Vila Boa. A second *bandeira*, led by João de Sousa Pereira Botafogo against Indian attackers in 1596 also seems to have reached Goiás; Botafogo's account is somewhat confused, but it seems that a group under Domingos Rodrigues Velho, detached from his large *bandeira*, reached the Rio Tocantins. What may have resulted from this expedition we do not know.[4]

There were still a few more *bandeiras* in search of precious metals after the turn of the century. In 1601 Governor-General Beringel, whom Escragnolle Taunay describes as belonging "to the great race of *el dorado* maniacs," sent one André de Leão with a large *bandeira* in search of silver mines. The expedition seems to have gone along the Rio Paraíba and possibly to the headwaters of the Rio São Francisco in search of the legendary silver mountain, Sabarabuçu, returning in 1602 without having found it. Nicolau Barreto set out at the end of 1602, reaching the Rio das Velhas and possibly the Paraná; he returned to São Paulo in 1604, unsuccessful.[5]

If we except these early expeditions, the *bandeira* movement, from the standpoint of objectives, may be divided into two periods: the slave-hunting and the prospecting; the former reached its height during the first half of the seventeenth century, the latter dominated after midcentury and into the eighteenth. It must be remembered that the Portuguese domain was under the crown of Spain from 1580 to 1640—during the apogee of slave-hunting—and that the policy of the Spanish crown was decidedly against the enslavement of Indians. A law of July 30, 1609, issued by Felipe III, declared all Brazilians free; yet such was the uproar upon its publication in Brazil that the king had to revoke it on January 10, 1611, and permit the taking of captives in just wars or for just motives and holding them in slavery for a period of ten years.[6]

Despite this concession, the order against *entradas* into the *sertão* still stood, albeit a dead letter; violations were common and continual. It must not be assumed that these *bandeiras* were composed of the dregs of society; we find, rather, that these slave-raiding *entradas* numbered among their ranks at one time or another nearly every able-bodied man in the captaincy of São Vicente; there were even men educated at the Jesuit college of São Paulo, municipal officials, and some of the clergy (excluding the Jesuits) in the ranks of the *bandeirantes*.[7] In 1623 we even find the *procurador* of the Indians himself, Fernão Dias, leading a *bandeira* of Portuguese and Indians into the backlands in search of the "remédio do Sertão", which Escragnolle Taunay terms "a euphemism characteristic of expeditions of prey."[8]

The first big slave-raiding *bandeira* was that led by Antônio Rapôso Tavares in 1629. Born in Beja, he had come to São Paulo with his father, who was captain-major of São Vicente, in 1622. The itinerary of the expedition is not known, but it seems to have proceeded in a southerly direction to the Paraná, where it may have met another *bandeira* led by Mateus Luís Grou. Tavares' force included 900 *mamelucos* armed with guns, swords, and hatchets, and some 2,200 Indians; the whole was divided into four companies. Upon reaching the Guairá country they assaulted the *aldea* of Encarnación and seized the Indians, refusing the plea of the superior to release two catechumens until a relief force of 1,200 Indians commanded by two padres appeared; the Portuguese agreed not to attack any more reductions and to confine their raiding to capturing savage Indians. The agreement was not kept, however, for Tavares soon attacked the reduction of San Antonio, taking a large number of prisoners despite the protests of Father Mola, who barely escaped assassination. One other column attacked another reduction, taking 1,500 men, but two gained none, suffering losses instead. The *bandeira* returned to São Paulo in May, where royal officials took the royal fifth of the slaves captured.[9]

The union of the crowns of Spain and Portugal actually facilitated these incursions, since the line of Tordesillas thereby lost much of its significance. Portuguese adventurers, serving the same king as the Spanish conquistadores, moved with relative ease back and forth across the line; Spain, concerned largely with Peru and its riches, did little to prevent it and, as we shall see, eventually lost a vast area through neglect. Royal officials in São Paulo behaved more as Brazilians or Paulistas than as loyal servants of His Catholic Majesty, and not only connived in the *bandeiras* but sometimes even took part in them. So great a threat were they to the Guaraní reductions along the Paraná that Viceroy Chinchón in a letter of May 24, 1632, emphasized to the king the necessity of protecting them and urged that strong measures be taken, even suggesting the incorporation of Brazil into the Spanish empire.[10] Nothing was done, and the raids continued.

Three years later a *bandeira* of some two hundred men under Fernão de Camargo, known as "the Tiger", and Luís Dias Leme operated in present-day Rio Grande do Sul, around the Lagoa dos Patos or Laguna; a small detachment penetrated into the interior, but was slaughtered by the Caaguaras. There is some evidence of the entry of a fleet into the Lagoa dos Patos, but documentation is very scanty.[11] Anticipating further incursions, the Jesuits resolved to defend the reductions to the end; a palisade was constructed around the *aldea* of Jesús María, and Indians were trained to fight by two former soldiers, Fathers Bernal and Cárdenas.

The expected attack came soon. In 1636, in January, a *bandeira* of 150 Portuguese and 1,500 Tupis, led by Antônio Rapôso Tavares, left São Paulo for the mission country.[12] After taking many captives along the Rio Taquari, Tavares reached the *aldea* in early December, attacked, met strong resistance, but took it with considerable losses of his own. A little later he seized the reductions of San Cristóbal and San Joaquín, but had to do battle with a force of 1,600 Spaniards and Indians; there were heavy losses on both sides. By the end of January, 1637, Tavares, fearing a revolt of his captives at his stockade, returned, spent four months there, and departed for São Paulo, apparently returning sometime in mid-1638.[13]

Meanwhile another *bandeira* departed from São Paulo in 1637, under the leadership of Francisco Bueno, who soon died leaving it to his lieutenant, André Fernandes, and the latter's brother Baltasar. Although the group numbered only three hundred men, they were able to take the large (25,000 population) *aldea* of Santa Teresa in late December, and proceeded to devastate the surrounding country, around the Rio Ijuí. Despite a subsequent defeat by a Hispano-Jesuit force, the Paulistas managed, by early 1638, to entrench themselves in Caasapamini, and defied an order to leave the jurisdiction of the bishop of Buenos Aires or suffer excommunication. Ultimately the *bandeira* returned to São Paulo early in 1639.[14] The Paulistas were generally unmoved by threats of excommunication or appeals to their Christian duty toward their fellow men, and even by threats of eternal punishment; they maintained that they were baptized Christians and believers—thus their salvation was assured.

Thus far we have considered expeditions whose primary purpose was the capturing of Indians to serve as slaves; the *aldeas* were attacked for the simple reason that it was easier to capture the more or less docile Indians living in considerable numbers in the reductions than to beat the bushes for the much more elusive savages. Whatever geographical knowledge was gained from these expeditions—and it was considerable—was incidental to the primary purpose; they were essentially to provide human labor at a time when the Dutch held part of northeast Brazil and Angola, cutting off the supply of Negro slaves. In 1640 Portugal separated from the crown of Spain; Angola was reconquered, and the Dutch were forced to relinquish their conquests. This had a dual effect in Brazil: it made Indian slaves, who were less desirable, less necessary, and it made the boundary between Portuguese and Spanish America more difficult to cross. But where was the boundary, this line of Tordesillas? Geographical notions were vague at that time, and there was also the desire to make the most of a good thing, so some Portuguese maps showed it as far west as the Río de la Plata; this concept was perhaps dictated by the belief then current that the Paraná and Amazon systems were connected, and that Brazil was an island.[15] What would be more logical, then, than that the whole of this island should be under one crown? By midcentury it had been quite well established that Brazil was not insular, but Portugal was determined to gain the Río de la Plata boundary nonetheless, and to expand into the Amazon valley. If the gold- and silver-bearing mines of the Andes could be annexed, so much the better, for there was a shortage of these precious metals in Portugal.

To investigate this area, Antônio Rapôso Tavares set out from São Paulo in May of 1648 at the head of a *bandeira* which numbered more than two hundred Portuguese and one thousand armed Indians. The exact itinerary of the expedition is not easy to fix; apparently it followed the Rio Tietê downstream to the Paraná, then the main force under Tavares struck out across country, probably to the present site of Corumbá, where it remained until April or May of 1649. Here the second force under Captain Antônio Pereira joined them, and the *bandeira* finally took form. Here again we are faced with a problem: just where did this "greatest *bandeira* of the greatest *bandeirante*" (as Jaime Cortesão terms it) go? Legend would have him scaling the Andes and striding into the Pacific with his sword held high; truth does not take him quite as far, but does reveal his as one of the most extensive exploring expeditions in the history of the continent, covering the territory from the Atlantic to the Andes, and from the Tropic of Capricorn to the equator. It would appear from extant accounts that the *bandeirantes* got lost somewhere in the swampy areas around the upper Río Paraguay, wandering with their clothes on their heads and their beards in the water; they attacked reductions savagely, yet treated captured priests with courtesy and civility; they crossed the Paraguay, reached the Gauporé, descended it and the Mamoré and the Madeira, reaching the Amazon. From this point the expedition seems to have penetrated into Quito, but there is no evidence of its reaching the Pacific. By now three years had elapsed since the *bandeira* left São Paulo; after a brief stay in Quito, Rapôso Tavares led his *bandeira* down the tributaries of the upper Amazon to the mighty river itself, perhaps following much the same route as Orellana had taken long before him. The descent was somewhat leisurely, since the great *bandeirante* took time to explore the various tributaries, especially the Rio Negro, as he journeyed to Belém. Presumably Rapôso Tavares and his group reached São Paulo sometime in 1652; so disfigured was he on his return that neither friend nor relative recognized him. He had traveled perhaps some 12,000 kilometers, and had given Portugal a good claim to much of the continent.[16]

Paulista expansion was by no means confined to the south and west. Early in the seventeenth century, in 1613, one Pêro Domingues led an expedition northward, down the Rio Araguaia to its confluence with the Tocantins; this is the earliest known penetration of the present state of Goiás. A Jesuit missionary, Father Antônio de Araújo, reported another exploring expedition of some thirty Paulistas, accompanied by as many Indians, who reached the headwaters of the Tocantins, a stream called Iabeberi or das Arraias, which they followed to its confluence with the Araguaia. Along the banks of the latter river the *bandeira* seems to have acquired some three thousand Caatingas Indians, who rebelled on the journey back to São Paulo, killing a number of Portuguese and their Tupi allies.[17]

While it could scarcely be said that the Goiás area was frequented by the *bandeirantes*, it was by no means deserted by them after this first *entrada*. In 1615 Antônio Pedroso de Alvarenga reached the banks of the Rio Raraupava, which Escragnolle Taunay identified positively as the Tocantins; in the same year, the *inventário* of Antônio de Oliviera states that he died in the *sertão* of the Rio Paraupava.[18] Within the next few years, large areas of present-day Goiás were crossed by *bandeiras* led by Manuel de Campos Bicudo, Bartolomeu da Silva (the first "Anhangüera"), Sebastião Pais de Barros, Pascoal Pais de Araújo, and Padre Antônio Rapôso. In 1625 the "apostolic *bandeira*" of Frei Crístovão de Lisboa reached the shores of the Tocantins. Eleven years later the first Jesuit explorer of Goiás, Padre Luís Figueira, was found on the Rio Cametá by the second, Padre Antônio Ribeiro.[19]

The land to the northeast of Goiás, the present-day Piauí, was crossed by various explorers in the early seventeenth century, the earliest apparently arriving through the valley of the Rio Parnaíba; among them were Pêro Coelho (1603), Martim Soares Moreno (1613), Frei Cristóvão Severim (1626), and various Jesuit missionaries who had been evangelizing the Piauí Indians since 1607. At least one *bandeirante* operated in the area; in 1662 or 1663 Domingos Jorge Velho was called in by the Bahian *sertanista*, Francisco Dias de Avila, to chase the Indians out of the pasturelands of the upper Rio São Francisco valley, a task which he doubtless carried out with enthusiasm.[20]

As interest in slave-hunting gradually died down after the middle of the seventeenth century, and the *bandeirantes* turned their attention again to prospecting for precious stones and metals. In 1665 Agostinho Barbalho Bezerra, who had been named governor of the mines of São Paulo by King Afonso VI in the previous year, made preparations for a prospecting *bandeira* into the captaincy of Espíritu Santo. He had the advantage of strong royal support in the enterprise, for the king had written to certain leading Paulistas—Fernão Dias Pais, Lourenço Castanho Taques, Fernão de Camargo, Guilherme Pompéu de Almeida, and Fernão Pais de Barros—seeking their cooperation with the new governor, and had ordered the viceroy of Brazil to assist him with all his forces. Supplied by Paulistas, he began a journey up the São Mateus River in 1666, but died before reaching the second cataract and the expedition returned.[21]

The failure of the Bezerra expedition did not dampen the enthusiasm of the Paulistas; rather it encouraged them to prospect for precious stones and metals as a sign of devotion to the crown.[22] Reference has already been made to the legendary silver mountain of Sabarabuçu; in 1671 Fernão Dias Pais volunteered to head an expedition equipped at his own expense to look for it. This man, one of the greatest of Brazilian explorers, was born in São Paulo in 1608, the son of Pedro Dias Leme and grandson of Fernão Dias Pais; he was one of the leading citizens of the city, and one of the wealthiest men in the captaincy. He was generous to the Church, and his devotion to the crown was beyond question; in 1640 he had outfitted at his own expense a party of soldiers to defend Santos against an anticipated Dutch attack, and he had paid for Bezerra's provisions at the king's request. He had also had experience as a *bandeirante*, having led a big *bandeira* into the south around Caasapaguaçu, destroying the reductions of Caaro and Caaguá.

It was not the silver mountain alone that lured Dias Pais on his greatest *bandeira;* there was also the prospect of finding emeralds. In the earlier days of prospecting—about 1614—Marcos de Azeredo had found some of these precious stones (albeit of inferior quality) in the valley of the Rio São Mateus; they had been sent to the king, whose experts were convinced that top-quality emeralds could doubtless be found in the same area. At least the prospects seemed sufficiently good to win for Azeredo admission to the Ordem de Cristo, but most unfortunately he died before revealing exactly where he had made his find. Now, almost sixty years later, Dias Pais proposed to seek out these riches; honors and rewards were promised if he were successful, and he was authorized to seek public and private support in the captaincy of São Vicente.[23]

Dias Pais was a firm believer in careful planning; for two years he prepared for the *bandeira*, raising money, recruiting men, and purchasing supplies. The governor had promised him 1,000 cruzados in 1672, but only 215 milreis actually reached him; he spent well over 6,000 cruzados in preparation, using his own funds and borrowing from others, and during the course of the expedition his wife and daughters sold their jewels to meet additional expenses. Plans were completed by mid-1674, and an advance party of whites, Indians, and Negroes, accompanied by two chaplains and a goldsmith, and led by Captain Matias Cardoso de Almeida, was dispatched ahead to prepare stopping places along the route. Dias Pais set out at the head of a small group of forty whites on July 21, accompanied by his son Garcia Rodrigues Pais and his son-in-law Manuel de Borba Gato; just before his departure his young wife, Maria Garcia Rodrigues Betim became very ill and implored him not to go, but he told her that even if she received the Last Anointing, he would have to leave right afterward. She did recover, however.[24]

How long the *bandeira* would be gone no one knew; absence was measured in years rather than months, and one *bandeira* was not heard of again until eighteen years after its departure. Consequently, as we have already seen with respect to Dias Pais' preparations, they were costly to equip. The *bandeirante* usually wore all his clothing—some type of head covering, stirrup stockings, cotton drawers, leather shoes, cloth coat and breeches—and carried the rest of his belongings in a leather chest. These nearly always included a hammock and pillow, a blanket, and at least a partial change of clothes, although some carried several changes. There were the simplest of kitchen utensils—tin plates, copper pots, gourds for drinking and for carrying salt, a knife, spoons, and bread wrapped in leaves which preserved it up to a year or more. Some *bandeirantes* carried medicines and first-aid equipment and one carried a deck of cards for amusement. But most important was the heavy equipment: guns and other weapons, axes, machetes, scythes, pans for gold-washing, mining tools, fishing equipment and very often cloth and trinkets for trading purposes. Thus laden the *bandeirante* was prepared for a long time in the *sertão*, ready to live off the land.[25]

Dias Pais and his group headed toward Sumidouro, some seventy or eighty leagues away, where Captain Cardoso de Almeida and his force were waiting; this was near the supposed location of the silver mountain, and presumably somewhere in the vicinity of Bezerra's emerald strike. For three years—perhaps four—they searched the area in vain. There was a plot to kill the commander, discovered in the nick of time; his illegitimate son José Pais was involved, and he did not hesitate to order the son's execution. There was further trouble; Dias Pais had forbidden the capture of Indians, so the majority of the party, under Cardoso de Almeida, deserted to engage in this more lucrative work. Despite the desertions, Dias Pais vowed that he would go on alone with his son, if necessary; he did continue on with Borba Gato and a few others across the *sertão* to Itamirindiba, where he set up a base and began searching for emeralds, in the belief that he had found the place where Azeredo had been. His efforts finally seemed crowned with success, for he found some green stones which he took to be emeralds, and headed back to São Paulo. He was never to return, for he died of fever, probably near the palisades of the Rio das Velhas, somewhere between March 27 and June 26, 1681. He had explored vast areas of present-day Minas Gerais hitherto unknown and thus contributed to the discovery of rich gold fields, but his family was ruined by the enterprise; his brother, Father João Leite de Silva had to petition the king for remuneration.[26]

The year after the death of Dias Pais we find the restless Paulistas again on the march, this time in the west into areas which seemed quite clearly to belong to the Crown of Castile. One of the early trespassers was Brás Mendes Pais, who in 1682 led a *bandeira* into the southern part of the present state of Mato Grosso; there he encountered a Spanish force whose commander demanded that Mendes Pais and his commanders sign a declaration stating that they recognized the rights of His Catholic Majesty over the land. Thoroughly intimidated, he prepared to sign, but one of his soldiers, Pedro Leme da Silva, denounced the proceedings, loudly claiming that the region legally belonged to the king of Portugal. The chorus of voices supporting Leme led him to withhold his signature; the Spaniards denounced him but left without fighting, and Mendes Pais continued his explorations without incident. Was this interpreted as a sign of weakness on the part of Spain? Perhaps so, for the *bandeirantes* grew more audacious and arrogant, claiming now that the silver mines of Potosí were in Portuguese territory; apparently they hoped to ship the precious metal downstream to their stronghold of Colônia do Sacramento on the Río de la Plata, and thence to Lisboa.[27]

The *bandeirantes* continued their exploring activities in the early part of the eighteenth century. The lure was still gold rather than slaves, and expeditions pushed into the vast interior of Brazil in search of it; how difficult a task it was may be seen from the experiences of the second "Anhangüera," Bartolomeu Bueno da Silva, son of the famous *bandeirante*. On July 3, 1722, his *bandeira* left São Paulo, headed for the Rio Grande (the upper part of the Paraná). With him were two Benedictine monks, Father Antônio da Conceição and Frei Luís de Sant'Ana, a Franciscan priest, Cosme de Santo André, 39 cavalry, 152 foot soldiers, and 20 Indians. Some of the men were Paulistas, others Portuguese; there was considerable rivalry among them and a good deal of suspicion of the leader himself. After nearly three weeks they reached the Rio Grande; Calógeras believes that they crossed this river at the Uberaba, crossed the Triangulo Mineiro, and reached the Rio Paranaíba at Pôrto Velho.[28]

Dissensions continued; Father Antônio accused Bueno da Silva of disloyal actions, a charge echoed in the log book of Silva Braga, who accused him of the greatest cupidity, of injustice in distributing supplies, and of continually postponing the promised accounting. The *bandeira* advanced through sterile areas, losing many from illness or privations, and from Indian attacks. Morale was very low, and exasperation with the commander so great that at one point some thought of assassinating him and replacing him with his brother Simão Bueno; Braga claims to have prevented it, but not out of any love for "Anhangüera," for on learning from him that the Amazon (or Maranhão, as he called it) was not far away, he set out with nineteen companions, deserting the expedition. After a long and arduous journey, they reached Belém.

Despite the defection of the chronicler, we are not without a record of the subsequent activities of the *bandeira*; another logbook, attributed to Urbano de Couto Meneses, which reports the low state of morale and the departure of Braga's group, relates how after three years of the greatest sufferings, Bueno finally reached the place he sought in Mato Grosso after passing through areas of Goiás where the Indians still remembered his terrifying father. Somewhere in Mato Grosso Bueno found gold, probably in the upper valley of the Rio das Mortes (or Rio Manso, as it is called today); but he had lost a great number of his men and many supplies; so there was nothing to do but return, bringing with him eight thousand oitavas of gold—about thirty kilograms.

Since nothing had been heard of Bueno for so long a time, speculation in São Paulo ran high; when word arrived that he had found something, and was remaining in the *selva* to continue the search, a relief expedition was sent out on April 1, 1725, but it ran into great financial problems, exhorbitant charges, and what was more important, desertions which rendered the enterprise futile. Then on October 21 to everyone's surprise, Bueno turned up in São Paulo, announcing the discovery of gold and producing his evidence. His reward was great; he was given some 14,000 square kilometers of land for three lifetimes, and was made Capitão-Mor and Regent of the Mines, with absolute civil and criminal jurisdiction.[29]

Bueno's success lured others into the vastness of Mato Grosso in search of wealth. In 1734 two brothers from Socaraba, Fernão and Artur Pais de Barros, organized a *bandeira* which pushed with great zeal into the western reaches of Mato Grosso, where they discovered a gold-bearing area near the confluence of the Galera and Guaporé rivers. Artur remained there, while Fernão returned to Cuiabá to announce the strike to the royal official there and to seek aid and equipment. The request was not granted, but Sergeant-Major Antônio Fernandes de Abreu was sent to return with Pais de Barros and examine the strike. Artur, meanwhile, had moved to another stream, the Maqueberé, with some success; his brother and Abreu, on their arrival, explored the area with considerable success, for Abreu was able to return with four *oitavas* of gold in 1735, causing great excitement in Cuiabá.[30] The following year Manuel Dias da Silva, one of the most important settlers of Cuiabá, who had mined previously with his wealthy father, Domingos Dias, decided to investigate the mines of Goiás, about which there were glowing reports. There he worked with some degree of success until a royal order called upon all Paulistas to join in an invasion of Paraguay to halt a possible Spanish invasion of Cuiabá. Because of the dangers involved in crossing the territory of the Caiapós (which lay between Goiás and Mato Grosso), Dias took a more southerly course, across the plains of Vacaria. Here he noticed the strange absence of horses and cattle usually found there; he learned that the Spaniards had driven them to the plateau of Maracajú, and eventually located their encampment near the Río Paraguay. Fearing to attack a force considerably larger than his own, he returned to Camapoã in Mato Grosso, and destroyed a Spanish *padrão* he found there, replacing it with one claiming Portuguese sovereignty over the *sertão* of Vacaria. Eventually Dias returned to Cuiabá, having explored a vast circle of territory north and west of São Paulo.[31]

Other explorers pushed into the regions to the south—present-day Paraná state—to complete the circle of Paulista exploration and expansion in all directions. Zacarias Dias Cortes, of Curitiba, explored the plains of Palmas, seeking the fabled gold-bearing hills of Ibituruba. Fidel Francisco Boloto, Gabriel Alves de Araújo, Francisco Xavier Pissarro, Francisco de Sousa de Faria, and Manuel Rodrigues da Mota explored south of the Rio Iguaçú into what is today the state of Rio Grande do Sul, while Bruno da Costa Figuera explored the whole course of the Iguaçú. After 1765 several *bandeiras* operated in the gold- and diamond-bearing areas along the Rio Tibagi, while the western part of the area, toward the Rio Paraná, was explored by Afonso Botelho de Sampaio e Sousa.[32]

There remains Amazonia. Into this vast area Paulistas came from the south, from the Rio Tocantins and its tributaries far west to the Rio Madeira. In 1741 two men, Jacinto São Paio Soares and João Pacheco do Couto, in all likelihood Paulistas, descended the Rio Tocantins from the Goiás area; Soares turned toward the east to explore the Rearim and the Pindaré, but both groups suffered from Indian attacks.[33] The following year, 1742, witnessed the navigation of the route from the Rio Guaporé via the Mamoré, the Madeira, and the Amazon to Belém. This feat was accomplished by Manuel Feliz de Lima, who disobeyed the royal order of October 27, 1733, which forbade navigation of the Rio Madeira to avoid disputes with the Spaniards in this area. As soon as the expedition reached Belém, Lima was seized by order of the captain-general, João de Abreu Castelo Branco, who sent him back to Portugal. It was scarcely an effective deterrent, for others made use of the same route soon after.[34]

Most notable of these was João de Sousa de Azevedo, who had not made the profit he expected in searching for gold near the headwaters of the Arinos. Deciding to engage in trade, he descended the Rio Tapajós to the Amazon, and then proceeded on to Belém, where he was not seized as Lima had been. After a considerable delay he was able to outfit a commercial fleet which reached Vila Bela on the Guaporé on July 10, 1749. The fleet had come by the same route Lima had used; when Azevedo decided to return to Belém the way he had come, he was seized by order of the captain-general, Gorjão, who forced him into the royal service. There this explorer-trader remained until 1752, when he agreed not to sail the Madeira again without a license.[35] In 1749 José Lemos do Prado went from Vila Bela to Belém in fifty-two days; his journey down the

Guaporé was responsible for the decision of the Spaniards to postpone their plans to occupy and settle the region on its eastern bank. The following year he turned up in Vila Bela again, this time as a guide for the second commercial fleet to sail upstream to Vila Bela.[36] From highway of the explorer, missionary, and slave-raider, the Amazon had now become an avenue of commerce.

In two centuries of exploration, audacious and intrepid *bandeirantes* had penetrated far into the distant reaches of modern Brazil—west into Mato Grosso, Rondônia, and the borderlands of Peru, north through Goiás and Piauí to the Amazon, south into Paraná, Santa Catarina, and the north of Rio Grande do Sul. Only the missionaries had penetrated as far. Their homeland, São Paulo city, benefited not at all from their wanderings; depopulated, it was shabby and utterly devoid of the refinements of urban living. Few of the *bandeirantes* came back possessed of great wealth. Why did they go? The prospect of great wealth from slaves and gold was ever present, of course, but there was another element. Quoting Diogo Grasson Tinoco's early epic of the *bandeirantes*, which pictures their wanderings through unexplored lands, virgin forests, unknown mountains and broad rivers, Escragnolle Taunay suggests that "the penetration of the *sertões* was frequently motivated more to satisfy a sportive instinct than to answer an economic necessity" and refers to "the craving to roam unknown lands." [37] It is of such stuff that explorers are made.

NOTES

1. The standard work on the *bandeirantes* is the monumental study by Affonso d'Escragnolle Taunay, *História geral das bandeiras paulistas*, 11 vols., (São Paulo, 1924–50), abridged as *História das bandeiras paulistas*, 2 vols. (São Paulo, 1954). There is a good chapter by Myriam Ellis in Sergio Buarque de Holanda, ed., *História geral da civilização brasileira*, (São Paulo, 1963), Vol. I, Pt. 1. In English there is the classic but outdated work of Robert Southey, *History of Brazil* (London, 1819), Vol. II; appropriate chapters in C. M. Boxer, *Salvador de Sá and the Struggle for Brazil and Angola, 1602–1686* (London, 1952), and his *The Golden Age of Brazil, 1695–1750* (Berkeley and Los Angeles, 1962); and the very useful work edited by Richard M. Morse, *The Bandeirantes: the Historical Role of the Brazilian Pathfinders* (New York, 1965). On the *coureurs-de-bois* see J. Bartlet Brebner, *The Explorers of North America, 1492–1806* (New York, 1933).

2. *Rapôso Tavares e a formação territorial do Brasil* (Rio de Janeiro, 1958), pp. 70-77 (cited in Morse, *op. cit.*, p. 22).

3. Affonso d'Escragnolle Taunay, *História das bandeiras paulistas*, Vol. I, p. 24.

4. *Ibid.*, Vol. I, p. 28, and Vol. II, p. 191.

5. *Ibid.*, Vol. I, p 31; Myriam Ellis, "As bandeiras na expansão territorial do Brasil," Chap 2, Bk. V, in Buarque de Holanda, *op. cit.* Vol. I, Pt. 1, pp. 290-91; Antonio Baião, Hernâni Cidade, and Manuel Múrias, eds., *História da expansão portuguesa no mundo* (Lisboa, 1940), Vol. III, pp. 144-45.

6. Escragnolle Taunay, *op. cit.*, Vol. I, p. 37.

7. *Salvador de Sá and the Struggle for Brazil and Angola, 1602–1686*, p. 24.

8. Escragnolle Taunay, *op. cit.*, Vol. I, p. 38; see also Couthey, *op. cit.*, Vol. II, pp. 305-7.

9. Escragnolle Taunay, *op. cit*, Vol. I, pp. 49-50; Myriam Ellis, *op. cit., loc. cit.*, pp. 286-87. See also Justo Mansilla and Simón Maceta, "The Atrocities of the Paulistas" in Morse, *op cit.*, pp. 81-91.

10. Rubén Vargas Ugarte, S.J., *Historia del Perú,* Vol. II, p. 234.

11. Escragnolle Taunay, *op. cit.,* Vol. I, p. 65

12. The names of thirty-seven of these *bandeirantes* are known; for a list see Pablo Pastells, S.J., *Historia de la Compañía de Jesús en la Provincia del Paraguay* (Madrid, 1912), Vol. I, p. 458, n. 1.

13. Escragnolle Taunay, *op. cit.,* Vol. I, pp. 65-67.

14. *Ibid.,* pp. 67-68.

15. See, for example, the map by João Teixeira Albernás, 1667, in Baião *et al., op. cit.,* Vol. II, p. 137.

16. See Escragnolle Taunay, *op. cit.,* Vol. I, pp. 98-100, and Jaime Cortesão, "The Greatest Bandeira of the Greatest Bandeirante," in Morse, *op. cit.,* pp. 100-13. Taunay based his findings on documents in the Archivo General de las Indias in Sevilla, Cortesão on Spanish and Portuguese documents, many of Jesuit origin, mostly unpublished.

17. Escragnolle Taunay, *op. cit.,* Vol. II, p. 191.

18. *Ibid.,* p. 192.

19. *Ibid.,* p. 193. The term "Anhangüera" ("Old Devil") was applied to Silva by the Indians after he had, by igniting oil or spirits poured on a river, overawed them by his seeming power to make water burn.

20. Southey (*op. cit.,* Vol. II, pp. 567-68) tells of Jorge's meeting with a *bandeira* operating in the interior of Pernambuco which had been sent by Domingos Afonso, "a Pernambucan of low fortunes", who had by hard work acquired a fazenda on the Rio São Francisco. The *bandeira* encountered Jorge in Piauí; the two groups talked joyfully, agreed that the land was big enough for both of them, and departed, taking separate courses.

21. Escragnolle Taunay, *op. cit.,* Vol. I, p. 155; Manoel Cardozo, "The Last Adventure of Fernão Dias Pais," *Hispanic American Historical Review,* XXVI (1946); 471-72, n. 21.

22. Such is the opinion of the great Paulista chronicler, Pedro Taques de Almeida Pais Leme, cited in Cardozo, *op. cit.,* p. 472.

23. Cardozo, *op. cit.,* pp. 473-74. On the silver mountain legend, see Basílio de Magalhães, "A lenda de Sabarabuçu" in Congresso do Mundo Português, *Publicações,* Vol. X, "Memôrias e comunicações apresentadas ao Congresso Luso-Brasileiro de Historia, VII Congresso" (Lisboa, 1940), pp. 57-66.

24. Cardozo, *op. cit.,* pp. 475-76. The incidents of the sale of the jewels and the illness of Dona Maria are related in Escragnolle Taunay, *op. cit.,* Vol. I, p. 161.

25. José de Alcântara Machado, "Life and Death of a Bandeirante," in Morse, *op. cit.,* pp. 70-73; Southey, *op. cit.,* Vol. II, p. 307. The usual fare was pine nuts (roasted or boiled), fish, and game.

26. Cardozo, *op. cit.,* pp. 476-79; Escragnolle Taunay, *op. cit.,* Vol. I, pp. 161-62.

27. Escragnolle Taunay, *op. cit.,* Vol. I, pp. 147, 150.

28. Calógeras' opinion is cited in Escragnolle Taunay, *op. cit.,* Vol. II, pp. 197-99.

29. *Ibid.,* pp. 199-205.

30. *Ibid.,* Vol. II, pp. 83, 101-2.

31. *Ibid.,* Vol. II, pp. 79-80.

32. *Ibid.,* Vol. I, pp. 199-200.

33. *Ibid.,* Vol. II, p. 272.

34. *Ibid.,* Vol. II, p. 271.

35. *Ibid.,* Vol. II, p. 272.

36. *Ibid.,* Vol. II, p. 271. Taunay confuses the man's name, referring to him as Francisco Leme do Prado at the head of the chapter, and as José Leme do Prado on p. 271. Artur Cézar Ferreira Reis, writing in Buarque de Holanda, *op. cit.* (Vol. I, Pt. 1, p. 264), refers to him as José Lemos do Prado.

37. "Os epos bandeirante e São Paulo vila e cidade" (*Ensaios paulistas,* São Paulo, 1958), translated as "Effects of the Bandeiras" in Morse, *op. cit.,* 182.

VII *The Struggle*
for the Amazon Valley

The great Brazilian statesman Joaquim Nabuco once remarked that "nothing in the conquests of Portugal is more extraordinary than the conquest of the valley of the Amazon." [1] By all norms of the time, the Amazon was indisputably Spanish; the discovery—whether by Vespucci, Pinzón, or Orellana—was under the flag of Castile, as was the ill-fated exploring expedition of Ursúa. What is more, the line of the Treaty of Tordesillas, by all commonly accepted demarcations, ran through the mouth of the great river at a point near the present city of Belém, leaving the river in its entirety within the Castilian sphere. In view of this, which assuredly should have made Spanish right in the valley incontestable, it is indeed singular that so vast an area should have been so easily lost.

At the root of the problem lay the wealth of Peru. So preoccupied was Spain with the fabulous riches of this viceroyalty that little effort was made to extend its jurisdiction up to the line of Tordesillas. This disregard of its legitimate interests was also occasioned by the union of the two crowns after 1580, which served to erase the line at least from the monarch's point of view. Consequently, when the English, Dutch, and French began to make their appearance along the coast to the north of the Amazon, it was to his Portuguese subjects that the king of Spain and Portugal looked for the defense of this part of his realm.

France had been interested in Brazil since the early part of the sixteenth century, and had founded a settlement at the present site of Rio de Janeiro in 1555. When this was captured by Mem de Sá in 1560, "Antarctic France" was effectively liquidated, and the French were constrained to turn their attention elsewhere—to that area along the northeast coast on either side of the mouth of the Amazon, where they planned to establish "Equinoctial France." A memorial to the Council of the

Indies from Captain Manuel de Sousa d'Eça related the presence of the French, and the Portuguese were directed to take steps to remove this menace. The fort of São Luís which they had constructed was taken by Captain Francisco Caldeira de Castelo Branco, who headed the captaincy of Rio Grande do Norte, in 1615; the success of this campaign led the military leaders in a meeting on December 13 to plan an advance on the Amazon.[2] An expedition was organized which numbered 150 men in three caravels, and included also Francisco Frias Mesquita, engineer-major of the state of Brazil, and two Frenchmen familiar with the region to serve as auxiliary pilots. The force got under way on Christmas day, 1615, and anchored in Guajará Bay on January 12, 1616, where they built a fort called Presépio (The Crib) and named the land Feliz Lusitânia. Fort Presépio would in time develop into the town of Santa Maria de Belém, the chief city of Amazonia. Castelo Branco notified São Luiz and Lisboa of his accomplishment, and André Pereira prepared for King Felipe his *Relaçam do que ha no rio das Amazonas novamente descoberto*.[3]

Years passed. While Fort Presépio held firm, the Spaniards were unable to dislodge the English and Dutch from the coast of Guiana, and so long as they could remain as a threat to the fort, all of Amazonia was in danger. In 1621, on November 4, it was decided in Madrid to end the restrictions against the Portuguese and in the face of a greater danger to entrust to them the task of holding the Amazon valley for the crown. Doubtless a memorial of Luís Aranha de Vasconcelos of June 21, 1621, sent to the court by order of Don García de Haro, may have influenced the court in this decision.[4] Two years later Aranha de Vasconcelos decided to confront the rivals of the crown and sailed over four hundred leagues up the Amazon, exploring the lower reaches and taking soundings; he discovered that the current divided into two branches 130 leagues from the sea, and that the Grão-Pará and the Amazon were one and the same river, a fact which had eluded earlier navigators. On the basis of this information Antônio Vicente Cochado, pilot-major of Pernambuco and leader in the expedition's exploring activities, made an exact map, the first chart of the region.[5] The enterprise was not restricted to exploring, however; an order of the king issued in Aranjuez on May 22, 1622, had specified that he be provided with items for purchasing the aid of the Indians—axes, knives, beads, combs fishhooks, etc.—at a cost of 80 milreis. And after taking on the pilot, Cochado, at Recife, Aranha had picked up fighting men and one thousand Indian archers recruited by the Franciscan Frei Cristóvão de São José. In his report to the king, he told of bringing many people under the king's dominion in the area he had explored, and related further an encounter with the Dutch and the English along the shores of the river. In this operation he destroyed two Dutch forts, taking the defenders prisoners, along with their Angolan

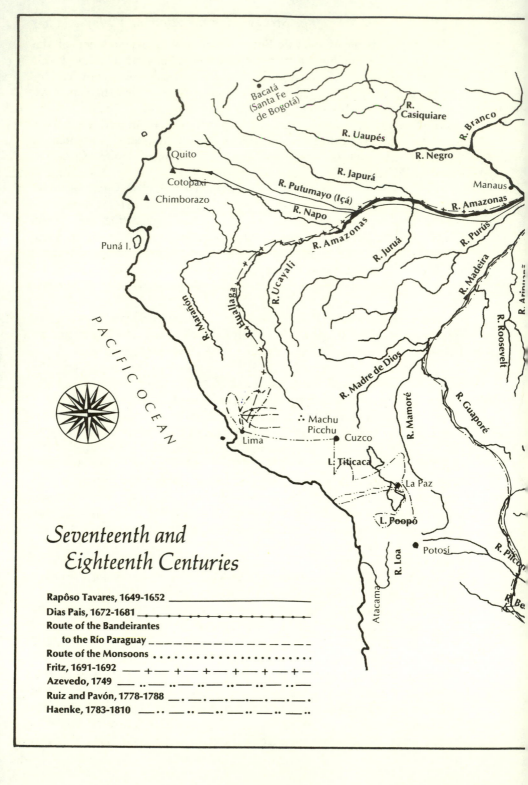

Bacatá
(Santa Fe
de Bogotá)

R. Casiquiare

R. Branco

R. Uaupés

R. Negro

Quito

Cotopaxi

▲ Chimborazo

R. Japurá

R. Putumayo (Içá)

Manaus

R. Napo

R. Amazonas

PACIFIC OCEAN

Puná I.

R. Marañón

R. Huallaga

R. Ucayali

R. Amazonas

R. Juruá

R. Purús

R. Madeira

R. Roosevelt

R. Ariquaz

Machu
Picchu

Cuzco

R. Madre de Dios

R. Mamoré

R. Guaporé

Lima

L. Titicaca

La Paz

L. Poopó

R. Loa

Potosí

R. Pilco

Seventeenth and
Eighteenth Centuries

Rapôso Tavares, 1649-1652 _____

Dias Pais, 1672-1681 _ . _ . _ . _ . _ . _ . _ . _ . _ .

Route of the Bandeirantes
  to the Río Paraguay _ _ _ _ _ _ _ _ _ _ _ _ _ _

Route of the Monsoons . . . .

Fritz, 1691-1692 —— + —— + —— + —— + —— + —— + —— + —

Azevedo, 1749 ___ .. ___ .. ___ .. ___ .. ___ .. ___

Ruiz and Pavón, 1778-1788 __ . __ . __ . __ . __ . __ .

Haenke, 1783-1810 __ .. __ .. __ .. __ .. __ .. __ ..

Atacama

R. Be

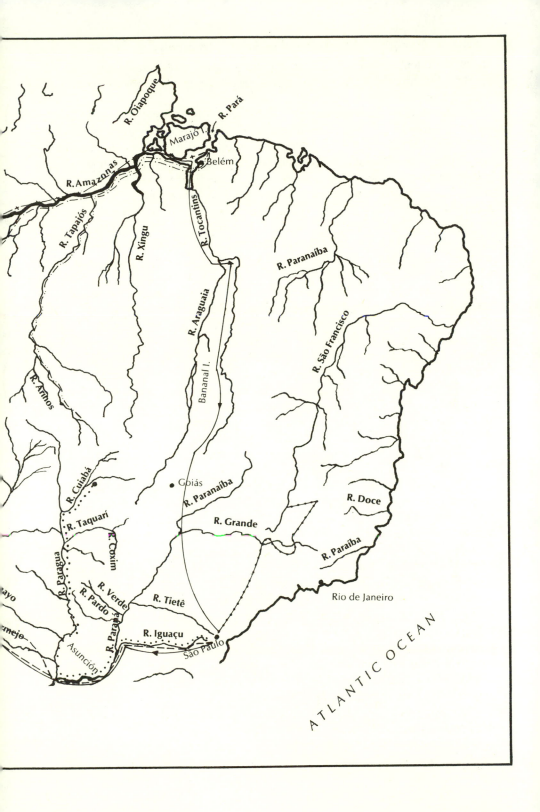

slaves, and sent one English ship to the bottom with the loss of "six English hidalgos." [6] Clearly the Portuguese did not intend to be dislodged from the lower Amazon.

While Aranha de Vasconcelos firmly established Portuguese authority at the mouth of the Amazon, and while his expedition explored the lower reaches of the river for a considerable distance, major credit for laying the foundation for Portuguese authority throughout the major portion of the valley belongs to Captain Pedro Teixeira. In 1615 he had participated in the Castelo Branco expedition; in 1623 he was with Aranha de Vasconcelos in his attack on the Dutch and English in the lower valley; in 1625, along with Pedro da Costa Favela and Jerônimo de Albuquerque he attacked new Dutch and English positions on the Xingu River and along the coast of Macapá, north of the mouth of the Amazon; in 1629 with Costa Favela he assaulted the fort of Torrego on the island of Tocoju.[7] His next enterprise would be an expedition traversing nearly the entire length of the Amazon.

In 1636, it will be remembered,[8] two Franciscan lay brothers had gone down the Río Napo and into the Amazon, proceeding on to Belém. The governor, Jácome Raimundo de Noronha, sent one of the friars, Andrés de Toledo, to Lisboa to make a report of their experiences while he organized at Belém an expedition of 80 Portuguese with some 1,200 Indians and Negroes in 47 canoes to explore the entire length of the river; this was by far the biggest expedition yet to navigate the Amazon. In command was Captain Pedro Teixeira; along as guides were two friars, Domingos Brieva, who had come down the river with Andrés de Toledo, and Agustín de las Llagas.

The expedition left Belém on October 28, 1637; despite the lack of a good river pilot, the explorers managed to progress upstream without serious difficulty and after several months reached the Río Napo, which they followed into the country of the Quijos Indians, where Gonzalo Pizarro had begun his search for cinnamon. By this time some of the Indians had deserted, and fearful lest the others would join them, Teixeira sent an Indian expert, Colonel Benito Rodríguez de Oliveira, with some soldiers and auxiliaries in eight canoes to find the way to Quito. On June 24, 1638, the colonel reached a Spanish outpost, Payamino, where he was provided with guides for the remainder of his journey. Teixeira, meanwhile, after stationing troops to guard his return, followed in the wake of his advance party, finally reaching Quito where he was well received by the authorities. Almost a full year had elapsed since the expedition left Belém.

The Spanish authorities in Quito were well aware of the significance of Teixeira's accomplishment, and its importance was not lost in Lima; when the viceroy received news of it, he immediately wrote to the king in Spain, and ordered his chief cosmographer to meet with the pilots and prepare a map of the route followed. A discussion was held in Lima to consider what use Spain might make of the voyage; the chief advantages seemed to be in the possible shipment of silver down the Amazon to Belém, from whence it could more quickly be shipped to Spain, avoiding the danger of pirates. The viceroy, the Conde de Chinchón, saw too many difficulties, however, and preferred the old route. The audiencia in Quito, meanwhile, decided to notify the governor in Belém and Teixeira as well that the latter had exceeded his authority in penetrating into lands not of the Portuguese crown (although it was still worn by Felipe IV of Spain); to avoid any inconvenience to him he was to be allowed to return by the same route he had come, and without delay enroute. Further, he was to take with him one or two persons who, on reaching Belém, would embark immediately for Spain to present to the king a complete account of what had transpired.[9]

Volunteers for this assignment were not wanting, "but he who, above all, displayed most ardent zeal in seeking new occasions of prosecuting the service of his King, which he had now done for thirty years, and his ancestors before him, was Don Juan Vasques de Acuña, a knight of Calatrava"[10] and corregidor of Quito, who offered to raise troops for the expedition and pay for them himself. Since his services as corregidor were more valuable to the Crown he was denied permission to go; instead, his brother, the Jesuit Padre Cristóbal de Acuña, received the assignment.[11] His instructions were precise: he was to "take particular care to describe, with clearness, the distance in leagues, the provinces, tribes of Indians, rivers and districts which exist from the first embarkation, to the said city of Para; informing yourself with all possible precision, of all things, that you may report upon them, as an eye witness, to the Royal Council of the Indies."[12]

The expedition departed from Quito on February 16, 1639, following the course of the Río Napo toward the Amazon. Acuña was awed by the great river he had been commissioned to explore, calling it "the largest and most celebrated river in the world" and pointing out that it waters a far more extensive region and supports more people than the Ganges, Tigris, or Nile: "it only wants, in order to surpass them in felicity, that its source should be in paradise, as is affirmed of those other rivers by grave authors."[13] The extensive system of tributaries in the upper part of the valley impressed him considerably; he went to some length to describe how the Amazon could be entered from Peru, Quito, and New Granada, and thus serve to carry the products of these areas directly to the Atlantic.[14]

The early part of the journey, down the Río Napo and into the upper Amazon, or Marañón, took them into the country of the Agua (or Omagua) Indians, whom Acuña described as the "most intelligent and best governed of any on the river," who went about "decently clothed" but had a deplorable custom of flattening the heads of their infants.[15] About one hundred leagues beyond the first settlement of the Aguas they found the weather so cool that they had to put on more clothes; according to the Indians, this phenomenon occurred during June, July, and August, and was caused by winds from the high sierras to the south. It occurred to Acuña that wheat might be grown here. Farther downstream, beyond the confluence of the Río Putamayo (or Içá), they came upon the mouth of the Juruá, the "river of Cuzco," [16] and heard tales of gold and of a land of giants "sixteen palms in height, wearing great plates of gold in their ears and noses" [17] some two months' journey away.

Since the Amazon, during the rainy season, inundates much of the land along its shores, Acuña was pleased to note that along that portion of the river the land was high enough not to flood and would, he thought, be suitable for pasture. The river widens considerably in this region; Acuña speaks of a series of lakes.

One of the largest of the Amazon's tributaries is the Rio Negro, a great river whose clear waters are in marked contrast to the muddy waters of the Amazon; so strong is the current of the Negro that its waters do not blend with those of the larger river for a considerable distance. Father Acuña was much impressed by this phenomenon; his almost poetic description of it is worthy of repetition: "though the Amazons opens its arms with all its force, the new river does not wish to become subject to it, without receiving some marks of respect, and it thus masters one half of the whole Amazons, accompanying it for more than twelve leagues, so that the waters of the two can be clearly distinguished from each other. At last the Amazons, not permitting so much superiority, forces it to mingle with its own turbulent waves, and recognize for a master the river which it desired to make a vassal." [18] But Acuña was also the very practical man; he had learned from the Indians of a connection between the Rio Negro and the Orinoco (the Río Casiquiare), and suggested the mouth of the Rio Negro, which controlled the route, as a good place for a fort.

The expedition's brief stay at the mouth of the Rio Negro very nearly was a cause of considerable trouble. On October 12, 1639, the Portuguese sailors, feeling that they had not been adequately rewarded for their two years of service, wanted to go upstream along the Rio Negro on a slave-hunting expedition. When they learned that the Captain-major was inclined to permit this, Acuña and his companion, Andrés de Artieda, drew up a formal paper pointing out that the audiencia of Quito had been assured that the expedition would be in Belém in two and one half months; eight months had elapsed thus far, and they were still six hundred leagues from their destination—further delay might postpone the fortification of the river, a matter of importance to His Majesty.

Furthermore, they pointed out, the Portuguese could not take slaves with a good conscience. They urged that the expedition proceed, and demanded, in the event that Teixeira intended to delay for such a purpose as this, that they be given arms and supplies and be allowed to proceed alone as His Majesty had ordered. Apparently Teixeira had a better conscience in this matter than his men; Acuña relates that the commander "was rejoiced to have us on his side" and ordered the expedition to proceed.[19]

Proceeding downstream from the Rio Negro, the expedition passed the mouth of the Rio Madeira and came upon the adjacent great island of the Tupinambás, who, Acuña relates, were refugees from the Portuguese conquest of Pernambuco. These Indians acquainted the explorers with two new myths: they told of two nearby nations, one of dwarfs as small as little children, the other of people "who all have their feet turned the wrong way, so that a person who did not know them, in following their footsteps, would always walk away from them." [20] And there was that persistent myth of the Amazons, the fabulous female warriors whom Orellana first mentioned. Acuña makes no judgment in the matter; he relates the usual story about them, and tells of a woman in Pasto who claimed to have been in their country, but cautions that "time will discover the truth." [21]

Below this island the river begins to narrow, eventually down to one-quarter of a league, above the entrance of the Rio Tapajós. From this point on, Acuña observed, the tides became noticeable. This region had been considerably worked over by Portuguese slave-hunters, who had abused and oppressed the Tapajosos Indians. Interesting is the mention of the earlier entrance of a large English ship, and the murder of its crew by the Indians. Farther downstream the expedition passed the Rio Ginipape,[22] which the Indians asserted would produce gold in such quantity as to rival Peru. Two leagues farther on the river divided into two arms; the expedition followed the right branch, proceeding past the Rio Tocantins to the fortress of Grão-Pará, which they reached on December 12, 1639. Acuña was not satisfied with the location of the fortress; he felt that the Island of the Sun, fourteen leagues closer to the sea, was a better location; it had a good harbor, he pointed out, and was but twenty leagues from where the Amazon enters the sea "by eighty-four mouths." [23]

Acuña was most faithful to the charge laid upon him in Quito. His description of the lands bordering the Amazon makes them seem desirable in the extreme; he tells us that "the river is full of fish, the forests of game, the air of birds, the trees are covered with fruit, the plains with corn, the earth is rich in mines, and the natives have much skill and ability." [24] Surely a lush paradise indeed! Nor is the account lacking in details; we learn that the river is 1,350 Castilian leagues in length,[25] that it varies in width from one to three leagues and more, and at its narrowest is but one-quarter of a league. A list of products of the area includes maize, yuca (or manioc), plantains, pineapples, guavas, chestnuts and coconuts; we are even told how the Indians brew a potent beverage from the roots of the yuca plant.

Among the fauna of the valley two aroused Acuña's particular curiosity; there was the manatee, or peguebuey, whose flesh could be roasted and preserved for a month and whose skin could be used for shields, and there was the electric eel, which "has the peculiarity that, while alive, whoever touches it, trembles all over his body, while a closer contact produces a feeling like the cold shivering of ague, which ceases the moment he withdraws his hand." [26]

The climate he found agreeable, describing it as temperate "so that the heat does not molest and the cold does not fatigue, neither is there a continual change of weather to annoy." [27] There were refreshing breezes and daily showers, and none of those things so feared by sixteenth- and seventeenth-century men, "harmful dews" and "pestilential airs." Only the plague of mosquitoes prevented it from being a paradise.

Amazonia seemed to Acuña to be a land of inexhaustible riches. There were the valuable medicinal drugs produced in the forests, useful in the healing arts and for many other purposes. There were huge cedars, ceiba trees, and ironwood trees, and naval stores in abundance; ships could be built there more cheaply than anywhere else, and the supply of timber could not be exhausted. There was cacao, cotton, tobacco which could be the best in the world, an excellent source of dye, and sugar, which could be cultivated in vast plantations along the river. What was more, the affluents drained the richest areas in the world, and the Amazon, the way of entry, "is the chief master of all those riches."

The Indians attracted Acuña's interest and solicitude. He spoke of more than 150 nations, each with its own language, constantly involved in wars. They were skilled hunters, using spears and hatchets, generally fashioned from bone. They worshiped idols, albeit without much ceremony, and were much influenced by sorcerers. For the most part he found them to be mild and generous, and felt that they might make good Christians. [28]

In a memorial appended to his account, Acuña urged the king not to delay in occupying Amazonia. The advantages of such action were many: it would provide Spain with a well-protected route for bringing the riches of Peru to the Atlantic, avoiding the danger of pirates in the Caribbean; it would be fairly easy to accomplish if the conquest were begun at the mouth rather than from Quito; it would keep the Portuguese, and what was worse, the Dutch, out of lands rightfully belonging to the Spanish Crown; it could end the Indian wars, reducing the rapid depopulation of the area; it presented a marvelous opportunity for converting the infidels.[29] But in 1640 Portugal became independent of the Spanish Crown, and the situation changed radically.

Acuña reached Spain and published his account, *New Discovery of the Great River of the Amazons*, in 1641, but the book was destined to enjoy only a minimal circulation. The editor of an early English translation believed that the king, in view of the Portuguese revolt, suppressed the book lest, being of no use now to Spain, it might be valuable to Portugal. Gomberville, a member of the French Academy, who edited the French translation, said that the only copies extant were the one he used and perhaps another copy in the Vatican Library.[30]

In 1655 Blaise François de Pagan, Comte de Merveilles, wrote a *Description de la rivière et pais des Amazones*,[31] based largely on Acuña's account; in a dedicatory letter to Mazarin, he proposed an "easy conquest" of the river—something the cardinal was not free at the time to undertake, although he did later try to plant colonies in several locations at the mouth of the river.

But if Acuña's work was wasted on Spain, as well as Pagan's attempt to turn it to France's advantage, there was still another with sufficient foresight to suggest it to his sovereign. In 1661 one William Hamilton made an English translation of Pagan's work, dedicated to King Charles II. He pointed out that the book had been prepared for Mazarin to induce him to attempt the conquest of the Amazon for France, but since nothing had been done "it comes now to me to beg your Majestie's favourable acceptance in the hope of that large retribution to your self, when your Majesty shall think fit to apply your thoughts to it, for which it was intended for another." It was, he said, "possest by the barbarous Natives only, except in two skirts; Brasile on the East, where the Portuguese pitched; and Peru upon the West, where the Spaniard is divided from the Inland by the tract of the Andes." The Spanish and Portuguese discoveries, he claimed, "were more to satisfy their curiosity, than that they could then hope for a conquest." Since neither power, nor France, had made any serious effort to occupy Amazonia, he felt that God in His providence seemed to have intended it for England.[32]

But Hamilton's efforts were as unavailing as those of Pagan in France or Acuña in Spain, for it was Portugal, now under a native dynasty, that proceeded slowly but surely to appropriate nearly the entire Amazon valley. For some time Portuguese Jesuits had been evangelizing along the southern shore of the Amazon, while Carmelite fathers preached to the Indians to the north; but the major Portuguese advances were not so peaceful, being the work of soldiers and adventurers who pushed up along the river from Grão-Pará in search of Indians for slaves. They built no settlements as they advanced along the shores, but merely informed the Indians that these lands were Portuguese territory and that they were subject to the Portuguese.[33]

This was, of course, clearly a violation of the Treaty of Tordesillas, for by no generous interpretation of its provisions could the line be presumed to give Portugal much of the lower Amazon, and assuredly it did not extend as far as the Rio Negro. Yet what is most singular is that Spain, certainly aware of what was going on as a result of Father Acuña's work, made no serious attempt, aside from the *entradas* of the missionaries, to extend its control over this vast area. The viceroy of Peru, the Conde de Chinchón, showed little enthusiasm for exploring the region; he felt that explorers exaggerated the advantages of their expeditions, which experience showed bore little fruit, that Spain simply lacked the manpower to maintain garrisons in newly discovered lands, and that entering under arms is hardly the best way to win over the Indians and convert them to Christianity.[34]

Despite this indifference, still one more effort was made to stem the Portuguese advance, and it was the work not of a Spaniard, but of a Jesuit missionary of the Bohemia province, Father Samuel Fritz. In 1685 an outbreak of smallpox in the country of the Cocama or Ucayali Indians led many of them to seek safety among the Omaguas (or Aguas) farther down the Amazon. The latter told them of Portuguese slave raids in their territories, so the Cocamas, by way of repaying their hospitality, invited them to return upstream with them to meet Father Juan Lorenzo Herrero, who, they felt, could help them. He urged them to become Christian and settle nearer to his mission, but pointed out that he could not leave his own charges and that he would send another missionary to them. The choice fell upon Father Fritz, a tall, spare, venerable-looking man with a curly beard, who had recently arrived from Germany.[35]

Fritz was received enthusiastically, and in three years had baptized them all, founding the mission of San Joaquín. The Jurimaguas, who lived farther downstream, heard of his work and invited him to preach to them, which he did with great success, founding the mission of Nuestra Señora de las Niebes. Fritz notes in his *Journal* that the women of the Jurimaguas and Aysuares fight with bows and arrows—probably the source of Orellana's story. Finally the missionary became gravely ill with dropsy and fever, and lay in bed, unable to move, for three months, dependent on Indians for food and drink when they could come. To add to his misery, it was flood season, and while the river passed almost alongside his bed, it was just beyond his mouth. His food was eaten by lizards and rats, and he was almost killed by a crocodile. Learning that the Portuguese were eight days' journey farther downstream, he decided to seek them out in the hope of obtaining a remedy for his ills, and left his mission on July 3, 1689.[36]

Eventually, after being assisted by a few missionaries he met along the way, Fritz found the Portuguese he had heard about—slave-raiders under Capitão-Mor Andrés Pinheiro and Padre João Maria Garzoni, who had heard extraordinary stories about him. The cures they attempted—bleeding for the fever and fumigation for dropsy—apparently were worse than the illnesses, for Fritz grew worse, and on August 15 Pinheiro decided to send him to Grão-Pará in the care of a soldier and a Jesuit lay brother. He reached there September 11, "more dead than alive," as he put it, but after two months' care in the Jesuit *colégio* there, recovered his health.[37]

His presence there created a problem for Governor Arturo Sá de Meneses; he was aware that Fritz had come solely for his health, yet, as Fritz put it, "conscience does not cease to be a restless monitor," and the Portuguese, well aware of their continual violations of the Treaty of Tordesillas, "began to suspect that I was an abandoned spy, sent by the Governor of Marañón in the service of Castile to investigate these advances."[38] So he placed Fritz under house arrest, claiming, in an attempt to justify himself, that the Omaguas, among whom Fritz was working, were subject to the Portuguese Crown.[39] For eighteen months the missionary was prevented from leaving, despite his appeals; ultimately he was successful, for the king of Portugal announced that he would have deposed Sá for this incident, had his term not ended, and he instructed the new governor, Antônio de Albuquerque, to send Fritz back to his mission—even to Quito, if necessary—at royal expense.

For the return trip Fritz would have preferred to be accompanied only by Indian rowers, so as not to alarm the tribes, but the governor insisted that the Crown required soldiers, and sent six and a surgeon to accompany the missionary and his Indians. After a three-month delay, the party set out July 6, 1691, in two canoes; the larger, assigned to Fritz, had a cabin astern. The trip was uneventful to August 2, when a storm nearly wrecked the canoes, but there were no further troubles of this nature. The party reached the narrowest part of the river on August 14, and Fritz corroborates Acuña's statement that it reached a width of only one-quarter of a league. After a stay at the Urubú mission, where Father Fritz heard accounts of the fantastic tales that had been told about him, the group pushed on; beyond the mouth of the Rio Madeira they passed a number of villages destroyed by an earthquake, which the Indians looked upon as divine disapproval of Fritz's detention. As they approached the Rio Negro, the missionary noticed the phenomenon which so intrigued Acuña and has interested travelers ever since—the division of the muddy waters of the Amazon and the clear, dark waters from the Rio Negro plainly visible in midstream.

Beyond the Rio Negro they came upon grim evidences of the slave-raiders—burned and deserted villages; even Fritz's mission, which they reached on October 13, was uninhabited. It was obvious that the Indians feared the Portuguese, and Fritz urged them to leave him and return to Grão-Pará, but they insisted on accompanying him to the outermost of the Omagua villages, which was likewise deserted. Here Captain Miranda finally revealed that his orders were to take possession of the lands of the Omaguas, and to tell Fritz to leave. Despite the missionary's assertion that these were undoubtedly Spanish lands, the Portuguese marked a tree as a sign of possession before they departed, indicating that they intended to return to settle there. Fritz did not doubt that they would; he knew their zeal in slave-hunting, "in addition to which," he continues, "they imagine that from here they can find a gate of entrance to El Dorado, that their dream is not very distant." [40] Proceeding on now without his Portuguese escort, Fritz continued up river, reaching the mission of San Joaquín on December 3, where he remained until proceeding on to Quito in February.

Determined now to warn the authorities of this new Portuguese encroachment, Fritz contemplated going to the audiencia in Quito, but was advised to lay the matter before the viceroy in Lima, the Conde de Monclova, who could bring such an urgent matter more quickly to the attention of the king. Proceeding via the Río Huallaga and the Río Paranapura, he reached the City of the Kings on July 2, 1692. While the viceroy was impressed with Fritz's accomplishments and summoned him several times to the viceregal palace, he displayed the same lack of interest as Chinchón; the Portuguese were Catholics too, he said, and Amazonia was not worth defending, since it yielded no fruits to the king. Besides, there was land enough in the Indies for both crowns. He would, however, inform the king and see what happened. If Father Fritz failed to impress the viceroy with the gravity of the situation, he did not come away completely empty-handed, for Monclova did authorize the expenditure of additional funds for the Amazon missions. The report was sent to the king, but unfortunately the count failed to apprise him of the gravity of the situation, which he himself, of course, did not grasp, and which Carlos II was incapable of understanding. [41]

On returning to the missions Fritz learned of further Portuguese advances. Traveling to Nuestra Señora de las Niebles, Fritz learned, upon reaching there, that only four days before the Portuguese had carried off many Indians, telling them that the river belonged to them. After attending to affairs of the other missions, he returned to Las Niebles on March 5, 1696, in answer to a call for help—the Indians had heard that the Portuguese were again coming up river in search of slaves. Fritz decided to intercept them, and after a three-day journey downstream met one Francisco Sousa, who said he had come only to buy cacao; since Fritz's departure from Belém, he told him, the king had forbidden the taking of captives unless they had killed a Portuguese. [42]

It soon became obvious to Fritz that the Portuguese were determined to take possession of the upper Amazon valley by one means or another.

In 1698 he encountered a party of Portuguese, whose coming he had learned of from the Indians, headed by Captain José Antunes da Fonseca and a Carmelite provincial, Father Manuel de la Esperança, who tried to oust Fritz from his mission on the grounds that the Indians had sent for them. Fritz later learned that Governor Albuquerque had inquired of the Indians in the locality whether they wanted a missionary. On being told that they had one who visited them from time to time, the governor told them that this missionary did not care for them or he would reside permanently with them; he promised to send one who would. The problem was settled peaceably when Fritz and the Portuguese agreed to part and go in opposite directions, but throughout the remainder of the year and 1699 he continued to learn of repeated Portuguese advances. In 1701 he went to Quito, where he was delayed by an illness; upon recovering he went downstream again, reaching the Amazon in May, and proceeded to the new settlement of the Jurimaguas, who had fled the Portuguese.[43]

The gravity of the situation caused the missionary to request soldiers, who arrived late in August—just in time to foil a plot to murder the fathers. Subsequently Fritz received a Portuguese Carmelite friar, who importuned him to urge the Indians to go back to their old homes and submit to the Portuguese; Fritz declared that they were not under Portuguese jurisdiction, and could do as they pleased. He did agree to accompany the Carmelite downstream; in the course of the voyage they heard of more slave-raiding, which the friar promised to try to halt. On his return, Fritz was met by some Portuguese whom he told to stay out of the area until the boundary was finally determined by the two crowns.[44] The remainder of the *Journal*, which carries the account down to 1723, is largely concerned with work in the missions and with continued Portuguese incursions; Fritz's exploring activities were considerably reduced, and he spent most of his time among the Jebaro Indians. There, on March 16, 1724, he remarked to a friend that he would not live to see his seventieth birthday (April 9); two days later he died, amid the great lamentation of his flock. One of the great fruits of his explorations was his map of the Amazon, prepared in 1691, a valuable contribution to cartography indeed. All that Fritz would claim for it was that it was the first one drawn with a proper survey of levels. It was ultimately brought to Paris by the French explorer La Condamine, who held it in high regard.[45]

The importance to the Portuguese of possession of the Amazon was to become even more apparent in the eighteenth century with the discovery of the Rio Madeira. This river, which forms a link between Belém and the mines of Mato Grosso, was first sighted by Captain-Major João de Barros Guerra in a punitive expedition against the Torazes Indians, who had been raiding canoes engaged in the cacao trade on the

Amazon. It was rumored that Europeans lived above the cataracts, and so Governor João de Maia da Gama sent Sergeant-Major Francisco de Melo Palheta with some soldiers to explore the river in 1722; he went around the cataracts, found some Spanish missionaries, and returned to Belém to make his report.[46] Palheta was unaware of the possibility of communicating with Mato Grosso via this route; it remained for Manuel Téllez and later Miguel da Silva and Gaspar Barbosa Lima to discover it some years later, beginning from Mato Grosso.[47] In 1742 Manuel Féliz de Lima organized an expedition which left Mato Grosso and proceeded to Belém by way of the Sararé, Guaporé, and Madeira rivers; most of the Portuguese in his party of fifty, discouraged by privations and inconveniences, deserted the expedition before it reached its destination. The others might well have done so also, for on arriving at Belém they were charged with breaking a law forbidding Portuguese nationals to enter foreign colonies (Did the governor consider at least part of the territory rightfully Spanish?). Lima and another were sent in custody to Lisboa; the third, Joaquim Ferreira Chaves, was put into the army, from which he promptly deserted and passed through Maranhão and Goiás, where he learned that the rivers there flowed toward Belém. In 1749 José Leme do Prado, after interrogating Chaves, followed the same route from Mato Grosso, establishing conclusively the connection between the Plata and Amazon basins.[48]

One more great tributary of the Amazon attracted the attention of Portuguese explorers at this time. In August, 1742, one Leonardo de Oliveira left Mato Grosso and finally reached, four months later, the Jesuit mission of São José near the mouth of the Tapajós. Five years later a miner, João de Sousa de Azevedo, left the mines of Mato Grosso to seek gold farther on; his search was rewarded, for he found it in the Rio Arinos, one of the headwaters of the Tapajós, as well as in the upper reaches of the latter river itself. His discoveries enriched him sufficiently to enable him to buy several *fazendas* (plantations) on his return to Belém, and they enriched Portugal by providing another route into the gold-bearing areas of the interior. And five years later, as we have seen, João de Sousa de Azevedo explored the upper reaches of the Rio Tapajós and the Rio Arinos in search of gold, and descended the Tapajós and the Amazon to Belém.[49]

These expeditions, accomplished without interference or objection on the part of the Spanish authorities, demonstrated plainly what was obvious long before: Spain was no longer interested in asserting its rights in Amazonia. The great river and its valley had been discovered by the Spaniards, and, even before, had been assigned to Spain by the Treaty of Tordesillas, an agreement to which, for the most part, the Spanish sovereigns had rigidly adhered. For more than a century it had been reconnoitered by intrepid explorers in the service of the Spanish Crown,

The Struggle for the Amazon Valley 131

and Spanish missionaries had begun, with some success, the work of evangelizing its Indian inhabitants. Yet, paradoxically, it was during the period when the crown of Portugal was worn by the Spanish kings that the area would be allowed to pass under Portuguese control with scarcely a finger lifted to prevent it. The Portuguese policy of unrelenting prodding and advance had paid off; seldom has so vast an empire been acquired at so little cost.

NOTES

1. Quoted in Artur C. Ferreira Reis, "A Expansão Portuguêsa na Amazônia nos Séculos XVII e XVIII," *Cultura* (Rio de Janeiro, December, 1948), p. 94.
2. On the French efforts in Brazil see Sergio Buarque de Holanda, ed., *História geral da civilização brasileira* (São Paulo, 1963), Vol. I, Pt. 1, Bk. IV, Chap. 4.
3. *Ibid.*, p. 259.
4. Pablo Pastells, S.J. *Historia de la Compañía de Jesús en la Provincia del Paraguay* (Madrid, 1912), Vol. I, pp. 324-26, Doc. No. 378.
5. Buarque de Holanda, *op. cit.*, p. 262; João Lucio d'Azevedo, *Os Jesuítas no Grão-Pará, sus missões e a colonização*, 2nd. rev. ed. (Coimbra, 1930), p. 29. Azevedo states that the map was made by Pedro Teixeira.
6. Buarque de Holanda, *op. cit.*, p. 261; "Informação de Luiz Aranha de Vasconcellos sobre o descobrimento do Rio das Amazonas. 30 de Abril de 1626." (Published in *Documentos para a História da Conquista e Colonisação da Costa de Leste-Oeste do Brasil*, pp. 391-94. Vol. XXIV of the *Anáis da Biblioteca Nacional*, Rio de Janerio, 1905. I am grateful to my teaching assistant, Srta. Marguita Bergman, of Rio de Janeiro, for furnishing me a copy of this document.)
7. Buarque de Holanda, *op. cit.*, p. 261.
8. See account in Chap. V, pp. 93.
9. A good brief account of Teixeira's journey to Quito may be found in Rubén Vargas Ugarte, S.J., *Historia del Perú* (Lima, 1954), Vol. I, pp. 235-37.
10. Cristóbal Acuña, *A New Discovery of the Great River of the Amazons* (London, Hakluyt Society, 1859), pp. 58-59.
11. *Ibid.* The Franciscan historian Arcila Robledo points out that this relationship effectively cut out the friars from any further activity in the upper Amazon valley. *Las Misiones Franciscanas en Colómbia*, p. 364.
12. "Clause of the Royal Provision which the Royal Audiencia of Quito issued, in the Name of His Majesty, As Authority for this Discovery," Acuña, *op. cit.*, pp. 45-46.
13. *Ibid.*, p. 61.
14. *Ibid.*, pp. 87-92.
15. *Ibid.*, pp. 95-96.
16. *Ibid.*, pp. 98-105. Actually the river does not rise anywhere near Cuzco; its headwaters, the Alto Yuruá, rise near the source of a small stream which flows into the Río Ucayali, nearly three hundred miles below Cuzco.
17. *Ibid.*, p. 107.
18. *Ibid.*, p. 109.
19. *Ibid.*, pp. 112-17.
20. *Ibid.*, p. 119.
21. *Ibid.*, pp. 121-23.
22. This river, which enters the Amazon from the north, between the mouths of the Tapajós and the Xingu, does not appear by name on Father Samuel Fritz's map, published in 1707, but may be identical with a small, unnamed stream in this area; it rises to the southeast of the mythical Lake of Parima, which Fritz locates

to the north of the mouth of the Rio Tapajós. Since this was the site of the fabled golden city of Manoa, it may well be that the Indians' tales of abundant gold have had their origin in this tale, which had lured many Spaniards and Sir Walter Raleigh into the interior.

23. *Op. cit.*, p. 133.

24. *Ibid.*, p. 62.

25. *Ibid.*, p. 64. This would mean a length of approximately 4,667 miles. Actually, according to the *World Almanac,* the length is 3,900 miles. Considering the limited information Acuña had, his estimate is surprisingly close.

26. *Ibid.*, p. 71.

27. *Ibid.*, p. 73.

28. *Ibid.*, pp. 80-87.

29. *Ibid.*, pp. 135-42.

30. *Voyages and Discoveries in South America* (London, 1698), p. v.

31. Paris, 1655.

32. Blaise Pagan, *An Historical and Geographical Description of the Great Country and River of the Amazons in America,* trans. by William Hamilton (London, 1661), 3rd and 4th pages (pages are not numbered in this edition).

33. Vargas Ugarte, *op. cit.*, Vol. II, pp. 433-35.

34. *Ibid.*, Vol. II, pp. 232-33.

35. Samuel Fritz, S.J., "Mission to the Omaguas, Jurimaguas, Aysuares, Ybanomas, and other Nations from the Napo to the Rio Negro (translation of the Evora MS.)," in *Journal of the Travels and Labors of Father Samuel Fritz in the River of the Amazons, between 1686 and 1723* (London: Hakluyt Society, 1922), pp. 52-53. On Father Fritz's appearance, see p. 80.

36. *Ibid.*, pp. 55-57, 59-63.

37. *Ibid.*, 63-66.

38. *Ibid.*, p. 66.

39. The Portuguese based this claim on a *cédula* of the audiencia of Quito in 1639 which permitted them to take possession of an Indian village they called the Aldeia de Ouro; a tree trunk was supposedly marked, but could not be located, so the Portuguese claimed it was in the Omagua country. *Ibid.*, p. 68.

40. *Ibid.*, p. 77. The account of the journey up the Amazon may be found on pp. 69-77.

41. *Ibid.*, pp. 79-86; Vargas Ugarte, *op. cit.*, Vol. II, pp. 436-37.

42. "Letter of Father Samuel to Father Diego Francisco Altamirano, Visitor of the Province of Quito . . . ," in Fritz, *op. cit.*, pp. 90-98.

43. "Journal of Father Samuel Fritz, in which he relates that which took place in this Mission from the year 1697 to the year 1703," in Fritz, *op. cit.*, pp. 100-9.

44. *Ibid.*, pp. 109-14.

45. Clements Markham in Fritz, *op. cit.*, pp. 143-48. A copy of the map appears in this volume.

46. Azevedo, *op. cit.*, p. 269.

47. Pastells, *Historia de la Compañía,* Vol. I, p. 270, n. 1.

48. Azevedo, *op. cit.*, pp. 270-71.

49. See Chapter VI, p. 113.

VIII *Mines and Monsoons*

By the beginning of the eighteenth century it was apparent that Brazil was rich indeed in the precious metals and stones so eagerly sought after by the early explorers, and which had so long eluded them. Much of the pioneer work of exploring the wealth-producing interior, which would later be called Minas Gerais (the General Mines), was accomplished by the great *bandeiras* of the seventeenth century, especially that of Fernão Dias Pais. But no gold had been found. Yet, by the end of the century, the yellow metal was much in evidence. There is no agreement as to who first discovered it; the honor may well belong to Manuel de Borba Gato, son-in-law of Dias Pais, who apparently found considerable alluvial gold near Sabará. He had the misfortune to become engaged in a clash with Rodrigo de Castelo Branco, in charge of the alluvial gold strikes in São Paulo and now seeking more in Minas; Castelo Branco was killed, and Borba Gato did not dare to return to civilization for twenty years, until a pardon came from the governor, contingent on his revealing the location of the gold he had found. Meanwhile, Antônio Rois de Arzão, heading a *bandeira* of fifty, seems to have found gold in this area, while a veteran of Dias Pais' group, Duarte Lopes, claimed to have found so much alluvial gold along a branch of the Guarapiranga that he was able to fashion some jewelry from it.[1]

By the following year, 1694, the existence of gold in the interior was definitely known along the coast; a letter of one Bento Correia dated July 29 of that year mentions the arrival in Rio de Janeiro of one Padre João de Faria Fialho and various of his relatives, who told of mines they had discovered in the interior. Word of such a discovery spreads with astonishing rapidity, and others were not long in making similar finds. In 1695, in April, Garcia Rodrigues Pais washed the first specks of alluvial gold in the *sertão* of Sabarabuçu; if one accepts the date 1695, frequently given as that of the discovery of gold in Minas Gerais, then this was probably the first discovery. In 1696, on June 16, the governor of Rio de Janeiro, Sebastião de Castro Caldas, wrote to Dom Pedro II telling him of the discovery of gold in the *sertão* of Taubaté; on January 1, 1697, he informed his sovereign that eighteen or twenty streams, rich in gold, had been discovered. The following year, an anonymous document inserted in the Códice Costa Matoso tells of the discovery by Paulistas of much gold in what they called the *sertão* of the Cataguases. Within the next decade, almost the whole interior of Minas Gerais had been explored in the quest for gold.[2]

The search did not stop in Minas Gerais. In 1700 João Góis de Araújo, a Paulista in Bahia, was sent by the governor-general, Dom João de Lencastre, to look for gold; with thirty volunteers he explored the headwaters of the Rio Pardo, the Doce, the Verde, and the Rio das Velhas, eventually crossing into the captaincy of Espíritu Santo. In the same year, Pedro Gomes da Franca, with one hundred volunteers, explored the upper Pardo district in Bahia. Two years later, a number of Indian deserters from the mining areas turned up in Espíritu Santo, to the great consternation of the settlers, whose fears were soon conquered by avarice when they learned of the discovery of veins of gold just across the boundary of the captaincy. The king had issued orders forbidding communication between different captaincies about mines (with the exception of São Paulo and Rio de Janeiro), which were obviously being violated in this case. Consequently Governor-General Luís César de Meneses ordered roads to the gold-bearing areas closed in accordance with the royal order, and violators were severely punished. Even so, this did not prevent the bold Domingos Luís Cabral from exploring the watershed of the Rio Manhuaçu (then called the Maiguaçu) somewhere around 1707; the Puri Indians, however, rather than the authorities, gave him trouble, killing several of his men. Not until 1733 did Cabral make another attempt, this time to explore a tributary of the Manhuaçu believed to be rich in gold; as was so often the case, the belief was illusory.[3]

The quest for gold would take adventurous men far beyond the limits of Minas Gerais into distant Goiás and Mato Grosso—to the heart of the continent. More precisely, it took them to the Planalto do Mato Grosso, that vast watershed directly east of modern Bolivia, whence innumerable streams flow toward the Amazon directly north or northwest via the Guaporé and Madeira, and south toward the Paraná and Río de la Plata via the Paraguay and its tributary, the Rio Cuiabá. The first person of European descent known to have sailed on the latter stream was Antônio Pires de Campos; as a youth he had accompanied his father, Manuel de Campos Bicudo, into this region in 1675, and in 1716, seeking the fabled Serra dos Martírios, he marked out the route to the Rio Cuiabá.[4]

Two years later Pascoal Moreira Cabral Leme, following the same route, found gold at the bar of the Rio Coxipó-Mirim, and proceeded up the river as far as Forquilha, where he found some Indians and took some gold objects from them as booty. Returning downstream, he and his companions built a camp at a place later called Aldeia Velha, where they assessed their discoveries. The group had no mining tools, so they agreed that each member could keep all he could dig with his hands; some of the more fortunate, or perhaps more energetic, managed to accumulate 100 oitavas or more, and none seemed to have less than 50.[5] Shortly afterward a *bandeira* headed by Antônio Antunes Maciel arrived at the settlement; as soon as they learned of the gold strike, they joined the discoverers. Antunes, it developed, was acting in the capacity of a government agent; he eventually left for São Paulo with some gold to show to the authorities, and was to return later with artisans and supplies sorely needed in this frontier settlement. Accompanying him to São Paulo was Fernão Dias Falcão, who, at the head of a *bandeira* of 130 men, had come upon the settlement about the same time as Antunes and had with him some supplies, particularly mining equipment and arms, which filled well the immediate needs of the miners. On April 8, 1719, law and order came to the community with the establishment of a junta headed by Cabral; it was determined that the settlement would be called Cuiabá. When Dias Falcão returned, he was chosen "cabo maior dos mineiros." [6]

As might be expected, news of gold in Cuiabá spread rapidly, and there was a gold rush from the captaincies of São Paulo, Rio de Janeiro, and Minas Gerais that, among other things, seriously depleted several garrisons and even included some of the unbeneficed clergy. The going was rough, and many never reached their goal; they died en route, victims of pestilence, starvation, and wild beasts. Of those who survived, some managed to find the wealth they sought, but few were as fortunate as a Paulista, Miguel Sutil, and his Portuguese associate, João Francisco, who were planting a garden along the Rio Cuiabá. They had sent two Carijó Indians to collect wild honey; when they were reproached for returning without it, one of them asked Sutil if he had come to look for gold or honey, and gave him twenty-three grains of gold. Early in the morning the Indians guided them to the site of the strike, where they found that they could literally scoop it up with their hands. In one day Sutil collected half an arroba, and Francisco 600 drams. Others arrived quickly, and within a month the strike had been exhausted—400 arrobas had been taken out.[7]

It became obvious to the governor of São Paulo, the Conde de Assumar, that a land route had to be established to the gold fields of Cuiabá; accordingly, in 1720, he made an agreement with Gabriel Antunes Maciel to open the route. The task appeared to be too difficult, however, and Antunes gave up in discouragement. In 1721 Bartolomeu Pais de Abreu "bravely and imprudently" offered to carry out the governor's plan, and left São Paulo for Cuiabá in 1721. On reaching the latitude of the Rio Grande he established three supply centers for vegetables and cattle, then returned to São Paulo to learn of the arrival of a new governor, Rodrigo César de Meneses, who took a dislike to him and revoked his route-finding commission.[8] Ultimately a land route was established, passing in a northwesterly direction from São Paulo, across the Rio Grande and Rio Paranaíba through the *triángulo mineiro*, northward to the present site of Anápolis, thence westward to Goiás (Vila Boa) and directly west to Cuiabá.

In the years immediately following, intrepid explorers seeking gold pushed into the remaining unexplored areas of the heart of the continent. Bartolomeu Bueno da Silva ("Anhangüera"—the "Old Devil") led a *bandeira* into Goiás, as we have already seen,[9] and two Paulista brothers, Fernando and Artur Pais de Barros, discovered the mines of Mato Grosso (then called Vila Bela), and reached the Rio Guaporé.[10] By 1730 nearly every important gold-bearing area in Brazil had been discovered.

Most of those who came to the gold fields of Mato Grosso, and most of their supplies, came from São Paulo by way of various rivers to Cuiabá in what were called the "monsoons" (*monções*). The term originated in the alternating winds which brought heavy rains to India, and which determined the sailings from Lisboa; ships left Portugal in March or April, reached India in September, and set out on the return trip in February. The departure of canoes from São Paulo to Mato Grosso was also characterized by periodicity, which is probably the origin of the term as applied to these voyages. The *monçoeiros* (members of the monsoon) set out in March or April, when the rivers ran high from the autumn rains; some, however, preferred the winter months—July to September, when the danger of fever was lessened. The journey took five to seven months (which, as Boxer points out, was as long as from Lisboa to Goa) and was filled with dangers of every description—malaria, poisonous insects, piranhas, rapids, and Indians. But the lure of gold was sufficient to cause many indeed to run the risks.[11]

Despite the number of monsoons that set out from São Paulo for Cuiabá, the water route, according to Buarque de Holanda, was never as widely used as its possibilities would seem to indicate (this could be said of all water routes in Brazil except the Amazon). Brazilians, he indicates, tended to consider rivers as obstacles much the same as swamps and mountains, and such roads as they had crossed rather than followed them. When Brazilians finally did take to the rivers, as the *bandeiras* of Rapôso Tavares and Dias Pais ultimately did, it was generally aboard rafts called *jagandas*. Later, various other types of water craft made their appearance. There were the larger, more elaborate rafts (*balsas*) made of logs and planks—the only way of crossing the turbulent Paraná. Where wood was scarce, a basinlike boat of leather stretched over a wood frame was used—the *pelota*; this curious craft was neither rowed nor poled, but was pulled through the water by a swimmer who held a rope in his teeth. This was no easy feat; frequently the passenger in the *pelota* was abandoned in midstream and had to be rescued. A more serviceable and dependable craft was the pirogue, or dugout, but its construction was a long and tedious process. More easily built was the bark canoe, which was easy to pull with a rope, easy to row, and could be discarded when no longer usable with no great loss. This canoe, usually propelled by two rowers, one at each end, was the most popular craft on the monsoon route—a fact which resulted in its being called a "paulista" elsewhere. These vessels were usually about twelve meters long, and one and one-half wide. On the Rio Madeira large dugouts capable of carrying twenty men and their baggage were frequently used in the eighteenth century. They were made from tree trunks as long as seventeen meters, had flat bottoms (usually reinforced) and were extremely pointed; so popular were they that the supply of trees sufficiently large for their construction was considerably reduced by the end of the century.[12]

The crews for the monsoons were usually a disreputable lot, often consisting of bums and criminals, or others who, in the words of Buarque de Holanda, "had little interest in any useful occupation." [13] Generally they rowed stripped to the waist, and usually anointed themselves with fat so that they could be held only with great difficulty when they attempted to flee. That this was commonplace may be seen from the fact that sentries were usually placed around the rowers at night to prevent their escape, and rowers were counted on entering and leaving the canoes. Nights on shore, at least among the crew, were usually spent in card-playing, dancing, fighting, merrymaking and drinking aguardente; frequently the night came to a riotous end, with little rest or sleep.[14]

The larger canoes carried a crew of seven or eight; at the tip of the prow stood the pilot, then the bowman, standing, and five or six rowers in the space free of cargo. Cargo was placed in the middle of the canoe, while the passengers were aft, under some kind of canopy as a shelter of sorts. Where there were dangerous rapids or falls, a pilot or two would be taken on to assist the pilot and bowman. The latter was the most important member of the crew, since he had the key to the provisions and gave the beat to the rowers by pounding with his heel. In descending rapids, it was his responsibility to maneuver the canoe, and many of them became quite skilled at this, able to tell at a glance, by a mere movement of the waters, the depth, the channel, and the presence of submerged rocks.[15]

The origin of the monsoons, of course, goes back to the discovery of gold along the Coxipó-Mirim, and the subsequent journey of Pascoal Moreira Cabral to São Paulo, where he organized, at his own expense, an expedition which departed for the gold country in 1719 with the artisans and necessities for operating a settlement and exploiting the mines. The return trip with supplies was no easy voyage, for, as Buarque de Holanda points out, "the first monsoons destined for Cuiabá constituted veritable leaps into the unknown." [16] In 1723 Dias Falcão and Antunes Maciel returned to Cuiabá with so much baggage and supplies (including six *arrôbas* of powder) that Dias had to go into debt to provide and transport all of it. With this voyage, the monsoons became a regular feature of life in Mato Grosso.[17]

The routes of the monsoons varied. The earliest, such as that of Dias Falcão and Antunes Maciel, followed the Rio Tietê from São Paulo to the Paraná as far as the Pardo, up the Pardo and its tributary the Anhanduí Guaçu, across a watershed only two and one-half leagues wide to the Sanguexuga, thence down the Aquidauana to the Paraguay, up the latter to the Cuiabá, following it upstream to the settlement and the gold country. After 1725 the monsoons generally followed the Pardo as far as possible, then portaged ten miles at Camapoã to the headwaters of the Rio Coxim, thence downstream to the Taquarí as far as the Paraguay, continuing from this point as before. An alternate route, sometimes used, made use of the Rio Verde, which enters the Paraná some distance above the Pardo; this required a twenty-five-day portage to the headwaters of the Rio Piqueri, which entered the Cuiabá directly. Still another route, not frequently used, led overland south into modern Paraná state to the Rio Tibagi, followed that stream to the Paranapamena and into the Rio Paraná; from this point the monsoon proceeded, a short distance below, up the Rio Ivinheima to the Paraguay via either the Vacaria and Aquidauana or the Brilhante and Miranda, with relatively short portages by either route.[18]

The entire journey from São Paulo to the mines of Cuiabá, following the usual Rio Pardo route, was 3,664 kilometers. There were 113 waterfalls and rapids along the route: 55 were on the Rio Tietê alone, 33 on the Pardo, 24 on the Coxim, and 1 on the Taquarí. The Coxim was considered to be the most dangerous stretch because of the great numbers of falls and rapids in its relatively short course, but the dangers were only slightly less along the other portions of the route. To make matters worse, all were greatly swollen in the rainy season, and one traveler, the astronomer Lacerda, reported in 1786 that the Paraguay had flooded so much that he spent seven days trying to find land where he could disembark. The Rio Paraná was particularly dangerous for small craft when there was a wind; for that reason the flotillas were pulled out of the water at night, lest they be wrecked by a sudden storm on the river.

The water was undrinkable, but the waters of the Pardo were clear and potable, as were those of the Coxim. Writing of the "pestiferous Paraná," Cândido Xavier stated that its "murky waters and epidemic vapor were a continual cemetery." [19]

A typical monsoon would depart from São Paulo sometime between May 20 and June 13, the most favorable time for sailing.[20] The long, pointed dugout canoes were favored, which carried up to twenty or thirty passengers and crew, and up to 300 or 400 *arrôbas* of merchandise over and above the food consumed en route. Food was allocated on the basis of one hundred grams of bacon, one liter of flour (corn or manioc) and one-half liter of beans per person; this was augmented en route by fish, game, fruit, and palm hearts, generally eaten either about sundown or just before departure in the morning. Merchandise, which included salt, fabrics, tools, etc., was stored with the food in the middle of the canoe, protected by a covering of cloth. Passengers were protected aft by an awning of sailcloth, duck, or baize stretched over a wooden framework consisting of horizontal bars resting on forked poles. Between 1720 and 1725 mosquito nets were introduced, which were a great protection at night, particularly against the malaria-carrying anopheles mosquito, but of little help against the daylight variety. Mosquitoes were one of the worst terrors of the journey; one traveler, Herbert Smith, compared them with jaguars and anacondas, but did admit that their bites were not as painful as those of the mosquitoes in the swamps of New Jersey.[21]

Some of the monsoons carried pharmacies well equipped with the best remedies known at the time, of both Portuguese and Indian origin, many of which are virtually unknown today. We do know something of monsoon therapeutics, which seemed to concentrate on prevention when possible, possibly with the idea that the stronger the remedy, the more effective it would be. Among the chief medicaments were *Pimenta malagueta* (a very hot red pepper) and ginger, also the spur of the horned screamer, used both as an antidote for poisons and as a charm. Then there was the cleaning rod, used as a rectal medication—enough to strike terror into any stout heart.[22]

Hostile Indians constituted another grave danger, and their depredations finally led to the establishment of a convoy system as a mode of maximum protection for the monsoons. Since they were difficult to organize and since the time for such an operation was relatively brief, only one convoy was sent out per year. They were well armed and prepared for war, but even so this was no guarantee of a safe arrival at Cuiabá. In 1720 a convoy left São Paulo, and all the passengers and crew were killed; in the following year there was considerable loss of life and baggage, but most of those who set out managed to reach their destination. Particularly troublesome were the Paiaguá Indians, who were fairly new in the area and who hid in inlets in small canoes which carried eight to ten well-armed warriors. They never attacked unless by complete surprise, and with deadly effect; in 1725 they killed all but two of a convoy of six hundred, and in 1730 they attacked a convoy on the Rio Paraguay, killing four hundred and seizing sixty *arrôbas* of gold, with a loss of only fifty Indians. Not until 1734 was this menace met effectively, when a Portuguese expedition surrounded a Paiaguá camp at dawn, killed or captured one thousand Indians and lost but three men. Seeing them thus weakened, a formerly allied tribe, the Guiacurús, took advantage of the situation to finish them off.[23]

Even had there been no problem of health and no hostile Indians, the navigation of the river route to Cuiabá would still have been fraught with grave danger from the natural obstacles alone. In the first hour and a half after departing from São Paulo, no less than three rapids had to be negotiated, a feat particularly difficult if the canoes were not at least half-loaded; nine more were to follow within six leagues distance from the first one. This sector of the route passed through a heavily wooded area, abounding in fish, game, and fruits. Below the rapids of Arranca Rabo was a stretch of calm water, known as the Rio Morto, which extended some eighty-one kilometers; here the aspect of the land changed, for while a wooded area bordered the left bank, the right bank was largely prairie. From Laje onward the journey was interrupted by more rapids and the high falls of Itapura, until finally the Paraná was reached. Here navigation was easier; after the 4.4 meter drop at Urubupungá no falls or rapids were encountered on this great river until Sete Quedas was reached; the main dangers were whirlpools and squalls, and the monsoons usually moved close to shore.[24]

It was perhaps only natural that many legends and tales should develop around this difficult stage of the journey. Some have a foundation in fact; others rest on conjecture or superstition. There was, for instance, the weird experience of a monsoon led by Sergeant-Major Teotônio José Juzarte. Early one morning on the Tietê they noticed what appeared to be a canoe moving through the dawn mist nearby; the uniformed leader was plainly visible, and the oarsmen and passengers could easily be counted. Despite repeated calls to the canoe, Juzarte received no answer; he called on them to halt, and was ignored. Finally he undertook pursuit, but the canoe silently and mysteriously disappeared into the mist. Who were the unknown silent navigators? Lively imaginations supplied the answers: they were Spaniards, or Paulistas, or Indians; or perhaps deserters or smugglers. Or, as the more superstitious would have it, the canoe was manned by the spirits of *monçoeiros* who had lost their lives along the way. Juzarte, as superstitious as any, was convinced that they were the spirits of the gold-hungry who, because of their lust for the yellow metal, had lost their lives and their salvation on the way to Cuiabá.[25]

Then there was Padre José Pompeu de Almeida, a secular priest of some means who, being at odds with his bishop, decided to leave São Paulo and organized a monsoon. The Tietê was descended without serious difficulty, but trouble developed during an overnight halt at an island in the Paraná. Dissatisfied with their master, who was rather testy, Padre José's Indians took off while he slept, leaving him no means of sustenance or escape; it is possible that he survived a few days on the fruit of the jatobá tree. Meanwhile Padre Belchoir de Pontes, superior of a Jesuit *aldeia* near São Paulo, was returning to his station one day in the company of some Indians; when they reached the Rio Pinheiros, he went into a thicket and told the Indians to wait for him, since he would return later. When he failed to do so they went in to look for him, and made a thorough search which included the surrounding territory. When they failed to find him they proceeded on, with his horse, to the *aldeia* to inform the fathers. They did not appear concerned, convinced that he would return, as he did a few hours later, telling them that he had been to the shores of the Paraná to hear the confession of Padre José Pompeu. This seemed almost incredible, since a journey of this nature would ordinarily take at least two months; yet some time later travelers came upon the island where the priest had been marooned, and found a rude altar and a grave marked with a wooden sign which read "Here lies buried Padre José Pompeu, confessed by Padre Pontes." [26]

There were, of course, assorted monsters inhabiting the rivers. Schmidel, it will be recalled,[27] mentioned that reliable witnesses had assured him that they had seen a serpent of enormous size in the Tietê. Juzarte mentioned immense earthworms with supposed supernatural powers (the *minhocaçus*), and also the dangerous passage below the falls of Avanhadava, which many believed to be inhabited by *um grande bicho*. Some attributed the great waves, which occasionally overturned canoes with considerable loss of life, to nymphs (the *mães-d'agua*) who lived in the depths of the river. Others attributed such accidents to a marine beast, also a denizen of the deep.[28] The monsoons, it would seem, were doing their part to enliven the folklore of Brazil.

Many accounts of the monsoons by contemporaries have survived; these logbooks bear eloquent testimony of the dangers to which the *monçoeiros* were continually subjected, and of the fortitude with which they met them and overcame them. One account is of particular interest, since it describes in considerable detail the largest known monsoon, that of Rodrigo César de Meneses, governor and captain-general of São Paulo. This expedition, which left São Paulo on Sunday morning, July 7, 1726, numbered 305 canoes, and carried 3,000 passengers and crew.[29] After a brief introduction describing the organization of the monsoon the account[30] describes the dangerous descent of the Rio Tietê, which began on Tuesday, July 16. With almost monotonous regularity we read of the many rapids negotiated "with great risk and effort," and of the frequent necessity of drawing the canoes on shore, and transporting the baggage around cataracts on the backs of the Negroes. When particularly dangerous stretches of the route are reached, we learn of the accidental deaths of predecessors—names which have survived only because of their untimely death in the river.

By Saturday, August 10, the monsoon, now divided into three sections, reached the Paraná (or Rio Grande, as the logbook calls it); they had been 26 days on the way, and had covered 520 leagues. On this broad stream the dangers were somewhat lessened and were different —great depths, whirlpools, rocks and, occasionally, hostile Indians. The expedition got under way again at dawn the following day, and after a two-hour sail reached the fazenda of one Manuel Homem, where additional provisions were taken on. On August 14, at nine o'clock in the morning, the monsoon left the Paraná and entered the Rio Pardo.

This stage of the voyage presented new problems. It was upstream, requiring considerable straining on the part of the rowers. The current was strong and dangerous. Many huge logs were floating downstream— a grave menace to navigation. By August 30 they reached the beginning of a series of falls and rapids which were always the major menace of the journey, and for several days it was necessary to unload the canoes and carry the baggage around the worst of them. This situation continued and grew worse until September 13, when it became necessary to abandon the Pardo and transport everything across the height of land to the tributaries of the Paraguay. There were two settlements in this area, and the travelers were able to replenish their dwindling supplies.

On September 30 the canoes were launched in the Rio Camapoão-Mirim. Here there was a new problem, for this river did not carry a great volume of water, and at times was nearly dry. Floating logs were also a nuisance, but the monsoon was able to escape damage from them. On October 5 they came across a large log on the shore, and beside it a partially decomposed corpse; from all indications it was probably that of a white man who had been a member of a troop which passed through this region the year before; a grim reminder of the dangers ever present. That same day they entered the Rio Quexeim, and after negotiating four series of rapids on the following day, made camp in a ravine, beneath a huge peak, having traveled some thirty-five leagues that day, in many places between cliffs so high that the sun never shone on them. During the next three days they traveled sixty leagues, facing the same perils of cataracts, rapids, treacherous currents, narrows, and rocks—surely a tribute to the skill of the crews.

The last peril of the Quexeim was as great as any of the previous ones; as they approached the bar of the Taquari-Assu, it was necessary to descend a cataract and go through a channel so narrow and strewn with huge rocks that, owing to the force of the water, the slightest brush against one of them was sufficient to capsize the canoe and drown the passengers and crew. Only one league could be covered that day, and with heroic effort. But the journey down the Rio Taquari-Assu compensated for this; the waters were clear and the navigation easy, and by October 16 they had covered one hundred leagues. Three days later, having traversed the short Taquari-Mirim, the monsoon entered the Paraguay.

The point of entry was a marshy area, clogged with *agopés*—a creeping grass which grows in the water, forming floating islands which impeded navigation somewhat, until they entered the mainstream of the Paraguay on October 21. Three days later they entered the Rio Xianés, after some unpleasant nights with mosquitoes, and on October 26 entered the Rio dos Porrudos, which led them to the Cuiabá, the last stage of the voyage.

On October 31 the monsoon put in at a settlement for reprovisioning, delivering a cargo of Negro slaves, and collecting the royal fifth on the cargo. On Friday, November 1, the expedition resumed its course, making a few stops at fazendas along the way. The dangers were behind them, and without further incident they arrived at their destination, the town of Bom Jesus or Cuiabá, on November 15, four months and one week since the departure from São Paulo.

Other *roteiros*, or logbooks, relate similar incidents. One of the earliest, that of Don Luis de Céspedes in 1628, maintains that any escape from the perils of the Tietê is nothing short of miraculous; Don Luis lost one of his canoes at Avanhandava, and he and his companions, their clothes torn from them, barely managed to save the others. He attributed their escape from death to the intervention of his patroness, Nuestra Señora de Atocha. And more than a century later, in 1751, Dom Antônio Rolim, Conde de Azambuja, describing his journey from Rio de Janeiro to Cuiabá in a letter to his cousin said: "How much land and water have I passed through! Rivers so torrential, forests so dense, grasslands so extensive that they excite awe, especially in one who comes from a land so constricted as our kingdom." [31]

Not only did the monsoons play a major role in the exploration of the Brazilian interior, but they also left an excellent legacy of maps, albeit few of real scientific value except for those of Francisco José de Lacerda e Almeida in 1789, an anonymous map of 1764, and an earlier one of Luis de Céspedes, which is the oldest known map showing the penetration of the interior.[32] Precise cartography, with respect to the Paraná-Paraguay basin, was yet to come, but a valuable beginning had been made.

Once again, the lure of gold played a dominant role in the opening of yet another vast area in the interior of the continent. As had the discoverers, conquistadores, missionaries, and *bandeirantes* before them, so did the *monçoeiros* assume and carry out, perhaps without even realizing it, the role of explorers. For they had gone where few or none had gone before them, into lands virtually unknown, frequently at great risk and subject to unknown perils. These hardy Paulistas penetrated far into the heart of the continent, found gold, and opened avenues of trade and settlement. Another frontier had been pushed back; another *terra incognita* had vanished from the map.

NOTES

1. Affonso d'Escragnolle Taunay, *História das bandeiras paulistas*, 2 vols. (São Paulo, 1954), Vol. I, pp. 215-16.
2. *Ibid.*; Myriam Ellis, "As bandeiras na expansão geográfica do Brasil" (Chap. 2, Bk. V, Pt. I of Vol. I of Sergio Buarque de Holanda, ed., *História geral da civilização brasileira*, São Paulo, 1963), pp. 295-96.
3. Escragnolle Taunay, *op. cit.*, Vol. I, pp. 353-54.
4. Ellis, *op. cit.*, p. 295; Buarque de Holanda, *Monções* (Rio de Janeiro, 1945), p. 67.
5. 100 oitavas of gold was worth approximately £8/6s in English currency of the seventeenth century—quite a tidy sum, given the purchasing power of such an amount at that time, for a few weeks' work. It should be pointed out that not all the gold was dug; some was taken from the Indians.
6. Escragnolle Taunay, *op. cit.*, Vol. II, p. 14; Buarque de Holanda, *Monções*, pp. 67-70.
7. C. R. Boxer, *The Golden Age of Brazil, 1695-1750* (Berkeley and Los Angeles, 1952), pp. 256-58; Buarque de Holanda, *Monções*, pp. 72-73. Sutil's discovery was made in 1722.
8. Escragnolle Taunay, *op. cit.*, Vol. II, p. 31.
9. See Chap. VI, p. 112, for the story.
10. Buarque de Holanda, *Monções*, pp. 94-95.
11. On the monsoons see especially Buarque de Holanda, *Monções*, and Escragnolle Taunay, *Relatos monçoeiros* (Vol. IX in *Biblioteca Histórica Paulista*), (São Paulo, 1952). Good briefer accounts may be found in C. R. Boxer, *op. cit.*, pp. 261 ff.; Escragnolle Taunay, *História das bandeiras paulistas*, Vol. II, pp. 21 ff.; and Buarque de Holanda, "As Monções," Chap. 4 in his *História geral da civilização brasileira*, Vol. I, Pt. I, Bk. V. (An English translation of this chapter appears in Richard M. Morse, ed., *The Bandeirantes*, New York, 1965, Chap. 10.)
12. Buarque de Holanda, *Monções*, pp. 19-45.
13. *Ibid.*, p. 112.
14. *Ibid.*, pp. 112-15.
15. *Ibid.*, pp. 124-25.
16. *Ibid.*, p. 94.
17. See Buarque de Holanda, "As Monções," *loc. cit.*, pp. 312-14.
18. Eee Escragnolle Taunay, *História das bandeiras paulistas*, Vol. II, pp. 21-22; Boxer, *op. cit.*, p. 263.

19. Escragnolle Taunay, *Relatos monçõeiros*, pp. 51-53. The quotation from Cândido Xavier appears in his *História das bandeiras paulistas*, Vol. II, p. 159.

20. Escragnolle Taunay, *Relatos monçõeiros*, p. 53.

21. *Brazil, the Amazon and the Coast* (London, 1879), p. 94. (Cited in Buarque de Holanda, *Monções*, pp. 107-8. On the preparation for a monsoon, see *ibid.*, 103-6 and his "As Monções," *loc. cit.*, pp. 315-18.)

22. Escragnolle Taunay, *História das bandeiras paulistas*, Vol. II, pp. 159-60.

23. Buarque de Holanda, "As Monções," *loc. cit.*, p. 314; Boxer, *op. cit.*, pp. 264-66.

24. Buarque de Holanda, *Monções*, pp. 126-38; Escragnolle Taunay, *História das bandeiras paulistas*, Vol. II, p. 109.

25. Escragnolle Taunay, *História*, Vol. II, p. 177.

26. *Ibid.*, pp. 178-79.

27. See Chap. III, p. 58-62.

28. Escragnolle Taunay, *História das bandeiras paulistas*, Vol. II, p. 181.

29. Boxer, *op. cit.*, p. 264.

30. The account, from the collection of Padre Diogo Juares, S.J. (*Códice da Biblioteca de Evora*) appears in Escragnolle Taunay, *Relatos monçõeiros*, pp. 101-13.

31. Escragnolle Taunay, *Relatos monçõeiros*, pp. 44-45. The quotation appears on p. 182, the entire *Relação* of Azambuja on pp. 182-202.

32. Escragnolle Taunay, *História das bandeiras paulistas*, Vol. II, pp. 183-84.

IX Challenge

and Response in the South

By the end of the seventeenth century, the region watered by the lower Paraná and Paraguay rivers, explored and settled by Spaniards despite Indian and Portuguese hostility, presented a scene of relative tranquillity and prosperity to visitors from the outside world. One of these, who recorded his impressions of his journey in a very informative account, was Monsigneur Acarete du Biscay. Having lived a long time in Spain and learned the language, he conceived a desire to see the Indies, and despite the fact that this was prohibited to foreigners, in 1687 he managed to go, he tells us, by concealing his origin.[1] The voyage in a vessel of 450 tons, took 105 days, and was not without its anxious moments even at the end. As the ship entered the Río de la Plata it had to fight off a French frigate, which was subsequently captured by a Dutch fleet leaving the estuary and its crew killed.[2]

The ship sailed upstream toward Asunción, making brief stops which enabled Acarete to go ashore, but never far. This center of Spanish power he found to be a thriving place; it was well populated, and its environs produced such necessities as corn, millet, sugar, tobacco, honey, cattle, sturdy oaks and pines for the construction of ships, and *yerba mate*. This herb particularly impressed him, since it was so important an item of trade; "without that Herb," he tells us, "(with which they make a refreshing Liquor with Water and Sugar, to be drunk lukewarm) the Inhabitants of Peru, Savages and others, especially those that work in the Mines, could not subsist, for the Soil of the Country being full of Mineral Veins, the Vapours that rise out of the ground suffocate them, and nothing but that Liquor can recover them again, which revives and restores them to their former Vigour."[3] A feature of Asunción life which he found unusual was the custom of sleeping in the streets at night because of the heat. On his return to the Río de la Plata, Acarete visited Buenos Aires and was much impressed by its appearance and its size (it contained more than four hundred houses), as well as the commercial activity in the port. The women in the city outnumbered the men; they were, he said, very beautiful and absolutely faithful to their husbands; but should the men fail in fidelity to their wives, they "are often punished with Poison or Dagger." [4]

A visit to the interior took him to Córdoba; en route he and his Indian guide were confronted by a swollen stream which could not be forded on horseback. Since Acarete was unable to swim, the Indian killed a bull, flayed the hide off, stuffed it with straw, put Acarete and his baggage on it, and swam across pulling it with a cord, in the manner of the Brazilian Indians and pioneers. He found the city to be almost as large as Buenos Aires; the people were rich in gold and silver, and bred and traded thirty thousand mules annually. Yet this was frontier country; neighboring Indians still killed and ate their enemies, fashioning their skulls into drinking bowls. And as an added danger, he mentions the "abundance of Tigers that are fierce and ravenous" on the way to Santiago del Estero, but curiously enough refers to "lions that are very gentle." [5] Ultimately, traversing forests, groves of date palms, fertile plains, cotton fields and vineyards, he reached the populous city of Potosí with its four thousand houses built of stone in the Spanish style. In this fabulous center of wealth, with its rich mines, his account ends.

Little more than a century and a half had passed since first the Spaniards had entered this land and subdued it. Thriving towns stood where before there had been only grass, forests, and promising valleys; the land had been made to yield its fruit, and descendants of the con-quistadores and new immigrants, with their slaves and their Indian wards, toiled, prayed, and raised their families where only wild beasts and occasional savages had roamed before. At a time when settlements in North America above Mexico were mainly huddled along the coast or the St. Lawrence River, when Henry Kelsey, La Salle, Marquette, Jolliet, and others were first exploring the vast interior of that continent, hoping to find a river flowing to the Pacific Ocean, when the Cumberland Gap had not even been discovered, Acarete could find thriving centers of civilization far in the interior of the southern continent—eloquent testimony of the magnitude and success of Spain's imperial endeavor.

Yet one need not stray far from these centers of Spanish life to find that not all the forests had been traversed, not all the Indians subdued, not all the land brought under cultivation. A few dozen leagues north of Asunción man could not be sure what he would find. The center of the continent, it is true, was yielding to probings from different directions; most successful of these, in the Paraguay area, were the establishment of the Guaraní missions and, to the northwest, in the eastern part of modern Bolivia, the missions among the Chiquitos Indians. Once these peoples had been converted to Christianity, it had been one of the aims of the missionaries to open a route from the Guaraní to the Chiquitos missions, which would reduce considerably the time for visiting this large province. In May of 1702 two Jesuit fathers, Francisco Hervás and Miguel de Yegros, left with forty Indians as guides, setting out to find the water route (if one existed) between the two mission areas. After many difficulties, having traversed forests, rugged mountains, marshes, and lakes, they came upon a river they took for the Paraguay, and planted a cross on its bank. There was much joy in the Chiquitos missions when they returned with the news, and the provincial sent five experienced missionaries and a brother to attempt to locate the route from the Río Paraguay. Departing from the reduction of Candelaria on May 10, 1703, they eventually reached Asunción on June 22, and departed four days later in a large bark, taking with them four rafts, two pirogues, and a canoe. After progressing forty leagues upstream, they entered Paiaguá country; these Indians had no desire to have anything to do with Spaniards, who had destroyed their countrymen near Buenos Aires, but when one of the missionaries left some beads suspended from a tree as an act of friendship, the Indians took it and left some woven mats in return, the start of several days of lively trade. The Indians soon tired of commerce, and turned on the Spaniards, who were saved by the timely arrival of some Christian Indians who joined to help drive them off. By August 7 the group reached the mouth of the Río Jejui Guazú, and two weeks later passed through more Payaguá territory, finally reaching the mouth of the Río Tepotii on August 30. Ahead of them was a row of reefs through which, at certain times, the current was strong enough to overturn their craft; at low water human footprints could be seen on one of the rocks—the Indians claimed they were those of the apostle St. Thomas.[6]

Beyond the reefs the missionaries found twelve high rocks in an area of great natural beauty; the Guayacurú Indians used them as sites for building fires to send smoke signals warning of the approach of an enemy. Farther upstream were several lakes, and the Cuñayegua mountains, where two missionaries had been killed earlier for insisting that monogamy was necessary if one would be a Christian. On September 29 they reached the point where the Paraguay divides, forming an island twenty leagues long, and proceeded upstream, passing through Lake Jaragui on October 17, and entering Lake Jarayes, which they took to be the source of the Paraguay, on October 31. A diligent search failed to reveal the cross indicating the route from the river to the Chiquitos reductions, so it seemed better to go on; after proceeding 100 leagues they came upon some Guaranís, baptized them, and founded a reduction.[7]

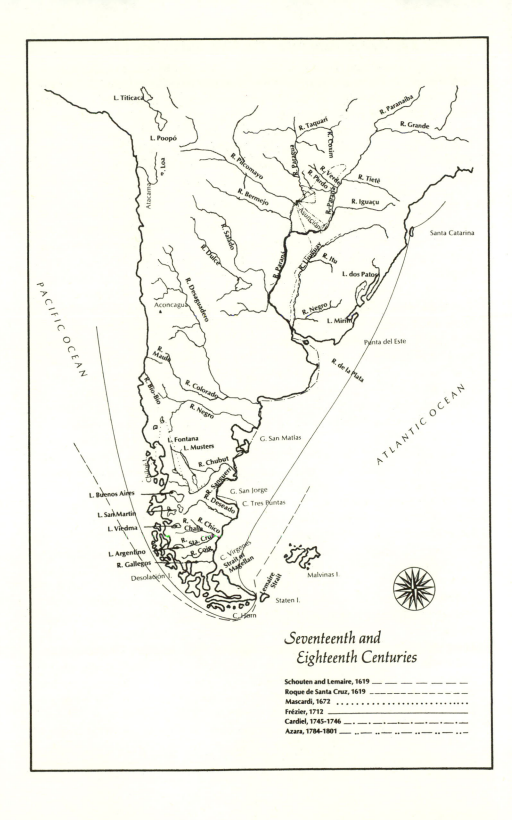

PACIFIC OCEAN

ATLANTIC OCEAN

L. Titicaca

R. Paranaíba

R. Taquarí

R. Grande

L. Poopó

R. Coxim

R. Pilcomayo

R. Verde

R. Tietê

R. Pardo

ª. Loa

R. Bermejo

R. Iguaçu

Asunción

Santa Catarina

R. Salado

R. Uruguay

R. Itu

R. Dulce

L. dos Patos

Atacama

R. Desaguadero

Aconcagua

R. Negro

L. Mirim

R. Paraná

Punta del Este

R. Maule

R. de la Plata

R. Bío-Bío

R. Colorado

R. Negro

G. San Matías

L. Fontana

L. Musters

R. Chubut

R. Senguerr

G. San Jorge

L. Buenos Aires

R. Deseado

C. Tres Puntas

L. San Martín

R. Chico

L. Viedma

R. Challa

R. Sta. Cruz

L. Argentino

R. Coig

C. Vírgenes

R. Gallegos

Strait of Magellan

Desolación I.

Malvinas I.

Lemaire Strait

Staten I.

C. Horn

Seventeenth and Eighteenth Centuries

Schouten and Lemaire, 1619 ⎯ ⎯ ⎯ ⎯ ⎯ ⎯

Roque de Santa Cruz, 1619 ⎯⎯⎯⎯⎯⎯⎯⎯

Mascardi, 1672 ·······························

Frézier, 1712 ⎯⎯⎯⎯⎯⎯⎯⎯⎯

Cardiel, 1745-1746 ⎯ · ⎯ · · ⎯ · ⎯ · · ⎯ ·

Azara, 1784-1801 ⎯ ·· ⎯ ·· ⎯ · ⎯ ·· ⎯ ··

Although this quest failed of its objective, the route was finally located late in 1715 by Fathers Joseph Arce and Bartolomé de Blende, closing the last gap between the Río de la Plata and the center of the continent.[8] Of great importance also was that this accomplishment interposed a Spanish line of communications across territory coveted by the Portuguese (who had not abandoned their hope of taking Potosí)—an achievement essential toward keeping this area under the Crown of Spain.

If the Portuguese were determined to extend the line of Tordesillas westward to the Río de la Plata, the Río Paraguay and even beyond, to the south there were intruders who could not have been less concerned with Spain's claims under the treaty. Among the earliest of these, after Drake's remarkable voyage of exploring and free-booting in 1577–78, was that of the Dutch navigators, Willem Cornelisz Schouten and Jacob Le Maire, early in the seventeenth century. Jacob's father, Isaac, dissatisfied with the monopoly accorded the East India Company, had organized the Southern Company, which was authorized in 1614 to undertake voyages under the Dutch flag. The following year the company equipped two vessels which sailed from Texel on June 14, under the command of Jacob Le Maire assisted by the experienced pilot Schouten. Not until the equator was crossed on October 25 was the crew informed of the purpose of the voyage—to find a new passage to the South Sea and India. Up to that time one reached India via the Cape of Good Hope or by sailing through the Strait of Magellan—and this could at times be a traumatic experience indeed. It was almost universally believed that Tierra del Fuego formed part of the vast continent which supposedly encircled the earth in the southern hemisphere, despite the doubts entertained by Magellan and Drake; it was these doubts that Le Maire determined to investigate.

Tragedy struck when the smaller of the two ships burned at Puerto Deseado on the Patagonian coast on December 19; not until January 13, 1616, was Le Maire able to proceed, after salvaging what he could. Sailing southeast along the coast of Tierra del Fuego, he reached a strait some eight leagues across on January 24; so strong was the current that he was convinced it flowed from the South Sea. After bestowing the name of Staten Island on the grassy land to his port side, he proceeded south, finally sighting the promontory which he felt certain marked the southern extremity of the continent, on January 29. This he named Cape Hoorn, for the town of Den Hoorn on Texel where the expedition had been organized; a council of pilots of the expedition on February 12 named the passage through which they had come for their leader, the Strait of Le Maire. Beyond lay the Pacific and the East Indies, where their ship was confiscated by the authorities and the officers and crew transferred to a Dutch squadron for the voyage home. Le Maire died en route, but Schouten and his companions returned to their homeland, having circumnavigated the globe and discovered a passage to the East which promised far less peril than Magellan's strait.[9]

The importance of this discovery was not lost on Spain, for it could easily jeopardize the kingdom's claim to exclusive jurisdiction over American waters. In the same year, 1617, the Council of the Indies organized an expedition to explore this new route; command was given to two skilled Galician pilots, Bartolomé García de Nodal and his brother Gonzalo de Nodal. Eight months were spent in readying the two caravels, which were manned by crews for the most part impressed from the arsenals of Lisboa; some Flemish pilots were hired, and copies of the diaries of Schouten and Le Maire, just published in the Netherlands, were obtained for their excellent charts and maps. The expedition departed from Lisboa on September 27, 1618, and reached Rio de Janeiro on November 15. Here the governor, pursuant to instructions from Madrid sent to all governors in South America,[10] rendered every assistance, even to locking up the crews in the city jail to prevent desertion.

By the middle of January, 1619, the expedition reached the entrance to the Strait of Magellan, and on the 22nd sailed through the Strait of Le Maire, finally rounding the Cape Horn on February 6. Inconvenienced only slightly by rain and hail, they entered the Strait of Magellan on February 25, revictualed while passing through, and entered the Atlantic on March 13, the first to have sailed around Tierra del Fuego. The voyage was a success in every respect, for on their return to Spain in July, the Nodal brothers could boast that not only had no one died on the expedition, but that those who had departed ill had returned well. And they had reached a farthest south point, having discovered a group of islands at 56° 40' south, which they named for their cartographer, Diego Ramírez. Yet for all its success, the effort was seemingly in vain; Spain did not make use of the new route until the eighteenth century.[11]

Not until late in the seventeenth century was there any serious French effort to intrude on Spain's hegemony in the New World. In 1695 Jean-Baptiste de Gennes founded a company for the purpose of establishing a colony on the Strait of Magellan; six vessels were equipped and the expedition set sail from La Rochelle on June 3; one of the members, a certain François Froger, has left us an interesting and detailed account of the voyage.[12] Apparently exploration was not its sole aim, nor the founding of a colony, for after reaching Madeira on June 21, it headed for the African coast, making a successful attack on a British-held fort on the Gambia River. After a considerable delay the expedition resumed its course to the south, arriving at Ascension Island on November 17, and Rio de Janeiro thirteen days later. The luxury and easygoing morals of the city appalled him; he seemed concerned over the material wealth and number of slaves possessed by the inhabitants; and of the clergy, with the exception of the Jesuits, he could find nothing good to say at all. The expedition did not tarry long here; continuing on south, it arrived at the Cape of the Virgins on January 11, 1696, and reached Tierra del Fuego eight days later. Entry into the strait was delayed by contrary winds, so the explorers had an opportunity to observe the Fuegans; Froger describes them as clad only in the skin of a "sea-wolf" thrown over their shoulders and, in view of the many tales of "Patagonian giants" we note with interest that he says that they saw none over six feet in height.[13] The delay also gave them an opportunity to observe the abundant marine life of the area; Froger mentions that along the Patagonian coast they found the sea so covered with red shrimp "that it might have been truly called the Red Sea. We took up about ten thousand of these animals in our buckets." [14]

Every effort of de Gennes to force a passage to the South Sea through the strait was frustrated by winds (an experience many after him were to share), so the attempt was finally abandoned on April 3 and the expedition sailed out of the strait into the Atlantic (or "North Sea," as Froger called it) on April 16, without making any effort to found a colony. Navigating northward, they reached Cabo Frio on May 16, and spent three days there observing the flora and fauna (recorded in splendid engravings in Froger's book) and an eclipse of the moon. There was another delay on reaching the Bahia de Todos os Santos on July 9, after which the expedition sailed north and northwest to Cayenne, where Froger was appalled by the poor condition of the slaves.[15] Resuming their course, the ships sailed past the Leeward and Windward islands before heading across the open sea, finally arriving at La Rochelle on April 21, 1697. Considerable information had been gathered although the major purpose was not accomplished.

The English challenge was renewed early in the eighteenth century. The death of the last Spanish Hapsburg, Carlos II, and the succession of Felipe V, second grandson of Louis XIV of France, as king of Spain and the Indies, ranged England against the Bourbon monarchies and made the Spanish empire fair game again, as it had been in the days of Elizabeth I. The prey was enticing: treasure ships might be seized, rich coastal towns taken and held for ransom, and perhaps even the rich Manila galleons might be captured. Consequently, English merchants were led to believe that "with a reasonable force, a very profitable expedition might be made into those parts, where the Buccaneers, with small vessels, and those ill provided, had performed such extraordinary things." [16] One of the first of these latter-day buccaneers to get into action was William Dampier, who headed an expedition of two ships of twenty-six guns each, the *St. George*, under his own command, and the *Fame*, under John Pulling, who deserted with his ship after a disagreement and was replaced by Charles Pickering commanding the *Cinque-Ports*, a smaller vessel carrying sixteen guns. The original plan was to seize two or three galleons believed to be in the Río de la Plata; when it was learned that they were at Tenerife, plans were changed: they would go to Peru.

The expedition left The Downs on April 30, 1703, and, sailing past the Canaries and the Cape Verde Islands, reached St. Anne's Island off the coast of Brazil early in December. Here Pickering died, and was replaced by Thomas Stradling; the vessels resumed their course, sailing near the "island of Sebald de Weert" [17] on December 29. A severe storm separated the vessels on January 4, 1704; the *St. George* sailed to nearly 60° south and, convinced that he had passed Cape Horn, Dampier headed north, finally reaching the Juan Fernández Islands, where he found the *Cinque-Ports* at anchor on February 10. There was a brief encounter with one French ship and a sighting of two more, but Dampier avoided an engagement, assuring everyone that he knew where he could get £500,000. This would obviously come from raiding rich coastal cities, but Dampier's attempts were unsuccessful and he had to content himself with taking two prizes which yielded not gold but several years' supply of flour, sugar, brandy, and cloth. One prize was taken into Sardinas Bay, where it was noticed that the rivers flowing into the bay smelled and tasted of musk, "occasioned by many alligators swimming in it," according to William Funnell, who accompanied Dampier and eventually assumed command. Despite the nauseous taste of the waters, Funnell assures us, "there are no instances of its doing any sort of prejudice to the constitutions of such as drink it." [18] There was an encounter with a Spanish man-of-war which proved inconclusive; nonetheless, the English succeeded in taking several prizes subsequently and, after raiding the coasts of Panama and Mexico, eventually returned home in 1706 via the Cape of Good Hope, bringing considerable detailed information on the South American coasts.[19]

In 1708 another expedition was organized by "gentlemen of Bristol" under Captain Woodes Rogers; there were two ships, the *Duke* and the *Duchess*, commissioned as privateers. Departing from England on June 15, the ships reached Ilha Grande on November 18, tarried a while in Brazil, then rounded Cape Horn and made for the islands of Juan Fernández. There a singular experience befell Rogers which was to lift his expedition out of the ordinary—the rescue of the original Robinson Crusoe, Alexander Selkirk. He had been master of the *Cinque-Ports*, and had been left ashore four years and four months earlier after a dispute with Captain Stradling. As he approached the islands, Rogers noticed a fire at night, and sent a pinnace ashore to investigate the following day; fearful that there might be a Spanish garrison on shore, he put out a signal for the boat, and showed a French ensign. "Immediately," he tells us, "our pinnace returned from the shore, and brought an abundance of cray-fish, with a man cloathed in goat-skins, who looked wilder than the first owners of them." [20]

Selkirk's story was fantastic. He was fortunate in having with him clothing and bedding, firelock, powder and bullets, tobacco, a hatchet, knife, kettle, mathematical instruments, and books, including his Bible. Melancholy and the terror of being left alone were his greatest problems at first; he managed to overcome them in part by keeping busy building two huts, one to live in, the other for keeping his food. Lack of salt deprived him of an appetite for some time, but eventually he grew accustomed to no salt, and subsisted quite well on crayfish, turnips (originally sown by some of Dampier's men), cabbage-palm hearts, pimientos, and goat flesh, which he either broiled over pimiento-wood or made into a broth. When his ammunition gave out, he was able to capture goats by sheer fleetness of foot. The serious problem of rats he finally overcame with the aid of several hundred cats which he tamed, winning their friendship with goat meat. When his clothes wore out, he fashioned some of goat skins, using a nail for a needle to stitch them together, and fashioned a skirt from linen cloth, sewed together with wool salvaged from old stockings. The island he knew intimately, and was able to give his rescuers detailed information concerning its geography, products, and relatively mild climate, which Captain Rogers duly recorded in his journal.[21] Following the rescue of Selkirk, Rogers managed to capture several prizes, seize the city of Guayaquil and hold it for ransom before continuing on to the Galápagos, Panama, Mexico, and Baja California (which he believed to be a peninsula, not an island) in a vain search for the Manila *galeón* which led him across the Pacific. The expedition returned home via the Cape of Good Hope in 1709.[22]

The success of these English privateering expeditions made it comparatively easy for a Frenchman, Amadée François Frézier,[23] to secure a commission from the Spanish king to visit Chile and Peru to conduct a study of their defenses against probable attacks by the enemies of the Bourbon monarchies. The voyage, judged by its activities, was essentially scientific, but in view of the stated purpose for which it was organized, it will engage our attention at this point. Two vessels were outfitted, the *Joseph*, of 350 tons (armed with thirty-six guns as a precautionary measure), and the *Mary*, 120 tons; they left St. Malo on Monday, November 23, 1711, but damage from a severe storm forced a return on December 20. On January 6, 1712, another attempt to get under way was made, and this met with success. They sailed southwest to Madeira, the Cape Verde Islands, and finally crossed the equator where, Frézier tells us, "the foolish ceremony of Ducking the Line, practis'd by all Nations, was not omitted." [24]

By April 5 the expedition had reached Santa Catarina Island, off the coast of Brazil; it anchored and remained a week to take on fruit, vegetables, and water. Soon after departing, the ships entered a thick fog, and it was necessary to fire the guns occasionally so that the *Mary* would not become separated. As the fog lifted, whales were sighted, and "new birds like Pigeons, their Plumage mix'd white and black, very regularly; for which Reason our Sailors call them *Damiers*, that is, Chequers." [25] On May 7 they reached Tierra del Fuego and coasted along the island to the Strait of Le Maire, which they entered on the following day; here they met "a strong and rapid Tide, as it were in a Torrent, which made us pitch so violently that the Boltsprit-Topsail dipp'd in the Water." [26] The Fuegan Indians Frézier found to be "quite naked, tho' in a very cold Country. Some of them cover their Privities with the Skin of a Bird, and others their Backs with that of some Beast. . . . They are almost as white as the Europeans. . . . They shew'd a strange Affection for any red Thing, and at the same time an extraordinary Boldness; for the first of them that came up, spying a red Cap on the Head of an Officer, who came to receive him, snatch'd it off daringly, and put it on his Arm . . . ; they would have taken away an Officer's red Breeches in the Boat: in short, they appeared robust, better shaped than the Indians of Chili: The Women they had with them, handsomer, and all of them great Thieves." [27]

One result of Frézier's explorations in the extreme south was to demonstrate the inaccuracy of existing maps; land had been sighted along the Patagonian coast where there was supposed to be none,[28] and the shape of Staten Island was found to be wrong. Later on, on his return voyage around Cape Horn, he dismissed the idea of "those Southern Lands, or *Terra Australis* generally laid down in the old Charts, as meer Chimeras." [29] His reasoning for this is interesting: no land had been found north of 63° south, from longitude 55° to 80° west. He did not, however, rule out the possibility of some land at the South Pole, for he had encountered icebergs, and was aware of the common belief that they were formed only of fresh water, which must run down from the land!

The voyage took Frézier as far as Lima; he has left us a detailed description of the mines along the coast, the cities, and the Indians, even describing a game, La Sueca, played by the Indians of Chile, which bears a striking resemblance to golf. On the return voyage he discovered a new channel in Tierra del Fuego, and took the trouble to correct his charts, suppressing "imaginary Lands" and adding new ones. Part of the confusion concerning the Patagonian coast he ascribed to some navigators touching the coast of "Sibald's Islands," which he felt were "certainly the same which Sir Richard Hawkins discover'd in 1593." [30] Heading north, the vessels touched at Salvador (Bahia), the Azores, and Gibraltar before docking at Marseille on August 16, 1714. The publication of the account of the voyage provided the most up-to-date description of the lands visited and of their resources, carefully gathered with the skill of the scientist. If these lands were not to be properly defended, it would not be because of any lack of knowledge of their possibilities.

The year 1739 found Great Britain and Spain involved in that conflict which bore the curious name of the War of Jenkins' Ear. Again Spain's empire came under attack; an expedition was organized under Commodore George Anson to prey on Spanish shipping and to seize the city of Panama. On September 18, 1740, a squadron of six armed vessels and two tenders sailed for the South Atlantic; it reached Santa Catarina Island on November 20, putting in for provisions and repairs, and departed on January 18, 1741. Meanwhile a Spanish squadron consisting of five vessels under Admiral José Pizarro, a descendant of the conquistador, had been sent to intercept the British; on February 7 it encountered the *Pearl*, a ship of forty guns, which had been separated from Anson's squadron by a gale on January 22. The British ship managed to slip away in the night, finally rejoining the others on February 17. The squadron put into the port of San Julián the following day, and Anson sent a longboat with two lieutenants to explore the region, and in particular to go to the salt-ponds about a league to the northwest; they returned with a considerable quantity of salt, but saw no one. The squadron sailed on February 27, sighted Tierra del Fuego on March 6, and entered the Strait of Le Maire on the following day. Little more progress was made before the weather began to grow very cold, gales sprang up, and rolling seas caused considerable distress, necessitating an eventual return to Brazil. Subsequently the squadron did manage to round Cape Horn, took several prizes in the vicinity of Acapulco and again near the Philippines, and returned to England in June of 1744 via the Cape of Good Hope. [31]

The presence of British vessels along the Patagonian coast caused considerable fear in Madrid that some attempts might be made by foreigners to found settlements; consequently when the procurador of the Jesuit fathers, Juan José Rico, sought permission to reconnoiter the coast with two or three missionaries with a view of converting the Indians, the Crown seized the opportunity and issued a *cédula* sending not two or three but ten Jesuits, among them Father José Quiroga, and a frigate "to reconnoiter the seacoast from Buenos Aires to the strait of Magellan." [32] Aside from determining whether the British were attempting to establish themselves along the coast, the real purpose was to investigate the possibility of establishing a colony at San Julián; the cost of making the Philippine sailing in two voyages from Spain to Veracruz and from Acapulco to Manila had become so high that the king was considering undertaking it directly via Cape Horn, with some port along the Patagonian coast—possibly San Julián—as a haven for passing the winter and awaiting a favorable time for continuing. Quiroga, who was skilled in navigation, was to make a map of the coast and add to the scanty knowledge of the region.

When the missionaries arrived in Buenos Aires, the governor, Domingo Ortiz de Rozas, arranged for the charter of a frigate, the San Antonio, commanded by Captain Joaquín de Olivares y Centeno, who had served under Admiral Pizarro in the unsuccessful expedition against Anson. After some delay in provisioning, the ship sailed on December 6, 1745, with three Jesuits, José Quiroga, José Cardiel, and Matías Strobel, who had been designated as superior of the Patagonian missions. At Montevideo they picked up twenty-five troops under Alférez Salvador Martín del Olmo, sailed on December 17, and arrived at Puerto Deseado on January 5; maps and acounts of earlier navigators in these regions were of great help to them. There they remained until January 11, making valuable zoological, botanical, archeological, and geographical observations. On January 16 they arrived at the latitude of San Julián, explored the coast, and finally entered the port on February 7. Hoping to find a suitable location for a reduction, Cardiel went into the interior with some soldiers, but returned drenched from storms, finding no wood or pasture necessary for a settlement. No Indians had been seen, but while seeking water they had come upon a cabaña which served as a burial place for three corpses; facing it were five dead horses, stuffed with straw and placed on logs as legs, to give the appearance of being alive. This evidence of human presence somewhere in the vicinity spurred them on to a further search, and a party of thirty-two men, provisioned for four days (in which they hoped to cover twenty-five leagues), explored the land carefully, but were unable to find a single Indian. They did, however, sight high mountains—the Andes—in the distance. Unsuccessful in their quest, they returned to San Julián, and after exploring other bays along the coast, the expedition returned to Buenos Aires on April 5, 1746.[33]

Shortly afterward the Jesuit provincial, Bernardo Nusdorffer, became interested in the idea of preaching to the hill peoples— the *serranos* —of Volcán (the name derives from the Indian Vuulcan), and chose Fathers José Cardiel and Thomas Falkner for the task. In August of 1746 they set out for Volcán, some one hundred leagues south of Buenos Aires, to find that the bulk of the *serranos* lived about two hundred leagues farther away, near the source of the Río del Sauce; the Indians further informed them that it was a six-day journey from there to the Strait of Magellan, and that the intervening land was heavily populated.[34] After founding the pueblo of Nuestra Señora del Pilar del Volcán, Cardiel followed the coast one hundred leagues south to the Río Colorado, where he made contact with the Puelches, who received him well. It was also his intention, after the pueblo had been founded, to investigate tales of the famous city of Los Césares, supposedly located somewhere in that vast area, but his pastoral duties prevented him from doing so.

On March 11, 1747, Cardiel left Buenos Aires accompanied by a student and four servants on another journey into the south. On April 20 they reached Nuestra Señora del Pilar, now under the care of Fathers Falkner and Strobel, and remained there until May 6, when they departed for the south with two *serrano* interpreters into a land where Europeans had never before ventured. Making six or seven leagues a day, they crossed several arroyos of varying depth, and turned toward the ocean on May 14, coming upon a rather sandy land which gave evidence of having had the vegetation recently burned off. Continuing on for six more days, they reached a country of low mountains; there the interpreters abandoned them, and they decided to return to the pueblo of Concepción de las Pampas via the beach. An encouraging picture of the land appears in Cardiel's account; the absence of marshes made the route passable for oxen and wagons; the arroyos could easily be forded, and the rivers crossed by placing baggage in a leather punt, pulled by a swimming horse, or by lashing the wagons together and floating them across, guided by swimming oxen. All the arroyos had drinkable water, as did the numerous lakes. Along the shore he found the sea "furious, with waves of five *varas* and more . . . , even in calm weather." [35] Cardiel was not a cartographer, yet he was able to prepare a very useful map, the first one made of this region.[36]

A much more elaborate description of Patagonia was that prepared by the English Jesuit Thomas Falkner. Much of it is based on personal experience, since he had traveled widely through the area; the remainder came from questioning Indians and Spaniards who had been their captives, especially a Captain Mancilla of Buenos Aires, prisoner of the Tehuelches for six years, who was a particularly valuable source. Falkner was perhaps one of the first to see Patagonia—or at least parts of it—as a region of potential value. The river valleys of the north, he suggested, were suitable for producing apples, peaches, plums, and cherries—the very fruits raised there today.[37] He recommended that a colony at the mouth of the Río Negro might be an extremely useful stopping place between Buenos Aires and the Strait of Magellan, particularly since the nearby forests would be useful; he had heard of one of the trees there that produced a gum resembling yellow wax, said to have a fragrant odor. But for the southern portion he held out little hope; the coast, he said, was dry, sterile, and devoid of any life, and he was unenthusiastic about the possibilities of settlement. Much of his account is given over to a detailed description of the Indians of Patagonia whom he found to be a sorry lot, quite prone to diseases introduced by Europeans because of their poor diet and lack of proper clothing and medicines.[38]

At this same time a French traveler, sailing aboard the *Marchand* on a voyage to Peru, gave his impressions of the southern reaches of the continent. Abbé Courte de la Blanchardière sailed from Brest on December 15, 1745, spent all of the next year in the North Atlantic, then crossed the equator in January of 1747, reaching Patagonia in March, and proceeding on to Tierra del Fuego. As they approached this stark land, they sighted a volcano which was spewing forth a considerable volume of smoke, although they were unable to see any flame. Proceeding onward, they passed by relatively flat land, taking soundings along the coast and noting the black and red pebbles which covered the sea bottom. The next day, Thursday, March 16, they hoisted sail at 5 A.M., hoping to sail close along the shore and make observations, but were driven off by contrary winds as they sailed past some snow-covered mountains. During a cold, snowy night they were forced to tack frequently, finally reaching the entrance to the Strait of Le Maire the next morning, only to be becalmed for six hours. The abbé observed that the land at the point of entrance is quite low, but that not far off it rose sharply, culminating in three mountains, snow-covered though only of medium height. The passage through the strait was without incident, and the expedition rounded Cape Horn and proceeded on to Peru.[39]

While the appearance of a vessel of an ally in these waters occasioned no alarm, the possibility that Great Britain might try to occupy a portion of the Patagonian coast presented the Spanish court with a real and ever present danger. The explorer of the northern and central portion of the cordillera, Jorge Juan, claimed to have discovered the intent of the British to establish a settlement somewhere along the coast, and stressed the importance of San Julián, in the extreme south, as a site for a Spanish settlement to act as a deterrent.[40] He needed to apply but little pressure on the Spanish minister Carvajal y Láncaster, who was already quite convinced of the importance of southern Patagonia; something of an Anglophile, he hoped that a friendly Great Britain might be most useful in protecting Spain's overseas empire, but was not so sanguine that he would neglect founding settlements on such a slim hope. Consequently, when the expedition of the Marqués de Valdelirios left to survey the boundary between Spanish America and Brazil, Carvajal instructed it to bring back information concerning the Patagonian coast as far as the Strait of Magellan. Valdelirios carried out his instructions, sending what data he could gather and two maps; his report seems to have been influenced by strong opinions in Buenos Aires concerning the necessity of founding a settlement—perhaps at San Julián, which could be made commercially profitable through the sale of salt found in the neighborhood. Much of the information was obtained from José Barnes, whom the Casa de Contratación had sent to Buenos Aires in 1752 to arrange to pick up a quantity of salt he had gathered and deposited at San Julián the year before. With the support of the Marqués and a *porteño* business man, Domingo Basavilbaso, Barnes sailed for San Julián late in 1753, loaded the salt, and returned with an evaluation of the port. On the basis of this and other information, Valdelirios recommended founding a town at the site (1) to aid in making Buenos Aires secure against Indian attack by allying with friendly Indians to the south against the savages of the pampas, (2) to provide a good stopping place for ships bound for the South Sea, incidentally keeping others away from the coast, and (3) as a base for attempting land communication with the Pacific ports.[41] Acting on this recommendation, which was in line with his own thinking on the matter, Carvajal y Láncaster directed that a settlement be established at the port.

During the following decade interest shifted to the island group known as the Malvinas, or Falklands, possession of which might be an important factor in controlling the sea lanes to the south. The discovery of these islands is shrouded in mystery. Credit has usually been given to John Davis, who was with the Cavendish expedition and supposedly reached the island group in the *Desire* on August 7, 1592,[42] but his priority has frequently been challenged. Paul Groussac, for example, believes that the honor should go to the Dutch navigator Sebald de Weerdt, whose discovery in 1598 seems to rest on more substantial ground.[43] At least, we find occasional reference to the "islands of Sebald de Weerdt" in the literature of eighteenth-century explorations, such as William Dampier's, and they appeared on Frézier's map in 1716, with a note that they were discovered by Sir Richard Hawkins in 1593! The first known landing was that of John Strong in the *Welfare* in 1690; he named the sound Falkland Sound after the First Lord of the Admiralty.[44]

But were the islands discovered before Davis? There is sufficient evidence—somewhat tantalizing, it must be admitted—to suggest the probability. The French explorer Louis de Bougainville, on the basis of a letter to Piero Soderini in 1504, gave the honor to Amerigo Vespucci.[45] The map by Portugal's leading cartographer, Pedro Reinel, discovered in Istanbul in 1938, and supposedly made in 1522 or 1523, shows the beginning of the Strait of Magellan and a group of islands which could be these. But who prepared it? It has been suggested that it could have been only Estêvão Gomes, a Portuguese who deserted Magellan at the strait and sailed for home.[46] Enrique de Gandía claims that the islands appeared, prior to the date given for the Reinel map, in a map made by

Pigafetta, which was well known in Spain in 1522.⁴⁷ But where did Pigafetta learn of them? When Gomes, commanding the *San Antonio*, deserted Magellan's expedition, he may have discovered the islands while sailing on a course from the Strait to the Cape of Good Hope *if*, Gandía cautions, he actually followed this route. If he had made such a discovery, why did he not mention it on his return? There was no mention until Elcano's return in 1522, which led Gandía to conclude that Pigafetta could have learned of the existence of the islands only from their discoverer, who must have been Duarte Barbosa, whom Magellan had sent in the *Victoria* to look for Gomes.⁴⁸ Gandía's thesis would certainly seem to establish a Spanish claim to the islands based on priority of discovery.

Regardless of any claims based on discovery, it seems quite clear that the first settlement was made by Bougainville in 1764. This explorer, a Parisian by birth, was only thirty-four years old at the time he set sail for the South Atlantic, yet he had some impressive accomplishments to his credit indeed. A mathematical prodigy, he had published a two-volume *Treatise on Integral Calculus* at the age of twenty-five. He had served as secretary of the French embassy in London. He served under Montcalm in Canada, then returned to Europe to fight the Prussians along the Rhine. After the Seven Years' War he devoted his energies to re-establishing the virtually defunct French navy, and rose to the rank of frigate captain.⁴⁹ In 1763 he sailed from St. Malo on September 15, stopping en route to the islands (by then known as the Falklands) at Montevideo, informing the local authorities that his destination was India. Resuming his course, Bougainville arrived at the islands on January 31, 1764, and planted a French flag at a place he named Port Louis. Taking possession of the archipelago in the name of Louis XV, he named them the Malouines after his home port. With the discovery that some of the turf would burn, the fuel problem was solved and a fort could be erected, with a small garrison to protect it. This accomplished, Bougainville sailed back to France.⁵⁰

Meanwhile, the authorities at Montevideo informed the court at Madrid of the presence of Bougainville's two ships in Spanish waters; the Spanish ambassador in Paris, Conde de Fuentes, pointed out to Choiseul that the route to India was not via Montevideo, and that the Family Compact (an alliance between the Bourbon powers of France and Spain) did not authorize French vessels in Spanish waters. Choiseul's defense—that Bougainville had merely stopped for repairs, and that his purpose was to discover an island as a base for rounding Cape Horn—did not impress Fuentes, who claimed the islands for Spain on the basis of their nearness to Patagonia. Rather than weaken the Family Compact, France transferred the islands to Spain in 1766 for a payment of £25,000 to Bougainville.⁵¹

Little more than two months after Bougainville left the Malouines (or Malvinas, as it was rendered in Spanish), a British expedition set sail for the South Atlantic. Three vessels—the *Dolphin* of twenty-four guns, the sloop *Tamar* with sixteen guns, and the provision ship *Florida*—left The Downs on June 21 under the command of Commodore John Byron, whose instructions were to make discoveries in the southern hemisphere and find a suitable place for a colony in the Malvinas, described as islands of His Britannic Majesty.[52] Scarcely had the fleet set sail when the *Dolphin* ran aground, necessitating putting into Plymouth for repairs; the bottom of the ship was sheathed with copper, which was described as "the first experiment of this kind that had ever been made on any vessel." [53] On July 3 they resumed course, stopping at Madeira to take on water and twenty pounds of onions for each man. More water was taken on at the Canaries, but by July 26 all of it was foul and had to be purified by a new method of forcing air through it by machine. A stop at the Cape Verde Islands from July 30 to August 2 provided them with additional water and fowl, lean goats, and monkeys, for which they traded old shirts, jackets, and similar items. By September 13 the fleet reached Guanabara Bay in Brazil, and anchored for three days, while the crew feasted on fresh meat and greens. Fourteen men were lost at Rio de Janeiro; Byron claimed that the Portuguese enticed them away from the shore, and got them so drunk that the ships sailed without them; he offered this intelligence "for the guidance of others." [54]

Foul weather plagued the expedition as it sailed south. In late October a gale of such force arose that Byron had to jettison several guns to ease the ships; November, although a spring month in the southern hemisphere, he found as cold as November in England, and as they progressed farther south in December he remarked that although it was now midsummer, yet "the weather was, in every respect, much worse than it is in the Bay of Biscay at the depth of winter." [55] After passing Cape Blanco, the expedition put in at Puerto Deseado (Port Desire), whose harbor was marked by a towering rock at the south of the entrance. Byron took a party ashore; they sighted some guanacos, "a very large Tyger" [jaguar], some wild pigs, and found some rhea eggs. They managed to shoot some wild ducks and hares, and "a little ugly animal which stunk so intolerably that none of us could go near him." The hares were another story, for they found their flesh "as white as snow, and nothing better can be tasted." [56]

After revictualing, the expedition set out in search of the mysterious "Pepys Island"; Byron strongly doubted its existence, and decided instead to search for the Malvinas, as he had been instructed to do. After passing through "the hardest gale at S.W. that I was ever in . . . ," Byron reached the Cape of the Virgins [57] and anchored nearby on December 20. An Indian horseman beckoned them ashore, an invitation which Byron accepted, bringing with him beads, ribbons, and the like. Others approached; the commodore described them as "of a gigantic stature, horribly painted," wearing skins draped over their shoulders with the hair inward, being otherwise naked except for boots with spurs of short, sharp sticks. They were not merely tall men, but well-proportioned "giants"; one of Byron's men, six feet two inches in height, is described as a "pygmy" in comparison.[58] Furthermore, we are informed that in order to put the beads around their necks, Byron had them sit on the ground, and "in this situation they were almost as high as the commodore when standing." [59] This attempt at establishing friendly relations proved to be almost too successful, for the Indians "were so delighted with the different trinkets, which hung around their necks, and fell down before on their bosoms, that the commodore could scarcely restrain them from caressing him, particularly the women, whose large and masculine features corresponded with the enormous size of their bodies." [60] When we consider that, according to this account, "their middle stature seemed to be above eight feet; their extreme nine and upward," the commodore must have had considerable cause for apprehension indeed.

An exploring excursion into the Strait of Magellan took Byron's fleet to Punta Arenas, where they anchored for Christmas; here he marveled to find "the ground covered with flowers of various kinds, that perfumed the air with their fragrance; and among them there were berries, almost innumerable, where the blossoms had been shed; we observed that the grass was very good, and that it was intermixed with a great number of peas in blossom." [61] Puzzling was the number of parrots and other birds, scarcely expected in so cold a climate; the area around Punta Arenas is protected from the winds by encircling mountains, which gives the port a moderate climate and may explain this phenomenon. No Indians were seen, although fires by deserted huts had scarcely gone out; on relighting one of them, Byron noticed that another was immediately lit in Tierra del Fuego across the strait.

Sailing out of the strait into the Atlantic on January 9, 1765, Byron sighted land ahead two days later, which he took to be the "islands of of Sebald de Wert," and was surprised to find a large bay, located in a low, flat island; nearby was a low, rocky island. He took possession of the group, which he called "Falkland's Islands," for King George III; convinced that they were the supposed "Pepys Island" (or Islands), he bestowed that name on an unknown island nearby. Leaving the group of islands on January 28, Byron sailed back to Puerto Deseado, that favorite stopping-place of non-Spaniards, to repair the rudder of the *Tamar*, then re-entered the Strait of Magellan on February 18. About two weeks later he saw some of the Indians who had eluded him earlier— four men, two women, and a boy in a poorly made bark canoe—"the poorest wretches I had ever seen. They were all naked, except a stinking seal skin that was thrown loosely over their shoulders." [62] Continuing onward, through "impenetrable fogs and incessant rain," the expedition finally entered the Pacific Ocean, whence it proceeded on to Saipan and Tinian, the South China Sea, through the Strait of Malacca, and home via the Indian Ocean and the Cape of Good Hope in 1766.

In that same year Samuel Wallis was ordered to take the *Swallow* and the *Prince Frederick* around the world. After loading supplies which included 3,000-weight of portable soup, a bale of cork jackets, and three large boxes of medicines, Wallis weighed anchor on August 19 and sailed for the South Atlantic. By November 12 he had reached latitude 30° south, and complained of the cold; a week later he mentioned an extraordinary phenomenon, a meteoroid "of extraordinary appearance . . . and it left a train of light behind it so strong, that the deck was not less illuminated than at noon-day." [63] Subsequent incidents are reminiscent of other eighteenth-century accounts; on December 8, near Penguin Island (south of Puerto Deseado), Wallis reported seeing so many red shrimp that "the sea was coloured with them"; on December 16, after rounding the Cape of the Virgins, he saw Byron's horseman on shore, inviting him to land. Coming ashore, Wallis presented the Indians with scissors, buttons, beads, and ribbons, but seemed unable to get across the idea that he wanted food in return. He noted that they wore boots with spurs, although one of them had Spanish brass spurs and stirrups and carried a scimitar. Measuring the Indians, he found that the tallest was six feet and six inches, and that most of them were from five feet ten inches to six feet; by European standards of the time, they were certainly tall, but these measurements are a far cry from Byron's nine feet and more.[64] Wallis' men were unable to converse with the Indians but as a patriotic gesture managed to teach them to say, "Englishmen, come on shore."

Passing through the strait, they encountered some Indians poorly dressed in the "stinking seal skins" described by Byron; to one of them they gave a fish just taken from the water, and he put on an astonishing performance: "The Indian took it hastily, as a dog would take a bone, and instantly killed it, by giving it a bite near the gills: He then proceeded to eat it, beginning with the head, and going on to the tail, without rejecting either the bones, fins, scales, or entrails." [65] Wallis made the same comment as Byron on the Indians' clothing—or lack of it: sealskins, which they wore loosely over the shoulders, and cast aside while rowing; he noted further that "they had all sore eyes, which we imputed to their sitting over the smoke of their fires, and they smelt more offensively than a fox, which perhaps was in part owing to their diet, and in part to their nastiness." [66]

Meanwhile, Bougainville had sailed from France on a voyage which was to take him around the world. On November 15, 1766, he sailed from Nantes in the twenty-six gun frigate *La Boudeuse*, which carried

214 officers and men and a distinguished supernumerary, the prince of Nassau-Sieghen; a store-ship, the *Etoile*, was to join him in the Malvinas. Crossing the equator on January 8, 1767, he reached Montevideo on February 28, then proceeded, after a delay, on a "rough and troublesome" voyage to the Malvinas, arriving March 23. After delivering the islands to the Spaniards on April 1, and waiting in vain for the *Etoile*, he returned to the agreed rendezvous, Rio de Janeiro, where he anchored on June 21, to find the supply ship had arrived a few days earlier. Bougainville got along very well with Dom Sebastião José de Carvalho, the king's lieutenant in the state of Brazil, who offered the French whatever they needed, even authorizing the purchase of a corvette. Taunay suspects that at the root of this bounty was the fact that the chaplain of the *Etoile* had been assassinated in the palace square, right below the viceroy's windows, and no one had been arrested.[67] Later, when Bougainville tried to protect a Spanish vessel after the Portuguese had seized a Spanish ship in Santa Catarina, he began to notice a growing hostility on the part of the viceroy, and decided to sail, departing on November 14. On December 2 he reached the Cape of the Virgins, but was unable to enter the strait because of contrary winds; not until November 7 was he able to enter, and then he had to seek anchorage in Possession Bay. On the following day, having proceeded to Boucalt Bay, he took a party ashore, where they encountered Indians who obviously had seen Europeans before. On measuring them he found their height to vary from five feet ten inches to six feet two inches; they appeared gigantic, he said, because "they had very broad shoulders, their heads were large, and their limbs thick." [68] So much for the myth of the Patagonian giants! Not until December 11 was Bougainville able to get under way again, and then he lost an anchor; five days later found him at Cape San Ysidro, the southernmost point of the continent, where he anchored, took on water, and remained for the rest of the month. Bad weather prevented any exploration of the peninsula, but he, the prince of Nassau, and two others were able to explore Tierra del Fuego from December 27 to 30. Resuming the passage through the strait on New Year's Day, they passed such evidences of British voyages as initials carved on trees, but were slowed by heavy rains; there was a particularly bad storm on January 17, with a thunderclap at high noon—the only one ever reported there to that time. Not until January 25 was Bougainville able to clear Cape Pilar, to continue his voyage around the world. He had been fifty-two days in the Strait of Magellan, whose length from the Cape of the Virgins to Cape Pilar he computed at 114 leagues. Despite the difficulties, he preferred this passage to trying to double Cape Horn.[69]

Much effort had been expended by Spain, and by its ally, France, in exploring and attempting to hold the Patagonian coast and the Malvinas for the Spanish Crown, and it was with difficulty, as we have seen, that

Spain was able to take and settle the Malvinas at all. They were rather hostile islands, and were in no way self-supporting. Bustards were the only edible native fowl, fishing was poor, and the governor of Buenos Aires had to send ships every three or four months to maintain the settlement; even the domestic animals he sent were so troubled by the cold, humidity, and sterility of the place that they refused to breed. Houses were made of sod; wood for fires had to be imported from Tierra del Fuego. There was ample water, and a good port, Soledad (the present Port Stanley), but even it had its limitations—it could be entered only with a north or northeast wind. Spain had sent two Franciscans and a governor to the islands; on seeing them, they were filled with melancholy, and the governor, Colonel Catán, said with tears in his eyes as the ships sailed for Buenos Aires that he considered those fortunate who were leaving, and as for himself, he would rejoice much to give his commission to another and return to Buenos Aires even if only as a cabin-boy.[70]

What of the mainland at this time? On February 22, 1783, the viceroy in Buenos Aires, Juan José de Vertiz, penned an answer to a letter he had received from the minister D. José de Gálvez, expressing the king's wish that expenses for the Patagonian establishments be reduced. It would be well, he said, to have ports along the coast as safe havens from storms, as sources of supplies, and place for repair of damage to vessels; the Patagonian ports, he stated, were of no use at all for these purposes. The Río Negro is dangerous to enter, and only small ships can cross the bar; the Río Colorado has been explored for twenty-five leagues, and has no wood other than small willows. Puerto Deseado has a narrow entrance and the current is strong, making entry and exit dangerous; San Julián is no better; to cross the bar, ships have to await the tide, and unfavorable winds make the prospect of shipwreck along the shores likely. The Río Santa Cruz, farther south, is useless. A colony in this region could not last long, he opined, without a constant flow of supplies from Buenos Aires; as to the danger from a possible foreign occupation, this, he felt, was minimal, for a foreign power, such as Great Britain, would face the same problems of sustaining the settlement. Such a settlement would not, even if established, be a threat to the security of Buenos Aires, for any force trying to invade by land would perish crossing the deserts. In the light of this, he had three recommendations: (1) abandon the settlement at San Julián, leaving a stone pillar bearing the royal arms; (2) reduce the Río Negro settlement to a fort and the small population it could protect; (3) abandon the port in the Bahía de San José, leaving a column as an indication of sovereignty.[71] Carvajal's fears, obviously, made small impression on his successors.

NOTES

1. *An Account of a Voyage up the River de la Plata, and thence over Land to Peru* (London, 1698), pp. 4-5. (This rare book has been reprinted by the Institute Publishing Co., North Haven, Conn. as part of its Mission Series, a collection of rare books on travel, discovery, and exploration in Latin America.)
2. *Ibid.*, pp. 5-6.
3. *Ibid.*, p. 10.
4. *Ibid.*, p. 22.
5. *Ibid.*, pp. 23-33.
6. Anthony Knivet, it will be recalled, reported hearing the same story in Brazil. See Chap. IV, p. 75.
7. The account of the voyage may be found in Juan Patricio Fernández, *Relación historial de las misiones de Indios Chiquitos que en el Paraguay tienen los padres de la Compañía de Jesús*, Vols. XII, XIII, in *Colección de libros raros o curiosos que tratan de América* (Madrid, 1895), Vol. XII, pp. 180-98.
8. *Ibid.*, Vol. XIII, p. 106.
9. Diego Barros Arana, *Historia jeneral de Chile* (Santiago, 1937), Vol. IV, pp. 151-53.
10. Portugal was under the Spanish Crown from 1580 to 1640, although the kingdoms were not united.
11. On this expedition, see Barros Arana, *op. cit.*, Vol. IV, pp. 154-57.
12. *Relation d'un Voyage à la Mer du Sud* (1715).
13. Froger, *op. cit.*, p. 106.
14. John Callander, ed., *Terra Australis Cognita, or Voyages to the Terra Australis, or Southern Hemisphere, during the 16th, 17th, and 18th Centuries* (Edinburgh, 1746–48), Vol. III, pp. 1-2.
15. *Ibid.*, pp. 154-57; several engravings in the volume illustrate Froger's complaints vividly.
16. *Ibid.*, p. 146
17. The Malvinas, or Falkland Islands.
18. Callander, *op. cit.*, Vol. III, pp. 160-61.
19. *Ibid.*, pp. 145-65, on this voyage.
20. *Ibid.*, p. 254.
21. *Ibid.*, pp. 254-64.
22. For the remainder of the voyage, see Callander, *op. cit.*, Vol. III, pp. 264-378.
23. Born in Chambery in 1682, he was a member of a family of English origin, the Frazers. Barros Arana, *op. cit.*, Vol. V, p. 525.
24. *A Voyage to the South-Sea, and along the Coasts of Chili and Peru in the Years 1712, 1713, 1714* (London, 1717), p. 15. This edition contains an interesting appendix by the famous astronomer Edmund Halley, defending himself against certain criticisms Frézier had made of one of his maps.
25. *Ibid.*, p. 18.
26. *Ibid.*, p. 32.
27. *Ibid.*, p. 32.
28. This was probably due to an error in longitude, not unusual in those days when this was a difficult problem indeed.
29. Frézier, *op. cit.*, p. 284.
30. *Ibid.*, p. 287.
31. On Anson's voyage see Callander, *op. cit.*, Vol. III, pp. 644-53. For Pizarro's attempts to intercept him, see Vicente Sierra, *Historia de la Argentina* (Buenos Aires, 1958), Vol. III, pp. 169-70.
32. Sierra, *op. cit.*, p. 195.
33. *Ibid.*, pp. 194-97.
34. *Ibid.*, pp. 197-98.

35. Cardiel's account may be found in Pedro de Angelis, ed., *Colección de viages, y expediciones a los campos de Buenos-Aires* (Vol. V of *Colección relativos a la historia del Río de la Plata*), (Buenos Aires, 1837), pp. 3-7.

36. This map reposes in the British Museum. Sierra, *op. cit.*, Vol. III, p. 199.

37. *Descripción de la Patagonia*, in Angelis, *op. cit.*, Vol. I, p. 5. The entire account appears in pp. 1-63 of this volume of Angelis.

38. *Ibid.*, p. 36.

39. René Courte de la Blanchardière, *Nouveau voyage fair au Pérou* (Paris, 1751), pp. 75-79.

40. "Sobre la necesidad y conveniencia de Poblar la Bahía de Sn. Julián y fortificar su gran Puerto en la Costa de Patagones" (No. 1 in vol. of MSS. *Viajes al Río de la Plata* in the Biblioteca del Palacio, Madrid, MSS. de América 2778, cited in Sierra, *op. cit.*, Vol. III, p. 243).

41. Sierra, *op. cit.*, Vol. III, pp. 243-44.

42. M. R. B. Cawkell, D. H. Maling, and E. M. Cawkell, *The Falkland Islands* (London, 1960), p. 1.

43. Raúl Menéndez, "Esquema del Descubrimiento de América del Sur," *Revista Geográfica Americana* XVI (Buenos Aires, October, 1941): 238.

44. Cawkell *et al.*, *op. cit.*, p. 10.

45. *Ibid.*, p. 1.

46. *Ibid.*, pp. 4-5. The Argentine Frigate Captain Héctor Ratto was of this opinion, which Enrique de Gandía defended in "Los Límites de la República Argentina," *Revista Geográfica Americana*, XIII (June, 1940): 366.

47. "Las Islas Argentinas de San Antonio," *Revista Geográfica Americana*, XXIV (November, 1945): 267.

48. *Ibid.*, *passim.* There still remains a puzzlement; early maps show the existence of the "islas Sansón" east of San Julián—apparently the Malvinas. Gandía, pointing out that nowhere in the toponymy of the Spanish empire can the name "Sansón" (Samson) be found, concludes that it must have been a misspelling of an abbreviation for "Islas San Antonio"—the name of Gomes' vessel—suggesting that the original mapmaker must have considered him to have been the discoverer (pp. 268-69). Cawkell *et al.* (*op. cit.*, pp. 3-4) cite the explanation of the sixteenth-century cosmographer Santa Cruz, who states that the islands were so named because a number of fat penguins, only half-feathered, reminded the sailors of the biblical hero Samson. This explanation, almost too far-fetched to be believed, is rejected by Gandía.

49. Affonso d'Escragnolle Taunay, *Rio de Janeiro de atanho: impressões de viajantes estrangeiros* (São Paulo, 1942), pp. 48-49.

50. Cawkell *et al.*, *op. cit.*, pp. 15-18; Sierra, *op. cit.*, Vol. III, p. 374.

51. *Ibid.*

52. Sierra, *op. cit.*, Vol. III, p. 376; Robert Kerr, ed., *A General History and Collection of Voyages and Travels* (Edinburgh, 1824), Vol. XII, pp. 1-2. Kerr reprinted the third edition of Byron's account, published in 1785. The narrative was also reprinted by the Hakluyt Society in 1962. It is interesting to note that Byron had as his objective in the Pacific the rediscovery of the Solomon Islands, which had been found by Medaña and subsequently "lost."

53. Kerr, *op. cit.*, p. 9, n. 1.

54. *Ibid.*, p. 13.

55. *Ibid.*, p. 17.

56. *Ibid.*, p. 22.

57. Which he erroneously called "Cape Virgin Mary"; Kerr, *op. cit.*, p. 27.

58. Kerr, *op. cit.*, pp. 29-32. Kerr, in a footnote (p. 29), dismisses this tale of "Patagonian giants" as "nonsense."

59. Edward Drake, ed., *A New Universal Collection of Authentic and Entertaining Voyages and Travels* (London, 1768), p. 646.

60. *Ibid.*

61. Kerr, *op. cit.*, p. 35.

62. *Ibid.*, p. 59.

63. *Ibid.*, p. 125.

64. Byron's story (the frontispiece of his book showed a huge Patagonian couple with a baby, standing beside a British sailor) was well accepted in England, since the ground had been prepared long ago by Pigafetta and Anthony Knivet; Wallis' account cast grave doubts on the story, and the Admiralty subsequently somewhat sheepishly admitted that no "giants" had ever been measured—which certainly created a credibility gap with respect to Byron's statements. Bougainville attacked him in an article, and, as we shall see, subsequently measured some Patagonians, with results similar to those of Wallis. This, plus the ridicule heaped on the story by Voltaire, finally served to discredit the story as a hoax. Cf. Percy G. Adams, *Travelers and Travel Liars, 1660–1800* (Berkeley, 1962), Chap. II, "The Patagonian Giants."

65. Kerr, *op. cit.*, Vol. XIII, pp. 152-53.

66. *Ibid.*, p. 153.

67. Taunay, *op. cit.*, p. 52.

68. Kerr, *op. cit.*, p. 485

69. Bougainville's full account is abstracted in Kerr, *op. cit.*, Vol. XIII, pp. 477-95.

70. Falkner, *op. cit.*, pp. 34-35.

71. Angelis, *op. cit.*, Vol. V, pp. 122-27. On Spain's attempt to colonize Patagonia, see James Stewart Cunningham, "Spanish Colonization in Patagonia," in *Greater America: Essays in Honor of Herbert Eugene Bolton* (Berkeley and Los Angeles, 1945), pp. 341-60.

X   *The Enchanted City*

and the Chilean Archipelago

With the exception of the Atlantic coast and the Strait of Magellan, Patagonia was still a relatively unknown land into the seventeenth century; few had seen anything of the interior, and the rugged coast of south Chile had been explored only in the most cursory fashion. Small wonder, then, that the story of the *ciudad encantada de los Césares* continued to grip the imagination of men in the seventeenth century and even into the eighteenth as it had in the sixteenth.[1] Had not Pedro de Oviedo and Antonio de Coba, survivors of the ill-fated expedition of the bishop of Palencia, seen this great city, fortified and closed at night? [2] And had not they and others issued sworn statements, testifying to the existence of this fabulous city? That it existed, many did not doubt; where it was, none could say with anything approximating certainty.

Even the origin of the myth, as we have seen, is uncertain. It seems to have begun with the voyage of Sebastian Cabot, who picked up survivors of the Solís expedition and heard from them wonderful stories of the interior. Cabot thereupon sent Francisco César to look for the rich lands of gold and silver they had described, and he seems to have found a district ruled by a friendly cacique. When the story was told by his soldiers, the town became known for them—"los Césares." [3] Then there was the tale of the founding of an idyllic community, in a country of beautiful lakes and meadows (the Argentine lake country?), by the survivors of the bishop of Placencia's expedition. Or, if one preferred a different version, it was founded by a group of Peruvians who migrated south, to build a city of great wealth and size, with stone houses whose roofs shone like gold, and with furnishings of gold and silver. A nearby mountain provided gold and diamonds, and there was an abundance of pearls. Disease was unknown in this city; death came only from old age. There was a magnificent church where religious services were conducted with much pomp and splendor. For protection, the city had been forti-fied and as an added precaution, the Indians in the neighborhood had been persuaded not to reveal its existence.[4] Small wonder, then, that men of the eighteenth century would come to refer to it as the "enchanted city."

In 1604 the first governor of the Río de la Plata province, Hernando Arias de Saavedra, led a force of eight hundred south across the pampas and beyond in search of the fabled city, but sickness among his men forced a return after four months, with nothing accomplished.[5] He had seen enough, however, to induce him in 1617 to write to the king recom-mending strongly the settlement of the area near the cordillera; he believed that it could sustain a population, serve as a base for future *entradas*, and would make possible the erection of watchtowers along the Pacific coast to warn of the approach of hostile ships. The king approved the idea, and in a royal *cédula* of August 10, 1619, directed the viceroy of Peru to see to the settlement of the slopes of the cordillera to the strait. To carry out the directive Saavedra chose his son-in-law, Jerónimo Luis de Cabrera, to lead a force of 250 men; they were to be assisted by support from Juan Ochoa de Zárate, a relative of Juan Alonso de Vera y Zárate, governor of Tucumán. The expedition, now four hundred strong, with two hundred carts and six thousand head of cattle, assembled at Córdoba and left late in 1620 or early in 1621 (details are lacking) for Mendoza, whence it was to head south. All that is known for certain is that the force crossed the Río Negro, where it was attacked by the Pehuenche Indians; most of the carts were burned, and since the expedition was not prepared to live off the land, Cabrera ordered a return.[6]

Meanwhile, the point of departure shifted to the west coast. In the same year, 1621, Diego Flores de León, lured by the legend of "los Césares," took a force of forty-six men across the cordillera via the Río Peulla and came upon the jewel of the Andes, Lake Nahuel Huapí, in February; lashing their canoes together, they explored the waters for a distance of eight leagues. Continuing south, they suffered much from hunger; meeting an Indian who told them he knew of a ship wintering in the strait, Flores de León was on the point of asking him to lead them when the Indian made it plain that there were numerous—and perhaps hostile—aborigines ahead. Since it was futile to continue, the expedition returned to Chile.[7]

For some years Nahuel Huapí would remain in comparative isolation. Then, about midcentury, Captain Luis Ponce de León, whose parents had been held captive by the Araucanians and who nursed a grudge against all Indians as a result, crossed the cordillera from Chile and took three hundred Indian captives, in violation of a peace earlier agreed upon. When the Indians complained, Governor Antonio de Acuña y Cabrera decided to send the illustrious Jesuit missionary, Diego de Rosales, to restore peace; he consented on the condition that the Indians who had been seized, including their cacique, Cantinaquel, be allowed to return, and that there be no more attacks. In October of 1650 Father Rosales crossed the cordillera, preached to the Indians, and promised no more attacks, a promise broken shortly after by the Salazar brothers, relatives of the governor. Not until the governor himself withdrew his protection from them did the Salazars give up; again Father Rosales crossed the cordillera, and on the shore of Lake Nahuel Huapí gave the Indians renewed assurance that attacks would end.[8]

Twenty years later an Italian Jesuit, Niccolò Mascardi, began preaching to the Poya Indians in the vicinity of Lake Nahuel Huapí. In 1671 he set out on a journey along the cordillera southward toward the strait, in the hope of finding the elusive city of "los Césares," which, he felt, by now must be a city totally without priests.[9] He seems to have reached latitude 44° south, without finding the city, but did discover a lake of considerable size in the middle of Patagonia—probably Lake Musters. In 1672 he departed from the island of Chiloé with four Indians and went directly to the lake, then eastward to the Atlantic coast, somewhere between Puerto Deseado and Santa Cruz, and south to the entrance to the Strait, at the Cape of the Virgins (Cabo Virgenes). Still there was no enchanted city. Once more, in late spring in 1673, Father Mascardi departed, this time accompanied by a few Indians and the friendly cacique Manqueunai, to make one more attempt to find "los Césares." This time, at about 47° south, disaster overtook the expedition; at a town of the Poyas, the explorers were attacked and killed at the instigation of the cacique Autullanca.[10] Mascardi's death at least served to revitalize missionary endeavor in Patagonia; another Jesuit, Diego Altamirano, pointed out that there was no one after Mascardi to carry out the work of evangelizing the Indians—work which would not only bring many to know their Creator, but might also have the happy effect of halting the Portuguese and others who might intrude in the lands toward the Strait of Magellan. As a result, the king issued a royal *cédula* providing four missionaries for the task, who, to avoid Mascardi's fate, would have troops under their command for protection.[11] The work of these missionaries was primarily pastoral, and they do not come to our attention as explorers.

Interest in the "enchanted city" (for as such would the eighteenth century know it) seemed to wane after Father Mascardi's untimely death, and for several decades no important expeditions set out either from Buenos Aires or from Chile in search of it, despite the fact that a map

published in Paris in 1703 by Guillaume de l'Isle, first royal geographer
of the Royal Academy of Sciences, plainly located "Cessares" just a little
to the east of Lake Fontana.[12] Attention shifted, rather, to exploring the
Chilean archipelagoes, not so much because this area was a convenient
starting point for seeking the "enchanted city" as because of the danger
of British occupation during the wars, or at least the use of the islands as
bases by British privateers. Little was done, oddly, during the wars; not
until 1769 was an important expedition sent out, that of Francisco Machado. Departing from the port of San Antonio de Chacao in the northern part of Chiloé Island, Machado explored the Guaiteca Islands south
of Chiloé, then entered the Archipiélago de los Chonos to the south,
explored the sizable Taitao Peninsula and the narrow isthmus of Ofquí
which ties it to the mainland. After reconnoitering the Gulf of San Estéban south of the peninsula, Machado proceeded as far as Campana
Island before returning to Chiloé.[13]

In the following year Governor Carlos de Beranger sent another
expedition to continue the work of exploring the archipelagoes. On
November 2, 1770, at 10 A.M., two artillerymen, Pedro Mancilla and
José Ríus, set out in two pirogues, equipped with masts and sails, from
the port of Queil in the island of Quinchao. All went well until November 6, when a sudden squall from the north nearly overturned their dugouts. After a two-day delay because of rain, they got under way again,
continuing to Yatablat Island, where they pulled their pirogues ashore
on a sandy beach; a sudden southeast wind of considerable force
with a high sea, kept all hands busy through the night lest the vessels
be damaged or lost. When the weather moderated, the expedition continued on its southerly course; on November 15 they entered Puliche
channel, and discovered a beautiful beach. Naming the place Puerto
Alegre ("Happy Port"), they raised a cross. Foul weather forced them to
remain there for a few days; subsequently they continued south, discovering another beach, this one covered with gravel; there was evidence
of earlier exploration—two crosses carved on oak trees. On November 21
they entered Diego Gallegos inlet, explored it, and carved a cross on a
cinnamon tree; weather permitting, they examined various inlets but were
unable to conduct any investigation of the land until November 29.
There was evidence of an earlier shipwreck and the establishment of a
brief settlement by the survivors—broken bottles, soles of shoes, and a
metal button; an Indian told them he had seen two bodies there years
before. Ríus, Mancilla, and their companions proceeded no further
south; reversing their direction, they began exploring the coastline with a
view to locating land fit for settlement, but could find none. The weather
was terrible; there were heavy rains (this is one of the wettest places in
South America), and to add to their apprehension a fireball fell and

burst near them. Several of the men were sick for a few days, but despite this and the almost constant rain and hail, they managed to reach Chiloé late in December.[14]

There were two subsequent expeditions of importance into the region explored by Ríus and Mancilla. The first of these was led by two Franciscans, Norberto Fernández, a Spaniard, and Felipe Sánchez, a Creole lay brother. Taking twenty-two men with them in two large pirogues, they left Chiloé on November 4, 1779, to explore the archipelagoes and the mainland; one of their objectives was to find a pass through the cordillera to see if there was any truth in the assertion that Europeans ("los Césares") were living in a city on the other side of the Andes. They carried out their task with thoroughness, exploring numerous islands and channels, and traversing a considerable part of the mainland. After eighty-two days they returned to Castro in Chiloé; they had added considerably to existing knowledge of the islands in their fruitless search for the city of "los Césares" and had discovered a route through the cordillera to the southern Patagonian plains.[15] In 1786 the viceroy, Teodoro Croix, dispatched Francisco Hurtado and José de Moraleda, officers in the navy, to make further explorations and complete the maps of the region of the archipelagoes. They left Callao on November 4 in the *Nuestra Señora de los Dolores*, sailed to the south, and remained in the region until 1790. On their return to Callao, Moraleda submitted a detailed journal and set of maps to the viceroy.[16]

Not long after the Franciscans Fernández and Sánchez reported their discovery of another pass through the cordillera, an expedition set out for the same region from the Atlantic. On November 7, 1782, Antonio Viedma, accompanied by León de Rosas, Joaquín Cundín, Ignacio Morales, Martín Chinchilla, and forty-four Toldos Indians under the cacique Julián Camelo left San Julián for the interior, taking with them fifteen horses and three mules to carry provisions. Other than occasional rain, there was no incident of consequence during the first week of their long journey, during which they averaged about three leagues per day. On November 15, led by three Indian guides, they reached a lake said by their guides to be the source of the Río Santa Cruz—one of their objectives; they were completely misinformed, since the Santa Cruz rises in Lake Argentino far to the southwest, and if there was a confusion between the Santa Cruz and the Río Chico, both of which enter the Atlantic at about the same point, the guides were also in error—the Chico rises in a lake far to the northwest, which they could have not reached in so brief a time. On November 16 they reached the Río Chico itself, and on the following day arrived at the banks of its tributary, the Río Chalía. Continuing to the west, Viedma's party arrived at "Laguna Grande," which another guide, Ocapán, assured him was the source of the Santa Cruz.[17] Apparently satisfied, Viedma spent several days in this pleasant location; early in the morning of November 23 he broke camp, beginning the return trip which continued without incident to the seacoast.[18]

We turn now to the explorations of that indefatigable Franciscan, Fray Francisco Menéndez. Having previously explored the archipelagoes south of Chiloé, he was directed to take over a particular task assigned to the Jesuits prior to their expulsion—to seek a convenient pass across the cordillera which would facilitate the exploration of the "Magellanic lands." It so happened that one of his parishioners, Miguel Barrientos, had done some exploring along the cordillera in April with his three sons, but had returned because of the lateness of the season; Menéndez felt they had been on the right track and arranged to go with them on another attempt. On December 15, 1783, they departed from Castro, on the island of Chiloé, and sailed to the Río Reremo, where they tied up their boat and prepared to attack the cordillera. Ten men went ahead to open a pathway, a difficult task since the slopes of the Andes were covered with canes, bamboos, oaks, and laurels, and there were many fallen trees to add to the difficulty. Menéndez, meanwhile, delayed at the river mouth to give the advance party a sufficient head start; there he said his Christmas Mass in a hut. On December 29 his party set out, following the course of the river in a southeasterly direction, but progressing slowly because of the delays in cutting a path. Heavy rains in early January soaked them, since their makeshift huts offered poor protection against a downpour, even though they were covered with ponchos. On the afternoon of January 9 they came to a river; by means of a fallen tree they were able to reach an island in the middle, and crossed to the other shore over the trunk of an oak tree which two of the men, who forded the river, cut down for the use of the others.

By January 11 they were ready to begin the ascent of the cordillera. Since a dense covering of small trees made progress directly up the slope all but impossible, they followed the river upstream and found it necessary to ford it again, in the process of which José Barrientos, one of Miguel's sons, cut his leg. They soon reached the snow line, and after some searching found a gorge which offered a way around the snow and brought them to the continental divide at the point where the Barrientos team had turned back with the coming of autumn on their earlier expedition. In vain they now looked for a way to descend the slope, but night finally overtook them and they slept fitfully, chilly under the open sky despite a fire they kept going. Incessant rain impeded their efforts the following day; not until January 14 did they find a pass, and then they could not proceed because of lack of supplies. Three men, led by Narciso Miranda, went off in search of supplies while the rest of the party explored the vicinity, but Miguel Barrientos' age and José's leg wound slowed them so much that they decided to return to the beach, where Fray Menéndez was afflicted by a painful swelling of his feet and a severe headache. Three had been left behind to continue exploring the region of the pass; on January 27 they reported having found a lake between two hills which was seven leagues long and contained six islands. After a few days' rest at the beach, the reunited party proceeded on to Chiloé, arriving February 6, 1784.[19]

Undismayed by the unsatisfactory results of his first expedition, Menéndez made another attempt in 1786. After spending some time with Miguel Barrientos recruiting for the expedition and securing a dugout, he left Chiloé on November 24 for the Chauqui Islands, west of the Tenaún peninsula, where foul weather delayed him until November 30. Departing again, they reached the Río Reremo on December 1, where they beached and secured their dugouts, unloaded their supplies, and stored them in a hut. There rain held them until December 8, when they were able to resume their journey, following the same route as before and camping at the snow line. About midnight they were startled by what seemed to be a clap of thunder, and discovered that a huge section of snow had slid off the mountain opposite and fallen into the gorge below. On December 21 the party reached the lake discovered on the previous expedition and found that the canoe they had used for exploring it was still there; making use of it and additional canoes made from larch trees, they went around the lake, noting much smoke to the north. At the north end they discovered that the lake discharged through a rocky gorge into another, and the party portaged to it, finding it to be four leagues long. As they sailed toward the south outlet on December 29, they noted three black peaks resembling cathedral towers; Menéndez recalled hearing that three such peaks marked the beginning of the pampas, where there was a settlement of Spaniards ("los Césares"?). On January 1 they explored the region around the lake, noting that much of it was badly scarred by fires. A week later they met Lorenzo Soto, who informed Menéndez that he and his small party had also been exploring the region, and had found an immense plain beyond the three peaks, crossed by three well-used roads; to the south he had seen an large lake which looked like the sea. Reports of hostile Indians in the vicinity, plus lack of water, led Menéndez once more to give up short of his objective, and the party returned to the island of Chiloé.[20]

In 1790 Father Menéndez went to Lima to inform the viceroy, Don Francisco Gil y Lemus, of what had been accomplished on the previous expeditions; Gil sent him back with instructions to find Lake Nahuel Huapí and "discover the Césares . . . who are supposed to exist east of the Archipelago."[21] On October 1, Menéndez embarked at Callao on the frigate *La Ventura*, arriving at Chiloé on November 17. In the middle of December he went to Castro, accompanied by another priest, Fray Diego del Valle, and thirty soldiers. On January 3 Menéndez left Castro with eighteen men in one pirogue, to meet the other at Callvuco. There they were joined by 60-year-old Sergeant Pablo Téllez, who knew the Indians at Nahuel Huapí. On January 10 the entire party embarked, arriving on the following day at the place where they had begun their inland journey before. After constructing a shed to protect their supplies, the party proceeded inland through a forest of oaks and laurels, finally reaching a gap from which they could see Lake Todos los Santos, on whose shores they established camp. On January 18 Sergeant Diego Barrientos and two others went out to look for signs of the old route, but accomplished nothing because of heavy rains which forced a removal of the camp as the lake rose. The rains ended on the 22nd, and with supplies brought up, a thorough exploration of the region could be begun. From January 25 to February 1 Menéndez and sixteen men examined the lake by dugout with great care; the following day they disembarked in a cove in the north, entered upon a meadow, and found a very deep, rather narrow river that led to another meadow which opened to the east through a valley. This, Menéndez was sure, would lead to Nahuel Huapí, in the event that Sergeant Tellez was unsuccessful in seeking a pass through the Vuriloche valley. A letter from the sergeant, who was seeking some of his men who had become separated, indicated that he had not found it. The friar then sailed along the lake shore to the south, finally finding signs of the old route, and followed a river to the place where supplies had been stored; there they found the missing men, who, seeking an opening to the east, had come upon the thermal springs of Vuriloche. When Téllez and his group arrived on February 13, they began, with the others, a detailed reconnaissance of the area, fording a river and coming upon a dwelling where probably the Jesuit Father Segismundo Guëll had lived in 1766.

A large and deep river, which flowed into Lake Todos los Santos, blocked further progress to the south, but by climbing a high mountain to the north they could see a pass in the distance, and decided to head in that direction. It was then February 17. The country was rough, and there was much rain; they passed more hot springs and a cane field, cut trees to cross rivers, and finally reached what they took to be the summit of the cordillera. To the north a great snow-capped mountain—Cerro Tronador—rumbled ominously, and openings in the hills appeared to the east and west. To the east they sighted the three spirelike peaks, and went in that direction to find a small lake, which drained to the north and east. But there was much scrub vegetation—*monte*—ahead, and Menéndez' men had no shoes and were fatigued; the days were growing shorter, and unless they intended to remain in the cordillera, prudence dictated an early return. There was still time for a little exploring on the way back, and the party made use of the opportunity. On March 11 they returned to Callvuco, the chief object of the journey unaccomplished.[22]

This was the last expedition sent out in search of the "enchanted city." That it would not be found we can accept as a forgone conclusion, but it is the nature of man often to believe what he wants to believe, and legends of great wealth, of lost cities and utopias die hard.[23] Without this legend as a stimulus, would these men have set out to explore the cordillera at this time? One wonders. Unsuccessful as they were in the attainment of their primary objective, these expeditions did bring back a substantial amount of information about the area, and others after them would be encouraged to explore it further. While sucessive expeditions along the east side of the cordillera failed to turn up the city of "los Césares," they did bring to light the spectacular Andean lakes, and again the profusions of nature showed themselves more various, more miraculous, even, than the myths of men.

NOTES

1. See Chap. III. An excellent account in English is that of Robert Hale Shields, "The Enchanted City of the Caesars, Eldorado of Southern South America," in *Greater America: Essays in Honor of Herbert Eugene Bolton* (Berkeley and Los Angeles, 1945), pp. 319-40. For an excellent account in Spanish, see Enrique de Gandía, *La ciudad encantada de los Césares* (Buenos Aires, 1933).

2. R. B. Cunninghame Grahame, *The Conquest of the River Plate* (London, 1924), p. 260.

3. Ricardo E. Latcham, "La Leyenda do los Césares: su orígen y su evolución," *Revista Chilena de Historia y Geografía* (Santiago, 1929), pp. 193-254.

4. John A. Zahm, *Through South America's Southland* (New York, 1924), pp. 353-55. (Based on Benjamin Vicuña Mackenna's "La Ciudad encantada de los Césares," in his *Relaciones históricos*, Santiago, 1877.)

5. Shields, *op. cit.*, p. 325; "Algunos aspectos de Patagonia," *Revista Geográfica Americana* XX (August, 1943): 99; Vicente Sierra (*Historia de la Argentina*, Buenos Aires, 1958, Vol. II, p. 206) believes that Saavedra, in mentioning an expedition "a los Césares" meant rather to indicate a direction—toward Neuquén—than to ascertain the truth of the legend. There is also the possibility that the term was used loosely to designate all Argentina.

6. Sierra, *op. cit.*, Vol. II, pp. 205-8; Shields, *op. cit.*, pp. 325-26.

7. *Ibid*, p. 208.

8. *Ibid.*, pp. 567-68.

9. "Carta del Dn. Valentin de Escobar Becerra, Deán de la iglesia de Buenos Aires, a S.M." Archivo General de las Indias, 75-6-9. Cited in Spain, Archivo general de las Indias (Pablo Pastells, S.J., ed.), *La Compañia de Jesús en la Provincia de Paraguay*, Madrid, Vol. III, p. 190. See also Sierra, *op. cit.*, Vol. II, pp. 569-70.

10. Sierra, *op. cit.*, Vol. II, p. 571.

11. "Real Cédula al Gobernador de Buenos Aires," Archivo General de las Indias, 75-6-33. Cited in Spain (Pastells), *op. cit.*, Vol. IV, pp. 40-42, No. 2334.

12. "Carta de Paraguay, du Chili, du Détroit de Magellan, &c.," reproduced in Guillermo Fúrlong Cárdiff, *Cartografía jesuítica del Río de la Plata* (Buenos Aires, 1936).

13. Fray Bernardino Izaguirre Ispizua, *Historia de las misiones Franciscanas y narración de los progresos de la geografía en el oriente del Perú* (Lima, 1924), Vol. IV, pp. 28-29.

14. *Ibid.*, pp. 30-46.

15. *Ibid.,* p. 27.

16. Rubén Vargas Ugarte, S.J., *Historia del Perú* (Buenos Aires, 1957), Vol. IV, p. 26.

17. Ocapán may also have erred. Was "Laguna Grande" the present Lake Viedma? Or did they reach Lake Argentino—in which case he was right?

18. On Viedma's journey see Ana Palese de Torres, "Las Exploraciones de Moyano en la cuenca del Santa Cruz," *Revista Americana Georgráfica* XXXVIII (Buenos Aires, December, 1954): 119-21.

19. Fray Francisco Menéndez, "Diario Primero," in Izaguirre, Vol. IV, pp. 81-92.

20. Menéndez, "Diario Segundo," in Izaguirre, Vol. IV, pp. 95-107.

21. Izaguirre, Vol. IV, p. 116.

22. For the complete account of the expedition, see Menéndez, "Diario para descubrir la Laguna de Nahuelhuapí" in Izaguirre, Vol. IV, pp. 115-43.

23. Even the twentieth century has lost cities; one, Machu Picchu, was found, and in search of another, a renowned explorer, Colonel Fawcett, lost his life.

Part Three

The Early Scientist-Explorers

XI *The Measurement of the Earth*

While explorers were charting the coasts of Patagonia and the islands, seeking Indians to convert, and searching for an enchanted city that never was, a controversy raged in the French Académie des Sciences that was to bring a new breed of man to explore the vast interior and the coasts of South America with a fervor equal to those who had gone before—the scientist. Briefly, the controversy dealt with the shape of the earth: was it an oblate spheroid (that is, slightly flattened at the poles) as Isaac Newton contended, or was it a prolate spheroid (slightly elongated at the poles and constricted slightly at the equator) as the Astronomer Royal of France, Jacques Cassini, held? At stake, from the French point of view, were Cassini's reputation and the national honor of France, and neither were served well when Jean Richter, who went to Guiana at Cassini's behest with one of the pendulum clocks invented by Christopher Huygens, found that the pendulum beat more slowly near the equator, a discovery that Newton, with much satisfaction, claimed was proof of the correctness of his position.

It was obvious that argument would never solve the problem, so the Académie decided to do what one would expect in that age of reason—solve it by investigation. They would measure the meridian of an arc of a degree of latitude in the Arctic and at the equator, and compare the results with measurements taken in France; if Newton were correct, the length would increase slightly toward the poles. The results, of course, would be of great value to navigation, for without such information, it was impossible to prepare accurate navigational charts. So in 1734 two expeditions were arranged; one to go to Lapland, the other to proceed to the province of Quito in the viceroyalty of Peru—the only place along the equator where scientists might conduct work of this nature. To head this expedition to the equator the Académie selected one of its members, Charles-Marie de La Condamine, mathematician, geodesist, and friend of Voltaire. This young aristocrat, who was born in 1701, belonged to a family which had acquired great wealth from John Law's speculative schemes; educated at the Collège de Louis le Grand, he developed an interest in mathematics that was to increase and develop during his years in the army. Such was his ability that he was elected to the Académie des Sciences at the age of twenty-nine, certainly an unusual accomplishment.

The decision for an expedition provided an unrivaled opportunity for La Condamine, and by careful lobbying and providing 100,000 livres toward expenses he was able to secure command of the equatorial expedition. With him would be an impressive array of talent: there were the astronomer Pierre Bouguer; the mathematician Louis Godin (who was charged with the direction of the work) and his cousin Jean Godin des Odonais; Joseph de Jussieu, the famous botanist; Captain Verguin, marine engineer; Morainville, engineer and draftsman; Dr. Jean Senièr-gues, physician; and Hugot, watchmaker and instrument technician. There was also young Couplet, whose presence can be explained by the fact that his uncle was the treasurer of the Académie. Since the audiencia of Quito lay within the domains of His Catholic Majesty, the King of Spain and the Indies, there was the problem of obtaining Spanish permission for the venture, and Spain had never felt any obligation to permit outsiders to roam through its empire. The fact that since the beginning of the century Spain also had a Bourbon king augured well; Louis XV sent Comte de Maurepas to the court of his uncle, Felipe V, in Madrid and permission was granted. Royal *cédulas* of August 14 and 20, 1734, required the viceroys and presidents of audiencias to give all help possible, even to supplying funds from the royal treasury; there was, however, one stipulation, to which France consented: one or two Spanish mathematicians were to accompany the expedition as equals.[1] As his representatives the king finally selected (on the recommendation of his chief minister, José Patiño) Jorge Juan y Santacilia, twenty-two years of age, and Antonio de Ulloa, nineteen years old. Young though they were, they were members of the *Guardias Marinas*, an organization comprised of young noblemen who were carefully schooled in navigation, astronomy, and mathematics; certainly their background fitted them well for the work ahead of them.[2]

On May 16, 1735, La Condamine and his companions left La Rochelle aboard a French naval vessel; they arrived at Martinique on June 22, and then continued on to Cartagena. Meanwhile, having been commissioned lieutenants in the navy, Juan and Ulloa embarked from Cádiz on May 26 in two vessels: Juan sailed in the ship of the line *Conquistador*, while Ulloa left in the frigate *Incendio*. Both made careful observations of longitude from Cádiz to Martinique, continuing this work as they sailed on to Cartagena via Curaçao and Santa Marta, finally reaching that great port on July 9.[3] Not until November 16 did the French party arrive, to receive a warm welcome at the hands of the Spaniards. During the months from July to November, Juan and Ulloa continued their scientific observations, but also found time to make a most detailed study of Cartagena, to which several chapters in their journal are devoted. There is a description of the bay, of the city and its agencies of government, and of the inhabitants from the pure Spaniards through various degrees of mixing to the Negro slaves and freemen. The young scientists were amazed by the widespread use of tobacco—used with a passion, they said, by men and women alike, usually in the form of little cigars. And there were the many dances, particularly the fandango, very popular among the lower classes, generally performed while drinking *aguardiente*, they noted, accompanied by indecencies.[4] There were many sicknesses, which could be divided into two types according to whether they affected only new arrivals or were common to all. Of the former type the most common was the *chapetonadas*, usually manifested as a cold or indigestion, followed by black vomiting (which usually preceded death); the disease was violent but brief; within three or four days the sufferer either recovered or died. Everyone in Cartagena, they found, had a propensity for the *mal de San Lázaro*, or leprosy, which some attributed, curiously enough, to eating pork, others to the climate.[5]

Withal it was a land of great beauty; palms and acacias and balsams, and the valuable cacao tree, from which came the chocolate sold by the street vendors (heavily adulterated with corn, according to Juan and Ulloa). And it was a land of bounty: corn, yuca, sugar cane, the fruits of the old world—grapes, oranges, medlars, and dates; and those of the new—pineapples, papayas, custard apples, guavas, mameys, plantains, and coconuts. A paradise indeed for those fortunate enough to survive!

To reach Quito the scientists had two choices. They could travel overland, via the Río Magdalena, but this would be most difficult in view of the amount and weight of their equipment, which might suffer severely from the long journey by muleback from the headwaters of the river to Quito. Or they could follow the convoy route to Puerto Bello on the isthmus of Panama, whence they could cross to Panama on the Pacific side and embark for the audiencia of Quito; this seemed to be the most practicable solution for them.

The voyage from Cartagena to Puerto Bello was accomplished without incident, and the scientists took advantage of the opportunity to make further observations concerning winds, currents, and the weather —information of considerable value in navigation. The port, a trading center of great importance, was populated largely by Negroes and mulattoes; Juan and Ulloa counted only thirty whites. Local customs appeared to them to be the same as in Cartagena, although the people seemed less open and free-spirited, and were of smaller stature. No doubt health conditions contributed to this; it was one of the unhealthiest ports in the Spanish empire: the heat was excessive, the climate enervating, and fever rampant. La Condamine's group might consider itself fortunate to have survived to a man even a brief stay there. Food was constantly in short supply, and therefore expensive; much of it came from Panama City and Cartagena.[6]

It was obviously inadvisable to linger in this unhealthful environment, so La Condamine's party left at 9 A.M. on December 22, 1735, arriving at the mouth of the Río Chagres in the late afternoon. Dugouts provided by the president of Panama were waiting, and the group began the ascent into the heart of the isthmus on the following day. They passed a variety of craft along this waterway, as well as a considerable number of caymans, and finally reached Cruces by midday of December 27, where they rested for two days before proceeding. At 11:30 on the morning of December 29 the earth-measurers left by mule for Panama, and arrived in the city that same evening, at 6:45 P.M. After paying their respects to the president, Martínez de la Vega, they learned that their ship would not sail for the province of Quito for some time; deciding to spend the intervening time profitably, they unpacked their gear and began to chart the bay of Panama, and to make careful notes about the people, the climate, and the products of the land.[7]

The last stage of the long sea voyage began on February 21, 1736, as the *San Cristóbal* set sail for Guayaquil. A thick fog made observations all but impossible, but it lifted after they reached the Bahía San Mateo in March, and it was possible to map the coast as they proceeded to the south and crossed the equator, entering the Bahía de Manta on March 9, where the vessel would take on water and provisions. The arid condition of the coast convinced La Condamine that this would be an ideal place to begin his observations; accordingly he and Pierre Bouguer decided to remain there, while the rest of the earth-measurers went on to Guayaquil. Unfortunately he was unaware of the *garúa*, that thick, heavy mist that hangs over the desert coast, obscuring the sun until late afternoon and greatly limiting the work that could be done. The *San Cristóbal* weighed anchor as soon as provisioning was completed, and entered the Gulf of Guayaquil on March 17, passed the mouth of the Río Tumbes, near where Pizarro had landed two centuries before, and reached the island of Puná on the 20th. Juan, Ulloa, and the Academicians made careful observations of the coast, depths, and currents, finally going ashore at Guayaquil on March 25 so as to be able to set up equipment for observing the eclipse of the moon due the following night.[8]

Fortunately, a break in the weather made it possible for La Condamine and Bouguer to view this eclipse from the coast, and from their observations they were able to map that portion of the coast with exactitude. Over the objections of Bouguer, who would have preferred going to Guayaquil, La Condamine insisted that they follow the shore north to the equator, where they could make the first of the observations necessary to achieve their objective. The journey north was through an arid coast broken only by occasional patches of green as a mountain stream found its way to the sea; by April they reached savanna country and stood on the westernmost projection of the South American coast. But now how to Quito? La Condamine, undaunted by the poor food and the constant annoyance of insects, wanted to go on farther north to seek the Río Esmeraldas and find a way to Quito from that quarter, Bouguer preferred joining their comrades in Guayaquil. Not until the appearance of Pedro Vicente Maldonado y Sotomayor, a young mathematician, cartographer, and explorer from Quito was the issue resolved: Bouguer would go to Guayaquil with the bulk of the instruments, La Condamine would accompany the Creole, who was much interested in establishing a Quito-Esmeraldas route, north to the river, and thence to Quito.[9]

The rest of the party, meanwhile, awaited La Condamine and Bouguer at Guayaquil, where they made preparations to ascend the cordillera to Quito, since the steamy atmosphere, as they found in trying to observe the eclipse of the moon and the satellites of Jupiter, was not suitable to scientific endeavor. The port lay along the Río Guayas, and was built on spongy land which became almost impassable during the rainy season from December to April or May; the terrible rains at that time, combined with the heat, insects, and other vermin, made life barely tolerable at that time of the year. And there were the fevers of the rainy season; these were treated with some degree of success through the use of *cascarilla* and *quina*. In the dry season the heat mitigated somewhat, and there was an abundance of fruits from which were made the punches of which the inhabitants of Guayaquil were extremely fond. The local diet also included breads, cereals, and meats, and there was an abundance of fish, particularly the *bagre* and the *roblado* (a kind of trout). The number of fish, Juan and Ulloa discovered, was kept down by the alligators, which were also very fond of human flesh. The alligator population was in turn kept down by the turkey buzzard, which was partial to alligator eggs.[10]

With the arrival of Bouguer, plans for the departure could be completed, and the party left Guayaquil aboard a large, flat-bottomed boat for Caracol, which they reached on May 14, and then to the Río Ojibar, the end of the road from the cordillera. All along the way they suffered greatly from mosquitoes day and night; mosquito netting proved to be of little help. Once on the road, the terrain began to change rapidly, and on the 16th they noticed that the air was growing cooler. From here too the going became more difficult; parts of the journey were over "dreadful precipices," with the road becoming extremely narrow. Crossing bridges was a traumatic experience, for "these structures, all of wood, and very long, shake in passing them; besides, their breadth is not above three feet, and without any rail; so that one false step precipitates the mule into the torrent, where it is inevitably lost; accidents, according to the reports of our guides, not uncommon. These bridges, by the rotting of the wood under water, are annually repaired towards winter, the only season when they are used; the rivers during the summer being fordable." [11]

On May 17 they reached Tariguagua; from here the road up the mountain was very steep, narrow, and full of holes which had to be repaired daily, since the rains filled them with slimy mud. The mules were most cautious going up; coming down they put their forefeet together, pulled up their hindfeet as if going to lie down, and slid down, as Ulloa remarked, "with the swiftness of a meteor." [12] Fallen trees were a great obstacle; no one ever removed them, and to pass, it was necessary to cut through the trunk—sometimes a yard in diameter. Not until they reached a narrow pass at Pacara were they out of this difficult country; there they were met by the corregidor, the alcalde, and a Dominican priest, and were entertained by a troop of dancing and singing *cholos* while they rested. Ahead, in the province of Chimbo, was a level, treeless plain with fields of wheat, barley, corn, and other grains. On May 22 their route took them across the desert of Chimborazo, where they suffered from wind and cold; the thermometer stood at the freezing point early the next morning. Passing the chasms around Mount Carguairaso and Mount Chimborazo, the scientists entered the plain of Tiopullo, then, on the 29th, the plain of Turabamba, which led them to Quito, where they arrived at 5 P.M., to receive an enthusiastic welcome from the governor and the president of the audiencia. [13]

While the scientists were making their way from the coast to their destination, La Condamine, with Maldonado as his guide, reached the small village of Esmeraldas, just a half-mile from the Pacific on the river bank, which he would use as a base for exploring and mapping the neighboring area during the ensuing month. On one of these side journeys he became acquainted with rubber, which he fashioned into a protective case for his quadrant. His report, incidentally, first made Europe aware of the possibilities of this product of the forest, and it was he who brought the first pieces of rubber to Europe. Their mapping completed, La Condamine and Maldonado embarked in a pirogue paddled by six zambos from the town; for five days they followed the course of the Río Esmeraldas upstream, mapping the river, collecting plants, and finding a new metal which was not recognized as platinum. Finally, at the confluence with the Río Toachi, they reached the town, deserted at the moment, which Maldonado had founded and enthusiastically named Puerto de Quito. It was then that the inhabitants emerged from the jungle to show themselves; they were the Colorado Indians, of short stature and brilliantly painted wtih red dye, who agreed to assist the explorers on their journey from the port to Quito. For two days these friendly Indians carried La Condamine's equipment through the forest, and then up the tangled lower slopes of the Andes to an elevation of three thousand feet, through continuous rain. There, at Maldonado's settlement of Tambo de la Virgen, these Indians, children of the lowland whom the chill of the altitude was already beginning to affect, were dismissed with gifts from the explorers' stock of supplies.

From this point onward the ascent was more marked; they were above the tropical rain forest now, in the cooler, fog-shrouded uplands, where stunted and twisted vegetation replaced the tall trees of the lowlands, finally reaching the crest of the Andes at twelve thousand feet—surely a difficult ascent for one who had never before been at high altitude! In this country they could get horses, and so they proceeded across the well-cultivated and well-populated plains to the ancient northern capital of the Incas.[14] There, of course, La Condamine shared in the round of visits, entertainment, and welcoming accorded the men who were to measure the earth.

The city of Quito was built on the slope of Mount Pichincha, above the place where the plains of Turubamba and Innu-Quito joined. Like all Spanish cities it had its central plaza, from which four broad streets led out; the rest were crooked and uneven, as might be expected because of the site. Juan and Ulloa notd that one-third of the inhabitants were Indians, one-third mestizos, and the remainder about equally divided between Spaniards and Negroes. There was a preponderance of women, for, as they said, males began to decay after reaching the age of thirty. Theft, drunkenness, and gambling were quite prevalent among the Quiteños. On the whole, the visitors found the climate mild and pleasant, with little variation in temperature throughout the year. Bright sunlight was the rule rather than the exception, although afternoons might bring on "dreadful and amazing tempests of thunder and lightning" which at least served the useful purpose of cleaning the streets. And cleaning they needed, for proper attention to problems of public health was not exactly a virtue in Quito. While there were not the mosquitoes and poisonous snakes of the lowlands, and few fleas, there was a good deal of spotted fever, pleurisy, *mal de valle* or *bicho* (probably gangrene of the rectum, for which the prescribed cure was the insertion of a pessary of gunpowder, guinea pepper, and a peeled lemon), venereal disease (very common; a cure was neglected because the climate checked its malignancy), catarrhs, and an inflammation, unknown in Europe, called simply *peste* (the symptoms were delirium and vomiting blood; one attack provided immunity thereafter).[15]

Scarcely any detail of life in the province of Quito, or any of its geographical features, escaped the attention of Juan and Ulloa. Their account presented a detailed description of the various jurisdictions of the province and its parishes; they investigated its early history and the many exploring expeditions that probed the remote areas far from Quito; they gave detailed accounts of everything that could be of use, from medicinal herbs and trees to the breeding of the *cochineal* insect, valued for its brilliant red dye. They knew of the venomous snakes and insects, and of the use of coca leaves. They discussed at length the lives of the Indians of the province, and their prodigious and licentious drinking bouts—seemingly the only thing to rouse them out of indifference—which lasted for days until all the *chicha* was downed. They told of the mines and of the methods of extracting the precious metals, and of their own belief that copper, tin, and lead would eventually be found. And they wrote of the ancient Indian monuments and ruins in the province, and of the magnificent workmanship in fitting the huge blocks of stone together. Scarcely a question could be asked about the province of Quito which could not be answered from the account of these young Spanish scientists.[16]

But now to the primary objective—the measurement of the earth. The first problem, finding a sufficiently level and large area for establishing base lines, was solved when Maldonado located a suitable place on the plain of Yarqui to the northeast. Thither the scientists departed, to discover on the way how costly their assignment could become when young Couplet died of the fever. The measurement would be accomplished by triangulation, which required mapping of the area and accurate measurement of the base lines; to this end the party divided, with Godin des Odonais and Verguin in the environs of Quito, Morainville and Bouguer to the north of the equator, and the rest of the group at Yarqui. This windswept, semidesert plain, eight thousand feet high, would be a great trial to the earth-measurers, with its fantastic variation between day and night temperatures, but the work must go on. To this was added the constant interference of the new president of the audiencia, José de Araujo y Río, which made it necessary for Juan and Ulloa to go all the way to Lima to secure a directive from the viceroy of Peru, which in effect told the president to mind his own business. This digression was time-consuming, of course, and it was already obvious that since the series of triangles would have to extend 3° from the base line, necessitating climbing mountains and exchanging signals in order to make simultaneous observations, the work was going to take years rather than months and would tax their endurance to the utmost. And death, this time by violence, would rob them of yet another, for the expedition's physician, Dr. Senièrgues, who had become more or less innocently involved (while the scientists were in Cuenca) in a dispute between the Quesada family and Diego de León, who had jilted their daughter Manuela, had found himself in the position in which peacemakers so often find themselves—misunderstood and scorned. One thing led to another, and in the heat of the controversy, in which all of Cuenca felt obliged to take sides, the good doctor was finally killed in the bull ring by an enraged crowd. To add to their troubles, Jussieu's mind snapped when the collection of plants he had so laboriously gathered with the greatest of effort was lost through carelessness.[17]

On September 24, 1740, a letter was delivered to Juan and Ulloa from the Marqués de Villa García, viceroy of Peru, requesting that they come to Lima with all possible speed; Commodore Anson's fleet [18] had appeared in the Pacific, and there was need of their professional knowledge for the defense of Callao. By September 30 they had left Quito for Guayaquil, and proceeded from there to the island of Puná, which they reached on November 3; two days later they arrived by *balsa* at Machala, on the south side of the gulf. Ulloa, injured in a fall, proceeded to Tumbes by canoe, landing at the uninhabited harbor of Salto on the night of November 7; the mosquitoes were a nuisance, and the nearby forest was the haunt of "tigers" [jaguars] "of the fury of which there are many melancholy examples," he related.[19] Two days later he reached Tumbes where he joined Juan who had arrived the previous day by horseback. Going south by way of Piura, they reached Trujillo, an important city located in a fertile oasis along the coast, near a river which provided ample water for irrigation. So hot and brilliant was the sun along the coast that they found it advisable to travel by night most of the way. By December 18 they entered Lima, which they described as "the queen of all the cities of South America." [20]

Again Juan and Ulloa indulged themselves in detailed description. We learn of the size and plan of this City of the Kings, of its wall and fortification, its churches and convents, the University of San Marcos, the hospitals and charitable foundations, the system of government, and the elaborate ceremonies attendant upon the entrance of the viceroy. Here there were nearly eighteen thousand whites, including the most distinguished nobility of Peru. Lima was a city of wealth, of ostentation in all classes, of men well-dressed in the current European style, of graceful, haughty women who were excessively fond of perfumes, who wore flowers in their long, dark hair, and whose short skirts scandalized new arrivals from Spain. Despite its location in the tropical zone, Lima's climate was moderate; summers were not hot, and the cool winters carried a chill at times because of the *garúa*—that heavy mist that hid the sun by day and the stars by night, but provided the verdure that made the city beautiful.[21]

There was, of course, the other side of the coin. For all its attractions, the city suffered from frequent earthquakes; Juan and Ulloa observed four in little more than a month in 1742, all lasting about a minute, and all occurring at half-ebb or half-flood tide. They began with a rumbling noise, about a minute before the shock; dogs howled, beasts of burden halted and spread their legs, and people rushed into the streets, at night often quite naked, shouting, screaming, and praying. The scientists could not accept the current explanation for this phenomenon—that an earthquake was due to the compression of air in the earth's pores and the consequent resistance to this compression. Noting that earthquakes followed the bursting of a new volcano, but not a second eruption, they concluded the cause was the intermixing of sulfurous and nitrous and other combustible substances by the action of subterranean water into a kind of paste, which fermented and exploded in the case of volcanoes, consuming all the sulfurous particles in the mountain. But in the case of earthquakes, the combustible items, present to a lesser degree and compressed, suddenly expanded through subterranean caverns and rent the earth, being unable to find a vent.[22]

For four months the two Spanish officers tarried in Lima, waiting for the attack that never came. Their time was not wasted, for they made use of the opportunity to amass encyclopedic information about Peru as they had about Quito. They wrote of the state of Peruvian agriculture: the fertility of the soil, the irrigation system which went back to Inca times and the abundant springs, the many fruits and vegetables and the superb olive groves which surpassed those of Spain; of the excellent but expensive food—the superb bread, the fine mutton, the excellent beef, the abundant poultry and pork, the great variety of excellent fish; and of the extensive trade carried on by the Limeños with Spain and the Spanish empire in America. They gathered information on the far reaches of the viceroyalty. We learn of the audiencia of Charcas, of Chuquisaca and its famous university, of Potosí and the mines, of lofty La Paz, Lake Titicaca, the Atacama Desert, of Santa Cruz and of Tucumán, of Asunción, Montevideo, and Buenos Aires.[23]

Convinced finally that Anson would not attempt to come around Cape Horn in the winter, Juan and Ulloa sought and obtained permission to return to Quito to continue their original purpose, and departed from Callao in a merchant ship bound for Guayaquil, finally joining their French companions in Quito. The reunion was not as amicable as might have been expected, for while the Spaniards were in Lima, La Condamine had been constructing pyramids at the extremities of the base line, each of which, when completed, was topped by a fleur-de-lis and bore an inscription in classical Latin testifying that the arc had been measured by La Condamine, Bouguer, and Godin. Ulloa was not offended, but Juan felt that the omission of their names and any reference to His Catholic Majesty was belittling to them and to Spain, and he immediately began legal action. Finally, after lengthy litigation, the audiencia handed down its decision on July 19, 1742: the pyramids could remain, subject to confirmation within two years from the Council of the Indies, and the names of Juan and Ulloa were to appear in the inscription, with their rank; furthermore, the fleurs de-lis were to be removed. Unfortunately the council subsequently (September 2, 1747) issued an order for the demolition of the pyramids; Juan and Ulloa had no part in this; rather, they exerted considerable pressure for a countermanding order, but in vain. So ended the pyramid controversy.[24]

By 1743 the last observations were completed, and the arc was finally measured, confirming, as had the Lapland expedition, the Newtonian position. Juan and Ulloa were no longer with the expedition; Commodore Anson had sacked the town of Paita in Peru on November 24, 1741 and on receiving news of this on December 5 the two representatives of the king made preparations to go to Guayaquil, departing December 16. They arrived at the port on December 24, and immediately took energetic measures for its defense, but to little avail; Anson went instead to Acapulco, so the Spanish officers sought leave to return to Quito. Since it was felt best to leave Juan in command at Guayaquil, Ulloa returned to Quito alone, arriving after a most difficult journey on January 19; three days later he had to depart again—the viceroy had ordered him and Juan to set out for Lima immediately, for Anson's squadron had put in at Juan Fernández Island. Before heading out toward Manila to intercept the galleon, and there was the possibility that he might return. Traveling night and day they reached the City of the Kings on February 26 and received their orders: Juan, commanding the frigate *Nuestra Señora de Belén*, and Ulloa, in the frigate *Rosa*, were to sail for Juan Fernández. For one reason or another the voyage was delayed; not until December 4, 1742 did they get under sail, finally reaching the island in the afternoon of January 7. They sailed through thick fogs, winter storms, and brief hurricanes until Ulloa began to question the aptness of the name "Pacific." One unshakable belief of Pacific pilots they found interesting enough to record: namely, a day or two before the north winds began to blow, the *quebrantahueso* birds would appear in numbers around the ships and along the shore—and at no other time; the birds would remain with the ship during the storm and until fair weather returned. The expedition remained at Juan Fernández until January 22—sufficient time for Juan and Ulloa to make a comprehensive report. Since Anson showed no signs of returning, they sailed for Concepción, arriving February 5.[25]

Again, these Spanish scientists took advantage of their stay in Chile to investigate everything and prepare a detailed report, in the manner of Peru and Quito, of the Captaincy-General of Chile. There are detailed descriptions of Concepción and its bay, of Santiago, of the entire area under the jurisdiction of the audiencia of Santiago, of Chilean commerce, and of the Araucanian Indians. After a long delay at Valparaíso, the ships departed on June 24, arriving at Callao on July 6. Since it was midwinter, it was extremely difficult to make observations at sea in the fog common at that time of the year. As soon as possible, Juan and Ulloa betook themselves to Quito, and joined Godin in observing a comet which they felt was the same one seen by Cassini in 1681 and Brahe in 1577.[26] This was their last work together; Juan and Ulloa departed for Callao, whence, having decided to sail separately, they left on October 22, 1744, in two French ships, the *Nôtre Dame de la Délivrance* and the *Lys*. The first of these arrived at Concepción on October 24, but the *Lys*, which had developed a leak, did not appear until January 6. Not wishing to delay in rounding Cape Horn, the captain of the *Délivrance* proceeded on his way, and to avoid the possibility of capture by the British, put in at Fernando de Noronha, made some necessary repairs, and departed on June 10, only to be picked up by British privateers in the Sargasso Sea, who took them to Louisbourg. Ulloa was subsequently taken to England, where he received many courtesies from the Royal Society (including the return of his papers), and was allowed to return to Spain.[27] Juan's voyage, via Montevideo and Puerto Rico, was less eventful; he sailed under convoy to France, where he was made a corresponding member of the Académie des Sciences, and finally joined Ulloa in Madrid.[28] Eleven years had passed since they had departed from Cádiz; they had measured the earth, they had brought back a detailed and lively account of their observations and adventures, and, what was known but to a few, a detailed private report on colonial administration and the treatment of the Indians, intended for the king—the famous *Noticias Secretas*, the contents of which were to be generally unknown until David Barry published in London a Spanish edition with his own preface, in 1826.[29]

Upon the departure of Juan and Ulloa from Quito, the French party of scientists also began to break up. Louis Godin had accepted a position as astronomer at the University of San Marcos in Lima; Jean Godin, who had married the attractive Isabel Grandmaison y Bruno at Guzmán in 1742, indicated that he would return by his own route, as did Bouguer; Hugot had married and settled in Quito, and Morainville was killed in a fall. For La Condamine, the return journey would almost equal what he had seen thus far, for he chose to go back by way of the Amazon, and to make an accurate map of this mighty river. Three possible routes from Quito presented themselves: via the Río Archidona and Río Napo, used by Teixeira and Acuña; via a narrow pass below Mount Tonguragua to Canelos, then via the Río Pastaza to the Marañón, the route preferred by the missionaries; via Jaén at the head of navigation of the Marañón, a difficult route because of almost continual rains, and the dangerous narrow pass of Pongo de Manseriche. It was to see this pass that La Condamine determined upon the latter route.[30]

Starting out on the Cuenca-Loja road, he detoured to Zaruma in order to put it on his map; learning that he was being pursued by some malcontents from Cuenca who wanted to kill him for prosecuting the assassins of Senièrgues, he managed to escape them by fording the swollen Río Los Jubones. La Condamine's journey had begun on May 11, 1743, from Tarqui; by June 3 he had reached Loja. It was not a long journey, but it was an arduous one, involving, as it did, the unsettling business of crossing several rivers over suspension bridges which would invariably begin to sway when the traveler reached midpoint and the wind was blowing; the Indians, he said, ran across laden with the baggage of the swimming mules, and laughed at travelers "who show less resolution than they." While in Loja he learned that the best *quinquina* grew there, and spent a day gathering specimens for the king's gardens in France. From Loja to Jaén the route lay over the lower hills of the cordillera, across many rivers, and through forests where the almost ceaseless rain made his hide-covered baskets "rot and stink intolerably." Finally he reached the "sorry village" of Jaén, located at the confluence of the Marañón and two other rivers; the town's port lay four days' journey ahead on the Río Chuchunga, which enters the Marañón below the falls; thither La Condamine went, crossing the river several times and at one time seeing his instruments and books soaked when his mules swam the river, necessitating drying the books and papers leaf by leaf. During this delay a raft was built for him to carry his baggage; even this was little better, for on July 8 he nearly lost everything when thrown by the current into a whirlpool below the pass of Cumbinama, where he remained for an hour until four Indians managed to throw lianas and pull him out. But the worst was to come.

Before Borja, the capital of the province of Maynas and the center of Spanish mission activity, was the Pongo de Manseriche, a passage through the cordillera with almost vertical walls. While his four Indians went to the town by stairs hewn in the rock, he waited on the raft in a creek opposite the river with a Negro slave; the river dropped with great rapidity during the night, when suddenly a branch of a large submerged tree came between the timbers of the raft. La Condamine managed to get off, with his precious records of eight years' work, just before being left suspended in midair. By noon of July 12 he managed to put off from shore on the salvaged raft and head into the Pongo, which narrowed from 1,500 to 150 feet; several times the craft struck rocks, but resisted the shock, and he did manage to avoid the whirlpool where the year before a missionary had spun around for two days before being rescued, almost dying of hunger.[31]

Below Borja a new world opened before him. The swift, turbulent Marañón had broken through the towering cordillera of the Andes to enter the broad, flat plain which would extend to the Atlantic; behind was a country of jagged rocks, ahead a flat world where the ground was completely covered with herbs and plants, and the Indians did not know of stone. At Borja La Condamine stayed with a Jesuit, Father Magnin, who treated him royally, gave him a map which he had made of the area, and agreed to accompany him as far as Laguna, beyond the mouths of the Pastanza, at the confluence of the Río Huallaga. There he met Pedro Maldonado, who had taken the second route and had waited for him for six weeks; together they would follow the course of the Amazon, and then go on to Europe.

On the morning of July 23 they set out in two large canoes, each three feet wide and about forty-four feet long, made from a single trunk, rowers in the front half, passengers and baggage aft under a roof of woven palm branches, much in the manner of the monsoons which left São P. ilo for the interior. En route La Condamine was preoccupied with the business of map-making—observing the compass, time, the tributaries, islands, breadth of the channel, etc.—a difficult task since they traveled day and night. On July 26 they reached the Río Ucayali, a tributary of such size that La Condamine speculated on which was the main stream. The following day brought them to the country of the Omaguas, who appeared to be descendants of Padre Fritz's converts; these Indians practiced the peculiar custom of squeezing the heads of newborn babes between two boards to make them resemble the full moon. La Condamine noted their use of the seeds of the *curupa* plant (described earlier by Feuilée), which they used to produce a hallucinogenic intoxicant sometimes powdered and inhaled through a Y-shaped reed inserted in the nostrils.[32]

The travelers reached the Río Napo on July 31—just in time to see the emersion of the first of Jupiter's satellites. After carefully checking the emersion of the satellite, La Condamine set about making observations to determine longitude, partly because of Portuguese pretensions even this far up the river, and partly to justify having carried a large telescope more than 150 leagues over rivers and mountains. He took the altitude of two stars to determine time, measured the intervals of observations by "a good watch," and calculated the difference between the meridian of Paris and that of the Napo as four hours and forty-five minutes—surprisingly accurate given the difficulties involved. Ten leagues beyond the Napo was the town of Pebas, whose missions were in a flourishing condition after being restored by the Jesuits of Quito; the area had been considerably depopulated since the day when Father Fritz founded missions in the area, and some languages were used by only a few families, remnants of once strong tribes.

After three days and nights of travel through an almost uninhabited country, La Condamine and Maldonado arrived at the Carmelite mission of São Paulo; they were now in Portuguese territory.[33] This mission was a surprise to them, for they found buildings of brick and stone, and women wearing shifts of British linen and using scissors, knives, mirrors, needles, and combs, all of which gave evidence of a lively trade with Belém, where cacao was exchanged for these items. The Portuguese canoes, they noted too, were considerably larger, up to sixty feet or more in length, with forty rowers and two masts.

Downstream they continued, the great river ever widening as one large tributary after another poured its waters into it—the Yutai, the Yuruca, the Tefé, and the Coari from the south, and the mighty Putamayo and Caquetá (or Içá and Japurá, as the Portuguese called them) from the north. La Condamine, recalling that Acuña and Fritz had referred to gold having been found in this region, believed this to be the origin both of the El Dorado and Lake Parima myths. But there was that other persistent myth—the Amazons. All the Indians told La Condamine the same story, which they had got from their parents, they said. One old Indian said that his grandfather had actually seen and spoken with some Amazons at the mouth of the Río Cuchivara, and knew their names. What is more, many of them had certain green stones which they said they got from the land of the women without husbands. La Condamine believed that most of the Indians were liars or credulous, but he wondered how so many different peoples got the same story, living apart from each other; and then there were the two governors of Venezuela, Diego Portales and Francisco de Torralba, both of whom accepted the story. He did not rule out the possibility that the story was at one time true, and that the women had given up their solitary existence.[34]

On August 20 La Condamine left Coari country, passed the mouth of the Japurá on the north and the Purus on the south, and entered the clear waters of the Rio Negro on August 23, going up several leagues to be sure that the river entered the Amazon from the north-west rather than the north, as Fritz's map showed. While visiting a Portuguese fort and mission, he learned of the connection between the Rio Negro and the Orinoco; this had actually appeared on old maps, but eighteenth-century cartographers believed it to be erroneous and left it out. La Condamine used every available map and account to ascertain the route; he was right about its existence, but his geography was faulty—he did not know that the connection was via the Río Casiquiare. He did make one valuable contribution, however, in laying low another myth—that of Lake Parima and its golden city, Manoa. The fable, he believed, had its origin in the capital of the Manaos Indians, who lived on a large lake, got gold from the Rio Yquiari (described by Fritz) and made plates from it; from this arose the story of golden roofs, an exaggeration which he attributes to "the greediness and prepossession of the Europeans, bent on finding, at any rate, what they were in search of; and, on the other hand, the natural propensity of the Indians to lye and exaggerate (which might be heighten'd by their being concern'd, in point of interest, to remove to a good distance from themselves, such troublesome intruders)." [35] Further discussion with Nicholas Horsman of Hildesheim, whom he was to meet in Belém, and who had also searched for Lake Parima, convinced him that this story, which had driven so many to a vain search, was indeed a fable.

Below the Rio Negro the Amazon changed; La Condamine found it to be a league wide at the least until it reached Fort Pauxis, where it was confined to a relatively narrow strait, little more than a mile across. At this point the tide could be felt, flowing in from the Atlantic at about twelve leagues per hour, creating two currents, one at the surface, and one below. The visitors were accompanied by the commandant half-way to Belém, after being shown every courtesy at the order of a minister interested in science. By September 4 mountains were visible to the north—the first they had seen since Pongo de Manseriche. Local legend placed the present home of the Amazons there, which agreed with stories La Condamine had heard farther up river. Ahead of the party was the mouth of the mighty Xingu, which flowed from the Brazilian mining country; to avoid danger of being swept away in the Amazon by the force of this new current, the explorers left the mainstream and entered the Xingu through a natural channel, re-entering the Amazon with the current. Below this point the river was so wide that it was impossible to see across it even if the absence of islands had permitted it. For some strange reason there were no more mosquitoes on the right bank, although the left bank was infested with them. Not far below the Xingu the Tacipuru branches off the Amazon to the south, around the great island of Marajó ("misrepresented on all the Maps"), becomes known as the Rio Pará, and finally receives the waters of the great Tocantins. The frequent overflow of the river brings many fish to lakes and marshes, which are easily caught when the waters recede; as La Condamine remarked, "Nature seems to have favour'd the general propensity of the Indians to laziness." He also learned of the many inhabitants of the jungle and the river —crocodiles, the "tygers" who gouge out their eyes, bears, monkeys, wild boars, porcupines, vampire bats, amphibious serpents twenty-five to thirty feet long, and the brilliantly colored parrots, the color of whose plummage the Indians were able to change by plucking a feather and rubbing the area with the blood of certain frogs.[36]

The journey was virtually at an end on September 19 when La Condamine and Maldonado arrived at "Grão Pará" (Belém); almost four months had elapsed since they had left Cuenca. Here, in this city "adorned with streets finely laid out, and handsome houses" they were very well received; in order to make several observations they tarried a while; the academician was interested, among other things, in determining whether the latitude of the city was exactly 0°, as the inhabitants stoutly maintained. It was not, but rather 1° 28' south, even farther than Fritz had put it. After a few journeys in the vicinity to improve his map, La Condamine determined to see the real mouth of the Amazon, north of Marajó Island, and then proceed on to Cayenne, returning to France from there rather than taking the Portuguese fleet sailing on December 3, 1743. It was necessary to remain until the end of the month because of an epidemic of smallpox which made it difficult to get Indian rowers, who were very prone to it. Having heard that a Carmelite missionary had inoculated his flock in 1728 and lost not one of them, La Condamine found it strange that no one was using this method in 1743.

On December 29 he embarked in a canoe with twenty-two rowers and a letter to the Franciscans at a mission on Marajó requesting that they provide new oarsmen. The island, he found, was some 150 leagues in circumference and not a group of small islands as generally depicted on maps. On reaching the northwest corner of the island, he crossed the broad Amazon to Macapá, an achievement that would have been almost impossible had not numerous islands provided some measure of safety for canoe traveling. Macapá lay 3' north of the equator, and the country north of it to the source of the Rio Oyapock was open and level, a fact which led La Condamine to conclude ruefully that he might have set out from Cayenne, 5° north, gone south to Macapá, almost on the equator, and measured the arc there rather than at Quito, saving several years. At least, though, he could accomplish one thing at Macapá; he could see the *pororoca*, that extraordinary tide which appeared at the three days nearest to the full and new moon. The sea then rose to a height in a minute or two instead of six hours, and made "a dreadful noise" which could be heard a league or two away; shortly after, "one mae see a liquid promontory, between twelve and fifteen foot in height, advance forewards; this is followed by a second, and that by a third, and sometimes a fourth upon the heels of each other, which takes up the whole breadth of the channel." Great blocks of earth with trees were sometimes carried away, and ships had to be anchored in a great depth of water to be safe. Not until the full moon was several days past would the Indian rowers resume the journey to take the explorers to Cayenne.[37]

Taking advantage of the opportunity to make observations all along the coast, La Condamine did not reach Cayenne until February 26, 1744. After waiting in vain for a French man-of-war for five months, he took advantage of an offer from the Dutch governor at Surinam of passage aboard a Dutch vessel with a safe-conduct pass in the event of war. He departed from Paramaribo on August 28 aboard a merchantman; twice they were attacked, once by a British privateer and once by a French, but finally arrived at Amsterdam on November 30. Two months more elapsed before passports could be arranged; La Condamine finally reached Paris on February 23, 1745, and made his report to the Académie. It was almost ten years since he had departed.[38]

Here we might write an end to the story of the earth-measurers were it not for the extraordinary odyssey of Godin and his wife. Jean Godin des Odonais, it will be remembered, had married the beauteous Isabel de Grandmaison y Bruno, who was thirteen at the time (1742); after the breakup of the expedition, he lingered in Quito, continuing his explorations and observations until 1749, when he decided to return to France, taking Isabel with him. Unwilling to risk her health and safety on the Amazon route, on which he had determined, without first testing it himself, he left Riobamba in March, arriving at Cayenne in July; there he wrote La Condamine of his intent; and also wrote the Minister of Marine, asking his assistance at the Portuguese court in arranging for him to ascend the Amazon and bring his wife and servants back with him. Portuguese officials were unduly suspicious of foreigners, and the request of Godin, who had come down the Amazon, to be permitted to go back up and return again apparently seemed to be too irrational to be believed. At any rate, there were interminable delay, and Godin finally hit upon an idea which might speed things—a letter to Choiseul suggesting how France might possess itself of the entire valley. Finally, in October of 1765, a small Portuguese vessel appeared in Cayenne with orders to take Godin up the Amazon into Spanish territory, despite the disapproval of the Conselho Ultramarino in Lisboa. For one reason or another Godin did not avail himself of the opportunity; it is possible that, having no reply from Choiseul, he believed the Portuguese had intercepted his letter and so this apparent kindness was in reality a ruse. Unable to wait any longer for Godin to make up his mind, the vessel departed, bearing a letter to Doña Isabel informing her that her husband was at Cayenne; the master of the ship was to await her reply and return with it.

Everything seemed to conspire against reunion. The Jesuits, to

Pedro de Valdivia, *conquistador* and governor of Chile, explorer of the Araucanian country. *(Photo courtesy of the Organization of American States)*

Diego de Almagro, associate of Pizarro in the conquest of Peru and first explorer of Chile. *(Photo courtesy of the Organization of American States)*

Francisco Pizarro, explorer of the northwest coast of South America and *conquistador* of Peru. *(Photo courtesy of the Organization of American States)*

Vasco Núñez de Balboa, discoverer of the Pacific Ocean. *(Photo courtesy of the Organization of American States)*

Strait of Magellan. Long-sought passage to Asia, discovered by Ferdinand Magellan. *(Photo courtesy of the Organization of American States)*

Iguaçu Falls, between Brazil and Argentina, discovered by Núñez Cabeza de Vaca on his expedition from Santa Catarina Island to Asunción. *(Photo courtesy of Pan American Airways)*

Sebastian Cabot, explorer of the Río de la Plata and the Paraná. *(Photo courtesy of the Organization of American States)*

Gonzalo Jiménez de Quesada, *conquistador* of the Chibcha kingdom, or the "New Kingdom of Granada." *(Photo courtesy of the Organization of American States)*

James Cook, explorer of the southern extremity of South America and the South Pacific in the eighteenth century. *(Photo courtesy of the Library of Congress)*

Alejandro Malaspina, leader of the Spanish expedition which explored the coasts of South America in the eighteenth century. *(Photo courtesy of Academia Nacional de Ciencias Exactas, Físicas, y Naturales de Buenos Aires)*

Angel Falls, highest waterfall in the world, in the Guiana highlands of eastern Venezuela. *(Photo courtesy of the Embassy of Venezuela)*

Hipólito Ruiz. Together with Pavón and Dombey, he conducted a detailed botanical survey of Peru in the eighteenth century. *(Photo courtesy of the Jardín Botánico de Madrid)*

Charles Darwin, member of the world cruise of H.M.S. *Beagle* and father of the theory of natural selection. *(Photo courtesy of the Library of Congress)*

Alexander von Humboldt, distinguished German scientist and explorer of Venezuela, Colombia, Ecuador, and Peru. *(Photo courtesy of the Organization of American States)*

Thaddeus Haenke, Bohemian botanist and member of the Malaspina expedition; after leaving the expedition, he made a detailed botanical survey of Upper Peru (Bolivia). *(Photo courtesy of Academia Nacional de Ciencias Exactas, Físicas, y Naturales de Buenos Aires)*

Pass of Quindiu in the cordillera of the Andes, Ecuador. Work of Alexander von Humboldt. *(Photo courtesy of the Organization of American States)*

Mt. Aconcagua. Highest mountain in the western hemisphere, in the Argentine Andes. First scaled by Mattiaz Zurbriggen, 1897. *(Photo courtesy of the Organization of American States)*

Lake Nahuel Huapí, in the central Argentine Andes; supposed location of the "Enchanted City of *los Césares.*" *(Photo courtesy of Moore-McCormick Lines)*

Alfred Russel Wallace, distinguished naturalist and explorer (with Bates) of the Amazon valley, nineteenth century. *(Photo courtesy of the Library of Congress)*

Louis Agassiz, American naturalist and member of the Thayer expedition into Brazil, nineteenth century. *(Photo courtesy of the Library of Congress)*

Candido Mariano da Silva Rondon. Noted Brazilian explorer, companion of Theodore Roosevelt in exploring the River of Doubt. *(Photo courtesy of the Organization of American States)*

P. H. Fawcett, explorer of the center of the continent, who lost his life searching for a "lost city" in Brazil. *(Photo from* Lost Trails, Lost Cities *by Percy Harrison Fawcett. Copyright 1953 by Funk & Wagnalls Co. Used with permission of the publisher, Funk & Wagnalls Co., Inc.)*

Cerro Fitz-Roy in the southern Andes, Argentina; the region explored by Steffen. (*Photo courtesy of the Pan American Union*)

whom the letter was to be entrusted at Las Lagunas, were expelled from the Spanish domains, and the letter itself was finally lost before it could be delivered. Its contents were known, however, and Doña Isabel, now almost on the verge of despair after twenty years, decided to make the journey herself, and join her husband in Cayenne. Elaborate preparations were made—perhaps too elaborate, for the party assumed the proportions of a full-scale expedition. In addition to Doña Isabel there were her two brothers, her young nephew, three Frenchmen (one a physician) from the South Sea who asked to go along, a Negro slave and a number of Indians. They were to go first to Canelos, where they could obtain canoes for the remainder of the trip, but this settlement had been wiped out by smallpox, and no canoes were available; they would have to continue with a raft and a dugout canoe. From here on the journey became a nightmare. The Indians deserted. One of the Frenchmen was drowned. The canoe struck a log and overturned with the loss of most of their food, whereupon they decided to pause on the banks of the Pastanza while the physician and the Negro took the canoe to seek help at the next mission. While they awaited rescue, their scanty food supply diminished rapidly, and the remaining Frenchman preyed on the servant women. Finally, after a month; Doña Isabel ordered a raft to be built and the journey continued; scarcely had they resumed their journey when the raft struck a log, and they were barely able to save themselves. Beset by hunger, sickness, and madness, one after another died in rapid succession; only Donã Isabel survived, to wander through the jungle for nine days until finding friendly Indians who took her to a mission. Meanwhile, her slave, Joaquín had returned, come upon the scene of death, and reported that all had perished. The missionaries at Loreto, however, immediately sent word of her safe arrival, and she was able to continue her journey to Cayenne aboard the Portuguese ship, reunited at last with her husband. When they went to Paris in 1773, the story of the earth-measurers was brought to a close; the last of them, after thirty-eight years, had returned home.[39]

When the expedition left France in 1735, no one, of course, could have foreseen or would have ventured to predict the almost incredible adventures and misadventures that would befall it. Nor, did it enter the minds of the sponsors and participants how much it would digress from its original purpose, or how widespread would be the explorations accomplished as a result of a decision to measure a portion of the earth in South America. What had begun as a geophysical expedition became an extensive study of a substantial part of the continent as the members dispersed and continued their investigations in various directions. It produced a detailed survey of one of the loftiest portions of the cordillera by skilled scientists and engineers. It revitalized interest in the Amazon valley, both because of La Condamine's detailed account and because of the poignant odyssey of Doña Isabel. What is more, it provided, to a great degree, the stimulus for the great scientific work of the nineteenth century.

NOTES

1. The primary sources for the expedition are La Condamine's *A Succinct Abridgement of a Voyage Made Within the Inland Parts of South-America* (Paris, 1745), and Antonio de Ulloa and Jorge Juan y Santacilia, *Relación histórica del viage a la América meridional*, 4 vols. (Madrid, 1748), (also published in an English translation by John Adams, *A Voyage to South America*, 2 vols., London, 1806). A good brief summary may be found in Rubén Vargas Ugarte, *Historia del Perú* (Lima, 1956), Vol. III, pp. 208 ff.; a more lengthy popular account, written in a lively style, appears in Victor Von Hagen, *South America Called Them* (New York, 1945), Chaps. I–IX. The best available life of Ulloa is Arthur Whitaker's "Antonio de Ulloa" in the *Hispanic American Historical Review* XV (1935): 155-94.

2. Whitaker, *op. cit.*, pp. 156-57.

3. An account of these observations may be found in Ulloa, *Relación histórica*, Vol. I, pp. 15-26.

4. *Ibid.*, pp. 41-56. The city and the bay are described on pp. 28-39.

5. *Ibid.*, pp. 60-61.

6. *Ibid.*, pp. 114-38.

7. *Ibid.*, pp. 145-70. The entire journey, with a description of Panama, its history and its commerce, comprise Bk. III of Ulloa's account.

8. *Ibid.*, pp. 189-96.

9. Cf. Von Hagen, *op. cit.*, pp. 28-33.

10. Ulloa, *op. cit.*, pp. 216-60.

11. Ulloa, *A Voyage to South America*, Vol. I, pp. 198-99.

12. *Ibid.*, p. 202.

13. *Ibid.*, pp. 199-206.

14. Cf. Von Hagen, *op. cit.*, pp. 32-42. La Condamine arrived June 4; Bouguer, who had taken the longer route, arrived six days later.

15. Ulloa, *Voyage*, Vol. I, pp. 248-81.

16. A complete description of the province appears in Bk. VI of Ulloa's *Voyage*, Vol. I, pp. 294-478.

17. Cf. Von Hagen, *op. cit.*, pp. 46-54.

18. See Chap. IX, p. 156.

19. *Voyage*, Vol. II, p. 5.

20. *Ibid.*, p. 29.

21. *Ibid.*, pp. 29-78 (Bk. VII, Chaps. 3-6).

22. *Ibid.*, pp. 78-94 (Bk. VII, Chap. 7).

23. *Ibid.*, pp. 94-173 (Chaps. 8-15).

24. On the Pyramid Controversy, see Lewis Hanke, "Dos Palabras on Antonio de Ulloa and the *Noticias Secretas,*" *Hispanic American Historical Review* XVI (1936): 481-86, and La Condamine, *A Succinct Abridgement . . .* , pp. 3-4.

25. Ulloa, *Voyage*, Vol. II, pp. 191-233 (Bk. VIII, Chaps. 1-4).

26. *Ibid.*, pp. 218-94 (Bk. VIII, Chaps. 5-11).

27. Ulloa's return voyage is described in *Voyage*, Vol. II, pp. 298-328, 336-56, 374 ff. (Bk. IX, Chaps. 1-2, 4-5, 7-9).

28. For Juan's return voyage, see Ulloa, *Voyage*, pp. 357-73 (Bk. IX, Chap. 6).

29. Lewis Hanke suggests that whatever Barry's motives may have been in publishing the work, it "is entirely possible that the publisher, at least, realized that Ulloa's revelations would have a sale in Spanish America" (*op. cit.*, p. 570). Arthur

P. Whitaker ("Jorge Juan and Antonio de Ulloa's Prologue to their Secret Report of 1749 on Peru," *Hispanic American Historical Review* XVIII [1938]; 506) points out that in suppressing Juan and Ulloa's preface and writing his own, "Barry was at best partly responsible for some of the rather serious misunderstandings that have grown up on the report and his own published version of it."

30. La Condamine, *A Succinct Abridgement* . . . , pp. 9-10.

31. For the first part of the journey, see La Condamine, *op. cit.*, pp. 10-23.

32. La Condamine, *op. cit.*, pp. 24-40

33. This was a temporary overextension of Portuguese authority; San Pablo de Loreto lies today well within Peruvian territory.

34. One feature of the story La Condamine could not accept and viewed as a European addition—the cutting off of the right breast. The cacique who warned him about them did not mention it, and a Coari Indian who claimed to have seen an Amazon nursing a baby would surely have noticed such a deformity, yet he made no mention of it. *Succinct Abridgement*, pp. 54-56.

35. *Ibid.*, p. 65. Again, we have some faulty geography but a correct conclusion.

36. For this part of the journey see *ibid.*, pp. 67-88.

37. *Ibid.*, pp. 93-98.

38. For this conclusion of the voyage, see *ibid.*, pp. 100-08.

39. For an absorbing account of the voyage of the Godins, see Von Hagen, *op. cit.*, pp. 70-81. A briefer account may be found in João Lucio d'Azevedo, *Os jesuitas no Grão-Pará*, 2nd ed. rev. (Coimbra, 1930), pp. 272-73.

XII Eighteenth-Century
Maritime Scientific Exploration

Maritime expeditions to the southern part of the South American continent hitherto discussed were, as we have seen, primarily of an exploratory nature, or were part of a freebooting enterprise or a voyage around the world. A number of eighteenth-century expeditions, however, might be properly termed scientific in the sense that they were specifically organized for the advancement of science and were equipped to that end.

The first truly scientific expedition to South America in that century was that of Père Louis Feuillée from 1707 to 1711. Born into a poor Provençal family in 1660, Feuillée joined the Order of the Minimes in 1680, where he was well educated in astronomy, natural history, and physics, for which he seemed to have a natural inclination. After a voyage to the Orient in 1700, Père Feuillée visited the new world from February of 1703 to June of 1706; his activities were confined to the Caribbean area, particularly Martinique. On his return to France he conceived the idea of a voyage to the coasts of South America; his purpose was to determine the coasts of Peru and Chile and thus ascertain the exact position of the continent.[1]

In preparation for his expedition, Feuillée set about procuring the finest instruments available for making observations in the fields of astronomy, meteorology, and natural history; among them was a hydrometer of his own invention. His plan of observations was worked out in conjunction with scientists from the Académie. After preparations were complete, the expedition sailed from Marseille on December 14, 1707.

After long delays in the islands en route, and in the Río de la Plata, Feuillée rounded Cape Horn at the end of 1708 and arrived at Concepción in Chile on January 20. There he remained a month, making numerous observations which enabled him to fix quite accurately the geographical location of the city, chart the southern skies, and gather a good collection of plants and animals. On February 21 he set sail for Valparaíso, where he remained twenty-eight days. The fruits of this visit were similar: he continued his astronomical and geographical observations, surveyed the bay, and prepared a view of the port and its fortifications. Subsequently his work took him to the coast of Peru and to the City of the Kings itself, where he was to hold a lucrative position. Early in 1711 he undertook the return trip to Europe, tarrying a while in Concepción, and returned to Brest on August 27 of the same year.[2]

Pére Feuillée wrote a lengthy account of his voyage in his *Journal des observations physiques, mathématiques et botaniques, faites par l'ordre du Roi sur les côtes orientales de l'Amérique Méridionale, et dans les Indes Occidentales, depuis l'année 1707 jusqu'à en 1712.*[3] For those curious about the events of the journey itself, this monumental work is something of a disappointment, for it is almost strictly a scientific account of observations of latitude and longitude, celestial observations, soundings, and descriptions and plans of cities. It is in the realm of natural history, however (if we except the elaborate descriptions of the flora at the end of the work), that the account may occasionally delight the casual reader. For Pére Feuillée was a careful observer and had a flair for finding the unusual. He describes, for example, an odd monstrous beast born in Buenos Aires on August 27, 1708; it had a single large eye, with a horn above it, ears resembling those of a horse on the side of its head, a human mouth, and a body like a cow.[4] And there is the account of a two-headed child with four arms seen in Lima in December of 1709.[5] In each case, Feuillée provided drawings to illustrate his description; these and the many other engravings of a less bizarre nature make the work extremely valuable.

War, perhaps more than anything else, discouraged any maritime expeditions of a scientific nature for several decades; not until the Treaty of Paris (1763) terminated the long series of great European wars and their colonial counterparts do we find any such enterprise undertaken again. In 1768 the Royal Society in London selected Captain James Cook to observe that rather rare astronomical event, a transit of Venus; he was further entrusted with the task of finding the southern continent, which thus far had eluded all who had sought it. A Yorkshireman, Cook had gone to sea as a young man, rose rapidly, and would have been in command of a collier had he not volunteered to serve in the Royal Navy. His service in the campaign against the

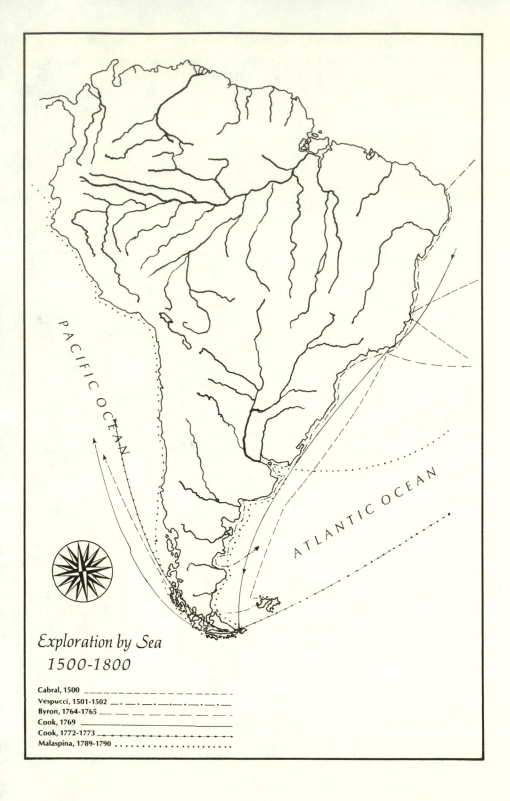

PACIFIC OCEAN

ATLANTIC OCEAN

Exploration by Sea
1500-1800

Cabral, 1500 — — — — — —
Vespucci, 1501-1502 — · — · — · — · — ·
Byron, 1764-1765 — — — — — —
Cook, 1769 ————————
Cook, 1772-1773 · · · · · · · · · · · ·
Malaspina, 1789-1790 · · · · · · · · · · · · · · ·

French in Canada and his work in surveying the eastern coasts of that country brought him to the attention of the Royal Society, and led to his selection for its important commission.

Cook chose his own ship for the voyage, a collier of 366 tons, named H.M. Barque *Endeavour* when purchased for the Royal Navy; J. Holland Rose opined that no better vessel had ever been selected for such a venture.[6] An excellent crew was chosen, and Cook had aboard as scientists two astronomers and the distinguished botanist, Joseph Banks. Preparations were thorough, and to combat the dread scurvy such antiscorbutics as lemons, oranges, raisins, and sauerkraut were taken on at London.[7] The *Endeavour* took on bread, beer, and water at Plymouth, and departed from that port on Friday, August 26, sailing to the South Atlantic via Madeira, and the Canaries, reaching the coast of Brazil on Tuesday, November 8. Six days later Cook anchored at Rio de Janeiro, where he took on beef and vegetables, rum and water.[8] On Thursday, December 8, the vessel weighed anchor and set sail for the southern extremity of the continent. Cook reports that at 38° 37′ south and 52° 5′ west the crew got drunk celebrating Christmas.[9]

Tierra del Fuego was sighted on Wednesday, January 11, 1769; the *Endeavour* continued southward toward the Strait of Le Maire, encountering squalls, hail, rain, and high tides. On Monday, January 16, the ship anchored in the Bay of Success and Cook took a party ashore, where they encountered some thirty or forty Fuegan Indians, who showed no fear of them. His description of them is worthy of repetition: "They are something above the Middle size of a dark copper Colour with long black hair, they paint their bodies in Streakes mostly Red and Black, their cloathing consists wholy of a Guanacoes skin or that of a Seal, in the same form as it came from the Animals back, the Women wear a piece of skin over their privey parts but the Men observe no such decency." His account of their manner of living brings to mind other contemporary descriptions: "Their Hutts are made like a beehive and open on one side where they have their fire, they are made of small Sticks and cover'd with branches of trees, long grass and cᵃ in such a manner that they are neither proff against wind, Hail, rain or snow, a sufficient proff that these People must be a very hardy race; they live chiefly on shell fish such as Muscles which they gather from the rocks along the seashore."[10] They were, he also observed, very fond of anything red.

Tragedy struck the expedition on Thursday, January 17; Banks reported the death of two Negro servants. It seems that they had advanced too far into the interior, halted, made a fire and, since they were in charge of the liquor, "made too free with it and stupified themselves to that degree that they either could or would not travel but laid themselves down in a place where there was not the last thing to shelter them from the inclemency of the night . . . ," and were found dead in the morning.[11]

On January 25, once again on their course, the crew excitedly reported sighting Cape Horn; in actuality it was the False Cape—the tip of the Hardy peninsula at the extremity of Isla Hoste. Cook sighted the true cape later; according to his account "It appeared not unlike an Island with a very high round hummock upon it."[12] Yet he could not be sure, for he was unable to determine with certainty whether it was an island or not; the latitude seemed proper, and his doubts were resolved when he rounded the cape on the following day and entered the Pacific Ocean. Cook had never been in the Strait of Magellan, but he remarked that from what he heard of it, he would much prefer the route around the cape.[13]

As the *Endeavour* entered the Pacific and swung to a northwesterly course, it sailed out of our field of study. Cook would accomplish his scientific purpose, for he observed the transit of Venus from Tahiti, and he would accomplish part of his other purpose—discovery —for he found an island group which he named the Society Islands for his sponsor. But the supposed great southern continent eluded him, although he would find New Zealand and Australia, spending months in exploring them, nearly losing the *Endeavour* when it struck a coral reef. Not until July of 1771 would he return to England, sailing by way of the Cape of Good Hope, to make his report.

The experience of the first voyage led Cook to state to the Admiralty his conviction that the best route for exploring the Pacific would be via the Cape of Good Hope to Australia and New Zealand. Acting on this advice, the Admiralty gave him in 1772 two ships, the *Resolution* and the *Adventure*, and directed him again to search for the southern continent. Sailing south from the Cape of Good Hope in the *Resolution*, Cook became the first to cross the Antarctic Circle, but he found no southern continent, nor was he able to find it by sailing close to 60° south to the longitude of New Zealand, where he put in to rest his crew. Sailing eastward and then far into the South Pacific he reached a latitude of 71° 10' south, navigated through an ice field, and returned again to Queen Charlotte Sound in New Zealand for a rest, convinced now that a large, temperate southern continent did not exist.

Yet he made one last attempt to be certain of his conclusion. Making what he believed to be the first Pacific crossing in the high latitudes of the south (he did not know that the *Adventure* had preceded him), he reached Cape Deseado on December 17 after passing through three days of stormy weather. The next day, sailing south by east, he passed Cape Noir, and on December 19, near an island he called Gilbert Isle, he passed another point of land he named Cape Desolation, for, as he said, "I have before observed that this is the most desolate coast I ever saw. It seems entirely composed of rocky mountains without the least appearance of vegetation. These mountains terminate in horrible precipices, whose craggy summits spire up to a vast height, so that hardly any thing in nature can appear with a more barren and savage aspect than the whole of this country." [14]

More barren, rocky isles appeared ahead. Desirous of taking on water, Cook searched for a harbor, finally locating an excellent one on what he believed to be the mainland of Tierra del Fuego, which he named "Devil's Bason." [15] One of the party, reconnoitering, discovered some terns' eggs and organized a hunting expedition which bagged fourteen "geese". Attracted by the sound of the shooting, Indians appeared in nine canoes—apparently the Pecheras of whom Bougainville had written. Cook was appalled by their destitute condition: "They are a little, ugly, half-starved, beardless race. I saw not a tall person among them. They are almost naked; their clothing was a seal-skin; some had two or three sewed together, so as to make a cloak which reached to the knees; but the most of them had only one skin, hardly enough to cover their shoulders, and all their lower parts were quite naked. The women, I was told, cover their nakedness with the flap of a seal-skin, but in other respects are clothed like the men." [16]

The Indians did not share in their visitors' Christmas dinner of "roast and boiled geese, goose-pye, etc." and Madeira wine; as Cook relates, "Indeed I believe no one invited them, and for good reasons; for their dirty persons, and the stench they carried about them, were enough to spoil the appetite of any European; and that would have been a real disappointment, as we had not experienced such fare for some time." But apparently the Christmas spirit welled up in them, for before departing on December 27, Cook and his men gave the Indians "some baize and old canvas to cover themselves." [17]

On the following day the *Resolution* sailed past the Ildefonso Isles, and sighted False Cape Horn. Later the vessel rounded Cape Horn itself; "it is known, at a distance," Cook reminds us, "by a high round hill over it." [18] Sailing on through the Strait of Le Maire, Cook tarried at Staten Island before setting a course across the South Atlantic for the Cape of Good Hope, returning to England in 1775.

By far the most comprehensive scientific survey of the coasts of South America was that undertaken by the Malaspina expedition from 1789 to 1794. Alessandro (or Alejandro, as he would be known to history) Malaspina was a Lombard noble who had entered the service of Spain as a young man, rose rapidly, and eventually commanded the frigate *Astrea* on its voyage around the world. Encouraged by this venture, and aware of the work of Cook and La Pérouse,[19] Malaspina, now commandant of Marines at Cádiz, conceived a new voyage which would follow up their work as well as visit and explore the coasts of the Spanish domains in America. The purpose of the expedition was to be twofold: to make hydrographic charts "for the most remote regions of America" and sea charts to guide the navigator, and to make observations concerning the political state of America relative to Spain and the other nations, the ease or difficulty of resisting possible foreign invasions, and the state and potentialities of commerce. He proposed to divide his investigations into two categories: (1) scientific, which would be published, and (2) secret information, which would include his political and economic assessment of the Spanish empire and, if the government desired it, information on the Russian establishments in California and the British in Botany Bay. He felt that the Royal Navy could furnish the personnel (except for two botanists and two drafts-men). The ships should combine safety, comfort, and economy, and each should have a complement of one hundred armed men.

The project, he said, would take three years, and he proposed that it should begin on July 1, 1789. This would allow eight months for preparations and time for preliminary studies, especially in practical astronomy. After departing from Cádiz, the ships would sail to Montevideo, then to the Malvinas, the Bahía del Buen Suceso in the Strait of Le Maire, around Cape Horn, and to Chiloé by the end of the year. He planned to spend the entire year 1790 on the Pacific coast, as far as Acapulco, then to Hawaii, the California coast, along the Alaskan coast and Kamchatka to Canton. The following year would be spent in the Philippines, the Marianas, Botany Bay in Australia, and New Zealand, then back to Spain via the Cape of Good Hope. In a letter of October 14, 1788, Minister of Marine Antonio Valdés, who was an enthusiastic supporter of the plan, informed Malaspina that the king had approved the project, that he was being relieved of his command in order to begin preparations, and that whatever was needed would be provided "to your entire satisfaction." [20]

Upon receiving Malaspina's request for ships, Valdés informed him that he could have the bomb ketch *Santa Rosa de Lima* and another ship to be constructed.[21] But upon receiving Malaspina's objections to a rehabilitated bomb ketch, the minister reassured him that His Majesty would not deny him anything necessary to the success of the expedition, and had authorized the construction of another corvette, according to his specifications.[22] Meanwhile, Malaspina outlined his plans to Antonio de Ulloa, now Lieutenant-General of the Fleet, indicating that he intended to chart as accurately as possible certain areas of the coast and the location of certain harbors and islands, especially the Malvinas. Relying on Ulloa's "vast knowledge" and "true love of solid progress in the sciences," he sought his advice on such diverse matters as icebergs, whaling possibilities in Patagonia, the best instruments for measuring water temperatures, studying the Patagonians, and on-shore reconnaissance.[23] In a second letter [24] he inquired as to the best items to use in trading with the Indians at Chiloé, the best time of the year to sail along the coast of Peru, how to avoid delays by being becalmed, whether the level of the Pacific Ocean was higher than that of the Atlantic, and whether it was worth while to seek the Northwest Passage through the Strait of Juan de Fuca—a project about which Malaspina had grave doubts.

In the selection of crews, Malaspina was given complete freedom —even to the selection of chaplains and surgeons.[25] From the letters written by Malaspina to José Salvaresa, royal physician to the fleet, we can form some estimation of the thoroughness with which he planned the expedition. There was much attention to the water supply and its renovation in the hold. The crew and some of the officers who had greater robustness and endurance, were selected from the northern, mountainous provinces. There were detailed specifications concerning the living quarters in the corvettes under construction, and a suggestion that vinegar could be used to eliminate foul air between the decks. Food consisted of four principal items—bread, soup, salted meat, and bacon—along with oil, vinegar, and wine. The bread, he insisted, must be made of good wheat, and the vegetables should include anti-scorbutics and must be the type which would dry but little aboard—rice, *garbanzos* (chick-peas), beans and lentils. He wondered whether he should take *gazpacho* (an Andalusian salad soup), and what its effect would be on northern sailors; should he insist that they eat it whether they liked it or not? Was a half-pint of wine enough? And what time of day should they drink it? [26]

Malaspina was particularly concerned about the problem of sickness at sea; assuming that the sailor was ordinarily healthy, he felt that sickness could be attributed to three causes alone: the quality of the food, the quality of the air, and rapid changes of temperature. Quite well informed concerning symptoms, curative remedies, and ways to prevent epidemics, Malaspina offered for comment some ideas of his own on the treatment of illness; the patient should immediately be given sauerkraut and malt, sudorifics with plenty of sugar, and oxygenated water, and he should be denied salt meat and given instead soups, broth tablets, or meat preserved in oil. [27] He inquired whether eating dried meat would lead to scurvy, and whether vegetables would be better preserved in oil or brine. He indicated that he favored much use of coffee and tea, since sugar is an antiscorbutic, and heat is good for the digestion, but he opposed the use of spices or fats, believing that pork lard was particularly harmful.[28] Malaspina remarked later on that he had followed Cook's policies with respect to health at sea, modifying his rules to suit the climate and conditions. With the exception of a few casks which spoiled because of lack of salt or introduction of air, the sauerkraut had lasted two years; weevils got into the bread and dried soup, but the flour was saved from them, especially that from Philadelphia, which, he said, maintained its excellent quality for two years. There was an abundant supply of orange and lemon juice, which Cook had found so important in preventing the dreaded scurvy.[29]

No detail escaped Malaspina's attention. In a letter to Captain Fermín de Sesma, sub-inspector of Arsenals at Cádiz, he made suggestions concerning rigging, cordage, masts, anchors, buoys, hawsers, cables, pulley blocks, sails, boatswain's and pilot's equipment, tools, and the duties of carpenters and calkers.[30] The question of discipline aboard concerned him: in a letter to his second in command, Don José Bustamente y Guerra, he indicated that he did not favor military discipline on a scientific expedition but, rather, the rule of reason. Captains, he felt, should be an example to their men if they were to preserve the "solidity of the structure" in the face of the "series of hardships and dangers" that would confront them. The great detail evident in Bustamente's instructions demonstrates even further the care with which Malaspina planned his expedition, for no detail, no matter how seemingly insignificant, was overlooked.[31]

Meanwhile, construction of the two corvettes, to be named the *Descubierta* and the *Atrevida*, proceeded satisfactorily in the arsenal of La Carraca in Cádiz, under Malaspina's careful supervision, and were finally deemed safe for the purposes of the voyage in tests undertaken in the presence of Ulloa. Preparations were completed by July of 1789, and the officers, crews, and passengers began to board the ships; 102 men were assigned to each vessel, with Malaspina commanding the *Descubierta* and Bustamente the *Atrevida*. Several specialists were to accompany the expedition; there were Lieutenant Colonel Antonio Pineda, a geologist to be in charge of natural history, the painters José del Pozo, José Guío and Eduardo Brambilla (the latter would join at Acapulco), and the botanists Louis Née and Thaddeus Peregrinus Haenke (who was also a violin virtuoso). Haenke missed the departure and had to proceed to Buenos Aires on a merchant vessel, joining the expedition there.

The *Descubierta* and the *Atrevida* departed from Cádiz on July 30 and reached Tenerife in the Canaries on August 3, where Malaspina determined its longitude by use of a chronometer and found Captain Cook's calculations to be erroneous. At this point four stowaways were found in the *Descubierta* and two in the *Atrevida*, despite all the precautions that had been taken to prevent such an occurrence. Resuming their course, the ships headed toward the equator, narrowly missing a hurricane in the vicinity of the Cape Verde Islands. On August 9 they met a British slaver, the *Philips Stevens*, and encountered more bad weather shortly afterward, which eventually ended as they approached the equator. On August 17 the two ships came together for reciprocal visits of the crews and a check of the chronometers; it was learned that on opening the storerooms, they had found the ship's biscuit infested with caterpillars. Antonio Pineda made detailed observations, even using a microscope, and concluded that the bread must have contained the eggs before being taken on board, and that heat had caused them to hatch. He pointed out that the biscuits were not toxic, but Malaspina pointed out that it was difficult to overcome one's natural repugnance to eating such bread.[32]

After crossing the equator on August 29, the vessels ran into strong winds which damaged the topmast of each. Better weather prevailed as they continued south, but after crossing the Tropic of Capricorn on September 10 they encountered severe storms, and then fog on September 18, with frequent flashes of lightning during the night. Under these somewhat inauspicious circumstances the expedition put into Montevideo on September 20, there to begin a two-month survey of the Río de la Plata. At first Malaspina had planned a survey to last only a few days, but a glance at the magnitude of his task led him almost to despair of accomplishing it. He did not want to start what he could not finish, nor did he wish to sacrifice time allotted for exploring and surveying the coasts of Patagonia and Tierra del Fuego. But it would be necessary to provision the ships and make some replacements in the crew; the complement of officers was intelligent and eager to participate, they had ample astronomical and geodesic instruments, and there was an observatory in Montevideo. Consequently, why not alter the schedule? It was quickly decided to explore the estuary from its broadest extension; Bustamente and others would take a *sumaca* (a small schooner for river use) to Buenos Aires and, with assistance from the viceroy, begin a survey from the capital to Cape San Antonio, while others under him would explore the northern coast to Maldonado, returning to Montevideo and then proceeding on to Colonia. Since weather did not permit sailing for Buenos Aires until September 28, a local botanical expedition consisting of Felipe Bausá, Pineda, and Née searched the reaches of Montevideo, finding an abundance of plants not well known.[33]

Bustamente and his group proceeded to Colonia by land, then took the mail ship to Buenos Aires, arriving on September 29 to meet the *sumaca*. Aided by the viceroy, the Marqués de Loreto, he began a series of observations, first determining latitude and setting up a base line on which a system of triangulation could be worked out. This survey, which was quite accurate, continued until October 12. Meanwhile another party surveyed the northern coast as far as Cape Santa María, assisted by

Frigate Captain Santiago Liniers (who would later distinguish himself in the defense of Buenos Aires against the British), and surveyed and fathomed the port. After October 13 the explorers met at Colonia, planning to survey the coast to the west, but found that the road turned inland, making this extremely difficult and time-consuming. Consequently the project was abandoned, and Malaspina contented himself with checking chronometers and sending out local botanizing expeditions, which collected some important specimens.[34]

By October 31 the various groups had returned, and Malaspina made preparations for continuing his voyage. The officers and crew were paid; the ungovernable, the sick, and the deserters were replaced, and three days leave was given to all who wanted it. Meanwhile, there were unusual opportunities for scientific observations—a partial eclipse of the moon, a good view of the largest satellite of Jupiter, and a transit of Mercury (unfortunately partially obscured by clouds). Difficulties beset departure plans. Winds were unfavorable. There were more desertions. Efforts to get voluntary replacements failed, and since the *Atrevida* scarcely completed its complement and the *Descubierta* was four short, they made a levy of vagrants. It was decided to sail on November 13, but Malaspina was advised that the omens in the southwest sky were unusually bad; no sooner had he countermanded his sailing orders than a storm came up of such force as to be a veritable hurricane. The next day was fair, and the ships sailed at dawn.[35]

Malaspina wanted to take advantage of the summer months and the latest advances in astronomy and physics to perfect the work of his predecessors. Consequently, as he progressed farther to the south, he lined up the corvettes and a brigantine equidistant apart, continually taking soundings and making observations. But the brigantine was sluggish and slowed them up considerably, so it was finally left behind. Shortly afterward there was a sudden shift of wind, the temperature and atmospheric pressure dropped, and they were buffeted by a severe storm for the better part of a day. By November 21 the storm abated and they could resume their course, sailing south along a barren coast, devoid of people, without tree or shrub, until they arrived at the Gulf of San Matías. For two days they explored the gulf and the so-called "Bahía sin Fondo" ("Bottomless Bay") along the San José (or Valdés) Peninsula; soundings showed a depth of seventy fathoms. The morning of November 26 was beautiful. The sea was calm; there were many whales and seals to be seen, and numerous aquatic birds of many species flew around the ships. So clear was the air that even small objects on shore could be easily seen; brilliant sunshine made possible exact astronomical observations. By the afternoon of November 30 they reached Puerto San Gregorio, passed through the channel between Isla Rasa and the Isla Leones into the Gulf of San Jorge. Malaspina was surprised at the extreme indentation of this gulf—a fact apparently unknown to either Anson or Byron. Since the coast was arid and stony, and there were many reefs, the expedition wasted no more time exploring it, but sailed south, past Cape Blanco (which marked the southern limit of the gulf) to Puerto Deseado, where a stone in the shape of a tower marked the somewhat difficult entrance to the port.[36]

As they approached the entrance, they were surprised to see the brigantine *Carmen* coming out to meet them; although it had been left behind, it was subsequently aided by favorable weather, and Captain de la Peña had made directly for the port. He recommended entering the port when the tide stopped, since it flowed with great force; by the next night both corvettes had managed to slip in. On December 3 a party went ashore with trinkets for trading, and soon met a Patagonian on horseback, to whom they offered a few items. On seeing this, the rest of the tribe, which was nearby, gathered quickly—some forty in all; of great interest is Malaspina's statement that "in general all, including women and children, were of gigantic stature." [37] In case we may tend to doubt this assertion in view of Bougainville's work two decades earlier, it must be understood that Antonio Pineda, a scientist whose honesty cannot be doubted, measured the "giants" and found them to be six feet ten inches in height. This is a far cry from the exaggerated proportions given by Byron, but they certainly measured considerably taller than those whom Bougainville had seen. Since we find no subsequent reports of "giants," it seems safe to assume that Malaspina simply came upon a few unusually tall Patagonians. The Spaniards managed to communicate with the Indians through signs and a few words, for the women were unusually adept at learning; Malaspina quickly won their confidence by dismissing an armed guard at their request and by inviting them aboard ship.

Meanwhile, there were the demands of science. While part of the crew busied themselves with hunting, fishing, and taking on water, the scientists made many astronomical and hydrographic observations and collected a variety of specimens of flora and fauna. A delay occasioned by a lost anchor, which was subsequently retrieved after considerable searching, provided the director of maps and plans, Felipe Bausá, with an opportunity of mapping the port and the subaltern of the *Atrevide*, Dionisio Galiano, with a chance to build a temporary observatory to determine longitude astronomically. Meanwhile the Indians returned for a visit after four days; the Spaniards continued their attempts at communication, managing to learn a little of the Indians' language and something of their religion and customs. Before their departure, Malaspina gave them considerable quantities of food to take back to the tribe. This presented something of a problem in transportation, for about the only material available for sacks was their clothing, a circumstance which provided an interesting anecdote concerning the modesty of Patagonian women. It seems that a young girl of fourteen, who had sat as a model for Malaspina's artists, had been particularly favored with gifts, which she intended to take back to her parents. Since the skin she wore was not big enough to contain all the gifts, she sought the advice of the others, who suggested that the larger shirtwaist she wore under the skin would be adequate. But this would necessitate stripping in the presence of the Spaniards; as Malaspina delicately put it, "in the struggle of modesty versus the advice of others, filial love won out, but she took off her shirt-waist with such skill and modesty that it gave great credit to her and to her sex in general." [38]

With the work in the port completed, Malaspina directed the brigantine to sail along the coast to explore the Santa Cruz and Gallegos rivers, while he set the corvettes on a course directly to the Malvinas, departing on the morning of December 14. Four days later they reached Port Egmont, and Malaspina found, as Byron had said, that a ship could anchor close to shore in twelve to twenty fathoms of water, protected from the wind. While the ships took on water, there was much else to do: the naturalists sought out the flora and fauna and climbed Mount La Virgía; an observatory was established to make observations of the sun and check the chronometers; and wild celery, which seemed to abound in the islands, was taken aboard to maintain the health of the crew. As a morale-booster Malaspina gave the crew shore leave on December 20, much to his regret; it seems that they "gave way to their natural instincts for disorder and destruction" and managed to set fire to some mounds of peat, creating a conflagration with which the fire-fighting equipment on the *Descubierta* could not cope; a column of smoke arose so dense that one ship was not visible from the other. Frustrated by the smoke and other difficulties which prevented accurate observations at sea despite excellent instruments, exact methods, and rigorous calculations, Malaspina decided to abandon further attempts in the Malvinas and head back for the mainland. [39]

The corvettes reached the Patagonian coast on Christmas day. Joining two packetboats, the *Eulalia* and the *Casilda*, they sailed south past Cape Virgenes on December 28 to the coast of Tierra del Fuego at Cape Espíritu Santo, making good use of Sarmiento's account of his voyage in these waters. Malaspina discovered that the coast of the island inclined more to the east than Cook's map indicated, and that the Nodal brothers had charted the area with a greater degree of accuracy. Bad weather caused a cessation of scientific activity, but by December 30 it was clear and pleasant so they continued to explore the coast, which was covered with abundant green vegetation against a backdrop of snow-topped mountains. Malaspina was anxious to determine exactly the longitude of Cape Horn, since Cook believed that he had possibly erred as much as one-quarter of a degree. Believing that the error would manifest itself at Cape Santa Inés on the island, if error there were, Malaspina carefully determined its latitude using chronometer 61, which he believed most accurate, and discovered that the Englishman had erred by placing the Cape 21′ too far to the west. His mapping of the coast of Staten Island, however, was found to be exact. Heavy seas forced a suspension of charting on December 31, but New Year's Day, 1790, was clear, the sea was calm, and the rounding of Cape Horn proved to be one of the most pleasant events of the voyage.[40]

After a pleasant meeting with a commercial frigate of Cádiz, the *Santa María Magdalena*, the corvettes pursued a westerly, northwesterly course into the Pacific Ocean, reaching the island of Chiloé on February 8. There they remained for eight days, subsequently making observations along the coast of Chile, stopping at Concepción, Valparaíso, Coquimbo, and Arica, arriving at Callao on May 20. To avoid demoralization of the crew, Malaspina arranged an extended shore leave for them, while the botanists Née and Haenke took advantage of the opportunity to seek new specimens in the vicinity. On September 2 the corvettes set sail for Guayaquil, carefully surveying the coast en route, eventually proceeding to Acapulco where Malaspina received orders to investigate the supposed discovery farther north of the "northwest passage" by Captain Ferrer Maldonado in 1588. A voyage as far as the Bering Sea revealed no passage, so the expedition returned to Acapulco, sailing from there on an extended voyage to the Philippines and the Marianas.[41]

Not until July 31, 1793, did the expedition return to Callao, where it was to lose several distinguished members. Because of susceptibility to asthma, Felipe Bausá and the hydrographer, Lieutenant José Espinosa were forbidden by the surgeons to make the return trip around Cape Horn; instead, they proceeded overland via Valparaíso and Santiago to Buenos Aires embarking there on a merchant vessel for Cádiz. Because there was so little botanical information on the interior of the continent, Haenke, with the approval of the viceroy, was sent to Buenos Aires via Huancavelica, Cuzco, and Potosí with instructions to collect botanical and zoological specimens; Jerónimo Arcángel was to accompany him as a taxidermist. Louis Née left the expedition at Concepción and botanized in the vicinity of Santiago and along the cordillera, finally proceeding to Buenos Aires.[42]

At the end of August a courier from Buenos Aires brought the "disagreeable news of the declaration of war" against the French republic; all commanders and governors were instructed to treat British vessels as allies. Malaspina's ships were poorly armed, a circumstance which augured ill for the success of his expedition, but it seemed very unlikely that, given the preponderance of allied sea power, the French would venture into the Pacific Ocean. The expedition divided at this point; the *Atrevida* was to explore Diego Ramírez Island south of Cape Horn, visit the Malvinas and the port of La Soledad, determine the true position of the Aurora Islands, then follow the coast north to Buenos Aires and Montevideo. The *Descubierta* would explore the west Patagonian coast from 46° south latitude to Cape Pilares, explore the outer coasts of Tierra del Fuego, and correct the location of Diego Ramírez Island.[43]

On October 16 the vessels weighed anchor. The *Atrevida* proceeded ahead and completed its mission without incident, but the *Descubierta* was held up at Concepción because of an epidemic of spotted fever on board. By early December the crew had convalesced, and the voyage could be resumed; Malaspina commented on an extra benefit from their stay—the residents of La Mocha had been so generous in giving wine to the crew that he suspended the daily ration of grog until the wine was all consumed. Progress was slow until December 16, for the weather had turned tempestuous and the sea was heavy, but this gave way to light winds and a serene sky. Two days later the corvette met an American whaler and sent a group aboard, chiefly to seek news, but the ship had left port six months earlier and its complement knew less of conditions in Europe than did the Spaniards. The weather changed for the worse on the following day, but Malaspina managed to keep from being driven toward the coast. Cook's route and descriptions were invaluable to him, and he marveled at the Englishman's exactitude; he was able to improve on the descriptions only where improved weather conditions enabled him to see what had been hidden from Cook. As they continued south, the Spanish scientists were fearful lest Diego Ramírez Island, which they wished to observe, might be obscured by dark clouds. They were very curious about the existence of the island, since among Spanish navigators only the Nodal brothers had seen it, and their description did not agree with later maps, including Cook's. By December 24 the clouds began to break up, and by afternoon Diego Ramírez—actually a small archipelago —was plainly visible to the northeast. Located at 56° 33' south, the island group seemed likely to be considered by future navigators as the true end of Tierra del Fuego, at least in Malaspina's opinion. And this, no doubt, was what impelled him to honor the Minister of Marine by naming the southernmost tip of the group Cape Valdés. Early on Christmas morning they sighted Cape Horn, and again rounded the "celebrated cape" on a calm sea, with excellent weather, but these ideal conditions did not last long enough to permit taking the latitude and longitude of the cape. But Cook had already done that under better circumstances, so the *Descubierta* continued on to Staten Island where, by another quirk of the weather, it was becalmed.[44]

When a wind sprang up on the morning of December 26, the *Descubierta* was able to sail toward the Strait of Le Maire, pausing to investigate two small bays on the coast of Staten Island, Buen Suceso and Valentín. Strong winds, however, made any attempt to anchor for the purpose of exploring the hinterland a risky business. Consequently Malaspina decided to pass by the island, and set a course for the Malvinas, putting in on arrival at Port Egmont. The early days of 1794 were spent in a careful exploration of the islands, shore leave for rest and recuperation, and scientific observations; the latter were concerned primarily with gravity, since the season was unfavorable for astronomical observations and the proper operation of the chronometers was impaired by humidity. There was also the incident of the American ships. There were several in port, including a small schooner unable to continue because of its bad state; Malaspina was fearful that if they remained much longer there was imminent danger of the destruction of all the seals on the islands, so energetic were they in hunting them. Consequently he summoned the captains of the ships and informed them of Spain's claim to the islands, telling them that he could not remain indifferent to their fishing, which was hostile to the national interest. The captains agreed to depart, after obtaining some badly needed ship's biscuit from Malaspina, with one exception: Captain White, of the disabled schooner, having neither money nor items of trade, put his ship at the disposal of the Spaniards for a week after repairs were made.[45]

On January 20, after the American ships had departed, the *Descubierta* set sail for Patagonia, arriving at the Gulf of San Jorge eight days later. There a temporary observatory was set up on shore, and marine clocks were brought in to determine longitude. Observations continued for three days, during which hunters were out to secure food for the table and specimens for the collection. By February 1 a change in the weather indicated that a departure was advisable; the corvette sailed north to the Río Colorado, arriving on February 9. Since he could find none of the rivers described by Cardiel and Quiroga, Malaspina continued north on the following day, making observations along the way. During the night of February 14, the *Descubierta* entered the harbor of Montevideo, and the voyage was ended.[46]

Malaspina had made elaborate plans for the publication of the results of the voyage, but a succession of unfortunate events prevented them from reaching fruition. It will be recalled that he was also to make political observations, and these proved to be his undoing. He felt it unwise to try to govern all parts of the empire—areas of great geographical diversity —in the same manner, proposing instead an autonomous system. There should be a "natural association" with Spain, but the deciding factor in all planning should be what is "useful to America." He favored ecclesiastical reform. He believed it erroneous to try to acclimate the Negro to the continent, believing that the Malay was best suited to live with Europeans. He indicated his belief that, because of resulting poverty and depopulation, the discovery of America had been a disaster for Spain. But it was his championing of the emancipation of the colonies, expressed in a letter to Padre Gil in 1795, that would be his undoing. Manuel Godoy, chief minister, seeing in him, from his point of view, a dangerous malcontent, had Malaspina arrested and imprisoned, and Padre Gil with him. Napoleon finally secured his release and exile to Milano, where the great explorer died in 1809. His collections were dispersed, most of the memoirs were lost, and the maps remained unpublished for thirty years. Yet, because of the magnitude of the enterprise, the great care with which it was conceived and carried out, the exactitude of the observations, the diversity of the collections, the precision of the illustrations and the maps, the expedition was of singular and lasting value. And perhaps it is well that it was so, for the wars of independence would soon part Spain and its empire forever. The New World would be thrown open to explorers of all nations, and when, later in the nineteenth century, Spain would again send a scientific expedition to the Americas, it would not enjoy the privileged position accorded to its predecessors.

NOTES

1. Diego Barros Arana, *Historia general de Chile*, 2nd ed. (Santiago, 1939), Vol. V, pp. 522-23.

2. *Ibid.*, pp. 523-34.

3. Paris, 1714.

4. *Journal des observations*, pp. 242-43.

5. *Ibid.*, pp. 480-87.

6. "Captain Cook and the South Seas" (reprinted from J. Holland Rose, *Man and the Sea, Stages in Maritime and Human Progress*, Cambridge, Eng., 1935), in Robert J. Albion, ed., *Exploration and Discovery* (New York, 1965), p. 87. See also John C. Beaglehole, *The Exploration of the Pacific* (London, 1934), Chap. X.

7. Albion, *op. cit.*, p. 88.

8. James Cook, *The Journals of Captain James Cook on His Voyages of Discovery*, ed. by John C. Beaglehole (Cambridge, Eng.: Hakluyt Society Extra Series, 1955), Vol. XXXIV, pp. 19-22.

9. *Ibid.*, pp. 34, 36.

10. *Ibid.*, pp. 44-45.

11. *Ibid.*, p. 46.

12. *Ibid.*, p. 49.

13. *Ibid.*, p. 58.

14. James Cook, "An Account of a Voyage Towards the South Pole and Round the World," in Robert Kerr, ed., *A General History and Collection of Voyages and Travels* (Edinburgh and London, 1824), Vol. XIV, pp. 1-96.

15. Actually it was on Isla Hoste, separated from the mainland of Tierra del Fuego by the Beagle Canal.

16. Cook, "An Account of a Voyage . . . ," in Kerr, *op. cit.*, Vol. XIV, p. 503.

17. *Ibid.*, pp. 504-5.

18. *Ibid.*, Vol. XV, pp. 1-2.

19. Jean-François Galaup de La Pérouse (or Lapérouse) headed an expedition which rounded Cape Horn in 1786, explored the entire Pacific Ocean, and was lost through shipwreck off the Santa Cruz Islands. Cf. *Voyage de La Pérouse autour du*

monde, ed. by L. A. Milet Moreau (Paris, 1797), Vol. II. This was the first and official published account.

20. For the plan and its proposal to the government see letter of Malaspina and Bustamente to the Minister of Marine, September 10, 1788, in Malaspina, *Viaje al río de la Plata en el siglo XVIII* (Buenos Aires, 1938), pp. 1-5.

21. Letter of November 17, 1788, in *ibid.,* p. 6.

22. Letter of December 9, 1788, in *ibid.,* pp. 7-8.

23. Undated letter, *ibid.,* pp. 15-21.

24. Cádiz, January 31, 1789, *ibid.,* pp. 22-29.

25. Letters of Valdés to Malaspina, December 9 and 30, 1788, *ibid.,* pp. 8-11.

26. Letter of December 23, 1788, *ibid.,* pp. 25-30.

27. Letter of February 1, 1789, *ibid.,* pp. 33-36.

28. Letter of February 5, 1789, *ibid.,* pp. 38-39.

29. *Ibid.,* pp. 116-17.

30. January 2, 1789. *Ibid.,* pp. 51-55.

31. April 1, 1789. *Ibid.,* pp. 58-80.

32. *Ibid.,* pp. 127-33.

33. *Ibid.,* pp. 138-43.

34. *Ibid.,* pp. 143-49.

35. *Ibid.,* pp. 149-52.

36. *Ibid.,* pp. 153-65.

37. *Ibid.,* p. 167.

38. *Ibid.,* pp. 169-77. The anecdote appears on pp. 176-77. The shirtwaist was apparently a simple type of poncho.

39. *Ibid.,* pp. 180-89.

40. *Ibid.,* pp. 190-98.

41. *Ibid.,* pp. 200-1; Vargas Ugarte, *Historia del Perú* (Buenos Aires), 1957, Vol. IV, pp. 24-25.

42. Malaspina, *op. cit.,* pp. 201-2; Vargas Ugarte, *op. cit.,* p. 24.

43. Malaspina, *op. cit.,* pp. 203-5.

44. *Ibid.,* pp. 207-20.

45. *Ibid.,* pp. 226-31.

46. *Ibid.,* pp. 232-40.

XIII   *Eighteenth-Century*
Continental Scientific Explorations

The surge of scientific interest in South America was by
no means limited to measuring the earth or surveying the coasts. Almost
from the beginning of settlement there was a keen interest in the
luxuriant vegetation of the new world; among the earliest writings on
Brazil are those dealing with its natural history. Missionaries of the
sixteenth and seventeenth centuries, well schooled in the science of their
times, carefully noted down their observations of the flora of the vast
areas in which they labored. But not until the eighteenth century were
botanical studies pursued in the New World solely for their own sake.

Spanish royal interest in botany goes back to the first of the Bourbon
monarchs, Felipe V, who installed a teacher of botany at the royal
medical college in Sevilla and issued a *cédula* requesting all state officials
in the Spanish empire to watch for unusual specimens of plants, animals,
and minerals and send them to Spain. During the reign of his successor,
Fernando VI, Secretary of State José de Carvajal learned that the great
Swedish botanist Linnaeus considered the plant life of the Spanish empire
extraordinarily rich and quite unknown, and managed to obtain from
him a botanist, Pehr Löfling. In 1754 Löfling accompanied an expedition
to Venezuela, finding some six hundred specimens, 250 of which were
completely unknown to Linnaeus, verifying his prediction. In the following year a botanical garden was founded at Migas Calientes, and its
botanists were quite productive of scholarly research. It remained for
the enlightened despot Carlos III to found the Royal Botanical Garden
in Madrid in 1774, which would take the lead in study and research. Two
years later a museum of natural history was founded to house the small
existing royal collection and another, belonging to an Ecuadorean, Pedro
Francisco Dávila, who became its first director. Officials of the empire

were advised to furnish the museum with such specimens as they were able to obtain, especially medicinal plants.[1]

In the hope of enlarging his collections, Carlos III sent out three expeditions to the new world: José Celestino Mutis to Nueva Granada; Hipólito Ruiz and José Pavón to Peru; Vicente Cervantes, Martín de Sessé and José Longino Martínez to Nueva España. Since Mexico lies outside the scope of this work, the latter expedition is not our concern here, and we shall confine our attention to the first two.

Father José Celestino Mutis (1732–1808), who was also a physician, became interested in botany while in Madrid in 1757, spent several years studying it, and finally secured an appointment as physician to Pedro Mesía de la Cerda, newly appointed viceroy of Nueva Granada, in order that he might study the little-known flora of the viceroyalty. Mutis left Madrid on Monday, July 28, 1760, for Cádiz, accompanied by Jaime Navarro, arriving Sunday, August 10, none the worse for having been thrown from his mule half a league out of the capital. Not certain whether he was to sail on the same ship as the viceroy, Mutis decided to call on him at his residence in Puerto Real, accompanied by the Riberó brothers, one of whom intended to offer the official his ship, the *Tetis*. On the way they met La Cerda, headed for Cádiz. He informed them that he was sailing aboard the *Castilla*, and allowed Mutis to go to Cádiz to pick up his baggage, then board the ship.[2]

The *Castilla* set sail on September 7. Although the sea was not rough, it took a while for the passengers to accustom themselves to this new element; Mutis reports that he and many others were seasick for two days. The voyage to the Canaries was uneventful; to provide some diversion, the crew scheduled entertainment on deck on the evening of Thursday, September 16, which somewhat shocked the sensibilities of the passengers, for Mutis reports that they saw "two Portuguese dance the most lewd and scandalous dance which human malice could invent; one of the dancers assured them that this was frequently done in Portugal."[3] Three days later they sighted land, and on September 20 docked in Tenerife.

The voyage continued without incident. On October 14 they saw a Dutch ship laden with sugar and coffee, and were informed that they were one hundred leagues east of Tobago. Two days later they sighted the island and continued on to Curaçao, arriving October 23. Six days later they were in port in Cartagena, where they remained a while before departing for Bogotá. Since the greater part of the journey to the capital would be up the Río Magdalena, Mutis would have an excellent opportunity to observe the flora and fauna en route. Early on the morning of January 8, 1761, Mutis and his party departed from the village of Mompós on the right bank of the river in a small boat, and proceeded upstream, making careful observations as they progressed. On

January 13, he tells us, "we had the satisfaction of killing a cayman from our small boat. The shot penetrated into his skull." While the Indians lunched on the beach, they took it aboard and cut off its head and one leg with an ax, noting with surprise that there was still movement although it had been half an hour since they killed it.[4]

Mutis had several opportunities to practice his surgical skill. He had noticed that one of the rowers had a large boil on the pectoral muscle, near the armpit, and in the belief that tortoise eggs were easily infected and might cause the boil to fester, had deprived himself of this good food. Mutis opened the boil on January 18, much to the Indian's eventual satisfaction. Four days later the canoe *San Antonio* was involved in a small accident which nearly cost one of the rowers his arm; he had the hawser in his left hand and it was suddenly jerked so violently as to break his middle finger and cut the ring finger to the bone. As Mutis set the finger and treated the cut, he concluded that the dangers involved in the navigation of the river, which often resulted in loss of life and property, were owing to the total lack of concern on the part of those who might have made the river more navigable. The narrows at Presidio particularly concerned him, for the passage there was extremely dangerous. Above this point he noticed a haze rising above the surface of the water, and learned from the Indians that it resulted from the pouring of the cool waters of the Río Mare into the warmer Magdalena. All along the route he was able to gather specimens of little-known plants, and was particularly pleased to obtain the *Aristoloquia*, highly prized as a remedy for snakebite.[5]

By February 18 the party arrived in Bogotá. Mutis found the vicinity excellent for botanical work, and he had many opportunities to practice medicine, except for a prolonged period of illness which confined him to bed from late May through June. He was particularly interested in some of the fantastic local medical lore he picked up: that excrement was a good cure for goiter, and that poisonous animals do not harm pregnant women. Although the latter was "attested" to by two women, Mutis had grave doubts, since he had also heard that they did not harm priests.[6] The years 1761 and 1762 were spent largely in botanizing in the vicinity of Bogotá, and Mutis' account is a mine of information concerning the great variety of specimens he was able to collect. Not only was he concerned with enlarging the king's collection, but also in devising new uses for known species. He displayed a particular interest, for example, in the possibility of raising cinnamon trees, and even of using the resin that could be drained from the trunk. His other scientific interests were not neglected; in February of 1762 he climbed the Cerro de Guadalupe to see how far the barometer would fall at the summit, and records spending a few chilly nights there.[7]

For the next few years the priest-physician attended to medical duties, occasionally collected specimens, and continued his correspondence with the great Swedish botanist, Linnaeus, which he had begun upon his arrival in America. His diary contains few entries; for the entire year 1766, for example, there is one only, for September 30, containing reflections to his visit to the mines—the "misery of the Indies." [8] Not until 1777 was Father Mutis able to undertake an extensive journey away from Bogotá; on October 1 he went to Minas del Sapo, where he would remain for more than a year, exploring the environs of the settlement and cataloging its profuse flora. But his attention was by no means confined to botany, for nothing that lived escaped his attention. He was intrigued by the flying ants, termites, worms, and carnivorous flies; he saw armadillos and anteaters, and devotes several pages to detailed descriptions of them. On "one of the most distinguished days in my diaries" he saw a rubber tree, and recalling La Condamine's mention of it, explains the method of extracting latex and making rubber.[9] On January 2, 1778, there was another occasion for rejoicing, for he found what he had sought in vain for many years—the saffron plant.

For most of that year, Mutis' diary is concerned with descriptions and discussions of a variety of plants and insects, and of his difficulties with two particularly troublesome species, woodborers (he tells of watching an army of them cross the floor as he wrote) and ants. He was interested particularly in glowworms, which he had not seen until reaching Cartagena and which he found in abundance in Minas del Sapo. There is one unhappy entry; on September 9 he tells of receiving a letter from his brother Julián containing "the saddest news I have received in my entire life"—Linnaeus had died on February 10. For eighteen years he had corresponded with that "varón inmortal" and had sent him cases containing 118 specimens.[10]

Since his arrival in the viceroyalty, Mutis' duties had prevented him from devoting as much time and energy to botany as he would have wished. He had been able to accomplish enough on his brief excursions into the interior to whet his scientific appetite, and he sought in vain to get royal support for an expedition. Not until 1782 would he be successful, when the new viceroy, Archbishop Antonio Caballero y Góngora, granted provisional authorization. In preparation Mutis visited the Llanogrande during March and April, which was very profitable from a botanical standpoint. Royal approval came the following year, and Mutis organized a small expedition which included the great naturalist Dr. Eloy Valenzuela.

On Tuesday, April 29, the group left Bogotá, reaching Basillas by evening. There they were delayed because several beasts of burden had disappeared (a regular occurrence, Mutis explained), so several days were spent exploring the immediate neighborhood. Continuing on April 30, they found that the road became difficult, necessitating a switch from horse to mule, and finally to foot travel, an inconvenience to which Valenzuela seemed oblivious in his zeal for collecting and his elation at seeing finally *chinchona* (the quinine-producing tree) in its native soil. On May 1 they reached a hospice, to be greeted by one D. Francisco Gutiérrez, who insisted that they accept the hospitality of his nearby hacienda. While there Father Mutis was called to baptize a three-day-old girl, severely ill with a virus. Resuming their journey, the botanists arrived at the Mesa de Juan Díaz, where they spent a month gathering a substantial collection of new specimens. Mutis also tested his thermometer, and an ivory aerometer made in China, giving a detailed summary of his tests. At the end of June the group transferred its operations to Mariquita, remaining in that locality from July 7 to August 13. The scientists were very fortunate in collecting an abundance of plants and flowers; Mutis' diary devotes some sixty pages to their descriptions. Leaving Mariquita, the expedition proceeded to Honda on the banks of the Magdalena, remaining there for the rest of the year. Mutis remarked that he enjoyed walking through this valley, remembering that Bouguer had trod the same ground before him.[11]

Early January, 1784, was spent at the pueblo of Cipacón in search of *quina* and cinnamon. Mutis had never been there before. Some specimens were found, but they gathered still more, including laurel, on their return to Bogotá. There they remained until April 19, botanizing and preparing illustrations. Considerable progress was made by the draftsmen, who were using a new method of coloring with inks imported from China. Once again Mutis' expedition departed for Mariquita, arriving April 22 in the rain. There were observations of temperature to make, papers to organize, and drawings to be made, followed by more excursions to observe birds and insects, and to gather additional botanical specimens. By June 22 Father Mutis had completed a catalog of the plants mounted in his cabinet—but might there not still be some he had missed? A one-day visit to Honda proved most rewarding, for he found a very beautiful specimen of *Huertaea*—and he had seen but one before, in 1781. On his return to Mariquita, he found that his *herbolarios*, Estéban and Pedro, had brought many more specimens, which indicated that a longer stay was in order. Mutis spent most of his time identifying and classifying the plants, but occasionally, "after the Christian obligations of the day were concluded," he would go out himself.[12]

For six more years Father Mutis sought out new specimens in Mariquita, the Parroquia de Bocaneme, and Honda, devoting much of his time to trees. While the work of identification and classification required many hours indoors, he spent as much time in the field as possible, for, as he said, "my continual confinement is not favorable to my health."[13] We learn little of his activities in these years, for his diary is primarily a prodigious list of specimens collected, with descriptions and classifications. Yet for all this, the bulk of his scientific work remains un-published, and reposes in the archives of Madrid, Sevilla, Bogotá, London, and Upsala. It was Humboldt and Bonpland who brought his work to the attention of Europe when they dedicated their *Equinoctial Plants* to this "Patriarch of Botany in the New World." And it remained for a twentieth-century botanist of Spain, Professor Francisco de las Barras of Aragón in his *La Flora de Bogotá* [14] to acclaim the work of this eighteenth-century priest-physician-naturalist as "superior." [15]

While Father Mutis labored in the viceroyalty of Nueva Granada, the second botanical expedition began and completed its work in Peru. This enterprise actually had its origin in France. Turgot, the finance minister, believing that a greater knowledge of natural history and geography would be beneficial to the French economy, requested permission from Carlos III to send a botanist to Peru, since this was the one area from which botanical specimens were singularly lacking in France. After some hesitation, José de Gálvez, minister of the Indies, consented to grant permission to Turgot's nominee, Joseph Dombey, with the stipulation that he be accompanied by two Spanish botanists and that a copy of his findings be deposited in Madrid. Two years had elapsed since Turgot made his request, and he had already fallen from office before the Spanish botanists were named in November of 1776.[16]

Gálvez' choice fell upon two relatively young men, Hipólito Ruiz López and José Antonio Pavón y Jiménez, both twenty-two years of age. Ruiz, a native of Old Castile, had come to Madrid at an early age to study the natural sciences while serving as an assistant to his pharmacist uncle. In 1772 his growing interest in botany took him to Migas Calientes, where he could study under Spain's greatest botanists. Pavón, an Extremaduran, had lived in Madrid since the age of eleven in the home of his uncle, a royal pharmacist. Developing an interest in botany as well as pharmacy, he too eventually went to Migas Calientes. Neither had the training or reputation of Dombey, who was twelve years their senior, a doctor of medicine from Montpellier, and a well-known botanist, but Gálvez chose to appoint Ruiz to head the expedition because it would operate on Spanish soil and because he had misgivings concerning the "French temperament." [17] Appointed also were two artists from Madrid, José Brunete and Isidro Gálvez.

The royal *cédula* appointing Ruiz indicated quite clearly the purpose of the expedition; it was to undertake "the methodical examination and identification of the products of nature of my American dominions . . . not only in order to promote the progress of the physical sciences, but also to banish doubts and adulterations that are found in medicine, painting, and the other important arts, and to increase commerce and to form herbaria and collections of the natural products, describing and making delineations of the plants found in those fertile dominions of mine to enrich my Cabinet of Natural History and the Botanical Garden of the Court." [18] The botanists were to spend four years in the vice-royalty of Peru—one year in Lima, then to the audiencia of Quito. All information was to be shared, and each discoverer of a plant was to list his name with the discovery in the diary. For their guidance they were to be provided with the works of Linnaeus, Markgraf, and Feuillée.[19]

The three botanists and their artists left Madrid for Cádiz on September 19, 1777, arriving October 2. After spending more than two weeks in equipping, they sailed on October 19 in H.M.S. *Peruano*, reaching Tierra del Fuego on February 7, and finally anchoring at Callao on April 8, 1778. Until they reached Pisco, near the end of their journey, they had seen only one ship—a rather unusual circumstance. Once in Lima, the party made contact with three men who would be of considerable assistance to them: Padre Francisco González Laguna, overseer of El Jardín de la Buena Muerte, Cosme Bueno, professor of medicine, mathematics, and cosmography at the University of San Marcos, and Hipólito Unanue, a serious student of natural history.[20]

After several months of organization and acquainting themselves with their new environment, Ruiz and his group began the first phase of their explorations in the vicinity of Lima. On July 22 the party started out for Arnedo (or Chancay), about forty miles northwest, along the coast. Ruiz and Pavón carried three months' pay in advance with them, a fact which apparently became known to a local bandit, Uracán, and his accomplices, who plotted to hold up the party. The botanists became suspicious, and surprised Uracán by pointing two pistols at his chest, effectively thwarting his plan. At their destination they were guests on the hacienda of Don Toribio Brabo de Castilla, who joined them and assisted them in the gathering and drying of specimens during July and August. In September they transferred their activities to the sugar-cane fields of Huaura, where they gathered some forty specimens which grew in the nearby desert areas, taking their moisture from the *garúa*, that very heavy mist which hangs over the coast of Peru at certain times of the year. By October 22 they were back in Lima, and then proceeded south to Lurín, some twenty miles away, for the early summer (December). [21]

From Lurín the group moved on to Surco, then returned to Lima on March 6, 1779. This first expedition had been quite fruitful, for they were able to load seventeen cases aboard the *Buen Consejo*; Ruiz and Pavón had packed 275 plants, seeds for 160 plants, and 242 drawings, plus assorted "natural curiosities" into ten of the cases, while Dombey shipped minerals and seeds and a herbarium of 284 plants in the remaining seven. There were also seventeen pots with living plants; Dombey had misgivings about shipping them around Cape Horn without the care of specialists, but the Spaniards had orders to do so, since the British had been fairly successful in their attempts.[22]

Aside from the major objectives of the expedition, Dombey had three in particular which had occupied his attention before coming to America. First of all, there was cinnamon; there was still hope in Spain that exploitation of the cinnamon trees Gonzalo Pizarro had sought in the sixteenth century might drastically reduce the peninsula's dependence on Dutch Ceylon, major source of the spice. The hope had been nourished by Pedro Maldonado, who had worked with La Condamine, but it proved to be illusory. Dombey found, on gathering specimens, that this was an entirely different species, and recommended abandoning the project. Then there was platinum. Because of its high melting point, which made it inseparable from gold, it was a nuisance in mining and could be fraudulently (from the point of view of those who did not know its real value) alloyed with gold and passed off as the yellow metal. As its real worth gradually became apparent (to some, at least) in Europe, Dombey got permission to send twenty pounds to France, acquiring most of it for twelve shirts and four Dutch linen sheets. His hopes of finding saltpeter, an ingredient necessary for gunpowder and found only in South Asia and Spain in appreciable quantities, did not turn out so well. He and Ruiz held out high hopes that it would be found along the coast of Peru, but samples sent to Spain proved to be only salt of an inferior quality. Early in 1779 the viceroy asked Dombey to analyze the mineral waters of Chinchín; on March 11 he left the group to go there with a lady of Lima, Señora Oydora, who was going to the baths.[23]

The years 1779–81 were spent in the Peruvian *montaña*. The party (with the exception of Dombey) left Lima on May 12, 1779, following the valley of the Río Rímac toward Tarma, their destination. The journey was anything but uneventful. At the outset, along the gorge of the river, they had to proceed up crumbling stone steps (no effort had been made to use binding material), a perilous undertaking. They saw one of their mules get stuck in the mud in the channel and drown near Pucará. They were able to save only the loads on the animal's back, and spent the next day drying out the books and clothing, all of which had become thoroughly tinted from the artists' colors that had been loosely packed in the chests. Consequently they did not reach Puente de la Oroya until 8:00 P.M. on May 20, and had to spend three hours by the light of *ichu* grass flares pulling themselves across this rawhide and vine suspension bridge in wicker baskets, along with the loads and saddles; the animals had to be driven across a ford, and one was drowned. Upon their arrival at the pueblo of Oroya at midnight, they were to lose another mule, stolen in the night. Resuming their journey the next day, May 21, they followed the river as it passed through a narrow and dangerous gorge; Ruiz was captivated by the almost continual waterfall—in some places raging and almost deafening, in others "so serene and beautiful that they charm and distract the imagination with the foamy, smooth water, which at a distance appears like pure snow that is always in movement or in total repose, forming extraordinary and beautiful designs." [24] As they continued, the botanists passed through a variety of climatic zones, collecting an abundance of specimens from each, many, according to Indian belief, a sure cure for some ailment or other. They discovered, for example, that the maw of *huacha* birds would dissolve a goiter; that shoots of *quiscar* boiled with water supposedly cured colds, or, mixed with urine, toothaches; that other plants would heal wounds, backache, hemorrhoids, and infertility, ease childbirth, or repel insects. In short, there was a cure for everything; one needed only the right plant. [25]

Ruiz, Pavón, and their group set up headquarters at Tarma, a town of about four thousand population at an elevation of ten thousand feet —a good location from which to send expeditions into the surrounding countryside. Ruiz and Gálvez, for example, went into the province of Xauxa, two leagues from Tarma, following the royal highway of the Incas part of the way, subsequently visiting the convent of Santa Rosa de Ocopa. At the end of September Dombey finally joined them, since Señora Oydora had decided to return to Lima from Chinchín; he claimed to have analyzed the waters and reported to the viceroy concerning their content, but Ruiz stated categorically that he did neither. Specimen-collecting now continued in earnest; Pavón and Brunete went toward Palca, gathering two chests of dried plants which they took to Lima, returning in November, while Ruiz, Dombey, and Gálvez headed for Huasihuasi. Five leagues from the town was Mount Churupallana, which they decided to climb, getting half-way up before nightfall and a rainstorm halted them. Just before dawn they heard mournful screams in the woods "that sounded as if they were made by people in conflict, and that put us all in a state of apprehension." [26] Soldiers later informed them that these were the cries of the birds called *almas perdidas* (lost souls). Dombey had slipped on the way up, and by November 1, the next day, he could barely walk; this, plus more rain, discouraged further attempts to climb. As luck would have it, they went down the mountain in bright sunshine. On the return trip to Lima, after leaving the pueblo of Oroya, Ruiz nearly suffered a disaster; the mule he was riding slipped into a gorge cut by the rain, but luckily it was tied to a horse, and Ruiz suffered only a scratch on the cheek from the horse's hoof. By January 23, 1780, they were back in Lima. [27]

After their return, the botanists had to spend some time in repackaging their specimens because of termite damage; the boxes were subsequently stored in the armory as a protective measure because of the war with Great Britain. At the end of April the party again set out for the *montaña*, reaching Huánuco, near the Río Huallaga, about a month later. Since the settlement had deteriorated, they made some suggestions for restoring its former prosperity, chief among which was the cultivation of *quina*, from which quinine was produced. By early July they were deep in the *quina* country and established a camp at Cuchero, some fifty miles northeast of Huánuco, where they found several varieties of *chinchona*, the quinine-producing tree. Ruiz was intrigued by the *zerbatana*, the blowpipe used by the local Indians for hunting, and provided a description: it was a two-and-one-half-yard tube, with a perfectly smooth bore, made from the black, hard wood of the *chonta* palm. Darts were dipped in poison from several milky plants called *vejucos*, which was boiled, dried, and then mixed with juice from yuca roots; unless extracted at once (as the monkeys do), the poisoned darts cause the blood to clot immediately, yet do not poison the game for food.[28]

From the standpoint of medicinal plants, the stay in Cuchero was most rewarding. While there the botanists learned how to make extract of quinine by shredding the bark and boiling it in water, finally reducing the liquid to a thick syrup, which retained its strength much longer than the bark. They became acquainted with coca leaves and their medicinal properties, and were much impressed by the maguey (agave), the leaves of which were used as a cure for ulcers and the roots for rheumatism and venereal diseases. But by the end of the month difficulties arose. The food which they had brought on the advice of the natives was insufficient and "not of the best," so that some days they were reduced to eating "salted meat half putrid, and boiled maize and roasted yuca instead of bread." Then on the night of August 1 they learned that their camp was surrounded by a horde of Chuncho Indians; Dombey and Pavón managed to slip out and go to Chinchao, but Ruiz, who was ill, remained with the rest. The arrival of fifteen more armed men to support the thirty in town was fortunate; they discharged a cannon, frightening away the Indians, who apparently had no motive other than to cause the botanists to flee, leaving their supplies to be raided. With no good reason to remain, Ruiz and his group left as soon as he was able.[29]

While Dombey and Pavón collected coca leaves in Chinchao, Ruiz and the others explored Huamalíes province, where they came upon the river that Fritz and La Condamine believed to be the Marañón.[30] The expedition was reunited at Huánuco early in October; Dombey produced a piece of rubber which an Indian had given him, and indicated his hope of organizing an expedition into the Amazon valley after their return to Lima. Meanwhile they learned of a serious local problem. It seemed that the seeds of the thorn-apple, which was very common in Huánuco, induced a state akin to drunkenness; the corregidor wanted to destroy all the plants (an almost impossible task) but the Indians, who used the leaves and seeds for a variety of remedies, effectivly forestalled him. In October Ruiz and Gálvez began exploring to the west but, discouraged by bad weather, returned, and activities were confined largely to the Huánuco area through the remaining spring and the summer months. With the beginning of autumn (March 22, 1781), the party gathered baggage and specimens for the return to Lima. The weather was foul; rains made the road so slippery that, as Ruiz recounts, "never before had I found myself in such imminent danger of losing my life." [31] And, as a result of their excursions into the countryside, Ruiz continues, "our legs were covered . . . with a kind of eruption that ended in very amazing and itching pimples, so that especially at night we passed whole hours scratching until our skin was raw." [32] In addition, Pavón was afflicted by a skin disease called *mayco*, "consisting of papules filled with matter which cover the hands and the buttocks and sometimes the neck, accompanied by some fever." [33] Fortunately a cure was available—roasted bunches of *albergilla* (a species of *Valeriana*) applied as hot as could be borne all over the afflicted areas; with this treatment Pavón was able to resume work in ten days.

Returning to Lima on April 16, 1781, the botanists remained until July 4, drying plants, finishing descriptions, and arranging plants by classes in packages. Dombey managed to borrow 2000 pesos to finance an expedition into Amazonia to search for rubber, but the uprising of Tupac Amaru [34] made this impossible. In the meantime they learned that the British had captured the *Buen Consejo*, which was carrying their plants to Spain, necessitating another expedition into the nearby hills and valleys to get replacements; Dombey did not go with them, since he had had the foresight to provide himself with duplicates. This was scarcely necessary, however, for when the British sold the cargo of the vessel at Lisboa, Spain bought it and ordered Dombey's collections sent to France. [35]

While in Lima the botanists heard much about Chile and determined to go if possible; since the war with Britain made the Atlantic crossing hazardous, the visitador-general was willing to extend their stay, and they sailed in January of 1782 aboard the *Nuestra Señora de Belén*. On January 26 they sighted the island of Santa María, and that well-known landmark, Las Tetas de Bíobío; they decided to enter the harbor of Talcahuano by moonlight, but the wind died down and they had to wait until morning. When the sail was hoisted, a sailor was knocked from the main topsail into the sea; a piece of wood was thrown to him and he was finally rescued. Entering the pueblo of Talcahuano, the scientists were guests of Colonel Ambrosio O'Higgins, Maestre del Campo of Concepción, [36] who invited them to join him at a parley with the Araucanian leaders. While at the conference, Ruiz had an opportunity to study the

Indians of the plains and the coast, both of whom were present, and to record a description of them. He found the men generally ugly and short; they wore jacket, breeches, poncho, and slouch hat. The women, generally not beautiful, wore a cotton blanket tied at the waist, other blankets to cover their backs, and silver earrings. All, he said, were fond of liquor, drinking *chicha* made of corn, apples, or quinoa. Men could marry as many wives as they could support; religion was confined to belief in Pillán, the supreme deity, and in the immortality of the soul. Pillán's will was interpreted by witches; Ruiz suspected that they sometimes used their position to settle scores by handing down interpretations damaging to those against whom they had grievances.[37]

The party was considerably impressed by Chile; Ruiz reported that "the kingdom of Chile is unquestionably, as might be inferred from its benign climate, its products, and the character of its inhabitants, one of the most pleasant and enviable countries in the world." [38] In order to make a comprehensive study of the flora, they remained until the spring of 1783; Dombey spent the winter months examining the mercury mines of La Serena at the behest of the audiencia, and returned with high hopes of increasing production, but subsequent operations were in vain.[39]

Their work in Chile now completed, the botanists returned to Peru aboard the *Nuestra Señora de las Mercedes*, and anchored in Callao on November 4. Two days later they took their cases of specimens to the customs-house; there were fifty-five cases of dried plants, boxes of gold and silver, animals and birds, dried fish, shells, rocks, curious natural products, and Indian clothing, plus eight hundred sketches of plants in natural colors and thirty-three tubs of trees and shrubs in heated cases. These were to be loaded aboard the *San Pedro de Alcántara* and the party remained in Lima until the ship sailed in April of 1784.[40] Dombey left the group at this time; he had been in failing health, and secured permission to return to Spain on *El Peruano*—the same ship that had brought them—with his seventy-three cases of specimens of all types. After a long and arduous journey around Cape Horn, which cost him his hair and nearly his life (thirty-two died en route), he finally reached Cádiz on February 22, 1785.[41]

After Dombey's departure, Ruiz and Pavón departed again, with their group, for Huánuco in May of 1784. Five days after they left Lima, Ruiz was troubled with a pain in the side, but managed to continue, with considerable discomfort. Crossing the cordillera on May 20, the party was forced to spend the night on the snow, and Ruiz records that "I thought I was going to die in that uninhabited place for lack of some warm nourishment and on account of the cold I suffered during the night. I was attacked by a terrible griping and thirst, and we had to break the ice to drink water." [42] Finally they reached Pasco;

after several days in bed and, so he believed, with the aid of lettuce salad and some apples, Ruiz felt much better, and with a few days additional rest, recovered completely. This period was very productive of results; despite problems created by wild beasts, skin infections, falling trees and the like, they were able to gather a wide variety of specimens. Ruiz was particularly fascinated by the papaya and the pineapple, and took the trouble to record a good recipe for pineapple candy. There are also descriptions of rather curious plants such as the *piñi-piñi*, the only plant Ruiz knew of with globular leaves, and the *yerba de golondrina*, the milk of which allegedly cured cataracts.[43]

While in Huánuco Ruiz and Pavón received two pieces of news: first of all, all their tubs of living plants on the *San Pedro de Alcántara* were lost in a storm off Chile, although fortunately the remaining boxes were safe; second, Gómez Ortega, superintendant of the royal botanical garden, felt that they should finish their work and return to Spain as quickly as possible, recommending that they take one or two men with them and train them to carry on the work. Father Gónzalez Laguna recommended Juan José Tafalla, who had studied pharmacy, and Francisco Pulgar, an artist. They seemed to work out quite well, so in June of 1785 the party re-entered the *montaña*. Tafalla and Pulgar soon proved to be a disappointment, complaining of illness, disobeying orders, and finally leaving on August 6. But this was only a minor misfortune; quite accidentally the roof of the botanists' house caught fire and flames raged through the structure, destroying the winter's collections, three years' diaries, and volumes of descriptions covering four years of work, along with books, clothing, food, and supplies. The only thing not destroyed (although badly damaged) was Ruiz' silver *pot de chambre*.[44]

There was nothing to do but rewrite descriptions for the plants stored in Huánuco, a task which took the better part of a month. After this, and five bouts with fever, Ruiz had had enough, and asked to return to Spain. By June of 1786 there was still no reply, but he and Pavón learned that the Minister of the Indies intended to relieve Tafalla and Pulgar (who had been ordered to rejoin the expedition) of their duties and abandon plans to continue the work. Not until the royal order on March 18, 1787, recalling Ruiz and Pavón to Spain, was this order reversed. In the meantime Tafalla and Pulgar were sent to Lima with fifty-six tubs of trees and shrubs in May of 1786, while Ruiz and Pavón went again to the *montaña*, staying at the hamlet of Muña until September, when they went back to Huánuco. There the artists proved to be temperamental, refusing to duplicate any of their work until there was certainty of loss. Brunete, one of them, decided to leave the expedition and return to Lima; on the way his mule fell down a precipice with two cases containing his personal effects. He was able to secure help in retrieving his things, but there was extensive damage, which bothered him considerably. Apparently suffering from exposure, he became ill, could breathe only with difficulty, and could barely walk; he failed to respond to treatment, and finally died on November 14.[45] In the meantime, the *San Pedro de Alcántara*, repaired in Rio de Janeiro, managed to sail to Portugal, only to ram the coast and sink with a loss of thirty-nine lives and all the plants—five years' work.[46]

But this last excursion could make up in part for the losses, for Pavón and Pulgar were able to take 73 boxes of dried plants, 18 pots containing live plants, and 586 drawings to Lima in January of 1787. In August the party left for the pueblo of Pillao, to the northeast of Huánuco, and in September stopped at Chacahuasí, which had a population of four; their stay was brief, for Ruiz described it as "that narrow, deep dungeon where the sun penetrates only at midday; . . . nothing could make us stay one single day." [47] On October 12 orders arrived for the return to Spain; after several months spent in packing, Ruiz and Pavón reached Lima on February 10, 1788, and departed for Callao at the end of March. For the sake of safety, the 29 boxes, 589 drawings, and 24 tubs of live plants were divided between two ships, *El Jasón* and *El Dragón*; Ruiz sailed on the latter, with the plant descriptions, while Pavón took duplicates aboard the former and triplicates were given to Tafalla to send later. They set sail on April 1, arrived at Cádiz on October 12 and, after being bedded down with fever for more than a week, departed separately for Madrid. On December 16, Ruiz wrote a simple end to their labors and disappointments of years: "I deposited the crates with my plants in the Botanical Gardens." [48]

In the same year of the return of Ruiz and Pavón, the government of Spain, it will be remembered,[49] was preparing an expedition around the world under Alejandro Malaspina, which included among its members the celebrated Bohemian naturalist Thaddaeus Peregrinus Haenke. Born in Trebitz in 1761, he received the doctorate of philosophy from Charles University in Prague in 1782, after completing his studies in mathematics, medicine, and natural sciences. His great interest in botany led him to explore the Riesengebirge, and to pursue advanced studies in geology and botany in Vienna, which led to his appointment to the Malaspina expedition, probably on the recommendation of Nicholas Jaquin, under whom he had pursued his botanical studies. In addition to his scientific accomplishments, Haenke was also a skilled musician, performing both on the clavichord and the violin.

After receiving permission from Emperor Josef II, Haenke left Vienna on June 26, 1789, arrived in Madrid July 20, where he remained a week, then proceeded on to Cádiz, arriving just a few hours after the *Descubierta* and *Atrevida* had sailed. In the hope of joining the expedition in Buenos Aires, he took passage on the *Nuestra Señora del Buen*

Viaje, which was shipwrecked on entering the Río de la Plata; Haenke managed to swim to shore, carrying his copy of Linnaeus and his papers in his nightcap. It was November 25, and Haenke learned that he had missed the expedition again; it had sailed for the Malvinas ten days earlier. Exhaustion and depression took their toll, for he was held up for three weeks in Montevideo by sickness. If he were to catch up with Malaspina now, there was only one course of action open: cross the continent to Chile, and join him there. With this in mind, he journeyed to Buenos Aires, arriving December 23, after botanizing a bit between Montevideo and Colonia.[50]

Haenke remained in Buenos Aires for two months making preparations for his journey, during which time he managed to obtain 800 pesos and the necessary papers from the new viceroy, Nicolás de Arredondo. He would have a unique opportunity, for no botanist had ever crossed the pampa, but he would cross it at the hottest time of the year by diligence, cart, and horse, with an almost complete absence of the amenities and the continual danger of ambush by the Indians. But it was now or not at all, so Haenke began his journey on February 24, 1790, arriving at Mendoza on March 17 a little the worse for having come so far with little rest. Four days later he was again on his way, and on April 2 arrived in Santiago, this time not too late. With him he brought 1,400 plants collected along the way, many hitherto unknown.[51]

During Malaspina's stay in Chile, Haenke botanized in Coquimbo, Copiapó, Arica, and Isla San Felipe as the *Descubierta* sailed north to Callao. Arriving in Peru, he spent several months collecting plants and studying the natural history of the viceroyalty before continuing north and across the Pacific. When the corvettes returned to Callao on July 23, 1793, it was decided, as we have seen, for medical and other reasons, that several of the scientific personnel should leave the vessels at various ports and continue by land. Haenke, with the approval of the viceroy, left the expedition in Lima to return to Buenos Aires via Huancavelica, Cuzco, and Potosí to make zoological and lithological as well as botanical studies along the way; Jerónimo Arcángel of the *Descubierta* was to accompany him as a taxidermist. Because of the importance of this work, he was permitted to delay his return to Buenos Aires as late as September or October of 1794.[52]

Now completely on his own, Haenke began a thorough exploration of Huancavelica province at the end of 1793, arriving in Cuzco in January of 1794. During the succeeding months he journeyed to Arequipa via Cambaja, exploring the region and investigating the thermal waters and mineral wealth. From Arequipa he headed north, skirted the south shore of Lake Titicaca, and arrived in La Paz in August, continuing on shortly afterward, exploring the *yungas* area in the region of the Beni and Mamoré rivers. From there his explorations took him south to Santa Cruz de la Sierra, Chuquisaca, and finally, in the following May, to Potosí. There Haenke continued his botanizing and also spent considerable time trying to improve the process for the extraction of silver and mercury; months later he was to concern himself with the exploitation of salt at Chiquitos. Later, in 1796, he returned to Potosí, then proceeded to Cochabamba, where he decided to remain.[53]

Haenke never returned to Spain or Bohemia. Through the influence of the governor, Francisco Viedma, he was able to obtain an extension of his status as royal botanist, and continued his botanical studies, particularly in the field of medicinal plants. There were variations from this routine; he gave music lessons, and on a visit to Tarapacá discovered nitrates, about which he became so enthusiastic that eventually he was commissioned to make powder for the defense of Buenos Aires against the British in 1806. The fate of Malaspina did not encourage Haenke to return to Spain, and when he was so ordered by Junta of Sevilla in 1810, he sought an extension of his commission on the grounds of his service to the state in Buenos Aires and the delicate condition of his health as the result of a fall. The petition was denied by Viceroy Cisneros, but he was soon deposed and after the virtual separation of the viceroyalty from Spain on May 25, Haenke was quite on his own. The rest of his life (he died in 1817) was spent largely on his estate in the mountains of Yuracaré, north of Cochabamba, botanizing, operating a small mine, practicing medicine, and raising mulberry trees in the hope of establishing a silk industry.[54]

The results of these last two botanical expeditions were gratifying and impressive indeed. The botanical garden in Madrid was greatly enriched by the collections of Ruiz and Pavón and Haenke, and since the Bohemian botanist was permitted to keep duplicates of all his discoveries, these eventually passed to the museum in Prague. In addition to the collections, Ruiz made a further important contribution in preparing the *Flora Peruana et Chilensis*, four volumes of which were published. And Tafalla, who had served with Ruiz and Pavón, founded a botanical garden at the request of the viceroy, Teodoro de Croix.

Portugal also showed an interest at this time in expanding its knowledge of its American realm. Upon the recommendation of the professor of natural history at the University of Coimbra, a young Brazilian doctoral candidate, Alexandre Rodrigues Ferreira, was chosen to head an expedition for scientific exploration in Brazil. Not until five years later did he arrive in Belém, accompanied by a botanist, Agostinho Joaquim do Cabo, and two draftsmen. For the next four years they explored the lower Amazon and that part of the Rio Negro, together with its tributaries, which flowed through Brazil. In 1789 they turned their attention southward, ascending the upper Rio Guaporé, then crossing over to the

Rio São Lourenço to descend the Rio Paraguai. Ferreira kept elaborate diaries and prepared detailed scientific records of his work; these and his extensive collections were sent to the director of the Real Gabinete de História Natural in Lisboa. Unfortunately, either through negligence or through maliciousness on the part of rivals, much of his collection deteriorated, and labels and numbers on the remainder were mixed. And if this were not enough, the French naturalist, Geoffroy de Saint-Hilaire, took advantage of the French invasion of Portugal to transport the remainder of the collection, along with Ferreira's diaries and records, to the Muséum d'Histoire Naturelle in Paris, where they remained until 1815.[55]

While Mutis, Ruiz, Pavón, Dombey, Haenke and Ferreira were about their labors in other parts of the continent, Félix de Azara was engrossed in explorations in the Paraná-Paraguay basin which would eventually consume twenty years—something of a record indeed for a Spanish explorer. Azara was not by training a naturalist, nor was he sent to South America to head a scientific expedition. A member of a brilliant family, he was born in Huesca province on May 18, 1746, and was educated at the University of Huesca and at the military academy in Barcelona. In 1775 he was commissioned a lieutenant, and during the landing at Argel in Africa he received a wound so severe that it required five years to heal. Meanwhile, prolonged negotiations over the boundary between Spanish and Portuguese territory in South America resulted in the Treaty of San Ildefonso of October 1, 1777. To demarcate the boundary, Spain and Portugal named commissions in 1780; Azara was appointed as one of the Spanish commissioners, and was made a lieutenant-colonel of Engineers, assigned to the Marine Corps.[56]

Orders received in San Sebastián directed Azara to go immediately to Lisboa and present himself to the Spanish ambassador, who directed him to proceed at once in a Portuguese vessel (because of Spain's involvement in the American Revolutionary War) to Buenos Aires, there to receive further instructions. With him went José Varela y Ulloa (a *capitán de navío*) and two other naval officers; on crossing the equator, Azara opened a dispatch from the king and found that he had been named a frigate captain, since it was judged best that all be officers of the fleet.[57] Upon arrival in Buenos Aires, Varela conferred with the viceroy, Vértiz, who informed him that the boundary would be broken into five segments, with Varela in charge of the nearest two segments, Azara the more distant, beyond Asunción. Each commission included engineers, surgeons, chaplains, an astronomer, overseers, and laborers, all well paid.[58]

Azara was first sent to meet the Portuguese commissioners at Rio Grande de San Pedro where they determined general ground rules for fixing the boundary from the arroyo of Chuy to the confluence of the Rio Guaporé and the Saroné. On returning to the Río de la Plata, he was ordered to proceed as soon as possible to Asunción and prepare to join the Portuguese commissioners in delimiting the fourth sector. Well aware of the opportunities for independent geographical and zoological investigations, Azara resolved to undertake them on his own rather than run the risk of having the viceroy turn down a request and refuse assistance or permission on the grounds that it might interfere with his primary work.[59] Events were to prove the wisdom of his choice, for there was ample time for him to pursue his objective of getting the most out of his efforts in the lands discovered and colonized by Spain.

Early in January, 1784, Azara departed by boat from the city of Santa Fe for his base of operations at Asunción. Little escaped his attention along the way; he noted that the surrounding lands abounded in anteaters as well as "lions and tigers," and reported a local belief that "tigers" when hungry preferred Negroes, then mulattoes and Indians, to Europeans. Passing through a wooded country with many carobs, willows, and ceibas (where he became sick from eating too much watercress), Azara entered the country of the Apibones with its many reductions, and finally reached Corrientes. Resting there several days, which gave him time for a detailed description of the city and province, he resumed his journey, continuing his detailed account of all that he saw until the party reached Asunción.[60]

On June 12, 1784, Azara departed from this ancient center of Spanish power on the first of seven journeys in demarcating the boundary; he was accompanied by Ignacio Pazos, a pilot of the Royal Navy. On the journey north, Azara noted the location of certain hills, made observations of latitude and longitude, described the Caranday palm (found only in the lowlands) and the prominent Cordillera de Caballero, which was said to have once belonged to the conquistador and explorer Irala. Map-making was his chief concern on this journey, and since it was impossible for him to set up base lines and execute triangles, he followed an alternate method. On reaching a prominent point, he determined its latitude carefully and marked it on his map, along with nearby hills and forests, whose direction was determined by compass. On reaching these points, he verified their latitude, set up triangles on paper, and determined the distances by trigonometry. By drawing lines from two points (whose latitude was known), using a compass, he was able to determine longitude by calculus.[61]

The second journey began from Recoleta, in this same area, on July 27; Azara was accompanied by the pilot Pablo Zizur and Juan Francisco Aguirre, frigate captain and chief of the fourth boundary division. This was primarily a mapping expedition, and ended at Capiatá in mid-August.[62] On August 20, Azara began his third journey, accompanied by Zizur and Ignacio Pazos, toward the mission country. Much of his account is given over to coordinates of places along the route, although there is an interesting and detailed description of the coconut palm, and of other flora and fauna encountered. An unexpected event was the full-dress reception accorded the explorers at the pueblo of Santa María on August 28, complete with drummers, buglers, flutists, the corregidor, the administrator, and the entire *ayuntamiento* (town government). There were long speeches in Guaraní; Azara was able to understand only the frequently repeated name of Carlos III. After the Magnificat was intoned, there were "sweets, beverages, and complimentary remarks." [63] The journey continued in the mission country, into a forested area which sloped toward the Paraná and which, in Jesuit times, contained some of the richest and most populous of the reductions. By the end of the month the rivers were swollen by heavy rains which, alternating with thick fog, created serious although not insurmountable difficulties for the explorers. On September 17 they stayed at a Portuguese ranch, marking their farthest advance; rain continued, and they began the return journey, arriving back at Asunción on September 25. An important result of this expedition was the mapping, for the first time, of the Río Tebicuary. [64]

A fourth journey in 1786 took Azara and Aguirre to San Estanislao and San Joaquín. Beginning January 14, they passed through the valley of Tapua—crossing the Río Salado, the Río Piribibui, and the Río Tobatituya—from a heavily forested land of red earth to a marshy area abounding in reeds and rushes. Proceeding on, they explored the vicinity of the Río Tacuarí, reaching the Río Paraguay on January 17 and arriving at San Estanislao soon afterward. Careful observations had been made all along the route, since the primary object of this journey was to make an accurate map; yet Azara did not fail to report so small a detail as the fact that the peons in the area used the roots of the *ysipo-yu* plant to give an orange color to food and fabrics. The explorers proceeded as far as San Joaquín, once a flourishing reduction of two thousand inhabitants; but since the expulsion of the Jesuits it had decreased to 854. Insects were a nuisance; in making their observations the group was considerably bothered by flies, gadflys, mosquitoes, and, Azara notes, three kinds of bees. By the end of the month the party had completed this stage of its work, and returned to Asunción. [65]

A fifth journey in April of 1786, which took him to Quiindí in the company of the engineer of the demarcation, Julio Ramón de César, was undertaken, Azara quite candidly states, to improve his ornithological as well as his cartographic knowledge. [66] In the following month Governor Melo de Portugal decided to visit Quaripotí, which he had founded, and asked Azara to accompany him. In the light of the many kindnesses he had received, the explorer could not refuse, and turned the journey to his own advantage by a series of careful observations along the way.⁶⁷ A seventh and last journey completed Azara's participation in the boundary demarcation. He had become quite interested in natural history and was particularly desirous of gaining more information concerning the birds and quadrupeds of the Laguna Yberá. Accordingly, when the chaplain of the boundary commission, Father Antonio Arcos y Matas, wanted to visit a friend at Candelaria, he found it easy to persuade Azara to accompany him there. The first night was spent at Yta, where the curate told them about the indigo plant, pointing out that sixty arrobas (some fifteen hundred pounds) were exported every year. A visit to nearby San Ignacio-guazú made it possible for Azara to visit and hunt with his only correspondent on the fauna of Paraguay, the local priest, D. Pedro Blas Noseda. In Candelaria, near Laguna Yberá, he found the second division of the boundary commission, working jointly with the Portuguese, and turned in a long list of observations of latitude and longitude, completing his part in the demarcation.⁶⁸

Recalled to Buenos Aires, Azara was given a command in the Pampas Indian country; at the conclusion of this mission he received permission from the viceroy to visit all the Spanish possessions south of the Paraná and Río de la Plata. This gave him the opportunity of mapping the region, a work in which he exercised the greatest care to ensure accuracy. In 1793 he returned to Paraguay, where he developed a great interest in the archives; the cabildo (municipal council), aware of his vast knowledge, asked him to devote his labors toward the preparation of a map. Three months later, on September 23, he presented his map and a large volume, the *Descripción histórica, física, política y geográfica escrita a instancias del Cabildo de la Asunción.* In gratitude the cabildo named him "most distinguished citizen of Asunción." Later he wrote the *Historia y descripción crítica de las Provincias del Paraguay y Río de la Plata* in two manuscript volumes, 1797–98. While preparing to go to Córdoba, he was recalled and given command of the entire eastern frontier because of war with Britain, with which Portugal was allied. This gave him an opportunity to prepare the first reliable map of the Río Uruguay from its cataracts to its mouth. Although, as he confessed, his primary interest was in the making of accurate maps, Azara had, during his long years of isolation, become a proficient naturalist; he was an avid reader of Buffon in a Spanish translation, and had developed a lively interest in zoology as a result of trying to devise a reliable means of preserving the skins of animals.⁶⁹

At the end of 1801 Azara sailed for Spain, never to return to South America. Writing occupied him immediately, and in 1802 he published his *Apuntamientos para la historia natural de los cuadrúpedes del Paraguay y Río de la Plata*; subsequently there would appear his *Apuntamientos para la historia natural de los pájaros del Paraguay y Río de la Plata,* the *Viajes*, and the *Geografía física y esférica de las provincias del Paraguay y misiones guaraníes*. Through his brother José Nicolás, ambassador to France, he achieved his ambition of meeting the great minds of the time, among them Geoffroy Saint-Hilaire and Cuvier. Carlos IV offered Azara the position of viceroy of Nueva España, but he declined it, preferring to remain in Spain. He was active in the war against Napoleon, but being of the liberal persuasion refused the restored Fernando VII's offer of the Grand Cross of the Order of Isabel la Católica. He remained in retirement at his birthplace, Barbuñales, until his death in 1821.[70]

Azara's name looms large in the history of the exploration of the Paraná-Paraguay basin. In his introduction to the *Viajes inéditos* of Argentina's soldier-statesman and historian Bartolomé Mitre remarks that "he was the first to concern himself with sound criticism of the primitive history of the Río de la Plata, studying it in the light of original documents and the indestructible testimony of nature, widening its horizons and disturbing the conventional foundations on which it was based. He was the first to give a scientific basis to the geography of the Río de la Plata, to whose history his name is everlastingly bound. He was the first to make known to the world under different aspects the regions watered by the Plata, the Uruguay, the Paraná, and the Paraguay." [71] His biographer, Guíllot Muñoz, credits Azara with propounding the germ of the evolutionary theory, based in part on his reading of Lamarck, Buffon, and Saint-Hilaire, but primarily resulting from "his own disciplined and reflective intelligence, aided by his acute intuition and his discerning method of classification." [72] He saw him as a careful observer of the struggle for existence, greatly interested in mutations of color, and anticipating the concepts of dominant and recessive traits. In this sense he serves, perhaps, as a strong link between his predecessors and contemporaries, and the great naturalists of the nineteenth century.

NOTES

1. Arthur R. Steele, *Flowers for the King: the Expedition of Ruiz and Pavón and the Flora of Peru* (Durham, N.C., 1964), pp. 28-43. Based on research in the archives of Spain and on original sources, especially Ruiz, *Relación histórica de viaje que hizo a los Reinos del Perú y Chile el Botánico D. Hipólito Ruiz en el año de 1777*, this book presents an interesting and balanced account of this expedition.

2. José Celestino Mutis, *Diario de observaciones* (Bogotá, 1958), Vol. I, pp. 1-34.

3. *Ibid.*, Vol. I, pp. 35-36.

4. *Ibid.*, Vol. I, pp. 66-67.

5. *Ibid.*, Vol. I, pp. 75-84.

6. *Ibid.*, Vol. I, p. 86.

7. *Ibid.*, Vol. I, pp. 87-143 *passim*.

8. *Ibid.*, Vol. I, p. 180.

9. *Ibid.*, Vol. I, pp. 208-9.
10. *Ibid.*, Vol. I, p. 355.
11. *Ibid.*, Vol. II, pp. 3-109.
12. *Ibid.*, Vol. II, pp. 113-542 *passim.*
13. *Ibid.*, Vol. II, p. 645.
14. Madrid, 1931.
15. Mutis, *Diario,* Vol. I, pp. v-vii.
16. Steele, *op. cit.,* pp. 50-51.
17. *Ibid.*, pp. 53-57.
18. Archives of Alcalá, Docket 2525, transferred to the Museo Nacional de Ciencias Naturales, Madrid. Quoted in Hipólito Ruiz, *Travels of Ruiz, Pavón, and Dombey in Peru and Chile* (1777–88), trans. by B. E. Dalghren (Vol. 21 in Botanical Series, Field Museum of Natural History), (Chicago, 1940), Appendix I, p. 279.
19. Steele, *op. cit.,* pp. 58-59.
20. Ruiz, *Travels,* pp. 9-11; Steele, *op. cit.,* pp. 66-73.
21. Ruiz, *op. cit.,* pp. 14-29. Ruiz gives a good description of the province of Chancay, as well as Lima and Luria, with a detailed catalog of the flora and the properties of the various plants.
22. *Ibid.*, pp. 30-32; Steele, *op. cit.,* pp. 85-86.
23. Steele, *op. cit.,* pp. 89-98; Ruiz, *op. cit.,* p. 32.
24. Ruiz, *op. cit.,* p. 38.
25. On this part of the journey see Ruiz, *op. cit.,* pp. 33-39, and Steele, *op. cit.,* pp. 99-100.
26. Ruiz, *op. cit.,* p. 57.
27. On the Tarma expedition, see Ruiz, *op. cit.,* pp. 49-60.
28. Ruiz, *op. cit.,* p. 72; see also Steele, *op. cit.,* pp. 102-6.
29. Ruiz, *op. cit.,* pp. 75-85; Steele, *op. cit.,* pp. 107-9.
30. In a marginal note, probably added in Spain, Ruiz states that the river rises in Lake Lauricocha, in the province of Tarma. See Ruiz, *op. cit.,* p. 80, n. 1.
31. *Op. cit.,* pp. 86-94.
32. *Ibid.*, p. 95.
33. *Ibid.*, p. 95.
34. A descendant of the last Inca, he led a revolt of the grossly exploited Indians in southern Andean Peru, 1780–81; he was defeated and brutally executed by the authorities.
35. Ruiz, *op. cit.,* p. 99; Steele, *op. cit.,* pp. 110-12.
36. A native of Ireland, he subsequently became captain-general of Chile and later viceroy of Peru. He was the father of the Chilean national hero, Bernardo O'Higgins.
37. Ruiz, *op. cit.,* pp. 110-21; Steele, *op. cit.,* pp. 115-18.
38. Ruiz, *op. cit.,* p. 121.
39. Steele, *op. cit.,* pp. 125-28.
40. Ruiz, *op. cit.,* pp. 105-6.
41. Steele, *op. cit.,* pp. 131-34.
42. Ruiz, *op. cit.,* p. 168.
43. Ruiz, *op. cit.,* pp. 169-206.
44. Ruiz, *op. cit.,* pp. 188-91. If this salvaged item seems odd, it should be noted that Ruiz took an incredible amount of personal baggage with him.
45. Ruiz, *op. cit.,* pp. 196-218.
46. Steele, *op. cit.,* p. 154.
47. Ruiz, *op. cit.,* p. 224.
48. Ruiz, *op. cit.,* p. 241.
49. See Chap. XII, pp. 209-220.
50. Lorenzo R. Parodi, "Thaddeus Peregrinus Haenke a dos siglos de su nacimiento," *Anales de la Academia Nacional de Ciencias Exactas, Fisicas, y Naturales de Buenos Aires* XVII (1964): 9-13.

51. *Ibid.,* pp. 14-15.
52. *Ibid.,* pp. 16-19.
53. *Ibid.,* pp. 19-20.
54. *Ibid.,* pp. 23-24.
55. Olivério Mário Oliveira Pinto, "Explorações Científicas," in Sergio Buarque de Holanda, ed., *História geral da civilização brasileira* (São Paulo, 1960), Vol. II, pp. 171-73.
56. Alvaro Guillot Muñoz, *La Vida y obra de Félix de Azara* (Buenos Aires, 1941), pp. 16-22.
57. *Ibid.,* p. 23.
58. *Ibid.,* p. 24; Diego de Alvear, "Diario de la Segunda División de Límites," in Pedro de Angelis, ed., *Colección Relativos a la historia del Río de la Plata* (Buenos Aires, 1837), Vol. IV, pp. 3-4; Vicente Sierra, *Historia de Argentina* (Buenos Aires, 1959, Vol. III), pp. 585-86.
59. Guillot Muñoz, *op. cit.,* pp. 24-25.
60. Félix de Azara, *Viajes inéditos* (Buenos Aires, 1873), pp. 20-58.
61. *Ibid.,* p. 89, note by Juan María Guitérrez; Guillot Muñoz, *op. cit.,* pp. 24-25.
62. Azara, *op. cit.,* pp. 94-116.
63. *Ibid.,* p. 133.
64. *Ibid.,* pp. 116-202.
65. *Ibid.,* pp. 202-33.
66. *Ibid.,* pp. 233-38.
67. *Ibid.,* pp. 238-47.
68. *Ibid.,* pp. 247-50.
69. Guillot Muñoz, *op. cit.,* pp. 33-38; Azara, *op. cit.,* pp. 15-17 (Introduction by Bartolomé Mitre).
70. *Ibid.,* pp. 42-43; Arthur Cezar Ferreira Reis, "A Viagem Filosófica e as Expedições Científicas na Ibero-América no Século XVIII," *Cultura*, Rio de Janeiro, December, 1952, p. 80.
71. P. 2.
72. *Op. cit.,* p. 66.

XIV *The New World*
of Alexander von Humboldt

       Among the many men of science who explored the South American continent in the nineteenth century, few names loom so large as that of Friedrich Heinrich Alexander, Baron von Humboldt. Linguist, biologist, astronomer, geologist, and explorer, he came perhaps nearer than any other to being the true *uomo universale* of the nineteenth century; Darwin later called him "the greatest scientific traveler who ever lived." [1] Humboldt was by no means the first scientific explorer of the continent, as we have seen, but the very magnitude of his work and the interest which it generated touched off a series of scientific explorations which would fill most of the gaps in man's knowledge of the continent by the end of the century.

       Born in Berlin in 1769, Humboldt developed an interest in science when young, and went on a scientific expedition up the Rhine at the age of twenty—an experience which determined him to become a scientific explorer. "I felt an increasing passion for the sea and distant expeditions," he tells us; "I was anxious to contemplate nature in all its variety of wild and stupendous scenery." [2] After six years of observations and preparation in Europe and the Near East, he learned of an expedition leaving France, under Captain Baudin, to visit Spanish South America and return by way of New Holland and the Cape of Good Hope. With great enthusiasm he and Aimé Bonpland, a young French botanist, joined the expedition as scientists, reserving the right to leave it when they so wished, but the War of the First Coalition forced France to withdraw funds, and the expedition did not sail. Subsequent attempts to go to Africa were equally unsuccessful, so Humboldt and Bonpland decided to winter in Spain. In the spring of 1799 it happened that they met Baron von Forell, the Saxon minister in Madrid and an amateur geologist, who suggested that the Minister of State, D. Mariano Luis de Urquijo, might arrange for them to visit Spanish America at their own expense. The idea bore fruit; they were authorized free use of instruments of physics and geodesy, and were permitted to make astronomical observations, measure the height of mountains, examine products of the soil, "and execute all operations which I should judge useful for the progress of the sciences." . . . "Never had so extensive a permission been granted to any traveller," Humboldt continued, "and never had any foreigner been honoured with more confidence on the part of the Spanish government." In all his five years of travel, he remarks, he never saw "the slightest sign of mistrust." [3]

Nearly three months were spent in Spain purchasing instruments and in visiting such eminent botanists as Ruiz, Pavón, and Née, who opened their collections to Humboldt. Arrangements were finally made to embark on the sloop *Pizarro*, and a letter was dispatched to Captain Baudin to arrange for a meeting in Montevideo, Chile, or in Lima. By June 5 all was in readiness, and the sloop sailed out of Coruña at 2 P.M., taking care to avoid the British blockade as it made for the Canaries, where it remained for a week. On June 25 the *Pizarro* left Santa Cruz for South America, and crossed the Tropic of Cancer two days later. Humboldt and Bonpland were entranced by the tropics. "From the time we entered the torrid zone," Humboldt wrote, "we were never wearied with admiring, every night, the beauty of the southern sky which, as we advanced toward the south, opened new constellations to our view. We feel an indescribable sensation when, on approaching the equator, and particularly on passing from one hemisphere to another, we see those stars, which we have contemplated from our infancy, progressively sink, and finally disappear. Nothing awakens in the traveller a livelier remembrance of the immense distance by which he is separated from his country, than the aspect of an unknown firmament." [4]

The crossing was more or less uneventful until they reached the Antilles, when the sighting of an "enemy squadron" caused considerable alarm until it turned out to be some rocks. There was also sickness aboard—possibly typhus—which affected a number of the crew and passengers; consequently Humboldt and the rest of the travelers were anxious to get off at Cumaná and proceed on another ship. Humboldt's intended stay of a few weeks expanded into a year; but for fever on board the *Pizarro*, he remarked later, he might never have reached the Orinoco, the Casiquiare, and the Negro rivers. And so, not far from Columbus' landfall three centuries earlier, on July 15, 1799, Alexander von Humboldt first set foot on the continent which would gain so much by his presence. [5]

There was much in Cumaná to interest the naturalists. There were few trees in the city; Humboldt believed that Spaniards cared little

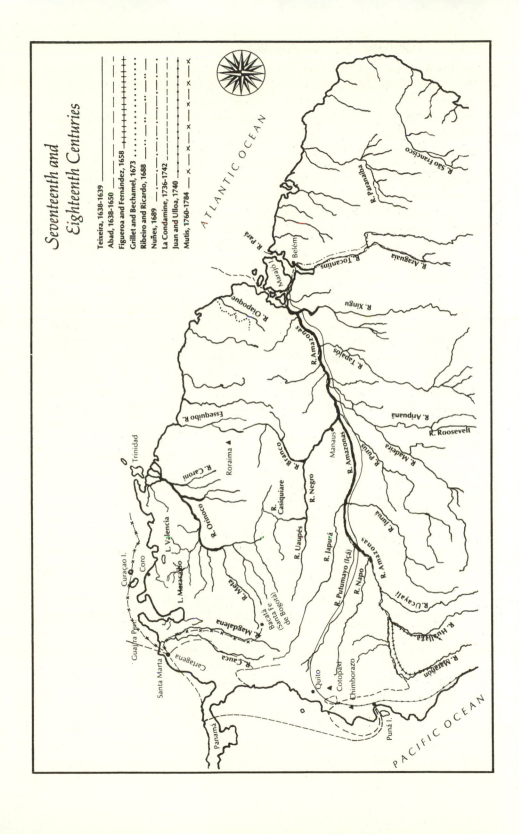

Seventeenth and
Eighteenth Centuries

Teixeira, 1638-1639
Abad, 1638-1650
Figueroa and Fernández, 1658
Grillet and Bechamel, 1673
Ribeiro and Ricardo, 1688
Nuñes, 1689
La Condamine, 1736-1742
Juan and Ulloa, 1740
Mutis, 1760-1784

for them, or for singing birds. Bathing was very popular; "the children," he commented, "pass, as it were, a part of their lives in the water; the whole of the inhabitants, even the women of the most opulent families, know how to swim." [6] The first weeks were spent in calibrating their instruments (which had arrived undamaged) and making astronomical observations; Bonpland gathered his first plant, a small shrub, *Avicennia tomentoso*, and they examined traces of the earthquake of 1797. The arrival of a Danish slave ship and the sale of its human cargo filled Humboldt with revulsion; at least in Cumaná, he remarked, the number of slaves was relatively low. There were excursions into the neighboring areas: Araya peninsula and a mountainous area called "the Impossible," since it was believed to offer a safe refuge for the people of Cumaná. Several things struck Humboldt during these journeys—the fact that "everything is gigantic," "the deep silence of these solitudes, the individual beauty and contrast of forms, or that vigour and freshness of vegetable life, which characterize the climate of the tropics." [7] In the settlement called Arenas, Humboldt learned of an extraordinary phenomenon, a man who, when his wife took sick was able to nurse their child with his own milk; he satisfied himself as to the veracity of this story by seeing the man himself. [8] He and Bonpland continued herbalizing at Rinconada, and investigated caverns there from which it was reported that flames sometimes rushed out at night; Humboldt suspected that they were of volcanic origin, and expressed his belief that the focus of volcanic activity came from deep within the earth.

During these excursions, and during most of their subsequent journeys, the scientists were usually the guests of the missionary friars at various settlements; Humboldt was gratified over their hospitality (especially since he was a Protestant); he was impressed with their collections of books and with their kind treatment of the Indians. At Caripe he found the Capuchins willing guides in exploring the large Cavern of the Guacharo (unknown in Europe), where they killed several *guacharo* birds hitherto unknown to naturalists, and found a number of subterranean plants. [9] Some days later they went by mule to the tableland of Guardia de San Agustín, and descended a steep incline—Humboldt took it to be almost 60°—back to the lowlands. This was their introduction to this sure-footed beast; Humboldt wrote that "the mules in going down draw their hind legs near their fore legs, and lowering their crupper, let themselves slide down at a venture. The rider runs no risk, provided he loosens the bridle, and leaves the animal quite free in his movements." [10]

The return to Cumaná nearly resulted in a disaster, for Bonpland was attacked and almost killed by a huge zambo (person of Indian/Negro ancestry) whose only explanation for his action was that he had been left on the coast by a French captain, and when he heard Bonpland speaking French, he decided to harm him in retribution. But there were natural phenomena soon after to make them forget the incident. There was a magnificent eclipse of the sun the following day, and on the day after a reddish vapor was noticed in the air, which thickened into a fog during succeeding days. Nights were stifling; the atmosphere seemed on fire and the ground was parched, dusty, and cracked. At 2 P.M. on November 4 two nearby mountains were enveloped by large black clouds extending up to the zenith; at 4 P.M. there was a burst of thunder, followed by two shocks that nearly threw Bonpland to the floor. This was followed by a violent blast of wind, electrical rain in great drops, and a spectacular sunset. "The sun appeared . . . on a firmament of indigo-blue. It's disk was enormously enlarged, distorted, and undulated toward the edges. The clouds were gilded, and fasciculi of divergent rays, which reflected the most brilliant colors of the rainbow, extended even to the midst of the heavens." [11]

The real work lay ahead. On November 16, 1799, Humboldt and Bonpland sailed for La Guaira, whence they would go to Caracas. It was their plan to remain there to the end of the rainy season, then cross the *llanos* to the Orinoco missions, follow the river to the Río Negro and the Brazilian frontier, returning to Cumaná via Angostura—seven hundred leagues in all. The *llanos* country was unknown to the inhabitants of Caracas and Cumaná, but the explorers were fortunate in meeting a Franciscan lay brother, "enlightened, highly intelligent, and full of spirit and courage," [12] who knew the land well and confirmed Humboldt in his desire to see "the much disputed bifurcation of the Oroonoko." [13] Humboldt found La Guaira to be one of the hottest places on earth, but the climate of Caracas was "a perpetual spring." He and Bonpland remained there two months, which gave them time to make many observations. One excursion took them to the twin peaks of the Silla de Caracas, which Humboldt insisted on climbing when he learned that it had not been properly surveyed; it was a dangerous climb, but the view from the top was magnificent, and there was ample opportunity for making valuable observations.

By February 7, 1800, Humboldt and Bonpland were ready to depart from Caracas and begin their journey to the Orinoco. Little escaped their attention; they noticed the great quantity of garnet disseminated in veins of gneiss where the road was cut through rock, the great number of coffee trees, the frequency of drunkenness among the Indians of the area, and the possibility of gold in the region. And there were the giant fig trees; Humboldt marveled how nutritious fluids could be raised 180 feet, without interruption, for perhaps a thousand years. In little more than a week they entered the vast estate of Conde Tovar, along the north shore of Lake Valencia, whose level, for some unexplained reason, seemed to be lowering. Deciding to visit the coast once more before going inland, Humboldt and Bonpland began the descent to Puerto Cabello, following a river of hot water. The area was one of considerable natural beauty, but their enjoyment of it was marred by the heat, which grew more stifling as they approached the coast. While in the port, where they made observations which Humboldt confesses were not dependable, they were guests of a French physician, M. Juliac, who was studying yellow fever; he had an excellent natural history collection, which doubtless excited the admiration, and perhaps envy, of his guests.

On March 1 they resumed their journey, stopping at the plantation of Barbula to investigate a phenomenon which excited their interest when they learned of it—the *palo de vaca*, or cow-tree. When the trunk is cut, Humboldt reported, "it yields an abundance of a glutinous milk, tolerably thick, destitute of all acrimony, and of an agreeable and balmy smell"; only its viscosity "renders it a little disagreeable." [14] He marveled at the bounty of nature; it furnished milk, bread (from the plantain and sago), clothing (from spathes of palms and the bark of trees), ladders (the interior cells of bamboo trunks), and furniture (from bamboo and other trees). Perhaps nature was too prodigal, for "In the midst of this lavish vegetation, so varied in its productions, it requires very powerful motives, to excite man to labour, to awaken him from his lethargy, and unfold his intellectual faculties." [15]

On March 6 the explorers left the valley of Aragua, skirted the southwest shore of Lake Valencia, and finally entered the *llanos* at the Mesa de Paja. The ground temperature was excessively hot; there was no breath of air, and yet, Humboldt recorded, "in the midst of this apparent calm, whirls of dust incessantly arose, driven on by those small currents of air, that glide over the surface of the ground." [16] The *llanos* fascinated him; he saw them as "real steppes" and speculated that had they and the *pampas* been filled with herds furnishing milk in abundance, the nomads tending them "would have subdued the civilized nations of Peru and New Granada, overturned the thrones of the Incas and of the Zaque, and substituted for the despotism, which is the fruit of theocracy, that despotism which arises from the patriarchal government of a pastoral people" [17] (given a series of droughts and floods which would have led these people to fight each other until one group gained dominance over all).

Humboldt found the *llanos* a place of wonderment even on a dark night. "There was no moonlight, but the great mass of nebulae, that decorate the southern sky, enlighten, as they set, a part of the terrestrial horizon. The solemn spectacle of the starry vault, which displays itself in its immense extent, the cool breeze which blows over the plain during the night; the waving motion of the grass, wherever it has attained any height; everything recalled to our minds the surface of the ocean." [17] The absence of any shade resulted in unusually high mean temperatures (30.6° C.) for a tropical country, where days and nights are of equal duration; this gave rise to mirages, which fascinated the scientists, particularly when the images were inverted.

At Calabozo Humboldt and Bonpland had two unexpected encounters involving electricity. Resident there was one Carlos del Pozo, who had built an "electrical machine" from batteries and parts purchased in the United States, and assembled from reading Sigaud de la Fond and Franklin. One can only imagine his surprise on viewing Humboldt's equipment—"instruments which he had not made, and which appeared to be copied from his own." [18] And there were the electric eels, or *gymnoti*. Humboldt had learned that they could be found in the vicinity, and was determined to have a specimen. There was difficulty in procuring one; the Indians were quite afraid of them, although they professed to believe that one could touch them with impunity while chewing tobacco. Specimens were finally obtained for the naturalists, caught by a method almost unbelievable. When the Indians located pools where the eels dug into the mud, they ran some thirty horses and mules into them; the noise of the hoofs excited the eels, which came out, crowded under the animals, and discharged. The frightened beasts were then driven back into the pools and the process repeated until the eels eventually tired and approached the edge of the pool, where they were taken by harpoons fastened to long cords which, being dry, were not conductors. A number of horses and mules were drowned in the process, which seemed extraordinarily wasteful. Humboldt was delighted with his specimens, and described the eels at considerable length in his narrative.[19]

Continuing south from Calabozo on March 24, the naturalists found that the ground became more dusty, and the trees disappeared by degrees. They occupied themselves in making many observations and in a careful study of the geology of the region, and even of the summer sleep of the caymans. Daytime temperatures hovered around 35° C. (95° F.), and the direct rays of the sun were quite oppressive. At one point they found a young Indian girl, lying on the savanna in a state of lethargy, and managed to revive her before her condition became critical. By March 29 they reached the capital of the Capuchin missions in the province, San Fernando de Apuré. The *llanos* journey had come to an end; for the next three months they would be on the rivers.

Although they were advised to proceed overland in a southeasterly direction to the Orinoco, Humboldt and Bonpland preferred to go by way of the Río Apuré in a *lancha*, a large boat, paddled by four Indians, with a palm-thatched cabin at the stern, furnished with a table and benches made of ox hides stretched across frames of brazilwood. They took enough provisions for themselves for a month, to which the head of the mission, Fray José María de Málaga, added sherry, oranges, and tamarinds. The Indians relied on their hooks and nets, since there was an abundance of fish, manatees, and turtles in the river. The journey was enlivened by the presence of the brother-in-law of the governor of the province of Barinas, Nicolás Soto, a man of "amiable disposition and gay temper." [20]

The voyage began in the late afternoon of March 30. On the following day they entered a land "inhabited only by tigers, crocodiles, and *chiguires*, a large species of the genus cavia of Linnaeus." [21] The wild beauty of the region reminded Humboldt of the traditions about the state of the primitive world, yet he noticed that the animals carefully avoided each other. "The golden age has ceased," he concluded, "and in this Paradise of the American forests, as well as everywhere else, sad and long experience has taught all beings, that benignity is seldom found in alliance with strength." [22] That night they stayed at a plantation owned by a dark-skinned man who amazed his visitors by regarding himself as a "caballero blanco"; that this man, who knew no shelter but the shade of a tree, could regard himself as a European, Humboldt found most singular.

The days on the Apuré were filled with fascination. There were vast numbers of flamingos, small jet-black monkeys, the bloodthirsty *caribito* fishes (relatives of the piranhas), many manatees, and the *zancudo* flies, which seemed to be able to pierce a hammock and the thickest garments. And there was the incredible noise that began nightly about 11 P.M., which the Indians described as the animals keeping the feast of the full moon. On April 5 the naturalists reached the point where the Apuré discharged into a river Humboldt described as being as broad as the Seine opposite the Tuileries: "it is not without emotion," he continued, "that we behold for the first time, after long expectation, the waters of the Oroonoko at a point so distant from the coast." [23]

The aspect of the terrain was totally different once they entered the Orinoco. Ahead of them the river, wide as a lake, stretched as far as they could see, its limits somewhat uncertain owing to mirages; here the forest did not reach to the water's edge, for the shores were lined with beaches. Humboldt estimated the width of the river at 3,714 meters, and found the temperature in the *Thalweg* (the main channel) to be a warm 29.2° C. Friendly Carib Indians advised them how to circumvent the great cataracts, and from them the explorers learned the Carib version of the Deluge. The waves of the sea beat against the rocks of Encaramada, according to the legend, and there were but two survivors, a man and a woman, who saved themselves on the high mountain of Tamanacu. Departing, they threw behind them the fruit of the mauritia palm, and from its seeds sprang men and women to repopulate the earth.[24]

That evening the party reached a populated island in the river and spent the night as guests of the resident missionary, who invited them to remain the next day for the harvest of the tortoise eggs, an event to which Humboldt devoted many pages of his narrative. Beyond the mouth of the Río Araucá and the mission of Concepción de Urbana the river narrowed some as mountains approached the east bank. The explorers found themselves wishing for spring water, for the water of the river seemed gelatinous, a phenomenon which the Indians attributed to the decaying hides of putrefied caymans. At Carichana they visited the missionaries, who were just recovering from the tertian fever. There they were able to buy a good canoe from the fathers—a necessity in portaging around the rapids ahead. Since their Indian pilot would not take them beyond that point, Fray Bernardo Zea, even though he was not yet fully recovered from the fever, agreed to accompany them as far as Brazil.

Using the mission as a base of operations, the naturalists made several excursions into the countryside, with considerable profit. Bonpland got a "rich harvest of plants" and Humboldt studied the bands on the mountains which indicated the ancient levels of the waters. Was the Orinoco, he wondered, "only the feeble remains of those immense currents of fresh water of a past era?" [25] Beyond Carichana were cataracts—the Raudal de Cariven—where the river poured through channels not five feet in width, requiring twelve hours of hard rowing. Ahead was the Río Meta; its volume was such (Humboldt compared it to the Danube) as to suggest that it could be an excellent route to the heart of Nueva Granada.[26]

The two main cataracts of the Orinoco, at Atures and Maipurés, presented a beautiful sight to Humboldt and a challenge of mystery as well; "beyond the Great Cataracts," he commented, "an unknown land begins." [27] There were, of course, missions in this "unknown land," for Jesuit priests and brothers, as well as various orders of friars, had labored there for generations, but other explorers were extremely rare. Passing through the one-time Jesuit mission of San Juan Nepomuceno de los Atures, Humboldt and Bonpland found it in "a deplorable state"; the Indian population, 320 before the suppression of the Jesuits, had diminished to 47—a phenomenon they were to find repeated, to a lesser degree, in the Franciscan missions ahead. What had caused it? Humboldt suggested that "what depopulates the Christian settlements is the repugnance of the Indians for the regulations of the missions, the insalubrity of a climate at once hot and damp, bad nourishment, want of care in the diseases of children, and the guilty practice of mothers of preventing pregnancy by the use of deleterious herbs." [28] In addition, there was infanticide; if twins were born, one was immediately destroyed for the curious reason that the parents might resemble rats, which have a litter. It was also believed that two children born at the same time could not possibly have the same father. Physically deformed babies were killed instantly by the father, and weak children who could not keep up with their parents were put to death. "Such is the candor and simplicity of manners," Humboldt mused, "such the boasted happiness of man in the *state of nature!*" [29] Abortion was also common to preserve the freshness and beauty of the women and permit them to concentrate on domestic and agricultural labor, having their children later in life. Humboldt deplored these practices on practical as well as moral grounds; he feared that the missions would become extinct, with the result that there would be no aid for travelers, no pilots for the rapids, and a virtual cessation of communication between Angostura [30] and the Río Negro.

Above the cataracts, in the hot and humid land where nighttime temperatures were only a little lower than those of the day, insects were a major problem. There were mosquitoes and *zancudos* which caused swollen hands, as well as a host of others of various species which tormented the travelers day and night. Humboldt even discovered that one variety succeeded another at fixed and invariable hours. So bothersome were they that Bonpland was finally forced to accept an Indian suggestion that he dry his plants in their *hormitos*, or ovens, from which the insects had been chased by burning wet wood, after which the door was closed. He dried hundreds of plants in this manner.

By the light of copal torches, Humboldt and Bonpland arrived on the night of April 18 at Father Zea's mission, San José de Maipurés. From this settlement they proceeded partly by water, partly by a portage through the jungle, eventually reaching the Río Negro. As Humboldt studied this route, designed to avoid the rapids on the Orinoco, he became convinced of the advisability of constructing a canal ten feet wide through the portage route to facilitate direct communication between the Orinoco and Amazon systems. Leaving Maipurés before sunrise on April 22, the naturalists proceeded toward San Fernando de Atabapo, where the Orinoco bends east, to ascend the Río Atabapo toward the portage. Despite the slight rain, the forest was beautiful and green; Bonpland found some aromatic cinnamon along the way, and Humboldt met an old Indian who assured him that he had seen "with his own eyes" the mysterious Rayas, dwellers of the unexplored forests of Sipapo, who had their mouths in their navels. Beyond the mission of San Fernando everything changed; the mosquitos were absent during the day and the *zancudos* few at night, there were no more crocodiles, manatees, howler monkeys, or crested pheasants, and the water itself was pure and agreeable to the taste. Viewing the incomparable scenery around him, Humboldt was convinced that "nothing can be compared to the beauty of the banks of the Atabapo. Loaded with plants, among which rise the palms crowned with leafy plumes; the banks are reflected in the waters; and the verdure of the reflected image seems to have the same vivid hue as the object itself directly seen." [31]

The portage route (which gave Humboldt and Bonpland an opportunity to study the rubber tree) was not overly difficult, except for one torrential downpour; it brought them to the Río Pinichín, which led them, on May 6, into the Río Negro. Proceeding downstream, past several missions, they arrived at the fort of San Carlos del Río Negro, near the Brazilian border, where they were told that it would be difficult to pass on to the Portuguese settlements.[32] While there they saw some green stones, reputed to have come from the country of women without husbands; Humboldt refused to reject the tradition of the Amazons entirely (in the light of La Condamine's careful collection of evidence), suggesting that perhaps some women, weary of slavery to men, had formed a fugitive community, or may have simply been women defending their homes while their husbands were hunting. But he did reject entirely another legend of long standing—that of Lake Parima—and presented ample evidence to disprove the story beyond doubt.

On May 10 they embarked on the Río Casiquiare, which joins the Orinoco and the Río Negro. Along the way Humboldt bought a toucan, and a macaw, which he added to their menagerie of seven parrots, two manakins, a motmot, two *guans*, two manaviris, and eight monkeys. These were a great source of concern to Father Zea, since, while some were caged, the rest had the run of the boat. The humidity and insects grew worse as they progressed, there was no wind, and the shores appeared as two vertical green walls, with vegetation so thick that it was impossible to land and step out of the boat. By May 21 they arrived at the point Humboldt had come so far to see (and with some misgivings, since its existence was still a matter of doubt in Europe), the bifurcation of the Orinoco. Here, below lofty mountains rising along the northern bank, the Orinoco divides; the main stream flows to the west, the branch—the Casiquiare—flows to the southwest 180 miles to the Río Negro. Humboldt had little concern that the Casiquiare might silt up, for it was "as broad as the Rhine"; he envisioned it as a great artery of commerce in the future.

At the solitary mission of Esmeralda, located above the bifurcation at the foot of the volcano Cerro Duida, Humboldt and Bonpland observed with interest the manufacture of curare from the *bejuco* liana, [33] watched the manufacture of fish flour, and attended a festival of the *juvias* (Brazil-nut trees), where they ate broiled skinned monkeys.

On May 23 they took leave of the mission, proceeding to the bifurcation to take observations, and then to the mission of San Fernando de Atabapo, where Humboldt discussed with the president of the Missions the evils of *entradas,* and expressed the hope that the lot of the Indians would be improved and they would be led to participate in the benefits of civilization. Resuming their journey, the naturalists passed beyond the Great Cataract at Maipurés to Puerto de la Expedición where they visited the cavern of Ataruipe, where some six hundred skeletons of the nearly extinct Atures nation were regularly arranged in baskets. Farther downstream, at the mission of Concepción de Urbana, the explorers studied the Otomac Indians, with whom earth-eating was almost an obsession, and who inhaled *niopo* powder which deprived them of reason for several hours and made them ferocious in battle.[34]

On June 7 Humboldt and Bonpland left their host, Fray Ramón Bueno, with much regret, and proceeded downstream to the mouth of the Apuré, where Nicolás Soto left them to return to his family. Two days later, on June 11, they arrived at Angostura and presented themselves to Governor Felipe de Ynciarte. Humboldt recalled the great pleasure they felt at seeing wheat bread on the governor's table.[35] There they remained a month, Bonpland studying specimens, Humboldt determining the coordinates of the city, when suddenly both were stricken by what Humboldt took to be typhus. A mixture of honey and Angostura bark, much recommended by the Capuchin missionaries, relieved Humboldt's fever, but Bonpland was in a sorry state for several weeks more, having also contracted dysentery.

By July 13 Bonpland had recovered, and they left Angostura for the Caribbean coast, intending to proceed to Nueva España, sail from Acapulco to Manila, and return home via Basra and Syria. On July 23 they arrived at the port of Nueva Barcelona after a journey across the *llanos* made arduous by the absence of a breeze. After a month in the port, the naturalists loaded their cages, collections, and instruments aboard a *lancha* bound for Cumaná, where they planned to get a ship bound for Vera Cruz. The *lancha* was soon captured by a privateer from Halifax, who showed little inclination to put Humboldt and Bonpland off, but fortunately the British sloop *Hawk* overhauled the privateer, took the explorers aboard, and dropped them at Cumaná. After a two-month delay because of the blockade, they were able to sail for Habana aboard a United States vessel on November 16, 1800.[36]

While in Cuba Humboldt received a newspaper notice in the mail telling that Captain Baudin's expedition had left France, and expected to be in Peru in a year. The planned journey to Vera Cruz was abandoned immediately, and Humboldt wrote Baudin that he and Bonpland would journey overland to Lima, and wait for him there. There was another piece of luck. In Habana they met the British explorer John Fraser, who had been shipwrecked off the coast of Cuba; he was awaiting passage to England, and agreed to take two cases of Bonpland's plants with him.[37]

Sixteen days after leaving Habana, Humboldt and Bonpland landed at the village of Zapote at the mouth of the Río Sinu, and were immediately taken with the wild beauty of the place. Humboldt wrote, "How beautiful this land appeared to us! such it must appear to the few travellers who, sensible to the charms of nature, at the aspect of a thick forest, crowned with palm-trees, do not measure their enjoyment by the civilization of the places where they disembark!" [38] Leaving Zapote on March 27, they sailed for Cartagena, experiencing a very severe storm that night, and arrived at their destination on March 30. After talking to Joaquín Fidalgo, who was about to set out on a survey of the coast, they decided to make the journey to Peru by land rather than by sea—little suspecting that this 600-league trip would consume eighteen months.

While in the vicinity of Cartagena during the month of April, 1801, Humboldt had hoped to visit the isthmus of Panama, navigate the Río Chagres, and offer a solution to the problem of a canal, but such a journey would take time, and there was the danger of missing Baudin in Peru, so he gave up the idea.[39] There was time, however, to pause at Turbaco on the way to the Magdalena to see the famous *volcanitos*, or air volcanos. These small cones, about eight inches in height, made of blackish clay, were filled with water, through which great quantities of air were discharged periodically after a hollow sound was heard in the earth.[40]

The journey up the Río Magdalena was made in a *bongo*—a long dugout extended on both sides by boards, with a *toldo* covering the stern. Careful observations were made, and a map of the river was prepared to the port of Honda, where the naturalists disembarked to take up the journey to Bogotá by mule. Word of their coming had preceded them, for the archbishop sent his own carriage to pick them up and bring them to the capital city of the viceroyalty.[41] But the chief purpose in their visiting Bogotá was to see Padre José Celestino Mutis, whose botanical expeditions, as we have seen, took him over much of the viceroyalty. Mutis was most pleased to see them; he gave Humboldt one hundred of his drawings, and recommended his pupil José de Caldas to accompany them to Quito. Indeed, Humboldt impressed all with whom he came in contact most favorably; Charles Cochrane, who traveled through the republic of Colombia later, remarked that "wherever I have followed the steps of the Baron Humboldt, I have heard the most friendly and anxious enquiries after him, and all unite in pronouncing an eulogy on his urbanity of manner, endearing conduct, and gentlemanly deportment." [42]

Humboldt, Bonpland, and Caldas left Bogotá on September 8, and proceeded south toward Quito via Pandi and Ibaque, through a forest of wax palms, tree ferns, orchids, passion flowers, and fuchsias.[43] In the middle of October they traversed the mountain of Quindín, descended to the western side of the cordillera, and passed through a country of bogs and bamboos. So badly were their shoes torn apart that they were reduced to going barefooted, since Humboldt could not bring himself to be carried on the back of an Indian.[44] Passing through Popayán, they paused at Pasto to celebrate Christmas, and entered the ancient city of Quito on January 6, 1802. There Humboldt received the disappointing news that Captain Baudin had changed his plans, and was sailing around the world via the Cape of Good Hope; but this would allow time to explore the volcanoes and Peru, and visit Mexico after all.

The audiencia of Quito boasted of some of the highest peaks in the Andes; among them was the volcano Chimborazo, which towered 20,577 feet above sea level and had never been climbed. Humboldt and Bonpland determined to attempt the conquest of the peak; several months were spent in preparation, which included climbing the smallest of the nearby volcanoes, Pichincha. Apart from testing their physical stamina, the ascent of this mountain furnished an opportunity for important scientific study. Humboldt had already learned that in advancing toward the poles, the mean temperature drops one degree Fahrenheit for each degree of latitude; in ascending Pichincha he found a decrease of one degree for each 300 feet of altitude. During the period of preparation they also managed to interest Carlos Montúfar, son of the Marqués de Aguirre y Montúfar, in joining them in attempting the ascent of Chimborazo.[45]

On June 9 the trio left Quito, and by the 22nd reached the foot of Chimborazo, spending the night in the hut of the alcalde of Calpi. At daybreak, accompanied by Indian guides, they began the ascent, which was relatively easy for the first six thousand feet, but became more difficult as they climbed higher. At the snow line all the guides but one deserted them, and to add to their difficulties there was a mist which made it all but impossible to see down the slope. By seventeen thousand feet the mist thickened so that they were unable to see the summit, and *soroche*—mountain sickness—began to affect them, especially Montúfar. A clearing of the mist finally enabled them to see the summit, but it also revealed ahead of them a chasm which Humboldt estimated as four hundred feet deep and forty feet wide. There seemed to be no way to cross the chasm, and the temperature was already below freezing. Reluctantly Humboldt decided to begin the descent. They had not reached the summit, but they had climbed to an elevation of 19,286 feet—the highest point man had yet attained. Even the descent presented great dangers; they were weak from loss of blood (a consequence of *soroche*, which is accompanied by bleeding from the nose and mouth), chilled to the bone, and had to contend with a violent hailstorm followed by a snowstorm on the way down. Despite these difficulties, Humboldt did think to bring some rocks from Chimborazo back with him, anticipating a demand for them when he returned to Europe.[46]

Returning to Quito, the party passed over the suspension bridge at Penipé, spanning the Río Chambo, 120 feet long and seven or eight feet broad, made of ropes some four inches in diameter fastened to a "clumsy framework" on each bank. Humboldt recommended that travelers cross such swaying structures one at a time, leaning forward, as quickly as possible; by no means should he look down at the water below, or stop in the middle, lest he be gripped by terror and be unable to move.[47] Once in Quito, Humboldt and Bonpland prepared to leave for Lima to observe the transit of Mercury. Resuming their journey, they proceeded to Riobamba to stay a few weeks with the corregidor, a brother of Carlos Montúfar. While there Humboldt became acquainted with some old manuscripts in the Purugayan tongue, which had been translated into Spanish; this got him interested in the Indian tongues in general, and he communicated what he was able to learn to his brother Karl Wilhelm, the eminent philologist.[48]

The road south led through Cuenca and Loja, where Bonpland was anxious to visit the *chinchona* forests and add to his collections. After a year at high altitudes, Humboldt wrote, "it is delightful to descend gradually through the more genial climate of the Cinchona or Quina Woods of Loxa, into the plains of the Upper Amazon. There an unknown world unfolds itself, rich in magnificent vegetation." [49] Going on to Jaén, where Condamine began his Amazon journey, the naturalists had to traverse a region of thick growth, following, down rainy slopes, a road which crossed the Río Guancabamba twenty-seven times. Finally reaching the banks of the great river, they remained seventeen days; Bonpland gathered specimens while Humboldt worked with his instruments to correct errors in Condamine's map.

Leaving the upper Amazon, they followed the Inca highway, which Humboldt felt was as imposing as any Roman road he had seen, past orange groves and the silver mountain of Gualgayoc, and across a series of *páramos*—those cold, windswept regions—where Humboldt finally located the magnetic equator. Ahead lay Cajamarca, where Pizarro had met Atahuallpa, located in what might have been the bed of an ancient lake, an extraordinarily fertile place with an agreeable climate. There a guide, son of the cacique, told them of hidden subterranean golden gardens of the Incas, with trees and birds exquisitely made of the purest gold; he would not dig to find them, lest success bring in invasion of gold-seekers, and bring down upon him the wrath of his people.[50]

After five days in Cajamarca, Humboldt and Bonpland, with new mules and guides, began the crossing of the cordillera, toward the Pacific. They descended by a zigzag road into the deep valley of the Río Magdalena, then ascended a steep wall of rock 5,116 feet high; the Indians told them that the sea would be visible from a nearby pass, but there was a heavy cloud cover. Humboldt's desire to behold the Pacific from the heights of the Andes, born when he first read of Balboa's exploit, was finally gratified when the sky cleared as they approached the Alto de Guanzamarce. "We now, for the first time, commanded a view of the Pacific," Humboldt wrote. "We saw it distinctly, reflecting along the line of the coast an immense mass of light, and rising in immeasurable expanse until bounded by the clearly-defined horizon." [51] They could only estimate the elevation of the Alto; in the excitement of the moment, they had forgotten to open the barometer.

As they visited the Chimu ruins along the coast, Humboldt concluded that it must not have rained appreciably for centuries for the remains to be in so remarkable a state of preservation. But the atmosphere was humid, clouds hung over the cordillera, and the skies seemed to portend rain. Yet it never came. Why? The mystery began to unfold when Humboldt took the temperature of the sea, and found the current to be cool and moving in a northerly direction. A visit to the island of Mazorca, covered with several hundred feet of *guano* (that nitrogen-rich fertilizer which the Incas used on their terraces), convinced him that it had not rained there for centuries. Obviously so vast a quantity had accumulated from millions of birds, who lived on the millions of fish swarming in the cold current. Returning to the mainland with samples of *guano* to send to Europe for analysis, Humboldt took the temperature of the water again at Callao—it was 60° F., while the temperature of the air over the land was 73°. Here was the answer! The cooler air from the sea was heated as it moved over land; this increased its capacity to carry moisture, which it absorbed out of the air—hence no rain.[52]

On November 9, 1802, Humboldt observed the transit of Mercury in Lima, completing his observations. There was little else to do; on January 2, 1803, he and Bonpland sailed out of Callao for Acapulco. As they entered the Río Guayas in the audiencia of Quito, they were thrilled to see Cotopaxi erupting; Humboldt would have gone to the rim had not Bonpland pointed out the risk of missing the sailing for Mexico. After a year's stay in Mexico, Bonpland returned to Europe, while Humboldt continued on to the United States, where he was an honored guest of President Jefferson in Washington and Monticello. He returned to France in 1804. Bonpland, receiving an invitation to become a professor in Buenos Aires, returned to South America; while on a botanical expedition in the Chaco region, he became a captive of the Paraguayan dictator, José Gaspar Rodríguez de Francia. Although he treated Bonpland with honor and allowed him to pursue his botanical studies, under surveillance, *El Supremo* resisted every effort of Humboldt, Pedro I of Brazil, and The Liberator himself, Simón Bolívar, to secure his release. Not until 1831—ten years after his capture —was he given his freedom. Despite this chilling experience, which Bonpland viewed philosophically, he remained in South America for the rest of his life.[53]

The contributions of Humboldt and Bonpland to an enlarged knowledge of South America are enormous. Together they had covered nearly two thousand leagues by land and water, exploring many areas, particularly in the region of the Orinoco, which were scarcely known, if at all, to Europeans, and collecting thousands of plants. Their journey, as Cutright remarks, "gave the world its first realistic picture of the great South American forest, and of the abundance and exuberance of life therein." [54] Humboldt's writings—his *Personal Narrative, Views of Nature, Researches Concerning the Institutions and Monuments of the Ancient Inhabitants of America*, and others—influenced naturalists and explorers throughout the nineteenth century. Scientific societies honored him, geographical features were named for him. But perhaps the greatest tribute came from Simón Bolívar, who, in his letter to Francia seeking Bonpland's release, wrote: "From the early years of my youth I had the honor of cultivating the friendship of Mr. Bonpland and Baron de Humboldt [*sic*], whose learning has done America more good than all of the conquerors." [55]

NOTES

1. Victor Von Hagen, *South America Called Them* (New York, 1945), p. 168.
2. Alexander von Humboldt, *Personal Narrative of Travels to the Equinoctial Regions of the New Continent during the Years 1799–1804* (London, 1814), Vol. I, pp. 34-35.
3. *Ibid.*, Vol. I, p. 42.
4. *Ibid.*, Vol. 1, pp. 240-42.
5. For a detailed description of the voyage, see Humboldt, *Personal Narrative*, Vol. I, pp. 59-353.
6. *Ibid.*, Vol. II, p. 373.
7. *Ibid.*, Vol. III, pp. 37-38.
8. *Ibid.*, Vol. III, pp. 47-49.
9. *Ibid.*, Vol. III, pp. 107-35.
10. *Ibid.*, Vol. III, p. 164.
11. *Ibid.*, Vol. III, p. 317.
12. *Ibid.*, Vol. III, p. 350.

13. *Ibid.,* Vol. III, p. 351.
14. *Ibid.,* Vol. IV, pp. 225-26. I have tried the milk of the *palo de vaca,* and can agree entirely with Humboldt's appraisal.
15. *Ibid.,* Vol. IV, p. 227.
16. *Ibid.,* Vol. IV, p. 292.
17. *Ibid.,* Vol. IV, p. 325.
18. *Ibid.,* Vol. IV, p. 344.
19. *Ibid.,* Vol. IV, pp. 345-76.
20. *Ibid.,* Vol. IV, p. 417.
21. *Ibid.,* Vol. IV, p. 420.
22. *Ibid.,* Vol. IV, p. 421.
23. *Ibid.,* Vol. IV, p. 456.
24. *Ibid.,* Vol. IV, pp. 472-75.
25. *Ibid.,* Vol. IV, p. 556.
26. Humboldt was not alone in this opinion; a twentieth-century traveler, Father John A. Zahm, followed the Río Meta route to Bogotá, and foresaw great possibilities for it. See his *Up the Orinoco and Down the Magdalena* (New York, 1910), p. 112. Fr. Antonio de Monteverde had also recommended it in the 17th century. See Chap. V.
27. Humboldt, *Personal Narrative,* Vol. V, p. 5.
28. *Ibid.,* Vol. V, p. 28.
29. *Ibid.,* Vol. V, p. 30.
30. The present Ciudad Bolívar.
31. Humboldt, *Personal Narrative,* Vol. V, p. 218.
32. What Humboldt did not know at the time was that an order had been issued by authorities in Brazil for his arrest and the seizure of his instruments; he and Bonpland were to be conducted to Belém, and thence to Lisboa. When the court learned of this order, it was reversed, with orders that he should be encouraged, and not disturbed. *Ibid.,* Vol. V, pp. 370-71.
33. The bark is bruised and ground, and placed in a filter of plantain leaves. Cold water is poured on it, and the yellowish juice filtered out is evaporated in a pot, and tasted to determine proper strength. The taste is bitter, and the poison is harmful only in contact with the blood. The juice of the *tiracaquero* tree is added to give it the color and consistency of tar, for use on darts and arrows. The Indians considered curare a good stomachic; it is harmless taken internally, and hence animals killed by poisoned darts and arrows are quite edible. Humboldt, *Personal Narrative,* Vol. V, pp. 514-22.
34. The powder was made from *mimosacea* pods which were wetted and fermented; the seeds were then kneaded into a paste, mixed with cassava flour and lime from helix shells, and roasted in small cakes, which were subsequently powdered. The powder was inhaled through a forked bone from a bird; this bone was believed to be essential. *Ibid.,* Vol. V, p. 662.
35. *Ibid.,* Vol. V, p. 692.
36. *Ibid.,* Vol. VI, pp. 84-105.
37. Helmut De Terra, *Humboldt, the Life and Times of Alexander von Humboldt* (London, 1935), pp. 115-17.
38. Humboldt, *Personal Narrative,* Vol. VII, p. 436.
39. De Terra, *op. cit.,* p. 118.
40. Humboldt, *Researches Concerning the Institutions and Monuments of the Ancient Inhabitants of America* (London, 1814), Vol. II, pp. 95-98.
41. On the journey to and stay in Bogotá, see Von Hagen, *op. cit.,* pp. 132-35.
42. *Journal of a Residence and Travels in Colombia* (London, 1825), Vol. II, pp. 391-92.
43. De Terra, *op. cit.,* pp. 121-22.
44. Humboldt, *Researches,* p. 65.
45. See De Terra, *op. cit.,* pp. 122-23; Charlotte Kellner, *Alexander von Humboldt* (London, 1963), p. 57; Von Hagen, *op. cit.,* 144-45.

46. Humboldt described the ascent of Chimborazo in a letter to his brother, Karl Wilhelm, which appears in Edward Whymper, *Travels Amongst the Great Andes of the Equator* (New York, 1892), pp. 428-30. His record stood for thirty years, until Boussingault reached an elevation of 19,700 on the same mountain in 1831. Whymper, who reached the summit of Chimborazo in 1879, had many misgivings concerning Humboldt's account, especially concerning his exact route and rate of descent, and some of his observations (pp. 27-33). He also quotes Charles Darwin who, after his experiences with altitude at the much lower level of 14,000 feet in the Portillo Pass in Chile, remarked: "It is incomprehensible to me how Humboldt and the others were able to ascend to the elevation of 19,000 feet." (*Narrative of the Surveying Voyages of His Majesty's Ships Adventure and Beagle*, III, 393, quoted on p. x). I am indebted to Professor Ronald Hilton of Stanford University for first calling this to my attention.

47. Humboldt, *Researches*, Vol. II, pp. 13-14.

48. De Terra, *op. cit.*, pp. 133-34.

49. Humboldt, *Views of Nature* (London, 1828), p. 390.

50. *Ibid.*, pp. 393-412.

51. *Ibid.*, p. 419.

52. De Terra, *op. cit.*, pp. 144-46; Von Hagen, *op. cit.*, pp. 154-56. The *guano*, when analyzed in Europe, was found to be thirty-three times more effective than ordinary manure; this created a fantastic demand, and *guano* became a mainstay in the economy of Peru for years to come. The cold current was later named for Humboldt, although he claimed that this was improper, since he had done no more than determine its temperature. It is also known today as the Peru Current.

53. Paul R. Cutright, *The Great Naturalists Explore South America* (New York, 1940), pp. 11-12.

54. *Ibid.*, p. 9.

55. Vicente Lecuna, ed., *Cartas del Libertador*, Vol. III, p. 264 (quoted in J. Fred Rippy and E. R. Brann, "Alexander von Humboldt and Simón Bolívar," *American Historical Review* LII (July, 1947): 701.

Part Four

The Great Age
of Scientific Exploration

XV   *The Great Naturalists*

Humboldt's journeys marked a watershed in the history of the exploration of South America. By 1800 exploration of the continent, in the traditional sense of the term, was all but complete; only a few remote areas had not been crossed by conquistadores, missionaries, *bandeirantes,* or eighteenth-century scientists. After Humboldt exploration took on a new dimension; the naturalist dominated, bringing to the museums of Europe and the United States thousands of specimens of the lush plant life, the insects, carnivores, amphibians, reptiles, and fishes of this bountiful continent. Though he seldom found himself on untrodden paths, the naturalist was no less an explorer than his predecessors. One of them, Louis Agassiz, commented: "The work of the naturalist, in our day, is to explore worlds the existence of which is already known; to investigate, not to discover. The first explorers, in this modern sense, were Humboldt in the physical world, Cuvier in natural history, Lavoisier in chemistry, La Place in astronomy. They have been the pioneers in the kinds of scientific work characteristic of our century." [1]

The nineteenth century was a time of intense activity by naturalists in South America. Many came on their own; others accompanied government-sponsored or privately sponsored expeditions. With one exception, we shall here be concerned with those whose work was unconnected with any sponsored projects, leaving the others for later consideration. One of the first of these independent naturalist-explorers was Charles Waterton. Born in Yorkshire, England, in 1782, he was educated at a Catholic college, traveled in Spain, and in 1804 went to British Guiana to oversee some family estates, remaining two years and then returning to England. Subsequently he made four journeys to South America over a ten-year period, recording them, somewhat apologetically, in a delightful book [2] frequently flavored with classical allusions and quotations from *Don Quixote.* For Waterton was a classics scholar; like a number of other nineteenth-century naturalists, he was self-taught in natural history.

Waterton set out on his first journey from Stabroek in Guiana in April of 1812 with two purposes in mind: to collect "a quantity of the strongest Wourali poison; and to reach the inland frontier fort of Portuguese Guiana." [3] Following the course of the Demerara River, he was awed by the magnificence of the tropical forest—the great trees, the wild fig trees, the bush-ropes, and the great variety of fauna which included jaguars, monkeys, anteaters, sloths, scarlet curlews, vultures, vampires, snakes, lizards, and a host of insects. At an Indian settlement he managed to procure some wourali (curare) poison and assured himself of its potency by trying it on a dog, which promptly died after being wounded in the thigh. On the night of May 1 he heard a strange, unexplainable noise, like several regiments firing muskets rapidly, which terrified the Indians; not until his return did he learn the cause—an eruption on St. Vincent Island. Entering the Essequibo River, Waterton was so moved by the beauty around him that he became almost lyrical in describing it. [4] In this he was like many of his fellow naturalists of the century, whose descriptions of scenery and natural wonders are at times almost pure poetry.

Entering the Apoura-poura River, Waterton reached a locality where legend had established a fabulous city. "According to the new map of South America," he related, "Lake Parima, or the White Sea, ought to be within three or four days' walk from this place." [5] But he was enough of a realist to view this legend with the same skepticism he reserved for other fantasies commonly believed by the Indians. When, a few days later, he reached Fort São Joaquim at the Brazilian frontier on the Rio Branco, the commandant told him that he had been forty years in Portuguese Guiana and had not met anyone who had actually seen the lake. While there Waterton procured some more curare from the Macoushi Indians, who, he said, made the most potent variety. He also learned of an antidote for the poison: an apparently dead animal was revived through artificial breathing for several hours by means of a bellows. [6]

Fearing a return of the fever which had attacked him prior to entering Portuguese territory, Waterton decided to return to Demerara by the same route he had come, and thus he returned to England. Four years later he was able to resume his work in the New World, arriving at Recife from Liverpool on March 19, 1816. The birds in the vicinity he found most attractive, and managed to collect fifty-eight specimens of them before the rainy season began. At first he considered going up the Amazon to the Rio Negro and thence to the source of the Essequibo, but changed his plans, going instead to the former scene of his labors, where the season for procuring birds of fine plumage had already begun. For six months he wandered through the forests of Demerara, collecting some two hundred specimens of fine hummingbirds, cotingas, campane-

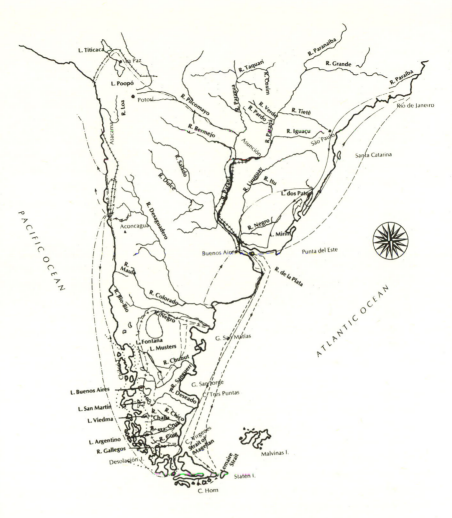

L. Titicaca
La Paz
L. Poopó
Potosí
R. Loa
Atacama
R. Pilcomayo
R. Bermejo
R. Salado
R. Dulce
R. Desaguadero
Aconcagua
R. Maule
R. Bío-Bío
R. Colorado
R. Negro
L. Fontana
L. Musters
R. Chubut
R. Senguerr
R. Deseado
L. Buenos Aires
L. San Martín
L. Viedma
R. Chico
Chalia
R. Santa Cruz
L. Argentino
R. Coig
R. Gallegos
Desolación I.
C. Horn

R. Taquari
R. Coxim
R. Paraguay
R. Verde
R. Pardo
R. Paraná
Asunción
R. Uruguay
R. Itu
L. dos Patos
R. Negro
L. Mirim
Buenos Aires
R. de la Plata
Punta del Este
G. San Matías
G. San Jorge
C. Tres Puntas
C. Vírgenes
Strait of Magellan
Le Maire Strait
Staten I.

R. Paranaíba
R. Grande
R. Paraíba
Río de Janeiro
R. Tietê
R. Iguaçu
São Paulo
Santa Catarina

Malvinas I.

PACIFIC OCEAN
ATLANTIC OCEAN

Nineteenth Century

Saint-Hilaire, 1820 ——————————

Orbigny, 1826 ——————————

Poeppig, 1827-1828 —x—x—x—x—x—x—

Orbigny, 1829 ·······································

Orbigny, 1830 ++++++++++++++++++++++++++++

Darwin, 1832-1833 — — — — — — — —

Darwin, 1834-1835 —·—·—·—·—·—·—·—·

Philippi, 1853-1855 ++++++++++++++++++++++++

Page, 1855 + + + + + + + + + + + +

Musters, 1869-1870 — + — + — + — + — + —

Moyano, 1880 — — — — — — — — —

Touar, 1883 — ·· — — ·· — — ·· — — ·· —

Steffen, 1892-1902 ·····························

ros, toucans, Guiana jays, ricebirds, woodpeckers, egrets, trumpeters, and other birds of beautiful plumage. For those who would follow him he gave some practical advice: take only what is necessary for comfort, but above all a sheet to suspend above one's hammock to keep off the rain, and wear only a hat, shirt, and light trousers; learn to walk bare-foot. Depend on one's own skill or the Indians for food, and do not worry about animals—snakes attack only if disturbed, and the few jaguars will flee; the worst insect bites cause only transient fever.[7] Surprising as this advice may seem, it served Waterton quite well.

In 1820 he returned to Demerara, and established himself in the ruined former home of an old friend; repairs made it at least an acceptable shelter. Fever attacked him in June; he treated it successfully with calomel, jalap, tea, and castor oil, and was soon able to study the profuse wild-life of the region: sloths, anteaters, armadillos, tortoises, caymans, and vampires. Waterton tried without avail to get one of the vampire bats to suck blood out of him; he was more fortunate in capturing a four-teen-foot constrictor which he successfully dissected. Anxious to capture a large cayman, he began a journey down the Essequibo in search of one. The scenery delighted him: "Nothing could be more lovely than the appearance of the forest on each side of this noble river. Hills rose on hills in fine gradation, all covered with trees of gigantic height and size. Here their leaves were of a lively purple, and there of the deepest green. Sometimes the caracara extended its scarlet blossoms from branch to branch, and gave the tree the appearance as though it had been hung with garlands." [8] And there were the sounds of this wondrous world—the "tolling" of the campanero bird, the roaring of the "tigers," and finally the noise of the cayman, a "singular and awful sound . . . like a suppressed sigh, bursting forth all of a sudden, and so loud that you might hear it above a mile off." [9] The cayman hunt was successful; the Indians built an instrument of barbed wooden sticks at the end of a long rope tied to a tree, and succeeded in capturing a sizable specimen, which Waterton carefully dissected and added to the collection he took back to England.

Three years later, in 1824, Waterton decided to make one last journey to South America. First he visited New York, Montreal, Québec, and Philadelphia, then set sail for the West Indies, visiting the Lesser Antilles before going to Demerara in Guiana. This expedition, which lasted until the onset of the rainy season at the end of December, netted him a sizable collection of birds, as well as a few monkeys.

A contemporary of Waterton, operating during these same years along the south coast of Brazil, was the French botanist, Auguste de Saint-Hilaire. A native of Orléans, he developed an early interest in natural history, beginning with entomology, and finally settling on botany. In 1816 he had the opportunity of accompanying the Duc de Luxembourg, newly appointed ambassador of France to Portugal and Brazil, to his new post and departed April 1. Before beginning his travels, he went to Uba, on the banks of the Rio Paraíba, and spent a month in the virgin forest. Europeans, he commented, accustomed to forests of pine, beech, and oak, could form only an imperfect idea of the virgin forests of South America, where nature seemed to have exhausted its forces in displaying such magnificence and variety.[10] Leaving Rio de Janeiro on December 7, 1816, he went to Minas Gerais, where he spent fifteen months wandering through the province, describing the caatingas (forest growth peculiar to relatively dry areas), the great forests, the Serra de Mantiquiera, the diamond area, and the great Rio São Francisco, the source of so much sickness because of the putrefying animals along its shores. After spending some time in São João del-Rei, he returned to Rio in March of 1818.

After putting his collections in order, Saint-Hilaire left in August of the same year for the province of Espiritú Santo, via the Rio Doce, as far as the city of Vitoria. The journey enabled him to enlarge his collections, particularly of the medicinal plants in the area. Rather than return by the same route, he took a ship to Rio de Janeiro in November, 1818.

A third journey took him back to São João del-Rei in January of 1819 to collect more medicinal plants, study the variations in vegetation at different altitudes, collect rare flowers, and visit the source of the Rio São Francisco. Saint-Hilaire proceeded as far as Vila Boa (the present Goiás) and the Rio Claro, then south to Santa Ana, where he studied the Chicriabas Indians, learning something of their language, which he found very systematic. The journey ended at São Paulo in October; the season was excessively dry, and there were few flowers to collect.

Leaving the collections he had made in the care of the president of São Paulo, he continued south in December, reaching Curitiba, where he became acquainted with *mate*, noting the differences between the Brazilian and Paraguayan types. Continuing on to Santa Catarina, he eventually reached Pôrto Alegre in Rio Grande do Sul, and was impressed by the beauty of its setting. On October 29 he arrived in Montevideo, noticing that there, in the Temperate Zone, flowers disappeared, as in France. Proceeding up the Río Uruguay, he visited the falls and the mission country, studied the Guaranís, and returned to Pôrto Alegre, whence he embarked for Rio de Janeiro in June, 1821.

In January of 1822 Saint-Hilaire paid one last visit to southern Minas Gerais, then proceeded to São Paulo to pick up the collections he had left there, remaining until May. The results of the five journeys were most gratifying: he had collected 2,005 birds, 6,000 insects, 125 quadrupeds, 35 reptiles, 58 fishes and shells, and 7,000 plants. The findings were published in several journals, and in a multivolume work.[11]

A third naturalist active in South America during this decade was the Englishman William Swainson, who came to Recife late in 1816. Like Waterton, he intended to explore on his own, but found himself limited to the immediate vicinity of the city because of revolutionary disturbances. Not until the middle of 1817 was he able to leave for the interior, going as far as Penedo, then returning to the coast at Salvador, where he explored the vicinity. In 1818 he went to Rio de Janeiro, where he remained several months, returning thereafter to England with a magnificent collection of specimens, both zoological and botanical.[12]

A few years later the Danish naturalist Peter W. Lund, advised to seek a warmer climate, made a journey to Brazil (1825–29) which enabled him to botanize extensively in the region around Rio de Janeiro. Returning in 1833 with Louis Riedel, he explored the provinces of São Paulo and Minas Gerais, settling finally in Lagoa Santa, where he remained until his death in 1880. In addition to sending large collections of flora and fauna to Copenhagen, he made a detailed study of fossils.[13]

The most extensive explorations of the decade were those undertaken by the German Eduard F. Poeppig. After visiting the United States, he sailed from Baltimore in 1827, rounding Cape Horn, continuing past the Chonos archipelago to Valparaíso. After exploring the vicinity to collect specimens, he went to the Río Aconcagua valley at the onset of spring, collecting specimens of plant and animal life, as well as making a thorough study of agriculture, stockraising, and arborculture in the vicinity. As summer approached, Poeppig went to Santiago, then to the Andes, across to Mendoza in Argentina, then back to Chile to study the mines at Coquimbo. Subsequently he went to study the southern provinces, wintering in Talcahuano. There, with his accustomed thoroughness, he undertook a detailed study of the area, observing not only its natural history but its economic resources and trade possibilities and manner of living as well. With the return of spring he began a journey through the Andes from Antuco, observing the various climate zones and the vegetation peculiar to them and collecting a variety of specimens. In addition, he studied the Indians with whom he came in contact on his journey as he progressed to the north.

Leaving Chile, Poeppig went to Lima, whence he made excursions to the Sierra de la Viuda, Casacancha, and various Inca ruins, botanizing extensively and seeing, finally, the wild potato in its native environment. Further travels took him to Cerro de Pasco, Huánuco, and finally into the *montaña*, where he was able to add extensively to his collections, including such novel items as coca plants and monkeys. The variety and wealth of plant life in this area were sources of great satisfaction to him; the *montaña* was a collector's paradise. Continuing his explorations, Poeppig came to the Río Huallaga, studying the Indians in the regions, especially the Jibitos and Maynas. This was the famous mission country of which he had read much, and he explored it extensively, botanizing and collecting specimens of the varied insect world. Reaching now the Marañón, or upper Amazon, Poeppig slowly descended the great river, continuing his scientific observations along the way to Belém. Returning to Germany, he was named to a professorship of zoology at Leipzig, where he published three major works on his explorations.[14]

Of all the great naturalists who visited South America, the outstanding name, of course, is that of Charles Darwin. His journey was not the longest, nor his explorations the most extensive; but the conclusions he reached from his observations, published in *The Origin of Species*, rocked the scientific world and established his reputation as one of the greatest scientists of his age. Unlike his predecessors in South America, Darwin did not come on his own initiative but as a member of a surveying expedition ordered by the British government. Yet his work was so separate and distinct from the chief work of the expedition, and his subsequent reputation as a naturalist so great, that it would seem inappropriate indeed not to discuss his work at this point.

In 1830 the two surveying ships, H.M.S. *Adventure* and H.M.S. *Beagle*, which the Admiralty had sent out to explore the coasts of South America, returned to England, bringing three Fuegan Indians with them in the hope that they might benefit from their exposure to British civilization.[15] The following year the Admiralty decided to return the Fuegans and complete the survey, and perhaps continue the journey to sail around the world. The *Beagle* was commissioned for the voyage and extensively modified; command was given to Captain Robert Fitz-Roy, who had brought the vessel back from the earlier mission, with its Fuegan guests.

Anxious to make the most of the opportunity of collecting useful information, Fitz-Roy suggested to the hydrographer "that some well-educated and scientific person should be sought for who would willingly share such accommodations as I had to offer, in order to profit by the opportunity of visiting distant countries yet little known." [16] Such an offer, which promised no financial remuneration, would scarcely attract established scientists and it did not. Through connections at Cambridge, he obtained the name of Darwin (like Waterton, trained in classics and self-taught in natural history), who agreed to go provided that he could leave the expedition when he thought proper and that he should pay a fair share of the expenses of Fitz-Roy's table.[17]

The *Beagle* sailed from Devonport on December 27, 1831. The object of the expedition, as Darwin records it, "was to complete the survey of Patagonia and Tierra del Fuego, commenced under Captain King in 1826 to 1830, to survey the shores of Chile, Peru, and some islands in the Pacific—and to carry a chain of chronometrical measurements round the World." [18] To accomplish this last end, twenty-two chronometers were taken aboard the ship. After an uneventful cruise with stops in the Canaries and Cape Verde Islands, which gave Darwin an opportunity to study marine life, the *Beagle* arrived at Salvador on February 29, 1832. There the young scientist was delighted to enter, at last, the tropical forest. But, as he expressed it, "delight itself . . . is a weak term to express the feelings of a naturalist, who, for the first time, has wandered by himself in a Brazilian forest. The elegance of the grasses, the novelty of the parasitical plants, the beauty of the flowers, the glossy green of the foliage, but above all the general luxuriance of the vegetation, filled me with admiration." [19]

Early in April the *Beagle* arrived in Rio de Janeiro, and for the next several months Darwin visited various localities in the vicinity, climbed Corcovado, observed the striking effects caused by the atmospheric haze (which Humboldt had noticed), and amassed a large collection of insects. On July 5 the expedition left Rio de Janeiro, and anchored at Montevideo on July 26. Darwin made his headquarters in nearby Maldonado, "a most quiet, forlorn, little town" [20] in whose vicinity he was able to collect a considerable number of birds, as well as some quadrupeds and reptiles, many of which were entirely unfamiliar to him.

After several months in the Río de la Plata area, the *Beagle* resumed its journey south, and finally on December 17 anchored in the Bahía de Buen Suceso in Tierra del Fuego. The following morning they made contact with some Fuegans, who appeared clad only in mantles of guanaco skins, just as earlier navigators had described them centuries before. Culturally backward though they might be, Darwin found them a friendly lot, and marveled at their skill in mimicry, recalling that the Fuegans with them, York Minster, Jemmy Button, and Fuegia Basket, had learned English quickly and had picked up some Spanish and Portuguese during their limited stay in Brazil and Argentina.

Exploring the island, Darwin found it covered on the east coast with a vast forest extending from the water's edge up to one thousand feet, where it was succeeded by a band of peat, and finally by snow at the 3000- to 4000-foot level. So thick was the forest that the only way he could explore the island was to follow the course of mountain torrents, eventually reaching the top of one of the hills, which afforded a wide view of the surrounding country. Although it was mid-summer, the weather was wretched; the sun was seldom seen, and snow and sleet were not uncommon. Darwin marveled at how the Fuegans survived in this climate. One day, at Wollaston Island, he saw six of them in a canoe, "the most abject and miserable creatures I anywhere beheld";

what surprised him most was to see a completely naked mother feeding her newborn child "whilst the sleet fell and thawed on her naked bosom, and on the skin of her naked baby!" [21] At the end of December Fitz-Roy set sail for the Beagle Channel (discovered on the earlier voyage) in order to deliver his Fuegan charges to their people. Mission completed, the *Beagle* returned to the Río de la Plata with a stop in the Malvinas (Falklands).

Leaving Maldonado on July 24, 1833, the *Beagle* reached the mouth of the Río Negro, some three hundred miles south, and anchored. The ship's party went ashore to the town of El Carmen (or Patagones), eighteen miles inland on the river—the southernmost point on the Atlantic coast at that time inhabited by civilized man. Learning that an Englishman resident there, a guide, and five gauchos were going to Bahía Blanca, which was the ship's next port, Darwin decided to accompany them. En route he saw the famed sacred tree of the Indians, slept under the stars on the pampas, and saw for the first time the guanaco and the agouti. At the Rio Colorado they came upon the camp of General Juan Manuel de Rosas, absent from Buenos Aires on a campaign against the Indians. Darwin met him, and was most favorably impressed; he felt Rosas would use his influence for the prosperity and advancement of his country—a prediction which, he admitted, turned out to be completely wrong during the general's subsequent dictatorship.[22]

The next night was spent at an exceptionally clean and neat post house, commanded by a Negro lieutenant whom Darwin described as one of the most civil and obliging men he had ever met. A day's ride took them to Bahía Blanca, a small fortified outpost, where they were to rejoin the *Beagle*. Riding to the harbor, some distance away, to see if the ship had arrived, Darwin and his companion descried what they took to be three Indian hunters in the distance. One of them rode out of sight; eyeing the other two cautiously, they made an attempt to evade them without being seen and return to the fort, when Darwin's companion burst out laughing—they were women, the wife and sister-in-law of the major's son, hunting ostrich eggs!

The *Beagle* arrived August 24. Since it was to sail for the Río de la Plata a week later, Darwin obtained Fitz-Roy's consent to proceed to Buenos Aires by land, giving him an opportunity to continue his investigations. There was much to interest him, particularly the fossilized remains of nine great quadrupeds previously found in the vicinity, and several more specimens he located himself. Of particular interest to him was the resemblance of some of these extinct species to living animals. There was also time to study the rhea, or South American ostrich, several smaller birds, and a number of reptiles, and to listen to horrendous tales of the barbarity on both sides in Rosas' war of extermination against the Indians.[23]

On September 8 Darwin, having hired a gaucho to accompany him, set out on his journey across the pampas to Buenos Aires. The trip was without incident, although he did miss by one day witnessing a singular event—a storm during which hail the size of small apples fell with such violence as to kill a great number of wild animals, which they saw being brought into the post-house. The two arrived in Buenos Aires on September 20, and a week later Darwin set out for Santa Fe, where he spent some time continuing his geological investigations, in the course of which he discovered a fossilized tooth of the extinct early American horse. Illness prevented further explorations on his part, so he took ship for Buenos Aires, observing the wildlife along the riverbanks, and speculating on what noble towns would be found along the river had the English been the first to enter the Río de la Plata.

Going to Montevideo, Darwin found that the *Beagle* would not sail for some time; consequently he went to Colonia del Sacramento, and leisurely probed for more fossils. So many were found that, as he remarked, "We may conclude that the whole area of the Pampas is one wide sepulchre of these extinct giant quadrupeds." [24] On December 6, Darwin exchanged the freedom of the plains for the cramped quarters aboard the *Beagle*, and braced himself for a return of the seasickness which plagued him during most of the voyage. The course now was south, to Puerto Deseado on the Patagonian coast. On one dark night he witnessed an unusual spectacle: "There was a fresh breeze, and every part of the surface, which during the day is seen as foam, now glowed with a pale light. The vessel drove before her bows two billows of liquid phosphorus, and in her wake she was followed by a milky train. As far as the eye reached, the crest of every wave was bright, and the sky above the horizon, from the reflected glare of these livid flames, was not so utterly obscure as over the vault of the heavens." [25]

The *Beagle* anchored December 23 at Puerto Deseado, near the ruins of the old Spanish settlement, deserted because of the dryness of the climate and occasional Indian attacks. The flora and fauna were very limited; there was little to observe other than the numerous guanacos. The geology Darwin found more interesting. As he noted the vast deposits of shells of extinct molluscs, and found more fossils of gigantic quadrupeds, he wondered what should cause some creatures to become extinct and others to survive. On April 13, 1834, the *Beagle* anchored in the mouth of the Río Santa Cruz, in the far south of Patagonia. So little was known about the river that Fitz-Roy decided to follow it as far as time would permit. A party of twenty-five was sent out in three whaleboats, with provisions for three weeks; so strong was the current that it was impossible to row or sail, and the boats had to be hauled upstream by tracking lines. After three days of monotonous plains, the nature of the landscape altered as they came upon a great basaltic platform through which the river flowed. There Darwin shot his first condor, a great bird with an eight-and-one-half-foot wingspread. Finally, on April 29, they caught sight of the cordillera, visible occasionally in white majesty as the clouds parted, but they were not to reach it. On May 4, at a distance of 140 miles from the Atlantic and 60 miles from the nearest arm of the Pacific, Fitz-Roy decided to go no farther, for their supplies were giving out and there was little prospect of reaching the mountains. The descent was rapid; they reached the *Beagle* on May 8, after a total journey of twenty-one days.

On March 16 the expedition returned to the Malvinas (Falklands), anchoring again in Berkeley Sound; there Darwin studied the local birds and the rather plentiful marine life. At the end of May, the *Beagle* again entered the Strait of Magellan, and on June 1 anchored at Port Famine. On going ashore, Darwin found a thick, dank forest, with little of interest other than a curious type of fungus which grew in vast numbers on beech trees and formed an important element in the diet of the Fuegan Indians. He found Tierra del Fuego poor in fauna; there were only a few species of birds and no reptiles at all; the waters around, by contrast, teemed with life. All of it, he noticed, depended on kelp, which provided food and shelter; without it the fish could not live, nor then the cormorants, seals, otters, and porpoises, "and lastly, the Fuegan savage, the miserable lord of this miserable land, would redouble his cannibal feast, decrease in numbers, and perhaps cease to exist." [26] Nature and habit, he felt, had fitted the Fuegans to this land, and any change in the balance would mean his end. On June 8 Fitz-Roy decided to leave via the recently discovered Magdalen Channel; the following day they passed towering Mount Sarmiento, and on June 10 the *Beagle* sailed into the open Pacific.

The expedition arrived in Valparaíso in the middle of the Chilean winter, on July 23; "after Tierra del Fuego," Darwin remarked, "the climate felt quite delicious—the atmosphere so dry, and the heavens so clear and blue with the sun shining brightly, that all nature seemed sparkling with life." [27] The next two months Darwin spent in traveling about central Chile, visiting the beautiful valley of Quillota, climbing Mount Campana for a magnificent view of the central valley and the Andes, visiting Santiago and the mines at the base of the Andes. Illness confined Darwin to bed after his return to Valparaíso, but he recovered in time to join the *Beagle* when it sailed for Chiloé Island and the Chonos archipelago on November 10.

Chiloé was cool and damp, and agriculture was limited to such growth as did not require much sunlight to ripen. For the next several weeks the *Beagle* cruised around the vicinity taking soundings. Captain Fitz-Roy decided to try to climb San Pedro mountain, but his party had to abandon the attempt; as Darwin explained, "the forest was so impenetrable, that no one who has not beheld it, can imagine so entangled a mass of dying and dead trunks." [28] On December 11 the *Beagle* sailed south into the Chonos archipelago, where it picked up five deserters from an American whaler, who had roamed the coasts for fifteen months in a vain attempt to reach civilization. As they explored the islands, Darwin found that the climate and vegetation resembled Tierra del Fuego more than Chiloé; the ground in the forests was covered with a thick, elastic peat rather than an elaborate growth of ferns and other plants. The zoology was poor, chiefly a few aquatic quadrupeds and petrels.

Upon leaving Chiloé on February 4, the *Beagle* sailed north to Valdivia, where Darwin was amazed at the seemingly endless apple orchards. Sixteen days later the *Beagle*'s complement were witnesses at Valdivia to the great earthquake which devastated Concepción and Talcahuano. The damage was not serious at Valdivia, and not until March 4, when Darwin and the others walked the rubble-strewn streets of Concepción, could they comprehend the extent of the destruction— not a house was left standing. The one thing that caused him to marvel was the fact that the greater number of the inhabitants escaped unhurt.

Leaving this scene of desolation, the expedition sailed again for Valparaíso, arriving March 11. Two days later Darwin set out for the Portillo Pass, which would take him across the Andes. Little escaped his attention on the way; he was particularly interested in the geology of the cordillera, which he came to believe was the result of a gradual rather than sudden upheaval, as was commonly thought. As he ascended the pass, he began to notice a tightness in the head and chest—the first symptoms of *soroche* (or *puna*, as the Chileans called mountain sickness)— which was forgotten as he found fossil shells on the highest ridge. Yet, he said, "Certainly the exertion of walking was extreme, and the respiration became deep and laborious. It is incomprehensible to me, how Humboldt and others were able to ascend to the elevation of 19,000 feet." [29] Descending the eastern slope of the cordillera, Darwin was struck by the difference in vegetation and quadrupeds on the two sides of the Andes, and by the fact that a great number of plants, animals, and insects were identical with or closely allied to those of Patagonia.

Scientific curiosity took the naturalist across the Río Luján and as far as the city of Mendoza before he decided to return to Chile via the Uspallata Pass—the route San Martín had followed in his campaign of liberation. At a height of seven thousand feet he was gratified to find some petrified trees, which told him that this was once the shore of the Atlantic Ocean, that the land had submerged to a great depth to be covered by sedimentary beds and great streams of submarine lava, then had been raised up again to its present level. The journey through the pass, although very cold, was uneventful, and on April 10 Darwin returned to Valparaíso after an absence of twenty-four days. "Never," he said, "did I more deeply enjoy an equal space of time." [30]

Arranging with Fitz-Roy to pick him up in Copiapó, Darwin proceeded to that port by land, stopping for a while at Coquimbo to make important geological observations and to visit the mining outposts in the desert. The change of climate, evident from the fossil remains he found, puzzled him: why was it so arid now, when obviously it had not been before? The rise of the cordillera, he felt sure, was slow; therefore the change of climate must have been slow, and the Indian remains he found about him, well preserved in the arid climate, must antedate it and thus be of greater antiquity than anyone had before imagined. On June 29, after a numbing night because of a gale, Darwin descended the cordillera for the coast, reaching Copiapó on July 1. Three days later the *Beagle* arrived at the port, eighteen miles distant (a precaution against pirates), and Darwin went to join it; the following morning it sailed for Iquique, which at that time was a Peruvian port.

A brief stay in port gave Darwin a chance to visit the saltpeter works, fourteen leagues away, and to experience the complete and utter desolation of this desert, strewn with the carcasses and bones of animals which had perished on it. "Excepting the Vultur aura, which preys on the carcasses," Darwin observed, "I saw neither bird, quadruped, reptile, nor insect." [31] On July 19 the *Beagle* anchored at Callao and remained for six weeks; because of political disturbances, Darwin saw little of the country, and what he did see he did not like. A cloud bank hung over the port and Lima, obscuring the Andes, and the visitors experienced for the first time the *garúa*—that heavy, thick mist which is almost rain but does not fall. Like Humboldt and others before him, Darwin was convinced that the ague, which afflicted many in the coastal cities, was caused by miasma. He might have looked for other causes, for he declared Callao to be "filthy" and "ill-built," populated by "a depraved, drunken set of people" and Lima to be "in a wretched state of decay; the streets are nearly unpaved; and heaps of filth are piled up in all directions, where the black gallinazos, tame as poultry, pick up bits of carrion." [32] Despite these conditions, and the political unrest, Darwin did have an opportunity to make significant geological observations along the coast.

His most significant observations, however, were made not on the continent but some five hundred miles out to sea, along the equator, in the Galápagos Islands. There nature presented herself in unusual aspects; vegetation was extremely poor and more typical of Arctic than equatorial flora, and the fauna seemed to be peculiar to the islands. There were the great land tortoises, which he believed to be aboriginal inhabitants of the islands; there were unusual lizards and fishes—most of them new species, as were the birds he saw. The plants were equally interesting; he found one hundred new species, which he believed to be peculiar to the islands. What was more, several of the islands had their own species of plants and animals, unknown on the other islands. Darwin could advance no satisfactory explanation for these phenomena, but along with the observations he had made on the continent they would give him much to ponder over as the *Beagle* continued around the world. Eventually it would become clear to him through the principle of natural selection, on which his fame would rest.

Two years after the *Beagle* returned to England, the Swiss naturalist Johann Jakob von Tschudi left Europe to explore Peru. Sailing from Le Havre February 27, 1838, aboard a merchant vessel, he found the voyage relatively uneventful until the high latitudes of the south were reached; the ship had to pass east of Staten Island rather than through the Strait of Le Maire, and continuing storms and a heavy sea delayed the vessel twenty-two days in rounding Cape Horn. On June 5, 1839, the *Edmond* anchored at San Carlos in Chiloé and remained for several weeks, giving Tschudi an opportunity to explore the island, frequently on foot into the thick forests Darwin had marveled at earlier. He was also impressed by the local method of treating fractures: the bone was set, and the limb bound with a broad band of slimy seaweed which, on drying, formed a firm bandage that would not move until soaked off.[33]

After further stops at Valparaíso and Juan Fernández, the *Edmond* arrived at Callao, at the moment under siege by the Chileans, who had taken Lima in their war with the Peru-Bolivia Confederation. Examining the coast, Tschudi agreed with Darwin that the land had risen in ages past, but challenged his belief that it had occurred since inhabited by man. On a visit to Lima, Tschudi was captured by the Chileans but managed to win his freedom in a strange manner indeed. An officer, much interested in phrenology, had met the naturalist in Chile and insisted that he read his head. Tschudi, who had no faith in such things, complied and suggested that he had much talent in mathematics. Now in Lima, the officer recognized him, told him that he had predicted correctly, since he had applied mathematics successfully to artillery, and gave him his freedom.[34]

Tschudi's stay in Lima gave him ample opportunity to study the city and its environs, and such interesting natural phenomena as the *garúa*, which, he found, ended abruptly a few miles from the sea, to be replaced by rain. The line of division, he discovered, could be determined with precision.[35] Leaving the capital, he proceeded toward the cordillera via Puente de Surco. Chaclacayo, and the Río Seco to Sucro and San Juan de Matucanas. The hazards were many: diseases such as the *verugas* (painful, oversize boils which caused great loss of blood on bursting, apparently caused by something in the spring water); stinging insects; a three-foot-wide suspension bridge without railings, from which he narrowly missed falling with his mule into the river below; narrow, treacherous paths; and filthy *tambos* (inns) scarcely fit for habitation. And there was the time when an Indian *regidor* demanded his passport; he discovered that he had lost it, and handed him a handbill from a Lima production of *Lucia di Lammermoor,* which the Indian inspected and then announced that his passport was in order.

At an elevation of 15,600 feet in the Pass of Antarangra, Tschudi found himself on the continental divide. Noting two ponds nearby, thirty paces apart, one draining to the Atlantic, one to the Pacific, he could not resist taking a cup of water from one and pouring it into the other. Continuing his journey to Pachachaca, he had to pass through La Oroya, reached by crossing a suspension bridge made from untanned leather ropes, branches, straw, and roots of the agave tree. Shattering as this experience must have been, at least he did not have to cross via a *huaro,* which he described as a thick rope to which is affixed a roller and a strong piece of wood resembling a yoke; the passenger is tied to the yoke, which he grasps firmly, crosses his feet over the thick rope, and Indians pull him across by small ropes attached to the yoke. Tschudi described this as "very dangerous," surely an understatement! [36]

In the eastern cordillera (to which he said the name "Andes" should properly—and exclusively—apply) Tschudi came upon some sandstone pyramids; he believed the fractures were the result of weather, although he mentioned Ulloa's surmise that they might have been made by some Indians who knew the art of melting stone. He saw numerous condors, llamas, alpacas, haunacus, and vicuñas on the dreary puna, as well as some very well-preserved sections of the old Inca highway. After a visit to Cerro de Pasco and neighboring mines, Tschudi began a journey (January 12, 1840) into what he termed "the wildest part of the Puna region." [37] The ice-covered summits of the cordillera rose on both sides; ahead were level areas, broken occasionally by ridges of hills. In this wild country, he said, it seemed as if "Nature had breathed out her last breath. Here life and death meet together as it were to maintain the eternal struggle between being and annihilation." [38] How true this was would soon be apparent; suffering from snowblindness, Tschudi finally found a cave, ate, and lay down to sleep. In the morning, finally opening his eyes, which were closed with coagulated blood, he found to his horror that his pillow had been a human corpse. Going in search of his mule, he discovered that the animal lay dead, having eaten the poisonous *garbancillo.* Fortunately, he was able to persuade some llama-herders to carry his baggage, and could resume his journey.

After spending some time with the Indians in the area, Tschudi descended into the *montaña.* There he saw sarsaparilla, *chinchona,* balsam and various gums, but as a zoologist he was primarily interested in the variety of fauna: monkeys, vampires, sloths, armadillos, anteaters, birds, tortoises, caymans, snakes, and a host of stinging insects. And, if one were credulous, there was the carbunculo, a foxlike beast (according to the Indians) seen only at night which, if followed, lets down a flap in its forehead, from which issues a brilliant and dazzling light, believed to come from a precious jewel. The Indians he found unsocial and gloomy, and remarkable for their longevity; he met one (in 1839) who was born in 1697, had drunk nothing but *chicha* for ninety years, had chewed coca three times daily since he was eleven, and lived on corn, quinoa, and barley, with meat on Sundays.

Tschudi's work was hailed by the *Westminster Review* as "the best of its kind that has come before us since the first appearance of Darwin's Journal, to which it may be considered a needful supplement." [39] The Peru journey did not mark the end of his explorations; subsequent trips took him into the southern Andes and into the Brazilian province of Minas Gerais. His accounts of these extensive travels fill five substantial volumes.[40]

In 1848 the German naturalist Karl Ferdinand Appun left for Venezuela to explore the Orinoco and the Río Negro as far as the Amazon, on the recommendation of Humboldt himself. As his ship approached La Guaira, Appun noticed that the offshore breeze carried the perfume of many flowers over the sea—surely a pleasant introduction to the land where he would spend the next twenty years. His early experiences demonstrated the extent of his lack of knowledge of this land. He bit into a red pepper, with disastrous results, in the belief that it was a tomato. While bathing in the river at a spot he felt was hidden from public gaze he suddenly spotted a cayman; unaware that it was a harmless kind, he grabbed his clothes and ran away in panic, unclad, to the amusement of the women washing their clothes on the opposite bank. His next attempt at bathing was equally unpleasant; thousands of minute fish surrounded him and bit him—a decidedly disagreeable experience.[41]

Appun's first explorations were along the coast of the Golfo Triste and the Río Yaracuy and its branch, El Chino. Here he marveled at the gigantic trees of the forest, the great variety of palms, the many bamboos and vanilla plants, and great number of caymans in the river. Despite the hordes of *zancudos*, he enjoyed the beauty of the tropical night with its clear air and millions of stars. Leaving the coast, he took the mountain road inland to the *llanos* of Carabobo, Tocuyito, and Valencia; there he finally settled down in a small cabin covered with palm leaves, which he named *La Soledad*, to observe and study the lush flora about him. He remained until early July, 1857, making frequent trips into the interior. The first of these was to the mission of El Baúl in February of 1850, by way of Carabobo, where Bolívar's victory in 1821 had assured Venezuelan independence. En route he had acquired an unsought guide known as "El Sabio", who promptly got lost and delayed their arrival at the mission. Appun made a detailed study of the natural history of the area and enlarged his knowledge through subsequent journeys.[42]

On July 20, 1857, Appun left Puerto Cabello for Curaçao. The ship's crew was entirely Negro, and he acclaimed them as the finest sailors anywhere. After a brief stay in Willemsted, he took passage on a Spanish schooner for "the beautiful city of Maracaibo." After exploring the vicinity, he embarked for La Ceiba on the southeast shore of Lake Maracaibo. En route they were entertained by a pretty Creole girl who played the guitar and sang on the deck after dinner. Appun was much taken with the beauty of the Creole women; they are beyond comparison, he affirmed, and "on seeing them it is difficult for a man to keep the temperature of his blood normal." [43] Before reaching La Ceiba he encountered three other hazards—a waterspout; a great cloud of mosquitoes which the ship swerved to avoid, since they could be deadly; and a hurricane. After disembarking, he got mules and muleteers for a trip to Trujillo, an "insignificant city," "tranquil and solitary," but a paradise for orchid collectors. He savored the delicious fruit of the tropics; he went into the *páramos* to an elevation of twelve thousand feet, making sketches and drawings of all he saw. Progressing as far as Barquisimeto, the largest interior city after Valencia, he returned to the coast and proceeded to the east, eventually reaching Ciudad Bolívar, the former Angostura.[44]

With a view toward exploring the Orinoco delta, Appun and two companions left Ciudad Bolívar early in the morning of March 26, 1859, with photographic apparatus, a bale of dry paper for specimens, cases for collections, cans for preserving in alcohol, and the other accoutrements of the naturalist. The beginning of the journey was inauspicious; the wind took them across the river, they sailed back almost to where they had started, were blown across again, finally resorting to oars—all in front of a crowd of onlookers who found it hilarious. Downstream they were nearly swamped by waves, and were finally rescued by a steamer from Oldenburg. Passing the mouth of the Río Caroní later, they followed its course as far as the cataracts, correcting Humboldt, who had not visited the falls but relied on the word of others as to their height. Proceeding on to the delta, the three explorers passed by enormous trees, marshes, many islands, and went hunting occasionally in nearby lagoons. Once in the delta, at Santa Catalina, they were guests of one Francisco Silva, who had come to the area as a young man, later married an Indian and became a sort of king in the tribe, to whom he taught his skills. He had considerable botanical knowledge, and Appun botanized in the neighborhood with Silva's sons. He was ecstatic about the results, claiming that the shores of the delta channels offered without doubt the most exuberant scenes of plant life in the world. Concluding his work, he returned to Ciudad Bolívar on May 30.[45]

After sending his abundant collections to Europe, Appun went to (the former) British Guiana, remaining there in the employ of the British government as a scientist. He traveled into the interior of the colony, and subsequently went on, via the Rio Branco and Rio Negro, to the Amazon, going up as far as the frontier outpost of Tabatinga. In his preface to his account of his travels, he said that he had done as much as one man could in going into immense forests among savage Indian tribes, discharging his difficult task with true devotion and the sacrifice of his physical forces and money, with great privations and many times in danger of death. His descriptions, he said, were faithful to what he actually saw.[46] Yet the British naturalist, Everard Im Thurn, who worked in this area later, claims that although Appun, who drew his pictures on the spot, was so skilled that even in his most crowded compositions it was possible to recognize the species of each plant, yet his pictures are not a true record of the scenery, since he only included the most striking plants, leaving out those resembling temperate flora.[47]

Two years before Appun began his explorations, an American amateur naturalist, William H. Edwards, made a journey to the Amazon. A graduate of Williams College, he had studied law, but in 1846 he succumbed to the lure of the tropics, and explored the lower Amazon as far as Manaus, from February to October, collecting plants and animals, and studying the people and climate of the region. The results of his explorations were published in 1847, after which he began the practice of law, eventually entering the mining and railroad business, and finally publishing also a great work on butterflies, his hobby for years. Of himself, Edwards was not an important naturalist-explorer, but his *A Voyage up the River Amazon* influenced two great British naturalists, Alfred Russel Wallace and Henry W. Bates, to explore the same area.[48]

Bates, a native of Leicester, born in 1825, had been designated by his family for a business career, but became interested in collecting insects. Wallace, born in 1823 in Monmouthshire, had been attracted to botany early in life, but after meeting Bates became interested in the latter's study of insects. Both read Edwards' account and decided to go to South America to gather facts toward solving the problem of the origin of species.[49] On May 26, 1848, they arrived at Belém and spent a year and a half there collecting. Entering the virgin forest in June, the naturalists marveled at the number and variety of trees, their great height, supported by buttresses, and the climbers that wound around them. They sought out insects, discovering that the morning and early afternoon were the best times, before the heat of the day reached its peak.[50] Since the Amazon is unrivaled with respect to insect population, they were able to amass a sizable collection, most of which were new to them. During June and July, they found, heavy showers fell on most afternoons, producing a refreshing effect. Each one followed a precise pattern. First there was a cool sea-breeze in late morning, which would finally die. Afterward "the heat and electric tension of the atmosphere would then become almost insupportable. Languor and uneasiness would seize on every one; even the denizens of the forest betrayed it by their motions. White clouds would appear in the east and gather into cumuli, with an increasing blackness along their lower portions. The whole eastern horizon would become almost suddenly black, and this would spread upwards, the sun at length becoming obscured. Then the rush of a mighty wind is heard through the forest, swaying the tree-tops; a vivid flash of lightning bursts forth, then a crash of thunder, and down streams the deluging rain. Such storms soon cease, leaving bluish-black motionless clouds in the sky until night. Meantime all nature is re-freshed." [51]

Vegetation improved in July, and they saw many beautiful blossoms and flowers to add to their collections. They saw mounds of earth thirty feet and more in length, ten and more in width, and three to four feet high—the work of *saúba* ants, which also strip trees completely of their leaves. They learned to eat monkeys, agoutis, and sloths. They spent several months exploring the lower Rio Tocantins by canoe, collecting insects, butterflies, and a large "frigate-bird pelican," but failing to get a blue macaw they saw. They saw their first alligator, several varieties of dolphins, rubber trees, birds of brilliant plumage, and tasted the delicious fruits of the tropics. There was almost a tragedy—a gun was accidentally discharged in the canoe, taking off a piece of Wallace's hand near the wrist. The wound became infected, and ultimately required two weeks' treatment after they returned to Belém.[52] On November 3 Wallace left for Mexiana Island, on the equator near Marajó, where he collected seventy specimens of birds, including eagles, herons, egrets, hawks, and a large yellow-billed toucan. Exploring the interior of the island, he followed a small stream to a lake through country the beauty of whose vegetation, he said, surpassed anything he had seen before. After collect-ing more specimens, he crossed to Marajó in January, remained a week, then returned to Belém to observe that great tidal wave, the *pororoca*, and explore the Rio Capim. In July, 1849, he was back in Belém to greet his brother, who had just arrived.[53] Bates, meanwhile, left on December 7 to visit Caripí, twenty-three miles from Belém, noted for the number and beauty of its insects and birds. He remained there until February 12, collecting hummingbirds, anteaters, and bats with the assistance of a German family who had formerly lived in Illinois, hunting with the Indians, and studying the white ants so numerous there.[54]

Late in July Wallace decided to go up the Amazon in a canoe which had discharged its cargo and was returning to Santarém. After purchasing a good store of provisions and borrowing some books, he left Belém early in August, spent several days in the narrow channels connecting the Rio Pará and the Amazon, finally entering the great river twelve days later. In another four weeks he arrived at Santarém, where he was the guest of a resident Scotsman. After a side trip to Montealegre, where he saw some picture-writing in a cave, Wallace returned to Santarém and proceeded to Obidos, where he met another British naturalist, Richard Spruce, with whom he had previously conversed in Santarém. After a visit with Padre Torquato, who had accompanied Prince Adalbert of Prussia up the Xingu, at Vila Nova, Wallace finally arrived at Manaus (then called Barra do Rio Negro) on the last day of 1849.[55]

Meanwhile Bates departed from Belém on September 5 aboard a schooner which proceeded through the complex channels west of Marajó Island and entered the Amazon on October 3. Bates left the ship at Obidos on October 11 and remained there until November 19, studying the spider monkeys and the bountiful insect life of the region. Resuming his journey as a passenger aboard a small trading vessel, Bates had an excellent opportunity to study the natural history of the Amazon during the numerous stops and while the vessel navigated through the channels of the great island of Tupinambarama and stopped at the mouth of the Madeira. Finally, on January 22, he arrived at Manaus, and met Wallace, whom he had missed in Serpa.[56]

The two naturalists explored the vicinity, finding the forest a very pleasant place; there were broad pathways through it, and one of them led through a beautiful section to a ten-foot waterfall, a favorite of the citizens, as well as of naturalists who had preceded them. Birds and insects were scarce, and they often had to spend all day and go a considerable distance for a few specimens. After a few weeks, Wallace and Bates decided to separate to explore the interior, Wallace concentrating on the Rio Negro, Bates on the Solimões or upper Amazon. On August 31 Wallace departed in a large dugout, with its afterdeck covered with a semicircular roof, high enough to sit under. Going upstream on the extremely broad Rio Negro, he passed the old capital of the province, Barcelos, eventually reaching São José on October 1; there it was necessary to transfer to two smaller canoes in order to go around the falls. Above this point Wallace managed to get twelve fine specimens of the cock-of-the-rock, and saw the curious figures painted on the rocks at the Serra de Cocoí. Leaving the canoes beyond the mouth of the Casiquiare, Wallace walked to the town of Yavita, only to find that he had arrived just at the end of the area's three-month-long summer. He was greeted by a downpour, which continued for several days. Nonetheless, he remained for forty days, collecting fish and forty new species of butterflies, which he found great difficulty in drying and preserving. Accordingly, he decided to return to Brazil, and by June 12, 1851, reached the Rio Uaupés, which he found so good for collecting live birds and animals that he abandoned a proposed Andean trip to return there in the hope of getting a white umbrella-chatterer. But first it would be necessary to return to Manaus to ship his collections; there was a long delay in getting a canoe (which enabled him to collect some fine orchids), but he finally reached the port on September 15.

Wallace and Spruce had hoped to go back to the Rio Uaupés together, but the available canoe was too small for both. The trip back was marked by the capture of a manatee, which Wallace skinned to prepare the skeleton for his collection, and by sickness, for he was quite ill with fever and ague on arriving at São Joaquim, where he remained for nearly three months. From mid-February to mid-April he was in the extreme northwestern part of Brazil, purchasing animals when he was unable to collect them himself. After a brief visit to the Rio Branco, he returned to Manaus on May 17. To his consternation he found that he had to pay a duty on every insect, bird, and animal collected, and in addition had considerable difficulty in getting a passport.

Nothing seemed to go right on the return trip to England. The canoe which Wallace had engaged at Manaus was nearly lost in a storm on the Amazon, and was saved only by drifting into some floating grass. On arriving at Belém, he learned that his brother Herbert, who had been collecting in the area, had died of yellow fever. After boarding the British brig *Helen* on July 12 (1852), Wallace again suffered a malaria attack, but was able to cure it. On August 6, seven hundred miles from Bermuda, the ship caught fire and had to be abandoned; all Wallace's collections were lost. For ten days the passengers and crew drifted in lifeboats, suffering from rain and sun, until rescued by a British ship bound for London; they endured two heavy gales before they reached the safety of the home port.[57]

After their decision to explore and collect separately, Bates left Manaus ahead of Wallace's departure, on March 26, 1850, for the town of Ega (now called Tefé) on the upper Amazon, or Solimões. Here he found many things to be different: the trade winds did not reach this far, the land was extremely flat, the vegetation more luxurious, with continual fruit and flowering, and, while the climate was healthy, "one lives here as in a permanent vapour bath."[58] Bates found this town of 1,200, which Father Fritz founded in 1688, so pleasant a place that he made it his headquarters during the years he spent on the upper Amazon. The lack of any racial bias in areas of mixed blood impressed him favorably, as did the prospects for real democracy at the local level.

Bates remained at Ega for a year, enlarging his collections considerably, then returned to Santarém, where he set up his headquarters for a three-and-one-half-year stay in November of 1851. There was much to attract him to this city: the climate, he said, was "glorious," with little rain from August to February and fresh breezes from the sea; there were no insect pests, the city was clean, and the food supply varied and adequate. To enlarge his collections, he made frequent trips up the Rio Tapajós, as far as the Irurá; he would have gone further, but could find no Brazilian willing to accompany him into the interior—they seemed to have no taste for exploration by land. His most extensive Tapajós journey was from June 8 to October 9, with a crew he managed to hire, as far as the falls of the Cuparí. On this journey he learned to fish with poison, collecting many specimens in this manner; he tamed a wild parrot, collected many new varieties of birds and insects, nearly had a disastrous encounter with a huge boa constrictor, and witnessed tides 530 miles from the Atlantic.[59]

Having completed his explorations of the lower Amazon, Bates returned to Ega in 1855 and settled down in a spacious cottage filled with his reference books, cages, notes, equipment, and collections. From here he made excursions into the surrounding area, sometimes as far as four hundred miles, on foot or by small boat. There was scarcely any danger at Ega; he mentioned a visit by a jaguar as "an extraordinary event," and even the alligators which appeared at the bathing places in the dry weather were a danger only to the incautious. On an excursion up the Rio Tefé he killed a huge cayman, went on a turtle-egg hunt, saw for the first time the rare umbrella-bird, and captured some electric eels. In November of 1856 Bates embarked on a steamer for the Indian settlement of Tunantins, 240 miles upriver, and made a very good collection of monkeys, birds, and insects. On the return trip he visited Fonte Boa, "a wretched, muddy, and dilapidated village," the "headquarters of mosquitos" which were bad enough in the town but in the forest formed a cloud around the person every step of the way.

Returning to Ega in January 25, 1857, Bates remained there until September 5, when he left again by steamer for the town of São Paulo de Olivença, 260 miles distant in a straight line, a journey of five days. The scenery was grand, and Bates had an opportunity of seeing flocks of aquatic birds, huge caymans, and numerous turtles on the way. He remained five months, but felt that five years would not suffice to exhaust the botanical and zoological treasures of the area. As on his previous journeys, he had ample opportunity to observe the Indians; he also heard tales of cannibalism, involving the eating of two young mameluco traders who had behaved improperly toward some Majerona women a few months before. Bates intended to explore the Amazon basin as far as the Andes, but an attack of the ague in his fourth month there forced him to change his plans. Since this sickness did not exist at São Paulo de Olivença, he felt it was the culmination of gradual deterioration of his health, which had been going on for several years, plus overwork and bad diet. When the steamer arrived in January of 1858, he returned to Ega; although the ague left him, he felt that his health was too weak to begin any more journeys. Leaving Ega February 3, 1859, he returned to Belém and sailed June 2 for England via New York.[60] With him went his vast collections of animals and birds, fish and amphibians, and fourteen thousand insects—one of the finest to come to Europe.

Bates's long residence in South America was equaled and surpassed by the British botanist Richard Spruce. Born in Yorkshire in 1817, he became a mathematics teacher at the Collegiate School in York, but developed a strong interest in botany which led him to spend ten months collecting in the Pyrenees, where he developed a special interest in mosses. After publishing the results of this trip, he went to London in 1848, and on learning of Wallace's and Bates's journey to South America, decided to go himself, sailing for Belém on June 7, 1849, accompanied by Robert King, who would go with him on the Amazon, and Wallace's brother Herbert. Arriving at Belém on July 12, Spruce and King remained for three months, botanizing in the vicinity with considerable success. At Tauaú, a farm owned by Archibald Campbell, a British resident, he saw the primeval forest for the first time: "There were enormous trees, crowned with magnificent foliage, decked with fantastic parasites, and hung over with lianas. . . . Intermixed with the trees, and often equal to them in altitude, grew noble palms; while other and far lovelier species of the same family . . . formed, along with shrubs and arbuscles of many types, a bushy undergrowth, not usually very dense or difficult to penetrate." [61]

Spruce decided to make his headquarters at Santarém, and arrived there October 27 with letters of credit, currency, and supplies. There he botanized for a while, seeing the magnificent *Victoria regia* water-lilies, four and one-half feet in diameter, and chanced to meet Wallace, with whom he engaged in lively conversation. In mid-November he left for the Rio Trombetas; an almost continuous drizzle made him fear for his collections, but he was told that fair weather—the *verano del niño*, as he put it—would come by Christmas. It never did, and on one expedition into the forest, King got separated from them during a heavy storm and was nearly lost; he had to spend the night in the damp forest, and suffered rheumatic pains for a week as a result. Nonetheless, the journey was productive in the botanical knowledge Spruce gained. Returning to Santarém, he remained there until October 8, 1850. The rise of the Amazon and Tapajós, higher than anyone could remember, enabled him to study a phenomenon which had puzzled him—the great floating-grass islands which sometimes attained a thickness of thirty feet; he discovered that they originated in riverside lakes which burst their banks during the flooding.

On October 8 Spruce departed for Manaus, stopping briefly at Vila Nova, where he met Padre Torquato, of whom Prince Adalbert, Wallace, and Bates had written so favorably. He saw the great pirarucú, "the monarch of the fishes of the Amazon" (it attained a length up to eight feet), and became acquainted with the guaraná plant, famed as a remedy for diarrhea. Arriving at Manaus on December 10, he made it his headquarters to November 14, 1851, exploring a relatively small area most thoroughly from a botanical standpoint. He kept no regular journal during this time, only a few scattered notes and sketches. Scarcely going more than five miles from the city, he added 750 specimens to the 110 already collected.[62]

In November Spruce left Manaus in a canoe with six men to go up the Rio Negro. The first stage, to São Gabriel, was not uneventful: he collected many unusual flowers, watched with amazement the Indian art of fishing with a bow and arrow, and heard the Indians making a frightful din one night to frighten the moon (which was in total eclipse) from running away. He remained in São Gabriel until August 21, then went on to explore the Rio Uaupés until March of 1853. Moving on, he went as far as the frontier, then returned and ascended the Rio Negro to San Carlos, where he remained until the end of November, collecting many specimens, including mosses.

Bates next decided to follow the Casiquiare connection to the Orinoco. Humboldt's journey had obviously made a great impression, for he met old Indians at Solano who had seen him, and along the Casiquiare he stopped at Pueblo de Ponciano, named for an Indian who had known Humboldt and Bonpland; his widow was still living. Entering the Orinoco, he stopped briefly at Esmeralda, which he called "an Inferno"; there were no signs of life, for the mosquitoes were so bad that the inhabitants went out only in early morning or late evening. He proceeded down the Orinoco as far as the Río Cunucunuma, and then returned, going up the Orinoco to a point near its source, and after that going back to San Carlos where he arranged and packed his collections, and botanized to mid-May. On a second journey in June, he explored the Río Guainia, went to Yavita and San Fernando de Atabapo, then to Maipures. There he fell ill with fever for three weeks and was cared for by a disagreeable old *zamba* who hated him. Returning to San Carlos, he set out for Manaus; on the first night out he overheard the Indians plotting to kill him, and foiled the scheme by slipping out of his hammock and into the boat, where he spent the night holding a gun in readiness. By December 22 he was back in Manaus, to wait for a steamer to Peru.[63]

On March 14, 1855, Spruce embarked for Iquitos, with stops at São Paulo de Olivença, Tabatinga, and Loreto, enabling him to find plants new to him amid the luxuriant vegetation of the forest. After a two-week delay in Iquitos, he proceeded by canoe with an English sailor, Charles Nelson, into the Huallaga and Napo rivers, and caught his first glimpse of the Andes. During the two years he spent along the eastern slope of the cordillera, Spruce kept no regular journal; information concerning his activities is found only in his letters to George Bentham and John Teasdale in London. He botanized chiefly around Tarapoto, the banks of the Río Huallaga, and the slopes of the Campana mountains, collecting many mosses and 1,094 species of flowering plants and ferns. From Tarapoto he journeyed to Baños in the company of two merchants of that town; apparently Nelson was left behind, for we hear no more of him. The rain was nearly constant; at one point, in a severe storm, the water rose so rapidly that the lianas used to secure the boats broke. Fortunately, the Indians were in the crafts, held on to branches, found more lianas and retied them, and remained standing in the canoes all night to guard against further damage. On June 12 Spruce reached Canelos; botanizing extensively, he collected specimens of the famous vegetable ivory plant and many fruits, which the Indians unfortunately ate, not knowing he intended to preserve them.

After crossing the Río Bombonasa, Spruce entered the *montaña*, and found himself in the mossiest place he had ever seen. There was much rain, causing the rivers to become swollen; only with great difficulty, and leaving his boxes of collections behind, was he able, with his Indians, to construct a bamboo bridge across the Río Topo. And to descend to the sandy beach of the Río Pastasa, Spruce had to climb 150 feet down a notched pole from a rock overhanging the river. This stream led him to the forest of Canelos, where Mme Godin des Odonais had wandered so long, and eventually into a cooler, cultivated area.[64]

From July, 1857, to September, 1860, Spruce wandered about the Ecuadorean Andes, collecting ferns and mosses, botanizing on the slopes of Chimborazo, in Baños, and in Riobamba. He climbed Pichincha, crossed the *páramo* of Mocha, enduring the *paramero*—that deadly cold wind "that withers every living thing it meets"—and was nearly attacked by condors when exhaustion drove him to rest. He saw the alubilla tree, which Indians feared to touch or walk in the shade of, lest their bodies swell all over, and demonstrated the falsity of the superstition. He spent a year gathering *chinchona* plants for the Indian government. He became deaf in one ear, and suffered a partial paralysis of the back and legs, which required several months' treatment, yet he continued to explore, partly on horseback, "partly dragging myself about by the aid of a long staff." [65]

Spruce's explorations in South America ended with a journey to the Pacific coast. On October 28, 1860, he left the farm near Riobamba for Guayaquil, where he loaded much of his collection for shipment. His collecting activities were somewhat limited by the condition of his health, and to add to his troubles, a bank failure in the port cost him $6,000—nearly all he had. Nonetheless, he continued his work; he saw the desert bloom from unexpected heavy rains in March, and expanded his collections as a result. The following year he sailed for Peru, where he remained for some time until he reached the painful decision that he could no longer continue his work, and returned to England via Panama in 1864. Having spent more time in the southern continent than any of the other naturalists, he was able to travel farther and accomplish much more, publishing the results of his studies in *The Palms of the Amazon Valley* and *The Hepaticae of the Amazon and the Andes of Peru.*[66]

In the north of the continent, H. Villiers Stuart, the ornithologist, spent part of 1858 and 1859 exploring Guiana. Leaving Paramaribo in November, 1858, he ascended the Surinam River into the interior, adding a number of beautiful birds to his collection, and progressed as far as the watershed of the Amazon basin before his crew refused to continue. Returning to Paramaribo, he heard that at Cayenne he would be able to find a steamer for Belém. He was able to reach the French port on a gunboat, and found it to be "a naturalist's paradise—birds of brilliant plumage, the most curious insects, the most exuberant vegetation." [67] Upon learning that to get to Belém he would have to go to Southampton first, Stuart decided to go instead to the Orinoco, and arrived finally at the port of Angostura, or Ciudad Bolívar. After exploring the area, he took ship, following Raleigh's route, for Port of Spain, and explored Trinidad.

Another ornithologist, Sir Everard F. Im Thurn, who had published a book on the birds of his native Marlborough, arrived in British Guiana in 1877 as curator of the Georgetown Museum. In the following year, accompanied by two countrymen and some Indians, he ascended the Essiquibo and Potaro rivers to the spectacular Kaieteur Falls. Along the way, the party was attacked by vampires, but Im Thurn was unable to induce any of them to bother him. There was trouble with a local medicine man, who threatened to kill the entire party, mentioning the order in which he would do it; later, all of them got the fever, in that order, and Im Thurn was convinced that the Indian was the cause of it. Climbing a hill near Quatata, he saw an area below that flooded to lake proportions in the wet season; glittering white clouds above, lighted by the sun, resembled a city of towers and temples—a possible source of the legend of Lake Parima and the city of Manoa. The coming of heavy rains brought an end to the expedition, and they returned to Georgetown.[68]

In October of 1878, Im Thurn made a second journey to the Kaieteur Falls, higher than Niagara and unknown until 1871. Upon finally reaching the site, no trace of water was seen—only a white mist; the falls were not dry, as the Indians suggested, but only flowing at half-width because of the dry season, and were only partially visible from below. Not until a subsequent visit in the rainy season would he see this great cataract in all of its splendor, "an indescribably, almost inconceivably, vast curtain of water—I can find no other phrase—some four hundred feet in width . . . ." [69] Visible from this region was the forbidding Mount Roraima, highest peak in the Guiana highlands, believed to be unclimbable because of perpendicular walls rising several thousand feet beyond the five-thousand-foot level. Im Thurn repeated the belief of many that the summit was inaccessible except to birds, and the speculation that it was still inhabited by some animals of a primitive type, who had undergone no modification since the mountain was isolated. The mysterious peak beckoned, but not until 1884 would Im Thurn return to challenge it.[70]

As Agassiz had suggested, these naturalists of the nineteenth century were as truly explorers as those who had gone before them. For the most part, they were not the first men in the areas they visited, nor were they far from some semblance of civilization during most of their investigations, yet their contribution to the sum total of man's knowledge was great indeed. For they explored the world of nature, collecting specimens, cataloging and categorizing them, discovering new species and variations of known ones, leading them to conclusions which would drastically alter man's concept of the world about him, and even of his own origin. From the limited beginnings in the eighteenth century, the study of natural history had come into full flower.

NOTES

1. Agassiz, *A Journey in Brazil* (Boston, 1868), p. 7.
2. Waterton, *Wanderings in South America* (London, 1895).
3. *Ibid.*, p. 1.
4. For this stage of Waterton's journey, see *Wanderings*, pp. 4-22.
5. *Ibid.*, p. 37.
6. *Ibid.*, pp. 51-75.
7. *Ibid.*, pp. 115-16.
8. *Ibid.*, p. 225.
9. *Ibid.*, pp. 227-28.
10. Saint-Hilaire, *Esquisse de mes voyages au Brésil et Paraguay* (in *Cronica Botanica*, Vol. X, No. 1, 1946, p. 24).
11. For a convenient summary of Saint-Hilaire's work, see *op. cit.*, pp. 24-61.
12. Olivério M. Oliveira Pinto, "Viajantes e Naturalistas" in Sergio Buarque de Holanda, *História geral da civilização brasileira* (São Paulo, 1967), Vol. V, p. 451.
13. *Ibid.*, pp. 457-58.
14. Eduard Poeppig, *Reise in Chile, Peru, und auf dem Amazonenstrom*, 2 vols. (Leipzig, 1835–36), *passim*. His other works were *Nova genera ac species plantarum*, 3 vols. (Leipzig, 1835–45) and *Illustrierte Naturgeschichte des Tierreichs*, 4 vols. (Leipzig, 1851).
15. For the account of this cruise, see Chap. XVI.
16. Robert Fitz-Roy, ed., *Narrative of the Surveying Voyage of H.M. Ships Adventure and Beagle, 1826–1836* (London, 1839), Vol. II, p. 18.
17. *Ibid.*, p. 19; Paul R. Cutright, *The Great Naturalists Explore South America* (New York, 1940), pp. 18-20. Cutright notes that Fitz-Roy nearly turned Darwin

down. Believing himself able to judge men's character by their facial contours, he felt that the young scientist's nose cast doubts on his energy and determination for the voyage.

18. Darwin, *The Voyage of the Beagle* (New York, 1958), p. 1. This "Bantam Classic" is a convenient reprint of an edition which varies somewhat from the original, published as Vol. III of Fitz-Roy's account, above. See also Vol. II of the same work, and Alan Villiers, "In the Wake of Darwin's Beagle," *National Geographic* 136 (October, 1969): 449-95.

19. Darwin, *The Voyage of the Beagle*, p. 10.

20. *Ibid.*, p. 33.

21. *Ibid.*, p. 183.

22. *Ibid.*, p. 62, n. 1 (1865).

23. *Ibid.*, Chap. V.

24. *Ibid.*, p. 133.

25. *Ibid.*, p. 139.

26. *Ibid.*, p. 207.

27. *Ibid.*, p. 217.

28. *Ibid.*, p. 241.

29. Fitz-Roy, ed., *Narrative of the Surveying Voyages* . . . , Vol. III (Darwin's account), p. 393.

30. *Voyage of the Beagle*, p. 290.

31. *Ibid.*, p. 314.

32. *Ibid.*, pp. 317-18.

33. Tschudi, *Travels in Peru during the Years 1838–1842* (London, 1854), pp. 1-20.

34. *Ibid.*, p. 56.

35. For a comprehensive account, see *ibid.*, pp. 59-227.

36. *Ibid.*, pp. 279-88.

37. *Ibid.*, p. 341.

38. *Ibid.*, p. 355.

39. October, 1846. The notice appears at the end of the volume of Tschudi's *Travels.* . . .

40. *Reisen durch Süd-Amerika* (Leipzig, 1866–69). See also his *Reise durch die Andes von Süd-Amerika von Cordova nach Cobija im jahre 1858* (Gotha, 1860), and *Die brasilianische provinz Minas Geraes* (Gotha, 1867).

41. Appun, *En los trópicos* (Caracas, 1961), pp. 17-75.

42. On this phase of his work, see Appun, *op. cit.*, pp. 90-283.

43. *Ibid.*, p. 314.

44. The Maracaibo-Barquisimeto portion of his travels is described in Appun, *op. cit.*, pp. 312-49.

45. On the Orinoço journey see Appun, *op. cit.*, pp. 352-428.

46. *Ibid.*, pp. 10-11.

47. Everard Im Thurn, *Among the Indians of Guiana* (London, 1883), pp. 87-88.

48. Cutright, *op. cit.*, pp. 22-23.

49. For firsthand accounts of their explorations see Bates, *The Naturalist on the River Amazons*, 2 vols. (London, 1863), republished in a single volume by the University of California Press, Berkeley and Los Angeles, 1962; and Wallace, *A Narrative of Travels on the Amazon and Rio Negro* (London, 1889). Curiously, Bates makes only a few scattered references to Wallace by name, and Wallace refers to Bates not at all by name, but only through the impersonal "we."

50. Wallace, pp. 11-23; Bates (1962 ed., cited hereinafter), pp. 25-39.

51. Bates, p. 34.

52. For the Tocantins journey, see Wallace, pp. 35-56, and Bates pp. 66-89.

53. Wallace, pp. 57-76.

54. Bates, pp. 103-30.

55. See Wallace, pp. 92-111. Later, Wallace went to Southeast Asia, and eventually formulated his theory of natural selection, for which he shares credit with Darwin.

56. See Bates, pp. 160-98.

57. On the Rio Negro and Rio Uaupés expeditions and the homeward voyage, see Wallace, pp. 112-279.

58. Bates, p. 290.

59. Bates, pp. 208-97.

60. On the Ega phase of his exploration, see Bates, pp. 288-461. On his return he published his absorbing account of his travels; later (1862) he became secretary of the Royal Geographical Society, serving in that capacity until his death in 1892.

61. Spruce, *Notes of a Botanist on the Amazon and Andes,* 2 vols. (London, 1901), Vol. I, p. 17. Spruce left no account of his journey; his notes were acquired by Wallace, who finally edited and published them, with an introduction.

62. Spruce, Vol. I, pp. 54-210.

63. *Ibid.,* pp. 259-504.

64. For the journey from Manaus into the *montaña,* see Spruce, Vol. II, pp. 1-170.

65. *Ibid.,* p. 260.

66. *Ibid.,* pp. 260-341.

67. Henry Windsor Villiers Stuart, *Adventures amidst the Equatorial Forests and Rivers of South America* (London, 1891), p. 42.

68. Im Thurn, *op. cit.,* pp. 4-55.

69. *Ibid.,* p. 75.

70. *Ibid.,* p. 82.

XVI   Government-Sponsored

Explorations: Early Nineteenth Century

Prior to the nineteenth century, as we have seen, a number of government-sponsored expeditions had increased man's knowledge of the South American continent by careful and thorough exploration of its coasts and interior. After the restoration of peace in Europe, following the Napoleonic wars, this type of exploration was resumed, and in this great century of natural history it is only to be expected that we should find naturalists prominent in such expeditions. Among the earliest of these were two Bavarians, the zoologist Johann Baptist von Spix (1781–1826) and the botanist Karl Friedrich Philipp von Martius (1794–1868), who in 1815 conceived a plan to go to Buenos Aires, then by land to Chile and north to Quito, returning to Europe via Caracas or Mexico. Difficulties caused postponement, but a way was soon found. In 1817 the Archduchess Leopoldina, daughter of the Austrian emperor, was to go to Brazil to marry Dom Pedro, son of King João VI of Portugal and Brazil; several scientists were sent in her suite, and the king of Bavaria, who happened to be in Vienna at the time, arranged for his two academicians to accompany them on "a literary tour into the interior of South America." [1]

The duties of the two scientists were laid down in considerable detail. Spix was to observe the inhabitants, both aboriginal and colonial, checking the different effects of climate on them, and was to observe the habits, instincts, geographical limits, and migrations of animals. Martius was to study the botanical families peculiar to the country, make climatic and geognostic observations, report on changes in plants, native and foreign, when exposed to certain external influences, and study their internal structure; he was to investigate the history of the soil and methods of cultivation in use, as well as Brazilian *materia medica*.

In addition, both were to make mineralogical observations, study the declination of the magnetic needle, and collect information on electricity, the seas, and the atmosphere. And finally, they were to study native languages and the history of the area.[2] Surely this was a comprehensive assignment!

On February 10, 1817, the Bavarian academicians arrived in Vienna, where they met and joined their Austrian colleagues, the botanist Johann Natterer (1787–1843) and the botanist and mineralogist, Johann E. Pohl, M.D. (1782–1834). After visiting the Johanneum (an institution for propagating practical knowledge in natural history) at Graz, they set out on their journey, sailing from Pola on April 10 and finally casting anchor in Guanabara Bay late in the afternoon of July 14.[3] They found their first night in Rio de Janeiro enchanting. "A delicate transparent mist hangs over the country," Spix relates, "the moon shines brightly amidst heavy and singularly grouped clouds, the outlines of the objects which are illuminated by it are clear and well-defined, while a magic twilight seems to remove from the eye those which are in shade. Scarce a breath of air is stirring, and the neighboring mimosas, that have folded up their leaves to sleep, stand motionless beside the dark crowns of the manga, the jaca, and the etherial jambos; or sometimes a sudden wind arises, and the leaves of the acajú rustle, the richly flowered grumijama and pitanga let drop a fragrant shower of snow-white blossoms . . . ."[4]

Spix and Martius made their first excursions in the vicinity of Rio, climbing Corcovado, collecting many plants, birds, and insects, observing the tall trees along the bay and in the Serra dos Orgãos, and enjoying the stark beauty of the mountains. Learning of the presence of other naturalists in the area, they decided to go to São Paulo, then, after studying the natural history of the south Temperate Zone, to Minas Gerais, the Rio São Francisco, Goiás, then overland to Belém or Salvador. Since the Austrian naturalists were ordered to remain longer in Rio, they obtained passports and went on alone. Leaving Rio on December 8, they arrived at São Paulo on the last day of the year; it rained much of the way, and yellow mold grew on their specimens, yet they managed to enlarge their collections. Since continuing rain drastically limited the number of excursions they could make, they left January 9, 1818, for the iron foundry of São João Ipanema, twenty leagues away. Passing through a forest on the way, they were able to collect 120 different kinds of wood in one day; unlike most Brazilians, their guide was able to give the name of each, its use, and the time of flowering and fruit.[5]

As soon as improved weather permitted, Spix and Martius continued collecting and shipped a considerable number of items to Rio de Janeiro. Resuming their journey, they entered Minas Gerais via Sorocaba and Itú, past rugged mountains of granite, through thick fog, and across rivers swollen by torrential rains, into the gold-washing area. As they traveled through a valley in country resembling the lower Alps, they were able to collect considerable quantities of mica, feldspar, and quartz, as well as botanical specimens which they dried and packed at every stop. Whenever possible, they followed unfrequented paths. As they crossed the height of land separating the north- from the south-flowing rivers, to São José and the Lagoa Dourado, the scenery reminded them of the Bavarian Alps, but with tropical luxurance. At every level of altitude they made a careful study of the flora and fauna as well as the mineralogy of the entire area. Their itinerary took them to Ouro Prêto— no longer the rich center of extensive gold mining, but still a fascinating city—and beyond to the land of the Coroado Indians, a lethargic people with only a dim awareness of past and future. For Spix and Martius, this area was a collectors' paradise: "the treasures of this beautiful mountain valley," they wrote, "keep the naturalist in a continued transport. The forms of the plants here are incredibly diversified and beautiful." [6] So large had their collections grown at this point that they found it necessary to send them to Rio for shipment to Bavaria.

With their investigations in central Brazil complete, the Bavarian naturalists went on to Belém, arriving August 16, 1819. While making preparations for a journey up the Amazon, they explored the vicinity of the port, botanizing, studying the Indians, and observing that singular tidal phenomenon, the *pororoca*. By August 21 all was in readiness, and they departed from Belém, spending two weeks on the Rio Pará and the complicated system of channels to the west of it before entering the main stream of the Amazon. The mosquitoes were a great trial to them as they progressed up river, but this proved to be a minor problem, for between Santarém and Obidos they suffered a canoe accident which nearly cost Martius his life. In gratitude for his survival, he later caused to be erected in Obidos a life-sized figure of Christ on the cross.[7]

As they continued their journey from Obidos to Manaus, they learned much about the Indians along the shores. There was the art of fishing by using the poisonous juices of certain plants, which stupefied the fish and brought them to the surface. There were the remains of the ancient inhabitants of Tupinambarama. There were Indian sorceries, and remedies such as *guaraná*, excellent for illnesses of the digestive tract. After arriving at Manaus, they spent some time in exploring the surrounding territory, observing local agriculture, collecting specimens from the bountiful insect life, including this time fireflies, seeing the many monkeys of the forest, and the caymans, dolphins, and multiple varieties of fish in the rivers. And they continued these observations as they resumed their journey past inundated woodlands to Ega (Tefé), where Bates would later spend so much time.[8]

At Ega, the pair parted temporarily, Spix continuing up the Solimões, or upper Amazon, as far as the frontier post of Tabatinga, making a careful study of the Indians he met, and finally returning to Manaus on February 3, 1820. Martius, meanwhile, explored the Rio Yupurá as far as the falls of Arara-Coara, making careful observations along the river and a detailed study of Indian life, especially of their knowledge of medicinal plants. Upon returning to Manaus, he left to make similar observations along the Rio Negro as far as the old provincial capital of Barcelos, returning February 26.[9]

Together again, the pair left Manaus to explore the Rio Madeira in March; the excursion was rather brief but productive of results, especially with respect to the astronomical observations they were able to make along the river into Mato Grosso. Returning finally to the Amazon, they went downstream to Belém, to sail for Europe on June 13, 1820. From the standpoint of scientific study, the journey of Spix and Martius was most successful. Their collections embraced 85 species of mammals, 350 of birds, 130 of amphibians, 116 species of fish, 2,700 species of insects, and 6,500 species of plants—truly a monumental collection! [10] In addition, their account of the journey is a mine of information on the Amazon and its tributaries, its Indians, its luxurious vegetation, and its teeming animal life.

But what of the other members of the Austrian expedition? The botanist and geologist Johann Emmanuel Pohl left Rio de Janeiro on September 8, 1818, via the old miners' road to São João del-Rei in Minas Gerais, remained there a week, then went on to Paracatu and Vila Boa (now Goiás) early in 1819. From there he explored the headwaters of the Rio Tocantins, descending into the province of Pará, returning to Goiás and pushing westward into Mato Grosso. In the latter part of 1820 he explored a considerable portion of the Rio São Francisco, returning finally to Rio de Janeiro on February 26, 1821. During his travels (which are described in his *Reise im Innern von Brasilien*, Vienna, 1832–37) he limited his studies to his specialties, and accumulated a substantial botanical collection which led to the publication of his *Plantarum Brasiliae icones et descriptiones hactenus ineditae* (Leipzig, 1827–31).[11]

The most extensive explorations were those made by Johann von Natterer. During the early part of 1818 he collected in the vicinity of Sapetiba, then moved to the environs of Rio de Janeiro until he received permission for a long journey into central Brazil and Amazonia. Leaving Rio on November 2, 1818, in the company of the expedition's hunter, Socher, he arrived in São Paulo on January 12, 1819, with extensive collections gathered along the way. Shortly afterward he departed for Ipanema, a place popular with naturalists, and remained there until July of 1820. Subsequent travels took him to Curitiba and

Paranaguá before he returned to Rio de Janeiro in February of 1821. A second journey, begun in September, took him to Ipanema again, which served as a base for explorations into the northern part of São Paulo province, western Minas Gerais and southern Goiás. From December of 1823 to January of 1825 he was at Cuiabá; he left for Mato Grosso in 1826, explored the Rio Guaporé leisurely, then returned to Cuiabá in October of 1827. Four months later he returned to the Guaporé, this time descending it by canoe to the Rio Madeira, exploring the vicinity of Borba, and finally arriving at Manaus in September of 1830. During the early months of the following year, Natterer explored the Rio Negro as far as the Río Casiquiare, then returned to investigate the eastern tributaries of the Negro. Returning of Manaus, he explored the lower Solimões (upper Amazon) from August of 1823 to July of 1835; during this period loneliness apparently got the better of him, for he became enamored of an Indian maiden who bore him a daughter. In July of 1835 he left for Belém, whence he sailed for Europe in September. His collections, which included 12,293 birds (embracing 1,200 species), 1,146 mammals, 3,349 amphibians and fishes, 1,942 ethnographic pieces from 72 tribes and 70 vocabularies of Indian languages mark him as one of the greatest collectors of his times. Unfortunately, fire destroyed the museum in Vienna during the Revolution of 1848, and nearly all of his manuscripts and the bulk of his diary were lost.[12]

Even Tsar Alexander I of Russia became interested in the exploration of South America. In 1821 Baron Georg Heinrich von Langsdorff, a German physician and diplomat in the Tsar's service, undertook, at Alexander's behest (and his own suggestion) an expedition into the interior of Brazil. He was no stranger to the country. In 1803 he had visited Santa Catarina as a member of a Russian expedition around the world, and in 1813 he settled in Rio de Janeiro, where he became acqainted with most of the naturalists who passed through the city. There was a long delay in starting the journey; not until 1824 did the Russian consul grant permission to depart, and not until 1825 did the expedition enter the interior. In 1826, at the Rio Tietê, the expedition divided into two groups, one to proceed to the Guaporé and thence to the Amazon via the Madeira, the other, under Langsdorff, to proceed to Diamantina, and reach the Amazon via the Rio Arinos and the Tapajós. Nearly everything went wrong. Langsdorff became a victim of mental illness, the artist Taunay drowned trying to cross the Guaporé in a violent storm, and the astronomer Rubzov died, a victim of beriberi. Nonetheless, the expedition did manage to assemble at Santarém, and went downstream to Belém, with some significant ethnographic collections which were sent to St. Petersburg. Hercules Florence, a French artist on the expedition, left an account of it in his *Viagem fluvial do Tieté ao Amazonas de 1825 a 1829* (republished in São Paulo, 1941).[13]

Shortly after Langsdorff won approval to begin his journey into the interior of Brazil, a French expedition was organized to explore the southern part of the continent. The Muséum d'Histoire Naturelle had conceived the project at a meeting in November of 1824, and early in the following year, Geoffroy Saint-Hilaire, a professor at the museum, asked Alcide d'Orbigny, who had been studying molluscs, to go to South America as a *naturaliste-voyageur*. Very flattered, Orbigny accepted. The museum granted him 6,000 francs per year for expenses, but the botanist Desfontaines told him not to go to America with so trifling a sum—"you will die of hunger." To augment the grant, Orbigny sought out the Duc de Rivoli, who was something of a science buff; he promised him 3,000 francs additional each year.[14]

On July 29, 1826, Orbigny sailed from Brest for South America, stopping at Madeira and the Canaries, and entered the harbor of Rio de Janeiro on September 24. "Nothing was lacking for my happiness," he wrote, ". . . I was in America." [15] After two weeks, his ship, the *Meuse,* sailed for Montevideo, under Brazilian convoy because of the war with Argentina, and arrived on October 30. There he learned of a spurious "great French naturalist, sent by the French government" who was selling perfumes in the area from boxes supposedly for specimens, and had run afoul of the authorities. This made it difficult for Orbigny, who was confused with him; President Rivadavia even refused to see him when he arrived in Buenos Aires (on January 21, 1827), despite his great interest in science. On February 14 he left Buenos Aires on a journey which took him up the Paraná to Rosario and Corrientes; he was fascinated by the brilliant flowers of the forest, the great variety of bird life, and the multitudes of insects, some of which proved to be a great nuisance. For more than a year Orbigny remained in the province of Corrientes, making occasional side trips into the Chaco and the Guaraní country; he was quite pleased to note that everywhere he went he was known as "Don Alcide" or *El naturalista.* He visited farms, saw the ruins of the missions, watched with great interest demonstrations of the use of the *bolas,* saw enormous caymans, and drank in the beauty of the forest. On December 26 he reached the frontier of Paraguay; he would like to have entered both for scientific reasons and to see Bonpland, still a prisoner of the dictator Francia, but decided not to risk it.[16]

During the month of January, 1828, Orbigny traversed the territory at last where Azara had labored, and which Nuflo de Chávez had explored centuries before. His collections grew rapidly, and he was very gratified to obtain a specimen of the rare *aguara-guazú,* a species of American red wolf. Resumption of hostilities between Argentina and

Brazil made a return to Buenos Aires unwise, so he tarried a while in Corrientes, and explored part of the Chaco. Deciding in April to leave Corrientes, he purchased a boat to ship his large collection; while sailing down the Paraná, he was told that certain banks of the river were covered with a species of sarsaparilla, and that in consequence the waters of the river had curative powers; he recalled that Humboldt had heard the same tale in Caracas and in Colombia. By May 28 he had reached the capital, and prepared his collections for shipment. There he spent the winter, making careful plans for a voyage to the south; his chief interest was in finding a line of demarcation between the animals brought by the Spaniards and the indigenous animals, and in seeking new specimens from a more moderate climate.[17]

On January 2, 1829, Orbigny departed for the Río Negro, arriving January 7. For nearly nine months he explored Patagonia, partly by ship, partly on foot or horseback; he visited the Tehuelche Indians, learning from them that the so-called Patagonian "giants" were but a myth; he enlarged his plant and bird collection considerably, and added to it a number of fossils; he saw the famed "sacred tree" of the Indians, with its branches covered with propitiatory offerings (for the Indians believed it to be a malevolent deity); he visited a *salina* (salt mine), went on an ostrich hunt, and saw the monotonous, sterile, semi-desert country farther south. At last, on September 1, he embarked for Buenos Aires with his collections, preparing them for shipment on arrival.[18]

Orbigny had hoped to go overland to Chile from Buenos Aires, but was fearful of the Araucanian Indians, who were on the warpath, as was also the *gaucho* leader, Facundo Quiroga. Consequently, despite the discouraging reports he had heard about sailing around Cape Horn, he decided to risk it, and embarked from Montevideo in December aboard a ship commanded by a twenty-three-year-old Catalan, "poorly educated, but a good fellow." Orbigny remarked that he was overly religious, requiring frequent prayers by the crew and passengers—a necessary precaution, the captain no doubt felt, in view of the dangers attendant upon such a voyage. After several delays because of storms around Tierra del Fuego and Staten Island, the captain successfully doubled the cape at 60° south latitude and sailed into the Pacific in beautiful but cold weather. He was able to determine latitude quite accurately, but did longitude solely by instinct, with an assist by Orbigny. Without further incident, the ship reached the harbor of Valparaíso on February 16.[19]

After a visit to Santiago, Orbigny returned to the port to receive from the French consul the good news that President Santa Cruz of Bolivia, "a friend of the sciences," requested his services in evaluating the unknown riches of his country. Being in rather strained financial straits, the naturalist looked on this as providential, and accepted at once. Embarking on April 8, he reached the port of Tacna April 22, where he engaged muleteers for the ascent of the cordillera. During the course of the crossing he gathered much geographical, biological, and geological information, and, of course, suffered from *soroche* at the summit. After his arrival in La Paz, where he managed to adjust to the altitude, Orbigny called on President Santa Cruz, who directed him to the *yungas*—that lush country embracing the slopes from the *altiplano* to the lowlands—and offered him protection, funds, assistants, and an army officer "that I might have respect." [20]

To reach this area required the crossing of the eastern cordillera, accompanied by another attack of *soroche*, which was forgotten as Orbigny viewed the magnificent scenery about him. Upon entering the humid valleys of the *yungas* he was impressed by the variety and abundance of plant life; this region, he felt, would do much to increase the prosperity of the country. His wanderings took him to Santa Cruz, which lay in lower country, with tall trees, jaguars, and, of course, mosquitoes again—he had all but forgotten them. And there was rain —rain in a deluge beside which the rains of Europe were as nothing. Orbigny spent two years in exploring the province, during which he made many trips on the tributaries of the Madeira in a pirogue, corrected maps, and made extensive zoological, geological, and ethnographic observations which would eventually fill five of the seven volumes describing his explorations, published after his return to Paris in 1833.

Orbigny's work in South America was not finished with the completion of his Bolivian survey. In 1841 he left Bordeaux on the brig *Jefferson* for the Antilles; beginning with Cuba, he visited the chain of islands reaching to the South American continent, then went to Surinam and finally to British Guiana, where he waited a month for passage to New Granada in vain. Instead he went to Venezuela, visiting Caracas, and then went up the Orinoco to see the *llanos*. After a stay at San Fernando on the Apure, he proceeded up the Orinoco to the mission of Yavita, portaged to the Río Negro, followed it to the Brazilian frontier, returned to the Orinoco via the Casiquiare, and went back to Angostura. Subsequent journeys in Venezuela took him to Valencia and Maracaibo, and before his return to France in the following year, he found time to ascend the Río Magdalena, visit Bogotá, and explore the highlands of Colombia.[21]

In the year when Orbigny began his journey to South America, two British vessels, H.M.S. *Adventure* and H.M.S. *Beagle*, sailed from Plymouth to undertake a survey of the coasts of that continent. In accordance with instructions issued by the Admiralty on May 16, 1826, differences in longitude were to be carefully checked all the way to

Montevideo, and the coast was to be surveyed from Cape San Antonio, at the entrance to the Río de la Plata, all the way, including Tierra del Fuego, to the island of Chiloé. All proceedings were to be communicated to the Admiralty, and each captain was instructed, "You are to avail yourself of every opportunity of collecting and preserving Specimens of such objects of Natural History as may be new, rare, or interesting. . . ." [22] The expedition was to be under the command of Captain Philip Parker King in the *Adventure;* Captain Stokes would command the *Beagle.*

After an uneventful voyage from Plymouth, the two vessels arrived at Montevideo in early October, and spent the next month surveying the coast between that city and Cape Santa María. Rather than begin the survey of the Argentine coast immediately, Captain King decided to go at once to the Strait of Magellan while the ships were in excellent condition, the crews healthy, and "while the charms of a new and difficult enterprize had full force." [23] Even at this favorable time of the year, the foul weather encountered in the high latitudes as they progressed toward the strait made King apprehensive for the crews' health, and delayed them considerably. The commander was well read on the literature of the strait, and his account gives an extensive history of the most important of the early voyages into the region. Encounters with the Indians aroused the same revulsion we find in other accounts; King described them as hideous, filthy, and stinking of seal oil mixed with red ochre, earth, and charcoal with which they smeared their bodies, apparently as a protection against the cold. They were inordinately fond of such trifles as buttons and beads; the men would willingly exchange their wives, children, canoes, and furniture for a few of them. There was, of course, the question of the "Patagonian giants"; King measured some of the men, and found that none exceeded 6 feet 1¾ inches. He did note that the tallest were the oldest, and speculated that perhaps they had degenerated into a smaller race.

After wintering in Rio de Janeiro, the two ships paid a return visit to the strait in January of 1828; King suspected that there might be another passage as yet unknown, but searched several months in vain for it. Winter arrived with gales and snow in June, and King gave the order to sail finally on July 25 after an outbreak of scurvy among the crews. Captain Stokes of the *Beagle,* who for some reason or other seemed to dread the survey work of the expedition, began to show signs of imbalance; finally, in a fit of despondency, he committed suicide. When the ships returned to Rio de Janeiro in October, Lieutenant Robert Fitz-Roy replaced him in command of the *Beagle.*

At the end of 1828 the expedition sailed for the south again, and very nearly came to grief when it ran into one of those severe storms coming out of Patagonia—the *pampero.* Extensive damage occurred in a twenty-minute period, and the *Beagle* nearly capsized. The voyage continued, and at Puerto Deseado they fell in with two British vessels; King decided to divide their work. The *Adventure*, along with one of them, the *Chanticleer*, would explore as far as Valparaíso, and the *Beagle*, with the *Adelaide*, would make an extensive survey of the strait area. The first two vessels reached the Chilean port without incident, and went south to Chiloé, where they were joined by the *Beagle* and the *Adelaide* on August 2, 1829. The *Beagle* left again for the strait on November 18, followed later by the *Adelaide*, which was undertaking a separate survey. While exploring the strait, Fitz-Roy had an unpleasant encounter with some Fuegans who had stolen one of his whaleboats. In the ensuing scuffle, one of the Indians, to Fitz-Roy's regret, was killed; the boat was never recovered, so the captain took three young Fuegans as hostages, eventually taking them to England to attempt to educate them. There were two young men and a younger girl, to whom Fitz-Roy, as we have already seen, gave the fanciful names of York Minster, Jemmy Button, and Fuegia Basket. By June 21 the Beagle had completed its explorations and set sail for the north, arriving at Rio de Janeiro on August 2, where it joined the *Adventure* to sail four days later for Plymouth.[24]

The second voyage of the *Beagle*, from 1831 to 1836, is well known, and we have earlier surveyed the work of its illustrious passenger, Charles Darwin. But, since Darwin was away from the *Beagle* for extended periods of time, it remains to be seen what the expedition accomplished during his absence. While Darwin was crossing the *pampas*, the *Beagle* was surveying the adjacent coast, accompanied by two schooners, the *Paz* and the *Liebre*, which Fitz-Roy had hired because the survey proved to be too big a task for one vessel. While surveying the Malvinas (or Falkland Islands) after returning his Indian guests to their homeland, Fitz-Roy became convinced of the need of another vessel. The *Beagle*, he felt, could not execute her task "before she, and those in her, would be so much in need of repair and rest that the most interesting part of her voyage—the carrying a chain of meridian distances around the globe—must eventually be sacrificed to the tedious, although not less useful, details of coast surveying."[25] Consequently, when the *Unicorn*, a sealer of 110 tons, made of oak with a copper bottom, came into port, he bought it from its owner-master, and somewhat nostalgically renamed it *Adventure*. Thus the survey was completed with greater dispatch, and the ships returned to the Río de la Plata in October.

On December 6 the *Beagle* and the *Adventure* sailed south with nine months' provisions; the *Adventure* returned briefly to the Malvinas, eventually rejoining the *Beagle* during its survey of Tierra del Fuego and the strait. Upon the completion of this work, after some delay resulting from bad weather, the ships sailed into the Pacific under full canvas on June 11, 1834, eventually arriving at Valparaíso on July 22. Unable to support the *Adventure* any longer on the funds available to him, Fitz-Roy sold it there, returning its crew to the *Beagle*. The winter was spent in the Chilean port, preparing charts of the expedition's work thus far. During the spring and summer of 1834–35, it will be remembered, a survey was made of the island of Chiloé and the Chonos archipelago, and the explorers witnessed the aftermath of the great earthquake at Concepción.[26]

Fitz-Roy now decided to refit his vessel and gather supplies for the Pacific crossing. During this time he was able to complete his survey in a borrowed ship, and returned with the *Beagle* to Valparaíso in June, after which he learned of the loss of H.M.S. *Challenger* and managed to find and rescue its crew. While Darwin was engaged in exploring the Atacama, Fitz-Roy remained behind on business and the *Beagle* proceeded slowly up the coast, picking up Darwin and proceeding to Callao. Fitz-Roy arrived there on August 9 in H.M.S. *Blonde*, which had been operating in the Pacific, and arranged for the completion of the coastal survey after his ship would depart for the South Sea. On September 7 the *Beagle* departed for the Galápagos, beginning the last stage of its memorable voyage which would lead to Tahiti and eventually home.[27]

Callao, the *Beagle's* point of departure, had the year before (1834) been the point of origin of a transcontinental journey of two British naval officers which began under the sponsorship of the Peruvian government. During the three-month stay of H.M.S. *Samarang* at Callao, one of its officers, Lieutenant William Smyth, became acquainted with one John Thomas, who invited him to see some the pre-Inca ruins, then suggested penetration of the *montaña* to Mayro, going down the Río Pachitea and the Ucayali to the Amazon. This, he said with assurance, would be a natural outlet for the products of the interior; moreover, Padre Manuel Plaza, who had been in that country for thirty-two years, had written in the *Mercurio Peruano* of the richness of the land and the navigability of the Pachitea up to Mayro. There was one problem: both sides of the river were inhabited by the Cashibo nation, who were cannibals. When Smyth showed an interest in the project, Consul-General Wilson succeeded in interesting Matías León, minister of foreign affairs, and General Villa Riestra, minister of war, in the idea, and they won the approval of President Orbegoso. In the face of such powerful support, Captain Paget of the *Samarang* could do little other than approve, and permit Smyth to take another officer of his choice, Lieutenant Frederick Lowe, with him. His superior officer, Commodore Mason of H.M.S. *Blonde*, added his approval. Wilson, meanwhile, persuaded the Peruvian government to support the expedition actively; the war ministry provided Colonel Clement Althaus to direct movements to Mayro, with Major Pedro Beltrán, and Lieutenant Ramón Azcarte of the navy to assist them as far as the confluence of the Ucayali and the Amazon. The archbishop of Lima provided a letter to Padre Plaza at Sarayacu, asking his assistance, and the expedition was ready to begin.[28]

Smyth and Lowe departed on September 20 with five cargo mules and two muleteers. Beltrán and Azcarte joined them after five days, and Colonel Althaus a day later. Despite the usual difficulties, crossing the cordillera was a minor problem compared with the difficulties Althaus faced in getting local authorities to furnish money for the expedition; they professed to believe that the order to furnish assistance did not include spending public funds. Much time was lost in going back and forth to secure convincing authorization. Roads were narrow and often clung to precipitous slopes. The road from Muña to Pozuzu was of corduroy, partly rotted and narrow, and at one point Major Beltrán's horse slipped and fell 1,500 feet; luckily he was able to catch the edge of the path with his hands and recovered his footing. By the time they reached Pozuzu, the explorers found themselves in a difficult situation; their Indians had taken off, and they could find no others willing to go on. Consequently a change of plans was necessitated; instead of proceeding directly from Pozuzu to Mayro, they would retrace their steps to Huánuco, go down the Río Huallaga, cross the Pampa del Sacramento by land to Sarayacu, and there get the assistance of Padre Plaza to go up the Ucayali and Pachitea to Mayro.

At Huánuco they learned that rich *hacenderos* were secretly opposing them, fearing that opening a route via Pozuzu would ruin the value of their estates in the Chinchao valley; this might possibly explain the difficulty in securing Indian assistance. The journey down the Río Huallaga was somewhat hazardous in view of the swiftness of the current, since the river was confined between hills, but it was accomplished with little difficulty except at the rapids. Finally, on February 2, 1835, the party met the famed Padre Plaza; the next day he set out with them for the Río Ucayali, which they reached at noon. Smyth and Lowe felt a sense of relief at seeing this majestic river, a mile and a half wide, flowing tranquilly across the plain, and a sense of exhilaration at being the first Englishmen to enter its waters.[29]

The party remained at the mission of Yapata for a month, waiting for Indians to accompany them on the next stage of their journey. At their request, Padre Plaza wrote an assessment of their resources for the journey for the benefit of the Peruvian government; he found them very short in men, funds, and provisions. He could advance them nothing, he said; while appreciating the value of the expedition, he pointed out that he had not heard from Lima in nine years until he had word of their coming; he received no salary, but supported the mission by meager trade with the neighboring towns, and seemed to be unable to rouse the government into doing something before the whole area relapsed into barbarism. So remote did the possibility of accomplishing their primary objective appear now to Smyth and Lowe that they decided to abandon their plans, and instead go down the Amazon to the sea.

On March 6 the explorers boarded one of Padre Plaza's canoes for the trip downstream. Before departing, he exchanged their trinkets for sarsaparilla and cotton cloth, which, he assured them, would have a greater trade value on the Amazon. Loaded also were the missionary's cargoes of sarsaparilla, *manteca*, and turtle oil for the mission of San Pablo; more would follow for other stations on rafts. After sending his nephew to go with them as interpreter, Padre Plaza bade farewell to his guests, who proceeded down the Ucayali to Tierra Blanca, where they waited a day to pick up the missionary's rafts. On March 15 they entered the Amazon and proceeded to Omaguas; there Smyth, to amuse himself, conducted an archery contest, and was astonished to find that the Indians' skill with the bow and arrow had been over-rated—no one could hit an eighteen-inch square of cardboard beyond forty-five feet. The Peruvians left them at Tierra Blanca, to return to Lima; now, at the town of San Pablo de Loreto, near Brazilian territory, Smyth and Lowe would have to leave the canoe, which the Indians had to take back to the Ucayali mission. For $30 and their sarsaparilla, Smyth and Lowe were able to buy a vessel with a cabin on its after-deck, and with the assistance of rowers hired at various points along the river (one group of them stole a roll of their cotton cloth), they managed to reach Manaus without difficulty. There was little opportunity for observation, for it was the height of the rainy season; consequently they continued their journey to Santarém and finally to Belém, arriving May 21 and thus completing the crossing of the continent. The chief purpose of their journey had failed of achievement, and even a lesser one—collecting specimens—availed little when most of the animals died on the way to England; nonetheless, Smyth was of the hope "that it may not prove altogether useless, and may in some respects add to the store of information previously possessed respecting the countries we traversed." [30]

Eight years passed before another important government-sponsored expedition set out to explore South America. In the year 1843 King Louis-Philippe of France authorized a scientific expedition to explore the continent of South America, and at the suggestion of the Duc d'Orléans, heir to the throne, named François de la Porte, Comte de

Castelnau (1812–80), to head it. The count by his own admission had long been interested in science and adventure; he had read the writings of such explorers as Captain James Cook, and he had studied natural sciences under such leading lights as Cuvier and Saint-Hilaire. When an opportunity came to visit North America, he made the most of it, traveling extensively for five years through the United States and Canada. In the course of his travels he met several prominent Americans who, knowing of his desire to visit South America, proposed in the name of the United States government, that he go to Lima on a diplomatic assignment. Castelnau could not accept such an appointment without the approval of his government, and went back to France to seek it. There he was well received by the Duc d'Orléans, who had a great interest in scientific geography; he reproached him for what he called "desertion," and suggested instead that he head a French expedition to that continent, an offer which Castelnau immediately accepted.

The chief aim of the expedition was to study, in all its aspects, the vast Amazon basin, which Europeans felt would play a great role in the future history of South America. It was proposed to cross the continent twice—first from Rio de Janeiro to Lima, then to the headwaters of the Amazon and down that mighty river to its mouth. It was planned to explore its tributaries, to investigate the possibility of establishing communications between its waters and those of the Paraguay, and to study the products of all the lands through which they would pass. The expedition would be limited to the zone between the equator and the Tropic of Capricorn—certainly an area large enough to excite the imagination of the explorer. Castelnau was most anxious to observe the contrasts between the two Americas: in North America, he recalled, with one of the most variable climates in the world, man was constantly active, especially in commerce, and had developed all the resources of his intellect; in South America, he felt, there would be less activity, and more admiration of the magnificent works of nature, which all bore the stamp of Divinity. It was "a bizarre effect of civilization," he mused, that the most beautiful parts of the world are forsaken by men and left to "tigers" and great reptiles.[31]

Once the government had decided to send an expedition, it was irritated by the many delays that occurred; since the work would involve astronomy, physical geography, and natural science, many instruments and arrangements for packing collections, considerable advance study, and a five-year period in unknown wildernesses where they would have to depend on what they brought with them, Castelnau did not wish to leave until the expedition was as well trained and well equipped as possible. Twenty times the expedition was on the point of being abandoned, and when the Duc d'Orléans was killed in a carriage accident,

Castelnau feared it was over; fortunately, the minister of public instruction, Villemain, appeared to be convinced that the work must be done, and the prime minister, Guizot, took a lively interest in it. Castelnau chose his companions for this long journey very carefully. There was Eugène d'Osery, nephew of General Moreau, a brilliant Polytechnique graduate, courageous and honorable, and one of France's most promising young scientists. The Muséum d'Histoire Naturelle furnished one of its members, the physician and botanist Dr. Hugues-A. Weddell, father of the celebrated navigator, and one of its young employees, Emile Deville, as preparator.

The expedition finally left Brest on April 30, 1843, in the navy brig *Dupetit Thouars*, bound for Tenerife, Goréa, and Dakar before crossing the Atlantic. On June 2 the vessel crossed the equator with the usual ceremonies, and on June 17 entered Guanabara Bay. For two months the explorers remained in Rio de Janeiro, botanizing and studying the animals in the environs, and making meteorological, magnetic, and geological observations. Upon leaving the capital, the party made its way through the province of Rio de Janeiro into Minas Gerais, to Ouro Prêto and the Rio São Francisco, and finally to Goiás, which Castelnau described as "one of the most pleasant places in Brazil." [32] He had long wanted to explore northern Goiás province, a region unknown to geographers and naturalists, and finally won the approval of the provincial president, who agreed to put at his disposal all means possible. The count's purpose was to go down the Rio Araguaia until it joined the Rio Tocantins, come up the latter river to the limit of navigation, then cross the wilderness back to the town of Goiás. The journey began on May 3; they passed through beautiful country, arriving on May 6 at Carretão, where they found to their surprise that the *capitão-mor* was a woman, appropriately nicknamed "Dona Potência." Eight days later they reached the town of Salinas, whence they would embark on the river; crews were secured from among the Chavantes Indians, who were Christian and nearly all friendly.

On June 11 they started out, progressing downstream to the great fluvial island of Bananal; they took the right *furo* to the end of the island, and finally entered the country of the Chamboias, who apparently had never seen a white man, for they opened the shirts of the explorers to see if their chests were the same color as their faces, which they believed were painted white. Descending some rapids beyond the Chamboia country, they reached the military outpost at the confluence with the Tocantins, packed their collections for shipment to Belém, and began the journey up the Tocantins. [33] At the point where the river makes a great bend, they followed the overland cut-off, and eventually proceeded according to plan to Goiás. After a week they resumed their journey, heading in a westerly direction across the wilderness to Cuiabá, from which they made an excursion north to locate the sources of the Río Paraguay and the Tapajós, then south on the Rio São Laurenço and the Paraguay to the frontier of Paraguay, or, as Castelnau called it, "the Republic of Francia." [34]

After an excursion into the Gran Chaco, the explorers went back up the Río Paraguay, crossed the great marsh of Xarayes, totally unknown to Europeans, in the company of the Guato Indians, passed through the pestilential town of Mato Grosso, and entered the country of the Chiquitos, once a great Jesuit mission area. In his introduction to his account, Castelnau suggested that the missionaries should be credited with almost all modern geographical discovery, "for it is very rare that the boldest traveler can boast of not having been preceded by these pioneers of evangelical civilization. First the priest, then the naturalist—such are, in the wilderness, the forerunners of the white race." [35]

When the group entered Bolivia, Dr. Weddell detached himself for an extensive journey through that republic, which took him south as far as Tarija, east to the upper reaches of the Río Pilcomayo, in the Chaco, then northwest to Cochabamba and La Paz, east of Lake Titicaca to the region north of it, and finally to Cuzco. [36] Castelnau and the others, meanwhile, went through Chuquisaca (the modern Sucre) to Potosí, where they visited the mines of that fabled city, then crossed the *altiplano* to La Paz. They visited the ancient ruins of Tiahuanaco and Lake Titicaca, then proceeded to Arequipa and the Pacific coast, taking ship for Callao and Lima. D'Osery, who left the party at Arequipa, made the journey overland along the coast.

Four months were spent in Lima, during which Weddell rejoined his fellow explorers. Sufficiently rested, they left for Cerro de Pasco to visit the mines, then journeyed to Tarma, Huancavelica, and Ayacucho, where independence had been won. They crossed the Inca suspension bridge over the Río Apurímac to Cuzco, then proceeded to the western cordillera, into the coca-growing area. Ready now for the great river voyage, the explorers embarked upon the Río Urubamba. At one encampment they were suddenly abandoned by their guides, porters and soldiers alike, left to attempt the descent of this dangerous river alone. In view of this circumstance, Castelnau decided to send one of the group to Lima to place their instruments and papers in safety before attempting the descent; he selected d'Osery, who never accomplished his mission—he was killed by his new guides on the way. The rest of the group then continued their journey in pirogues to the mission of Sarayacu, and managed to cross the dangerous Pampa del Sacramento and reach the Amazon. [36]

Castelnau found the last stretch, the descent of the Amazon, the least trying part of the entire journey, and was able to make a constant and careful study of its products and peoples as they progressed toward Belém. From that port the group sailed to Cayenne, thence to the West Indies, where they secured passage on a ship bound for England, arriving in 1847. Returning to Paris, Castelnau rested a year, then returned to his beloved South America in 1849 as consul in Salvador da Bahia. Most of the written records of the expedition were lost when d'Osery was murdered—the official journal, d'Osery's own journal, the register of astronomical, meteorological, and magnetic observations, and the notes on zoology. Fortunately a portion of these records was recovered, but the most complete records were irretrievably lost. Despite this, Castelnau was able, using the journals of Weddell and Deville, notes sent by d'Osery to his father, several hundred drawings and sketches, and his own memory, to reconstruct the account as we have it today. It was well that he could do so, for his was possibly the most extensive exploration of tropical America since the almost legendary expedition of that great *bandeirante,* Antônio Rapôso Tavares, more than two centuries earlier.[37] Few indeed were the explorers of South America who covered so much of the continent.

NOTES

1. J. B. Spix and K. F. Martius, *Travels in Brazil in the Years 1817–1820,* 2 vols. (London, 1824); only two volumes of the original German edition appear in an English translation.
2. *Ibid.,* Vol. I, pp. 4-7.
3. For the preparations and the journey to Rio de Janeiro, see Spix and Martius, *Travels,* Vol. I, pp. 7-124.
4. *Ibid.,* Vol. I, p. 160.
5. On their work in the vicinity of Rio de Janeiro and the São Paulo journey, see Spix and Martius, *Travels,* Vol. I, pp. 131-327, and Vol. II, pp. 1-102.
6. *Ibid.,* Vol. II, p. 283. For the account of their journey through Minas Gerais, see *ibid.,* Vol. II, pp. 103-286.
7. Spix and Martius, *Reise in Brasilien* (München, 1831), Vol. III, pp. 887-1054.
8. *Ibid.,* Vol. III, pp. 1100-81.
9. *Ibid.,* Vol. III, 1197-1304.
10. *Ibid.,* Vol. III, p. 1387.
11. Olivério M. Oliveira Pinto, "Viajantes e Naturalistas," in Sergio Buarque de Holanda, ed., *História geral da civilização brasileira,* Vol. V, p. 455.
12. *Ibid.,* pp. 455-57.
13. *Ibid.,* pp. 444-47; Egon Schaden and João Borges Pereira, "Exploração antropológica," in Buarque de Holanda, *op. cit.,* Vol. V, p. 429.
14. Alcide d'Orbigny, *Voyage dans l'Amérique Méridionale* (Paris, 1835-47), Vol. I, pp. 3-6.
15. *Ibid.,* Vol. I, p. 20.
16. For this portion of his journey, see Orbigny, *Voyage dans l'Amérique Méridionale,* Vol. I, pp. 7-239.
17. *Ibid.,* Vol. I, pp. 240-477.
18. *Ibid.,* Vol. II, pp. 1-319.
19. *Ibid.,* Vol. II, pp. 319-33.
20. *Ibid.,* Vol. II, pp. 334-422.

21. For this second expedition, see Orbigny's *Voyage dans les deux Amériques,* Nouvelle ed. (Paris, 1853).

22. Robert Fitz-Roy, ed., *Narrative of the Surveying Voyage of H.M. Ships Adventure and Beagle, 1826–1836* (London, 1839), Vol. I, p. xvii. For the purpose of the voyage and complete instructions, see pp. xi-xix.

23. *Ibid.,* Vol. I, p. 1.

24. For this first voyage, see *ibid.,* Vol. I.

25. *Ibid.,* Vol. II, pp. 273-74.

26. For this portion of the voyage, see Fitz-Roy, *op. cit.,* Vol. II, pp. 316-424.

27. See *ibid.,* Vol. II, pp. 425-82.

28. William Smyth and Frederick Lowe, *Narrative of a Journey from Lima to Peru across the Andes and down the Amazon* (London, 1836), pp. 1-14.

29. For this stage of the journey, see Smyth and Lowe, *op. cit.,* pp. 16-107.

30. *Ibid.,* p. 305. For the journey through the lowlands, see pp. 108-305.

31. Castelnau's account, *Expédition dans les Parties Centrales de l'Amérique du Sud* (Paris, 1850), is a multivolume work of which the first six constitute the "Histoire du voyage." For the background of the expedition, see Vol. I, pp. 1-12.

32. Castelnau, Vol. I, p. 327.

33. The first stage of the journey, to the confluence of the Rio Araguaia and the Rio Tocantins, is covered in Vol. I of Castelnau's account.

34. José Gaspar Rodríguez de Francia was, of course, the dictator of Paraguay. Vol. II of Castelnau's account covers his expedition from the confluence of the Araguaia and the Tocantins to the Paraguayan frontier.

35. Castelnau, Vol. I, p. 26. This portion of the journey is treated in Castelnau, Vol. III.

36. For the journey from Lima to the Amazon, see Castelnau, Vol. IV.

37 See above, Chap. VI, p. 107.

XVII   Government-Sponsored

Explorations: Later Nineteenth Century

By the middle of the nineteenth century, the government of the United States had become interested in the exploration of South America. In 1836 Congress had authorized the United States Exploring Expedition for the purpose of surveying and exploring the Pacific Ocean and the South Seas. Lieutenant Charles Wilkes, U.S.N., was placed in command. Not until 1838 did the expedition get under way; during that year and the following one it was in South America, stopping at Rio de Janeiro, El Carmen, Patagonia, Tierra del Fuego, Valparaíso, and Callao. The expedition's scientists found little that was new, and the surveys made around the southern extremity of the continent were not spectacular, yet the expedition did serve to interest the government in the possibilities of such exploration.[1]

In 1847 a German astronomer, C. L. Gerling, suggested, as a means of measuring more accurately the distance of the sun from the earth, that observations be made of the retrograde motions of Venus from the Naval Observatory in Washington and from an observatory set up in the same latitude in South America. The Naval Observatory had been completed in 1844, and was largely the work of Lieutenant James Melville Gilliss (who had replaced Wilkes as head of the Navy Depot of Charts and Instruments in 1836). Lieutenant Matthew Fontaine Maury, however, had been named to head the observatory in 1842, so Gilliss became much interested in the plan, hoping to set up the southern observatory. During the latter part of 1847 Gilliss lobbied effectively for his project, securing the support of the Academy of Arts and Sciences, the American Philosophical Society, and the Smithsonian Institution. Secretary of the Navy Mason, while impressed by the recommendations, had doubts concerning his authority to authorize it, so the matter was laid before Congress, which appropriated $5,000 for an expedition to

Chile to make astronomical observations, and a complete report on Chile as well (Congress intended to get its money's worth).

As his associates in the venture, Gilliss named Edmond R. Smith (who immediately proceeded to learn something of Spanish, natural history and mineralogy) and two midshipmen, Archibald MacRae and S. L. Phelps. The assistants left Baltimore on July 11, 1849, for Valparaíso via Cape Horn, arriving October 30; Gilliss sailed from New York to go via Panama on August 16, arriving in Valparaíso on October 25 after a five-day stop at Callao and Lima. Gilliss had been advised in Washington to seek a site near Santiago rather than Chiloé Island; the Chilean government assisted him in locating and provided three Chileans, whom Gilliss taught astronomy. The expedition accomplished its purpose, and much more; many specimens were collected, and an exchange of plants and seeds was worked out between the government greenhouse in Washington and the National Botanical Garden in Santiago. Having no funds for this purpose, Gilliss was at times obliged to use his own.

After the conclusion of his work in 1852, Gilliss sold the observatory to Chile, enabling him to send MacRae home via the Andes and Buenos Aires to make magnetic and other observations. Damaged instruments made the value of his longitudinal observations doubtful, so he agreed to repeat them at his own expense if the government supplied instruments, which was done. Smith left the expedition to see more of Chile, and went to study the Araucanians. Gilliss and Phelps returned to Washington, where Gilliss sold to the Smithsonian Institution such natural history specimens as he had collected at his own expense; he also learned, to his chagrin, that Maury had failed, for one reason or another, to make the simultaneous astronomical observations in Washington, rendering much of the work useless. Yet much was accomplished; Gilliss' observations and his reports on Chile comprise six volumes, four of which were published in 1855 and after as *The United States Naval Astronomical Expedition to the Southern Hemisphere, During the Years 1849-'50-'51, '52.*[2]

The interest of the United States in South America was by no means confined to Chile. Maury had for some time been interested in the possibility of colonizing the Amazon valley with whites and their slaves from southern United States, both as a possible simple solution of the slavery problem (it could then be prohibited in the South) and to forestall Great Britain, which he believed was entertaining the idea that this region could be developed into a great cotton-producing area. It would be quite unlikely that the Brazilian government would be interested in approving an expedition for such a purpose as this, but if one could be sent for the purpose of increasing knowledge of the river, the navigability of its affluents, its agricultural possibilities and commercial prospects, surely information relevant to Maury's idea could be gleaned as well.

Presenting his idea to the secretary of the navy, Maury secured approval for one or two naval officers of the Pacific Squadron to return through South America, descending the Amazon on their way; his choice for the mission fell upon his cousin, Lieutenant William Lewis Herndon, then aboard the *Vandalia* at Valparaíso.[3]

Herndon received his orders in August of 1850, but because of the death of President Taylor had to wait for additional instructions. During that time he improved his Spanish and collected information on the Bolivian tributaries of the Amazon. In January he left for Lima, and on April 4, 1851, Lieutenant Lardner Gibbon arrived with detailed instructions concerning the information he was to gather, as well as seeds and plants which might be introduced into the United States. The choice of route was his, so he decided to go via Peru, sending Gibbon through Bolivia to join him on the Amazon. To accompany them, Herndon selected a master's mate, Richards, from the frigate *Raritan* and an interpreter. The party left on May 21; Herndon had difficulty in getting Peruvians to accompany him, since they could not believe he would leave on the day he proposed to do so. Their route took them through the pass of Morococha, where Richards, very ill with *soroche*, had to be left behind, then through Tarma, Chanchamayo, and back to Tarma, where Gibbon set out for Bolivia. Herndon left for Cerro de Pasco; on the way he passed through Carhaumayo, where, he tells us, "I saw the only really pretty face I have met within the Sierra and bought a glass of *pisco* from it." [4] Upon leaving Cerro de Pasco, situated at an elevation of fourteen thousand feet, he crossed the highest part of the cordillera and made the precipitous descent into the *montaña*, much impressed by the sudden transition from no cultivation to a zone of tropical vegetation.

Upon reaching the Río Huallaga, Herndon crossed it to Acomayo, where he saw a tree bearing a large, bell-shaped flower, the *floripondo*: "It gives out a delicious fragrance at night," he commented, "which accompanied, as I have known it, by soft air, rich moonlight and gentle company makes bare existence a happiness." [5] Leaving these idyllic surroundings, he crossed the Cerro de Carpis to Chinchao, descended the valley, and finally reached the confluence of the Río Chinchao and the Huallaga on July 30. Two days later he was at Tingo María, where he secured two large dugout canoes for the trip downstream. During the river journey Herndon witnessed two unusual sights—a lemon tree completely covered with a spider web, and a fishing party using the mashed pulp of the *barbasco* root to poison the fish. Passing through the lake country, he noticed that his Indians blew loudly on a horn; they believed that the lakes were inhabited by a great serpent capable of raising a tempest, which would answer them and warn them of its presence. Below Laguna, on September 3, they reached the mouth of the Huallaga, at the Amazon; there they halted to fit their boats with decks and cov-

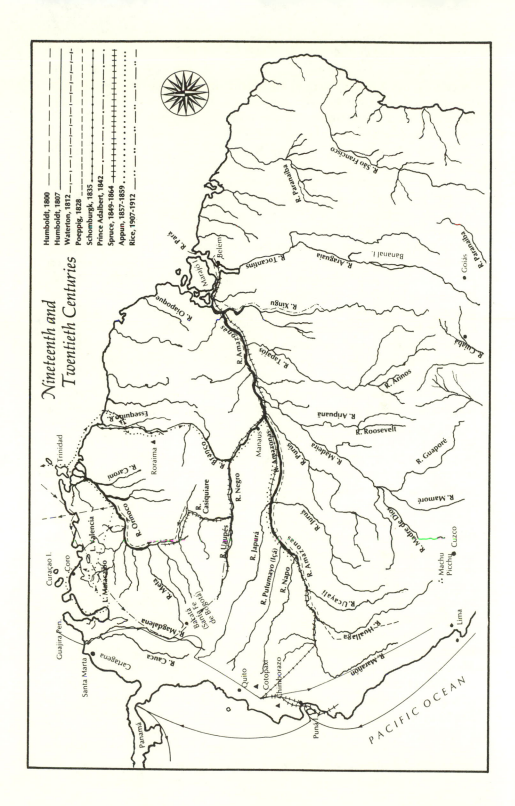

Nineteenth and Twentieth Centuries

Humboldt, 1800
Humboldt, 1807
Waterton, 1812
Poeppig, 1828
Schomburgk, 1835
Prince Adalbert, 1842
Spruce, 1849–1864
Appun, 1857–1859
Rice, 1907–1912

Trinidad

Curaçao I.
Coro
Guajira Pen.
Santa Marta
Cartagena
Panamá

L. Valencia
L. Maracaibo

R. Caroni
Roraima ▲

R. Orinoco
R. Meta
R. Magdalena
Bogotá (Santa Fe de Bogotá)
R. Cauca

R. Essequibo
R. Branco
R. Casiquiare
R. Negro
R. Uaupés
R. Japurá
R. Putumayo (Içá)
R. Napo

R. Pará
Belém
Marajó I.
R. Oiapoque
R. Amazonas
R. Tapajós
R. Xingu
R. Tocantins
R. Araguaia
Bananal I.

R. Arinos
R. Arinuanã
R. Roosevelt
R. Madeira
R. Guaporé
R. Mamoré
R. Madre de Dios

R. São Francisco
R. Paranaíba
Goiás
R. Paranaíba
R. Cuiabá

Manaus
R. Purus
R. Juruá
R. Amazonas
R. Ucayali
R. Huallaga
R. Marañón

Quito
Cotopaxi ▲
Chimborazo ▲
Puná I.
Machu Picchu
Cuzco
Lima

PACIFIC OCEAN

erings, hoisted a small American flag, and entered the great river on September 25. Within an hour the party reached the Ucayali (which disappointed Herndon—it was only half as wide as the Amazon) and spent the next twenty-three days exploring it. At Sarayacu Herndon became ill, and was nursed back to health by the missionaries, who dissuaded him from attempting to reach the Pachitea without a sufficiently large protective force.[6]

Back at Nauta again, near the mouth of the Ucayali, Herndon reentered the Amazon, progressed downstream to Iquitos, then to Pebas, below the mouth of the Río Napo, where he decided to stay a while to recover his strength. While there, he was a guest of the missionary, Padre Valdivia, a mestizo, eventually going with him to his mission of San José de los Yaguas. It was in a sorry state: "The priestly vestments were in rags," wrote Herndon. "The lavatory was a gourd, a little earthen pitcher, and a jack towel of cotton. It grieved me to see the host taken from a shaving box and the sanctified wine poured from a vinegar cruet." [7] While there he managed to acquire a number of additional animals for his collection, got some poisonous milk from the *catao* tree, as well as milk from the *palo de vaca*—the "cow-tree" which had so interested Humboldt.

The first stop in Brazil was the frontier post of Tabatinga. Herndon was carefully watched, lest he might be making a map or drawing; he could no longer fly the American flag, but was given a Brazilian one' instead, and the commandant insisted on exchanging boats with him so that he could say he was traveling in a Brazilian boat—foreign vessels were prohibited. As he proceeded downstream, Herndon saw the Indians making *manteiga* oil by crushing turtle eggs—a process which he was sure would eventually render the turtle extinct. At Manaus he learned of the *cedro*, a type of oak much in demand because it was the only wood of any value which could be floated to sawmills. At Obidos he visited a cacao plantation, then went on to Santarém, arriving March 1; there he found what he called "tokens of an increased civilization"—a marble monument in the cemetery and a billiard table. The remainder of the voyage was uneventful; what impressed Herndon most was the unerring accuracy with which his pilot steered through the maze of channels between the main course of the Amazon and the Rio Pará—even when he could not see the shore because of rain. After a month in Belém, Herndon returned to the United States; his report, and Gibbon's from Bolivia and the Rio Madeira, contributed not at all toward the solution of the slavery question, but provided a wealth of information to justify the $5,000 appropriated for the expedition.[8]

In the year of Herndon's return, 1852, Justo José de Urquiza, who had been named provisional director of the Argentine Confederation following his ouster of the dictator Rosas, opened the Paraná and

Uruguay rivers to the free navigation of all nations—a decree that led to another United States expedition to South America. The background of this expedition is interesting, involving as it does two men of quite different station and temperament: Carlos Antonio López, dictator of Paraguay, and Lieutenant Thomas Jefferson Page, U.S.N. López had let it be known that he would welcome the flag of the United States on the Río Paraguay, since commercial relations with the United States would be preferable, from his point of view, to relations with either France or Great Britain. Page's connection is less obvious. He had been serving in Chinese waters, and had got into discussions with United States businessmen in the Far East on the dangers to navigation in those waters; it occurred to him that accurate surveys would benefit trade, and he submitted the idea to the Navy, which approved it. Unfortunately, he was outranked for a command in the Pacific, but the secretary felt somewhat obligated to him for the idea and decided to send another expedition to the Río de la Plata in view of López' interest and Urquiza's decree. Page was offered the command of the *Water Witch*, assigned for the task, and accepted. The mission was to be purely scientific—this was the understanding of the Paraguayan government—a definition which Maury broadened to include sending home everything produced in Paraguay which could possibly be of interest to trade, including plants and seeds.[9]

The *Water Witch* arrived in Buenos Aires on May 25, 1853—the day on which the new constitution of the Confederation was proclaimed—to find the city under siege, since it would not join the Confederation. Urquiza was at that moment ready to depart for Entre Ríos, and Page's first assignment was to convey him to the town of Gualaguaychu, whence he departed for his nearby *estancia* to conclude negotiations on a treaty governing the navigation of the channel. Continuing upstream, the *Water Witch* paused at the city of Paraná, capital of the Confederation, and later docked at Corrientes for three days. Page was very impressed with the Argentine Mesopotamia, and believed it held great promise for European settlement; Nature, he said, "seems to have exhausted her bounty upon these Argentine States. They have the products of temperate and tropical zones; their woods and flora are rarely equaled; the climate is neither enervating nor severe, and the atmosphere is never laden with miasma." [10]

Twenty miles above Corrientes the Río Paraguay joins the Río Paraná; at the confluence lies the island of Atajo, claimed by Argentina, but the site of a Paraguayan base with a squadron of five ships under an officer with the pretentious title of Admiral of the Navy of the Republic of Paraguay. He came aboard the *Water Witch* and assured them of a cordial reception in Asunción. There López, after some argument, consented to navigation as far as Bahía Negra, conceded by both Paraguay and Brazil to be Bolivian territory. As he continued his journey north, Page envisioned a great future for this territory, which, he conceded, with the exception of the Mississippi valley, was "the fairest unbroken extent of cultivatable land in the world." [11] Upon crossing the Brazilian frontier at Fort Coimbra, Page was told by the commandant that he could go as far as Corumbá instead of only to Albuquerque, as had originally been agreed. Since the water was falling rapidly, Page did not tarry at Corumbá, but returned to Coimbra, where he was given some animals and rare birds which, he hoped, might become the nucleus of a national zoological collection. Upon re-entering Paraguay, Page sensed something was wrong, and finally learned that the government was disturbed at his entry into Brazil, fearing that Brazil would now expect the same favor granted the United States. Believing that he had smoothed things over, Page left the *Water Witch* at Asunción for extensive repairs, and prepared to continue exploring the vicinity in the *Pilcomayo*, a small vessel built for him of Paraguayan cedar.

The *Pilcomayo* left Asunción on May 18, 1854, to explore the Bermejo, going through flat country where the highest elevation was a four-foot ant hill. Page had hoped to go as far upstream as the river's depth would permit, but boiler trouble after 122 miles forced him to return to Asunción. Shortly afterward relations with López deteriorated over an incident involving the United States consul in the capital, and the dictator issued a decree closing Paraguayan waters to foreign ships; he further refused to ratify a treaty of commerce already ratified by the United States. Consequently, Page confined his explorations to Argentine waters, cruising in the *Pilcomayo* while the *Water Witch* was on its way to Montevideo for money and supplies. On January 1, 1855, he visited the *estancia* of Aimé Bonpland near Restauración. Bonpland was now eighty-two years of age, married to a Spanish-American woman and the father of many children.[12]

At the end of January, Page sent the *Water Witch*, under Lieutenant Jeffers, up the Paraná to determine the character of the rapids at Apipé Island. En route, with an Argentine pilot, the ship stuck on a sandbar in six feet of water. While trying to get it afloat, Jeffers saw a boat coming from the Paraguayan fort; he was handed a note, but returned it, stating that he could not read Spanish. The pilot finally got the *Water Witch* afloat, explaining the accident by saying that the channel was near the Paraguayan shore, so he had tried to stay as close to the Argentine shore as possible and had miscalculated the depth. At this point, the fort fired three blanks, then a shot which cut away the wheel and killed the helmsman. Jeffers returned fire, with some damage and loss of Paraguayan lives resulting. The fort fired again, but scored no hits, and Jeffers was able to drift past the fort to safety. When Page learned of the attack, he went to Montevideo to get two large-shell guns, intending to attack the fort. Finding the U.S.S. *Germantown* there, he tried to arrange to tow it up the Paraná to destroy the fort, but Captain Lynch would not agree and instructed him to halt all exploration in that area until further notice.[13]

Accordingly, Page altered his plans and on April 24, 1855, left Buenos Aires on an expedition to explore the Río Uruguay, which took him almost as far as the head of navigation at Salto Grande; he felt that a short canal there would open the river for several hundred more miles. The journey was rewarding: many soundings were taken, and, near Mercedes, fossil remains of giant quadrupeds were found.[14] On his return to Buenos Aires, Page chartered a small steamer, which had been assembled from American-made parts, to explore the Río Salado. The journey began on July 13 from the upriver town of Santa Fe; three days and twenty miles later Page was astonished to find himself in a completely uninhabited land. ". . . There is not a vestige of civilization or the track of a human being"; he wrote, "even the footprint of an Indian is nowhere visible; but the manifestations of animal life are extraordinary." [15] All about him were lofty quebracho trees, jaguars, armadillos, ducks, geese, swans, plovers, guanacos, ostriches, hares, and gulls, with the waters teeming with fish. But the river level fell rapidly, and at Monte Aguara he could go no farther. Cutting the letters "U.S." in a large *guaranina* tree, he buried a bottle giving the coordinates and names of the ship's crew, shot a magnificent jaguar, and returned on August 8. A second journey by land took him farther up the Río Salado, but it was cut short in November by spring rains. On returning to Buenos Aires through Salta, Tucumán, Santiago del Estero, Córdoba, and Rosario, Page found a letter of recall. Departing from Montevideo on February 3, 1856, he returned to the Washington Navy Yard on May 8. His report, while exaggerating the commercial possibilities of Paraguay, covers a wide range of observations, and is by far the best of the mid-century American explorers.[16]

The Civil War, of course, brought an interruption to the exploring and research activities of the United States in South America. During that hiatus we find Spain once more active in this area. More than sixty years had elapsed since the Malaspina expedition;[17] Spain's empire in the New World had all but disappeared, and there was a lack of up-to-date data and specimens from this area in her universities and museums. As a result, the government in 1862 decided to unite a scientific expedition with a good-will naval mission to South America, planned in 1860, consisting of the frigates *Resolución* and *Triunfo* and the schooner *Covadonga*. That this mission would eventually end in a war between Spain and its former dependencies, Peru and Chile, probably never entered the minds of those involved, yet there was fear in South America. Peru sent an agent to intercept Admiral Pinzón at Buenos Aires and question him; some Spanish papers had called for the occupation of the "Spanish" guano islands, but *La América* assured everyone that the only conquests would be scientific data, permanent friendship, and the "beautiful Peruvian women." [18] Furthermore, the fleet would visit only certain ports, and was to be at sea on local patriotic holidays.

The mission left Cádiz on August 10, 1862, with the scientific expedition headed by Patricio María Paz y Membiela, a retired naval captain and naturalist. On September 9 they reached Salvador, where the scientists spent several days collecting plants and animals, and studying the Indians. Upon their return to the *Triunfo*, friction developed between them and the ship's complement, which would heighten as time went on and make their stay aboard decidedly uncomfortable. On October 6 the expedition reached Rio de Janeiro, where the emperor Dom Pedro II granted them two audiences. There was ample opportunity for their own collecting, and they were able to buy a collection of 160 species of hummingbirds from a French naturalist resident there.

The expedition split up at the end of the year at Montevideo; because of his feud with the naval officers, Paz refused to go on by sea, and the expedition split. Part of it would continue by sea, the rest would go overland to Santiago; that Paz chose his personal friends to go by land is obvious—he took a conchologist with him, and sent a botanist by sea. Visiting Buenos Aires preparatory to their transcontinental journey, the land party met President Mitre and also the special Peruvian envoy, to whom Admiral Pinzón, who had arrived, made plain Spain's friendly intentions but also its firmness with respect to grievances it had against Peru. The overland trip was made by stagecoach into Chile, finishing by rail to Santiago; en route, the party got two pampas hares, which were the first ever sent to Europe, and saw the ruins of Mendoza, destroyed by an earthquake in 1861. The remainder of the party arrived at Valparaíso early in May of 1863, joined their companions in Santiago, and explored the countryside, augmenting their collections of insects and frogs. Proceeding to Coquimbo, they met an Englishman who had collected thousands of molluscs for shipment to England, and was kind enough to open his cases and give them 742 items representing 34 species. At Cobija, in what was then Bolivia, they visited mines and arranged to have their collections, including now a half-ton copper nugget, sent back to Spain. On July 11 the scientists, who were aboard the *Covadonga*, docked in Callao, rejoining the two frigates.[19]

A land party [20] left Tacna, Peru, on June 18 for La Paz in Bolivia, where they remained for nine days, exploring and botanizing, then left to see the pre-Inca remains at Tiahuanaco before going on to Lake Titicaca and Puno. To avoid the danger of too long a mule train—a target for bandits—the party separated: Manuel Almagro y Vega, the anthropologist, went to Cuzco, then joined the geologist and entomologist Fernando Amor y Mayor, second in command, to Ayacucho, Huancayo and Lima, while Juan Isern y Batlló, the botanist, went to Arequipa, and joined the others later.

Meanwhile the fleet had been well received, and was ready to depart when the dispute between Paz and the captain of the *Triunfo* reached a climax. Paz resigned from the expedition, to return to Spain by commercial vessel, and turned over command to the young naturalist Francisco de Paula Martínez y Sáez instead of Amor, who was very ill. After a stop at Guayaquil, they sailed on to Taboga Island in the Gulf of Panama and then to San Francisco, California, where Amor died in October. On the return trip, the scientists went ashore in Peru, collecting plants, Inca remains, and other specimens in complete freedom and safety, and then went on to Chile. At the end of March, 1864, Pinzón informed the scientists that they would have to leave the ship, since the destination of the squadron made it impossible for them to remain; they were to return to Spain, he said, aboard a commercial vessel departing in a few days. They protested, claiming that only the minister of public works, who had sent them, could recall them, and wrote him requesting authorization to return via the Amazon. Meanwhile, the fleet departed and seized Peru's guano islands—the Chinchas—as a reparative measure over Peru's refusal to pay certain Spanish claims, and war broke out. Lest Chile should join Peru, Pinzón sailed to Valparaíso and bombarded that defenseless port, then withdrew. Quite naturally this compromised the position of the scientists, who were believed to be spies, but Chilean scientists protected them and they were able to enlarge their collections considerably. At the end of July they received authorization for the *gran viaje* via the Amazon—and 12,000 pesetas. Marcos Jiménez de la Espada, the zoologist and the outstanding member of the expedition, then went to collect animals with Isern while the others went to Guayaquil to set up headquarters.[21]

The expedition was now reduced to four; Puig, the taxidermist, married the daughter of a wealthy landowner, and Castro, the photographer, was not well enough to be up to a long journey by mule and canoe. For several months the expedition remained in Ecuador, gathering specimens, making futile attempts to climb Chimborazo and Cotopaxi, but successfully climbing Antisana and Pichincha, where Espada went into the crater and found evidence of life there—a thing both La Condamine and Humboldt believed impossible. After lengthy preparations for the Amazon journey were completed, they left Quito in February, 1865, and crossed the cordillera despite rain, humidity, insects, and dysentery. Yet they could study the Indians, collect a variety of plants unknown in Spain, hummingbirds, and a live vampire. By May 19 they had progressed down the Río Napo to Aguano, where they had to wait six weeks for two large balsa rafts to be built; Almagro took advantage of this to go into the Jívaro country, and observe their interesting art of head-shrinking. After extensive explorations in the vicinity, as far as Coca, they finally got underway again on July 17, and proceeded to the Amazon.[22] On reaching the Brazilian frontier post of Tabatinga, they paid off their Indians, and waited twenty-eight days for a steamer. There was constant rain, and their health and collections deteriorated. On September 19 they finally boarded a Peruvian steamer and learned that the war was over. This stage of the journey had strained their resources so much that on arrival in Manaus they tried to conceal their identity, so poor were they, and, after paying for the collections, could only afford steerage tickets to Belém where, fortunately, they chanced to meet the new Spanish minister to Brazil, who congratulated them and gave them 90,000 pesetas. Their debts paid off, the party embarked for Spain, returning in late December. The expedition, despite the difficulties which beset it, was certainly a success; they had brought back more than eighty thousand specimens, each completely identified, and something which introduced a new dimension into exploration—three hundred glass-plate negatives.[23]

Two years later the United States re-entered the scene with an expedition sponsored by the Smithsonian Institution, which would essentially duplicate the *gran viaje* of the Spanish expedition. Headed by Professor James Orton of the University of Rochester, the expedition arrived in Guayaquil on July 19, 1867, and as soon as practicable began the ascent to Quito. Emulating Espada, Orton climbed Pichincha, on October 22, and descended into the crater; on climbing out he sang Psalm 100 ("Praise God from Whom all blessings flow") and remarked, "We doubt whether that famous tune and glorious doxology was ever sung so near to heaven." [24]

An excursion into the Oriente enabled Orton to study the Indians there, particularly the Napos and the Jívaros; while among the latter he observed their head-shrinking activities and learned that the Jívaro women go into the woods alone to bear their children, following which the husband goes to bed for eight days and is served choice dainties by his wife. Returning to Quito, the party made preparations for the Amazon journey, collecting supplies for five men for forty-two days. On October 30 the party left Quito and struck out to the east, once again entering the Oriente and the tropical rain forest that so impressed Orton. Descending the Río Napo, they entered the Amazon on December 11 and visited Iquitos, now boasting a population of 2,000 instead of the mere 227 of Herndon's time. Orton commented that the daytime temperature reached only 83° F., while the nights were cool—a blanket was needed on the lower river. Upon reaching the Rio Negro they paused at Manaus, where Orton met some United States southerners who had settled there since what they described as "the late unpleasantness." [25] At Santarém some 160 Confederates had settled, but many had left:

"many of them, however, were soon disgusted with the country," Orton remarked, "and, if we are to believe reports, the country was disgusted with them." [26] The expedition did not follow the Amazon to its mouth, but followed the usual procedure of navigating the maze of channels west of Marajó Island to the Rio Pará, and thence to Belém. The expedition, while generally uneventful, was highly successful; many specimens were gathered, extensive studies were made of the Indians, and detailed notes were assembled on plants (especially the medicinal varieties) and animals of Amazonia.

The Third French Republic also became active in South American exploration. In 1879 Dr. Jules Crevaux was sent by the Ministry of Public Instruction to explore the upper Río Paraguay and reach the Amazon. Upon his arrival in Buenos Aires, he was interviewed by the president of the Instituto Geográfico Argentino and two representatives of the Bolivian government who urged him to explore the Pilcomayo. Crevaux had been interested in this river even before his arrival in South America, and had discussed with his colleagues the belief that the river lost itself in the Chaco. Accordingly he decided to go. The Argentine government gave him free rail passage and two marines, and by January 16, 1882, they had reached the Bolivian frontier, where they were set upon by an armed band but fortunately were unharmed. On March 8 he met at Tarija Father Doroteo Gianeccini, prefect of the Italian missions there, who offered to accompany him to the mission of San Francisco de Solano del Pilcomayo, where he could get all he would need for his expedition. With them they took Yalla Petrona, a young Toba Indian girl, whom they planned to send ahead to facilitate their passage, since they would have to go through Toba country. Upon learning that the Indians of Caíza had gone to war with the Tobas, Father Doroteo suggested that they slow up so as not to enter Toba country until he could arrange for an armed escort. Upon arriving finally at Caíza, they met the subdelegate with his guard; Crevaux asked him, should he have any Toba prisoners, to send them to him at San Francisco de Solano so that he could return them to their people as a gesture of good will. All was well when the explorers reached the mission. There they received a letter from the missionary of Tarairi inviting them to his mission, where he would give them enough planks to construct some small boats.[27]

On March 30 Caíza people returned from their war; they had killed about a dozen Noctenes, allies of the Tobas, and had brought back seven children. Father Doroteo was fearful lest the parents try revenge; Crevaux, on the other hand, felt that the Indians would not maltreat a foreigner not a party to their quarrels, and gave the children gifts. On April 4 he and the priest sent the eldest girl captive, laden with gifts, back to her people in the care of Yalla, with instructions to assure her parents and people of Crevaux's friendly intentions. Shortly after this the Tobas and Noctenes attacked a nearby mission, but Crevaux determined to go on—nothing risked, nothing discovered. The boats were ready on April 18, and although Yalla had not returned, Crevaux and his party pushed off. All went well at first, and in Toba country the Indians provided an escort on both banks. Then, on April 24, the Indians invited the party ashore to eat; suddenly the explorers found themselves surrounded by Indians, who began killing them with clubs. Three managed to jump into the river, but were captured when they swam ashore. Two of them were tied to trees to serve as targets, the other was ransomed after six months through the efforts of Father Doroteo, one of the few survivors of a party of twenty-one. It was ironic that the party had gone ashore without arms; Crevaux had kept them under lock and key to avoid any appearance of hostility, and now lay murdered on the beach.[28]

While this grisly business was going on, another French expedition fared much better in the south. In 1882 the *Romanche* sailed from Cherbourg under the command of Frigate-Captain Louis-Ferdinand Martial, with instructions to make a scientific study of the southern extremity of the continent. After arriving at Montevideo, the expedition headed south, entered the Strait of Magellan, and explored as far as Punta Arenas. Subsequently it departed for the Malvinas (Falklands), then returned to explore the Beagle Channel, Tierra del Fuego, and Cape Horn. The six-volume account of the expedition's work contains detailed accounts of hydrographic studies and a wealth of ethnological information.[29]

In 1883 another French explorer, Arthur Thouar who was in Santiago, Chile, received via the French chargé d'affaires a message from the minister of foreign affairs directing him to seek out survivors of the ill-fated Crevaux expedition. Reports had come of some prisoners seen among the Pilcomayo Indians—perhaps some of them had been with Crevaux. Leaving as soon as possible, Thouar arrived in Arica and took a train to Tacna, where, he said, "an earthquake that night reminded me that without doubt, I was in Peru." [30] Only inexperience, he remarked, would lead him to attempt to cross the Andes in late autumn poorly equipped, but he succeeded, arriving May 28 in La Paz. There, in an interview with the foreign minister, he learned that, contrary to rumors in France, Bolivia had offered Crevaux a force of two hundred men, which he had refused, and on learning of the massacre, had sent a force of two hundred on an unsuccessful mission to punish the malefactors.[31]

To guard against a repetition of the massacre, the government provided Thouar with an escort of two hundred troops on his journey south. On the way he spent two weeks at Tarija, climbed Mount Aguairenda, and visited the Chiriguano Indians who, he was astonished to learn, kill or bury alive deformed babies and, if twins are born, kill one of them unless the mother opposes it—a rare occurrence. On July 2 1 he entered Caíza; a month later he set out for the Pilcomayo, and came upon the ruins of the mission of Santa Barbara, which he renamed Colonie Crevaux and began to fortify. Entering Toba country, Thouar found some planking from Crevaux's boats. He began to be convinced by now that he would find no survivors. On September 2 3 his party en-countered a group of Indians armed from head to foot, who refused to let them proceed until Thouar's guard, under Colonel Estensorro, drew up in battle array; the Indians quickly dropped their menacing attitude and agreed to serve as guides. But while this immediate threat was dis-sipated, there was more trouble ahead. On October 3, Thouar was attacked by some one thousand Tobas and Tapietis; the battle raged two days, until Thouar was finally able to arrange a parley with the chief, who was willing to conclude peace.

Thouar now determined to proceed with the exploration of the Pilcomayo, and crossed to the other side of the river. By October 1 3 he could follow it no further, since it divided into many channels and flowed through a marsh. The heat grew more intense, and water and pasturage became scarce; not until October 1 8 did they come upon a water supply of any size—a small lake he named Laguna de la Providencia. Hoping that the Río Paraguay was not far ahead, Thouar determined to push forward. Things grew worse; they walked through marshes where they were tormented by mosquitoes, many of their mules died and baggage had to be abandoned, their clothing was in tatters and their bodies infested with vermin, fever racked them, the heat was in-tense, and only with considerable difficulty did Thouar dissuade one of his men from committing suicide. Finally they encountered a Paraguayan hunter and his son, who informed them that only the Laguna de Ñaro separated them from the Paraguay. It was decided immediately that Thouar, Dr. Campos and Colonel Estensorro should go ahead as quickly as possible to Villa Hayes. Unable to procure supplies for their comrades there, they hastened to Asunción, where President Caballero himself received them and directed that a Paraguayan warship pick up the rest of the party. In early December Thouar somewhat regretfully left his brave comrades and went to Buenos Aires. There President Roca received him, as did the president of the Instituto Geográfico Argentino, who installed a bust of Crevaux and made Thouar a corresponding member of the Instituto. On Christmas day Thouar departed for France, arriving January 2 0, 1 8 8 4.[32]

In the following year Thouar returned to Argentina, and in the company of a young French adventurer, Wilfrid Gillibert, set out to explore the Pilcomayo delta. Between July 31 and December 1 3, despite Toba raids, they managed to make hundreds of observations and map the course of the river, an accomplishment hitherto considered impossible.[33] On December 2, 1886, after a journey from Salta to Sucre, where he visited Colonel Estensorro, Thouar set out to explore the possibility of using the Pilcomayo as an outlet to the sea, since the War of the Pacific had deprived Bolivia of her Pacific seacoast. Father Doroteo joined the expedition en route, and his knowledge of the country was of considerable value. Entering the Toba country, they met Yalla, who had been with Crevaux, and learned that she had apparently told the Indians that the French explorers would deprive them of their right to fish on the Pilcomayo, and that there were no Bolivian soldiers with them—an open invitation to an attack. They also learned the names of Crevaux's assassins, and used this information to gain from the Tobas a pledge of no hostilities; one false move, and Thouar would deal with them as assassins, and without pity. Even so, the Indians attacked on August 19, and Thouar defended his group successfully with no losses. From this point on the expedition was plagued by the same problems that beset Thouar's earlier venture, and especially by lack of water. Only the arrival of a relief expedition saved them from disaster. Returning to Colonie Crevaux, Thouar left for Caíza and Sucre, where he recommended a railroad as the only solution to Bolivia's problem, pointing out that before this could be accomplished the administrative system of the Chaco colonies would have to be modified and the boundary delimited with Paraguay. His mission accomplished, Thouar departed for Buenos Aires and returned to France.[34]

During the last decade of the nineteenth century the Chilean boundary commission sponsored a series of expeditions in western Patagonia which not only materially assisted in delineating the boundary with Argentina but added considerably to the store of geographical knowledge concerning the southern Andes, the valleys, and the fiords along the coast. In December of 1893 Hans Steffen set out with an expedition to the Gulf of Reloncaví, Chiloé, the Gulf of Corcovado, and finally the Río Palena, which afforded them entry into the interior. Following the river and its continuation, the Carrileufu (or Carrenleufú, as it appears on Argentine maps), they were able to confirm the existence of spacious and fertile valleys in this region, and covered for the first time all the space between them and the coast. In addition, they demonstrated the possibility of communication between the coast and these valleys, since the Palena was suitable for steam navigation to the point of the confluence with the Río Claro. The geological structure of the valley was determined wherever possible. It had been hoped that this study could be carried as far as Lake Nahuel Huapí, but the attitude of the Argentine government, which arrested one group of the party that had inadvertently crossed the frontier and forced it to go six hundred kilometers to Junín de los Andes before being allowed to recross into Chile, made this impossible.[35]

During the summers of 1895 and 1896, Steffen led two expeditions to the Río Puelo, which is near to Puerto Montt and a settled area, and so quite important; the government wanted it and its tributary the Río Manso explored up to the watershed. As a result of their work, Steffen and his associates determined that the upper valley of the Manso was suitable for agriculture, and especially stock-raising, and suggested this valley as a route of communication with the Argentine settlements in Chubut and around Nahuel Huapí.[36]

In late December of 1896, Steffen led another expedition—this time with passports approved by the Argentine chargé d'affaires—to explore the valley of the Río Aisén. Ascending its broad estuary, they made numerous topographical observations, and explored the various tributaries, one of which Steffen patriotically named Río Emperador Guillermo. Continuing their course across the cordillera, the explorers eventually reached Lake Fontana and the Río Senguerr, and finally the Río Chubut. With no hindrance from the Argentine authorities this time, they were able to visit Lake Nahuel Huapí, Lake Todos los Santos, and finally Lake Llanquihue before returning to Puerto Montt.[37]

A year later Steffen was directed to explore the valley of the Río Cisnes and find the divide between Lakes La Plata and Fontana and the rivers tributary to the Pacific, studying also the hydrography of the Río Félix Frías. This work again took him across the cordillera into the valley of the upper Senguerr, where he made extensive meteorological observations and was amazed by the extraordinary force of the wind in this locality. The observations completed, the party returned to Puerto Montt via Lake Nahuel Huapí, the Peulla valley and the lakes, as before.[38] Steffen later repeated much of this journey while serving on the British arbitral commission in 1902.[39]

As the nineteenth century drew to a close, Steffen was called upon to make an extensive survey of one of the least-known sections of the continent, the region of the fiords between 46° and 48° south latitude. Only three maps were of any value: those from the expedition of the *Beagle*, Enrique Simpson's Chilean naval expedition of 1872–73, and the naval expedition headed by Adolfo Rodríguez in 1888. Setting out from Puerto Montt on November 27, 1898, Steffen's party explored the coast from the Bahía de los Exploradores to the southeast corner of the Seno de Elefantes, then to the Darwin Channel and on to the Strait of Magellan. During their journey, which lasted until May 18, 1899, they discovered the Río Baker and explored its valley, conducted extensive explorations around Lake Cochrane and the mesetas of southern Patagonia, and prepared a series of accurate maps and charts of the area which were of great value to navigation. With the completion of Steffen's work, little remained to be discovered and few areas remained to be mapped in this long-neglected part of the world.[40]

The accomplishments of these government-sponsored explorations were, of course considerable. From the standpoint of the biological sciences alone, the results had been most gratifying, not only for the immense amount of information gathered, but especially for the size and variety of the collections sent back to Europe and, to a lesser degree, to the United States. Geophysical observations continued and amplified the work begun by La Condamine, while geographical investigations took scientists into regions that had not seen a European since the great age of the missions. Two interesting phenomena emerge from a study of these explorations. First is their number—far in excess of any government-sponsored explorations of past centuries—which might well be attributed to the great growth of interest in scientific studies and also to the existence of a prolonged period of relative peace which made such things possible. Second, it bacomes apparent that government sponsorship is no longer restricted to the major European powers traditionally interested in such activity. Bavaria and Russia enter the scene, and Spain returns after an absence of many decades. Most of all, it marks the coming of age of the New World in this area of endeavor, as the United States and Chile enter the ranks of exploring powers.

NOTES

1. On the Wilkes expedition and subsequent United States explorations, see John P. Harrison, "Science and Politics: Origins and Objectives of Mid-Nineteenth Century Government Expeditions," *Hispanic American Historical Review* XXV (1955): 175-202.

2. See above, also Wayne D. Rasmussen, "The United States Astronomical Expedition to Chile," *Hispanic American Historical Review* XXXIV (1954): 103-13.

3. See Harrison, *op. cit.*, and Hamilton Basso's introduction in William L. Herndon, *Exploration of the Valley of the Amazon* (New York, 1952); the original edition was published in two volumes in Washington, 1853.

4. Herndon, *op. cit.*, p. 50.

5. *Ibid.*, pp. 65-66.

6. For this stage of the river journey, see Herndon, *op. cit.*, pp. 60-128.

7. *Ibid.*, p. 138.

8. For the voyage down the Amazon, see Herndon, *op. cit.*, pp. 129-95.

9. See Harrison, *op. cit.*, and Page, *La Plata, the Argentine Confederation and Paraguay* (New York, 1859), pp. xix-xxii, 1-26.

10. Page, *op. cit.*, p. 97.

11. *Ibid.*, p. 164.

12. Bonpland was the beneficiary of a sudden order of Francia to release him; he was put in a canoe, taken across the Paraná to Corrientes, and left there with nothing but a few clothes. Page, *op. cit.*, p. 299.

13. Page, *op. cit.*, pp. 303-14. López justified the attack, alleging that the *Water Witch* was taking measurements near the fort, and was on a fighting expedition.

14. The Uruguay journey is described in Page, *op. cit.*, pp. 318-30.

15. Page, *op. cit.*, p. 335.

16. For the Río Salado expedition see Page, *op. cit.*, pp. 332-431. For one wishing a neutral appraisal of the work of the missionaries in this area, Chaps. 27-30 are especially valuable.

17. See Chap. XII, pp. 209-220.

18. The scientific mission is described in the writings of some of the Spanish participants, but the best account is that by Robert Ryal Miller, *For Science and National Glory: the Spanish Scientific Expedition to America, 1862–1866* (Norman, Oklahoma, 1968). For the background of the mission, see pp. 1-20; *La América's* comment is on p. 20.

19. For the journey from Spain to Peru, see Miller, *op. cit.*, pp. 23-80.

20. Almagro, Amor, and Isern, who had left Valparaíso in June.

21. For the Pacific stage of the expedition, see Miller, *op. cit.*, pp. 81-113.

22. Almagro had made a side trip as far as Iquitos; he remarked that Peru was trying to develop it, but predicted, quite inaccurately, that it would fail.

23. For the *gran viaje* through Ecuador and down the Amazon, see Miller, *op. cit.*, pp. 114-66.

24. James Orton, *The Andes and the Amazon* (New York, 1876), p. 140.

25. *Ibid.*, p. 246. Orton's comments on the Amazon temperatures may come as a surprise to many, but from two experiences on the Amazon, in Belém in December and Leticia in Colombia in June, I can attest to the accuracy of his account.

26. *Ibid.*, p. 251.

27. This portion of the expedition is described in Arthur Thouar, *Explorations dans l'Amérique du Sud* (Paris, 1891), pp. 33-36.

28. *Ibid.*, pp. 36-45.

29. France, Ministère de la Marine et d'Instruction Publique, *Mission Scientifique du Cap Horn, 1882–1883*, 6 vols. (Paris, 1888). Vol. I covers the history of the voyage, written by Captain Martial.

30. Thouar, *op. cit.*, p. 4.

31. *Ibid.*, pp. 11-12.

32. For the expedition on the Pilcomayo, see Thouar, *op. cit.*, pp. 20-114.

33. On the Pilcomayo delta expedition, see Thouar, *op. cit.*, pp. 119-76.

34. On this last mission, see Thouar, *op. cit.*, pp. 257-417.

35. Hans Steffen, *Viajes de esploracion i estudio en la Patagonia occidental, 1892-1902* (Santiago, 1909), Vol. I, pp. 165-320.

36. *Ibid.*, Vol. I, pp. 323-24, 397.

37. *Ibid.*, Vol. II, pp. 89-180.

38. On this see Steffen, *op. cit.*, Vol. II, pp. 474-540.

39. *Ibid.*

40. *Ibid.*, Vol. II, pp. 275-471.

XVIII *Private and Privately*

Sponsored Nineteenth-Century Explorations

In addition to the extensive work done under government sponsorship, much of the exploration of South America in the nineteenth century was accomplished by private individuals operating on their own or under private sponsorship. Those naturalists among them whose work was unsponsored have already been discussed; it remains here to consider the activities of the other explorers, including those naturalists who were sent under the auspices of an individual or of a private organization.

One of the earliest of these was a German, Prince Maximilian of Wied-Neuwied, who, after a distinguished military career, took up the study of anthropology and decided to go to Brazil, which, he felt, would afford him excellent opportunities for observation and study. Arriving in Rio de Janeiro in July of 1815, he was joined by Friedrich Sellow and Georg Wilhelm Freyreiss. As soon as practicable they left the capital to explore the coastal region to the east and northeast, studying the Puri and the Botocudo Indians. Sellow left him in November, preferring to remain in Vitória; Wied and Freyreiss continued north, exploring toward Salvador and inland as far as the frontier of Minas Gerais. Returning to the valley of the Jequitinhonha, Wied made an intensive study of the Botocudos, preparing an extensive vocabulary of their language. When he returned to Göttingen in 1817, he took a number of the members of this tribe with him. His *Reise nach Brasilien in den Jahren 1815 bis 1817*,[1] describing primarily these people, has been acclaimed as the first truly scientific monograph about a primitive Brazilian tribe.[2]

A decade later the scene changes to Peru, where an Englishman was preparing to cross the continent. For some time British merchants in Lima had been anxious to obtain information concerning the practicability of a route across Peru to the Amazon. The British consul-general, Ricketts, had arranged to explore the area with a Peruvian navy captain, but his return to England put an end to the plan. At that time Lieutenant Henry Lister Maw, R.N., who had learned of the proposal, saw an opportunity to earn a promotion by carrying it out. His ship was due to return to England, but he was able to persuade the senior officer to consent to the idea, which incidentally, he intended to carry out at his own expense. The Peruvian government was enthusiastic, and not only gave him a passport but also requested everyone along his route to aid him. After reading and interviewing extensively (and getting much contradictory advice) and purchasing necessary supplies and equipment, Maw was ready, and on December 4, 1827, he arrived at Huanchaco, the port of Trujillo, where he planned to make his start.[3]

Six days later he began his journey from Trujillo, ascended the Andes and arrived at Cajamarca, where he tried in vain to get his chronometer repaired—it had apparently stopped from the motion of the mules. The rarefied air exhilarated him, and the magnificent scenery entranced him: "I cannot conceive," he wrote, "that anything on earth or water could exceed the grandeur of the scenery, nor do I believe any person capable of describing it justly."[4] As he proceeded across the several cordilleras, there were harrowing experiences—such as crossing rickety bridges without rails and later nearly going over the brink of a narrow path when his horse slipped; and there were amusing ones—being mistakenly welcomed as a priest by those who took the anchor on his cap for a cross and shunned by those who took him for a Peruvian officer looking for troops. On December 27 he entered the *montaña*, and found the road so steep at times that he had to lie across the back of his mount: "I do not hesitate to say of this passage across the Montaña, that, had I not been a witness to the contrary, I could scarcely have believed it possible for any animal to have carried a human being over it alive."[5] Finally, on January 2, he reached Balsa Puerto, near the Río Huallaga, and made preparations for the fluvial part of his journey. Interviewing the local governors as he progressed, he gathered much information on the products of the country—balsam, almonds, gum, wax, pitch, indigo, cascarilla, etc.—and from a priest learned that the Indians had nearly destroyed the sarsaparilla industry by careless harvest and failure to replant the vines. On January 21 Maw entered the Marañón, and was pleased to think of himself as the first British officer ever to embark on this part of the largest river in the world. Four days later we find him giving some fishhooks to a stocky, elderly missionary who had not been paid in nine years —without a doubt this was the same missionary whom Smyth and Lowe would meet later—Padre Plaza.

By January 31 Maw and his party reached Tabatinga, where they were asked many questions about the revolution in Peru; the Brazilians there feared that Bolívar would make himself master of Spanish South America and invade their country. Consequently, since they were foreigners who were entering from Peru, the commandant was somewhat hesitant about letting them proceed, and only reluctantly did so after a delay. There were more such delays, for trivial reasons, as they progressed downstream. Maw discovered that there were three currents in the Amazon—one down each bank, and a third toward the channel; the latter was the slowest, while the most rapid one ran along the most broken bank. At Ega he heard tales of an enormous river serpent inhabiting the adjacent lakes—the same tale told by other explorers, it will be remembered. A priest there told him of having seen a serpent track in the *montaña* apparently made by a snake as big around as a man's waist is high; at Belém he talked with a man whose friend on Marajó Island had seen something large moving across a partially submerged bridge—both its head and its tail were unable to be seen.[6] There was a further delay at Manaus, but the commandant finally agreed to let them proceed rather than wait any longer for their licenses from Barcelos, where the provincial *senado* (senate) still sat. At Santarém the explorers were arrested, the commandant charging that they were not British, that they had not come from "Espanha" (Peru) but possibly Chile or Mexico, and that they had been making a plan of the fortifications (an old, overgrown, decaying fort with no guns). The commandant refused to honor their passports and professed doubt about the authenticity of their British papers. Not until Maw threatened to make an international incident of it would he clear them for passage to Belém, where they finally arrived on April 19.[7] In concluding his *Journal*, Maw strongly denounced the treatment of the Indians by the Brazilian *branco* (white), claiming that there were "uncontroled enormities" as a result of which the Indians "acquire his vices." [8] The Spanish system, he felt, was much better; the only friend the Amazon Indian had in Brazil was the missionary.

Brazil continued to hold an attraction for German explorers. After Prince Maximilian came the Austrian expedition, and between 1827 and 1832 Poeppig made his descent of the Amazon. A decade later, Prince Adalbert of Prussia appeared in Rio de Janeiro. He had long wished to make a lengthy sea voyage, and his attraction to the tropics led him to Brazil. Guanabara Bay enthralled him. He wrote: "Neither Naples, nor Stamboul, nor any other spot I have seen on earth, not even the Alhambra, can compare with the strange and magic charm of the entrance to this Bay." [9] From September 27 to October 30 he explored the province of Rio de Janeiro, visiting the Puri Indians, stopping at fazendas, and marveling at the great forest: "Every object here is colossal, everything seems to belong to a primeval world: we feel ourselves to be in disproportion to all around us, and to pertain to quite another period of existence." [10] On October 30 the prince and his companions, Count Oriolla and Count Bismarck, left Rio for Belém, and on November 22 began their Amazon journey in an *igarité*—an open boat roofed with palm leaves at the stern. Six days later they entered the main stream of the Amazon, whose width astonished them, and on November 30 Adalbert recorded: "We now turned sharp to the left, round a wooded sandy point, and again an ocean seemed to open before us,—it was the Xingu." [11] Two days later they reached Souzel, where the young missionary Padre Torquato Antônio de Souza agreed to join them on their journey up the river.

The Xingu, one of the greatest of the Amazon's large tributaries, was the scene of the prince's explorations. To avoid wasting twenty to forty days going around the great curve of the river against the current, Padre Torquato advised that they take the old overland cut-off, which the Jesuits had built and he had repaired. They followed his advice; rain and ants were the only problem. On reaching the Xingu again, they bathed in its waters despite warnings about piranhas, and were unmolested. Their journey upstream took them above the cataracts into Indian country, where they traded with the aborigines until they found no more settlements. Going downstream, the prince decided not to use the cut-off despite the rapids, and managed to reach Souzel without difficulty. After collecting various curios, the explorers re-entered the Amazon on December 23; as they entered the channels leading toward Belém, Prince Adalbert made careful studies of the currents, which convinced him that the Rio Pará was actually a part of the Amazon. From Belém the party went aboard the same vessel which had brought them, and disembarked at Salvador on January 17, 1843, whence they returned to Europe in the Sardinian vessel that had brought them.[12]

The interior of Brazil was explored more extensively two decades later by General José Vieira Conto de Magalhães, who had served as president of several provinces of the empire and was chiefly interested in ethnographic and linguistic studies. In 1862 he explored the province of Goiás, publishing his findings in *Viagem ao Araguaia*,[13] and in 1864 transferred his endeavors to the large province of Mato Grosso, still largely unexplored at that time; his *O Selvagem* [14] abounds in information about the Tupis, and contains a grammar of their language.[15]

Of especial importance during this decade was the Thayer expedition, which had as its objectives a study of the distribution of freshwater fish in the rivers of Brazil and the collection there of everything that could be of use for a museum of natural history. The organizer and driving force behind the expedition was the famed American naturalist Louis Agassiz. His interest in Brazil went back many years. At the age of twenty he was employed by Karl von Martius, on the death of Spix, to describe the fishes they had brought back. Subsequently he conceived the idea of a zoological museum in the United States; Dom Pedro II of Brazil had sent him collections for it, which stimulated his desire to go to Brazil himself to collect all the additional specimens he would need. This dream became a reality when the wealthy Nathaniel Thayer offered to send him with six assistants at his expense. In addition to those selected, seven volunteers, among them the philosopher William James, went at their own expense. The expedition received an additional bonus when Allen McLane, president of the Pacific Mail Steamship Company offered the whole party free passage to Brazil aboard the S.S. *Colorado*, which was sailing for San Francisco almost empty. Secretary Welles offered the assistance of the U.S. Navy if needed, and Secretary Seward recommended the expedition to the United States minister to Brazil. Surely an auspicious beginning! [16]

On the way to Brazil, Agassiz gave a series of lectures on the purposes of the expedition, dutifully recorded in his journal by his wife. He hoped to throw some light on how the organic world came to be as it is: "How did Brazil come to be inhabited by the animals and plants now living there? Who were its inhabitants in past times? What reason is there to believe that the present condition of things in this country is in any sense derived from the past?" [17]

The expedition reached Rio de Janeiro on April 23, 1865, and received a royal welcome indeed, for Dom Pedro himself visited the *Colorado*. During their stay in the capital, Agassiz and the others visited Juiz da Fora in Minas Gerais, Petrópolis, and Tijuca, gathering specimens, studying termite mounds, and finally obtaining specimens of coffee-tree larvae, which Agassiz had long sought. Mrs. Agassiz, who wrote this portion of the journal, also recorded that they received simultaneously the news of Lee's surrender and Lincoln's assassination. On July 25 Agassiz departed from Rio for Belém with James Burkhardt, the artist, Major Coutinho, M. Bourget, a collector and preparator, and two of his volunteers, Walter Hunnewell and William James. At Salvador two more of the volunteers, Dexter and S. V. K. Thayer, joined them with their collections. The party arrived in Belém August 11, and immediately began collecting in the environs. The local people were of considerable help, and one of them, Pimenta Bueno, put one of his company's steamers at their disposal for a month.[18]

Agassiz's group left Belém on August 20 aboard the *Icamiaba*, accompanied by a young Brazilian, Talisman, who joined them there; at Santarém he, Dexter, and James left to explore the Tapajós, while the rest of the party proceeded to Manaus after a week-long side trip by canoe to collect fish—a very successful venture, owing to the assistance of Indians along the way. At Manaus, specimens were prepared and packed for shipment, there was more collecting, and on September 2 the naturalists left for Tabatinga aboard another steamer, but still as guests. Dexter, James, and Talisman had returned from the Tapajós, and were with them. As they approached the Peruvian frontier, Agassiz was torn between going up to the Andes and collecting more fish in the Amazon. When he found a small fish with a mouthful of young, the issue was easily resolved—he remained with part of the group and sent Talisman and James up the Içá (Putamayo) and the Jutaí, where they would find themselves following in the footsteps of Bates. The group reassembled at Tefé (formerly Ega) on October 21, packed thirty barrels, boxes, and kegs, and returned to Manaus October 24.[19]

Through the kindness of the emperor, a Brazilian government vessel, the *Ibicuí*, was placed at the disposal of the naturalists and took them up the Rio Negro as far as Pedreira. While Dexter and Talisman went collecting up the Rio Branco, Agassiz studied racial mixing among the Indians and took many photographs. His observations led him to some rather confused notions concerning several human species. On January 15, 1866, they left Manaus to return to Belém, stopping frequently: at Vila Bela and the Rio Ramos they botanized, at Santarém they saw the crucifix that Martius had erected, they collected many specimens in the forest near Monte Alegre and many fish near the Xingu. Upon reaching Belém on February 4, Agassiz expressed his complete satisfaction with his researches. The Amazon, he reported, had more species of fish than the entire Atlantic, and twice as many as the Mediterranean. On March 26 the expedition left for Ceará, visited there to April 2, then returned to Rio de Janeiro.

While Agassiz was on the Amazon, a second group—the geologist Orestes St. John, with George Sceva, the preparator, and the volunteer Thomas Ward—went into Minas Gerais to the Rio São Francisco; Sceva gathered paleontological specimens to take back to Rio, while Ward, leaving his companions at Barbacena, went to the headwaters of the Tocantins, followed it to the Amazon and Belém, and returned home. St. John, joined by the ornithologist John Allen, planned further explorations, but Allen's health broke, necessitating his departure for Salvador, while St. John proceeded on through Teresina, Caxias, and São Luis to Belém, where he joined Agassiz. Frederick Hartt, the geologist, and the volunteer Edward Copeland, meanwhile, explored through Minas Gerais, Vitória and part of Bahia, studying the geological structure and collecting a variety of specimens. With the exception of Ward, the expedition reassembled in Rio to depart for the United States on July 2. Thayer had every reason to be satisfied with the results of his expedition. Not only had a magnificent collection been brought back, but the expedition's studies were to be a great contribution to scientific progress in Brazil.

While Agassiz's group was traversing much of the empire of Brazil, the British consul in Santos, who was none other than the famous explorer Sir Richard Burton, was wearying of inactivity. Having managed to visit Mecca disguised as a Moslem and, later, sought the headwaters of the Nile, it is understandable that he would find his present position a little less than exciting. Finally, "after eighteen dull months," he managed to get a leave of absence, and left with his wife on June 12, 1867, to explore the interior. His purpose was twofold: (1) to visit the gold mines, prairies and highlands of central Minas Gerais as a sort of holiday excursion, and (2) to go down the entire length of the Rio São Francisco to the Paulo Afonso falls, and then to the sea. "In this second act of travel, which is not a holiday excursion, the diamond diggings were to be inspected." [20]

The first part of the journey, to the highlands of Minas Gerais, being a "holiday excursion," need not concern us here. On September 18 Burton began his journey downstream, after having completed his inspection of the diamond mines around Diamantina. He was a careful observer, noting down everything of interest, as, for example, his detailed description of the carnaúba palm, "the most valuable palm of the Sertão." [21] Burton was aware of a proposal to create a new inland province of São Francisco, and assessed the prospects of such a move. Below Cabrobó, the rapids began, the course of the river turned to the southeast, and it began to narrow considerably. Below the rapids of Surubabé, down which they had to ease the raft carefully with ropes and poles, the river became calm again, flowing through a mountainous area; Burton found this to be the most interesting section. The river now turned to the east, and at Várzea Redonda the journey ended: ahead were the falls of Paulo Afonso. To reach that point, Burton hired mules and muleteers. They followed the river, which at one point narrowed so much that one could vault over it in the dry season. Finally they reached Paulo Afonso, where the river fell 250 feet into a gorge fifty-one feet wide at the narrowest; Burton was spellbound, he admitted, by this " 'realized' idea of power, of power tremendous, inexorable, irresistable." [22] He noted the incorrectness of British maps, which picture the river falling over a prolongation of the Serra da Borborema, when it actually falls over the edge of a "rotting plain, out of which rise detached blocks." [23] After viewing the falls from various locations, he proceeded down the lower Rio São Francisco in a leisurely fashion, stopped at Maceió, took a ship to Rio de Janeiro, where he rejoined his wife, and returned to Santos. His journey into the interior was scarcely spectacular, but it provided considerable information of the resources of the country, and a detailed study of the river and the falls.

In 1870 a second American expedition arrived in Brazil, under the leadership of Charles F. Hartt, who had been with the Thayer expedition. In 1867 he had returned to Brazil to explore the coast from Pernambuco to Rio de Janeiro, publishing the results of his work in his *Geology and Physical Geography of Brazil*.[24] Back in Boston in 1870, Hartt organized an expedition to explore the lower part of the Amazon and to try to refute some theories of Agassiz concerning past glaciation of the area, which he strongly doubted. He managed to secure the support of the local financier Junius Spencer Morgan, and named the expedition in his honor. Numbering among its membership such great names as Orville Derby, Herbert H. Smith and John Casper Branner, the Morgan Expedition accomplished much in the decade or so during which it operated in Brazil. Extensive geological surveys were made; Hartt shaped up the Imperial Geological Commission and headed it from 1874 until his death from yellow fever in 1878 (to be succeeded by Branner), and Derby became director of the geological section of the National Museum.[25] Smith spent most of his time collecting, and as a result of a second and third journey to Brazil, he was able to send six thousand specimens to the American Museum of Natural History in New York, and described his investigations and activities in *The Amazon and the Coast*.[26]

One of the last great foreign explorers of Brazil in the nineteenth century was the German ethnologist Karl von den Steinen. In 1884, accompanied by Otto Clauss, he explored the Xingu as far as Piranhaquara, the farthest point reached by Prince Adalbert coming from the other direction; there they found tribes which had never before seen a white man. In 1887 Steinen returned with an expedition which included the anthropologist Paul Ehrenreich, the geographer Peter Vogel, and the artist Wilhelm von den Steinen, his cousin, to explore the same area more extensively. The result of his work was a considerable increase in scientific knowledge of the Indians of the more remote sections of central Brazil, published in two substantial works.[27]

One more important area of tropical South America remains to be considered. Scant attention had been given to Guiana since the days of Waterton; not until 1803 did Britain gain full control of the Essequibo and Demerara colonies (which it united in 1812) and not until 1831 was Berbice added to form British Guiana. There was considerable speculation about the possibilities of the colony and its inhabitants, so an expedition was organized in 1835 to explore the interior, financed by the Royal Geographical Society. Chosen to head the expedition was the German-born Robert Hermann Schomburgk, whose survey of the coasts of one of the Virgin Islands had much impressed the Society earlier that year. He was given a grant of £900, and was permitted to keep all the specimens he might collect with the exception of one set, which the Society intended to present to the British Museum.

On October 1, 1835, Schomburgk's party of twenty-two began its journey up the Essequibo. After eight days they reached the Yaya Hills, which, according to Schomburgk's reckoning, put them at a place only eight miles from the Demerara River. Rapids were an occasional problem but dysentery proved to be a worse hazard, so Schomburgk spent the entire month of November at Annay to permit his crew to regain its health, while he collected and preserved specimens, prepared a map, and made a number of observations. The rainy season began in December, making progress difficult and bringing the added hazard of intermittent fever; nonetheless, the expedition accomplished a good deal, and Schomburgk was able to make a side trip to the Corona Falls and to visit Lake Amucu, supposed site of the fabled Lake Parima. At the end of February, 1836, the party began the ascent of the Essequibo from the mouth of the Rupunoony; by March 5 it reached its destination, a large cataract to which Schomburgk gave the name of King William's Cataract, since it had no Indian name. Being twenty-four feet high, in two stages, the cataract effectively blocked any attempt to reach the upper river other than building a camp and constructing a path around it. Unwilling to do this, Schomburgk turned back, March 5, and began the descent to Georgetown. The Essequibo, swollen from the rains, proved more difficult to negotiate than before, and at the Etaballly Falls one boat was lost, with the entire geological collection and some tree specimens—fortunately with no loss of life. At the end of March Schomburgk returned to Georgetown and made his report to the governor; he did not believe the Rupunoony River area fit for colonization, but only for the herding of wild horses and cattle—only the upper Essequibo offered hope for human settlement.[28]

In September of 1836 Schomburgk set out with the ornithologist Vieth, the draftsman Heraut, and three volunteers to explore the upper reaches of the Corentyn, easternmost of the three major rivers of British Guiana. After a slow start on the river, attributable in part to difficulty in procuring provisions and trouble with the Caribs, the explorers reached the falls of the Corentyn on October 18. Again there was the old problem: the upper river could be reached only if a path could be found around the falls, and to cut one would take almost two months. Schomburgk finally learned that a path existed, but the Caribs had concealed it from him, since they intended to use it for slave-raiding expeditions into the interior. Rather than force the Indians to reveal its location, he decided instead to explore the nearby Berbice, the other major river. He had at least seen enough of the Corentyn to prove that it was a major river, far longer than heretofore supposed. Returning to the coast, he began making preparations for a journey up the Berbice, and left for the interior on November 25. Many difficulties beset this expedition; Indians, fearful of going above the cataracts, deserted; they narrowly escaped an attack by thousands of ants; they were charged by stampeding hogs and escaped only by taking to the trees; overgrown vegetation slowed them on the river; and fresh food became scarce. On January 28, 1837, Schomburgk accidentally found the path to the Essequibo, and sent part of the party to that river while he walked to the Berbice, proving that the Demerara was shorter than believed, since he did not cross it. Proceeding down the Berbice, he detoured below to the falls of the Demerara, then went overland to the Corentyn, completing his survey of that river.[29]

In 1840 Schomburgk returned to England to accept an award from the Royal Geographical Society, and proposed that a settlement of the Guiana boundary be made as soon as possible. Accordingly, the government decided to act on his recommendation, and named him boundary commissioner. From 1841 to 1843 he surveyed from the northwest to the Corentyn River, an accomplishment which won him knighthood in 1844.[30] The result of his work was the establishment of the "Schomburgk Line" between Venezuela and British Guiana.

Robert Schomburgk's brother Richard was also active in British Guiana between 1840 and 1844. After recovering from a nearly fatal attack of yellow fever, he began a series of expeditions which, like his brother's work, took him on nearly every important river in the colony; he also went to the mouth of the Orinoco, and while on an expedition on the upper Essequibo, crossed into Brazil and visited São Joaquím on the Rio Branco. He made an attempt to climb Mount Roraima, the highest mountain in the Guiana highlands, but was unable to find a way up the sheer walls, which rise about half-way up, reaching to its flat top. A noted naturalist, his travels resulted in the gathering of a wide variety of specimens of natural history.[31]

Exploration of a private nature in the second half of the nineteenth century was largely confined to temperate South America, primarily Patagonia. Interest in this remote area was probably sparked by J. H. Gardiner who, in 1867, took command of a small expedition from Pavón Island into the interior when its leader, McDugall, quit on the fourth day out and returned to their base. Following the south bank of the Río Santa Cruz, the party traveled inland for sixteen days, reached a big lake, whose south shore they explored for the next several days, then returned to Pavón.[32]

More significant by far were the explorations of George Chaworth

Musters. Born in 1841, he was orphaned at the age of three and was raised by an uncle who had served on the *Beagle*. He served later as an officer on the *Stromboli*, spending three years in South American waters. When his naval service ended in 1869 he returned on business and conceived the idea of making a longitudinal journey through Patagonia from the Strait of Magellan to the Río Negro. Arriving at Punta Arenas in April, Musters joined a military party searching for some escaped prisoners. This took him as far as the Río Gallegos, where he managed to engage the services of a Tehuelche, who had been in the Malvinas (Falklands) where he had learned English and acquired the curious name of Sam Slick, to guide him to Santa Cruz. Musters learned the simple pattern of Tehuelche life: they went north in August, hunting along the way and finally trading hides and feathers along the Río Negro, then returned, hunting and trading, to Santa Cruz. He determined to travel with them rather than return with the Chilean party, and settled down for the winter at their camp, where he learned how to hunt the ostrich and guanaco, and how to make and use the *bolas*.[33]

Musters won acceptance by the Indians and was treated as their equal as they journeyed north in August. When, on August 23, 120 miles out of Santa Cruz, a young girl reached the age of puberty, he was allowed to witness the dancing and celebrations, and managed to overcome his repugnance to horsemeat by joining in the special banquet of cooked mare's meat and blood. Continuing in a northwesterly direction, the group sighted the cordillera on September 1, and crossed what he took to be the Río Chico,[34] through floating ice. Periodically fights broke out among the rather contentious Tehuelches, sometimes resulting in deaths. Indeed, of the eighteen Indians who left Santa Cruz only eight reached the Río Negro—and only a few deaths were from natural causes. On September 8 the party reached a settlement Musters called Amakaken (doubtless the present Tamel Aike), some thirty miles from the Andes, where they rested for four days.

From this point, the group followed a northerly course parallel to the cordillera. One day they heard what sounded like cannon fire coming from it and saw black smoke; the Indians told Musters that it came from some hidden city, which they had never found. The legend of "la ciudad encantada de los Césares" apparently was still very much alive. Early in October the group stopped to camp at a place called Tele, "close to a large lagoon," Musters wrote, "covered with waterfowl, into which flowed a beautiful stream issuing from the hill; along the margin of the clear pure water grew a profusion of a sort of green cress, and at sunset flights of flamingoes and rose-coloured spoonbills came to the lagoon to feed." [35] East of this place his map shows a large lake; he was apparently unaware of the existence of a second lake near to this one, which would one day be named for him.

During early November a large group of northern Tehuelches joined them, joined in a few days by another pampas group; the combined force now numbered two hundred, and recognized Casimiro, father of Sam Slick, as their leader. The march was now to the northeast, across a plain where the armadillo and ostrich were seen much more frequently than the guanaco. Soon they came upon a camp of twenty-seven Araucanians in ponchos, white linen drawers, and vests—quite a contrast to the skin-clad and painted Tehuelches. The two groups joined forces and continued northeast. More Araucanians were encountered as they progressed, and Musters was kept busy writing messages in Spanish as the leaders of various groups met ceremonially to delineate their spheres of influence. Conditions grew worse; it was April now, winter had made an appearance and game was scarce, and, what was more, an epidemic of fever had taken the lives of several children.

Finally the party reached the port of Carmen de Patagones on the Río Negro; Musters was the guest of a Welsh family there, and was finally able to get a haircut and a new suit of clothes, and buy gifts for his departing Indian friends. For those who might later be inclined to emulate his experience, he wrote: "Never show distrust of the Indians; be as free with your goods and chattels as they are to each other. Don't ever want anything done for you; always catch and saddle your own horse. Don't give yourself airs of superiority, as they do not understand it—unless you can prove yourself better in some distinct way. Always be first . . . in crossing rivers, or any other difficulties; they will learn to respect you; in a word, as you treat them, so will they treat you." [36]

During the next two decades, the exploration of Patagonia became the work of Argentine explorers. The greatest of these, without a doubt, was Carlos María Moyano, a naval officer from Mendoza, who was recalled from sea duty to serve in 1877 with Francisco P. Moreno's mapping expedition into the lake region. After a quick journey to Monte León, the party started up the Río Santa Cruz on January 15, 1878, following the map made by Fitz-Roy. The river was at maximum height, and they navigated without serious difficulty to a large lake which was its principal source, and named it Lake Argentino. On February 25 they headed north, coming upon a lake known to the Indians as "Kelta," later to be known as Lake San Martín, and the larger Lake Viedma. A change of direction to the west brought them to the cordillera, where they made observations and explored some of the peaks, then to Lake Argentino, whence they returned to Santa Cruz.[37]

In 1879 Moyano set out on another journey up the valley of the

Río Chalia to find a level pass which would afford easy communication with the Pacific—especially valuable should the land be populated with cattle. By January 8, 1880, he had reached Lake San Martín, and noticed a great iceberg, which apparently had come from another part of the lake. Going around the lake, he climbed to the summit of the nearby mountains and discovered what he took to be another lake, completely unknown (actually a portion of the extensive Lake San Martín on the Chilean side). Returning to his camp, he speculated concerning the fall of the level of the lake since he had last seen it: Did it drain into the Pacific? Convinced that the pass he sought must be to the north, if it existed, and unable to proceed in search of it in that direction, Moyano returned to the Río Santa Cruz on January 19.

At the end of of 1880 Moyano set out on another expedition up the Río Chico toward the pre-cordillera, then more or less along Musters' route to the Río Chubut. His purpose was to seek a route for transporting cattle to the utmost parts of the territory, since he was convinced that this was an excellent area for stockraising. The expedition departed on October 14 from the town of Santa Cruz, organized so that he could take care of almost anything that might come up. By October 25 the party reached the Río Deseado; Moyano and two companions explored the vicinity for a few days, and came upon a large, unmapped lake which he named Lake Buenos Aires. Thus far, Moyano had followed the trail of Musters, and supplied in detail the topographical information his predecessor could not give, since Musters had been traveling with a superstitious tribe whom scientific instruments might frighten. Proceeding through good pasture country, Moyano finally came upon the Río Senguerr, which took him to his destination, the Río Chubut. This journey was especially valuable for the wealth of topographical details and geographical information which it supplied.[38] Moyano had chosen the inland route on this expedition because of the need of finding adequate pasturage for cattle. In 1882 he surveyed the coastal route from August 28 to September, finding an easy way of land communication between Santa Cruz and Deseado, with adequate water all the way.

There still remained the question of a pass to the Pacific. On November 3, 1883, Moyano left Santa Cruz with twelve men, sixty-five horses, thirty hunting dogs, and nine loads of arms, instruments, and materials for constructing boats on the lakes. His direction was southerly, across the Río Coig (Coyle) to the Río Gallegos, which the party reached November 14. Because of its spaciousness and its port, Moyano felt this valley was much more suitable for colonization than the Coig. Following the valley westward, Moyano found some small shrubs he had never seen before, which bore a delicious small dark-red fruit; also he found many insects, especially bees, and some birds not seen on the coast, but no shrubs which could be used for wood. Eventually they entered a wooded area, and then a level region he took to be the Plains of Diana, which would put him not more than thirty miles from the Pacific. Here might be the pass—almost level—and perhaps a very careful interpretation of the boundary treaty with Chile might give Argentina a Pacific port! Heading for the Skyring Inlet, which led to the Pacific, Moyano hoped to take back with him a bottle of water from that ocean, but so thick was the forest and the undergrowth toward the shore that it was impossible to get through on horseback or on foot, and he had to abandon the idea. During the month of January, 1884, the expedition explored the headwaters of the Río Gallegos and the Río Coig, built boats on the shore of Lake Argentino, and explored it carefully. On February 8 the group returned to Santa Cruz, having proved the feasibility of communication between Argentine Patagonia and the Pacific, located the geographical position of the lakes accurately, and made extensive observations directed toward the possibility of colonization.

One other expedition into Patagonia deserves mention here, although strictly speaking it might be termed official. In May of 1885, Lieutenant Colonel Luis Jorge Fontana arrived in the province of Chubut as its first governor. A month later one Juan Thomas, representing a group of Welsh colonists who had established themselves in the Chubut valley twenty years earlier, approached him about the possibility of an expedition to the west, and was informed that an official expedition would be undertaken and that the colonists would be assigned to it. So enthusiastic were the colonists that they collected 6,000 pesos and made preparations. The money was offered to Governor Fontana, who got quick official permission for something which would cost the government nothing. Twenty-six of the colonists (seven of them named Jones) volunteered; they carried Remington rifles, had 260 horses, food and supplies for three months, and scientific instruments.

The expedition set out on October 4 from Rawson and followed the north bank of the Chubut, reaching the Valley of the Martyrs on October 23 and Paso de Indios, in the center of the province, on November 3. There the river had to be crossed; after two days spent in a futile attempt to ford it in the face of a *vendaval* (a strong wind from the sea), a raft was built and the crossing accomplished. Before the party finally returned to Rawson early in 1888, they had explored as far as the Río Carrenleufú, which flows along the base of the cordillera, and several Andean valleys.[39]

The last third of the century, then, saw Patagonia explored, surveyed, and mapped as it had not been for many years. The major river valleys had been penetrated, in some cases to their sources, and the lakes explored and mapped. Three longitudinal crossings accomplished the important mission of awakening the nation to the importance of the region for the raising of livestock, which would eventually become the basis of its prosperity.

That so much could have been accomplished by expeditions under private sponsorship is a tribute not only to the pluck of the explorers themselves but also to the generosity and breadth of vision of their sponsors. That the Royal Geographical Society should be among the sponsors occasions no surprise. What is of particular interest here is that men of wealth, particularly in the United States, were willing to provide the funds necessary for extensive exploration and scientific investigation. In an earlier age, the explorer in need of funds had, generally, to seek to interest his government in the project, and perhaps be prepared to beg private funds to augment a niggardly appropriation. Now it was possible to secure sufficient support from private funds exclusively, as men of wealth turned patrons of learning and scientific inquiry. It augured well for the future of exploration.

NOTES

1. Frankfurt-am-Main, 1820–21.
2. Cf. Egon Schaden and João Baptista Borges Pereira, "Explorações antropológicas," p. 427, and Olivério M. Oliveira Pinto, "Viajantes e Naturalistas," pp. 497-98, in Vol. V of Sergio Buarque de Holanda, *História da civilização brasileira* (São Paulo, 1967).
3. As a protection against pirates, many cities along the Pacific coast were built inland, and were served by a small port. Maw described his journey in his *Journal of a Passage from the Pacific to the Atlantic, Crossing the Andes in the Northern Provinces of Peru and Descending the River Marañón or Amazon* (London, 1829).
4. *Ibid.*, p. 45.
5. *Ibid.*, p. 79.
6. Maw did not believe these stories, and only included them in his journal under direction. He also noted that the Indians would not enter the lake without blowing a horn, and retreated if they heard a hollow sound. *Ibid.*, p. 276.
7. See Maw, *op. cit.*, pp. 343-62, on his difficulties at Santarém.
8. *Ibid.*, p. 417.
9. Adalbert, Prince of Prussia, *Travels of H.R.H. Prince Adalbert of Prussia* (London, 1849), Vol. I, p. 219. The first volume describes in detail his voyage to Brazil aboard the Sardinian frigate *San Michele*, and the city and environs of Rio de Janeiro.
10. *Ibid.*, Vol. II, p. 15.
11. *Ibid.*, Vol. II, p. 205.
12. For the exploration of the Xingu, see Adalbert, *op. cit.*, Vol. II, pp. 208-350.
13. Goiás, 1863.
14. Rio de Janeiro, 1876.
15. Schaden and Pereira, *op. cit.*, pp. 434-35.
16. Louis Agassiz, *A Journey in Brazil* (Boston, 1868), pp. v-ix. For a brief description of the journey, see Pinto, *op. cit.*, pp. 462-64.
17. Agassiz, *op. cit.*, p. 8.

18. For the work of the expedition in Rio de Janeiro and the journey to Belém see Agassiz, *op. cit.*, pp. 46-150.

19. For the journey up the Amazon and back to Manaus, see Agassiz, *op. cit.*, pp. 152-250.

20. Sir Richard F. Burton, *Exploring the Highlands of Brazil* (London, 1869), Vol. I, p. 19.

21. *Ibid.*, Vol. II, p. 309.

22. *Ibid.*, Vol. II, p. 444.

23. *Ibid.*, Vol. II, p. 448.

24. Boston, 1870.

25. In 1878 he went to São Paulo as Director of the Geological and Geographical Commission, and in 1907 he headed the Geological and Mineralogical Service in Rio de Janeiro.

26. New York, 1878. For the work of the Morgan Expedition, see the writings cited; a good brief summary may be found in Pinto, *op. cit.*, pp. 464-66.

27. Karl von den Steinen, *Durch Zentralbrasiliens* (Berlin, 1886), and *Unter den Naturvo elkern Zentralbrasiliens* (Berlin, 1884). See also Steinen, "O rio Xingu," *Revista da Sociedade de Geografía do Rio de Janeiro*, Vol. IV (1888), pp. 189-212. There is a good brief summary in Schaden and Pereira, *op. cit.*, pp. 436-37.

28. For the 1835-36 expedition see Robert H. Schomburgk, "Report of an Expedition into the Interior of British Guyana, in 1835-6," *The Journal of the Royal Geographical Society of London* VI (1836): 224-84.

29. See Schomburgk, "Diary of an Ascent up the River Corentyn in British Guyana in October, 1836," *The Journal of the Royal Geographical Society of London* VII (1837):285-301, and "Diary of an Ascent of the River Berbice, in British Guyana, in 1836-7," *The Journal of the Royal Geographical Society of London* VII (1837): 302-50.

30. See Schomburgk, "Journal of an Expedition from Pirara to the Upper Corentyn, and from thence to Demerara, Executed by Order of Her Majesty's Government," *The Journal of the Royal Geographical Society of London* XV (1845): 1-104.

31. See Moritz Richard Schomburgk, *Richard Schomburgk's Travels in British Guiana, 1840-44*, 2 vols. (Georgetown, B.G., 1922-23).

32. See Ana Palese de Torres, "Las exploraciones de Moyano en la Cuenca del Santa Cruz," *Revista Geográfica Americana* 38 (Buenos Aires, December, 1954): 124.

33. Musters has written two accounts of his explorations: "A Year in Patagonia," *The Journal of the Royal Geographical Society of London* XLI (1871): 59-77, and *At Home with the Patagonians* (London, 1873). See also Alfredo Rey Balmaceda, "El primer cruce longitudinal de la Patagonia," *Revista Geográfica Americana* 39 (May-June 1955): 253-56.

34. Probably the Chaliá; he did not know that it lay between the Santa Cruz and the Chico, flowing east.

35. Musters, *At Home with the Patagonians*, p. 95.

36. *Ibid.*, p. 188.

37. The best source for this is Moyano's *Viajes de exploración a la Patagonia* (Buenos Aires, 1931). For a good brief summary see Ana Palese de Torres, "Las exploraciones de Moyano en la Cuenca del Santa Cruz," *Revista Geográfica Americana* 38 (December, 1956): 125-28.

38. There is an excellent compilation of these details in Moyano, *op. cit.*, pp. 79-88.

39. See Lorenzo Amaya, "La expedición Fontana a la Cordillera del Chubut," *Revista Geográfica Americana* 4 (October, 1933): 255-69.

XIX   *The Mountains and the Desert*

Ever since Alexander von Humboldt attempted to conquer Mount Chimborazo and failed, this towering peak, long believed to be the highest mountain in the world, challenged the skill and intrepidity of those who dare to do the difficult. In 1813 a Frenchman, Jean-Baptiste Boussingault, made the attempt. For ten years he had been in South America, making a variety of observations in the cordillera, and it occurred to him that the study could end in no better way than by making a special study of Chimborazo. Actually, the base would have sufficed, but he got the idea of obtaining the mean temperature at an extremely high station. He normally would not approve of so dangerous an undertaking, but this was in the interest of science, which, he felt, justified it.[1]

There are two routes for climbing the mountain: via Arenal the slope is steep and the snow broken by many trachyte peaks; via Chillapullu, not far from Mocha, the slope is less steep but longer. This is the route Boussingault chose, and on December 14, 1831, he spent the night, accompanied by his friend Colonel Hall and a Negro porter, in the hacienda of Chimborazo. In the morning, the climb began; Indian guides took them to the snow line, but could provide no information on the route beyond. By noon they had reached an elevation equal to the height of Mont Blanc; the snow was at times waist-deep, making progress so difficult that they abandoned the climb by this route and returned to the hacienda. The next day they set out across the Arenal, following Humboldt's route, and began the ascent from that direction. The route led across hardened snow, and as they ascended they found it increasingly difficult to obtain a firm foothold. Finally, after cutting footholds, they arrived at a vertical wall several hundred meters high —and they were only at elevation 5,680 meters, lower than the point

Humboldt had reached. Reconnoitering from a high rock outcrop, they found a way around the wall, only to be stopped again—this time at the foot of a great prism of trachyte, whose upper base formed the summit. They were at 6,004 meters—the highest elevation anyone had reached in the Andes, and they could go no further. Above them were huge icicles; the air was clear and calm, the view magnificent. Unlike Humboldt and Bonpland, Boussingault suffered no effects of *soroche*—doubtless, he felt, the result of long residence in the high Andes. They made some experiments to determine the amount of oxygen in the air at this altitude, but by midafternoon heard thunder below and determined to descend quickly before rain fell and made the route all but impassable. As they entered the clouds below, snow began to fall; when they reached their tethered mules, hail fell violently, mixed with rain farther down. As night fell, they reached the hacienda, and returned to Riobamba the following day. All that he had seen confirmed Boussingault's previous ideas on the nature of these trachyte mountains; there was no sign of lava.[2]

Chimborazo would be conquered, but not until nearly a half-century had passed. Edward Whymper, the celebrated British mountain-climber, who, in 1865, after six failures, was first to conquer the Matterhorn, had become much interested in the phenomenon of mountain sickness. He had found that higher climbs seemed possible in Europe without illness than in South America, and it occurred to him that perhaps vegetation had some effect upon the air. He had hoped to test this theory in the Himalayas, but frontier problems made it inadvisable, and the beginning of the War of the Pacific ruled out the major portion of the Andean cordillera. He finally decided on Ecuador as the best place left, and Chimborazo as the site of his study. Arriving in Guayaquil on December 9, 1879, he left as soon as possible for the cordillera; December 27 found him encamped at Chimborazo. His comments on his experiences in traveling in Ecuador offer some extremely valuable advice: "We travelled through Ecuador unarmed, except for passports which were never exhibited, and with a number of letters of introduction which for the most part were not presented; adopting a policy of non-intervention in all that did not concern us, and rigidly respecting the customs of the country, even when we could not agree with them; and traversed that unsettled Republic without molestation, trusting more to our wits than to our credentials, and believing that a jest may conquer where force will fail, that a *bon-mot* is often better than a passport."[3]

Contrary to what he had expected, Whymper was unable to see the Andes until he had reached an elevation of ten thousand feet; the slopes of the Pacific range, he discovered, were wooded up to their crests on the Pacific side, and almost devoid of vegetation on the eastern side. On December 21 he first saw Chimborazo, and noted with surprise that there were two summits, although Humboldt and Boussingault had mentioned only one; moreover, there were numerous glaciers, and yet Humboldt said he had seen no glaciers in the tropics. Local officialdom nearly became a problem before he started; the *Jefe político* and Commissary of Police informed him that they knew that he *said* he was going to climb Chimborazo, but that was impossible, so he must really be looking for treasures buried on the slope, and surely he would not forget them. When Whymper offered them half the treasure found for sharing half the expenses, the matter was dropped.

Whymper decided that the eastern summit was the higher one, and chose a southwest approach—the one used by Humboldt and Boussingault—and a crossover to the higher peak. With him were Louis and Jean-Antoine Carrel, cousins, and an Englishman, Perring. On December 26 the party left Guaranda to begin the ascent, seeking the least fatiguing route. By the time they reached their second camp, Whymper and the Carrels were feverish, suffering intense headaches and afflicted with a great thirst, since they could get enough air only through their open mouths. Perring, although weakest in constitution, was unaffected; the problem was not one of exhaustion or deficiency of strength, Whymper wrote; the cause was solely the rarity of the air. Whymper found relief, he believed, from potassium chlorate, while Jean-Antoine Carrel would take only warmed red wine with a little spice and sugar, which, he assured them, was good for anything. In truth, there was no way to tell if they were effective—they might have done as well without anything.

By January 3 they had become somewhat accustomed to the altitude, and resumed their climb and reached the southern wall of the dome that same day, but the wind was too strong and they returned to their base. On January 5 Whymper and the Carrels started from their camp at 5:30 A.M. They made considerable progress at first, but tired as the day went on. By 10:00 A.M. they passed the highest exposed rocks, at 19,400 feet; an hour later they were half-way around the western dome at 20,000 feet. Clouds began to form, and they found the ground snowy and so soft that it was necessary to beat down the snow and crawl—and even then they sank occasionally. Not until 3:45 P.M. did they reach the western summit, where they discovered, as Whymper had thought, that it was lower. Returning to the plateau, they crossed it —this time on hard snow—and reached the eastern summit. Taking as many observations as possible—they found that the barometer dropped to fourteen inches—the group began the descent with little more than an hour of daylight left, finally reaching camp in utter darkness at 9:00 P.M. Although they had experienced a two-inch drop in pressure, they experienced no fever, nausea, headache, or gasping.[4]

Whymper had calculated the height of Chimborazo at 20,608 feet (which was very close—it is actually 20,561 feet), 817 feet lower than Humboldt's calculations. In view of this, he determined to go up again to check his measurements, and began the second ascent January 6. At 18,400 feet he reached the place where he believed Humboldt had stopped; both the German explorer and Boussingault said they had gone higher,[5] yet here was the southern wall, which one reaches by the Arenal approach, which they had taken, and the altitude was lower. The speed with which both descended was a puzzlement to Whymper too; he did not believe it possible, and suggests that they must have noted the time incorrectly. At the wall the weather turned bad, and the Carrels refused to go any higher; they descended to the base camp, where Whymper constructed a base line for making angles and drawing a map, and finally left on January 12.[6]

Rather than try another assault on Chimborazo at this time, Whymper decided instead to scale Cotopaxi, which apparently had been ascended for the first time by Dr. W. Reiss of Berlin in 1872. There was a large slope of ash at the apex of the terminal cone, at altitude 19,500 feet, high enough for the collection of additional data in preparation for future climbs several thousand feet higher. Accompanied by Louis Carrel, he set out for the volcano on February 14, from Machachi. Volcanic dust proved to be a nuisance; it was so fine that it penetrated everywhere. The ascent was relatively easy, since it involved no climbing —only walking up a ridge. Because the volcano was emitting clouds of steam, Whymper decided against camping on the edge. The slope was exposed, and it was necessary to dig out a site and secure the tent ropes to blocks of lava. A squall nearly carried the tent away during the night. When that was over, they noticed a smell of rubber, and discovered that one corner of the tent floor was beginning to melt— the temperature at that point was 110° F. During twenty-six hours on the summit, they experienced no *soroche*—only lassitude; obviously, one could camp safely at such a height. Whymper did achieve one of his primary objectives: he crawled to the edge of the cone at night and looked into the fire below.[7]

During March and April, Whymper and the Carrels ascended several other of Ecuador's towering peaks—Cayembe, Sara-Urcu, Cotocachi, Sincholagua, Antisana, and Pichincha, gathering additional valuable information concerning the effects of altitude. But Chimborazo beckoned a second time, and on June 25 Whymper, the Carrels, and four Ecuadoreans left Riobamba to attempt the ascent, this time from the north-northwest approach. The climb began at 5:15 A.M. on July 1; the sky was bright, and they had a magnificent view of Cotopaxi in eruption. By 11:00 A.M. they were in the direct rays of the sun, and it was very hot; they reached the plain between the summits without difficulty,

352

and at 1:00 P.M. saw the tattered flag they had put on the eastern summit on the first ascent. But their stay had to be brief, for the cloud from Cotopaxi had already obscured the other summit (which they named Pointe Veintemilla for Ecuador's president), and dust was making breathing difficult and drinking impossible. By 2:30 it was so dark that they decided to descend, and returned to camp without incident, dust still falling.[8]

Whymper's explorations of the Andes of Ecuador proved to be quite valuable. He found an important range between Chimborazo and the coast, discovered glaciers on Chimborazo, unreported by either Humboldt or Boussingault, and he determined the height of the mountain with a greater degree of accuracy than his predecessors. He made extensive botanical collections, finding twenty orders above 15,000 feet and one at 18,500 feet. He collected various insects, moths, butterflies and crustaceans, and found earthworms up to 15,871 feet; he also cast grave doubts on the authenticity of the story Humboldt repeated about a species of fish ejected by the thousands from the craters and fissures of volcanoes, which supposedly reached the plains below alive. But from his own point of view, the most important achievement was his study of mountain sickness. The basic cause, he determined, was atmospheric pressure, which lessened the value of the air breathed in, or caused air or gas in the body to expand, pressing on internal organs. To counteract this, he recommended a gradual ascent, with a careful check on pulse and temperature.[9]

To the south of Peru lies the vast Atacama Desert, six hundred miles long, which Almagro had crossed for the first time in 1537. Despite the fact that rain is seldom if ever recorded there, this desert is a source of great wealth by virtue of its vast nitrate fields. Maps of the desert were poor, and information on it was scattered and often contradictory. Consequently, in 1853 the government of Chile decided to send an expedition to explore it, and chose as its leader the German scholar Rudolph Amand Philippi, who had been living in Chile for some time and was professor of botany and zoology in the Instituto Nacional and director of the national museum. Leaving Valparaíso on November 22, Philippi went to the port of Coquimbo, Caldera, and then proceeded by train to Copiapó to complete his preparations and gather all the information he possibly could. Luckily one old desert hand, Diego de Almeida, seventy-three years of age (his friends said he was ninety), agreed to accompany them for twenty ounces of gold.[10]

Preparations were complete by December 7, and the expedition set out for the valley of the Río Salado. Philippi discovered that the animal kingdom (consisting chiefly of insects) was more extensive than the vegetable, and that while there was fairly abundant vegetation at an elevation of 230 meters, at 650 meters there was none at all. He was using a map prepared for President Ballivián of Bolivia which showed the Río Salado entering the sea at Paposo; to his surprise he found that it did not exist there, and that the river apparently began nowhere and went nowhere. By December 24 he was at Cobre, where he found the land completely sterile; everything needed had to be brought in. Three days later the group embarked for Isla Blanca, which Philippi discovered, had been erroneously depicted by Fitz-Roy as a peninsula; the island was completely devoid of life, and was covered with a thick layer of yellow guano overlaid with a thinner white layer. On December 31 Philippi climbed the Morro de Mejillones, and found evidences of animal life. The only explanation he could offer for this was that winter fogs must produce some ephemeral vegetation.

The months of January and February, 1854, were spent in the major work of the expedition, crossing the Atacama. A shortage of mules was nearly disastrous; the party could not walk, nor could they leave any equipment behind and still carry out their purpose—but the problem was solved when Almeida succeeded in borrowing three mules. The journey itself was relatively uneventful, other than for the inconveniences one might expect. Water usually had to be obtained by digging and, while not salty, it was turbid. The only fuel available was mule excrement. Nights were surprisingly cool for midsummer, and frequently cold, with freezing temperatures. Daytime heat and dust brought on eye inflammation, which caused one man to break the barometer accidentally. It was frequently difficult to find food for their mules, as vegetation became scarce or nonexistent, and the ground was perforated by innumerable rat-holes, making it quite dangerous for their beasts. From time to time they were able to follow the old Inca road, but frequently this disappeared, or was extremely difficult to traverse. By February 22 the worst was over, and they came upon a small oasis, with trees and a house. Philippi wrote: "I cannot describe the sentiments which the view of this grove and house in the middle of a vast desert awoke in my spirit—things which I had not seen for 22 days." They stayed at the house, sat at a table, ate bread again, a rice stew, and "the most delicious grapes in the world." [11] By now they were approaching fairly settled country; they explored the mining areas, visited some mines, and finally returned home. Philippi was quite satisfied with the results; much information had been gathered and organized, not only the Ballivián map but also Orbigny's had been corrected, and they were able, on the basis of their observations, to contemplate the possibility of cultivating the desert.

East and southeast of the Atacama lie the highest peaks of the Andes, nine of them towering more than 22,000 feet above sea level, and more than two dozen of them rising higher than any peak outside Asia. As we have already seen, exploration of this portion of the cordillera was intermittent, and was chiefly concerned, before the nineteenth century, with finding a way across rather than with a study of any individual mountain or mountains. In the nineteenth century, before the great work of Steffen in the south, we do find a number of European travelers who crossed the cordillera between Argentina and Chile, and whose experiences and impressions are of sufficient interest to merit mention here. First among these is Charles Brand, who arrived in Rio de Janeiro on June 7, 1827, and after a variety of experiences reached Buenos Aires on June 30, filled with a desire to cross the continent into Chile. During the month of July he crossed the pampas, spending the nights in post-houses, which were generally filthy after leaving Santa Fé; the sight of a door in one of them surprised him— he considered it a rarity "when it is taken into consideration that some of them are as far removed as three hundred miles from anything like a tree." [12] Despite the filthy condition of the *gauchos,* and their irritable dispositions, which often led to bitter fights, he found that he could admire their skill, dignity, manners, and humor. On August 14 he left Mendoza to begin the ascent of the Andes, surely a daring undertaking in winter. On the way he found carcasses of animals in a perfect state of preservation, but appearing to be thoroughly dried out—apparently the result of the rarefied atmosphere. This, together with increasing snow and cold, almost discouraged him at the Uspallata Pass, until he met a Chilean courier who had got through. Putting on snow boots made of sheepskin, Brand pushed through the pass, losing eventually all his mules, his wine and cooking pot, suffering from cold and the rarefied air and the danger of snowblindness, until by sheer courage and intrepidity he reached the warm valleys of Chile.[13]

In 1833, shortly after Darwin crossed the cordillera, a Frenchman, the famed orientalist Théodore Pavie, crossed the Andes along the route Brand had followed. His leisurely journey through the pampas gave him considerable opportunity to meet and talk with some of the soldiers of the *gaucho* leader Facundo Quiroga, and to study the life and customs of the slowly vanishing Indians. Finally he arrived at Uspallata, where, he tells us, "the Andes appeared in all their majesty." [14] The guards who examined his passport and books (the illustrations in a volume of Shakespeare particularly interested them) told him that they had seen only three travelers during that seven-month period when the pass was closed. They were astounded when they learned that he intended to cross the cordillera; Pavie quotes the comment of one: "He wants to cross the Cordillera, that fellow! Impossible! What have we here—an Englishman, a *chapetón* [Spaniard]? There is not a crag, not a ravine, not a precipice, not a slope that I do not know; the stranger who ventures into the Andes in such a winter will find there his grave." [15] Nonetheless, with seven men in the party (two of them guides, one a courier) and nine mules, Pavie did not take quite so dim a view, and started across. The journey was very difficult, with much snow, and he began to realize their terrible isolation and how dependent he was on his guides, whom he viewed as extraordinarily competent. Finally they reached the summit, and in the far distance ahead could see trees. Even then they were not safe from danger; an avalanche above them, started by some guanacos, was nearly a disaster. A sack of mail from Argentina was almost lost, but was recovered by one of the guides. This was the last point of danger, it developed. The remainder of the journey to the valley of Chile was accomplished without incident, and Pavie went on to Santiago whence he continued his journey into Peru.

Another foreign traveler crossed the cordillera from west to east. In early January of 1837, Platon Alexandrovich Chikhachev, a Russian aristocrat whose interest in geography was nourished by reading Humboldt, Darwin, and Orbigny, arrived at Valparaíso aboard a British vessel from Guayaquil. He was no novice as a traveler, having begun, at the age of twenty-three, a journey which took him through Canada, the United States, Mexico, Ecuador, and Peru before boarding the British frigate; he would (or so was his plan) board that same vessel in Buenos Aires to return to Europe. Going to Santiago, he spent a few days in seeing the city, whose people impressed him very much—particularly the women: "But the women—the women!! There are no women in the world more charming than the Spanish women born under the tropical heavens." [16] Despite the fears of the proprietress of his hotel, who felt he would be lost, he started out with a guide, three mules, some linens, money, a compass, and a few books and thermometers. With the exception of the uncomfortable results of eating a bite of his guide's proffered red-pepper sandwich, Chikhachev found the first stage of his journey anything but unpleasant or difficult. The night enchanted him: "Twilight in these latitudes is barely discernible. Hardly has the last edge of the sun disappeared beyond the horizon when darkness descends. Here there is not the delightful *chiaroscuro,* the dreamer, one will find in Spain and Italy, but the night is sure to console him for every wonderful thing he left behind in Europe. Even the most fertile, the most ardent imaginations cannot conceive the magnificence of the tropical skies, bright with the twinkling lights of millions of worlds lost in the immeasurable limits of the universe. The soul instinctively rises to the Creator of all marvels, and the Southern Cross, that majestic competitor of Orion, accepts the humble offering of the traveler's prayer." [17]

Since it was midsummer, Chikhachev and his guide were not troubled with snow as Pavie had been, but the narrow, zigzag trail, whose average incline was 30°, presented a hazard that gave him some anxious moments. On the second day they reached the summit of the pass, where the Russian hastily checked the boiling point of water by melting some snow—for here it was cold, and the snow was all around them. The first part of the descent, with the exception of the near loss of a mule in the Río de las Vacas, was not overly difficult; the worst was yet to come. Ahead was the Ladera de las Vacas, an extremely steep and narrow slope, with huge boulders overhanging above, and the river thundering in the abyss below. Only by giving the mules free rein could the path be safely negotiated. But one more hurdle remained, the summit of Paramillo, highest point of the eastern chain; it was crossed with comparative ease, and the travelers descended to the spa of Villa Vicencio, and finally arrived at Mendoza. The rest of the journey, to Buenos Aires, need not detain us here. Chikhachev did meet the British frigate and return to Europe aboard it. In view of the many dangers which he overcame on his American trip, it is ironic that most of his manuscripts and notes should be stolen from his hotel room in Paris; only excerpts remained, from which, aided by his memory, he was able to reconstruct his journey.

The southern Andes, as we have already seen,[18] were quite thoroughly explored in the last decades of the century by Colonel Luis Fontana and Hans Steffen in journeys a decade apart which took them through much of this picturesque region. Steffen, for example, explored in the area around Lake Todos los Santos in 1893, exploring the valley of the Río Peulla and measuring the volcano Osorno and the triple peak of Cerro Tronador.[19] For his work in exploring Chubut province and the southern cordillera, and for his subsequent efforts in delimiting the boundary with Chile, a grateful Argentine government gave Fontana twenty-five thousand acres of land; subsequently he returned it to form the nucleus of the impressive Nahuel Huapí national park.

Not until nearly the end of the century was the highest peak of the Andes conquered. Little was known of Aconcagua other than its supposed location, and nothing of its approaches; it was believed to be unclimbable. In 1883 Dr. Paul Güssfeldt made an attempt on February 21 with two inexperienced Chileans; one collapsed with frozen feet and had to be left behind; Güssfeldt and the other Chilean, with but 1,300 feet to go, were driven back by snow and sleet. A second attempt on March 5 had to be abandoned because of a snowstorm; Dr. Güssfeldt never reached the summit of Aconcagua.[20]

Not until 1896 was another attempt made, this time by the British mountain climber Edward A. Fitz Gerald. Learning of Güssfeldt's failure while climbing in the Austrian Tirol, he became ambitious to succeed in such a venture. Climbs in New Zealand and writing delayed him, and not until 1896 could he turn his attention to the Andes. Arriving in Buenos Aires from Southampton, he left for Mendoza, bringing with him one hundred large crates of equipment, weighing eight tons.[21] Although Aconcagua lies on the Argentine side of the frontier, so great is its height (22,834 feet—Fitz Gerald assumed it to be 23,080 feet) that it can be seen from the harbor of Valparaíso. Fitz Gerald decided to approach from the east, through Uspallata Pass; he found the writings of Darwin and the report of the U.S. Navy Astronomical Expedition of much value in making preparations.

After exploring the Vacas valley with his Swiss guide, Matthias Zurbriggen, who had been with him in New Zealand, Fitz Gerald decided that this route was unsuitable and sent his guide off in search of another one. Four days later Zurbriggen returned. He had found another route, and climbed up to nineteen thousand feet, where he discovered one of Güssfeldt's buried visiting cards—this would be the best route. There was need to hurry, for they had learned that the German Athletic Club in Santiago was planning a climb; it would, however, take them a week to cross the cordillera and reach the mountain. On December 23 Fitz Gerald and Zurbriggen set out with four porters, two horses, and ten mules up the Horcones valley. At sixteen thousand feet they made camp. The night was very cold, but they slept well in sleeping-bags. The next day, however, many things went wrong. There was trouble with the stove, and coffee could be made only with difficulty. They felt weak; one Swiss porter was ill, and had to be sent to the lower camp. Fitz Gerald began to show signs of *soroche* and could not sleep. The next day, Christmas, they could not cook, and opened cans of Irish stew, which served only to nauseate them. With fresh supplies from below they regained some of their strength, and pushed up to nineteen thousand feet, where they suffered more from *soroche* and decided to go down lower to recuperate. Making a fresh start, they again reached their previous height, but were unable to make a fire. Zurbriggen developed frozen feet at this point—only prompt rubbing and brandy saved him. On January 1 the party managed to reach twenty thousand feet, and found that from there to the summit they would have to go over loose, rolling stones. Cooking was impossible, and that terrible condition which made Aconcagua so difficult—sudden winds of almost hurricane force—plus low, chilling temperatures and *soroche* forced them back to the valley camp for rest and a good meal. To add to their problems, Zurbriggen was twice in the same day nearly killed by a mule rolling over.

Not until January 9 could they make another attempt. The weather was warmer, they had plenty of good food, and an adequate supply of firewood. But that night a terrible windstorm nearly tore their tent loose; Zurbriggen's injured shoulder pained him, and morning found them tired, only able to drink coffee. Not until 9:00 A.M., when the sun was high enough for some warmth, did they start again, reaching twenty-one thousand feet when Fitz Gerald fell, got sick, and they had to return to camp. Since Zurbriggen, who had reconnoitered ahead, had found a good route which would lead to the higher of the two peaks, they decided to try for the summit the next day, January 14. After a good start, Fitz Gerald developed nausea again, and decided to return to camp with two of the Swiss porters, sending his guide to try to finish the ascent. Zurbriggen succeeded, and planted an ice-ax on the summit, then stumbled weakly back to camp. The conquest of Aconcagua was complete.[22]

It would be expecting too much of human nature to think that Fitz Gerald would give up without having stood on the summit himself. He started out again with Stuart Vines on January 19, but *soroche* and extremely foul weather forced them back to camp, where they learned that the Germans had given up their attempt. Once again, on February 7, they set out for another try. Since cooking was most difficult at high altitude, they gave careful attention to food, and found that port wine with half a dozen eggs shaken in each bottle provided very adequate nourishment. By February 13 they had reached twenty thousand feet, and found it necessary to wear all the clothes they had. At this point Fitz Gerald was seized with a violent attack of nausea, and collapsed. At his direction Vines and one of the porters, Lanti, went on, passed Güssfeldt's cairn, and finally stood on the summit at 5:02 P.M. Building a cairn, Vines noted down that he and Lanti, representing the Fitz Gerald Expedition, had stood at the summit. Taking up Zurbriggen's ice-ax, he replaced it with Fitz Gerald's, and returned to camp at 8:00 P.M.[23] Fitz Gerald went on in 1897 to climb Catedral and Tupungato successfully, but never returned to Aconcagua.[24]

One more "unclimbable" peak remains for our consideration. Mount Roraima, at the meeting-point of Brazil, Venezuela, and Guyana, rises only 9,094 feet and is a pigmy in comparison with the giants of the Andes. Rising at first in a somewhat conical form, it becomes suddenly almost vertical at about the half-way mark, with sheer sides and a nearly flat top. Small wonder that Sir Arthur Conan Doyle should people it with dinosaurs in his *Lost World*. Many had made the attempt to scale this mountain; all had failed. But no mountain remains unclimbable, for inevitably someone with the strength, agility, daring, and perseverence will make the attempt, and succeed. So it was with Roraima. Everard Im Thurn, who had failed once before, finally was able to crown his efforts with success. In 1885, after much searching, he succeeded in finding a steep and narrow way up the face of the mountain and reached the top.[25] Years later, in 1938, his feat would be duplicated by Paul Zahl, a distinguished American entomologist, who succeeded in reaching the summit after a long, dangerous, and arduous climb. The flat summit he found to be rough and broken; so cold and dangerous was it that he dared not risk spending a night there, but descended through the encircling mists as rapidly as possible.[26] Roraima did not easily submit to conquest.

The nineteenth century was the great age of mountain climbing. Indians may have viewed the mysterious peaks as the abode of spirits; early explorers probably viewed them as obstacles, but nonetheless inspiring views. For the men of the nineteenth century, they presented a challenge; not unthinkingly do men say that they climb mountains "because they are there." One success led to another. So well did these men do their work that by the close of the century they had left virtually no more worlds to conquer. While for some the satisfaction of success may have been enough, each conquest accomplished, more than so limited a result. As each peak was vanquished, one more small segment of the vast map of the continent could be filled in or corrected. And with each ascent, man's knowledge of the effects of high altitude was considerably broadened. Through such small steps does the larger pattern eventually unfold.

NOTES

1. Boussingault, *Viajes científicos a los Andes ecuatoriales* (Paris, 1849), pp. 205-8. It is interesting to note that thirty Andean peaks tower over Chimborazo.

2. *Ibid.*, 208-24.

3. Edward Whymper, *Travels Amongst the Great Andes of the Equator*, 2nd ed. (London, 1892), p. xiv.

4. For the first ascent, see Whymper, *op. cit.*, pp. 23-75.

5. Humboldt, 19,286 feet, Boussingault, 19,698 feet.

6. For the second attempt, see Whymper, *op. cit.*, pp. 75-81.

7. On the ascent of Cotopaxi see Whymper, *op. cit.*, pp. 120-56.

8. For the second ascent to the summit, see Whymper, *op. cit.*, pp. 310-34.

9. *Ibid.*, pp. 383-84.

10. The expedition is described in Rudolph Amand Philippi, *Viage al desierto de Atacama, hecho del orden del gobierno de Chile en el verano 1853–1854* (Halle, Saxony, 1860).

11. *Ibid.*, p. 87.

12. Charles Brand, *Journal of a Voyage to Peru*, p. 39.

13. For the Andean crossing, see Brand, *op. cit.*, pp. 96-161.

14. Théodore Pavie, *Fragments d'un voyage dans l'Amérique méridionale en 1833* (Angers, 1840).

15. *Ibid.*, p. 115.

16. Platon Alexandrovich Chikhachev, *A Trip Across the Pampas of Buenos Aires (1836–1837)*, p. 21. This delightful account, a translation by Jack Weiner of *Poezdka chrez buenos-airesskia pampy*, appears as Occasional Publications Number Eight, Center of Latin American Studies, University of Kansas, Lawrence, 1967.

17. *Ibid.*, pp. 26-27.

18. See Chaps. XVII and XVIII.

19. Steffen, *Viajes de esploracion i estudio en la Patagonia occidental, 1892–1902* (Santiago, 1909), Vol. I, pp. 90-164.

20. For his expedition, see Edward A. Fitz Gerald, *The Highest Andes* (London, 1899), pp. 7-14.

21. The amount might seem excessive, but he had less than six hundred pounds left over at the end.

22. Fitz Gerald, *op. cit.,* pp. 45-83.

23. *Ibid.,* pp. 84-126.

24. For these subsequent climbs, see Fitz Gerald, *op. cit.,* pp. 132-45, 166-219.

25. See Im Thurn, "The Ascent of Mount Roraima," *Proceedings of the Royal Geographical Society* (New Series), VII (London, 1885): 497-521.

26. Zahl, *To the Lost World* (New York, 1939), pp. 248-54.

XX *Twentieth-Century*
Explorations

Basically, the main purpose of exploration in South America in the twentieth century was to fill in the gaps that still remained in man's knowledge of the continent despite the thorough work of the preceding century. We might expect, then, that twentieth-century exploration would be primarily scientific, which, in essence, it was; yet there was a decidedly romantic quality in several of the expeditions —a harking back, as it were, to earlier centuries when men firmly believed in El Dorado and lost cities and actively and relentlessly sought them out in every quarter of the continent.

If we exclude Hans Steffen's work on the Argentine-Chilean boundary, which was essentially a continuation of work begun in the previous century, the earliest of the important twentieth-century explorers of South America, and perhaps the greatest, was the American Dr. A. Hamilton Rice. A graduate of Harvard, Rice served for some time as Surgical Officer in Massachusetts General Hospital, then turned to exploring and received a diploma in surveying from the Royal Geographical Society. In 1897 he began a series of travels that took him to Spitzbergen, Russia, and the Caucasus; in 1899 he visited the west coast of Hudson Bay. Two years later we find him in South America, duplicating Orellana's voyage down the Amazon. In 1907 he followed Bolívar's route from Caracas to Bogotá, whence he journeyed to the source of the Río Uaupés and followed it to the Río Negro. He made a detailed study of the Indians in this region, and discovered that while diseases of the eye were common among them, they seemed to be singularly free from cancer, syphilis, and appendicitis.[1] Rice returned to this part of the Amazon basin in 1912 on a mission primarily topographical— to identify the rivers and ascertain the character of the country—but which produced a wealth of information concerning the Indians, especially from a medical point of view, and the natural history of the area.[2]

Five years elapsed before Hamilton Rice returned to Amazonia. In January of 1917 he went to the Río Negro with three purposes in mind: to make as complete a map as possible, including the Casiquiare, to test the practicability of receiving radio signals from Arlington, Virginia, in order to simplify the determination of differences of longitude between Washington (as a prime meridian) and field stations (as secondary and tertiary meridians), and to investigate diseases along the river. The expedition terminated three months later and, while quite productive, did not succeed in mapping the Casiquiare.[3]

In 1919 Rice set out to complete the unfinished work of this expedition—the mapping of the Río Casiquiare from the Río Negro to the Orinoco. On September 16, 1919, his party left Manaus in a launch, explored the back areas along the way in canoes, and finally entered the Casiquiare in the launch on December 13. Seven days later they entered the Orinoco, having logged 272.14 miles—considerably more than Humboldt's estimate of 180 miles. While in the shallow upper Orinoco in January, 1920, they were attacked by the savage Guaharibos, who indicated their intention of killing and eating them, but they managed to slip by successfully after firing toward the Indians.[4]

Rice's last expedition, from August 1924 to June 1925, was concerned primarily with surveying and mapping the Rio Branco and its western affluent the Uraricuera, following the latter to its source in the Sierra Parima to ascertain whether any path or passage existed between its headwaters and the Orinoco. Secondary considerations were studies of the geology—and especially the physiography—of the region as a whole, and to make anthropological, ethnological, and medical studies. The expedition was marked by the use of special radio apparatus, and a hydroplane for some of the surveying work. The latter innovation proved to be quite successful. Rice gathered considerable information on the flora, fauna, and topography of the Rio Branco region, and was surprised to find some quite light-skinned Indians. The major survey was unproductive of positive results; upon reaching the summit of the Sierra Parima, Rice found it impossible to cross overland to the headwaters of the Orinoco.[5]

Three years after Rice emulated Orellana's expedition which took him down the Amazon, two Frenchmen embarked on a journey which would cover substantially the same territory. On September 30, 1904, the Delebecque brothers left Panama for Guayaquil; upon arriving, they decided to save time in getting to Quito by taking a river steamer to Durán, and going the rest of the way by train. This railroad, with its numerous tunnels, bridges, and switchbacks, is one of the marvels of railroad construction, and had by that time reached the town of Colta; from there to Quito the brothers proceeded by diligence. After a few weeks in what they described as a lethargic capital, they set out to visit the Oriente, making a journey by horseback along precipitous trails to the town of Baños; there they met Père Alflans, who was astonished to meet countrymen in so remote a place. After a brief side trip into the Amazon forest, the Delebecques proceeded back to Guayaquil by way of the *páramos* of Chimborazo, and at the end of October left for Peru. Some weeks were spent in Lima making preparations to cross the cordillera, and in obtaining letters of introduction, which were always of use.

On November 22 the brothers departed by train to Oroya, the highest railway station in the world at that time (4,300 meters), then proceeded by mule down into the *montaña*, with its flowers, beautiful birds, and butterflies. Fresh mules arrived on November 26, and they advanced into the somber silent forest—a bit more civilized now, since they could cross rivers on bridges. By December 6 they were able to embark in a canoe on the Río Pichis for Puerto Bermúdez where, they were assured, an Irishman named "Bobby" Crawford, who employed a number of Indians, could assist them in getting canoes and crews for the remainder of their journey. Bobby told them that their projected trip—a descent of the Río Pachitea—was not possible, and suggested that they accompany him to Santa Zita; no rowers or canoes would be available. At Santa Zita Bobby rented them a canoe loaded with freight, and they proceeded down the Río Pichis to where it becomes the Pachitea. On December 15 they arrived at La Boca, two miles from the Ucayali, where they boarded the launch *Napo* for the Ucayali. From this point to Belém, their journey was by launch and steamer. Despite the civilized accommodations, they still remained essentially explorers rather than tourists, as the careful observations in their journal indicate.[6]

While the Amazon was becoming civilized, vast areas to the south of it were scarcely known except to the Indians who inhabited them; the only settlements to be found were in a thin line along the rivers. In 1907 the Brazilian government decided to build telegraph lines to the settlements on the Río Madeira, and selected Colonel Cândido Rondón to go into the unknown region north of Cáceres in Mato Grosso to map the courses of the rivers which run from the divide into the upper Tapajós and Madeira. Rondón was an excellent choice for the job. Descended from the Paulistas on his father's side, he was orphaned at the age of one and was raised on his uncle's cattle ranch near Cuiabá. After completing his studies at the government school there, he went to Rio de Janeiro, enlisted in the army, and was sent to the military

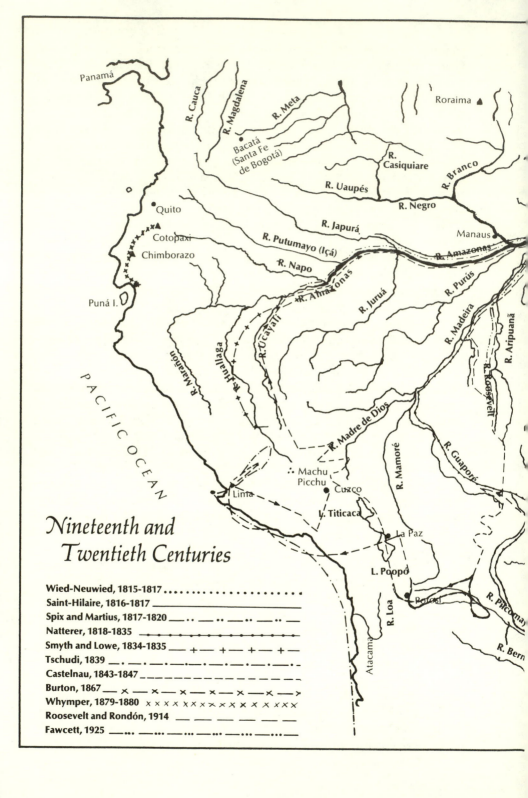

Panamá

R. Cauca

R. Magdalena

R. Meta

Roraima ▲

Bacatá
(Santa Fe
de Bogotá)

R.
Casiquiare

R. Branco

R. Uaupés

R. Negro

Manaus

Quito

R. Japurá

Cotopaxi

R. Putumayo (Içá)

R. Amazonas

Chimborazo

R. Napo

R. Amazonas

R. Purús

R. Juruá

R. Madeira

R. Aripuanã

Puná I.

PACIFIC OCEAN

R. Marañón

R. Huallaga

R. Ucayali

R. Roosevelt

R. Madre de Dios

R. Mamoré

R. Guaporé

Machu
Picchu

Cuzco

Lima

L. Titicaca

La Paz

Nineteenth and Twentieth Centuries

L. Poopó

R. Loa

Potosí

R. Pilcomayo

Atacama

R. Bermejo

Wied-Neuwied, 1815-1817	·················
Saint-Hilaire, 1816-1817	————————
Spix and Martius, 1817-1820	—··—··—··—··
Natterer, 1818-1835	·—·—·—·—·—
Smyth and Lowe, 1834-1835	—+—+—+—+—
Tschudi, 1839	—·—·—·—·—·—
Castelnau, 1843-1847	————————
Burton, 1867	—×—×—×—×—×—×
Whymper, 1879-1880	×××××××××××××
Roosevelt and Rondón, 1914	—— —— —— ——
Fawcett, 1925	—···—···—···—···

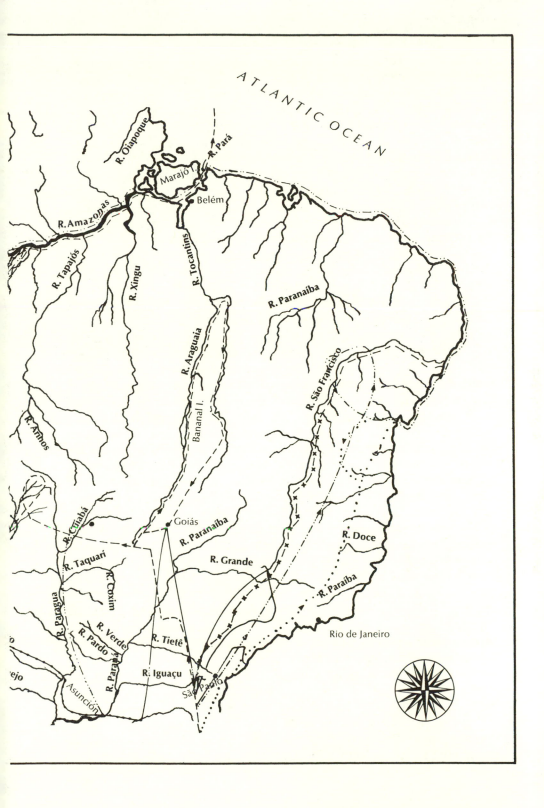

ATLANTIC OCEAN

R. Oiapoque
R. Pará
Marajó I.
Belém
R. Amazonas
R. Tapajós
R. Xingu
R. Tocantins
R. Paranaíba
R. Araguaia
Bananal I.
R. São Francisco
R. Arinos
R. Cuiabá
Goiás
R. Paranaíba
R. Doce
R. Taquari
R. Grande
R. Coxim
R. Paraguai
R. Verde
R. Pardo
R. Tietê
R. Paraná
R. Paraíba
Rio de Janeiro
R. Iguaçu
São Paulo
Asunción
ejo

school, where he taught mathematics after his graduation. Later he served with the army engineers, and finally was sent to Mato Grosso, where his exploring career began. Three times he penetrated into this vast, little-known area, and was away a year or two at a time, accompanied by members of the army and civilian scientists. The dangers were great; several of the party died of beriberi, and several were killed or wounded by Indians. Nevertheless, Rondón, by his fearlessness, resolution, and sheer force of personality succeeded in making friends of the Indians, and eventually they guarded the telegraph lines and assisted the soldiers. On his earlier explorations during this period Rondón mapped the Rio Sepotuba and the Juruena, and found that the Jiparaná was mapped 2° out of its proper location.

On May 3, 1909, Rondón began his longest and most important exploring trip thus far. Leaving Tapirapoan, he headed for the Rio Jiparaná, intending to descend it to the Madeira; the upper part of the river was little known. By August his party had exhausted all of its food, and lived for four months on game, fruit, and wild honey. They reached the river with no baggage; one-third of the group was so weak that they could barely crawl. Barely able to handle a canoe, the weakest were put in one the others had built, and headed downstream; the remainder built another canoe, taking with them a man they had found who had been lost for four months, had managed to live on Brazil nuts and grubs, and was scarcely able to walk. By Christmas both canoes had reached the Madeira, with their personnel worn out from fatigue, exposure, and semistarvation. Rondón had made one significant discovery on this expedition: namely, running northwest between the Juruena and the Jiparaná, a hitherto unmapped river, flowing through a region unknown to civilized man. Since all knowledge of it was pure conjecture, he named it the Río da Dúvida (River of Doubt).[7]

Rondón returned to the Río da Dúvida in 1913 as a member of perhaps the most spectacular expedition of the century, the Roosevelt-Rondón Scientific Expedition. The initiator of this enterprise, oddly enough, was neither of the men whose names it bore, but one Father John A. Zahm, C.S.C., a scientist from the University of Notre Dame and a man of many parts, who had become acquainted with President Theodore Roosevelt and formed a firm friendship with him based in part on their common interest in Dante, history, and science. Father Zahm was an inveterate traveler, who for some time had been following the trail of the conquistadores. While visiting the president in the White House in 1908, he proposed a trip up the Río Paraguay into the interior, but Roosevelt had already planned to go to Africa. After his return, the project was discussed from time to time, but other commitments interfered. Finally, in 1913, the former president decided to accept invitations to lecture in Argentina and Brazil, and resolved to make the trip into the interior also. Shortly afterward he went to the American Museum of Natural History to lunch with the curator of ornithology, Frank Chapman, and was surprised to see Father Zahm there; the priest, unaware of Roosevelt's decision, had thought of going alone, and was seeking a naturalist to accompany him—he was delighted to go with Roosevelt. To accompany them they chose George K. Cherrie, an experienced naturalist and something of a revolutionist, who had spent twenty years in South America; Leo Miller, another naturalist then in Venezuela; Anthony Fiala, a former Arctic explorer; Frank Harper, Roosevelt's secretary; Joseph Sigg, who served as cook and nurse; and the former president's son Kermit, who would join them in Brazil.[8]

The Roosevelt party divided upon reaching Rio de Janeiro; Father Zahm accompanied the former president on his speaking tour, while the rest of the group continued on to Buenos Aires, there to take a river steamer for Corumbá on the Paraguay, making occasional side trips in the Gran Chaco and elsewhere to collect unusual specimens. The original purpose of the journey—to go up the Paraguay and down the Tapajós to the Amazon—had been changed. Foreign Minister Lauro Müller had suggested to Roosevelt that the expedition could be more useful if it would descend and map Rondón's Rio da Dúvida, a proposal certainly appealing to the former president's spirit of high adventure. Rondón's work was by no means unknown to Roosevelt, and before they left New York, the former president and Father Zahm had thought that it would be desirable to secure his services, a matter which was arranged by the Brazilian ambassador in Washington through Foreign Minister Müller.

After completing his lecture tour, Roosevelt and his party proceeded to Asunción, where the gunboat-yacht of the president of Paraguay was put at their disposal for the journey upstream to Brazil. At the Brazilian border they were met by Colonel Rondón, and held animated discussions with his group concerning piranhas, caymans, jaracaras, and pumas, which the Americans viewed as the greatest dangers before them. Rondón, however, felt that the real dangers were swarming insects, fever, and dysentery. The party started up the river, visiting a Paraguayan hamlet on the right bank where Father Zahm baptized two children—no priest had been there in three years. By the next afternoon they were wholly within Brazilian territory, and arrived at Corumbá on December 15, where they were joined by Miller and Cherrie, who had been exploring the Río Pilcomayo.[9] The following day the entire party visited the fazenda of Senhor de Barros on the Taquarí, where a hunt was arranged for Roosevelt.[10]

After returning to Corumbá the expedition again set out upriver, diverting again to the Rio Cuiabá where, on another fazenda, Roosevelt had the satisfaction of killing a peccary with a spear. By the time they returned to the Paraguay, the rainy season had begun, and the journey, which took them now through the forest, began to give some evidence of the difficulties ahead: soaking downpours, mosquitoes, fire-ants, and terrible heat. Out of the marsh country at last, the party reached São Luís de Cáceres—the last town before the fringes of the Amazon. Going by canoe up the Sepotuba, Roosevelt had extraordinary success on a hunt and achieved his great ambition—to shoot a jaguar and a tapir. On July 13 they broke camp and set out upstream for Tapirapoan; ants were troublesome along the way, eating holes in Miller's mosquito netting and nearly finishing off his socks. At their destination, a small town gaily decked out in American and Brazilian flags in honor of the expedition, the explorers took time to pack their skins and specimens for shipment to the American Museum of Natural History, and sent forward a Canadian canoe, a motor, kerosene, and one hundred sealed tins containing in each a day's rations for six men, prepared in New York under Fiala's direction.

From Tapirapoan their course took them northwest across the *planalto*, first through dense forests, then up to the top of the Parecís plateau, across the divide into the Amazon basin, where they camped and awaited the auto-vans which would take them to Utiariti falls on the Rio Papagaio. They rode, through many heavy rains, across "endless flats of grass and of low open scrubby forest" which included "bastard rubber trees and dwarf palmetto; if the latter grew more than a few feet high their tops were torn and disheveled by the wind." [11] There were many high ant hills, and they say some of the inhabitants—leaf-carrying ants, which also cut up and carried off garments, and the poisonous black ants. There was also the sign of civilization—the telegraph line which Rondón had constructed, and on which the local Indians worked. The road ended at Salto Belo, the beautiful falls of the Rio Sacre; from there they had to proceed on foot to the falls of Utiariti, which were twice as high and wide as Salto Belo, and almost as big as Niagara. At this point the expedition was diminished by two: Father Zahm, who had already gone down the Amazon and was primarily interested in the lands of the conquistadores, did not care to make the trip again; Sigg left also to join friends in Paraguay.[12]

On February 3 the expedition started across the land of the Nhambiquaras with a mule train and six oxcarts; Fiala and Lieutenant Lauriadó (who came with Rondón) remained behind to descend the Papagaio, and then the Juruena and the Tapajós—an experience that nearly cost them their lives. For the others, a routine was developed: they were awakened early by a bugle, and had coffee; there was a heavy breakfast at eight; they rode until about four, then made camp for the night and cared for the animals. At night they sat around a bonfire, discussing history, literature, and science, and Roosevelt often entertained them with tales of his adventures. Fiala and Lauriadó rejoined them at the Juruena before continuing their descent, as did a party of Nhambiquaras, who seemed happy to see Rondón, whom they knew. On February 24 they reached a camp that Captain Amilcar, one of Rondón's party, had established on a brook that flowed into the River of Doubt; there the party divided, for Rondón said that all of them could not descend the Dúvida, and recommended that part of the group descend the Jiparaná to the Madeira.[13]

Miller volunteered to let Cherrie accompany Roosevelt, while he joined four of the Brazilian explorers and some thirty *camaradas* (Indian porters) to descend the Jiparaná and map it, gathering specimens as they proceeded. The journey to the Jiparaná took them down the Río Conmemoração, a beautiful stream with the forest in many places coming down to the edge of the water, and then past the Pimentá, where a near tragedy occurred when a seven-foot bushmaster fell into Amilcar's canoe and everyone jumped out, nearly drowning. Generally they kept to the middle of the stream to keep away from swarming insects, and they managed to continue their journey with no difficulties other than fever, which left the crew sick most of the way. Finally they entered the Madeira, where they were guests at the home of an owner of a rubber camp. Miller tarried a while to explore the back country, where he found beautiful flora, much game, and many insects and other interesting fauna in the swampy country. The last stage of the journey was by steamer to Manaus, where they awaited the arrival of the Roosevelt party.[14]

The former president and his group started down the River of Doubt about noon on February 27, 1914, with little idea of what was in store for them. "It was interesting work," Colonel Roosevelt wrote, "for no civilized man, no white man, had ever gone down or up this river or seen the country through which we were passing." [15] By March 5 they had passed the first rapids safely, and found that their main problem was insects: bees, horseflies, piums, borshuda flies, sandflies, ants (which made off with part of the lining of Roosevelt's helmet), and termites (which chewed one leg off his underwear). After fifteen days they had passed three more rapids, lost two canoes, and had to cut a tree and make one large canoe—work which was finished in a downpour. Cherrie took inventory of their food. They had enough for thirty-five days—and in fifteen days they had covered only thirty-seven out of a possible four hundred kilometers. The next day, as they approached more rapids, a sudden whirlpool caught their canoe; one of the *camaradas* was thrown into the rapids and killed; Roosevelt and his son Kermit were pulled into the whirlpool and nearly drowned, and Kermit's rifle was gone. Ten days' food supply was lost. A few days later, the new canoe was lost. They had, in eighteen days, used up one-third of their food, and had covered perhaps one-fifth of the distance. Another new river was discovered, which Rondón named the Río Kermit; the following day he raised a sign indicating that since the Dúvida was a large river, by order of the Brazilian government it would henceforth be known as the "Rio Roosevelt." [16]

To replace the lost canoes, new ones were again constructed and the expedition was ready to continue its journey downstream on March 22. As before, rapids constituted the major problem and occasioned numerous delays which further reduced their supplies. On March 27 the new canoes were nearly lost in some rapids, and in the salvage operation Roosevelt got a severe cut on the shin. At one point it took three days of extremely hazardous and laborious work to reach the bottom of a gorge so they could resume their journey, and in the process it was found necessary to reduce baggage to the absolute minimum. Fortunately, Cherrie's years of experience in tropical wilderness were of great benefit in seeking out wildlife for food. There was further trouble with termites and ants, which continued to eat into and damage their clothing. There was rain. There were more rapids. There was declining morale, as the *camaradas* in particular began to wonder if they would get out alive. Rondón himself was wondering if they might not have to abandon the canoes and let every man fight his way through the forest himself. Worst of all, Roosevelt was in poor shape; his health had not been good since the loss of the first canoe—he suffered from fever and dysentery—and now he had an ulcerated leg. His heart was affected, and he had to stop frequently to rest.[17]

Tragedy struck in another form a few days later. One of the men, a worthless scoundrel named Júlio, had been caught stealing food by one of the *camaradas*, Paixão, who punished him; Júlio thereupon picked up his gun, shot Paixão through the heart, and then disappeared into the forest. Rondón did not pursue him, since he could not legally shoot him, and simply could not ask his weakened men to guard him, if caught, to prevent another shooting. Subsequently he was seen on the shore, offering to surrender, an offer which was rejected. The men continued to grow weaker. Kermit Roosevelt had a very high fever, and the former president, feeling he could not reach civilization, announced his determination to remain behind, and urged the rest to get out without him—something no one would hear of.[18] Still more rapids were ahead of them, and they spent several days unloading, portaging, and reloading, with at least half the party in very poor health. Not until April 13 were they able to make long runs; by then the rapids were behind and the river was smooth. Two days later they found year-old rubber cuttings and a newly built but unoccupied house. Further on was a house of palm thatch. It was occupied, but the inhabitants fled, fearing an Indian raid, since the explorers had come from the north. Finally, however, they returned and made friendly overtures. They explained that the river, which they called the Castanho, was the west branch of the Aripuanã, a tributary of the Madeira.[19]

The physical condition of the party began to improve somewhat. Cherrie and Kermit recovered, and Roosevelt's abscess was opened and began to drain, enabling him to hobble a bit. They could make longer journeys now, for while there were yet more rapids ahead, the channels were known and the portage paths cut—and the rubber-men were most generous with their assistance. By April 26 they reached the mouth of the river, where they found the tent of Lieutenant Pyrineus of the Brazilian group, who had been waiting for them for a month. The explorers had been two months on the river, and until meeting the rubber-men had not seen another human being; they had traversed some 750 kilometers, and had not begun at the source of the river; it could be a thousand kilometers in length, Roosevelt felt. Leaving Rondón and his group to take observations, the former president went down the Madeira to the Amazon, and then to Manaus. Miller, who had been waiting, was astounded at his appearance: ". . . he had wasted to a shadow of his former self; but his unbounded enthusiasm remained undiminished."[20] In evaluating the work of the expedition, Roosevelt was of the belief that zoologically it had been a great success; Cherrie and Miller had collected over 2,500 birds, some 500 mammals, and a number of reptiles and birds—many new to science. But most important was the geographical work, the exploration and mapping of a river as big as the upper Rhine or Elbe, perhaps a thousand kilometers in length, totally unknown, completing Rondón's work of the previous six years.[21]

Two years after Rondón discovered his unknown river, an American scholar and explorer, Hiram Bingham, of Yale University, went to Peru with a dual purpose: to climb Mount Coropuna and ascertain whether it was indeed higher than Aconcagua, as reputed; and to seek not a lost river, but a lost city—the last capital of the Incas. Arriving in Arequipa in June of 1911, he decided not to risk the climb in winter, and went instead into the *montaña*, north of Cuzco, to the valley of the Río Urubamba. Somewhere in the cordillera of Uilcapampa, Manco II had established his capital, Uiticos; various stories of ruins circulated, but the best opinions fixed the capital somewhere in the valleys of the Vilcabamba and Urubamba rivers. Old maps were of little help, for names appeared on some and not others, or sometimes were changed: Uiticos became Viticos, and finally disappeared from the map, while Uilcapampa became Vilcabamba. Of all the tales of ruins, the most promising one told of those at Huayna Picchu, or Machu Picchu, mountains in the Urubamba valley. There Bingham determined to search.[22]

Bingham's route took him through the terraced valley of Yucay and past the gardens of Ollantaytambo, with its ancient fortifications above. At Salapunco in the Urubamba valley he saw the ruins of a small, ancient fortress; at Torontoy he entered the terraced Grand Canyon of the Urubamba, and camped on a sandy beach. The owner of a nearby hut, Melchor Arteaga, confirmed the tales of Huayna Picchu and Machu Picchu; the next morning, July 24, Bingham persuaded Arteaga to take him there for a *sol*. After a walk of forty-five minutes they left the main road, crossed the river on a primitive bridge of logs lashed together with vines, went through the jungle to the bottom of a precipitous slope, and then spent an hour and twenty minutes climbing to the top, past cultivated terraces dating back to Inca times. Noticing the fine stonework on some of them, Bingham's excitement grew. Guided now by a boy, he crossed the terraces, went through a nearby forest, and came upon a maze of granite houses, magnificent masonry, and some of the finest structures he had seen in Peru. The discovery astonished him: here was a semicircular temple, reminiscent of the Temple of the Sun at Cuzco; here was a great staircase, and a beautiful masonry wall with three windows, which he took to be a ceremonial structure. Was this Uiticos? If so, where was the white stone over a spring, mentioned in all the tales of the last capital? Important as Machu Picchu must have been, it was not, apparently, Manco II's capital. The search must continue.[23]

At Huadquiña Bingham learned of "important ruins" a few days' journey down the Urubamba—and there was mention of a white stone. But this proved to be a false lead; "Yurak Rumi" was apparently the ruins of nothing more impressive than a small Inca storehouse. Bingham resumed his search, going now to Quillabamba to consult D. Pedro Duque, said to be the best-informed man in the province. Through him he learned of one Evaristo Mogrovejo, lieutenant-governor of a village in the valley, whose brother had found some ruins while hunting for buried treasure in 1884. He agreed to take Bingham in search of ruins, and was promised one *sol* for each one, with two if they were really interesting. There were many ruins—even interesting ones, but they were not Uiticos—the true Yurak Rumi. Finally they saw on a hill a structure which seemed to have been built for a royal Inca, so impressive a fort it was. Could this be the locality? The second day Mogrovejo showed him a large white boulder, but there was no spring. Following a watercourse to an open place called Ñusta Isppana, Bingham stopped suddenly—ahead of him was a great white rock over a spring, with the ruins of a temple beside it. Was it Uiticos? Bingham could be reasonably certain that it was; subsequent explorations revealed no other site so marked.[24]

After the discovery of Machu Picchu and a possible Uiticos, the ascent of Coropuna proved to be an anticlimax. Accompanying Bingham were H. L. Tucker (who had planned the Mount McKinley ascent in 1910); the English naturalist Casimir Watkins, who took charge of the base camp; F. Hinckley of the Harvard Observatory at Arequipa; and Corporal Gamarra, an Indian. Hinckley was soon thrown from his mule, suffered a leg injury, and had to return to Arequipa. At Chuquibamba the party received an aneroid barometer from England, whereby they could determine altitude. They inspected Coropuna from Mount Calvario to determine where to begin the climb. Their "guide" proved to be of little real assistance, and the muleteers demanded extra pay before they would consent to unload at the snow line; they had a superstitious dread of the peak. Gamarra was persuaded to accompany Bingham and Tucker to the peak for a bonus, and they departed from the base camp located at the 17,300-foot level. Frostbite—which had plagued so many mountaineers—was no problem to them, since they had adequate warm clothing, but they did suffer from *soroche*, which slowed them considerably. On October 14, aided by sugar cubes to restore energy and snow-creepers to eliminate much step-cutting, they reached the summit after six and one-half hours. The mountain had proved to be not one peak but three, and not until they reached the summit did they know that they had scaled the highest one. Despite faulty barometer readings, it was evident that this peak was inferior to Aconcagua. In the end, even Bingham's cherished belief that at least it was the second highest peak in the hemisphere would be shattered, for later surveys indicated that it ranks only nineteenth among the Andean peaks.[25]

While Bingham explored Peru, and indeed even while Rondón was blazing a trail through the trackless forests of Mato Grosso, a British explorer, Major P. H. Fawcett, was laboring in the wilds of northeastern Bolivia to delimit the boundary with Brazil. Fawcett had been selected for this task (on the basis of his army course in such work) by the Royal Geographical Society, which the Bolivian government had asked to serve as a referee. Bored with service in home stations, he had accepted, and in May of 1906 set out for Bolivia by way of New York, Colón, Mollendo, and Lake Titicaca. After a chilling journey across the *altiplano*, staying in miserable *tambos*, Fawcett finally arrived at Riberalta in a crude boat called a *batelón*, which nearly sank on the way. General Pando, a former president, greeted him on his arrival and briefed him on his work. Then Fawcett went on to Cobija to pick up his instruments, only to find that the only serviceable instrument had been stolen. Eventually acquiring what he needed, he surveyed and mapped the area up to the Río Acre, undergoing an Indian attack, and shooting an anaconda that measured, he said, sixty-two feet in length. Fawcett was appalled at the unhealthy conditions in the rubber towns, and noted the cheapness of life there; if a man fell ill on a voyage, he was ridiculed by the others, and there was considerable hilarity on his death. On the completion of his survey, he reported to President Montes in La Paz, who asked him to stay on the boundary commission to mark the boundary with Paraguay. He agreed, if his government would grant permission, and returned to England late in 1907.[26]

Permission was granted, and Fawcett was eager to start out again in March, 1908—he found he had grown nostalgic for the jungle. Arriving in Buenos Aires, he took a steamer for Asunción. En route he learned of a cave at Villa Rica with curious inscriptions in an unknown language. Had there been another ancient civilization in the continent? By July he had finished his work in the Corumbá area, and moved north, passing through the dismal town of San Matías, where everyone seemed to have killed someone, to the old town of Vila Bela de Mato Grosso, virtually depopulated by the plague. By October 3 he had located the source of the Río Verde, completing that portion of the boundary. Nearby he saw the mysterious, flat-topped Ricardo Franco Hills, which he photographed.[27] The president of Bolivia was very satisfied with his work, and both boundary commissions agreed to return under Fawcett the following year to erect markers. Not until July 1, 1909, did he catch up with the Brazilian Commission, with whom he had worked in the Corumbá area, and begin the work of demarcation with boundary stones, which was satisfactorily completed. To return to La Paz to file his report, Fawcett decided to go down the Río Paraguay to the Paraná and Buenos Aires, then through the Strait of Magellan and to Mollendo by steamer, completing the journey by train and lake steamer as before. President Villazón, obviously pleased with his work, asked Fawcett to undertake the survey of the Peruvian boundary. To do so, he would have to retire from the army, which would give him no more leave; but promotions had been slow, and the War Office had cut his pension because he had served a foreign government, so he made the decision to leave the service.[28]

Between the years 1910 and 1912, Fawcett conducted extensive surveys in the *altiplano* to determine with accuracy the Peruvian-Bolivian frontier. Periodically he heard stories of remains of ancient civilizations, and he became fired with an ambition to investigate. When a dispute over the boundary arose between the two countries, Fawcett resigned from the commission. He was free now for private exploration. After a year in England, Fawcett returned to Bolivia, where he became enthusiastic over a project to seek out the source of some queer metal figures he had seen in a market—a plan which came to naught. After concluding some business in Santa Cruz, he headed north for the town of Mato Grosso, and became immediately curious about the lighter color of the Indians there, and the tint of red in their hair. Were they descendants of an earlier, higher civilization? Early in September he learned of the outbreak of the First World War, and returned to England.[29]

After the conclusion of the war, in which Fawcett rose to the rank of colonel, he found that he could no longer abide the tranquillity of the English countryside. Moreover, he had become entranced by tales of lost cities, in particular one in the northeast of Brazil, described in an old document in Rio de Janeiro, dated 1753.[30] Soon afterward he came into possession of a small stone idol which he said sent an electric current up one's arm when it was held in the hand. He was convinced that it came from one of the lost cities. Upon consulting several psychometrists, who claimed to be able to interpret this "current," he was led to believe that this idol revealed an amazing tale of a vast continent across the present South Atlantic Ocean, sundered in a vast cataclysm. Convinced that he had the city's bearings, Fawcett would not listen to contrary opinions. When a Frenchman told him that he had seen the "city"—a sandstone formation greatly exaggerated—Fawcett, a teetotaler, dismissed the man's testimony because he drank, although years later his son Brian was inclined to believe that it was true. After several false starts and many disappointments, Fawcett managed to secure support from the North American Newspaper Alliance for a small expedition consisting of himself, his son Jack, and Jack's friend Raleigh Rimell; taking any animals was out of the question because of lack of pasture and the problems of insects and vampires. Their goal was the lost city, designated simply as "Z." In April of 1925 Fawcett wrote from São Paulo that he had additional information about "Z"; its buildings and statues were of quartz! With high enthusiasm and the fervor of a true zealot, Fawcett led his small party into the interior of Brazil. At the end of May, after writing from his camp deep in northeast Mato Grosso that "you need have no fear of failure," he and his young companions boldly entered the wilderness to the east and were never heard from again.[31]

Nothing, of course, can quite excite the imagination like an unsolved mystery. In the years following there were several credible sightings of Fawcett, or someone resembling him, but not until 1928 was a relief expedition sent out under Commander George Dyott. Following Fawcett's trail to a village of the Anauquas, he learned from the cacique Aloique (who wore a brass plate obviously taken from one of Fawcett's cases) that the expedition had proceeded eastward and had been massacred by the Suyás some five days later; the bones were still there, he assured them. That evening one of Dyott's men overheard Aloique telling some friends that he intended to kill Dyott as he had killed Fawcett, and take everything he had. Dyott managed to slip out in the night, throwing nearly everything but his transmitter overboard to lighten the load and gather speed in his boat, and was finally able to reach safety. He reported as certain that Fawcett and his party had met death at the hands of hostile Indians, but also mentioned seeing ornaments which "definitely indicated a culture new to South America." [32] A further expedition headed by Peter Fleming in 1933, following Dyott's trail, reached the same conclusion: Fawcett and his companions had been killed shortly after leaving their last camp.[33]

Colonel Fawcett was the last of that long line of romantic explorers who had sought lost cities and gilded men since the sixteenth century in all quarters of the South American continent. After him, with the exception of the Dyott and Fleming parties and the accidental discovery, by the American flyer Jimmy Angel, of the world's highest waterfall (Angel Falls), no name has appeared to capture the imagination or excite the interest of the world. Exploration, of course, has continued, for there is always work for the adventurous and the inquisitive, and man's curiosity knows no bounds. But it has been scientific exploration —careful, detailed, unspectacular, and prosaic. Such, very likely, is the wave of the future, and many of us will doubtless lament that it will probably wash much of the romance out of our lives.[34]

NOTES

1. Hamilton Rice, "The Río Uaupés," *Geographical Journal* 35 (1910): 682-700. The expedition covered the period July 26, 1907, to April 1, 1908.

2. Rice, "Further Explorations in the N.W. Amazon Basin," *Geographical Journal* 44 (1914): 137. The expedition left Bogotá in February and returned in July.

3. Rice, "Notes on the Rio Negro (Amazonas)," *Geographical Journal* 52 (1918): 204-15.

4. Rice, "The Rio Negro, the Casiquiare Canal, and the Upper Orinoco, September 1919-April 1920," *Geographical Journal* 58 (1921): 321-43.

5. Rice, "The Rio Branco, Uraricuera, and Parima: Surveyed by the Expedition to the Brazilian Guayana from August 1924 to June 1925," *Geographical Journal* 71 (1928): 113-42, 209-23, 345-56.

6. The journey is described in J. Delebecque, *A Travers l'Amérique du Sud* (Paris, 1907).

7. Theodore Roosevelt, *Through the Brazilian Wilderness* (New York, 1914), pp. 125-49, 204, 227-28, 345-56.

8. Roosevelt, *op. cit.*, pp. 3-7. On the expedition, see also John A. Zahm, *Through South America's Southland* (New York, 1916); George K. Cherrie, *Dark Trails: Adventures of a Naturalist* (New York, 1930); and Leo A. Miller, *In the Wilds of South America* (New York, 1919).

9. Roosevelt, *op. cit.*, pp. 9-38; Cherrie, *op. cit.*, pp. 262-65; Miller, *op. cit.*, pp. 204-17; Zahn, *op. cit.*, pp. 419-20.

10. Roosevelt, *op. cit.*, pp. 49-90; Cherrie, *op. cit.*, pp. 271-72.

11. Roosevelt, *op. cit.*, p. 178.

12. Roosevelt, *op. cit.*, pp. 150-94; Zahn, *op. cit.*, pp. 498-502; Miller, *op. cit.*, pp. 225-28.

13. Roosevelt, *op. cit.*, pp. 219-31; Cherrie, *op. cit.*, pp. 274-75; Miller, *op. cit.*, pp. 239-40.

14. On the Jiparaná descent, see Miller, *op. cit.*, pp. 240-63.

15. Roosevelt, *op. cit.*, p. 235.

16 For the first stage of the descent, see Roosevelt, *op. cit.*, pp. 233-70; Cherrie, *op. cit.*, pp. 284-95.

17. Roosevelt, *op. cit.*, pp. 271-89. The former president said nothing on the state of his health at this point; see Cherrie, *op. cit.*, pp. 251-53, 305-8.

18. Roosevelt, *op. cit.*, pp. 290-302. He mentions a "bruise on the leg" here, but minimizes it.

19. Roosevelt, *op. cit.*, pp. 290-306.

20. Miller, *op. cit.*, p. 264.

21. Roosevelt, *op. cit.*, pp. 309-25.

22. Bingham described his adventures in several books and articles. See especially his *Inca Land* (Boston, 1922).

23. On the discovery of Machu Picchu, see Bingham, *op. cit.*, pp. 315-23.

24. The discovery was made on August 9, 1911. See Bingham, *op. cit.*, pp. 217-60.

25. Bingham calculated the elevation at 21,703 feet; actually it is 21,079 feet.

26. P. H. Fawcett, *Lost Trails, Lost Cities* (New York, 1953), pp. 23-116. With respect to the sixty-two-foot anaconda, I can only assume that Fawcett was badly mistaken or exaggerated grossly. Mr. Mike Tsalickis, who deals in animals and reptiles in Leticia, Colombia, told me there is no verified account of any anaconda in excess of thirty-eight feet. Most of them are considerably shorter.

27. Later he showed the photograph to Sir Arthur Conan Doyle, and believed that it furnished him with the locale for his *Lost World*. Fawcett, *op. cit.*, pp. 131-32.

28. On the Paraguay-Brazil survey, see Fawcett, *op. cit.*, pp. 118-48.

29. *Ibid.*, pp. 151-224.

30. For a translation of this document, see Richard Burton, *Exploration of the Highlands of Brazil* (London, 1869), Vol. II, pp. 459-63.

31. Fawcett, *op. cit.*, pp. 1-20, 228-315. The final portions were written by his son Brian.

32. Dyott, "The Search for Col. Fawcett," *Geographical Journal* 74 (1929): 541.

33. Peter Fleming, *Brazilian Adventure* (New York, 1934), 1962.

34. I am indebted to Professor Charles A. Bacarisse of the University of Houston for this happy phrase.

Epilogue

Four and one-quarter centuries separate Columbus and Colonel Fawcett. During those many years, explorers have penetrated relentlessly into the South American continent, forcing it to give up its secrets. Men of vastly different backgrounds, training, ability, and purpose, they have gradually lifted the veil and have made known to the world the nature of this vast land whose existence had not even been suspected. Nothing has been neglected, from the broad outlines of the continent down to the tiniest creatures that inhabit it. What led these men—these explorers—to do this? A new land mass had been found, and it lay athwart the route which was to take the Iberian peoples to the riches of the East. How did they react to it? For some, it was an obstacle to be overcome, and they sought with determination the strait that must exist which would take them around it to their destination. For others, it was a land to be exploited: gold, silver, pearls and emeralds indicated that this New World was possibly as rich as the lands they sought, and there was an abundant supply of labor to be pressed into service. For yet others, the millions of Indians were a rich potential harvest of souls; they must be baptized, taught useful arts, and protected from those who would exploit them. In the early decades, then, we find our explorers among the discoverers, the conquistadores, the adventurers, the gold-seekers, the slave-hunters, and the missionaries. Men of almost incredible endurance and resolution, endowed with an amazing ability to endure privations, they accomplished the phenomenal. They discovered a New World and subdued it, conquering vast and powerful empires; they found wealth beyond their wildest dreams, baptized the aborigines, and crossed and recrossed a vast continent whose perils they could not have imagined.

That the promise of gain, the hope of spiritual conquests, and the love of adventure (always a strong lure for the Spaniard) would lead them on was, of course, to be expected. Yet the fantastic, as we have seen, proved to be an equally strong attraction. In an earlier century the Portuguese, their enthusiasm fired by the legend of Prester John, dared to sail beyond Cape Bojador—and began the exploration of Africa. In South America men poured out their lives and fortunes in a vain search for El Dorado and the White King, the silver mountain of Sabarabuçu, the golden city of Manoa, and the Enchanted City of the Caesars. These were intelligent and brave men. Why did they risk so much for such a fantasy? Must we dismiss all this solely as an aberration of a more credulous age? Must we assume that these explorers were visionaries who were gullible beyond belief? So simple an answer is not the solution. It must be remembered that the height of the Middle Ages came late to Spain, and that medieval influences were very strong at the close of the fifteenth and the early part of the sixteenth centuries. Medieval literature was filled with tales of wonder, and the early explorers were quite prepared to encounter marvels of many kinds in a world of which they had no prior knowledge. These legends fired the imagination and provided a goal; for the avaricious, gold and gems beyond all expectation; for the missionaries, to convert the Indians or to bring again the solace of the sacraments to those whose priests had long ago died; for the curious and adventurous, wonders to marvel at. The New World had produced already so much that had not been imagined; might it not produce more?

By the time the last expedition set out in search of the Enchanted City, toward the end of the eighteenth century, the age of wonder was already giving way to the age of reality. This was the age of enlightenment, and myth and legend would have to give way to the cold, hard facts of science. The explorer of this era was still a man of curiosity, adventurous in spirit and endowed with great physical stamina, but his goals had changed. Instead of seeking treasures he sought knowledge; he mapped the coasts and rivers, measured the earth, delimited boundaries, studied the aborigines, and made a notable beginning in the study of natural history, especially botany.

With the advent of Alexander von Humboldt, the domination of science was assured. From the early stirrings under humanist missionaries and a period of development in the eighteenth century, scientific study made enormous strides under Humboldt and his successors. The nineteenth-century explorer, as we have seen, was basically a scientist, whether by training or by vocation. He was endowed with the same hardihood as his predecessors, for most of them, despite the greatest privations, lived to be past eighty; he had his same zest for adventure and curiosity about the unknown. But his interest lay in exploring the world of nature, and with indeed impressive results. Many of the great naturalists of the age may be counted among the explorers of South America.

It is curious, then, that in a sophisticated twentieth century, legend should again attract explorers into the interior of the continent. Men sought lost cities, and they even partially drained Lake Guatavita in search of the treasure of El Dorado. But this was not typical, although it was spectacular. More characteristic is the scientific work of Dr. Rice, and the expeditions of the Smithsonian Institution, the great scientific and geographic societies, and the universities, among others. Bit by bit the frontier of knowledge has been pushed back, and man's understanding of the continent, so small at first, has become very extensive.

For the most part, the work has been done. Few areas exist where civilized man has not at some time or other trod. He has navigated the rivers and mapped the coasts, traversed forest and desert, scaled the mountains and plumbed the depths of the surrounding seas. And where he has not actually traversed the land, he has seen it and mapped it from the air. No cities of gold or silver have been found, no lost communities revealed. Instead, new sources of wealth have been tapped: oil, coal, aluminum, copper, iron, and uranium. Highways and railroads have been built into the interior, and rivers have been bridged; new cities have been constructed in the once empty regions beyond the coasts. And more will be accomplished, as the metallurgists, highway engineers, and petroleum experts become the explorers of the future. Despite the great accomplishments of the past, exploration will not end, for man's curiosity is without limit. It merely changes, as it has before.

Bibliography

I. DOCUMENTARY SOURCES AND EARLY
CONTEMPORARY HISTORICAL WORKS

Anghiera, Pietro Martire d'. *The Decades of the Newe World, or West India.* English trans. by Richard Eden. London, 1555. A more recent English translation, by F. A. MacNutt under the title *De orbo novo* was published in New York in 1912. The best edition is the Spanish translation by Joaquín Torres Asensio, published in Buenos Aires in 1944 as Anglería, Pedro Mártir de, *Décades del Nuevo Mundo.*

Casas, Bartolomé de las. *Historia de las Indias.* This valuable work by the best of the early historians has appeared in many editions; the best, a three-volume edition edited by Agustín Millares Carlo with a bibliographical study by Lewis Hanke, was published by the Biblioteca Americana, México, D.F., 1951.

Cieza de León, Pedro. *The Incas of Pedro de Cieza de Leon.* Trans. by Harriet de Onís. Edited with an Introduction by Victor W. Von Hagen. Norman: University of Oklahoma Press, 1959. Excellent translation of the valuable *Chronicle of Peru,* with maps and illustrations.

López de Gómara, Francisco. *Historia de las Indias.* Appears as Vol. 2 of Andrés González de Barcia Carballido y Zuñiga, *Historiadores primitivos de las Indias Occidentales,* Madrid, 1749. Written in 1552; primarily concerned with the conquest of Mexico.

Jerez, Francisco de. *Verdadera relación de la conquista de Perú y provincia de Cuzco.* This account by one of the early chroniclers of the conquest appears as Vol. 26 in the *Biblioteca de Autores Españoles,* Madrid, Ediciones Atlas, 1947.

Oviedo y Baños, José. *Historia de la conquista y población de la provincia de Venezuela.* This early source for Venezuelan history appears as Vol. 107 of the *Biblioteca de Autores Españoles.* 1958.

Oviedo y Valdes, Gonzalo Fernández de. *Historia general y natural de las Indias.* Extensive, critical study by a contemporary of the conquest who traveled widely in America. Appears as Vols. 117 through 121 in the *Biblioteca de Autores Españoles,* Madrid, 1959.

Pastells, Pablo, S.J. *El descubrimiento del Estrecho de Magallanes.* Madrid, Sucesores de Rivadeneyra (s.a.) Artes gráficas, 1920. A collection, in two vols. of documents dealing with the discovery and early exploration.

Spain, Ministro de Ultramar, Archivo General de Indias. *Colección de documentos inéditos relativos al descubrimiento, conquista, y colonización de las posesiones españoles en América y Oceania.* 1st series, 42 vols.; 2nd series, 22 vols. Madrid 1895–1922. Fragments of the vast collections in the Archivo General de las Indias, chiefly for the sixteenth century, selected by Juan Bautista Muñoz. Some inaccuracies, but has the advantage of availability.

Spain, Ministro de Ultramar, Archivo General de Indias. *Historia de la Compañía de Jesús en la provincia del Paraguay segun los documentos originales del Archivo General de Indias.* 8 vols. in 9. Madrid, Suárez. This useful and valuable collection was edited by the Jesuit historian Pablo Pastells.

Trevisano, Agnolo. Letter written in 1501 or 1502 on the discoveries of Columbus. Known as the Sneyd-Thacher MS., this letter may be found in the Rare Book Room of the Library of Congress, Washington, D.C.

Zárate, Agustín de. *Historia del descubrimiento y conquista del Perú.* This account by an early historian may be found in Vol. 3 of Barcia Carballido y Zuñiga, *Historiadores primitivos de las Indias occidentales*, Madrid, 1749, and has been published more recently as Vol. 26 of the *Biblioteca de autores españoles*, Madrid, Ediciones Atlas, 1947.

2. COLLECTIONS

Angelis, Pedro de, ed. *Colección de obras y documentos relativos a la historia antigua y moderna de las provincias del Río de la Plata.* 6 vols. Buenos Aires: Imprenta del Estado, 1837. A good collection of contemporary accounts.

Barcia Carballido y Zuñiga, Andrés González de. *Historiadores primitivos de las Indias Occidentales.* 3 vols. Madrid, 1749. An excellent collection of the works of the earliest historians of the Indies.

Callander, John, ed. *Terra Australis Cognita: or, Voyages to the Terra Australis, or Southern Hemisphere, during the Sixteenth, Seventeenth, and Eighteenth Centuries.* 3 Vols. Edinburgh, 1746–48. An excellent collection, covering the major voyages to the southern hemisphere from Vespucci to Byron.

Churchill, Awnshan, ed. *A Collection of Voyages and Travels, Some Now First Printed from Original MSS., Others Now First Published in England.* 3rd ed., 6 vols. London: Lintot and Osborn, 1744. An excellent, useful collection.

Colección de libros raros o curiosos que tratan de América. 10 vols. Madrid, 1892. A collection of various books, bound together, of considerable interest.

Colección de viages y expediciones a los campos de Buenos-Aires y a las costas de Patagonia. Vol. 5 in the Angelis collection, above. Contains much on many little-known expeditions.

Drake, Edward Cavendish. *A New Universal Collection of Authentic and Entertaining Voyages and Travels, from the Earliest Accounts to the Present Time.* London: J. Cooke, 1768. Similar to Churchill, but much briefer.

Escragnolle Taunay, Affonso de, ed. *Relatos monçoeiros.* São Paulo: Libraria Martins Editôra, 1953. Valuable collection of contemporary source materials on the "monsoons."

Hakluyt, Richard, ed. *The Principall Navigations, Voyages, Traffiques and Discoveries of the English Nation.* 12 vols. Glasgow: James Mac Lehose & Sons, 1904. The classical collection, first published in 1589. Despite its title, it also includes several Spanish and Portuguese accounts.

Jesuits. *Cartas avulsas* (1550–68). Rio de Janeiro: Imprenta Nacional, 1887; and Oficina Industrial Graphica, 1931. Useful collection of letters from missionaries in South America.

Jesuits. *Cartas del Amazonas, escritas por los misioneros de la Compañía de Jesús de 1705 a 1754.* Ed. rev. por Juan B. Bueno Medina. Bogotá: Prensas de la Biblioteca Nacional, 1942. A brief (77 pp.) but valuable collection of letters from missionaries in South America.

Jesuits. *Voyages et travaux des missionaires de la Conpagnie de Jésus publiés par les pères de la même Compagnie pour servir de complément aux Lettres Edifiantes.* Paris, 1857. Very valuable for a study of the missions in French Guiana.

Kerr, Robert, ed. *A General History and Collection of Voyages and Travels, Arranged in Systematic Order.* 17 vols. Edinburgh: Wm. Blackwood; and London: T. Cadell, 1824. Similar to Churchill, but far more extensive. Contains lengthy accounts of some of the early historians.

Lettres édifiantes et curieuses. 2 vols. in 1. Paris: Receuil, 1702–3. A collection of letters from French Jesuit missionaries.

Navarrete, Martín Fernándes de, ed. *Colección de los viajes y descubrimientos que hicieron por mar los españoles desde el fin del siglo XV, con varios documentos inéditos concernienties a la historia de la marina castellana y los establecimientos españoles en Indias.* 5 vols. Madrid: Imprenta Real, 1829–59. A superb collection of the most important documents. Republished in Buenos Aires, 1945–46, and as Vols. 75-77 of the *Biblioteca de Autores Españoles*, Madrid, Ediciones Atlas, 1954 (u. 75) 1955.

Purchas, Samuel, ed. *Hakluytus Postumus, or Purchas His Pilgrimes.* 20 vols. Edinburgh, 1905–7. A continuation of Hakluyt, originally published in London in 1625.

Voyages and Discoveries in South America. London: S. Buckley, 1698. A brief but useful volume.

3. PERSONAL AND OFFICIAL NARRATIVES

Acarete du Biscay. *An Account of a Voyage up the River de la Plata and thence over Land to Peru, with Observations on the Inhabitants, as well as Indians and Spaniards, the Cities, Commerce, Fertility, and Riches of that Part of America.* London: Samuel Buckley, 1698. This brief but valuable account forms a part of *Voyages and Discoveries in South America* (above), and was reprinted in 1969 by the Institute Publishing Co., North Haven, Conn.

Acuña, Cristóbal de, S.J. *A New Discovery of the Great River of the Amazons.* Madrid: Royal Press, 1641. Also appears in Clements R. Markham, ed. *Expeditions into the Valley of the Amazons.* London: Hakluyt

Society, 1859. A more recent edition is available in Spanish as *Nuevo descubrimiento del gran río del Amazonas, por el P. Cristóbal de Acuña* . . . . Quito: Instituto Ecuatoriano de Cultura de Amazonas, 1944. Superb account by a member of the Teixeira expedition.

Adalbert, Prince of Prussia. *Travels of H.R.H. Prince Adalbert of Prussia.* 2 vols. London: D. Bogue, 1849.

Agassiz, Louis. *A Journey in Brazil.* Boston: Ticknor & Fields, 1868. Contains good woodcuts.

Appun, Karl Ferdinand. *Unter den tropen. Wanderungen durch Venezuela am Orinoco durch Britisch Guyana und am Amazonenstrome in den Jahren 1849–68.* 2 vols. Jena: H. Costenoble, 1871. Also published in a one-volume Spanish translation by Federica de Ritter as *En los trópicos,* Caracas, Universidad Central de Venezuela. Ediciones de la Biblioteca, 1961. A lively, interesting account.

Azara, Félix de. *Viajes inéditos de D. Félix de Azara desde Santa-Fe a la Asunción, al interior del Paraguay, y a los pueblos de misiones.* Introduction by Bartolomé Mitre. Buenos Aires: Imprenta y Librería de Mayo, 1873. Personal account by a member of the boundary commission in the late eighteenth century, turned explorer and naturalist.

Bates, Henry W. *The Naturalist on the River Amazons.* Berkeley and Los Angeles: University of California Press, 1962. A reprint, abridged somewhat, of this engaging and valuable work which was originally published in two vols. in London, 1863.

Bingham, Hiram. *Inca Land.* New York: Scribners, 1922. One of Bingham's several accounts of the discovery of Machu Picchu.

Boussingault, Jean Baptiste Joseph Dieudonné, *Viajes científicos a los Andes ecuatoriales.* Paris: Librería Castellana, 1849. A series of scientific monographs, concerning flora, resources, etc.

Brand, Charles, *Journal of a Voyage to Peru* (n.p., n.d.). Lively account by a nineteenth-century traveler.

Burton, Sir Richard F. *Exploration of the Highlands of Brazil.* 2 vols. London: Tinsley Bros., 1869. Written by the great explorer of Arabia and Africa while serving as consul in São Paulo. The appendix in Vol. 2 contains a translation of an old MS. reporting the discovery of a lost city in 1753.

Carvajal, Gaspar de. *The Discovery of the Amazon According to the Account of Friar Gaspar de Carvajal, and Other Documents.* Introduction by José Toribio Medina. Trans. from the Spanish by Bertram T. Lee, edited by H. C. Heaton. New York: American Geographical Society, 1934. The classic account of the discovery, with a 164-page introduction by the editor, the most productive of all archivists and researchers.

Castelnau, Francis de. *Expedition dans les Parties Centrales de l'Amérique du Sud.* 6 vols. Paris: P. Bertrand, 1850. The complete account of the expedition, with a folio supplement of illustrations.

Cherrie, George K. *Dark Trails: Adventures of a Naturalist.* New York: Putnam, 1930. A colorful account of his explorations in South America; Part 6 covers the Roosevelt-Rondón expedition.

Chikhachev, Platon Alexandrovich. *A Trip across the Pampas of Buenos*

Aires (1836–1837). Trans. from the Russian by Jack Weiner. Center of Latin American Studies, Occasional Publications No. 8. Lawrence: University of Kansas, 1967. An interesting and little-known account.

Cochrane, Captain Charles Stuart, R.N. *Journal of a Residence and Travels in Colombia during the Years 1823 and 1824*. 2 vols. London: Henry Colburn, 1825. Good description.

Colón, Fernando. *The Life of the Admiral Christopher Columbus, by his Son, Ferdinand*. Trans. by Benjamin Keen. New Brunswick, N.J.: Rutgers University Press, 1959. The original Spanish version, *Historia del almirante Don Cristóbal Colón . . . escrita por Don Fernando Colón, su hijo*, 2 vols., may be found in Vols. 5–6 of the *Colección de libros raros o curiosos que tratan de América*, above.

Cook, James, *The Journals of Captain James Cook on his Voyages of Discovery*. Edited by John C. Beaglehole. Vols. 34–36 in the Hakluyt Society Extra Series. Cambridge, Eng., 1955–67. An excellent edition with a superb introduction.

Courte de la Blanchardière, René. *Nouveau voyage fait au Pérou*. Paris: Imprimérie de Delaguette, 1751. A rare firsthand account.

Cruz, Luis de la. *Viage, a su costa, del alcalde provincial del muy ilustre cabildo de la Concepción de Chile, D. Luis de la Cruz, desde el Fuerte de Ballenes hasta la Ciudad de Buenos Aires*. Vol. 1 in Angelis, *Colección relativos a la Historia del Río de la Plata*, above.

Darwin, Charles. *Voyage of the Beagle*. There are many editions of this classic. Convenient is the recent paperback edition, New York: Bantam Books, 1958.

Delebecque, J. *A Travers l'Amérique du Sud*. Paris: Plon-Nournit, 1907. Interesting twentieth-century account.

Diario de la segunda division de limites, al mando de D. Diego de Alvear . . . . Vol. 4 of Angelis, *Colección relativos a la Historia del Río de la Plata, above*. Good description of the country Azara explored.

Dyott, George. "The Search for Col. Fawcett." *Geographical Journal* 72 (1928): 443-48, and 74 (1929): 513-40.

Falkner, Thomas, S.J. *Descripción de Patagonia y de las partes adyacentes de la América Meridional*. Vol. 1 in the Angelis collection, above; first Spanish translation of the *Description of Patagonia and the Adjoining Parts of South America*. Hereford, 1774. Indispensable for a study of Patagonia.

Fawcett, Percy Harrison. *Lost Trails, Lost Cities . . . .* From his Manuscripts, Letters and Other Records, Selected and arranged by Brian Fawcett. New York: Funk & Wagnalls, 1953. (Published in England as *Exploration Fawcett.*) The complete story of all of Fawcett's explorations, edited by his son.

Feuillée, Louis. *Journal des observations physiques, mathématiques, et botaniques*. Paris: *Pierre Giffart, 1714*. A useful account of early scientific exploration.

Fitz Gerald, Edward. *The Highest Andes*. London: Methuen, 1899. Describes the conquest of Aconcagua.

Fitz Roy, Robert, ed. *Narrative of the Surveying Voyage of His Majesty's*

Ships Adventure and Beagle between the Years 1826 and 1836. 3 vols. London: H. Colburn, 1839. By the captain of the *Beagle*; provides much information beyond the work of Darwin.

Fleming, Peter. *Brazilian Adventure.* New York: Scribners, 1960. Describes his search for Colonel Fawcett. Verifies Dyott's conclusions.

France, Ministère de la Marine et de l'Instruction Publique. *Mission scientifique du Cap Horn, 1882–1883.* 6 vols. Paris: Gauthier-Villars, 1888. The official account; comprehensive.

Frézier, Amadée François. *A Voyage to the South-Sea and Along the Coasts of Chili and Peru in the Years 1712, 1713, and 1714. . . . Postscript by Dr. Edmund Halley . . . and an Account of the Settlement, Commerce, and Riches of the Jesuits in Paraguay.* London: Jonah Bower, 1717. Especially valuable for excellent maps and contemporary illustrations, thirty-seven in number.

Fritz, Samuel, S.J. *Journal of the Travels and Labours of Father Samuel Fritz in the River of the Amazons between 1686 and 1723.* London: Hakluyt Society, 1922. The absorbing account of the work of this great missionary and explorer.

Froger, François. *Relation d'un voyage de la mer du Sud, détroit de Magellan, Brésil, Cayenne, et les isles Antilles, Amsterdam, l'Honoré, etc.* Chatelain, 1715. Very rare work.

Grillet, Jean, S.J., and Bechamel, François, S.J. *A Journal of the Travels of John Grillet and Francis Bechamel into Guiana in the Year 1674 in Order to Discover the Great Lake of Parima . . . .* London: Samuel Buckley, 1698. Included in *Voyages and Discoveries in South America,* above.

Guillot Muñoz, Alvaro. *La Vida y la obra de Félix de Azara: un sabio formado en el desierto.* Buenos Aires: Atlantida, S.A., 1941. The first part of this brief work is an account of Azara's life, the remainder consists of excerpts from his writings.

Herndon, William L. *Exploration of the Valley of the Amazon, under Direction of the Navy Department.* 2 vols. Washington, D.C.: Robert Armstrong, 1853. Republished in abridged form, New York, McGraw-Hill, 1952. A well-written, interesting account.

Humboldt, Alexander. *Personal Narrative of Travels to the Equinoctial Regions of the New Continent during the Years 1799–1804.* 5 vols. Trans. from the French by Helen Maria Williams. Philadelphia: M. Carey, 1815; London, 1814. One of the greatest pieces of travel literature; a superb account in every respect.

————. *Researches Concerning the Institutions and Monuments of the Ancient Inhabitants of America.* 2 vols. London: Longman, 1814. Describes some of Humboldt's experiences in Peru.

————. *Views of Nature, or Contemplation on the Sublime Phenomena of Creation.* Trans. from the German by E. C. Otté and H. G. Bohn. London: George Bell & Sons, 1878. Contains some reflections on his South American experiences.

Im Thurn, Sir Everard. *Among the Indians of Guiana.* London: K. Paul, Trench & Co., 1883. Work of an English ornithologist.

La Condamine, Charles Marie de. *A Succinct Abridgement of a Voyage*

Made Within the Inland Parts of South-America. Paris, 1745. (English trans. of *Relation abrégée d'un voyage fait dans l'interieur de l'Amérique méridionale,* Paris, 1745; the entire account appears in *Journal du voyage fait par ordre du roi à l'équateur,* Paris, 1751.) A very useful abridgment of this indispensable work, entirely satisfactory for nearly all purposes.

Lapérouse, Jean François. *The First French Expedition to California. Lapérouse in 1786.* Trans., Introduction, and Notes by Charles N. Rudkin. Los Angeles: Glen Dawson, 1959. This translation is only of those sections dealing with California; the introduction is of value.

Malaspina, Alessandro. *Viaje al río de la Plata en el siglo XVIII; reedición de los documentos al viaje de las corbetas Descubierto y Atrevida e informas de sus oficiales sobre el virreinato, extraídos de la obra de Novo y Colson.* Buenos Aires: Librería y editorial "La Facultad," Bernabó y cía., 1938. A satisfactory abridgment of Novo y Colson's fuller account.

Maw, Henry Lister, R.N. *Journal of a Passage from the Pacific to the Atlantic, crossing the Andes in the Northern Provinces of Peru and descending the River Marañón or Amazon.* London: Murray, 1829. A very readable and entertaining account.

Milet de Moreau, Louis Marie-Antoine Destouff, Baron de. *Voyage de La Pérouse autour du monde.* Paris: Imprimerie Nationale, 1797. The official account.

Miller, Leo E. *In the Wilds of South America: Six Years of Exploration in Colombia, Venezuela, British Guiana, Peru, Bolivia, Argentina, Paraguay, and Brazil.* New York: Scribners, 1919. Chaps. 13–16 cover the Roosevelt-Rondón expedition.

Moyano, Carlos M. *Viajes de exploración a la Patagonia, 1877–90.* Buenos Aires, 1931. An excellent account by one of Argentina's greatest explorers.

Musters, George C. *At Home with the Patagonians.* London: J. Murray, 1873. Lively account of his experiences.

––––––. "A Year in Patagonia," *Journal of the Royal Geographical Society* 41 (1871): 59–77. Briefer summary of Musters' expedition.

Mutis, José Celestino. *Diario de observaciones de José Celestino Mutis (1760–1790).* 2 vols. Bogotá: Editorial Minerva Ltda., 1958. A valuable reprint of Mutis' work, carefully annotated and with a good introduction by Guillermo Hernández de Alba.

Nowell, Charles E., ed. *Magellan's Voyage Around the World. Three Contemporary Accounts.* Evanston, Ill.: Northwestern University Press, 1962. Carefully edited and annotated accounts of Antonio Pigafetta, Maximilian of Transylvania, and Gaspar Corrêa.

Núñez Cabeza de Vaca, Alvar. *Comentarios.* Appears in Vol. 1 of Barcia Carballido y Zuñiga, *Historiadores primitivos de las Indias,* and in Vol. 22 of the *Biblioteca de Autores Españoles,* Madrid, Ediciones Atlas, 1946.

Orbigny, Alcide D. d'. *Voyage dans l'Amérique méridionale éxécuté pendant les années 1826, 1827, 1828, 1829, 1830, 1831, 1832, et 1833.* 11 vols. Paris: Chez Pitois-Levrault et Cie., 1835–47. The comprehensive and definitive account of his early expedition.

––––––. *Voyage dans les deux Amériques.* Nouvelle ed. Paris: Furne, 1853. Supplements the above; covers Orbigny's later travels.

Orton, James. *The Andes and the Amazon, or Across the Continent of South America.* New York: Harpers, 1870. Useful account of the Smithsonian Institution expedition.

Pagan, Blaise François de. *An Historical and Geographical Description of the Great Country and River of the Amazons in America.* Trans. by William Hamilton. London: J. Starkey, 1661. Excellent and absorbing seventeenth-century account.

Page, Thomas Jefferson, U.S.N. *La Plata, the Argentine Confederation, and Paraguay. Being a Narrative of the Exploration of the Tributaries of the River La Plata and Adjacent Countries during the Years 1853, '54, '55, and '56 under Orders of the U.S. Government.* New York: Harper, 1859. The account of the *Water Witch* incident, by the commander of the expedition.

Pavie, Théodore. *Fragments d'un voyage dans l'Amérique méridionale en 1833.* Angers: Imprimerie de V. Pavie, 1840. Author was an orientalist, widely traveled.

Philippi, Rudolph Amand. *Viage al desierto de Atacama, hecho de orden del gobierno de Chile en el verano 1853–54.* Halle, Saxony: Eduard Anton, 1860. Published under government auspices. Philippi was director of the national museum.

Poeppig, Eduard F. *Reise in Chile, Peru, und auf dem Amazonen Ströme während der Jahre 1827–32.* 2 vols. in 1. Leipzig: F. Fleischer, 1835–36. A new edition was published in Stuttgart, Brockhaus, 1960, containing excellent plates and a map.

Pons, François Raymond Joseph de. *Travels in South America.* 2 vols. London, 1807. Covers the years 1801–4.

———. *A Voyage to the Eastern Part of Terra Firma, or the Spanish Main, in South America, during the Years 1801, 1802, 1803, 1804 . . . .* 3 vols. London, 1805. A lengthier account.

Rice, Hamilton. "Further Explorations in the N.W. Amazon Basin." *Geographical Journal* 44 (1914): 137-68.

———. "Notes on the Rio Negro (Amazonas)." *Geographical Journal* 52 (1918): 204-15.

———. "The Rio Branco, Uraricuera, and Parima. Surveyed by the Expedition to the Brazilian Guayana from August 1924 to June 1925." *Geographical Journal* 71 (1928): 113-42, 209-23, 345-56.

———. "The Rio Negro, the Casiquiare Canal, and the Upper Orinoco September 1919-April 1920." *Geographical Journal* 58 (1921): 321-43.

———. "The Río Uaupés." *Geographical Journal* 35 (1910): 682-700.

Roosevelt, Theodore. *Through the Brazilian Wilderness.* New York: Scribners, 1914. Since the former president was a modest man, this should be supplemented by Cherrie, Miller, and Zahm.

Ruiz, Hipólito. *Travels of Ruiz, Pavon, and Dombey in Peru and Chile (1777–1788) with an Epilogue and Official Documents Added by Agustín Jesús Barreiro.* Trans. by B. E. Dahlgren. Vol. 21 in Botanical Series, Field Museum of Natural History, Chicago, 1940. A very useful abbreviated account of their travels.

Saint-Hilaire, Auguste de. "Esquisse de mes voyages au Brésil et Paraguay."

(Introduction to his *Histoire des plantes les plus rémarquables du Brésil et du Paraguay*. Paris: A. Belin, 1824.) No. 1 in Vol. 10, *Chronica Botanica*, Waltham, Mass., Spring, 1946.

Schmidel, Ulrich. *Viaje al Río de la Plata*. 2nd ed. Buenos Aires: Emecé, 1945. A recent edition of this colorful, sixteenth-century eyewitness account.

Schomburgk, Moritz Richard. *Richard Schomburgk's Travels in British Guiana*, 2 vols. Georgetown, B.G.: Daily Chronicle Office, 1922–23. English trans. of *Reisen in Britisch Guiana in den Jahren 1840–44*. 3 vols. Leipzig: J. J. Weber, 1847–48. Third volume not translated. The German edition has better maps.

Schomburgk, Robert H. "Diary of an Ascent of the River Corentyn in British Guayana in October 1836." *Journal of the Royal Geographical Society* 7 (1837): 285-301.

_____. "Diary of an Ascent of the River Berbice in British Guayana, in 1836–7." *Journal of the Royal Geographical Society* 7 (1837): 302-50. Map follows p. 350.

_____. "Expedition to the Lower Parts of the Barima and Guiania Rivers, in British Guiana." *Journal of the Royal Geographical Society* 12 (1842): 169-78.

_____. "Excursion up the Barima and Cuyuni Rivers in British Guiana in 1841." *Journal of the Royal Geographical Society* 12 (1842): 178-96.

_____. "Journal of an Expedition from Pirara to the Upper Corentyne, and from thence to Demerara, executed by order of Her Majesty's Government." *Journal of the Royal Geographical Society* 15 (1845): 1-104.

_____. "Journey from Esmeralda on the Orinoco to San Carlos and Moura on the Rio Negro, and thence by Fort San Joaquim to Demerara, in the spring of 1839." *Journal of the Royal Geographical Society* 10 (1841): 248-67.

_____. "Journey from Fort San Joaquim on the Rio Branco to Roraima, and thence by the rivers Parima and Mereweri to Esmeralda on the Orinoco in 1838–9." *Journal of the Royal Geographical Society* 10 (1841): 191-247.

_____. "Report of an Expedition into the interior of British Guayana in 1835–6." *Journal of the Royal Geographical Society* 6 (1836): 224-83.

_____. "Visit to the Sources of the Takutu, in British Guiana, in the Year 1842." *Journal of the Royal Geographical Society* 13 (1843): 18-75.

Smyth, William, and Lowe, Frederick. *Narrative of a Journey from Lima to Para across the Andes and down the Amazon*. London: J. Murray, 1836. An extremely interesting account.

Spix, Johann Baptista von, and Martius, C. F. *Travels in Brazil in the Years 1817–20. Undertaken by Order of H.M. the King of Bavaria*. 2 vols in 1. London: Longman, Hurst, Reed, Orme, Brown & Green, 1824. A valuable study with several excellent illustrations.

Spruce, Richard. *Notes of a Botanist on the Amazon and Andes*. 2 vols. London: Macmillan, 1908. Valuable source, edited and condensed by Alfred Russel Wallace.

Staden, Hans. *The True History of His Captivity, 1557*. Trans. and edited by

Malcolm Letts. London: George Routledge & Sons, 1928. An excellent edition of this colorful tale.

Steffen, Hans. *Viajes de esploracion i estudio en la Patagonia occidental 1892–1902.* 2 vols. Santiago: Imprenta Cervantes, 1909. Comprehensive; contains valuable maps.

Steinen, Karl von den. *Durch Central-Brasilien.* Leipzig: Brockhaus, 1886. Contains valuable plates and maps.

Steinen, Carlos von den. "O rio Xingu." *Revista de Sociedade de Geografia do Rio de Janeiro* 4 (1888): 189-212.

Stuart, (Henry Windsor) Villiers. *Adventures amidst the Equatorial Forests and Rivers of South America.* London: J. Murray, 1891. Good illustrations.

Thouar, Arthur. *Explorations dans l'Amérique du Sud.* Paris: Hachette, 1891. Very interesting account, with numerous illustrations and maps.

Tschudi, Johann Jakob von. *Reisen durch Süd-Amerika.* 5 vols. Leipzig: Brockhaus, 1866–69. Vols. 1–2, on Brazil, north and central, are bound together; Vols. 3–4–5, covering southeast Brazil, Argentina, Chile, and Peru are bound as a second volume. Good maps, illustrations.

———. *Travels in Peru during the Years 1838–42, 1854.* Trans. from the German by Thomasin Ross. London: D. Bogue, 1847. Translation is somewhat faulty.

Ulloa, Antonio de, and Juan y Santacilia, Jorge. *Relación histórica del viage a la América meridional hecho de orden de S. Mag.* 4 vols. Madrid: Antonio Marín, 1748. English trans. by John Adams as *A Voyage to South America.* 2 vols. London: Lockyer Davis, 1772. Another edition, published in 1808 by Stockdale, London, contains a note dedicating the republication to Sir Home Popham in honor of his capture of Buenos Aires, which the publisher expected would remain "one of the richest Jewels in the United Crown." This is a work of detailed and careful observation.

Valdivia, Pedro de. *Cartas de Pedro de Valdivia que tratan del descubrimiento y conquista de Chile.* Appears in Vol. 131 of the *Biblioteca de Autores Españoles,* above. An English trans. is available in the Appendix to Robert B. Cunninghame Graham's *Pedro de Valdivia,* below.

Vespucci, Amerigo. *El nuevo mundo. Cartas relativas a sus viajes y descubrimientos.* Textos en italiano, español, y inglés. Estudio preliminar de Roberto Levillier. Buenos Aires: Editorial Nova, 1951. Invaluable for any study of Vespucci. Carefully edited, with maps, by one of the outstanding authorities on the subject.

Wallace, Alfred Russel. *A Narrative of Travels on the Amazon and Rio Negro.* London: Ward & Locke, 1889. A new edition, entitled *Travels on the Amazon,* corrected and enlarged, was published in 1911.

Waterton, Charles. *Wanderings in South America.* London: Dent, and New York: Dutton, 1895. Everyman's Library No. 772. Despite the author's apology for it, this delightful book has gone into several editions.

Whymper, Edward. *Travels amongst the Great Andes of the Equator.* 2nd ed. London: J. Murray, 1892. A solid, well-written account by a great mountaineer.

Zahl, Paul A. *To the Lost World.* New York: Knopf, 1939. The ascent of Mount Roraima, by a naturalist.

4. SECONDARY WORKS

Abreu, João Capistrano de. *O descubrimento do Brasil.* Rio de Janeiro: Edição da Sociedade Capistrano de Abreu, Annuario do Brasil, 1929. A good critical study, based on contemporary and good standard sources.

An Account of the Spanish Settlements in America. Edinburgh: A. Donaldson & J. Reid for the author, 1762. Based on original sources.

Adams, Percy G. *Travelers & Travel Liars, 1660–1800.* Berkeley and Los Angeles: University of California Press, 1962. The chapter on the Patagonian giants is definitive.

Albion, Robert J., ed. *Exploration and Discovery.* New York: Macmillan, 1965. A brief paperback containing useful excerpts from standard works.

"Algunas aspectos de la Patagonia." *Revista Americana Geográfica* 20 (Buenos Aires, August, 1943): 98-100.

Anderson, Charles L. G. *Life and Letters of Vasco Núñez de Balboa.* New Jersey: Fleming H. Revell Co., 1941. Good critical study.

Aparicio, Francisco de. "Descubrimiento del territorio argentino. La 'entrada' de Diego Rojas." *Revista Histórica Americana* (México, D.F.), December, 1952.

Arcila Robledo, Gregorio. *Las misiones franciscanas en Colombia. Estudio documental.* Bogotá: Imprenta Nacional, 1950. Very good on the Amazon missions.

Arciniegas, Germán. *Germans in the Conquest of America: a 16th Century Venture.* Trans. by Angel Flores. New York: Macmillan, 1943. Useful, good acount, with an anti-German bias.

Amaya, Lorenzo. "La expedición Fontana a la cordillera del Chubut, 1885." *Revista Geográfica Americana* 4 (Buenos Aires, October, 1935): 255-69.

Azevedo, João Lucio d'. *Os jesuítas no Grão-Pará, suas missões e a colonização.* 2nd ed., rev. Coimbra: Imprensa da Universidade, 1930. Best on the subject.

Baião, Antônio; Cidade, Hernâni; Múrias, Manuel de. *História da expansão portuguesa no mundo.* 3 vols. Lisboa: Editorial ática, 1940. A collaborative venture, with many excellent accounts and superb illustrations and maps.

Baker, John N. L. *A History of Geographical Discovery and Exploration.* New ed., rev. New York: Cooper Square Publishers, 1967. Latest edition of this excellent standard work.

Ballesteros y Beretta, Antonio. *Cristóbal Colón y el descubrimiento de América.* (Vols. 4 and 5 in Ballesteros, ed., *Historia de América.*) Barcelona: Salvat Editorial, 1945. An excellent account, thoroughly documented, by one of Spain's leading historians. The second volume deals with the third and fourth voyages.

————. *Historia de España.* 12 vols. Barcelona: Salvat Editorial. 1948. The most complete and extensive scholarly treatment.

Ballesteros Gaibrois, Manuel. *Historia de América.* Madrid: Pegaso, 1946. A useful, well-written, brief account.

Barclay, William S. *The Land of Magellan.* New York: Brentano's, 1926. A useful study.

Barros Arana, Diego. *Historia general de Chile.* 11 vols. 2nd ed. Santiago: Editorial Nascimente, 1937. By one of Chile's most distinguished historians.

Beaglehole, John C. *The Exploration of the Pacific.* London: A. & C. Black, 1934. Good survey of exploration from Magellan to Cook.

Borda, José Joaquín. *Historia de la Compañía de Jesús en la Nueva Granada.* 2 vols. Poissy, 1872. Good survey of Jesuit activities in Colombia.

Boxer, Charles R. *The Golden Age of Brazil, 1695–1750.* Berkeley and Los Angeles: University of California Press, 1962. A well-written, carefully documented account of the period. The best study in English.

––––––. *Salvador de Sá and the Struggle for Brazil and Angola 1602–1686.* London: University of London, the Athlone Press, 1952. A first-rate study of a neglected epoch.

Brazil, São Paulo, Comisão para as Comemorações do "Dia de Anchieta." *Anchietana.* São Paulo: Secretaria de Educação e Cultura, 1965. An excellent collection of papers and monographs on Padre Anchieta.

Buarque de Holanda, Sérgio. *História geral da civilização brasiliera.* Vols. 1- . São Paulo: Difusão Européia do Livro, 1963– . An outstanding collaborative history of Brazil, well-balanced between the colonial and later periods.

––––––. *Moções.* Coleção Estudos Brasileiros, 3 Serie A. Rio de Janeiro, 1945. Best monograph on the subject.

Cardozo, Manoel S. "The Last Adventure of Fernão Dias Pais (1674–1681)." *Hispanic American Historical Review* 26 (1946): 467-79. Lively account of the last effort of this great *bandeirante*.

Cawkell, M. B. R.; Maling, D. H.; Cawkell, E. M. *The Falkland Islands.* London: Macmillan, 1960. Best on the subject, but should be balanced by Enrique de Gandía's writings, below.

Cortesão, Armando. *Cartografia e cartágrafos portugueses dos séculos XV e XVI.* 2 vols. Lisboa: Edição da "Seaca Nova," 1935. Very useful account, if one excepts the attempt to prove that Columbus was a Portuguese.

Cortesão, Jaime. *Brasil.* (Vol. 18 in Ballesteros, *Historia de América.*) Barcelona: Salvat Editorial, 1956. Concentrates on the colonial period.

––––––. *A carta de Pêro Vaz de Caminha.* Rio de Janeiro: Edições Livros de Portugal, 1943.

––––––. *Os descobrimentos portugueses.* 2 vols. Lisboa: Editoria Arcâdia, 1962. An excellent work by one of Portugal's leading historians, with superb maps and illustrations.

Cutright, Paul Russell. *The Great Naturalists Explore South America.* New York: Macmillan, 1940. Part I is historical, with good biographical sketches; the remainder consists of descriptions of specific fauna.

Davies, Arthur. "The 'First' Voyage of Amerigo Vespucci in 1497–98." *Geographical Journal* 108 (September, 1952): 331-37.

Descola, Jean. *The Conquistadors.* Trans. by Malcolm Barnes. London: Allen & Unwin, 1954. A good popular account.

De Terra, Helmut. *Humboldt. The Life and Times of Alexander von Humboldt, 1769–1859.* New York: Knopf, 1955. By a geologist and explorer. Based on primary sources; well written.

Escragnolle Taunay, Affonso de. *História das bandeiras paulistas.* 2 vols. São Paulo: Edições Melhoramentos, 1953. A condensation of his monumental *História geral das bandeiras paulistas*, 11 vols., São Paulo, 1924–50, the standard and classical work on the subject.

————. *Rio de Janeiro de antanho. Impressões de viajantes estrangeiros.* São Paulo: Companhia Editora Nacional, 1942. Includes accounts by a number of explorers and others.

Esteve Barba, Francisco. *Descubrimiento y conquista de Chile.* (Vol. 11 in Ballesteros, *Historia de América.*) Barcelona: Salvat Editorial, 1946. An excellent study, based on carefully selected sources.

Fernández, Juan Patricio. *Relación historial de las misiones de Indios Chiquitos que en Paraguay tienen los Padres de la Compañia de Jesús.* 2 vols. Asunción, 1896. (In *Colección de libros raros o curiosos* . . . , above, Vols. 12 and 13.)

Ferreira Reis, Arthur Cezar. "A viagem filosófica e as expedições científicos na Ibero-América no século XVIII. *Cultura* (Rio de Janeiro, 1952): 94-103.

Figueroa, Francisco de. *Relación de las misiones de la Compañía de Jesús en el país de los Maynas.* Madrid, 1904. Original title was *Ynforme de las misiones de el Marañón, Gran Pará, e Río de las Amazons.*

Friede, Juan. "Geographical Ideas and the Conquest of Venezuela." *The Americas* 16 (October, 1959): 145-59.

Fúrlong Cárdiff, Guillermo. *Cartografía jesuítica del Río de la Plata.* Buenos Aires: Talleres s.a. Casa Jacobo Penser ltda., 1936. An excellent work, with superb maps.

Gandía, Enrique de. *La ciudad encantada de los Césares.* Buenos Aires: A. García Santos, 1933. The definitive account.

————. *Historia de la conquista del Río de la Plata y del Paraguay, 1535–1556.* Buenos Aires: Lib. de García Santos, 1932. An excellent study by one of Argentina's leading and most productive historians.

————. "Las Islas Argentinas de San Antonio." *Revista Geográfica Americana* 24 (Buenos Aires, November, 1945): 265-70.

————. "Los límites de la República Argentina." *Revista Geográfica Americana* 13 (Buenos Aires, June, 1940): 360-69.

Graham, Robert B. Cunninghame. *The Conquest of the River Plate.* London: William Heinemann, 1924. The standard account in English; well written.

————. *Pedro de Valdivia, Conqueror of Chile.* New York: Harper, 1927. About one-half is text, followed by an appendix containing Valdivia's letters to Emperor Charles V.

Greenlee, William Brooks. *The Voyage of Pedro Alvarez Cabral to Brazil and India, from contemporary Documents and Narratives.* Trans. with Introduction and Notes by W. B. Greenlee. London: Haylukt Society, 1938. Proposes that Cabral, following a different course to save time, reached Brazil accidentally.

Hanke, Lewis. "Dos Palabras on Antonio de Ulloa's *Noticias Secretas*." *Hispanic American Historical Review* 16 (1936): 481-86. Covers the pyramid controversy, and the purpose behind publication of the *Noticias Secretas.*

Harrison, John P. "Science and Politics: Origins and Objectives of Mid-

Nineteenth Century Government Expeditions to Latin America." *Hispanic American Historical Review* 35 (1955): 175-202. An excellent introduction to the subject.

Harrisse, Henry. *John Cabot, the Discoverer of North America, and Sebastian, his Son.* London: B. F. Stevens, 1896. An excellent work by the outstanding authority on the Cabots.

Haskins, Caryl P. *The Amazon.* New York: Doubleday, 1943. An interesting, popular survey of exploration.

Irving, Washington. *A History of the Life and Voyages of Christopher Columbus.* 4 vols. London: J. Murray, 1828. Based on early historical writings; superseded by more recent works, but still of value.

Izaguirre Ispizua, Bernardino. *Historia de las misiones franciscanas y narración de los progresos de la geografía en el oriente del Perú . . . 1619–1921.* 14 vols. in 13. Lima: Tipográficos de la Penitenciaría, 1922–29. Contains many accounts of the missionaries themselves, as well as useful maps and tables.

Jouanen, José, S.J. *Historia de la Compañía de Jesús en la antigua Provincia de Quito.* 2 vols. Quito: Editorial Ecuatoriana, 1941–45. Definitive study, dividing at 1696.

Kellner, Charlotte. *Alexander von Humboldt.* London: Oxford University Press, 1963. By a physicist, based on excellent primary sources.

Kirkpatrick, Frederick A. *The Spanish Conquistadores.* London: A. C. Blade, 1934. The best general account.

Latcham, Ricardo E. "La leyenda de los Césares: su orígen y su evolución." *Revista Chilena de Historia y Geografía* (1929): 193-254. A very interesting and useful article.

Leite, Duarte. *Brasil.* Barcelona: Salvat, 1956. Well-documented, useful study.

Levene, Ricardo. *A History of Argentina.* Trans. by William S. Robertson. Chapel Hill: University of North Carolina Press, 1947. A good single-vol. history.

Levillier, Roberto. *America la bien llamada.* 2 vols. Buenos Aires: Editorial Guillermo Kraft, 1948. An excellent study by an outstanding authority on Vespucci, who accepts all four of the voyages.

Lodares, Baltasar de. *Los Franciscanos Capuchinos en Venezuela.* 3 vols. Caracas, 1929–30. Contains a brief account of the 1720–21 expedition in search of El Dorado.

López, Vicente F. *Historia de la Republica Argentina. Su orígen, su revolución y su desarrollo político hasta 1852.* Nueva ed. Buenos Aires: Librería la Facultad, de Juan Roldán, 1911. An outdated standard work, but useful.

Magalhães, Basilio de. "A lenda de Sabarabucu." *Congresso do Mundo Portugues, Publicações* 10 (Lisboa, 1940): 55-66. One of the few writings available on this subject.

Marcondes de Souza, Thomas O. *Amerigo Vespucci e suas viagens.* Facultade de Filosofia, Ciências e letras, Universidade de São Paulo. Boletim No. CV, *História da Civilização Brasileira*, No. 10. São Paulo: Universidade de São Paulo, 1949. A second edition appeared in the Coleção "Pasquale

Petraccone" de estudos italos-brasileiros No. 2, São Paulo, Instituto Cultural Italo-Brasileiro, 1954. A competent, scholarly work supporting Magnaghi's thesis that Vespucci made two, not four voyages.

Markham, Sir Clements R. *Early Spanish Voyages to the Strait of Magellan.* London: Hakluyt Society, 1911. A competent, scholarly study, with good illustrations, facsimiles, and maps.

––––––. *Expeditions into the Valley of the Amazons, 1539–40, 1639.* London: Hakluyt Society, 1859. A competent, scholarly work.

Melón, Amando. *Los primeros tiempos de la colonización. Cuba y los Antillas. Magallanes y la primera vuelta al mundo.* (Vol. 6 in Ballesteros, *Historia de América.*) Barcelona: Salvat Editores, 1952. A very detailed and accurate account.

Menéndez, Raúl. "Esquema del Descubrimiento de América del Sur." *Revista Geográfica Americana* 16 (Buenos Aires, October, 1941): 238-51.

Métraux, Alfred. "The Contribution of the Jesuits to the Exploration and Anthropology of South America." *Mid-America,* July, 1944.

Miller, Robert A. *For Science and National Glory: the Spanish Scientific Expedition to America, 1862–66.* Norman: University of Oklahoma Press, 1968. An excellent, well-written, and well-documented work.

Morison, Samuel Eliot. *Admiral of the Ocean Sea: A Life of Christopher Columbus.* 2 vols. Boston: Little, Brown & Co., 1942. An outstanding biography, concerned chiefly with Columbus as a navigator.

––––––. *Portuguese Voyages to America in the 15th Century.* Cambridge, Mass.: Harvard University Press, 1940. An excellent critical study, with good illustrations and maps.

Morse, Richard M. *The Bandeirantes: the Historical Role of the Brazilian Pathfinders.* New York: Knopf, 1965. A carefully edited collection of selections from outstanding authorities, with a good introduction.

Nowell, Charles E. "Aleixo Garcia and the White King." *Hispanic American Historical Review* 26 (November, 1946): 450-66. An excellent essay on the first European to reach Inca country.

––––––. "The Discovery of Brazil—Accidental or Intentional?" *Hispanic American Historical Review* 16 (August, 1936): 311-38. Presents arguments for the discovery of Brazil by the Portuguese before 1492, and for Cabral's discovery as intentional.

––––––. "The Discovery of the Pacific: a Suggested Change of Approach." *Pacific Historical Review* 16 (February, 1947): 1-10. Suggests that the Pacific was discovered by a Portuguese from the East Indies a year ahead of Balboa.

––––––. *The Great Discoveries and the First Colonial Empires.* Ithaca, N.Y.: Cornell University Press, 1954. A brief, scholarly, and valuable survey.

––––––. "Levillier: América la bien llamada." *Hispanic American Historical Review* 30 (November, 1950): 450-66.

––––––. "Reservations Regarding the Historicity of the 1494 Discovery of South America." *Hispanic American Historical Review* 22 (February, 1942): 205-10.

Ogden, Adele, and Sluiter, Engel, eds., *Greater America: Essays in Honor of Herbert Eugene Bolton.* Berkeley: University of California Press, 1945. Several essays are pertinent.

Parodi, Lorenzo R. "Thaddeus Peregrinus Haenke a dos siglos de su nacimiento." *Anales de la Academia Nacional de Ciencias Exactas, Físicas y Naturales de Buenos Aires* 17 (1964): 9-13. A brief but valuable article.

Parr, Charles M. *So Noble a Captain. The Life and Times of Ferdinand Magellan.* New York: Crowell, 1953. Contains a good list of sources and their location. An excellent biography, but it leaves a number of questions unanswered.

Penrose, Boies. *Travel and Discovery in the Renaissance, 1420–1620.* Cambridge, Mass.: Harvard University Press, 1952. A valuable study, especially useful on cartography.

Peres, Damião. *História dos descobrimentos portugueses.* Pôrto: Portucalense Editoria S.A.R.L., 1943. The best single-vol. account, by an outstanding Portuguese historian.

Pohl, Frederick J. *Amerigo Vespucci, Pilot Major.* New York: Columbia University Press, 1944. An excellent critical biography; accepts the Magnaghi thesis.

Portugal, Ministério de Ultramar. *A Náutica dos descobrimentos.* 2 vols. Lisboa: Agência Geral do Ultramar, 1951. An excellent and useful work, edited by Admiral Gago Coutinho.

Prescott, William H. *The Conquest of Peru.* This classic has appeared in many editions; for the purposes of this study, a useful one is that partly abridged (the sections on the civil wars are omitted) and revised by Victor W. Von Hagen, New York, New American Library, 1961.

Rasmussen, Wayne D. "The United States Astronomical Expedition to Chile, 1849–1852." *Hispanic American Historical Review* 34 (1954): 103-13. A very useful summary.

Restrepo, Daniel, S.J. *La Compañía de Jesús en Colombia.* Bogotá: Imprenta del Corazón de Jesús, 1940. A good, standard account.

Rey Balmaceda, Alfredo. "El primer cruce longitudinal de la Patagonia." *Revista Geográfica Americana* 39 (Buenos Aires, May-June, 1955): 253-56.

Rippy, J(ames) Fred, and Brann, E. R. "Alexander von Humboldt and Simón Bolívar." *American Historical Review* 52 (July, 1947): 697-703.

Rippy, J(ames) Fred. *Crusaders of the Jungle.* With Jean Thomas Nelson. Chapel Hill: University of North Carolina Press, 1936. An excellent, sympathetic, scholarly study.

Rubio, Julián María. *Exploración y conquista del Río de la Plata. Siglos XVI y XVII.* (Vol. 8 in Ballesteros, *Historia de América,* above.) Barcelona: Salvat Editores, 1942.

Sierra, Vicente. *Historia de la Argentina.* Vols. 1– . Buenos Aires: Unión de Editores Latinos, 1956– . An excellent collaborative work.

Southey, Robert. *History of Brazil.* 3 vols. London, 1819. Very good on the colonial period, although considerably outdated.

Steele, Arthur Robert. *Flowers for the King: the Expedition of Ruiz and Pavón and the Flora of Peru.* Durham: Duke University Press, 1964. Best on the subject, carefully researched and written.

Terra, Helmut de. *Humboldt: The Life and Times of Alexander von Humboldt, 1769–1859.* New York: Knopf, 1955. An excellent, well-written biography.

Torres, Ana Palese de. "Las exploraciones de Moyano en la Cuenca del Santa Cruz." *Revista Geográfica Americana* 38 (December, 1954): 125-28.

Vargas Ugarte, Rubén, S.J. *Historia del Perú.* Vols. 1– . Lima: Librería y Imprenta Gil, and Buenos Aires: López, 1949– . An excellent comprehensive history.

Varnhagen, Francisco Adolfo. *História geral do Brasil.* 4th ed., 5 vols. São Paulo: Cia. Melhoramentos de São Paulo, 1927.

Vasconcellos, Luiz Aranha de. "Informação de Luiz Aranha de Vasconcellos sobre o descubrimiento do Rio de Amazonas, 30 de Abril de 1626." In *Documentos para a História da Conquista e Colonisação da Costa de Leste-Oeste do Brazil.* (Vol. 24 of the *Anáis da Biblioteca Nacional.*) Rio de Janeiro, 1905, pp. 391-94.

Vidal de la Blache, Paul M. *La rivière Vincent Pinzon. Etude sur la cartographie de la Guyane.* Paris: Félix Alcon, 1902. A careful study by an eminent French geographer.

Villiers, Alan, "In the Wake of Darwin's *Beagle.*" *National Geographic* 136 (October, 1969): 449-95.

Von Hagen, Victor W. *South America Called Them.* New York: Knopf, 1945. A good, popular, colorful account of several eighteenth- and nineteenth-century scientific explorations, based on reliable primary sources.

Whitaker, Arthur P. "Antonio de Ulloa." *Hispanic American Historical Review* 15 (1935): 155-94. A good, brief biography.

––––––. "Jorge Juan and Antonio Ulloa's Prologue to their Secret Report of 1749 on Peru." *Hispanic American Historical Review* 18 (1938): 507-13. A careful editing of this controversial work.

Wilgus, Alva Curtis. *Maps Relating to Latin America in Books and Periodicals.* Washington, D.C.: Pan American Union, 1933. A very useful work.

Wilson, William Jerome. "The Historicity of the 1494 Discovery of South America." *Hispanic American Historical Review* 22 (February, 1942): 192-205. An attempt to prove, on the basis of the Sneyd-Thatcher MS., that South America was discovered on Columbus' second voyage.

Ybot León, Antonio. *La iglesia y los eclesiásticos españoles en la empresa de Indias.* 2 vols. Barcelona: Salvat, 1954 and 1963. A valuable, lengthy, scholarly account.

Zahm, John A., C.S.C. (H. J. Mozans, *pseud.*). *Along the Andes and down the Amazon.* New York: Appleton, 1923. A delightful book of considerable value.

––––––. *The Quest of El Dorado.* New York: Appleton, 1917. A charming account of Zahm's travels along the route of the conquistadores.

––––––. *Through South America's Southland.* New York: Appleton, 1916. Includes an account of the Roosevelt-Rondón expedition, in which Zahm participated.

––––––. *Up the Orinoco and Down the Magdalena.* New York and London: Appleton, 1910. An account of Zahm's explorations in Venezuela and Colombia, following the Orinoco-Meta-Magdalena route.

Index